OPERATIONS RESEARCH

OPERATIONS RESEARCH

FOURTH EDITION

S Kalavathy

Professor, Department of Mathematics

RMD Engineering College, Kavaraipettai, Thiruvallur district, Tamil Nadu

VIKAS®

VIKAS PUBLISHING HOUSE PVT. LTD.

VIKAS® PUBLISHING HOUSE PRIVATE LIMITED
E-28, Sector-8, Noida-201301 (UP), India
Phone: +91-120-4078900 • Fax: +91-120-4078999
Registered Office: A-27, 2nd Floor, Mohan Co-operative Industrial Estate, New Delhi-110044
E-mail: helpline@vikaspublishing.com • Website: www.vikaspublishing.com

SALES AND MARKETING OFFICES OF VIKAS® AND S CHAND AND COMPANY LIMITED

Chennai	:	Ph: 044-2363 2120, chennai@schandpublishing.com
Guwahati	:	Ph: 0361-2738 811, 2735 640, guwahati@schandpublishing.com
Hyderabad	:	Ph: 040-4018 6018, hyderabad@schandpublishing.com
Jalandhar	:	Ph: 0181-4645 630, jalandhar@schandpublishing.com
Kolkata	:	Ph: 033-2335 7458, 2335 3914, kolkata@schandpublishing.com
Lucknow	:	Ph: 0522-4003 633, lucknow@schandpublishing.com
Mumbai	:	Ph: 022-2500 0297, mumbai@schandpublishing.com
Patna	:	Ph: 0612-401 1400, patna@schandpublishing.com

All rights reserved. No part of this publication may be reproduced or copied in any material form (including photo copying or storing it in any medium in form of graphics, electronic or mechanical means and whether or not transient or incidental to some other use of this publication) without written permission of the copyright owner. Any breach of this will entail legal action and prosecution without further notice.

***Jurisdiction**: All disputes with respect to this publication shall be subject to the jurisdiction of the Courts, tribunals and forums of New Delhi, India only.*

Operations Research
ISBN: 978-93259-6347-4

Product Code: V6OPR61ORSR10ENAD13O

Fourth Edition 2013
Reprinted several times between 2013 and 2022, 2023 (Twice), 2024 (Fourth)
Reprint 2025

VIKAS® is the registered trademark of Vikas Publishing House Private Limited
Copyright © Vikas Publishing House Private Limited, 2013

PRINTED IN INDIA
By Vikas Publishing House Private Limited, Plot 20/4, Site-IV, Industrial Area Sahibabad, Ghaziabad-201010 and Published by Vikas Publishing House Private Limited, E-28, Sector-8, Noida-201301

Disclaimer: The publishers have taken all care to ensure highest standard of quality as regards typesetting, proofreading, accuracy of textual material, printing and binding. However, neither they nor the author accept responsibility for any loss occasioned as a result of any misprint or mistake found in this publication.

To my beloved students
past and present

Acknowledgements

It is my duty to remember and acknowledge the encouragement and support provided by (Late) Smt. Manjula Munirathnam, Chairperson, RMD Engineering College, Kavaraipettai.

I express my sincere thanks to Sri R S Munirathinam, Chairman, Mr R M Kishore, Vice-Chairman, Mr Yalamanji Pradeep, Secretary, and Mr R Jodhi Naidu, Director, R M D Engineering College, Kavaraipettai, for their multidimensional support and encouragement throughout the period. I would like to thank the Principal, Dr K Sivaram; Dean, Dr K Dharmalingam; HOD (S&H), Dr Maria Susai Immanuel, R M D Engineering College, for their support. I would also like to thank Dr R M Suresh, Principal, Jerusalem College of Engineering, for his help in bringing out this book successfully.

Sincere thanks are also due to the esteemed faculty members who have reviewed the book and given valuable suggestions—Prof Milu Acharya, Department of Mathematics, SOA University, Bhubaneswar, and Professor CV Chandrashekhar, Professor and Head, Department of Mechanical Engineering, JSS, Noida.

Suggestions for improvement are welcome.

S Kalavathy

Preface to the Fourth Edition

This book has been conceived and written with the objective of providing students with a comprehensive textbook on the subject of Operations Research. It follows a simple algorithmic approach to explain the concept of each method by giving different steps. This approach stems from the author's experience in teaching undergraduate and postgraduate students of Madras University and Anna University, Chennai, over many years.

One of the highlights of this book is the solved-problems approach, as each chapter in the book is substantiated with a large number of solved problems. Many of the questions that have been incorporated are from previous examination papers of various universities. In addition, each chapter has numerous exercise problems at the end and a section on short questions with answers.

The fourth edition has been thoroughly revised and updated. It includes a new chapter on Non-linear Programming to cater to the revised ME and MCA syllabus of Anna University. Another method - the stepping stone method - which can solve the problem of degeneracy in the transportation problem, has been included.

S Kalavathy

Preface to the First Edition

This book *Operations Research* is the outcome of my teaching mathematics to engineering students for over 13 years. It is designed to meet the requirements of students of a wide variety of courses, particularly, engineering, computing and management courses (BE, MCA and MBA).

One of the highlights of this book is the solved-problems approach. The book has a large number of solved examples in each chapter. The solution to many problems are from previous University questions. In addition, each chapter has numerous exercise problems at the end, and a section on short questions with answers.

I am extremely grateful to Dr. S. Jagathrakshagan, Chairman, Bharath Institute of Science and Technology (BIST) for encouraging and supporting my efforts in writing this book. I thank Dr. P. Vajravelu, Principal, and Prof. T. Rangarajulu, Director of BIST for providing me with adequate facilities, and for their interest and encouragement at all times.

I also thank Vikas Publishing House Pvt. Ltd for the interest, effort and cooperation in bringing out this book.

S Kalavathy

Contents

Chapter 1 Basics of Operations Research

1.1 INTRODUCTION

The term 'operations research' was coined in 1940 by McCloskey and Trefethen in a small town of Bawdsey in England. It is a science that came into existence in a military context. During World War II, the military management of UK called on scientists from various disciplines and organized them into teams to assist it in solving strategic and tactical problems relating to air and land defence of the country. They were required to formulate specific proposals and plans for aiding the military commands to arrive at decisions on optimal utilization of scarce military resources and efforts and also to implement the decisions effectively. This new approach to the systematic and scientific study of the operations of the system was called Operations Research (OR), or operational research. Hence OR can be termed as 'an art of winning war without actually fighting it.'

1.1.1 Definitions

Operations Research has been defined in various ways and it is perhaps still too young to be defined in some authoritative manner. There have not been any instance of uniformly acceptable definitions of it as yet. Some prominent ones proposed so far are given below. These definitions have also been improving with the development of the subject.

Operations Research is a scientific method of providing executive departments with a quantitative basis for decisions regarding the operations under their control. [Morse and Kimball (1946)]

Operations Research is the scientific method of providing executive with an analytical and objective basis for decisions. [P.M.S. Blackett (1948)]

Operations Research is the art of giving bad answers to the problems to which otherwise worse answers are given. [T.L. Saaty (1958)]

Operations Research is a systematic method-oriented study of the basic structures, characteristics, functions and relationships of an organization to provide the executive with a sound, scientific and quantitative basis for decision making. [E.L. Arnoff & M.J. Netzorg]

Operations Research is a scientific approach to problem solving for executive management. [H.M. Wagner]

Operations Research is an aid for the executive in making his decisions by providing him with the quantitative information based on the scientific method of analysis. [C. Kittel]

Operations Research is the scientific knowledge through interdisciplinary team efforts for the purpose of determining the best utilization of limited resources. [H.A. Taha]

The various definitions given above bring out the following essential characteristics of operations research:

(*i*) System orientation.
(*ii*) Use of interdisciplinary terms.
(*iii*) Application of scientific method.
(*iv*) Uncovering new problems.
(*v*) Quantitative solutions.
(*vi*) Human factors.

1.2 SCOPE OF OPERATIONS RESEARCH

There is a great scope for economists, statisticians, administrators and technicians working as a team to solve the problems of defence by using the OR approach. Besides this, OR is useful in various other important fields like:

(*i*) Agriculture
(*ii*) Finance
(*iii*) Industry
(*iv*) Marketing
(*v*) Personnel Management
(*vi*) Production Management
(*vii*) Research and Development
(*viii*) Military Operations

1.3 PHASES OF OPERATIONS RESEARCH

The procedure to be followed in the study of OR generally involves the following major phases:

(*i*) Formulating the problem
(*ii*) Constructing a mathematical model
(*iii*) Deriving the solution from the model
(*iv*) Testing the model and its solution (updating the model)
(*v*) Controlling the solution
(*vi*) Implementation

1.4 MODELS IN OPERATIONS RESEARCH

A model in OR is a simplified representation of an operation, or is a process in which only the basic aspects or the most important features of a typical problem under investigation are considered. The objective of a model is to identify the significant factors and interrelationships. The reliability of the solution obtained from a model depends on the validity of the model representing the real system.

A good model must possess the following characteristics:

(*i*) It should be capable of taking into account new formulation without having any change in its frame.
(*ii*) Assumptions made in the model should be as few as possible.
(*iii*) Variables used in the model must be less in number ensuring that it is simple and coherent.
(*iv*) It should be open to parametric type of treatment.
(*v*) It should not take much time in its construction for any problem.

1.4.1 Advantages of a Model

There are certain significant advantages of using a model. These are:

(*i*) Problems under consideration become controllable through a model.
(*ii*) A model provides a logical and systematic approach to the problem.
(*iii*) A model clearly shows the limitations and scope of an activity.
(*iv*) It helps in finding useful tools that eliminate duplication of methods applied to solve problems.
(*v*) It helps in finding solutions for research and improvement in a system.
(*vi*) It provides an economic description and explanation of either the operation, or the systems it represent.

1.4.2 Characteristics of a Good Model

(*i*) The number of variables used should be as few as possible.
(*ii*) The number of assumptions should be as few as possible.
(*iii*) It should be easy and economical to construct.
(*iv*) It should assimilate the system environmental changes without change in the framework.
(*v*) It should be adaptable to parametric type of treatment.

1.5 CLASSIFICATION OF MODELS

Classification of models is a subjective problem. Models may be distinguished by:

1. Degree of abstraction,
2. Function,
3. Structure,
4. Nature of an environment,
5. The extent of generality.

1.5.1 Models by Function

These models can further be classified as (*i*) Descriptive models (*ii*) Predictive models and (*iii*) Normative models.

(*i*) *Descriptive models:* They describe and predict the facts and relationships among the various activities of the problem. They do not have an objective function as a part of the model to evaluate the decision alternatives. Through them, it is possible to get the information on how one or more factors change as a result of changes in other factors.

(*ii*) *Predictive models:* These models are used in predictive analysis involving a variety of statistical techniques used to analyze the current and historical facts to make predictions about future events. Predictive models use patterns found in historical and transactional data to find various risks and opportunities. Statistical techniques include data mining, game theory and machine learning. Predictive models can be used in various areas like marketing, financial services, telecommunication, etc.

(*iii*) *Normative or Optimization models:* They are prescriptive in nature and develop objective decision rule for optimum solutions.

1.5.2 Models by Structure

These models are represented by (*i*) Iconic models (*ii*) Analogue models and (*iii*) Symbolic models.

(*i*) *Iconic or physical models:* These are the pictorial representations of real systems and have the appearance of the real things. An iconic model is said to be scaled down or scaled up according to the dimensions of the model, which may be smaller or greater than that of the real item, e.g., city maps, blueprints of houses, globe and so on. These models are easy to observe and describe, but are difficult to manipulate and are not very useful for the purpose of prediction.

(*ii*) *Analogue models:* They are more abstract than the iconic model as there is no similarity between these models and real life items. The models in which one set of properties is used to represent the another set of properties called analogue models. After the problem is solved, the solution is reinterpreted in terms of the original system. These models are less specific and concrete, but easier to manipulate than iconic models.

(*iii*) *Mathematical or symbolic models:* They are the most abstract in nature and employ a set of mathematical symbols to represent the components of the real system. These variables are related together by means of mathematical equations to describe the behaviour of the system. The solution of the problem is then obtained by applying most appropriate mathematical techniques to the model.

The symbolic model is usually the easiest to manipulate experimentally and it is also the most general and abstract. Its function is more explanatory than descriptive.

1.5.3 Models by Nature of an Environment

These models can be classified into (*i*) Deterministic models and (*ii*) Probabilistic models.

(i) Deterministic models: In these models all parameters and functional relationships are assumed to be known with certainty when the decision is to be made. Linear programming and break-even models are good examples of deterministic models.

(ii) Probabilistic or Stochastic models: These models have at least one parameter or decision variable as a random variable. These models reflect to some extent the complexity of the real world and the uncertainty surrounding it.

1.5.4 Models by the Extent of Generality

These models can be categorized as

(*i*) Specific models and (*ii*) General models.

When a model represents a system at some specific time, it is known as a *specific model*. In these models if the time factor is not considered, they are termed as *static models*. An inventory problem of determining economic order quantity for the next period assuming that the demand in planning period would remain the same as that of today is an example of static model. *Dynamic programming* may be considered as an example of *dynamic model*.

Simulation and *Heuristic models* fall under the category of general models. These models are used to explore alternative strategies which have been overlooked previously.

1.6 USES AND LIMITATIONS OF OPERATIONS RESEARCH

1.6.1 Uses

(*i*) It provides a logical and systematic approach to the problem.

(*ii*) It allows modification of mathematical solutions before they are put to use.

(*iii*) It suggests all the alternate courses of action for the same management.

(*iv*) It helps in finding avenues for new research and improvement in the system.

(*v*) It facilitates improved quality of decision.

(*vi*) It leads to optimum use of managers' production factor.

(*vii*) It makes the overall structure of the production problem more comprehensible and helps in dealing with the problem as a whole.

(*viii*) It aids in preparation of future managers by improving their knowledge and skill.

(*ix*) It indicates the scope as well as limitation of a problem.

1.6.2 Limitations

Models are the only idealized representations of reality and cannot be regarded as absolute in any case.

The validity of a model, for a particular situation, can be ascertained only by conducting experiments on it.

Mathematical models are applicable to only specific categories of problems as they do not take qualitative factors into account. All influencing factors, which cannot be quantified, find no place in mathematical models.

Operations Research requires huge calculations which cannot be handled manually and require computers, resulting in heavy costs.

As it is a new field, there is a resistance from the employees to the new proposals.

The implementation of OR mainly depends on the person (*or* the input) who provides the solution and the person (manager) who uses the solution.

1.7 OPERATIONS RESEARCH AND DECISION-MAKING

Operations research or management science, as the name suggests, is the science of managing, which is concerned with making decisions most of the times. It is thus a decision science that helps the management to make 'better decisions', a pivotal word in managing.

Decision-making can be improved and in fact there is a wide scope for such improvements. The essential characteristics of all decisions are:

(*i*) Objectives (*ii*) Alternatives

(*iii*) Influencing factors (constraints)

Once these characteristics are known, we can work towards improving the decisions.

In OR, scientific quantification is used in order to make better management decisions.

Thus, in OR, the essential features of decisions, namely, objectives, alternatives and influencing factors are expressed in terms of scientific quantifications or mathematical equations.

Operations research helps to overcome the complexity of the decision-making mode as it provides the management with the most needed tools for improving their decisions.

Chapter

2

Linear Programming

2.1 INTRODUCTION

Linear programming deals with the optimization (maximization or minimization) of a function of variables known as *objective functions*. It is a subject consisting of a set of linear equalities and/or inequalities known as *constraints*. Linear programming is a mathematical technique which involves the allocation of limited resources in an optimal manner, on the basis of a given criterion of optimality.

In this chapter, properties of Linear Programming Problems (LPP) have been discussed. The graphical method of solving an LPP is applicable where two variables are involved. The most widely used method for solving LPP problems consisting of any number of variables is called *simplex method*, developed by G. Dantzig in 1947 and made generally available in 1951.

2.2 FORMULATION OF LP PROBLEMS

The procedure for mathematical formulation of a LPP consists of the following steps:

Step 1 To write down the decision variables of the problem.

Step 2 To formulate the objective function to be optimized (maximized or minimized) as a linear function of the decision variables.

Step 3 To formulate the other conditions of the problems such as resource limitation, market constraints, interrelations between variables, etc. as linear inequations or equations in terms of the decision variables.

Step 4 To add the non-negativity constraints from the considerations so that the negative values of the decision variables do not have any valid physical interpretation.

The objective function, the set of constraints and the non-negative restrictions together form a Linear Programming Problem (LPP).

2.2.1 General Formulation of LPP

The general formulation of the LPP can be stated as follows:

In order to find the values of n decision variables $x_1\ x_2 \ldots x_n$ to maximize or minimize the objective function.

$$Z = c_1x_1 + c_2x_2 + \ldots + c_nx_n \qquad (1)$$

and also satisfy m-constraints

$$\left.\begin{array}{l} a_{11}x_1 + a_{12}x_2 + \cdots + a_{1n}x_n \ldots b_1 \\ a_{21}x_1 + a_{22}x_2 + \cdots + a_{2n}x_n \ldots b_2 \\ \vdots \\ a_{i1}x_1 + a_{i2}x_2 + \cdots + a_{in}x_n \ldots b_i \\ \vdots \\ a_{m1}x_1 + a_{m2}x_2 + \cdots + a_{mn}x_n \ldots b_m \end{array}\right\} \quad (2)$$

where constraints may be in the form of inequality ≤ or ≥ or even in the form of an equation (=) and finally satisfy the non-negative restrictions

$$x_1 \geq 0, x_2 \geq 0 \ldots x_n \geq 0 \quad (3)$$

2.2.2 Matrix Form of LP Problem

The LPP can be expressed in the matrix form as follows:

Maximize or
Minimize $Z = cx \longrightarrow$ Objective function
Subject to, $Ax\ (\leq = \geq)\ b$ Constraint equation
$b > 0, x \geq 0$ Non-negativity restrictions

where, $x = (x_1\ x_2\ \cdots\ x_n)$
$c = (c_1\ c_2\ \ldots\ c_n)$

$$b = \begin{pmatrix} b_1 \\ b_2 \\ \vdots \\ b_m \end{pmatrix}_{m \times 1} \qquad A = \begin{pmatrix} a_{11}\ a_{12} & \cdots a_{1n} \\ a_{21}\ a_{22} & \cdots a_{2n} \\ \vdots & \\ a_{m1}\ a_{m2} & \cdots a_{mn} \end{pmatrix}_{m \times n}$$

Example 2.1 A manufacturer produces two types of models M_1 and M_2. Each model of the type M_1 requires 4 hours of grinding and 2 hours of polishing; whereas each model of the type M_2 requires 2 hours of grinding and 5 hours of polishing. The manufacturer has 2 grinders and 3 polishers. Each grinder works 40 hours a week and each polisher works for 60 hours a week. Profit on M_1 model is ₹ 3.00 and on model M_2 is ₹ 4.00. Whatever is produced in a week is sold in the market. How should the manufacturer allocate his production capacity to the two types of models so that he may make the maximum profit in a week?

Solution

Decision variables: Let x_1 and x_2 be the number of units of M_1 and M_2 models.

Objective function: Since the profit on both the models are given, we have to maximize the profit viz.

$$\text{Max } Z = 3x_1 + 4x_2$$

Constraints: There are two constraints — one for grinding and the other for polishing.

Numbers of hours available on each grinder for one week is 40. There are 2 grinders. Hence the manufacturer does not have more than 2 × 40 = 80 hours of grinding. M_1 requires 4 hours of grinding and M_2 requires 2 hours of grinding.

The grinding constraint is given by

$$4x_1 + 2x_2 \leq 80$$

Since there are 3 polishers, the available time for polishing in a week is given by 3 × 60 = 180 hours of polishing. M_1 requires 2 hours of polishing and M_2 requires 5 hours of polishing. Hence we have $2x_1 + 5x_2 \leq 180$.

Finally we have,

Max $Z = 3x_1 + 4x_2$

Subject to,

$$4x_1 + 2x_2 \le 80$$
$$2x_1 + 5x_2 \le 180$$
$$x_1, x_2 \ge 0.$$

Example 2.2 A company manufactures two products *A* and *B*. These products are processed in the same machine. It takes 10 minutes to process one unit of product *A* and 2 minutes for each unit of product *B* and the machine operates for a maximum of 35 hours in a week. Product *A* requires 1 kg and *B* requires 0.5 kg of raw material per unit, the supply of which is 600 kg per week. Market constraint on product *B* is known to be minimum of 800 units every week. Product *A* costs ₹ 5 per unit and sold at ₹ 10. Product *B* costs ₹ 6 per unit and can be sold in the market at a unit price of ₹ 8. Determine the number of units of *A* and *B* per week to maximize the profit.

Solution

Decision variables: Let x_1 and x_2 be the number of products *A* and *B* respectively.

Objective function: Cost of product *A* per unit is ₹ 5 and selling price is ₹ 10 per unit.

∴ Profit on one unit of product $A = 10 - 5 =$ ₹ 5

x_1 units of product *A* contributes a profit of ₹ $5x_1$, profit contribution from one unit of product

$$B = 8 - 6 = ₹\,2$$

x_2 units of product *B* contribute a profit of ₹ $2x_2$

The objective function is given by,

$$\text{Max } Z = 5x_1 + 2x_2$$

Constraints: Time requirement constraint is given by,

$$10x_1 + 2x_2 \le (35 \times 60)$$
$$10x_1 + 2x_2 \le 2100$$

Raw material constraint is given by,

$$x_1 + 0.5x_2 \le 600$$

Market demand of product *B* is 800 units every week

$$\therefore \quad x_2 \ge 800$$

The complete LPP is

Max $Z = 5x_1 + 2x_2$

Subject to,

$$10x_1 + 2x_2 \le 2100$$
$$x_1 + 0.5x_2 \le 600$$
$$x_2 \ge 800$$
$$x_1, x_2 \ge 0.$$

Example 2.3 A person requires 10, 12 and 12 units of chemicals *A*, *B* and *C*, respectively for his garden. A liquid product contains 5, 2 and 1 units of *A*, *B* and *C*, respectively, per jar. A dry product contains 1, 2 and 4 units of *A*, *B*, *C* per carton. If the liquid product is sold for ₹ 3 per jar and the dry product is sold for ₹ 2 per carton, how many units of each product should be purchased, in order to minimize the cost and meet the requirements?

Solution

Decision variables: Let x_1 and x_2 be the number of units of liquid and dry products.

Objective function: Since the cost for the products are given, we have to minimize the cost.

$$\text{Min } Z = 3x_1 + 2x_2$$

Constraints: As there are 3 chemicals and their requirements are given, we have three constraints for these three chemicals.

$$5x_1 + x_2 \geq 10$$
$$2x_1 + 2x_2 \geq 12$$
$$x_1 + 4x_2 \geq 12$$

Finally the complete LPP is

Min $Z = 3x_1 + 2x_2$

Subject to,

$$5x_1 + x_2 \geq 10$$
$$2x_1 + 2x_2 \geq 12$$
$$x_1 + 4x_2 \geq 12$$
$$x_1, x_2 \geq 0.$$

Example 2.4 A paper mill produces two grades of paper namely X and Y. Owing to raw material restrictions, it cannot produce more than 400 tons of grade X and 300 tons of grade Y in a week. There are 160 production hours in a week. It requires 0.2 and 0.4 hours to produce a ton of products X and Y, respectively with corresponding profits of ₹ 200 and ₹ 500 per ton. Formulate the above as an LPP to maximize profit and find the optimum product mix.

Solution

Decision variables: Let x_1 and x_2 be the number of units of two grades of paper of X and Y.

Objective function: Since the profit for the two grades of paper X and Y are given, the objective function is to maximize the profit.

$$\text{Max } Z = 200x_1 + 500x_2$$

Constraints: There are 2 constraints, one referring to the raw material, and the other to the production hours.

Max $Z = 200x_1 + 500x_2$

Subject to,

$$x_1 \leq 400$$
$$x_2 \leq 300$$
$$0.2x_1 + 0.4x_2 \leq 160$$

Non-negative restriction $x_1, x_2 \geq 0.$

Example 2.5 A company manufactures two products A and B. Each unit of B takes twice as long as to produce one unit of A and if the company is to produce only A, it would have time to produce 2000 units per day. The availability of the raw material is sufficient to produce 1500 units per day of both A and B combined. Product B requiring a special ingredient, only 600 units can be prepared per day. If A fetches a profit of ₹ 2 per unit and B, a profit of ₹ 4 per unit, find the optimum product mix by graphical method.

Solution Let x_1 and x_2 be the number of units of the products A and B respectively.

The profit after selling these two products is given by the objective function,

$$\text{Max } Z = 2x_1 + 4x_2$$

Since the company can produce at the most 2000 units of the product in a day and type B requires twice as much time as that of type A, production restriction is given by

$$x_1 + 2x_2 \leq 2000$$

Since the raw materials are sufficient to produce 1500 units per day, if both A and B are combined, we have

$$x_1 + x_2 \leq 1500$$

As B requires special ingredients, there can be a maximum of 600 units from B so we have $x_2 \leq 600$.

Also, since the company cannot produce negative quantities, $x_1 \geq 0$ and $x_2 \geq 0$.

Hence the problem can be finally put in the form:

Find x_1 and x_2 such that the profits,

$$Z = 2x_1 + 4x_2 \text{ is maximum}$$

Subject to,

$$x_1 + 2x_2 \leq 2000$$
$$x_1 + x_2 \leq 1500$$
$$x_2 \leq 600$$
$$x_1, x_2 \geq 0.$$

Example 2.6 A firm manufacturers 3 products A, B and C. The profits are ₹ 3, ₹ 2 and ₹ 4 respectively. The firm has 2 machines and given below is the required processing time in minutes for each machine on each product

Machines	***Product-wise processing time (min)***		
	A	***B***	***C***
M_1	4	3	5
M_2	3	2	4

Machines M_1 and M_2 have 2000 and 2500 machine minutes respectively. The firm must manufacture 100 units of A's, 200 units of B's and 50 units of C's but not more than 150 units of A's. Set up an LPP to maximize the profit.

Solution Let x_1, x_2, x_3 be the number of units of the products A, B, C respectively.

Since the profits are ₹ 3, ₹ 2 and ₹ 4 respectively, the total profit gained by the firm after selling these three products is given by,

$$Z = 3x_1 + 2x_2 + 4x_3$$

The total number of minutes required in producing these three products at machine M_1 is given by $4x_1 + 3x_2 + 5x_3$ and at machine M_2, it is given by $3x_1 + 2x_2 + 4x_3$.

The restrictions on the machine M_1 and M_2 are given by 2000 minutes and 2500 minutes.

$$4x_1 + 3x_2 + 5x_3 \leq 2000$$
$$3x_1 + 2x_2 + 4x_3 \leq 2500$$

Also, since the firm manufactures 100 units of A's, 200 units of B's and 50 units of C's but not more than 150 units of A's the further restriction becomes

$$100 \leq x_1 \leq 150$$
$$200 \leq x_2 \geq 0$$
$$50 \leq x_3 \geq 0$$

Hence the allocation problem of the firm can be finally put in the form:

Find the value of x_1, x_2, x_3 so as to maximize

$$Z = 3x_1 + 2x_2 + 4x_3$$

Subject to the constraints, $x_1, x_2 \geq 0$

$$4x_1 + 3x_2 + 5x_3 \leq 2000$$
$$3x_1 + 2x_2 + 4x_3 \leq 2500$$
$$100 \leq x_1 \leq 150, \quad 200 \leq x_2 \geq 0, \quad 50 \leq x_3 \geq 0.$$

Example 2.7 A farmer has a 100 acre farm. He can sell all tomatoes, lettuce or radishes and can get a price of ₹ 1.00 per kg for tomatoes, ₹ 0.75 a heap for lettuce and ₹ 2.00 per kg for radishes. The average yield per acre is 2,000 kg of tomatoes, 3,000 heaps of lettuce and 1,000 kg of radishes. Fertilizers are available at ₹ 0.50 per kg and the amount required per acre is 100 kg each for tomatoes and lettuce and 50 kg for radishes. Labour required for sowing, cultivating and harvesting per acre is 5 man-days for tomatoes and radishes and 6 man-days for lettuce. A total of 400 man-days of labour are available at ₹ 20 per man-day. Formulate this problem as a linear programming model to maximize the farmer's total profit.

Solution Let x_1, x_2, x_3 be the area (*in acre*) of his farm to grow tomatoes, lettuce and radishes, respectively. The farmer produces $2000x_1$ kg of tomatoes, $3000x_2$ heaps of lettuce and $1000x_3$ kg of radishes.

∴ The total sales of the farmer will be

$$= ₹(1.00 \times 2000x_1 + 0.75 \times 3000x_2 + 2 \times 1000x_3)$$

∴ Fertilizer expenditure will be $0.5 \times [100\,(x_1 + x_2) + 50x_3]$

Labour cost= ₹ $20 \times (5x_1 + 6x_2 + 5x_3)$

∴ Farmer's profit will be

$$\begin{aligned} Z &= \text{Sale (in ₹)} - \text{Total expenditure (in ₹)} \\ &= (2000x_1 + 0.75 \times 3000x_2 + 2 \times 1000x_3) \\ &\quad - 0.5 \times [100\,(x_1 + x_2) + 50x_3]\ \text{(Fertilizer)} \\ &\quad - 20 \times (5x_1 + 6x_2 + 5x_3)\ \text{(Labour)} \\ Z &= 1850x_1 + 2080x_2 + 1875x_3 \end{aligned}$$

Since the total area of the farm is restricted to 100 acres

$$x_1 + x_2 + x_3 \leq 100.$$

Also, the total man-days labour is restricted to 400 man-days.

$$5x_1 + 6x_2 + 5x_3 \leq 400$$

Hence, the farmers allocation problem can be finally put in the form.

Find the value of x_1, x_2 and x_3 so as to maximize

$$Z = 1850x_1 + 2080x_2 + 1875x_3$$

Subject to,

$$\begin{aligned} x_1 + x_2 + x_3 &\leq 100 \\ 5x_1 + 6x_2 + 5x_3 &\leq 400 \\ x_1, x_2, x_3 &\geq 0. \end{aligned}$$

Example 2.8 An electric appliance company produces two products: refrigerators and ranges. Production takes place in two separate departments I and II. Refrigerators are produced in department I and ranges in department II. The company's two products are sold on a weekly basis. The weekly production cannot exceed 25 refrigerators and 35 ranges. The company regularly employs a total of 60 workers in the two departments. A refrigerator requires 2 man-weeks labour while a range requires 1 man-week labour. A refrigerator contributes a profit of ₹ 60 and a range contributes a profit of ₹ 40. How many units of refrigerators and ranges should the company produce to realize the maximum profit? Formulate the above as an LPP.

Solution Let x_1 and x_2 be the number of units of refrigerators and ranges to be produced.

Each refrigerator and range contribute a profit of ₹ 60 and 40, respectively.

∴ The objective function is to maximize $Z = 60x_1 + 40x_2$

There are 2 constraints which are imposed on weekly production and labour.

Since the weekly production cannot exceed 25 refrigerators and 35 ranges.

$$x_1 \leq 25$$
$$x_2 \leq 35$$

A refrigerator requires 2 man-weeks of labour and a range requires 1 man-week of labour and the total number of workers is 60.

$$2x_1 + x_2 \leq 60$$

Non-negativity restrictions: Since the number of refrigerators and ranges produced cannot be negative, we have $x_1 \geq 0$ and $x_2 \geq 0$.

Hence the problem can be finally arranged in the form:

Find the value of x_1 and x_2 so as to maximize

$$Z = 60x_1 + 40x_2$$

Subject to,

$$x_1 \leq 25$$
$$x_2 \leq 35$$
$$2x_1 + x_2 \leq 60$$

and,

$$x_1, x_2 \geq 0.$$

2.3 SENSITIVITY ANALYSIS

The term sensitivity analysis often known as post-optimality analysis refers to the optimal solution of a linear programming problem, formulated using various methods. Here, you will learn how sensitivity analysis helps to solve repeatedly the real problem in a different form. Generally, these scenarios crop up as an end result of parameter changes due to the involvement of new advanced technologies and the accessibility of well-organized latest information for key (input) parameters or the ' what-if ' questions. Thus, sensitivity analysis helps to produce the optimal solution of simple perturbations for the key parameters. For the optimal solutions, consider the simplex algorithm as a ' black box ' which accepts the input key parameters to solve LPP as shown below:

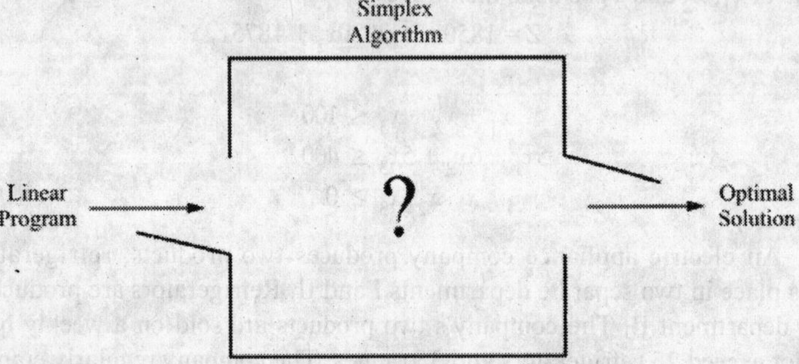

Example 2.9 Illustrate sensitivity analysis using simplex method to solve the following LPP:

Maximize

$$Z = 20x_1 + 10x_2$$

Subject to,

$$x_1 + x_2 \leq 3$$
$$3x_1 + x_2 \leq 7$$

And

$$x_1, x_2 \geq 0.$$

Solution Sensitivity analysis is done after making the initial and final tableau using the simplex method. Add slack variables to convert it into equation form.

Maximize $Z = 20x_1 + 10x_2 + 0S_1 + 0S_2$

Subject to, $x_1 + x_2 + S_1 + 0S_2 = 3$

$3x_1 + x_2 + 0S_1 + S_2 = 7$

Where $x_1, x_2 \geq 0.$

To find basic feasible solution, we put $x_1 = 0$ and $x_2 = 0$. This gives $Z = 0$, $S_1 = 3$ and $S_2 = 7$. The initial table will be as follows:

Initial table

	C_j		20↓	10	0	0	
C_B	B	x_B	x_1	x_2	S_1	S_2	Min $\frac{x_B}{x_i}$
0	S_1	3	1	1	1	0	3/1 = 3
←0	S_2	7	(3)	1	0	1	7/3 = 2.33 ←
	Z_j	0	0	0	0	0	
	$Z_j - C_j$		–20	–10	0	0	
			↑				

Find $\frac{x_B}{x_i}$ for each row and also find minimum for the second row. Here, $Z_j - C_j$ is maximum negative (–20). Hence, x_1 enters the basis and S_2 leaves the basis. It is shown with the help of arrows.

Key element is 3, key row is second row and key column is x_1. Now convert the key element into the entering key by dividing each element of the key row by key element using the following formula:

$$\text{New element} = \text{Old element} - \left[\frac{\text{Product of elements in the key row and the key column}}{\text{Key element}}\right]$$

The following is the first iteration table:

	C_j		20↓	10	0	0	
C_B	B	x_B	x_1	x_2	S_1	S_2	
←0	S_1	2/3	0	(2/3)	1	–1/3	$\frac{2}{3}/\frac{2}{3} = 1$ ←
20	x_1	7/3	1	1/3	0	1/3	$\frac{7}{3}/\frac{1}{3} = 7$
	Z_j	140/3	20	20/3	0	20	
	$Z_j - C_j$	–	0	–10/3	0	20/3	
				↑			

Since $Z_j - C_j$ has one value less than zero, i.e., negative value hence this is not yet the optimal solution. Value –10/3 is negative, hence x_2 enters the basis and S_1 leaves the basis. Key row is upper row.

	C_j		20	10	0	0
C_B	B	x_B	x_1	X_2	S_1	S_2
10	x_2	1	0	1	3/2	–1/2
20	x_1	2	1	0	–1/2	1/2
	Z_j	50	20	10	0	25
	$Z_j - C_j$		0	0	5	5

$Z_j - C_j \geq 0$ for all, hence optimal solution is reached, where $x_1 = 2,\ x_2 = 1, Z = 50$.

2.3.1 Shadow Price

The price or value of any item is its exchange ratio which is relative to some standard item. Thus, we may say that shadow price, also known as marginal value of a constraint *i*, is the change it induces in the optimal value of the objective function due to the result of any change in the value, *i.e.,* on the right-hand side of the constraint *i*.

This can be formulazied assuming,

Z = objective function

b_i = right-handed side of constraint i

π^* = standard price of constraint i;

At optimal solution

$Z^* = v^* = b^T \pi^*$ (Non-degenerate solution)

Under this situation, the change in the value of Z per change of b_i for small changes in b_i is obtained by partially differentiating with objective function Z, with respect to the right-handed side b_i, which is further illustrated as:

$$\frac{\delta z}{\delta b_i} = \pi_i^*$$

where,

π_i^* = price associated with the right-handed side.

It is this price, which was interpreted by Paul Samuelson as shadow price.

2.3.2 Economic Interpretation

We have often seen that shadow prices are being frequently used in the economic interpretation of the data in linear programming.

Example: To find the economic interpretation of the shadow price under non-degeneracy, you will need to consider the linear programming to find out minimum of objective function $z, x \geq 0$, which is as follows:

$$Min\ Z = -x_1 - 2x_2 - 3x_3 + x_4$$

$$x_1 + 2x_4 = 6$$

$$x_2 + 3x_4 = 2$$

$$x_3 - x_4 = 1$$

Now, to get a optimal basic solution, we can calculate the numericals:

$$x_1 = 6,\ x_2 = 2,\ x_3 = 1,\ x_4 = 0,\ z = -13.$$

The optimal solution for the shadow price is:

$$\pi^*_1 = -1,\ \pi^*_2 = -2,\ \pi^*_3 = -3,$$

as, $z = b_1\pi_1 + b_2\pi_2 + b_3\pi_3$, where $b = (6, 2, 1)$;

it denotes,

$$\frac{\partial z}{\partial b_1} = \pi_1 = -1,\quad \frac{\partial z}{\partial b_2} = \pi_2 = -2,\quad \frac{\partial z}{\partial b_3} = \pi_3 = -3.$$

As these shadow prices and the changes take place in a non-degenerate situation so, they do not impact the small changes of b_i. Now, if this same situation is repeated in a degenerate situation, we will have to replace $b_3 = 1$ by $b_3 = 0$; thereby $\partial z/\partial b_3^+ = -3$, only if the change in b_3 is positive. However, we need to keep in mind that if, b_3 is negative, then x_3 will drop out of the basis and x_4 transcends as the basic and the shadow price may be illustrated as;

$$\pi^\circ_1 = -1,\ \pi^\circ_2 = -2,\ \pi^\circ_3 = \partial z/\partial b_3^- = -9.$$

Here, we see that the interpretation of the dual variables π, and dual objective function υ corresponds to column *j* of the primal problem. So, the goal of linear programming (Simplex method) is to determine whether there is a basic feasibility for optimal solution, in the most cost-effective manner.

Thus, after iteration t, υ is the total cost of the objective function and this can be illustrated as:

$$\upsilon = \pi^T b = \sum_{i=1}^{m} \pi_i\, b_i$$

here, π_i = simplex multipliers which are associated with the basis *B*.

So, we may say that the prices of the problem of the dual variables are selected in such a manner, that there is maximization of the implicit indirect costs of the resources that are consumed by all the activities. Whenever any basic activity is conducted, it is performed at a positive level and all non-basic activities are kept at a zero level.

Hence, if the primal—dual variable system is utilized, then the slack variable is maintained at a positive level in an optimal solution and the corresponding dual variable is equal to zero.

EXERCISES

1. A company manufactures 3 products *A*, *B* and *C*. The profits are ₹ 3, ₹ 2 and ₹ 4 respectively. The company has two machines and given below is the required processing time in minutes for each machine on each product.

Machines	***Products-wise processing time (min)***		
	A	***B***	***C***
I	4	3	5
II	2	2	4

Machines I and II have 2000 and 2500 minutes respectively. The company must manufacturer 100 *A*'s, 200 *B*'s and 50 *C*'s but not more than 150 *A*'s. Find the number of units of each product to be manufactured by the company to maximize the profit. Formulate the above as a L.P. Model.

[**Ans.** Max $Z = 3x_1 + 2x_2 + 4x_3$ Subject to, $4x_1 + 3x_2 + 5x_3 \le 2000$; $2x_1 + 2x_2 + 4x_3 \le 2500$; $100 \le x_1 \le 150$, $200 \le x_2 \ge 0$, $50\ x_3 \ge 0$

2. A company produces two types of leather belts *A* and *B*. *A* is of superior quality and *B* is of inferior quality. The respective profits are ₹ 10 and ₹ 5 per belt. The supply of raw material is sufficient for making 850 belts per day. For belt *A*, a special type of buckle is required and 500 pieces are available per day. There are 700 buckles available for belt *B* per day. Belt *A* needs twice as much time as that required for the belt *B* and the company can produce 500 belts if all of them were of the type *A*. Formulate a L.P. Model for the above problem.

[**Ans.** Max $Z = 10x_1 + 5x_2$; Subject to, $x_1 + x_2 \le 850$; $x_1 \le 500$; $x_2 \le 700$; $2x_1 + x_2 \le 1000$; $x_1, x_2 \ge 0$ where, x_1, x_2 are the number of belts of the two types *A* and *B* respectively produced per day.]

3. The standard weight of a special purpose brick is 5 kg and it contains two ingredients B_1 and B_2, B_1 costs ₹ 5 per kg and B_2 costs ₹ 8 per kg. Strength considerations dictate that the brick contains not more than 4 kg of B_1 and a minimum of 2 kg of B_2 since the demand for the product is likely to be related to the price of the brick. Formulate the above problem as a L.P. Model.

[**Ans.** Min $Z = 5x_1 + 8x_2$; Subject to, $x_1 \le 4$; $x_2 \ge 2$ (Strength constraint); $x_1 + x_2 = 5$ (Availability constraint); $x_1, x_2 \ge 0$ where, $x_1, x_2 \ge 0$, x_1, x_2 are the quantities of B_1 and B_2 in kg in the brick.]

4. Egg contains 6 units of vitamin *A* and 7 units of vitamin *B* per gram and costs 12 paise per gram. Milk contains 8 units of vitamin *A* and 12 units of vitamin *B* per gram and costs 20 paise per gram. The daily minimum requirement of vitamin *A* and vitamin *B* are 100 units and 120 units respectively. Find the optimal product mix.

[**Ans.** Min $Z = 12x_1 + 20x_2$; Subject to, $6x_1 + 8x_2 \ge 100$; $7x_1 + 12x_2 \ge 120$; $x_1, x_2 \ge 0$ where, x_1 and x_2 are the number of units of egg and milk respectively.]

5. In a chemical industry two products *A* and *B* are prepared involving two operations. The production of *B* also results in a by-product *C*. The product *A* can be sold at ₹ 3 profit per unit and *B* at ₹ 8 profit per unit. The by-product *C* has a profit of ₹ 2 per unit but it cannot be sold as the destruction cost is ₹ 1 per unit. Forecasts show that upto 5 units of *C* can be sold. The company gets 3 units of *C* for each unit of *A* and *B* produced. Forecasts show that they can sell all the units of *A* and *B* produced. The manufacturing times are 3 hours per unit for *A* on operation one and two respectively, 4 hours and 5 hours per unit for *B* on operation one and two respectively. Because the product *C* results from producing *B*, no time is used in producing *C*. The available times are 18 and 21 hours of operation one and two respectively. How much of *A* and *B* need to be produced keeping *C* in mind, to make the highest profit. Formulate the above problem as LP Model.

[**Ans.** Maximize $Z = 3x_1 + 8x_2 + 2x_3$; Subject to, $3x_1 + 4x_2 \le 18$; $3x_1 + 5x_2 \le 21$; $x_1 + x_2 + 3x_3 \le 5$; $x_1, x_2, x_3 \ge 0$ where, x_1, x_2, x_3 are the number of units produced of product *A*, *B* and *C* respectively.]

6. A company produces two types of hats. Each hat of the first type requires twice as much labour time as the second type. If all hats are of the second type only, the company can produce a total of 500 hats per day. The market limits daily sales of the first and second types to 150 and 250 hats. Assuming that the profits per hat are ₹ 8 for type *A* and ₹ 15 for type *B*, formulate the problem as a linear programming model in order to determine the number of hats to be produced of each type so as to maximize the profit.

[**Ans.** Maximize $Z = 8x_1 + 5x_2$; Subject to, $2x_1 + x_2 \le 500$; $x_1 \le 150$; $x_2 \le 250$; $x_1, x_2 \ge 0$ where, x_1 and x_2 are the number of units of hats of type *A* and type *B* respectively.]

7. A company desires to devote the excess capacity of the three machines, lathe, shaping and milling machine to make three products *A*, *B* and *C*. The available time per month for these machines is tabulated below.

Machine	*Lathe*	*Shaping*	*Milling*
Available time/month	200 hours	100 hours	180 hours

The time taken to produce each unit of the products *A*, *B* and *C* on the machines is displayed in the table below.

Machine	Time taken (hours)		
	Lathe	Shaping	Milling
Product A	6	2	4
Product B	2	2	—
Proudct C	3	—	3

The profit per product would be ₹ 20, ₹ 16 and ₹ 12 respectively on products *A*, *B* and *C*. Formulate a LPP to find the optimum product mix.

[**Ans.** Maximize $Z = 20x_1 + 16x_2 + 12x_3$; Subject to, $6x_1 + 2x_2 + 3x_2 \leq 200$; $2x_1 + 2x_2 \leq 100$; $4x_1 + 3x_3 \leq 180$; $x_1, x_2, x_3 \geq 0$.
where, x_1, x_2, x_3 are the number of units of products *A*, *B* and *C*, respectively that are produced per month.]

8. An animal food company must produce 200 kg of a mixture consisting of ingredients x_1 and x_2 daily. x_1 costs ₹ 3/- per kg and x_2 ₹ 8 per kg. Not more than 80 kg of x_1 can be used and at least 60 kg of x_2 must be used. Formulate an LP model to minimize the cost.

[**Ans.** Min $Z = 3x_1 + 8x_2$; Subject to, $x_1 + x_2 = 200$; $x_1 \leq 80$; $x_2 \geq 60$; $x_1, x_2 \geq 0$.
where, x_1, x_2 are the ingredients in the mixture as expressed in kg.]

9. What is a sensitivity analysis?
10. What is the purpose of sensitivity analysis?
11. What is the difference between uncertainty and sensitivity analysis?
12. A company manufactures two products, *A* and *B*, on two machines *I* and *II*. It has been determined that the company will realize a profit of $3 on each unit of product *A* and a profit of $4 on each unit of product *B*. To manufacture a unit of product *A* requires 6 min on Machine *I* and 5 min on Machine *II*. To manufacture a unit of product *B* requires 9 min on Machine *I* and 4 min on Machine *II*. There are 5 hr of machine time available on Machine *I* and 3 hr of machine time available on Machine *II* in each work shift.
    (*a*) Find the range of values that the contribution to the profit of a unit of product *A* can assume without changing the optimal solution.
    (*b*) Find the range of values that the contribution to the profit of a unit of product B can assume without changing the optimal solution.
    (*c*) Find the range of values that the resource associated with the time constraint on Machine *I* can assume.
    (*d*) Find the range of value that the resource associated with the time constraint on Machine *II* can assume.
    (*e*) Find the shadow price for the resource associated with each constraint.
13. The Perth Mining Company operates two mines for the purpose of extracting gold and silver. The Saddle Mine costs $14,000 per day to operate, and it yields 50 ounces of gold and 3000 ounces of silver each day. The Horseshoe Mine costs $16,000 per day to operate and it yields 75 ounces of gold and 1000 ounces of silver each day. The management of the company has set a target of at least 650 ounces of gold and 18000 ounces of silver.
    (*a*) How many days should each mine be operated so that target can be met at a minimum cost to the company?
    (*b*) Find the range of values that the cost of operating the Saddle Mine per day can assume without changing the optimal solution.
    (*c*) Find the range of value that the cost of operating the Horseshoe Mine per day can assume without changing the optimal solution.
    (*d*) Find the range of values that the requirement for gold can assume.
    (*e*) Find the range of values that the requirement for silver can assume.
    (*f*) Find the shadow prices for each requirement.
14. Kane Manufacturing has a division that produces two models of fireplace grates— model *A* and model *B*. To produce each model *A* grate required 3 lbs of cast iron and 6 min of labour. To produce each model *B* grate requires 4 lbs of cast iron and 3 min of labour. The profit for each model *A* grate is $2 and the profit for each model *B* grate is $1.50. If 1000 lbs of cast iron and 20 hr of labour are available for the production of grates

each day, how many grates of each model should the division produce per day in order to help maximize Kane's profits?

(*a*) Use the method of corners to solve the problem.
(*b*) Find the range of values that the coefficient of x can assume changing the optimal solution.
(*c*) Find the range of values that the coefficient y can assume without changing the optimal solution.
(*d*) Find the range of values that the resource for cast iron can assume without changing the optimal solution.
(*e*) Find the range of values that the resource for labour can assume without changing the optimal solution.
(*f*) Find the shadow prices for each resource.
(*g*) Identify the binding and non-binding constraints.

15. Deluxe River Cruises operates a fleet of river vessels. The fleet comprises two types of vessels — a type-*A* vessel has 60 deluxe cabins and 160 standard cabins whereas a type-*B* vessel has 80 deluxe cabins and 120 standard cabins. Under a charter agreement with the Odyssey Travel Agency, Deluxe River Cruises is to provide Odyssey with a minimum of 360 deluxe and 680 standard cabins for their 15-day cruise in May. It costs $44,000 to operate a type-*A* vessel and $54,000 to operate a type-*B* vessel for that period.

(*a*) How many of each type of vessel should be used in order to keep the operating costs to a minimum?
(*b*) Find the range of values that the cost of operating a type-*A* vessel can assume without changing the optimal solution.
(*c*) Find the range of values that the requirement for deluxe cabins can assume.
(*d*) Find the shadow price for the requirement of deluxe cabins.

Chapter 3

Graphical Method

Simple linear programming problems with two decision variables can be easily solved by graphical method.

3.1 PROCEDURE FOR SOLVING LPP BY GRAPHICAL METHOD

The steps involved in graphical method are as follows:

Step 1 Consider each inequality constraint as an equation.

Step 2 Plot each equation on the graph, as each equation will geometrically represent a straight line.

Step 3 Mark the region. If the inequality constraint corresponding to that line is $\leq$, then the region below the line lying in the first quadrant (due to non-negativity of variables) is shaded. For the inequality constraint $\geq$ sign, the region above the line in the first quadrant is shaded. The points lying in the common region will satisfy all the constraints simultaneously. The common region thus obtained is called the '*feasible region*'.

Step 4 Assign an arbitrary value, say zero, to the objective function.

Step 5 Draw a straight line to represent the objective function with the arbitrary value (i.e., a straight line through the origin).

Step 6 Stretch the objective function line till the extreme points of the feasible region. In the maximization case, this line will stop farthest from the origin, passing through at least one corner of the feasible region. In the minimization case, this line will stop nearest to the origin, passing through at least one corner of the feasible region.

Step 7 Find the co-ordinates of the extreme points selected in step 6 and find the maximum or minimum value of Z.

Note: As the optimal values occur at the corner points of the feasible region, it is enough to calculate the value of the objective function of the corner points of the feasible region and select the one that gives the optimal solution. That is, in the case of maximization problem, the optimal point corresponds to the corner point at which the objective function has a maximum value, and in the case of minimization, the optimal solution is the corner point which gives the minimum value for the objective function.

Example 3.1 Solve the following LPP by graphical method.

$$\text{Minimize } Z = 20x_1 + 10x_2$$

$$\text{Subject to, } x_1 + 2x_2 \leq 40$$

$$3x_1 + x_2 \geq 30$$

$$4x_1 + 3x_2 \geq 60$$

$$x_1, x_2 \geq 0$$

Solution Replace all the inequalities of the constraints by equation

$x_1 + 2x_2 = 40$ If $x_1 = 0 \Rightarrow x_2 = 20$

If $x_2 = 0 \Rightarrow x_1 = 40$

$\therefore$ $x_1 + 2x_2 = 40$ passes through (0, 20) (40, 0)

$3x_1 + x_2 = 30$ passes through (0, 30) (10, 0)

$4x_1 + 3x_2 = 60$ passes through (0, 20) (15, 0)

Plot each equation on the graph.

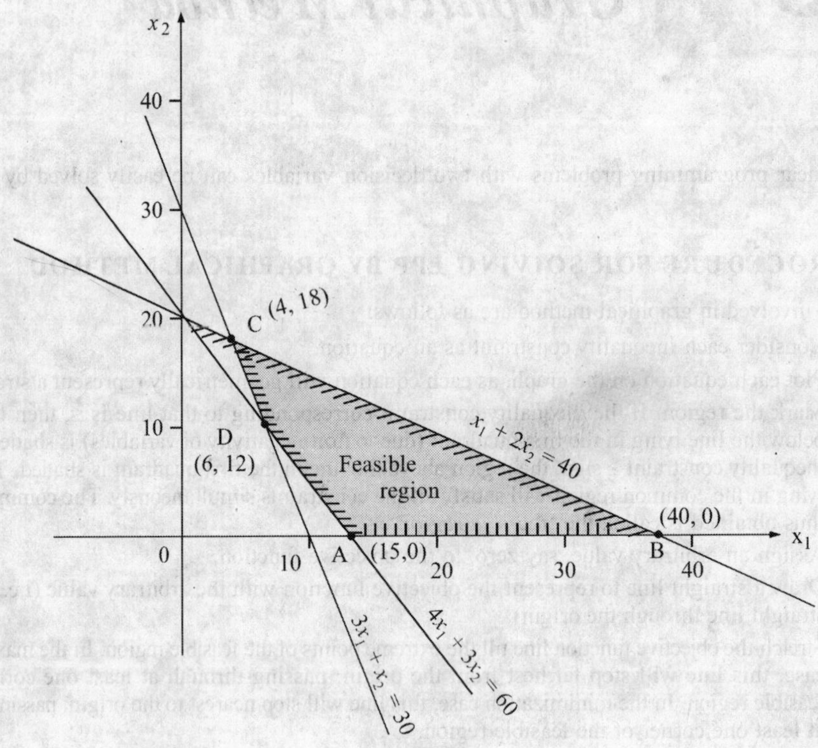

The feasible region is *ABCD*.

C and *D* are points of intersection of lines.

C intersect $x_1 + 2x_2 = 40, 3x_1 + x_2 = 30$

and, *D* intersect $4x_1 + 3x_2 = 60, 3x_1 + x_2 = 30$

$C = (4, 18)$

$D = (6, 12)$

Corner points	*Value of* $Z = 20x_1 + 10x_2$
A (15, 0)	300
B (40, 0)	800
C (4, 18)	260
D (6, 12)	240 (Minimum value)

$\therefore$ The minimum value of *Z* occurs at *D* (6, 12). Hence, the optimal solution is $x_1 = 6, x_2 = 12$.

Example 3.2 Find the maximum value of $Z = 5x_1 + 7x_2$

Subject to the constraints,

$$x_1 + x_2 \le 4$$
$$3x_1 + 8x_2 \le 24$$
$$10x_1 + 7x_2 \le 35$$
$$x_1, x_2 \ge 0$$

Solution Replace all the inequalities of the constraints by forming equations

$x_1 + x_2 = 4$ passes through (0, 4) (4, 0)

$3x_1 + 8x_2 = 24$ passes through (0, 3) (8, 0)

$10x_1 + 7x_2 = 35$ passes through (0, 5) (3.5, 0)

Plot these lines on the graph and mark the region below the line as the inequality of the constraint as ≤ which is also lying in the first quadrant.

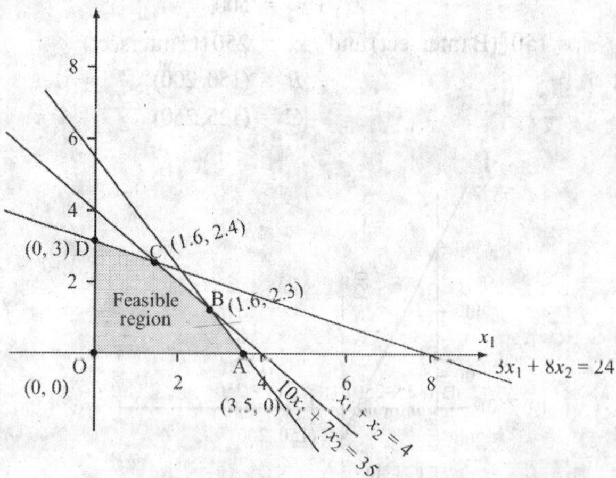

The feasible region is *OABCD*.

B and *C* are the points of intersection of lines

B intersect $x_1 + x_2 = 4$, $10x_1 + 7x_2 = 35$

and *C* intersect $3x_1 + 8x_2 = 24$, $x_1 + x_2 = 4$.

On solving we get, $B = (1.6, 2.3)$

$C = (1.6, 2.4)$

Corner points	*Value of* $Z = 5x_1 + 7x_2$
O (0, 0)	0
A (3.5, 0)	17.5
B (1.6, 2.3)	24.1
C (1.6, 2.4)	24.8 (Maximum value)
D (0, 3)	21

∴ The maximum value of *Z* occurs at *C* (1.6, 2.4) and the optimal solution is $x_1 = 1.6, x_2 = 2.4$.

Example 3.3 A company produces 2 types of hats *A* and *B*. Every hat *A* requires twice as much labour time as the second hat *B*. If the company produces only hat *B* then it can produce a total of 500 hats per day. The market limits daily sales of hat *A* and *B* to 150 and 250 respectively. The profits on hat *A* and *B* are ₹ 8 and ₹ 5 respectively. Solve graphically to get the optimal solution.

Solution Let x_1 and x_2 be the number of units of type *A* and type *B* hats respectively.

$$\text{Max } Z = 8x_1 + 5x_2$$

$$\text{Subject to, } 2x_1 + x_2 \leq 500$$
$$x_1 \leq 150$$
$$x_2 \leq 250$$
$$x_1, x_2 \geq 0$$

First rewrite the inequality of the constraint into an equation and plot the lines on the graph.

$2x_1 + x_2 = 500$ passes through (0, 500) (250, 0)

$x_1 = 150$ passes through (150, 0)

$x_2 = 250$ passes through (0, 250)

We mark the region below the lines lying in the first quadrant as the inequality of the constraints are ≤. The feasible region is *OABCD*. *B* and *C* are the points of intersection of lines

$$2x_1 + x_2 = 500,$$

$x_1 = 150$ (B intersect) and $x_2 = 250$ (C intersect)

On solving, we get $B = (150, 200)$

$C = (125, 250)$

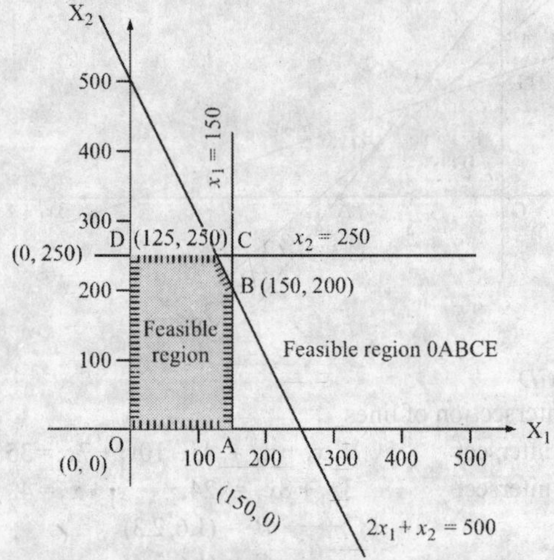

Corner points	*Value of* $Z = 8x_1 + 5x_2$	
$O(0, 0)$	0	
$A(150, 0)$	1 200	
$B(150, 200)$	2200	
$C(125, 250)$	2250	(Maximum $Z = 2250$)
$D(0, 250)$	1250	

The maximum value of Z is attained at $C(125, 250)$

∴ The optimal solution is $x_1 = 125, x_2 = 250$.

i.e., The company should produce 125 hats of type *A* and 250 hats of type *B* in order to get the maximum profit of ₹ 2250.

Example 3.4 By graphical method solve the following LPP.

$$\text{Max } Z = 3x_1 + 4x_2$$

$$\text{Subject to, } 5x_1 + 4x_2 \leq 200$$

$$3x_1 + 5x_2 \leq 150$$

$$5x_1 + 4x_2 \geq 100$$

$$8x_1 + 4x_2 \geq 80$$

and

$$x_1, x_2 \geq 0$$

Solution

Replacing the inequality by equality

$5x_1 + 4x_2 = 200$ passes through (0, 50), (40, 0)

$3x_1 + 5x_2 = 150$ passes through (0, 30), (50, 0)

$8x_1 + 4x_2 = 80$ passes through (0, 20), (10, 0)

$5x_1 + 4x_2 = 100$ passes through (0, 25), (20, 0)

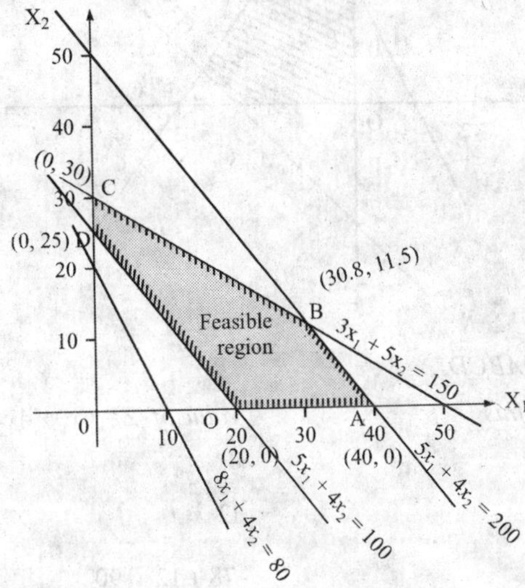

Feasible region is given by *OABCD*.

Corner points	*Value of* $Z = 3x_1 + 4x_2$
$O(20, 0)$	60
$A(40, 0)$	120
$B(30.8, 11.5)$	138.4 (Maximum value)
$C(0, 30)$	120
$D(0, 25)$	100

$\therefore$ The maximum value of Z is attained at B (30.8, 11.5)

$\therefore$ The optimal solution is $x_1 = 30.8, x_2 = 11.5$.

Example 3.5 Use graphical method to solve the LPP.

$$\text{Maximize } Z = 6x_1 + 4x_2$$

$$\text{Subject to, } -2x_1 + x_2 \leq 2$$

$$x_1 - x_2 \leq 2$$

$$3x_1 + 2x_2 \leq 9$$

$$x_1, x_2 \geq 0$$

Solution

Replacing the inequality by equality

$$-2x_1 + x_2 = 2 \text{ passes through } (0, 2), (-1, 0)$$
$$x_1 - x_2 = 2 \text{ passes through } (0, -2), (2, 0)$$
$$3x_1 + 2x_2 = 9 \text{ passes through } (0, 4.5), (3, 0)$$

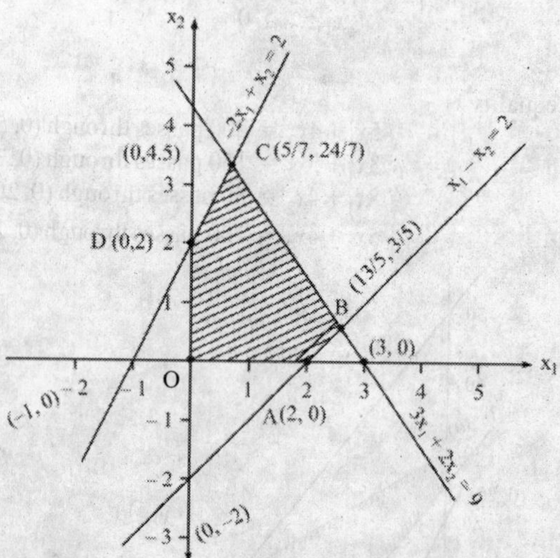

Feasible region is given by *OABCD*.

Corner points	*Value of* $Z = 6x_1 + 4x_2$
$O(0, 0)$	0
$A(2, 0)$	12
$B(13/5, 3/5)$	$\frac{78+12}{5} = \frac{90}{5} = 18$ (Maximum value)
$C\left(\frac{5}{7}, \frac{24}{7}\right) = \frac{126}{7} = 18$ (Maximum value)	
$D(0, 2) = 8$	

The maximum value of Z is attained at $B(13/5, 3/5)$ or at $C(5/7, 24/7)$.

$\therefore$ The optimal solution is $x_1 = 13/5, x_2 = 3/5$, or $x_1 = 5/7, x_2 = 24/7$.

Example 3.6 Use graphical method to solve the LPP.

$$\text{Maximize } Z = 3x_1 + 2x_2$$
$$\text{Subject to, } 5x_1 + x_2 \geq 10$$
$$x_1 + x_2 \geq 6$$
$$x_1 + 4x_2 \geq 12$$
$$x_1, x_2 \geq 0$$

Solution

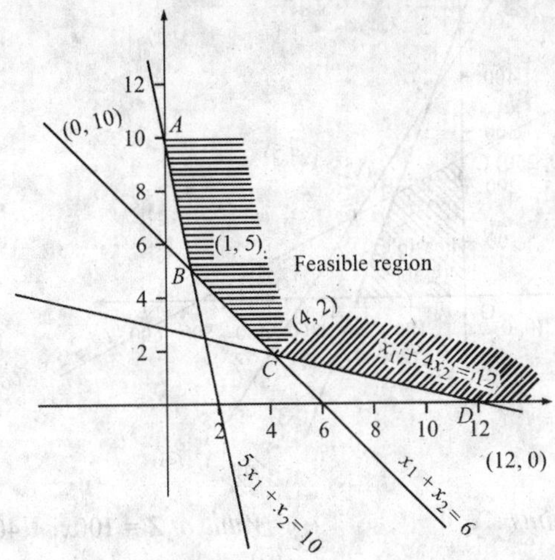

Corner points	*Value of* $Z = 3x_1 + 2x_2$
$A(0, 10)$	20
$B(1, 5)$	13 (Minimum value)
$C(4, 2)$	16
$D(12, 0)$	36

Since the minimum value is attained at B (1, 5) the optimum solution is $x_1 = 1, x_2 = 5$.

Note: In the above problem if the objective function is maximization, then the solution is unbounded, as the maximum value of Z occurs at infinity.

3.1.1 Some More Cases

There are some linear programming problems which may have,

(*i*) a unique optimal solution
(*ii*) an infinite number of optimal solutions
(*iii*) an unbounded solution
(*iv*) no solution.

The following examples will illustrate these cases.

Example 3.7 Solve the LPP by graphical method.

$$\text{Maximize } Z = 100x_1 + 40x_2$$

$$\text{Subject to, } 5x_1 + 2x_2 \leq 1{,}000$$

$$3x_1 + 2x_2 \leq 900$$

$$x_1 + 2x_2 \leq 500$$

and, $$x_1, x_2 \geq 0$$

Solution

The solution space is given by the feasible region *OABC*.

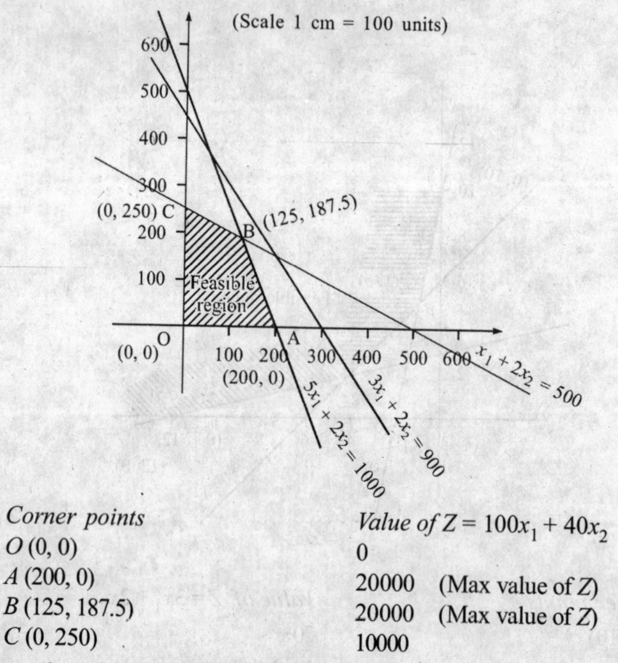

Corner points	*Value of* $Z = 100x_1 + 40x_2$
O (0, 0)	0
A (200, 0)	20000 (Max value of Z)
B (125, 187.5)	20000 (Max value of Z)
C (0, 250)	10000

∴ The maximum value of Z occurs at two vertices A and B.

Since there are infinite number of points on the line joining A and B it gives the same maximum value of Z.

Thus, there are infinite number of optimal solutions for the LPP.

Unbounded Solution

Example 3.8 Solve the following LPP.

$$\text{Max } Z = 3x_1 + 2x_2$$

Subject to,

$$x_1 - x_2 \geq 1$$
$$x_1 + x_2 \geq 3$$
$$x_1, x_2 \geq 0$$

Solution The solution space is unbounded. In fact, the maximum value of Z occurs at infinity. Hence, the problem has an *unbounded solution.*

No feasible solution

When there is no feasible region formed by the constraints in conjunction with non-negativity conditions, then no solution to the LPP exists.

Example 3.9 Solve the following LPP.

$$\text{Max } Z = x_1 + x_2$$

Subject to the constraints,

$$x_1 + x_2 \le 1$$
$$-3x_1 + x_2 \ge 3$$
$$x_1, x_2 \ge 0$$

Solution There being no point (x_1, x_2) common to both the shaded regions, we cannot find a feasible region for this problem. So the problem cannot be solved. Hence, the problem has no solution.

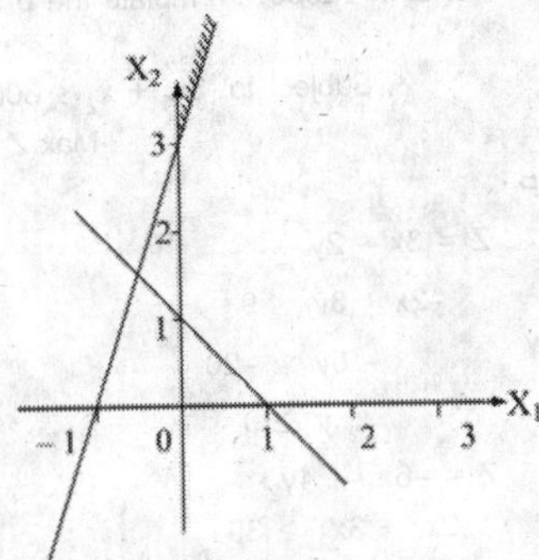

For this problem, no feasible region in found, hence is given as infeasible solution.

EXERCISES

1. Solve the following by graphical method.

Max $Z = x_1 - 3x_2$

Subject to,

$$x_1 + x_2 \le 300$$
$$x_1 - 2x_2 \le 200$$
$$2x_1 + x_2 \le 100$$
$$x_2 \le 200$$
$$x_1, x_2 \ge 0$$

[**Ans.** Max $Z = 205$, $x_1 = 200$, $x_2 = 0$]

2. Max $Z = 5x + 8y$

Subject to,

$$3x + 2y \le 36$$
$$x + 2y \le 20$$
$$3x + 4y \le 42$$
$$x, y \ge 0$$

[**Ans.** Max $Z = 82$, $x = 2$, $y = 9$]

3. Max $Z = x + 3y$

Subject to,

$$x + y \le 300$$
$$x - 2y \le 200$$
$$x + y \le 100$$
$$y \ge 200$$

and, $x, y \ge 0$

[**Ans.** Max $Z = 700$, $x = 200$ $y = 100$]

4. An egg contains 6 units of vitamin *A* and 7 units of vitamin *B* per gram and costs 12 paise per gram. Milk contains 8 units of vitamin *A* and 12 units of vitamin *B* per gram and costs 20 paise per gram. The daily minimum requirement of vitamin *A* and vitamin *B* are 100 units and 120 units respectively. Find the optimal product mix.
[**Ans.** Min $Z = 205$, $x_1 = 15$, $x_2 = 1.25$]

5. Solve graphically the following LPP.

Max $Z = 20x_1 + 10x_2$

Subject to,

$$x_1 + 2x_2 \le 40$$
$$3x_1 + x_2 \ge 30$$
$$4x_1 + 3x_2 \ge 60$$

and, $x_1, x_2 \ge 0$

[**Ans.** Max $Z = 240$, $x_1 = 6$, $x_2 = 12$]

6. A company produces two different products, *A* and *B* and makes a profit of ₹ 40 and ₹ 30 per unit respectively. The production process has a capacity of 30000 man-hours. It takes 3 hours to produce one unit of *A* and one hour to produce one unit of *B*. The market survey indicates that the maximum number of units of product *A* that can be sold is 8000 and those of *B* is 12000. Formulate the problem and solve it by graphical method to get maximum profit.
[**Ans.** Max $Z = 40x_1 + 30x_2$
Subject to, $3x_1 + x_2 \le 30000$; $x_1 \le 8000$; $x_2 \le 12000$; $x_1, x_2 \ge 0$
Max $Z = 600000$, $x_1 = 6000$ and $x_2 = 12000$]

7. Solve graphically the following LPP

Min $Z = 3x - 2y$

Subject to,

$$-2x + 3y \le 9$$
$$x - 5y \ge -20$$
$$x, y \ge 0$$

8. Min $Z = -6x_1 - 4y_2$

Subject to,

$$2x_1 + 3x_2 \ge 30$$
$$3x_1 + 2x_2 \le 24$$
$$x_1 + x_2 \ge 3$$
$$x_1, x_2 \ge 0$$

[**Ans.** Infinite number of solutions with min $Z = -48$
(*i*) $x_1 = 81$, $x_2 = 0$; (*ii*) $x_1 = \frac{12}{5}$, $x_2 = \frac{42}{5}$, etc.]

9. Max $Z = 3x_1 - 2x_2$

Subject to,

$$x_1 + x_2 \le 1$$
$$2x_1 + 2x_2 \ge 4$$
$$x_1, x_2 \ge 0$$

[**Ans.** No feasible region]

10. Max $Z = -x_1 + x_2$

Subject to,

$$x_1 - x_2 \ge 0$$
$$-x_1 + x_2 \ge 3$$
$$x_1, x_2 \ge 0$$

[**Ans.** No feasible region so no solultion]

3.2 GENERAL FORMULATION OF LPP

The general formulation of the LPP can be stated as follows:

Maximize or Minimize

$$Z = C_1x_1 + C_2x_2 + ... + C_nxs_n \quad ... \qquad (1)$$

Subject to m constraints

$$\left.\begin{array}{ll} a_{11}x_1 + a_{12}x_2 + \ldots + a_{1j}x_j + \ldots + a_{1n}x_n & (\le\ =\ \ge)\ b_1 \\ a_{21}x_1 + a_{22}x_2 + \ldots + a_{2j}x_j + \ldots + a_{2n}x_n & (\le\ =\ \ge)\ b_2 \\ \vdots & \\ a_{i1}x_1 + a_{i2}x_2 + \ldots + a_{1j}x_j + \ldots + a_{in}x_n & (\le\ =\ \ge)\ b_i \\ \vdots & \\ a_{m1}x_1 + a_{m2}x_2 + \ldots + a_{mj}x_j + \ldots + a_{mn}x_n & (\le\ =\ \ge)\ b_m \end{array}\right\} \quad (2)$$

In order to find the values of n decision variables $X_1\ X_2 \ldots X_n$ to maximize or minimize the objective function and the non-negativity restrictions

$$x_1 \ge 0, x_2 \ge 0 \ldots x_n \ge 0 \ldots \quad (3)$$

3.3 MATRIX FORM OF LPP

The linear programming problem can be expressed in the matrix form as follows:

Maximize or Minimize $Z = CX$

Subject to $$AX \begin{pmatrix} \le \\ = \\ \ge \end{pmatrix} b$$

$$X \ge 0.$$

where, $x = \begin{pmatrix} x_1 \\ x_2 \\ \vdots \\ x_n \end{pmatrix}$, $b = \begin{pmatrix} b_1 \\ b_2 \\ \vdots \\ b_m \end{pmatrix}$, $C = (C_1\ C_2 \ldots C_n)$

and, $$A = \begin{pmatrix} a_{11} & a_{12} & \cdots & a_{1n} \\ a_{21} & a_{22} & \cdots & a_{2n} \\ \vdots & & & \\ a_{m1} & a_{m2} & \cdots & a_{mn} \end{pmatrix}.$$

SOME IMPORTANT DEFINITIONS

1. A set of values $x_1, x_2 \ldots x_n$ that satisfies the constraints (2) of the LPP is called its *solution.*
2. Any solution to a LPP, which satisfies the non-negativity restrictions (3) of the LPP is called its *feasible solution.*
3. Any feasible solution, which optimizes (minimizes or maximizes) the objective function (1) of the LPP is called its *optimum solution.*
4. Given a system of m linear equations with n variables ($m < n$), any solution that is obtained by solving for m variables keeping the remaining n–m variables zero is called a *basic solution.* Such m variables are called *basic variables* and the remaining are called *non-basic variables.*

   The number of basic solutions $= \le \dfrac{n!}{m!(n-m)!}$

5. A *basic feasible* solution is a basic solution which also satisfies (3), that is all basic variables are non-negative. Basic feasible solutions are of two types:
   (*a*) *Non-degenerate*: A non-degenerate basic feasible solution is the basic feasible solution that has exactly *m* positive x_i (i = 1, 2 ... *m*) i.e., None of the basic variables are zero.
   (*b*) *Degenerate*: A basic feasible solution is said to degenerate if one or more *basic variables* are zero.
6. If the value of the objective function *Z* can be increased or decreased indefinitely, such solutions are called *unbounded solutions.*

3.4 CANONICAL OR STANDARD FORMS OF LPP

The general LPP can be classified as canonical or standard forms.

In *standard form*, irrespective of the objective function, namely, maximize or minimize, all the constraints are expressed as equations. Moreover RHS of each constraint and all variables are non-negative.

3.4.1 Characteristics of the Standard Form

Following are the characteristics of Standard form of LPP.

(*i*) The objective function is of maximization type.
(*ii*) All constraints are expressed as equations.
(*iii*) Right hand side of each constraint is non-negative.
(*iv*) All variables are non-negative.

In *canonical form,* if the objective function is of maximization type, all the constraints other than non-negative conditions are '≤' type. If the objective function is of minimization type, all the constraints other than non-negative condition are '≥' type.

3.4.2 Characteristics of the Canonical Form

Following are the characteristics of Canonical form of LPP.

(*i*) The objective function is of maximization type.
(*ii*) All constraints are of (≤) type.
(*iii*) All variables x_i are non-negative.

Notes:

(*i*) Minimization of a function Z is equivalent to maximization of the negative expression of this function, i.e., Min Z = – Max (– Z)

(*ii*) An inequality in one direction can be converted into an inequality in the opposite direction by multiplying both sides by (–1).

(*iii*) Suppose we have the constraint equation,

$$a_{11} x_1 + a_{12} x_2 + \ldots + a_{1n} x_n = b_1$$

This equation can be replaced by two weak inequalities in opposite directions,

$$a_{11} x_1 + a_{12} x_2 + \ldots + a_{1n} x_n \leq b_1$$

and, $$a_{11} x_1 + a_{12} x_2 + \ldots + a_{1n} x_n \geq b_1$$

(*iv*) If a variable is unrestricted in sign, then it can be expressed as a difference of two non-negative variables, i.e., if x_1 is unrestricted in sign, then $x_1 = x_1' - x_1''$, where x_1', x_1'' are ≥ 0.

(*v*) In standard form, all the constraints are expressed in equation, which is possible by introducing some additional variables called 'slack variables' and 'surplus variables' so that a system of simultaneous linear equations is obtained. The necessary transformation will be made to ensure that $b_i \geq 0$.

DEFINITIONS

(*i*) **Slack Variables:** If the constraints of a general LPP be

$$\sum_{j=1}^{n} a_{ij}x_j \le b_i \quad (i = 1, 2 \ldots m).$$

Then the non-negative variables S_i, which are introduced to convert the inequalities (≤) to the equalities,

$\sum_{j=1}^{n} a_{ij}x_j + S_i = b_i$ $(i = 1, 2 \ldots m)$ are called 'slack variables'.

Slack variables are also defined as the non-negative variables that are added in the LHS of the constraint to convert the inequality '≤' into an equation.

(*ii*) **Surplus Variables:** If the constraints of a general LPP be

$$\sum_{j=1}^{n} a_{ij}x_j \ge b_i \quad (i = 1, 2 \ldots m).$$

Then the non-negative variables S_i, which are introduced to convert the inequalities ≥ to the equalities

$\sum_{j=1}^{n} a_{ij}x_j - S_i = b_i$ $(i = 1, 2 \ldots m)$ are called surplus variables.

Surplus variables are defined as the non-negative variables that are removed from the LHS of the constraint to convert the inequality (≥) into an equation.

□□□

Chapter 4

Simplex Method

4.1 INTRODUCTION

Simplex method is an iterative procedure for solving an LPP in a finite number of steps. It provides an algorithm, which consists of moving from one vertex of the region of feasible solution to another in such a manner that the value of the objective function at the succeeding vertex is less or more, as the case may be, than at the previous vertex. This procedure is repeated and since the number of vertices is finite, the method leads to an optimal vertex in a finite number of steps or indicates the existence of unbounded solution.

4.1.1 Definitions

(*i*) **Cost Vector:** Let X_B be a basic feasible solution to the LPP.

$$\text{Max } Z = CX$$

Subject to, $AX = b$

and, $X \geq 0$. Such that it satisfies $X_B = B^{-1}b$

where B is the basis matrix formed by the column of basic variables.

The vector $C_{Bj} = (C_{B1}, C_{B2} \cdots C_{Bm})$ where C_{Bj} are the components of C associated with the basic variables, called the *cost vector* associated with the basic feasible solution X_B.

(*ii*) **Evaluation:** Let X_B be a basic feasible solution to the LPP.

$$\text{Max } Z = CX \text{ where,}$$
$$AX = b \text{ and } X \geq 0.$$

Let C_B be the cost vector corresponding to X_B. For each column vector a_j in A_1, which is not a column vector of B, let

$$a_j = \sum_{i=1}^{m} a_{ij}\, b_i$$

Then the number $Z_j = \sum_{i=1}^{m} C_{Bi}\, a_{ij}$

is called the *evaluation* corresponding to a_j and the number $(Z_j - C_j)$ is called the *net evaluation* corresponding to j.

4.2 SIMPLEX ALGORITHM

For the solution of any LPP by simplex algorithm, the existence of an initial basic feasible solution is always assumed. Various steps for the computation of an optimum solution are as follows:

Step 1 Check whether the objective function of the given LPP is to be maximized or minimized. If it is to be minimized then we convert it into a problem of maximization by

$$\text{Min } Z = -\text{Max } (-Z)$$

Step 2 Check whether all b_i $(i = 1, 2 \cdots m)$ are positive. If any b_i is negative then multiply the inequation of the constraint by -1 so as to get all b_i to be positive.

Step 3 Express the problem in standard form by introducing slack/surplus variables to convert the inequality constraints into equations.

Step 4 Obtain an initial basic feasible solution to the problem in the form $X_B = B^{-1}b$ and put it in the first column of the simplex table. Form the initial simplex table as given below:

		$C_j = C_1$		C_2	C_3	..	..	0	0	 0
C_B	S_B	x_B	x_1	x_2	x_3	x_4	..... x_n	S_1	S_2	..... S_m
C_{B1}	S_1	b_1	a_{11}	a_{12}	a_{13}	a_{14}	..... a_{1n}	1	0	 0
C_{B2}	S_2	b_2	a_{21}	a_{22}	a_{23}	a_{24}	..... a_{2n}	1	0	 0

Step 5 Compute the net evaluations $Z_j - C_j$ by using the relation $Z_j - C_j = C_B\,(a_j - c_j)$
Examine the sign of $Z_j - C_j$

(*i*) If all $Z_j - C_j \geq 0$, then the initial basic feasible solution x_B is an optimum basic feasible solution.

(*ii*) If at least one $Z_j - C_j < 0$, then proceed to next step as the solution is not optimal.

Step 6 (To find the entering variable, i.e., key column)
If there are more than one negative $Z_j - C_j$, choose the most negative of them. Let it be $Z_r - C_r$ for some $j = r$. This gives the entering variable x_r and is indicated by an arrow at the bottom of the rth column. If there are more than one variables having the same most negative $Z_j - C_j$ then, any one of them can be selected arbitrarily as the entering variable.

(*i*) If all $a_{ir} \leq 0$ $(i = 1, 2 \ldots m)$ then there is an unbounded solution to the given problem.

(*ii*) If at least one $a_{ir} > 0$ $(i = 1, 2 \ldots m)$ then the corresponding vector x_r enters the basis.

Step 7 (To find the leaving variable or key row)
Compute the ratio $(x_{Bi}/a_{ir},\ a_{ir} > 0)$
If the minimum of these ratios be x_{Bi}/a_{kr}, then choose the variable x_k to leave the basis called the *key row* and the element at the intersection of key row and key column is called the *key element.*

Step 8 Form a new basis by dropping the leaving variable and introducing the entering variable along with the associated value under C_B column. Convert the leading element to unity by dividing the key equation by the key element and all other elements in its column to zero by using Gauss Elimination Method on the formula

$$\text{New element} = \text{Old element} - \left[\frac{\text{Product of elements in key row and column}}{\text{Key element}}\right]$$

Step 9 Go to step (5) and repeat the procedure until either an optimum solution is obtained or there is an indication of unbounded solution.

Example 4.1 Use simplex method to solve the LPP.

Max $Z = 3x_1 + 2x_2$

Subject to, $x_1 + x_2 \le 4$

$x_1 - x_2 \le 2$

$x_1, x_2 \ge 0$

Solution By introducing the slack variables S_1, S_2, convert the problem in standard form.

Max $Z = 3x_1 + 2x_2 + 0S_1 + 0S_2$

Subject to, $x_1 + x_2 + S_1 = 4$

$x_1 - x_2 + S_2 = 2$

$x_1, x_2, S_1, S_2 \ge 0$

Writing in martix form $AX = 6$

$$\begin{bmatrix} x_1 & x_2 & S_1 & S_2 \\ 1 & 1 & 1 & 0 \\ 1 & -1 & 0 & 1 \end{bmatrix} \begin{bmatrix} x_1 \\ x_2 \\ S_1 \\ S_2 \end{bmatrix} = \begin{bmatrix} 4 \\ 2 \end{bmatrix}$$

An initial basic feasible solution is given by

$$x_B = B^{-1} b,$$

where, $B = I_2,\ x_B = (S_1\ S_2)$.

i.e., $(S_1\ S_2) = I_2\,(4, 2) = (4, 2)$

Initial simplex table

$$Z_j = C_B\, a_j$$

$$Z_1 - c_1 = C_B\, a_1 - c_1 = \begin{pmatrix} 0 \\ 0 \end{pmatrix} \begin{pmatrix} 1 \\ 1 \end{pmatrix} - 3 = -3$$

$$Z_2 - c_2 = C_B\, a_2 - c_2 = \begin{pmatrix} 0 \\ 0 \end{pmatrix} (1 - 1) - 2 = -2$$

$$Z_3 - c_3 = C_B\, a_3 - c_3 = \begin{pmatrix} 0 \\ 0 \end{pmatrix} (1\,0) - 0 = -0$$

$$Z_4 - c_4 = C_B\, a_4 - c_4 = \begin{pmatrix} 0 \\ 0 \end{pmatrix} (0\,1) - 0 = -0.$$

		C_j	3	2	0	0		
C_B	Basis	x_B	x_1	x_2	S_1	S_2	Min $\frac{x_B}{x_1}$	
0	S_1	4	1	1	1	0	4/1 = 4	←
←0	S_2	2	(1)	–1	0	1	2/1 = 2	
	Z_j	0	0	0	0	0		
	$Z_j - C_j$		–3	–2	0	0		
			↑					

Since there are some $Z_j - C_j < 0$, the current basic feasible solution is not optimum.

Since $Z_1 - C_1 = -3$ is the most negative, the corresponding non-basic variable x_1 enters the basis. The column corresponding to this x_1 is called the *key column*.

$$\text{To find the ratio } = \text{Min}\left\{\frac{x_{Bi}}{x_{ir}}, x_{ir} > 0\right\}$$

$$= \text{Min}\left\{\frac{4}{1}, \frac{2}{1}\right\} = 2, \text{ which corresponds to } S_2.$$

$\therefore$ The leaving variable is the basic variable S_2. This row is called the *key row*. Convert the leading element x_{21} to units and all other elements in its column n i.e. (x_1) to zero by using the formula or Gauss Elimination:

$$\text{New element} = \text{Old element} - \left[\frac{\text{Product of elements in key row and key column}}{\text{Key element}}\right]$$

To apply this formula, first we find the ratio, namely

$$\frac{\text{The element to be zero}}{\text{Key element}} = \frac{1}{1} = 1$$

Apply this ratio for the number of elements that are converted in the key row. Multiply this ratio by key row elements as shown below.

$$1 \times 2$$
$$1 \times 1$$
$$1 \times -1$$
$$1 \times 0$$
$$1 \times 1$$

Now subtract this element from the old element. The element to be converted into zero is called the *old element row*. Finally we have,

$$4 - (1 \times 2) = 2$$
$$1 - (1 \times 1) = 0$$
$$1 - (1 \times -1) = 2$$
$$1 - (1 \times 0) = 1$$
$$0 - (1 \times 1) = -1$$

$\therefore$ The improved basic feasible solution is given in the following simplex table

First iteration

	C_j		3	2	0	0		
C_B	Basis	x_B	x_1	x_2	S_1	S_2	Min $\frac{x_B}{x_2}$	
←0	S_1	2	0	(2)	1	–1	2/2 = 1	←
0	x_1	2	1	–1	0	1	—	
	Z_j	6	3	–3	0	0		
	$Z_j - C_j$		0	–5	0	0		
				↑				

Since $Z_2 - C_2$ is most negative, x_2 enters the basis.

To find $\text{Min}\left(\frac{x_B}{x_{i2}}, x_{i2} > 0\right)$

$$\text{Min}\left(\frac{2}{2}, \frac{2}{-1}\right) = 1. \qquad (\because \text{ negative or zero value are not considered})$$

This gives the outgoing variables. Convert the leading element into one. This is done by dividing all the elements in the key row by 2. The remaining elements should be made zero using the formula as shown below.

$-\frac{1}{2}$ is the common ratio. Put this ratio 5 times and multiply each ratio by key row elements.

$$\left(-\frac{1}{2}\right) \times 2$$
$$\left(-\frac{1}{2}\right) \times 0$$
$$\left(-\frac{1}{2}\right) \times 2$$
$$\left(-\frac{1}{2}\right) \times 1$$
$$\left(-\frac{1}{2}\right) \times -1$$

Subtract this result from the old element. All the row elements that are converted into zero, are called the *old element*.

$$2 - \left(-\frac{1}{2} \times 2\right) = 3$$
$$1 - \left(-\frac{1}{2} \times 0\right) = 1$$
$$-1 - \left(-\frac{1}{2} \times 2\right) = 0$$
$$0 - \left(-\frac{1}{2} \times 1\right) = \frac{1}{2}$$
$$1 - \left(-\frac{1}{2} \times -1\right) = \frac{1}{2}$$

Second iteration

	C_j		3	2	0	0
C_B	***Basis***	x_B	x_1	x_2	S_1	S_2
2	x_2	1	0	1	1/2	–1/2
3	x_1	3	1	0	1/2	1/2
	Z_j	11	3	2	5/2	1/2
	$Z_j - C_j$		0	0	5/2	1/2

Since all $Z_j - C_j \geq 0$, the solution is optimum. The optimal solution is Max $Z = 11$, $x_1 = 3$, and $x_2 = 1$.

Example 4.2 Solve the LPP

$$\text{Max } Z = 3x_1 + 2x_2$$

Subject to,

$$4x_1 + 3x_2 \leq 12$$

$$4x_1 + x_2 \leq 8$$

$$4x_1 - x_2 \leq 8$$

$$x_1, x_2 \geq 0$$

Solution Convert the inequality of the constraint into an equation by adding slack variables S_1, S_2, S_3,.

$$\text{Max } Z = 3x_1 + 2x_2 + 0S_1 + 0S_2 + 0S_3$$

Subject to,

$$4x_1 + 3x_2 + S_1 = 12$$

$$4x_1 + x_2 + S_2 = 8$$

$$4x_1 - x_2 + S_3 = 8$$

$$x_1, x_2, S_1, S_2, S_3 \geq 0$$

$$\begin{bmatrix} x_1 & x_2 & S_1 & S_2 & S_3 \\ 4 & 3 & 1 & 0 & 0 \\ 4 & 1 & 0 & 1 & 0 \\ 4 & -1 & 0 & 0 & 1 \end{bmatrix} \begin{bmatrix} x_1 \\ x_2 \\ S_1 \\ S_2 \\ S_3 \end{bmatrix} = \begin{bmatrix} 12 \\ 8 \\ 8 \end{bmatrix}$$

Initial table

	C_j		3	2	0	0	0	
C_B	*Basis*	x_B	x_1	x_2	S_1	S_2	S_3	$Min \frac{x_B}{x_1}$
0	S_1	12	4	3	1	0	0	12/4 = 3
0	S_2	8	4	1	0	1	0	8/4 = 2
←0	S_3	8	(4)	−1	0	0	1	8/4 = 2
	Z_j	0	0	0	0	0	0	
	$Z_j - C_j$		−3	−2	0	0	0	
			↑					

$\because$ $Z_1 - C_1$ is most negative, x_1 enters the basis. And the min $\left(\frac{x_B}{x_{il}}, x_{il} > 0\right) = \min(3, 2, 2) = 2$ gives S_3 as the leaving variable.

Convert the leading element into 1, by dividing key row element by 4 and the remaining elements into 0.

First iteration

	C_j		3	2	0	0	0	
C_B	*Basis*	x_B	x_1	x_2	S_1	S_2	S_3	*Min* $\frac{x_B}{x_2}$
0	S_1	4	0	4	1	0	–1	4/4 = 1
←0	S_2	0	0	⓶	0	1	–1	0/2 = 0
3	x_1	2	1	–1/4	0	0	¼	—
	Z_j	⑥	3	–3/4	0	0	¾	
	$Z_j - C_j$		0	–11/4 ↑	0	0	¾	

$$8-\left(\frac{4}{4}\times 8\right)=0 \qquad 12-\left(\frac{4}{4}\times 8\right)=4$$

$$4-\left(\frac{4}{4}\times 4\right)=0 \qquad 4-\left(\frac{4}{4}\times 4\right)=0$$

$$1-\left(\frac{4}{4}\times -1\right)=2 \qquad 3-\left(\frac{4}{4}\times -1\right)=4$$

$$0-\left(\frac{4}{4}\times 0\right)=0 \qquad 1-\left(\frac{4}{4}\times 0\right)=1$$

$$1-\left(\frac{4}{4}\times 0\right)=1 \qquad 0-\left(\frac{4}{4}\times 0\right)=0$$

$$0-\left(\frac{4}{4}\times 1\right)=-1 \qquad 0-\left(\frac{4}{4}\times 1\right)=-1$$

Since $Z_2 - C_2 = -\frac{11}{4}$ is the most negative, x_2 enters the basis.

To find the outgoing variable, find $\text{Min}\left(\frac{x_B}{x_{i2}}, x_{i2} > 0\right)$

$$\text{Min}\left(\frac{4}{4}, \frac{0}{2}, -\right) = 0$$

First iteration

Therefore, S_2 leaves the basis. Convert the leading element into 1 by dividing the key row elements by 2 and make the remaining elements in that column as zero using the formula.

$$\text{New element} = \text{Old element} - \left[\frac{\text{Product of elements in key row and key column}}{\text{Key element}}\right]$$

	C_j		3	2	0	0	0	
C_B	*Basis*	x_B	x_1	x_2	S_1	S_2	S_3	*Min* $\frac{x_B}{S_3}$
←0	S_1	4	0	0	1	−2	①	4/1 = 4
2	x_2	0	0	1	0	1/2	−1/2	—
3	x_1	2	1	0	0	1/8	1/8	$\frac{2}{1/18} = 16$
	Z_j	6	3	2	0	11/8	−5/8	
	$Z_j - C_j$		0	0	0	11/8	−5/8	
							↑	

Second iteration

Since $Z_5 - C_5 = -5/8$ is most negative, S_3 enters the basis and

$$\text{Min}\left(\frac{x_B}{S_{13}}, S_{i3}\right) = \text{Min}\left(\frac{4}{1}, 16\right) = 4.$$

Therefore, S_1 leaves the basis. Convert the leading element into one and remaining elements as zero.

Third iteration

	C_j		3	2	0	0	0
C_B	*Basis*	x_B	x_1	x_2	S_1	S_2	S_3
0	S_3	4	0	0	1	−2	1
2	x_2	2	0	1	1/2	−1/2	0
3	x_1	3/2	1	0	−1/8	3/8	0
	Z_j	17/2	3	2	5/8	1/8	0
	$Z_j - C_j$		0	0	5/8	1/8	0

Since all $Z_j - C_j \geq 0$, the solution is optimum and it is given by $x_1 = 3/2$, $x_2 = 2$ and Max $Z = 17/2$.

Example 4.3 Using simplex method solve the LPP.

$$\text{Max } Z = x_1 + x_2 + 3x_3$$

Subject to,

$$3x_1 + 2x_2 + x_3 \leq 3$$

$$2x_1 + x_2 + 2x_3 \leq 2$$

$$x_1, x_2, x_3 \geq 0$$

Solution Rewrite the inequality of the constraints into an equation by adding slack variables.

$$\text{Max } Z = x_1 + x_2 + 3x_3 + 0S_1 + 0S_2$$

Subject to,

$$3x_1 + 2x_2 + x_3 + S_1 \leq 3$$

$$2x_1 + x_2 + 2x_3 + S_2 \leq 2$$

Initial basic feasible solution is,

$$x_1 = x_2 = x_3 = 0$$

$$S_1 = 3, S_2 = 2 \text{ and } Z = 0$$

$$\begin{bmatrix} x_1 & x_2 & x_3 & S_1 & S_2 \\ 3 & 2 & 1 & 1 & 0 \\ 2 & 1 & 2 & 0 & 1 \\ 1 & 1 & 3 & 0 & 0 \end{bmatrix}$$

	C_j		1	1	3	0	0	
C_B	Basis	x_B	x_1	x_2	x_3	S_1	S_2	Min $\frac{x_B}{x_3}$
0	S_1	3	3	2	1	1	0	3/1 = 3
←0	S_2	2	2	1	(2)	0	1	2/2 = 1
	Z_j	0	0	0	0	0	0	
	$Z_j - C_j$		–1	–1	–3 ↑	0	0	

Since $Z_3 - C_3 = -3$ is the most negative, the variable x_3 enters the basis. The column corresponding to x_3 is called the *key column.*

To determine the key row or leaving variable, find $\text{Min}\left(\frac{x_B}{x_{i3}}, x_{i3} > 0\right)$ $\text{Min}\left(\frac{3}{1}, \frac{2}{2}\right) = 1$

Therefore, the leaving variable is the basic variable S_2, the row is called the *key row* and the intersection element 2 is called the *key element.*

Convert this element into one by dividing each element in the key row by 2 and the remaining elements in that key column as zero using the formula

$$\text{New element} = \text{Old element} - \left[\frac{\text{Product of elements in key row and key column}}{\text{Key element}}\right]$$

First iteration

	C_j		1	1	3	0	0
C_B	Basis	x_B	x_1	x_2	x_3	S_1	S_2
0	S_1	2	2	3/2	0	1	–1/2
3	x_3	1	1	1/2	1	0	1/2
	Z_j	3	3	3/2	3	0	3/2
	$Z_j - C_j$		2	1/2	0	0	3/2

Since all $Z_j - C_j \geq 0$, the solution is optimum and it is given by $x_1 = 0, x_2 = 0, x_3 = 1$, Max $Z = 3$.

Example 4.4 Use simplex method to solve the LPP.

$$\text{Min } Z = x_2 - 3x_3 + 2x_5$$

Subject to,

$$3x_2 - x_3 + 2x_5 \leq 7$$
$$-2x_2 + 4x_3 \leq 12$$

$$-4x_2+3x_3+8x_5 \le 10$$

$$x_2, x_3, x_5 \ge 0$$

Solution Since the given objective function is of minimization, we shall convert it into maximization using Min Z = –Max(–Z) = –Max Z^*

$$\text{Max } Z^* = -x_2+3x_3-2x_5$$

Subject to,
$$3x_2 - x_3 + 2x_5 \le 7$$
$$-2x_2+4x_3 \le 12$$
$$-4x_2+3x_3+8x_5 \le 10$$

We rewrite the inequality of the constraints into an equation by adding slack variables S_1, S_2, S_3 and the standard form of LPP becomes.

$$\text{Max } Z = -x_2+3x_3-2x_5+0S_1+0S_2+0S_3$$

Subject to,
$$3x_2 - x_3 + 2x_5 + S_1 = 7$$
$$-2x_2+4x_3+S_2 = 12$$
$$-4x_2+3x_3+8x_5+S_3 = 10$$
$$x_2, x_3, x_5, S_1, S_2, S_3 \ge 0$$

∴ The initial basic feasible solution is given by $S_1 = 7$, $S_2 = 12$, $S_3 = 10$. ($x_2 = x_3 = x_5 = 0$)

Initial table

		C_j	–1	3	–2	0	0	0	
C_B	Basis	x_B	x_2	x_3	x_5	S_1	S_2	S_3	Min $\frac{x_B}{x_3}$
0	S_1	7	3	–1	2	1	0	0	—
←0	S_2	12	–2	(4)	0	0	1	0	12/4 = 3
0	S_3	10	–4	3	8	0	0	1	10/3 = 3.33
	Z_j	0	0	0	0	0	0		
	$Z_j - C_j$		1	–3	2	0	0	0	
				↑					

Since $Z_2 - C_2 = -3 < 0$, the solution is not optimum.

The incoming variable is x_3 (key column) and the outgoing variable (key row) is given by,

$$\text{Min}\left(\frac{x_B}{x_{i3}}\ x_{i3} > 0\right) = \text{Min}\left(-, \frac{12}{4}, \frac{10}{3}\right) = 3.$$

Hence, S_2 leaves the basis.

First iteration

		C_j	−1	3	−2	0	0	0	
C_B	B	x_B	x_2	x_3	x_5	S_1	S_2	S_3	$Min\ \frac{x_B}{x_2}$
←0	S_1	10	(5/2)	0	2	1	1/4	0	$\frac{10}{5/2}=4$
3	x_3	3	−1/2	1	0	0	1/4	0	—
0	S_3	1	5/2	0	8	0	−3/4	1	2/5
	Z_j	9	−3/2	3	0	0	3/4	0	
	$Z_j - C_j$		−1/2	0	2	0	3/4	0	
			↑						

Since $Z_1 - C_1 < 0$, the solution is not optimum. Improve the solution by allowing the variable x_2 to enter into the basis and the variable S_1 to leave the basis.

Second iteration

		C_j	−1	3	−2	0	0	0
C_B	B	x_B	x_2	x_3	x_5	S_1	S_2	S_3
−1	x_2	4	1	0	4/5	2/5	1/10	0
3	x_3	5	0	1	2/5	1/5	3/10	0
0	S_3	11	0	0	10	1	− 1/2	1
	Zj	11	− 1	3	2/5	1/5	8/10	0
	$Z_j - C_j$		0	0	12/5	1/5	8/10	0

Since all $Z_j - C_j \geq 0$, the solution is optimum.

∴ The optimal solution is given by Max $Z^* = 11$

$$x_2 = 4, x_3 = 5, x_5 = 0$$

∴ $\text{Min } Z = -\text{Max }(-Z) = -11$

∴ $\text{Min } Z = -11, x_2 = 4, x_3 = 5, x_5 = 0.$

Example 4.5 Solve the following LPP using simplex method.

Max $Z = 15x_1 + 6x_2 + 9x_3 + 2x_4$

Subject to,
$$2x_1 + x_2 + 5x_3 + 6x_4 \leq 20$$
$$3x_1 + x_2 + 3x_3 + 25x_4 \leq 24$$
$$7x_1 + x_4 \leq 70$$
$$x_1, x_2, x_3, x_4 \geq 0$$

Solution Rewriting the inequality of the constraint into an equation by adding slack variables S_1, S_2 and S_3, the standard form of LPP becomes.

Max $Z = 15x_1 + 6x_2 + 9x_3 + 2x_4 + 0S_1 + 0S_2 + 0S_3$

Subject to,
$$2x_1 + x_2 + 5x_3 + 6x_4 + S_1 = 20$$

$$3x_1 + x_2 + 3x_3 + 25x_4 + S_2 = 24$$
$$7x_1 + x_4 + S_3 = 70$$
$$x_1, x_2, x_3, x_4, S_1, S_2, S_3 \geq 0$$

The initial basic feasible solution is $S_1 = 20$, $S_2 = 24$, $S_3 = 70$ ($x_1 = x_2 = x_3 = x_4 = 0$ non-basic)

The initial simplex table is given by

	C_j		15	6	9	2	0	0	0	
C_B	Basis	x_B	x_1	x_2	x_3	x_4	S_1	S_2	S_3	$Min\ \frac{x_B}{x_1}$
0	S_1	20	2	1	5	6	1	0	0	20/2 = 10
←0	S_2	24	(3)	1	3	25	0	1	0	24/3 = 8←
0	S_3	70	7	0	0	1	0	0	1	70/7 = 10
	Z_j	0	0	0	0	0	0	0	0	
	$Z_j - C_j$		–15	–6	–9	–2	0	0	0	
			↑							

∴ As some of $Z_j - C_j \leq 0$ the current basic feasible solution is not optimum. $Z_1 - C_1 = -15$ is the most negative value and hence x_1 enters the basis and the variable S_2 leaves the basis.

First iteration

	C_j		15	6	9	2	0	0	0	
C_B	Basis	x_B	x_1	x_2	x_3	x_4	S_1	S_2	S_3	$Min\ \frac{x_B}{x_2}$
←0	S_1	4	0	(1/3)	3	– 32/3	1	– 2/3	0	$\frac{4}{1/3} = 12$
15	x_1	8	1	1/3	1	25/3	0	1/3	0	$\frac{8}{1/3} = 24$
0	S_3	14	0	– 7/3	– 7	– 172/3	0	– 7/3	1	—
	Z_j	120	15	5	15	125	0	5	0	
	$Z_j - C_j$		0	– 1	6	123	0	5	0	
				↑						

Since $Z_2 - C_2 = -1 < 0$ the solution is not optimal therefore, x_2 enters the basis and the basic variable S_1 leaves the basis.

Second iteration

	C_j		–5	6	9	–2	0	0	0
C_B	B	x_B	x_1	x_2	x_3	x_4	S_1	S_2	S_3
6	x_2	12	0	1	9	–32	3	–2	0
15	x_1	4	1	0	–2	57/3	–1	1	0
0	S_3	42	0	0	14	–132	7	–7	1
	Z_j	132	15	6	24	93	3	3	0
	$Z_j - C_j$		0	0	15	91	3	3	0

Since all $Z_j - C_j \geq 0$, the solution is optimal and is given by,

$$\text{Max Z} = 132, x_1 = 4, x_2 = 12, x_3 = 0, x_4 = 0.$$

Example 4.6

Max $Z = 3x_1 + 2x_2 + 5x_3$

Subject to
$$x_1 + 2x_2 + x_3 \leq 430$$
$$3x_1 + 2x_3 \leq 260$$
$$x_1 + 4x_2 \leq 420$$
$$x_1, x_2, x_3 \geq 0$$

Solution Rewrite the constraint into equation by adding slack variables S_1, S_2, S_3. The standard form of LPP becomes

Max $Z = 3x_1 + 2x_2 + 5x_3 + 0S_1 + 0S_2 + 0S_3$

Subject to,
$$x_1 + 2x_2 + x_3 + S_1 = 430$$
$$3x_1 + 2x_3 + S_2 = 460$$
$$x_1 + 4x_2 + S_3 = 420$$
$$x_1, x_2, x_3, S_1, S_2, S_3 \geq 0.$$

The initial basic feasible solution is,

$$S_1 = 430, S_2 = 460, S_3 = 420 \; (x_1 = x_2 = x_3 = 0)$$

Initial table

	C_j		3	2	5	0	0	0	
C_B	B	x_B	x_1	x_2	x_3	S_1	S_2	S_3	Min $\frac{x_B}{x_3}$
0	S_1	430	1	2	1	1	0	0	430/1 = 430
←0	S_2	460	3	0	(2)	0	1	0	460/2 = 230
0	S_3	420	1	4	0	0	0	1	
	Z_j	0	0	0	0	0	0	0	
	$Z_j - C_j$		−3	−2	−5	0	0	0	
					↑				

Since some of $Z_j - C_j \leq 0$, the current basic feasible solution is not optimum. Since $Z_3 - C_3 = -5$ is the most negative, the variable x_3 enters the basis. To find the variable leaving the basis find,

$$\text{Min}\left(\frac{x_B}{x_{i3}}, x_{i3} > 0\right) = \text{Min}\left(\frac{430}{1}, \frac{460}{2}, -\right) = 230.$$

$\therefore$ the variable S_2 leaves the basis.

First iteration

	C_j		3	2	5	0	0	0	
C_B	B	x_B	x_1	x_2	x_3	S_1	S_2	S_3	$Min \frac{x_B}{x_2}$
←0	S_1	200	–1/2	(2)	0	1	1/2	0	200/2 = 100
5	x_3	230	3/2	0	1	0	1/2	0	—
0	S_3	420	1	4	0	0	0	1	420/4 = 105
	Z_j	1150	15/2	0	5	0	5/2	0	
	$Z_j - C_j$		9/2	–2	0	0	5/2	0	
				↑					

Since $Z_2 - C_2 = -2$ is negative, the current basic feasible solution is not optimum. Therefore, the variable x_2 enters the basis and the variable S_1 leaves the basis.

Second iteration

	C_j		3	2	5	0	0	0
C_B	B	x_B	x_1	x_2	x_3	S_1	S_2	S_3
2	x_2	100	–1/4	1	0	1/2	–1/4	0
5	x_3	230	3/2	0	1	0	1/2	0
0	S_3	20	2	0	0	–2	1	1
	Z_j	1350	7	2	5	1	+2	0
	$Z_j - C_j$		4	0	0	1	2	0

Since all $Z_j - C_j \geq 0$, the solution is optimum and is given by $x_1 = 0, x_2 = 100, x_3 = 230$ and Max $Z = 1350$.

EXERCISES

1. Using the simplex method, find non-negative values of x_1, x_2 and x_3, which Maximize $Z = x_1 + 4x_2 + 5x_3$

   Subject to the constraints,

   $3x_1 + 6x_2 + 3x_3 \leq 22$

   $x_1 + 2x_2 + 3x_3 \leq 14$

   and, $3x_1 + 2x_2 \leq 14$

   [**Ans.** Max $Z = 650$, $x_1 = 0$, $x_2 = 100$, $x_3 = 50$]

2. Maximize $Z = x_1 + x_2 + 3x_3$

   Subject to, $3x_1 + 2x_2 + x_3 \leq 2$

   $2x_1 + x_2 + 2x_3 \leq 2$

   $x_1, x_2, x_3 \geq 0$

   [**Ans.** Max $Z = 3$, $x_1 = x_2 = 0$, $x_3 = 1$]

3. Max $Z = 10x_1 + 6x_2$

   Subject to, $x_1 + x_2 \le 2$

   $2x_1 + x_2 \le 4$

   $3x_1 + 8x_2 \le 12$

   $x_1, x_2 \ge 0$ **[Ans.** Max $Z = 20$, $x_1 = 2$, $x_2 = 0$]

4. Max $Z = 30x_1 + 23x_2 + 29x_3$

   Subject to the constraints,

   $6x_1 + 5x_2 + 3x_3 \le 52$

   $6x_1 + 2x_2 + 5x_3 \le 14$

   $x_1; x_2, x_3 \ge 0$ **[Ans.** Max $Z = 161$, $x_1 = 0$, $x_2 \Rightarrow x_3 = 0$]

5. Max $Z = x_1 + 2x_2 + x_3$

   Subject to, $2x_1 + x_2 - x_3 \ge -2$

   $-2x_1 + x_2 - 5x_3 \le 6$

   $4x_1 + x_2 + x_3 \le 6$

   $x_1, x_2, x_3 \ge 6$ **[Ans.** Max $Z = 10$, $x_1 = 0$. $x_2 = 4$, $x_3 = 2$]

6. A manufacturer is engaged in producing 2 products x and y, the contribution margin being ₹ 15 and ₹ 45 respectively. A unit of product x requires 1 unit of facility A and 0.5 unit of facility B. A unit of product y requires 1.6 units of facility A, 2.0 units of facility B and 1 unit of raw material C. The availability of total facility A, B and raw material C during a particular time period are 240, 162 and 50 units respectively.

   Using the simplex method find out the product mix that will maximize the contribution margin.

   [Ans. Max $Z = 15x_1 + 45x_2$; Subject to, $x_1 + 1.6x_2 \le 240$; $0.5x_1 + 2x_2 \le 162$; $x_2 \le 50$; $x_1, x_2 \ge 0$. Also, Max $Z =$ ₹ 1815, $x_1 = 18.4$, $x_2 = 35$]

7. A firm has availability of 240, 370 and 180 kg of wood, plastic and steel respectively. The firm produces two products A and B. Each unit of A requires 1, 3 and 2 kg of wood, plastic and steel respectively. The corresponding requirements for each unit of B are 3, 4 and 1 respectively. If A is sold for ₹ 4, and B for ₹ 6, determine how many units of A and B should be produced in order to obtain the maximum gross income. Use the simplex method.

   [Ans. Max $Z = 4x_1 + 6x_2$; Subject to, $x_1 + 3x_2 \le 240$; $3x_1 + 4x_2 \le 370$; $2x_1 + x_2 \le 180$; $x_1, x_2 \ge 0$. Max $Z = 540$, $x_1 = 30$, $x_2 = 70$]

Chapter

5 Artificial Variables Technique

5.1 INTRODUCTION

The LPPs in which constraints may also have ≥ and = signs after ensuring that all $b_i \geq 0$ are considered in this section. In such cases basis matrix cannot be obtained as an identity matrix in the starting simplex table, therefore we introduce a new type of variable called the *artificial variable.* These variables are fictitious and cannot have any physical meaning. The artificial variable technique is merely a device to get the starting basic feasible solution, so that the simplex procedure may be adopted as usual until the optimal solution is obtained. To solve such LPPs there are two methods.

(*i*) The Charne's Big-*M* Method or Method of Penalties.

(*ii*) The Two-Phase Simplex Method.

5.2 THE CHARNE'S BIG-*M* METHOD

The following steps are involved in solving an LPP using the Big-*M* method.

Step 1 Express the problem in the standard form.

Step 2 Add non-negative artificial variables to the left side of each of the equations corresponding to constraints of the type ≥ or =. However, addition of these artificial variables causes violation of the corresponding constraints. Therefore, we would like to get rid of these variables and would not allow them to appear in the final solution. This is achieved by assigning a very large penalty (–*M* for maximization and *M* for minimization) in the objective function.

Step 3 Solve the modified LPP by simplex method, until any one of the three cases may arise.

(i) If no artificial variable appears in the basis and the optimality conditions are satisfied, then the current solution is an optimal basic feasible solution.

(ii) If at least one artificial variable is there in the basis at zero level and the optimality condition is satisfied, then the current solution is an optimal basic feasible solution (though degenerated).

(iii) If at least one artificial variable appears in the basis at positive level and the optimality condition is satisfied, then the original problem has no feasible solution. The solution satisfies the constraints but does not optimize the objective function, since it contains a very large penalty *M* and is called *pseudo optimal solution.*

Note: While applying simplex method, whenever an artificial variable happens to leave the basis, we drop that artificial variable and omit all the entries corresponding to its column from the simplex table.

Example 5.1 Use penalty method to

Maximize $Z = 3x_1 + 2x_2$

Subject to the constraints,

$$2x_1 + x_2 \le 2$$
$$3x_1 + 4x_2 \ge 12$$
$$x_1, x_2 \ge 0$$

Solution By introducing slack variable $S_1 \ge 0$, surplus variable $S_2 \ge 0$ and artificial variable $A_1 \ge 0$, the given LPP can be reformulated as:

Maximize $Z = 3x_1 + 2x_2 + 0S_1 + 0S_2 - MA_1$

Subject to, $2x_1 + x_2 + S_1 = 2$

$$3x_1 + 4x_2 - S_2 + A_1 = 12$$

The starting feasible solution is $S_1 = 2$, $A_1 = 12$.

Initial table

	C_j		3	2	0	0	$-M$	
C_B	B	x_B	x_1	x_2	S_1	S_2	A_1	$\frac{x_B}{x_2}$
$\leftarrow 0$	S_1	2	2	(1)	1	0	0	2/1 = 2
$-M$	A_1	12	3	4	0	–1	1	12/4 = 3
	Z_j	$-12M$	$-3M$	$-4M$	0	M	$-M$	
	$Z_j - C_j$	–	$-3M - 3$	$-4M - 2$	0	M	0	
				↑				

Since some of the $Z_j - C_j \le 0$, the current feasible solution is not optimum. Choose the most negative $Z_j - C_j = -4M - 2$.

$\therefore$ x_2 variable enters the basis, and the basic variable S_1 leaves the basis.

First iteration

	C_j		3	2	0	0	$-M$
C_B	B	x_B	x_1	x_2	S_1	S_2	A_1
2	x_2	2	2	1	1	0	0
$-M$	A_1	4	–5	0	–4	–1	1
	Z_j	$4 - 4M$	$4 + 5M$	2	$2 + 4M$	M	$-M$
	$Z_j - C_j$		$5M + 1$	0	$4M + 2$	M	0

Since all $Z_j - C_j \ge 0$ and an artificial variable appears in the basis at positive level, the given LPP does not possess any feasible solution. But the LPP possesses a *pseudo optimal solution.*

Example 5.2 Solve the LPP.

Minimize $Z = 4x_1 + x_2$

Subject to,

$$3x_1 + x_2 = 3$$
$$4x_1 + 3x_2 \geq 6$$
$$x_1 + 2x_2 \leq 4$$
$$x_1, x_2 \geq 0$$

Solution Since the objective function is minimization, we covert it into maximization using,

Min $Z = -\text{Max}(-z) = -\text{Max } z^*$ $(\because \quad Z^* = -Z)$

Maximize $z^* = -4x_1 - x_2$

Subject to,

$$3x_1 + x_2 = 3$$
$$4x_1 + 3x_2 \geq 6$$
$$x_1 + 2x_2 \leq 4$$
$$x_1, x_2 \geq 0$$

Convert the given LPP into standard form by adding artificial variables A_1, A_2, surplus variable S_1 and slack variable S_2 to get the initial basic feasible solution.

Minimize $Z^* = -4x_1 - x_2 + 0S_1 + 0S_2 - MA_1 - MA_2$

Subject to,

$$3x_1 + x_2 + A_1 = 3$$
$$4x_1 + 3x_2 - S_1 + A_2 = 6$$
$$x_1 + 2x_2 + S_2 = 4$$
$$x_1, x_2, s_1, s_2, A_1, A_2 \geq 0$$

The starting feasible solution is $A_1 = 3$, $A_2 = 6$, $S_2 = 4$.

Initial solution

		C_j	-4	-1	$-M$	0	$-M$	0	
C_B	B	x_B	x_1	x_2	A_1	S_1	A_2	S_2	Min $\frac{x_B}{x_1}$
$-M$	A_1	3	(3)	1	1	0	0	0	3/3 = 1
$-M$	A_2	6	4	3	0	-1	1	0	6/4 = 3/2
$\leftarrow 0$	S_2	4	1	(2)	0	0	0	1	4/1 = 4
	Z_j	$-9M$	$-7M$	$-4M$	$-M$	$-M$	M	$-M$	
	$Z_j - C_j$		$-7M + 4\uparrow$	$-4M + 1$	0	$-M$	$2M$	$-M$	

Since some of the $Z_j - C_j \leq 0$, the current feasible solution is not optimum. As $Z_1 - C_1$ is most negative, x_1 enters the basis and the basic variable A_1 leaves the basis.

First iteration

		C_j	−4	−1	−M	0	−M	0	
C_B	B	x_B	x_1	x_2	A_1	S_1	A_2	S_2	Min $\frac{x_B}{x_1}$
−M	A_1	3/2	5/2	0	1	0	0	−1/2	3/5
← −M	A_2	3/2	(5/2)	0	0	−1	1	−3/2	3/5
−1	x_2	3/2	1/2	1	0	0	0	1/2	3
	Z_j	−3M − 3/2	−5M − 1/2	−1	−M	+M	−M	2M − 1/2	
	$Z_j - C_j$		−5M + 7/2	0	0	M	0	2M − 1/2	
			↑						

Since $Z_1 - C_1$ is negative, the current feasible solution is not optimum. Therefore, x_1 variable enters the basis and the artificial variable A_2 leaves the basis.

Second iteration

		C_j	−4	−1	−M	0	0	
C_B	B	x_B	x_1	x_2	A_1	S_1	S_2	Min $\frac{x_B}{x_2}$
← −M	A_1	0	0	0	(1)	1	1	0
−4	x_1	3/5	1	0	0	−2/5	−3/5	—
−1	x_2	6/5	0	1	0	−1/5	4/5	6/5
	Z_j	−18/5	−4	−1	−M	−M +9/5	−M +8/5	
	$Z_j - C_j$		0	0	0	−M +9/5	−M +8/5	
					↑			

Since $Z_4 - C_4$ is most negative, S_1 enters the basis and the artificial variable A_1 leaves the basis.

Third iteration

		C_j	−4	−1	0	0	
C_B	B	x_B	x_1	x_2	S_1	S_2	Min $\frac{x_B}{x_2}$
← 0	S_1	0	0	0	1	(1)	0
−4	x_1	3/5	1	0	0	−1/5	—
−1	x_2	6/5	0	1	0	1	6/5
	Z_j	−18/5	−4	−1	0	−1/5	
	$Z_j - C_j$		0	0	0	−1/5	
						↑	

Since $Z_4 - C_4$ is most negative, S_2 enters the basis and S_1 leaves the basis.

Fourth iteration

	C_j		−4	−1	0	0
C_B	B	x_B	x_1	x_2	S_1	S_2
0	S_2	0	0	0	1	1
−4	x_1	3/5	1	0	1/5	0
−1	x_2	6/5	0	1	−1	0
	Z_j	−18/5	−4	−1	1/5	0
	$Z_j - C_j$		0	0	1/5	0

Since all $Z_j - C_j \geq 0$, the solution is optimum and is given by $x_1 = 3/5$, $x_2 = 6/5$, and Max $Z = -18/5$

$\therefore$ Min $Z = -$ Max $(-Z) = 18/5$.

Example 5.3 Solve by Big M method.

Maximize $Z = x_1 + 2x_2 + 3x_3 - x_4$

Subject to,

$$x_1 + 2x_2 + 3x_3 = 15$$
$$2x_1 + x_2 + 5x_3 = 20$$
$$x_1 + 2x_2 + x_3 + x_4 = 10$$

Solution Since the constraints are equations, introduce artificial variables $A_1, A_2 \geq 0$. The reformulated problem is given as follows.

Maximize $Z = x_1 + 2x_2 + 3x_3 - x_4 - MA_1 - MA_2$

Subject to,

$$x_1 + 2x_2 + 3x_3 + A_1 = 15$$
$$2x_1 + x_2 + 5x_3 + A_2 = 20$$
$$x_1 + 2x_2 + x_3 + x_4 = 10$$

Initial solution is given by $A_1 = 15$, $A_2 = 20$ and $x_4 = 10$.

	C_j		1	2	3	−1	−M	−M	
C_B	B	x_B	x_1	x_2	x_3	x_4	A_1	A_2	Min $\frac{x_B}{x_3}$
−M	A_1	15	1	2	3	0	1	0	15/3 = 5
← −M	A_2	20	2	1	(5)	0	0	1	20/5 = 4 ←
−1	x_4	10	1	2	1	1	0	0	10/1 = 10
	Z_j	−35M −10	−3M − 1	−3M − 2	−8M − 1	−1	−M	−M	
	$Z_j - C_j$		−3M − 2	−3M − 4	−8M − 4 ↑	0	0	0	

Since $Z_3 - C_3$ is most negative, x_3 enters the basis and the basic variable A_2 leaves the basis.

First iteration

	C_j		1	2	3	−1	−M	
C_B	B	x_B	x_1	x_2	x_3	x_4	A_1	$Min \frac{x_B}{x_2}$
← −M	A_1	3	−1/5	(7/5)	0	0	1	$\frac{3}{7/5} = \frac{15}{7}$
3	x_3	4	2/5	1/5	1	0	0	$\frac{4}{1/5} = \frac{20}{1}$
−1	x_4	6	3/5	9/5	0	1	0	$\frac{6}{9/5} = \frac{30}{9}$
	Z_j	$-3M+6$	$\frac{1}{5}M+\frac{3}{5}$	$-\frac{7}{5}M-\frac{6}{5}$	3	−1	−M	
	$Z_j - C_j$		$\frac{1}{5}M-\frac{2}{5}$	$-\frac{7}{5}M-\frac{16}{5}$	0	0	0	
				↑				

Since $Z_2 - C_2$ is most negative, x_2 enters the basis and the basic variable A_1 leaves the basis.

Second iteration

	C_j		1	2	3	−1	
C_B	B	x_B	x_1	x_2	x_3	x_4	$Min \frac{x_B}{x_1}$
2	x_2	15/7	$-\frac{1}{7}$	1	0	0	—
3	x_3	25/7	3/7	0	1	0	25/3
← −1	x_4	15/7	($\frac{6}{7}$)	0	0	1	15/6
	Z_j	$\frac{90}{7}$	$\frac{1}{7}$	2	3	−1	
	$Z_j - C_j$		−6/7	0	0	0	
			↑				

Since $Z_1 - C_1 = -6/7$ is negative, the current feasible solution is not optimum. Therefore, x_1 enters the basis and the basic variable x_4 leaves the basis.

Third iteration

		C_j	1	2	3	−1
C_B	B	x_B	x_1	x_2	x_3	x_4
2	x_2	15/6	0	1	0	1/6
3	x_3	15/6	0	0	1	3/6
3	x_1	15/6	1	0	0	7/6
	Z_j	15	1	2	3	3
	$Z_j - C_j$		0	0	0	4

Since all $Z_j - C_j \geq 0$, the solution is optimum and is given by $x_1 = x_2 = x_3 = 15/6 = 5/2$, and Max $Z = 15$.

Example 5.4 Use penalty method to solve the following LPP:

Minimize $Z = 5x + 3y$

Subject to,

$$2x + 4y \leq 12$$
$$2x + 2y = 10$$
$$5x + 2y \geq 10$$
$$x, y \geq 0$$

Solution First we convert the objective function from minimization to maximization using

Min $Z = -\text{Max}(-Z)$.

Rewrite the given LPP into standard form by adding slack variable $S_1 \geq 0$, surplus variable $S_2 \geq 0$ and the artificial variables $A_1, A_2 \geq 0$.

Maximize $Z = -5x - 3y + 0S_1 + 0S_2 - MA_1 - MA_2$

Subject to,

$$2x + 4y + S_1 = 12$$
$$2x + 2y + A_1 = 10$$
$$5x + 2y - S_2 + A_2 = 10$$
$$x, y, S_1, S_2, A_1, A_2 \geq 0$$

Initial feasible solution is given by $S_1 = 12$, $A_1 = 10$ and $A_2 = 10$

Since all $Z_j - C_j \geq 0$ (see Table 5.1) and no artificial variable is in the basis, the solution is optimum and is given by:

$x = 4, y = 1$, Max $Z = -23$

Min $Z = -\text{Max}(-Z) = 23$

Table 5.1

		C_j	-5	-3	0	$-M$	0	$-M$	
C_B	B	x_B	x	y	S_1	A_1	S_2	A_2	$Min \frac{x_B}{x}$
0	S_1	12	2	4	1	0	0	0	12/2 = 6
$-M$	A_1	10	2	2	0	1	0	0	10/2 = 5
← $-M$	A_2	10	(5)	2	0	0	-1	1	10/5 = 2
	Z_j	$20M$	$-7M$	$-4M$	0	$-M$	M	$-M$	
	$Z_j - C_j$		$-7M + 5$↑	$-4M + 3$	0	0	M	0	
									$Min \frac{x_B}{y}$
← 0	S_1	8	0	(16/5)	1	0	2/5		$\frac{8 \times 5}{16} = 5/2$
$-M$	A_1	6	0	6/5	0	1	2/5	—	30/6 = 5
-5	x	2	1	2/5	0	0	$-1/5$	—	10/2 = 5
				↑					

	C_j		-5	-3	0	$-M$	0	$-M$	
C_B	B	x_B	x	y	S_1	A_1	S_2	A_2	$Min \frac{x_B}{x}$
	Z_j	$-6M-10$	-5	$-6/5\,M-2$	0	$-M$	$-2/5\,M+1$	—	
	$Z_j - C_j$		0	$-6/5\,M+1\uparrow$	0	0	$-\frac{2}{5}M+1$		
									$Min \frac{x_B}{S_2}$
-3	y	$5/2$	0	1	$5/16$	0	$1/8$	—	20
$\leftarrow -M$	A_1	3	0	0	$-3/8$	1	$-1/4$	—	12
-5	x	1	1	0	$-1/8$	0	$-1/4$	—	—
	Z_j	$-3M-25/2$	-5	-3	$-3/8M$ $-5/16$	$-M$ 0	$+7/8$ $-1/4M$	—	
—	$Z_j - C_j$		0	0	$3/8M$ $-5/16$	0	$7/8$ $-M/4\uparrow$	—	
-3	y	1	0	1	$1/2$	—	0	—	
0	S_2	12	0	0	$-3/2$	—	1	—	
-5	x	4	1	0	$-1/2$	—	0	—	
	Z_j	-23	5	-3	1		0		
	$Z_j - C_j$		0		1		0	—	

EXERCISES

Use penalty method to solve the following LPP

1. Minimize $\quad Z = 12x_1 + 20x_2$

   Subject to,
   $$6x_1 + 8x_2 \geq 100$$
   $$7x_1 + 12x_2 \geq 120$$
   $$x_1, x_2 \geq 0$$
   [**Ans.** $x_1 = 15$, $x_2 = 5/4$ and Min $Z = 205$]

2. Maximize $\quad Z = 2x_1 + x_2 + 3x_3$

   Subject to,
   $$x_1 + x_2 + 2x_3 \leq 5$$
   $$2x_1 + 3x_2 + 4x_3 = 12$$
   $$x_1, x_2, x_3 \geq 0$$
   [**Ans.** $x_1 = 3$, $x_2 = 2$, $x_3 = 0$ and Max $Z = 8$]

3. Minimize $\quad Z = 4x_1 + 3x_2 + x_3$

   Subject to,
   $$x_1 + 2x_2 + 4x_3 \geq 12$$
   $$3x_1 + 2x_2 + x_3 \geq 8$$
   $$x_1, x_2, x_3 \geq 0$$
   [**Ans.** $x_1 = 0$, $x_2 = 10/3$, $x_3 = 4/3$ and Min $Z = 34/3$]

5.3 THE TWO-PHASE SIMPLEX METHOD

The two-phase simplex method is another method to solve a given LPP involving some artificial variables. The solution is obtained in two phases.

Phase I

In this phase, we construct an auxiliary LPP leading to a final simplex table containing a basic feasible solution to the original problem.

Step 1 Assign a cost –1 to each artificial variable and a cost 0 to all other variables and get a new objective function $Z^* = -A_1 - A_2 - A_3...$ where A_i are the artificial variables.

Step 2 Write down the auxiliary LPP in which the new objective function is to be maximized, subject to the given set of constraints.

Step 3 Solve the auxiliary LPP by simplex method until either of the following three cases arise:

(*i*) Max $Z^* < 0$ and at least one artificial variable appears in the optimum basis at positive level.
(*ii*) Max $Z^* = 0$ and at least one artificial variable appears in the optimum basis at zero level.
(*iii*) Max $Z^* = 0$ and no artificial variable appears in the optimum basis.

In case (*i*), given LPP does not possess any feasible solution, whereas in cases (*ii*) and (*iii*) we go to phase II.

Phase II

Use the optimum basic feasible solution of phase I as a starting solution for the original LPP. Assign the actual costs to the variable in the objective function and a zero cost to every artificial variable in the basis at zero level. Delete the artificial variable column that is eliminated from the basis in phase I from the table. Apply simplex method to the modified simplex table obtained at the end of phase I till an optimum basic feasible solution is obtained or till there is an indication of unbounded solution.

Example 5.5 Use two-phase simplex method to solve,

Maximize $Z = 5x_1 + 3x_2$

Subject to,
$$2x_1 + x_2 \leq 1$$
$$x_1 + 4x_2 \geq 6$$
$$x_1, x_2 \geq 0$$

Solution We convert the given problem into a standard form by adding slack, surplus and artificial variables. We form the auxiliary LPP by assigning the cost –1 to the artificial variable and 0 to all the other variables.

Phase I

Maximize $Z^* = 0x_1 + 0x_2 + 0S_1 + 0S_2 - 1.\,A_1$

Subject to,
$$2x_1 + x_2 + S_1 = 1$$
$$x_1 + 4x_2 - S_2 + A_1 = 6$$

Initial basic feasible solution is given by $S_1 = 1, A_1 = 6$.

C_B	B	x_B	x_1	x_2	S_1	S_2	A_1	$Min\ \frac{x_B}{x_2}$
	C_j		0	0	0	0	–1	
← 0	S_1	1	2	(1)	1	0	0	1/1 = 1
–1	A_1	6	1	4	0	–1	1	6/4 = 1.5
	Z_j	–6	–1	– 4	0	1	–1	
	$Z_j - C_j$		–1	– 4↑	0	1	0	
0	x_2	1	2	1	1	0	0	
–1	A_1	2	–7	0	– 4	–1	1	
	Z_j	–2	7	0	4	1	–1	
	$Z_j - C_j$		7	0	4	1	0	

Since all $Z_j - C_j \geq 0$, an optimum feasible solution to the auxiliary LPP is obtained. But as Max $Z^* < 0$, and an artificial variable A_1 is in the basis at a positive level, the original LPP does not possess any feasible solution.

Example 5.6 Use two-phase simplex method to solve,

Minimize $\quad Z = x_1 - 2x_2 - 3x_3$

Subject to, $\quad -2x_1 + x_2 + 3x_3 = 2$

$$2x_1 + 3x_2 + 4x_3 = 1$$

$$x_1, x_2, x_3 \geq 0$$

Solution Convert the objective function into maximization using,

Minimize $\quad Z = -\text{Max}\,(-Z)$

Maximize $\quad Z = -x_1 + 2x_2 + 3x_3$

Introducing the artificial variables $A_1, A_2 \geq 0$, the constraints of the given problem become,

$$-2x_1 + x_2 + 3x_3 + A_1 = 2$$

$$2x_1 + 3x_2 + 4x_3 + A_2 = 1$$

$$x_1, x_2, x_3, A_1, A_2 \geq 0$$

Phase I

Assigning a cost –1 to the artificial variables A_1 and A_2, and cost 0 to other variables, the objective function of the auxiliary LPP is,

Maximize $Z^* = 0x_1 + 0x_2 + 0x_3 - 1 \,.\, A_1 - 1 \,.\, A_2$, subject to the given constraints.

	C_j		0	0	0	−1	−1	
C_B	B	x_B	x_1	x_2	x_3	A_1	A_2	Min $\frac{x_B}{x_3}$
−1	A_1	2	−2	1	3	1	0	2/3
← −1	A_2	1	2	3	(4)	0	1	1/4
	Z_j	−3	0	−4	−7	−1	−1	
	$Z_j - C_j$		0	−4	−7↑	0	0	
−1	A_1	5/4	−7/2	−5/4	0	1	−3/4	
0	x_3	1/4	1/2	3/4	1	0	1/4	
	Z_j	−5/4	7/2	5/4	0	−1	3/4	
	$Z_j - C_j$		7/2	5/4	0	0	7/4	

Since all $Z_j - C_j \geq 0$, an optimum basic feasible solution to the auxiliary LPP has been attained. But since max Z^* is negative and the artificial variable A_1 appears in the basis at positive level, the original problem does not possess any feasible solution.

Example 5.7

Maximize $Z = 5x_1 - 4x_2 + 3x_3$

Subject to,

$$2x_1 + x_2 - 6x_3 = 20$$
$$6x_1 + 5x_2 + 10x_3 \leq 76$$
$$8x_1 - 3x_2 + 6x_3 \leq 50$$
$$x_1, x_2, x_3 \geq 0$$

Solution Introducing slack variables $S_1, S_2 \geq 0$ and an artificial variable $A_1 \geq 0$ in the constraints of the given LPP, the problem is reformulated in the standard form.

Initial basic feasible solution is given by $A_1 = 20$, $S_1 = 76$ and $S_2 = 50$.

Phase I

Assigning a cost −1 to the artificial variable A_1 and cost 0 to other variables, the objective function of the auxiliary LPP is,

Maximize $Z^* = 0x_1 + 0x_2 + 0x_3 + 0S_1 + 0S_2 - 1 \,.\, A_1$

Subject to,

$$2x_1 + x_2 - 6x_3 + A_1 = 20$$
$$6x_1 + 5x_2 + 10x_3 + S_1 = 76$$
$$8x_1 - 3x_2 + 6x_3 + S_2 = 50$$
$$x_1, x_2, x_3, S_1, S_2, A_1 \geq 0$$

	C_j		0	0	0	−1	0	0	
C_B	B	x_B	x_1	x_2	x_3	A_1	S_1	S_2	$Min \frac{x_B}{x_1}$
−1	A_1	20	2	1	−6	1	0	0	20/2 = 10
0	S_1	76	6	5	10	0	1	0	76/6 = 12.66
←0	S_2	50	(8)	−3	6	0	0	1	50/8 = 6.25
	Z_j	−20	−2	−1	6	−1	0	0	
	$Z_j - C_j$		−2	−1	6	0	0	0	
			↑						

	C_j		0	0	0	−1	0	0	
C_B	B	x_B	x_1	x_2	x_3	A_1	S_1	S_2	$Min \frac{x_B}{x_2}$
←−1	A_1	15/2	0	(7/4)	−15/2	1	0	−1/4	30/7
0	S_1	77/2	0	29/4	11/2	0	1	−3/4	154/29
0	x_1	25/4	1	−3/8	3/4	0	0	1/8	—
	Z_j	−15/2	0	−7/4	15/2	−1	0	1/4	
	$Z_j - C_j$		0	−7/4↑	15/2	0	0	1/4	
0	x_2	30/7	0	(1)	−30/7	4/7	0	−1/7	
0	S_1	52/7	0	1	256/7	−29/7	1	2/7	
0	x_1	55/7	1	0	−6/7	3/4	0	1/14	
	Z_j	0	0	0	0	0	0	0	
	$Z_j - C_j$		0	0	0	0	1	0	

Since all $Z_j = C_j \geq 0$, an optimum solution to the auxiliary LPP has been obtained. Also Max $Z^* = 0$ with no artificial variables in the basis. We go to phase II.

Phase II

Consider the final simplex table of phase I. Consider the actual cost associated with the original variables. Delete the artificial variable A_1 column from the table as it is eliminated in phase I.

	C_j		5	−4	3	0	0
C_B	B	x_B	x_1	x_2	x_3	S_1	S_2
−4	x_2	30/7	0	1	−30/7	0	−1/7
0	S_1	52/7	0	0	256/7	1	2/7
5	x_1	55/7	1	0	−6/7	0	1/14
	Z_j	155/7	5	−4	90/7	0	13/4
	$Z_j - C_j$	0	0	0	69/7	0	13/14

Since all $Z_j - C_j \geq 0$, an optimum basic feasible solution has been reached. Hence, an optimum feasible solution to the given LPP is $x_1 = 55/7$, $x_2 = 30/7$, $x_3 = 0$ and Max $Z = 155/7$.

Example 5.8 Solve by two-phase simplex method

Maximize $Z = -4x_1 - 3x_2 - 9x_3$

Subject to
$$2x_1 + 4x_2 + 6x_3 \geq 15$$
$$6x_1 + x_2 + 6x_3 \geq 12$$
$$x_1, x_2, x_3 \geq 0$$

Solution Convert the given LPP into the standard form by introducing surplus variables S_1, S_2 and artificial variables A_1, A_2. The initial solution is given by $A_1 = 15$, $A_2 = 12$.

Phase I

Construct an auxiliary LPP by assigning a cost 0 to all the variables and –1 to each artificial variable subject to the given set of constraints, and it is given by

Maximize $Z^* = 0x_1 + 0x_2 + 0x_3 + 0S_1 + 0S_2 - 1A_1 - 1A_2$

Subject to,
$$2x_1 + 4x_2 + 6x_3 + S_1 + A_1 = 15$$
$$6x_1 + x_2 + 6x_3 - S_2 + A_2 = 12$$

	C_j		0	0	0	0	0	–1	–1	
C_B	B	x_B	x_1	x_2	x_3	S_1	S_2	A_1	A_2	$Min \frac{x_B}{x_3}$
–1	A_1	15	2	4	6	1	0	1	0	15/6
← –1	A_2	12	6	1	(6)	0	–1	0	1	12/6
	Z_j	–27	–8	–5	–12	1	1	–1	–1	
	$Z_j - C_j$		–8	–5	–12↑	1	1	0	0	
										$Min \frac{x_B}{x_2}$
–1	x_1	3	–4	(3)	0	–1	1	1	[1	3/3 = 1
0	x_3	2	1	1/6	1	0	–1/6	0	1/6	$\frac{2}{1/6} = 12$
	Z_j	–3	4	–3	0	1	–1	–1	1	
	$Z_j - C_j$			–3↑	0	1	–1	0	2	
0	x_2	1	–4/3	1	0	–1/3	1/3	1/3	–1/3	
0	x_3	11/6	22/18	0	1	1/18	–4/18	–1/18	4/18	
	Z_j	0	0	0	0	0	0	0		
	$Z_j - C_j$		0	0	0	1	1	1		

Since all $Z_j - C_j \geq 0$, the current basic feasible solution is optimal. Since Max Z* = 0 and no artificial variable appears in the basis, we go to phase II.

Phase II

Consider the final simplex table of phase I; also consider the actual cost associated with the original variables. Delete the artificial variables A_1, A_2 column from the table as these variables are eliminated from the basis in phase I.

	C_j		−4	−3	−9	0	0	
C_B	B	x_B	x_1	x_2	x_3	S_1	S_2	$Min\ \frac{x_B}{x_1}$
−3	x_2	1	− 4/3	1	0	−1/3	1/3	—
← −9	x_3	11/6	(22/18)	0	1	1/18	−4/18	3/2
	Z_j	−39/2	−7	−3	−9	1/2	1	
	$Z_j - C_j$		−3↑	0	0	1/2	1	
−3	x_2	3	0	1	12/11	−3/11	−1/11	
−4	x_1	3/2	1	0	18/22	1/22	−4/22	
	Z_j	−15	−4	−3	−72/11	7/11	1	
	$Z_j - C_j$		0	27/11	7/11	1	1	

Since all $Z_j - C_j \geq 0$, the current basic feasible solution is optimal.

∴ The optimal solution is given by Max $Z = -15$, $x_1 = 3/2$, $x_2 = 3$, $x_3 = 0$.

EXERCISES

Use two-phase method to solve the following LPP.

1. Maximize $Z = 2x_1 + x_2 + x_3$

   Subject to,
   $4x_1 + 6x_2 + 3x_3 \leq 8$
   $3x_1 - 6x_2 - 4x_3 \leq 1$
   $2x_1 + 3x_2 - 5x_3 \geq 4$
   $x_1, x_2, x_3 \geq 0$ [**Ans.** Max $Z = 64/21$, $x_1 = 9/7$, $x_2 = 10/21$, $x_3 = 0$]

2. Minimize $Z = -2x_1 - x_2$

   Subject to,
   $x_1 + x_2 \geq 2$
   $x_1 + x_2 \leq 4$
   $x_1, x_2 \geq 0$ [**Ans.** Min $Z = -8$, $x_1 = 4$, $x_2 = 0$]

3. Maximize $Z = 5x_1 - 2x_2 + 3x_3$

   Subject to,
   $2x_1 + 2x_2 - x_3 \geq 2$
   $3x_1 - 4x_2 \leq 3$
   $x_2 + 3x_3 \leq 5$
   $x_1, x_2, x_3 \geq 0S$ [**Ans.** Max $Z = 85/3$, $x_1 = 23/3$, $x_2 = 5$, $x_3 = 0$]

4. A company possesses two manufacturing plants, each of which can produce three products X, Y, Z from common raw material. However, the proportions are different in each plant and so are the plants' operating cost per hour. Data on production per hour and costs are given below, together with current orders in hand for each product.

	Product X	Y	Z	Operating cost per hour (`)
Plant I	2	4	3	9
Plant II	4	3	2	10
Order in hand	50	24	60	

Use simplex method to find the number of production hours needed to fulfil the orders in hand at a minimum cost. [**Ans.** Min $Z = 9x_1 + 10x_2$; Subject to, $2x_1 + 4x_2 \geq 50$; $4x_1 + 3x_2 \geq 24$; $3x_1 + 2x_2 \geq 60$; $x_1, x_2 \geq 0$. Also Min $Z = 195$, $x_1 = 35/2$, $x_2 = 15/4$]

5.4 DEGENERACY

The phenomenon of obtaining a degenerate basic feasible solution in a LPP is known as degeneracy. Degeneracy in LPP may arise:

(*i*) at the initial stages.

(*ii*) at any subsequent iteration stage.

In case of (*i*), at least one of the basic variables should be zero in the initial basic feasible solution. Whereas in case of (*ii*) at any iteration of the simplex method, more than one variable is eligible to leave the basis, and hence the next simplex iteration produces a degenerate solution in which at least one basic variable is zero, i.e., the subsequent iteration may not cause improvements in the value of the objective function. As a result, it is possible to repeat the same sequence of simplex iteration endlessly without improving the solution. This concept is known as *cycling* (tie).

5.4.1 Methods to Resolve Degeneracy

The following systematic procedure can be utilized to avoid cycling due to degeneracy in LPP.

Step 1 First find out the rows for which the minimum non-negative ratio is the same (tie); suppose there is a tie between first and third row.

Step 2 Now rearrange the columns of the usual simplex table so that the columns forming the original unit matrix come first in proper order.

Step 3 Find the minimum of the ratio,

$$\left(\frac{\text{Elements of the first column of the unit matrix}}{\text{Corresponding elements of key column}}\right)$$

only for the tied rows, i.e., for the first and third rows.

(*i*) If the third row has the minimum ratio then this row will be the key row and the key element can be determined by intersecting the key row with the key column.

(*ii*) If this minimum ratio is also not unique, then go to the next step.

Step 4 Now find the minimum of the ratio, only for the tied rows. If this minimum ratio is unique for the first row, then this row will be the key row for determining the key element by intersecting with key column.

$$\left(\frac{\text{Elements of the second column of the unit matrix}}{\text{Corresponding elements of key column}}\right)$$

If this minimum is also not unique, then go to the next step.

Step 5 Find the minimum of the ratio. The above step is repeated till the minimum ratio is obtained so as to resolve the degeneracy. After the resolution of this tie, simplex method is applied to obtain the optimum solution.

$$\left(\frac{\text{Elements of the third column of the unit matrix}}{\text{Corresponding elements of key column}}\right)$$

Example 5.9

Maximize $Z = 3x_1 + 9x_2$

Subject to,

$$x_1 + 4x_2 \le 8$$
$$x_1 + 2x_2 \le 4$$
$$x_1, x_2 \ge 0$$

Solution Introducing slack variables $S_1, S_2 \ge 0$, we have

Maximize $Z = 3x_1 + 9x_2 + 0S_1 + 0S_2$

Subject to,

$$x_1 + 4x_2 + S_1 = 8$$
$$x_1 + 2x_2 + S_2 = 4$$
$$x_1, x_2, S_1, S_2 \ge 0$$

		C_j	3	9	0	0	
C_B	B	x_B	x_1	x_2	S_1	S_2	$Min \frac{x_B}{x_2}$
0	S_1	8	1	4	1	0	8/4=2 } tie
0	S_2	4	1	2	0	1	4/2=2 } tie
	Z_j	0	0	0	0	0	
	$Z_j - C_j$		−3	−9↑	0	0	

Since the minimum of the ratio is not unique, the slack variables S_1, S_2 leave the basis. This is an indication for the existence of degeneracy in the given LPP. So we apply the above procedure to resolve this degeneracy (tie).

Rearrange the columns of the simplex table so that the initial identity matrix appears first.

		C_j	0	0	3	9	
C_B	B	x_B	S_1	S_2	x_1	x_2	$Min \frac{S_1}{x_2}$
0	S_1	8	1	0	1	4	1/4
← 0	S_2	4	0	1	1	(2)	0/2 = 0
	Z_j	0	0	0	0	0	
	$Z_j - C_j$		0	0	−3	−9↑	

Using Step 3 of the procedures given for resolving degeneracy, we find

$$\text{Min}\left(\frac{\text{Elements of first column}}{\text{Corresponding elements of key column}}\right) = \text{Min}\left(\frac{1}{4}, \frac{0}{2}\right) = 0$$

Hence, S_2 leaves the basis and the key element is 2.

	C_j		0	0	3	9
C_B	B	x_B	S_1	S_2	x_1	x_2
0	S_1	0	1	–2	–1	0
9	x_2	2	0	$\frac{1}{2}$	$\frac{1}{2}$	1
	Z_j	18	0	$\frac{9}{2}$	$\frac{9}{2}$	9
	$Z_j - C_j$		0	$\frac{9}{2}$	$\frac{3}{2}$	0

Since all $Z_j - C_j \geq 0$, the solution is optimum. The optimal solution is $x_1 = 0, x_2 = 2$, Max $Z = 18$.

Example 5.10

Maximize $\quad Z = 2x_1 + x_2$

Subject to,

$$4x_1 + 3x_2 \leq 12$$
$$4x_1 + x_2 \leq 8$$
$$4x_1 - x_2 \leq 8$$
$$x_1, x_2 \geq 0$$

Solution Introducing the slack variables $S_1, S_2, S_3 \geq 0$, the given problem can be reformatted as shown below:

Maximize $\quad Z = 2x_1 + x_2 + 0S_1 + 0S_2 + 0S_3$

Subject to,

$$4x_1 + 3x_2 + S_1 = 12$$
$$4x_1 + x_2 + S_2 = 8$$
$$4x_1 - x_2 + S_3 = 8$$

	C_j		2	1	0	0	0	
C_B	B	x_B	x_1	x_2	S_1	S_2	S_3	$Min \frac{x_B}{x_1}$
0	S_1	12	4	3	1	0	0	12/4 = 3
0	S_2	8	4	1	0	1	0	8/4 = 2 } tie
0	S_3	8	4	–1	0	0	1	8/4 = 2 }
	Z_j	0	0	0	0	0	0	
	$Z_j - C_j$		–2↑	–1	0	0	0	

Since the minimum ratio is same for 2nd and 3rd rows, it is an indication of degeneracy. Rearrange the columns in such a way that the identity matrix comes first.

	C_j		0	0	0	2	1		
C_B	B	x_B	S_1	S_2	S_3	x_1	x_2	$Min\ S_1/x_1$	$Min\ S_2/x_1$
0	S_1	12	1	0	0	4	3	1/4	0/4
0	S_2	8	0	1	0	4	1	0/4	1/4
← 0	S_3	8	0	0	1	4	– 1	0/4	0/4
	Z_j	0	0	0	0	0	0		
	$Z_j - C_j$	0	0	0	0	– 2↑	– 1		

Using the procedure of degeneracy, find

$$\text{Min}\left\{\frac{\text{Elements of first column of unit matrix}}{\text{Corresponding elements of key coulmn}}\right\}$$

for 2nd and 3rd rows. Min {0/4, 0/4} which is unique.

So again compute,

$$\text{Min}\left\{\frac{\text{Elements of first column of unit matrix}}{\text{Corresponding elements of key coulmn}}\right\}$$

for 2nd and 3rd rows. Min {– , 1/4, 0/4} = 0, which occurs corresponding to the third row. Hence, S_3 leaves the basis.

	C_j		0	0	0	2	1	
C_B	B	x_B	S_1	S_2	S_3	x_1	x_2	$Min\ \frac{x_B}{x_2}$
0	S_1	4	1	0	–1	0	4	4/4 = 1
← 0	S_2	0	0	1	–1	0	(2)	0/2 = 0
2	x_1	2	0	0	1/4	1	–1/4	—
	Z_j	4	0	0	1/2	2	–1/2	
	$Z_j - C_j$		0	0	1/2	0	–3/2↑	$Min\ \frac{x_B}{S_3}$
← 0	S_1	4	1	–2	(1)	0	0	4/1 = 4
1	x_2	0	0	1/2	–1/2	0	1	—
2	x_1	2	0	1/8	1/8	1	0	$\frac{2}{1/8} = 16$
	Z_j	4	0	3/4	–1/4	2	1	
	$Z_j - C_j$		0	3/4	–1/4↑	0	0	
0	S_3	4	1	–2	1	0	0	
1	x_2	2	$\frac{1}{2}$	–1/2	0	0	1	
2	x_1	3/2	–1/8	3/8	0	1	0	
	Z_j	5	$\frac{1}{4}$	1/4	0	2	1	
	$Z_j - C_j$		1/4	1/4	0	0	0	

Since all $Z_j - C_j \geq 0$, the solution is optimum and given by $x_1 = 3/2$, $x_2 = 2$, and Max $Z = 5$.

EXERCISES

1. Solve the following LPP

Maximize $Z = 5x_1 - 2x_2 + 3x_3$

Subject to,

$$2x_1 + 2x_2 - x_3 \geq 2$$
$$3x_1 - 4x_2 \leq 3$$
$$x_2 - 3x_3 \leq 5$$
$$x_1, x_2, x_3 \geq 0$$

$\left[\textbf{Ans.}\ \text{Max } Z = \frac{85}{3}, x_1 = \frac{23}{3}, x_2 = 5, x_3 = 0\right]$

2. Maximize $Z = 2x_1 + 3x_2 + 10x_3$

Subject to,

$$x_1 + 2x_3 = 0$$
$$x_2 + x_3 = 1$$
$$x_1, x_2, x_3 \geq 0$$

[**Ans.** Max $Z = 3$, $x_1 = 0$, $x_2 = 1$, $x_3 = 0$]

3. Maximize $Z = x_1 + 2x_2 + x_3$

Subject to,

$$2x_1 + x_2 - x_3 \leq 2$$
$$-2x_1 + x_2 - 5x_3 \geq -6$$
$$4x_1 + x_2 + x_3 \leq 6$$
$$x_1, x_2, x_3 \geq 0$$

[**Ans.** $x_1 = 0$, $x_2 = 4$, $x_3 = 2$, Max $Z = 10$]

5.5 UNBOUNDED SOLUTION

In some LPP, the solution space becomes unbounded, so that the value of the objective function also can be increased indefinitely without a limit. However, it is not necessary that an unbounded feasible region should yield an unbounded value for the objective function. The following example will illustrate these points.

Example 5.11 (Unbounded optimal solution)

Maximize $Z = 2x_1 + x_2$

Subject to,

$$x_1 - x_2 \leq 10$$
$$2x_1 - x_2 \leq 40$$
$$x_1, x_2 \geq 0$$

Solution By introducing slack variables $S_1, S_2 \geq 0$ the standard form of LPP becomes:

Maximize $Z = 2x_1 + x_2 + 0S_1 + 0S_2$

Subject to,

$$x_1 - x_2 + S_1 = 10$$
$$2x_1 - x_2 + S_2 = 40$$
$$x_1, x_2, S_1, S_2 \geq 0$$

	C_j		2	1	0	0	
C_B	B	x_B	x_1	x_2	S_1	S_2	$Min \frac{x_B}{x_1}$
← 0	S_1	10	(1)	–1	1	0	10/1 = 10
0	S_2	40	2	–1	0	1	40/2 = 20
	Z_j	0	0	0	0	0	
	$Z_j - C_j$		–2↑	–1	0	0	$Min \frac{x_B}{x_2}$
2	x_1	10	1	–1	1	0	—
← 0	S_2	20	0	(1)	–2	1	20/1 = 20
	Z_j	20	2	–2	2	0	
	$Z_j - C_j$		0	–1↑	2	0	
2	x_1	30	1	0	–1	1	
1	x_2	20	0	1	–2	1	
	Z_j	80	2	1	–4	3	
	$Z_j - C_j$		0	0	–4↑	3	

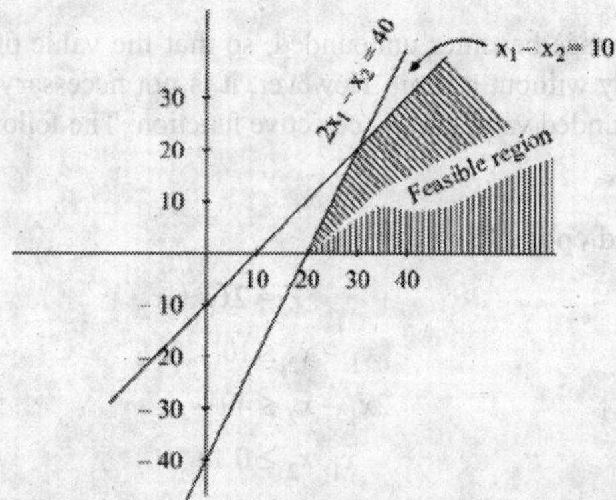

Since $Z_3 - C_3 = -4 < 0$, the solution is not optimum. But all the values in the key column are negative which is the indication of unbounded solution.

The feasible region is unbounded since it has all x_2 negative. Hence, Z can be made arbitrarily large and the problem has no finite maximum value of Z. Therefore, the solution is unbounded.

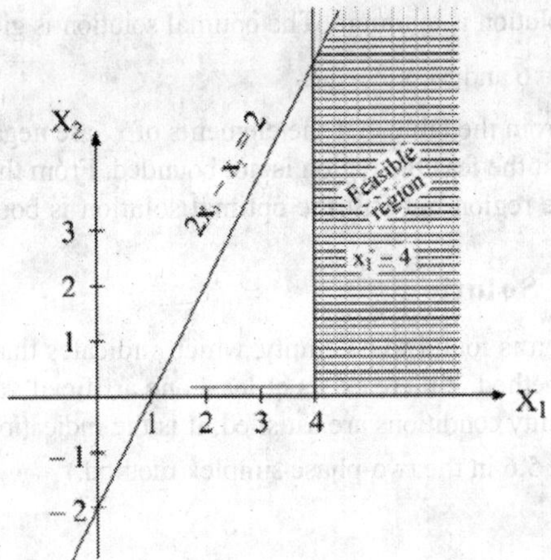

Example 5.12 (Unbounded feasible region but bounded optimal solution)

Maximize $Z = 6x_1 - 2x_2$

Subject to,

$$2x_1 - x_2 \le 2$$
$$x_1 \le 4$$
$$x_1, x_2 \ge 0$$

Solution By introducing slack variables S_1, S_2 the standard form of LPP is,

Maximize $Z = 6x_1 - 2x_2 + 0S_1 + 0S_2$

Subject to,

$$2x_1 - x_2 + S_1 = 2$$
$$x_1 + S_2 = 4$$
$$x_1, x_2, S_1, S_2 \ge 0$$

Initial solution is given by $S_1 = 2$, $S_2 = 4$

	C_j		6	−2	0	0	
C_B	B	x_B	x_1	x_2	S_1	S_2	$Min \frac{x_B}{x_1}$
← 0	S_1	2	(2)	−1	1	0	2/2 = 1
0	S_2	4	1	0	0	1	4/1 = 4
	Z_j	0	0	0	0	0	
	$Z_j - C_j$		−6↑	2	0	0	$Min \frac{x_B}{x_2}$
6	x_1	1	1	−1/2	1/2	0	—
← 0	S_2	3	0	(1/2)	−1/2	1	$\frac{3}{1/2} = 6$
	Z_j	6	6	−3	3	0	
	$Z_j - C_j$		0	−1↑	3	0	
6	x_1	4	1	0	0	1	
−2	x_2	6	0	1	−1	2	
	Z_j	12	6	−2	2	2	
	$Z_j - C_j$		0	0	2	2	

Since all $Z_j - C_j \geq 0$, the solution is optimum. The optimal solution is given by,

$$x_1 = 4, x_2 = 6 \text{ and Max } Z = 12.$$

It is now interesting to note from the table that the elements of x_2 are negative or zero (-1 and 0). This is an immediate indication that the feasible region is not bounded. From this we conclude that a problem may have unbounded feasible region but still the optimal solution is bounded.

Non-Existing Feasible Solution

In this case the feasible region is found to be empty, which indicates that the problem does not have a feasible solution. In simplex method, if there exists at least one artificial variable in the basis at positive level and even though optimality conditions are satisfied, it is the indication of non-feasible solution.

(Refer to examples 5.5 and 5.6 in the two-phase simplex method.)

Chapter 6

Duality in Linear Programming

6.1 INTRODUCTION

Every LPP (called as primal problem), can be transformed into a dual problem (called its dual), which provides an upper bound to the optimal value of the primal problem.

The importance of the duality concept is because of two main reasons:

(*i*) If the primal contains a large number of constraints and a smaller number of variables, the labour of computation can be considerably reduced by converting it into the dual problem and then solving it.

(*ii*) The interpretation of the dual variables from the cost or economic point of view, proves extremely useful in making future decisions in the activities being programmed.

6.2 FORMATION OF DUAL PROBLEMS

For formulating a dual problem, first we bring the problem in the canonical form. The following changes are used in formulating the dual problem:

(*i*) Change the objective function of maximization in the primal into minimization in the dual and vice versa.

(*ii*) The number of variables in the primal will be the number of constraints in the dual and vice versa.

(*iii*) The cost coefficients $C_1, C_2, ..., C_n$ in the objective function of the primal will be the RHS constant of the constraints in the dual and vice versa.

(*iv*) In forming the constraints for the dual, we consider the transpose of the body matrix of the primal problem.

(*v*) The variables in both problems are non-negative.

(*vi*) If a variable in the primal is unrestricted in sign, then the corresponding constraint in the dual will be an equation and vice versa.

6.3 DEFINITION OF THE DUAL PROBLEM

Let the primal problem be,

$$
\begin{aligned}
\text{Max} \quad & Z = C_1 x_1 + C_2 x_2 + ... + C_n x_n \\
\text{Subject to,} \quad & a_{11} x_1 + a_{12} x_2 + ... + a_{1n} x_n \le b_1 \\
& a_{21} x_1 + a_{22} x_2 + ... + a_{2n} x_n \le b_2 \\
& \vdots \\
& a_{m1} x_1 + a_{m2} x_2 + ... + a_{mn} x_n \le b_m \\
& x_1, x_2, ..., x_n \ge 0
\end{aligned}
$$

Dual The dual problem is defined as,

$$\begin{aligned}
\text{Min} \quad & Z' = b_1w_1 + b_2w_2 + \ldots + b_mw_m \\
\text{Subject to,} \quad & a_{11}\, w_1 + a_{21}\, w_2 + \ldots + a_{m1}\, w_m \geq C_1 \\
& a_{12}\, w_1 + a_{22}\, w_2 + \ldots + a_{m2}\, w_m \geq C_2 \\
& \vdots \\
& a_{1n}\, w_1 + a_{2n}\, w_2 + \ldots + a_{mn}\, w_m \geq C_n \\
& w_1, w_2 \ldots w_m \geq 0
\end{aligned}$$

where, $w_1, w_2, w_3 \ldots w_m$ are called *dual variables.*

Example 6.1 Write the dual of the following primal LP problem.

$$\begin{aligned}
\text{Max} \quad & Z = x_1 + 2x_2 + x_3 \\
\text{Subject to,} \quad & 2x_1 + x_2 - x_3 \leq 2 \\
& -2x_1 + x_2 - 5x_3 \geq -6 \\
& 4x_1 + x_2 + x_3 \leq 6 \\
& x_1, x_2, x_3 \geq 0
\end{aligned}$$

Solution Since the problem is not in the canonical form, we interchange the inequality of the second constraint.

$$\begin{aligned}
\text{Max} \quad & Z = x_1 + 2x_2 + x_3 \\
\text{Subject to,} \quad & 2x_1 + x_2 - x_3 \leq 2 \\
& 2x_1 - x_2 + 5x_3 \leq 6 \\
& 4x_1 + x_2 + x_3 \leq 6 \\
\text{and,} \quad & x_1, x_2, x_3 \geq 0
\end{aligned}$$

Dual Let w_1, w_2, w_3 be the dual variables.

$$\begin{aligned}
\text{Min} \quad & Z' = 2w_1 + 6w_2 + 6w_3 \\
\text{Subject to,} \quad & 2w_1 + 2w_2 + 4w_3 \geq 1 \\
& + w_1 - w_2 + w_3 \geq 2 \\
& - w_1 + 5w_2 + w_3 \geq 1 \\
& w_1, w_2, w_3 \geq 0
\end{aligned}$$

Example 6.2 Find the dual of the following LPP.

$$\begin{aligned}
\text{Max} \quad & Z = 3x_1 - x_2 + x_3 \\
\text{Subject to,} \quad & 4x_1 - x_2 \leq 8 \\
& 8x_1 + x_2 + 3x_3 \geq 12 \\
& 5x_1 - 6x_3 \leq 13 \\
& x_1, x_2, x_3 \geq 0
\end{aligned}$$

Solution Since the problem is not in the canonical form, we interchange the inequality of the second constraint.

$$\begin{aligned}
\text{Max} \quad & Z = 3x_1 - x_2 + x_3 \\
\text{Subject to,} \quad & 4x_1 - x_2 + 0x_3 \leq 8 \\
& - 8x_1 - x_2 - 3x_3 \leq -12 \\
& 5x_1 + 0x_2 - 6x_3 \leq 13 \\
& x_1, x_2, x_3 \geq 0
\end{aligned}$$

Max $Z = Cx$

Subject to, $Ax \le B$

$x \ge 0$

$$C = (3\ \ -1\ \ 1) \times \begin{pmatrix} x_1 \\ x_2 \\ x_3 \end{pmatrix} \quad b = \begin{pmatrix} 8 \\ -12 \\ 13 \end{pmatrix}$$

$$A = \begin{pmatrix} 4 & -1 & 0 \\ -8 & -1 & -3 \\ 5 & 0 & -6 \end{pmatrix}$$

Dual Let w_1, w_2, w_3 be the dual variables. The dual problem is,

Min $Z' = b^T W$

Subject to, $A^T W \ge C^T$ and $W \ge 0$

i.e., $$\text{Min } Z' = (8 - 12\,13)\begin{pmatrix} w_1 \\ w_2 \\ w_3 \end{pmatrix}$$

$$\text{Subject to, } \begin{pmatrix} 4 & -8 & 5 \\ -1 & -1 & 0 \\ 0 & -3 & 6 \end{pmatrix}\begin{pmatrix} w_1 \\ w_2 \\ w_3 \end{pmatrix} \ge \begin{pmatrix} 3 \\ -1 \\ 1 \end{pmatrix}$$

Min $Z' = 8w_1 - 12w_2 + 13w_3$

Subject to,

$$4w_1 - 8w_2 + 5w_3 \ge 3$$
$$-w_1 - w_2 + 0w_3 \ge -1$$
$$0w_1 - 3w_2 + 6w_3 \ge 1$$
$$w_1, w_2, w_3 \ge 0$$

Example 6.3 Write the dual of the following LPP.

Min $Z = 2x_2 + 5x_3$

Subject to,

$$x_1 + x_2 \ge 2$$
$$2x_1 + x_2 + 6x_3 \le 6$$
$$x_1 - x_2 + 3x_3 = 4$$
$$x_1, x_2, x_3 \ge 0$$

Solution Since the given primal problem is not in the canonical form, we interchange the inequality of the constraint. The third constraint is also an equation and can be converted into two inequations.

Min $Z = 0x_1 + 2x_2 + 5x_3$

Subject to,

$$x_1 + x_2 + 0x_3 \ge 2$$
$$-2x_1 - x_2\ \ 6x_3 \ge -6$$
$$x_1 - x_2 + 3x_3 \le 4$$
$$x_1 - x_2 + 3x_3 \ge 4$$
$$x_1, x_2, x_3 \ge 0$$

Again on rearranging the constraints, we have

Min $Z = 0x_1 + 2x_2 + 5x_3$

Subject to,

$$x_1 + x_2 + 0x_3 \geq 2$$
$$-2x_1 - x_2 - 6x_3 \geq -6$$
$$x_1 - x_2 + 3x_3 \geq 4$$
$$-x_1 + x_2 - 3x_3 \geq -4$$
$$x_1, x_2, x_3 \geq 0$$

Dual Since there are four constraints in the primal, we have four dual variables namely w_1, w_2, w_3', w_3''

Max $Z' = 2w_1 - 6w_2 + 4w_3' - 4w_3''$

Subject to,

$$w_1 - 2w_2 + w_3' - w_3'' \leq 0$$
$$w_1 - w_2 - w_3' + w_3'' \leq 2$$
$$0w_1 - 6w_2 + 3w_3' - 3w_3'' \leq 5$$
$$w_1, w_2, w_3', w_3'' \geq 0$$

Let $w_3 = w_3' - w_3'$

Max $Z' = 2w_1 - 6w_2 + 4(w_3' - w_3'')$

Subject to,

$$w_1 - 2w_2 + (w_3' - w_3'') \leq 0$$
$$w_1 - w_2 - (w_3' - w_3'') \leq 2$$

Finally, we have, $0w_1 - 6w_2 + 3\,(w_3' - w_3') \leq 5$

Max $Z' = 2w_1 - 6w_2 + 4w_3$

Subject to,

$$w_1 - 2w_2 + w_3 \leq 0$$
$$w_1 - w_2 - w_3 \leq 2$$
$$0w_1 - 6w_2 + 3w_3 \leq 5$$
$$w_1, w_2 \geq 0, w_3 \text{ is unrestricted.}$$

Example 6.4 Give the dual of the following problem:

Max $Z = x + 2y$

Subject to,

$$2x + 3y \geq 4$$
$$3x + 4y = 5$$
$$x \geq 0 \text{ and } y \text{ unrestricted.}$$

Solution Since the variable y is unrestricted, it can be expressed as $y = y' - y''$, $y', y'' \geq 0$. On reformulating the given problem, we have

Max $Z = x + 2\,(y' - y'')$

Subject to,

$$-2x - 3\,(y' - y'') \leq -4$$
$$3x + 4\,(y' - y'') \leq 5$$
$$3x + 4\,(y' - y'') \geq 5$$
$$x, y', y'' \geq 0$$

Since the problem is not in the canonical form, we rearrange the constraints.

Max $Z = x + 2y' - 2y''$

Subject to,

$$-2x - 3y' + 3y'' \leq -4$$
$$3x + 4y' - 4y'' \leq 5$$
$$-3x - 4y' + 4y'' \leq -5$$

Dual Since there are three variables and three constraints in the primal, we have three variables, namely, w_1, w_2', w_2''

Min $Z' = -4w_1 + 5w_2' - 5w_2''$

Subject to,

$$-2w_1 + 3w_2' - 3w_2'' \geq 1$$
$$-3w_1 + 4w_2' - 4w_2'' \geq 2$$
$$3w_1 - 4w_2' + 4w_2'' \geq -2$$
$$w_1, w_2', w_2'' \geq 0$$

Let $w_2 = w_2' - w_2''$, so that the dual variable w_2 is unrestricted in sign. Finally the dual is,

Min $Z' = -4w_1 + 5(w_2' - w_2')$

Subject to

$$-2w_1 + 3(w_2' - w'') \geq 1$$
$$-3w_1 + 4(w_2' - w'') \geq 2$$
$$3w_1 + 4(w_2' - w'') \geq -2$$

i.e., Min $Z' = -4w_1 + 5w_2$

Subject to,

$$-2w_1 + 3w_2 \geq 1$$
$$-3w_1 + 4w_2 \geq 2$$
$$3w_1 - 4w_2 \geq -2$$
$$w_1 \geq 0 \text{ and } w_2 \text{ is unrestricted.}$$

i.e., Min $Z' = -4w_1 + 5w_2$

Subject to,

$$-2w_1 + 3w_2 \geq 1$$
$$-3w_1 + 4w_2 \geq 2$$
$$-3w_1 + 4w_2 \leq 2$$

i.e., Min $Z' = -4w_1 + 5w_2$

Subject to,

$$-2w_1 + 3w_2 \geq 1$$
$$-3w_1 + 4w_2 = 2$$
$$w_1 \geq 0 \text{ and } w_2 \text{ is unrestricted.}$$

Example 6.5 Write the dual of the following primal LPP.

Min $Z = 4x_1 + 5x_2 - 3x_3$

Subject to,

$$x_1 + x_2 + x_3 = 22$$
$$3x_1 + 5x_2 - 2x_3 \leq 65$$
$$x_1 + 7x_2 + 4x_3 \geq 120$$
$$x_1 + x_2 \geq 0 \text{ and } x_3 \text{ is unrestricted.}$$

Solution Since the variable x_3 is unrestricted, $x_3 = x_3' - x_3''$. Also bring the problem into canonical form by rearranging the constraints.

Min $Z = 4x_1 + 5x_2 - 3(x_3' - x_3'')$

Subject to,

$$x_1 + x_2 + (x_3' - x_3'') \leq 22$$
$$x_1 + x_2 + x_3' - x_3'' \geq 22$$
$$-3x_1 - 5x_2 + 2(x_3' - x_3'') \geq -65$$
$$x_1 + 7x_2 + 4(x_3' - x_3'') \geq 120$$
$$x_1, x_2, x_3' - x_3'' \geq 0$$

Min $Z = 4x_1 + 5x_2 - 3x_3' + 3x_3''$

Subject to,

$$x_1 + x_2 + x_3' - x_3'' \geq 22$$
$$-x_1 - x_2 - x_3' + x_3'' \geq -22$$
$$-3x_1 - 5x_2 + 2x_3' - 2x_3'' \geq -65$$
$$x_1 + 7x_2 + 4x_3' - 4x_3'' \geq 120$$
$$x_1, x_2, x_3', x_3'' \geq 0$$

Dual Since there are four constraints in the primal problem, in dual there are four variables namely w_1', w_1'', w_2, w_3, so that the dual is given by

Max $Z' = 22(w_1' - w_1'') - 65w_2 + 120w_3$

Subject to,

$$w_1' - w_1'' - 3w_2 + w_3 \leq 4$$
$$w_1' - w_1'' - 5w_2 + 7w_3 \leq 5$$
$$w_1' - w_1'' + 2w_2 + 4w_3 \leq -3$$
$$-w_1' + w_1'' - 2w_2 - 4w_3 \leq 3$$
$$w_1', w_1'', w_2, w_3 \geq 0$$

Let $w_1 = w_1' - w_1''$, i.e., the variable w_1 is unrestricted

i.e. Max $Z' = 22(w_1' - w_1'') - 65w_2 + 120w_3$

Subject to,

$$w_1' - w_1'' - 3w_2 + w_3 \leq 4$$
$$w_1' - w_1'' - 5w_2 + 7w_3 \leq 5$$
$$-(w_1' - w_1'') - 2w_2 - 4w_3 \geq 3$$
$$-(w_1' - w_1'') - 2w_2 - 4w_3 \leq 3$$

i.e. Max $Z' = 22w_1 - 65w_2 + 120w_3$

Subject to,

$$w_1 - 3w_2 + w_3 \leq 4$$
$$w_1 - 5w_2 + 7w_3 \leq 5$$
$$-w_1 - 2w_2 - 4w_3 \geq 3$$
$$-w_1 - 2w_2 - 4w_3 \leq 3$$

Finally we have,

Min $Z' = 22w_1 - 65w_2 + 120w_3$

Subject to,

$$w_1 - 3w_2 + w_3 \leq 4$$
$$w_1 - 5w_2 + 7w_3 \leq 5$$
$$-w_1 - 2w_2 - 4w_3 = 3$$

$w_2, w_3 \geq 0$ and w_1 is unrestricted.

6.4 IMPORTANT RESULTS IN DUALITY

(*i*) The dual of the dual is primal.

(*ii*) If one is a maximization problem, then the other is of minimization.

(*iii*) The necessary and sufficient condition for any LPP and its dual to have an optimal solution is that both must have feasible solutions.

(*iv*) Fundamental duality theorem states, if either the primal or dual problem has a finite optimal solution, then the other problem also has a finite optimal solution and also the optimal values of the objective function in both the problems are the same, i.e., Max Z = Min Z'. The solution of the other problem can be read from the $Z_j - C_j$ row below the columns of slack or surplus variables.

(*v*) Existence theorem states that, if one of the problem has an unbounded solution then the other problem has no feasible solution.

(*vi*) Complementary slackness theorem states that:

(*a*) If a primal variable is positive, then the corresponding dual constraint is an equation at the optimum and vice versa.

(*b*) If a primal constraint is a strict inequality then the corresponding dual variable is zero at the optimum and vice versa.

Example 6.6 Find the maximum of $Z = 6x + 8y$

Subject to,
$$5x + 2y \leq 20$$
$$x + 2y \leq 10$$
$$x, y \geq 0 \text{ by solving its dual problem.}$$

Solution The dual of this primal problem is given below. As there are two constraints in the primal, we have two dual variables namely, w_1 and w_2.

Min $Z' = 20w_1 + 10w_2$

Subject to,
$$5w_1 + w_2 \geq 6$$
$$2w_1 + 2w_2 \geq 8$$
$$w_1, w_2 \geq 0$$

We solve the dual problem using the Big-M method. Since this method involves artificial variables, the problem is reformulated and we have,

Max $Z' = -20w_1 - 10w_2 + 0S_1 + 0S_2 - MA_1 - MA_2$

Subject to,
$$5w_1 + w_2 - S_1 + A_1 = 6$$
$$2w_1 + 2w_2 - S_2 + A_2 = 8$$
$$w_1, w_2, S_1, S_2, A_1, A_2 \geq 0$$

		C_j	−20	−10	0	0	−M	−M	
C_B	B	x_B	w_1	w_2	S_1	S_2	A_1	A_2	Min $\frac{x_B}{w_1}$
← −M	A_1	6	(5)	1	−1	0	1	0	6/5 = 1.02
−M	A_2	8	2	2	0	−1	0	1	8/2 = 4
	Z_j	−14M	−7M	−3M	M	M	−M	−M	
	$Z_j - C_j$		−7M + 20	−3M − 10	M	M	0	0	
			↑						
−20	w_1	6/5	1	1/5	−1/5	0	—	0	6/5 × 5/1 = 6
← −M	A_2	$\frac{28}{5}$	0	8/5	2/5	−1	—	1	28/5 × 5/8 =7/2
	Z_j	$\frac{28}{5}M - 24$	−20	− 4 − 8/5M	4 − 2/5 M	M	—	−M	
	$Z_j - C_j$		0	$\frac{8}{5}M + 6$	$4 - \frac{2}{5}M$	M	—	0	
				↑					

(Contd...)

	C_j		-20	-10	0	0	$-M$	$-M$	
C_B	B	x_B	w_1	w_2	S_1	S_2	A_1	A_2	$Min \frac{x_B}{w_1}$
-20	w_1	$\frac{1}{2}$	1	0	-1/4	$\frac{1}{8}$	—	—	1/2
-10	w_2	$\frac{7}{2}$	0	1	1/4	$\frac{-5}{8}$	—	—	—
	Z_j	-45	-20	-10	5/2	15/4	—	—	
	$Z_j - C_j$		0	0	5/2	15/4			

Since all $Z_j - C_j \geq 0$, the solution is optimum. Therefore, the optimal solution of dual is,

$$w_1 = 1/2,\ w_2 = 7/2,\ \text{Min } Z' = -45$$

The optimum solution of the primal problem is given by the value of $Z_j - C_j$ in the optimal table corresponding to the column surplus variables S_1 and S_2

$$\therefore \quad x = \frac{5}{2},\ y = \frac{15}{4}$$

$$\text{Max } Z = 6 \times \frac{5}{2} + 8 \times \frac{15}{4} = 45$$

Example 6.7 Apply the principle of duality to solve the LPP.

Max $\quad Z = 3x_1 + 2x_2$

Subject to,

$$x_1 + x_2 \geq 1$$
$$x_1 + x_2 \leq 7$$
$$x_1 + 2x_2 \leq 10$$
$$x_2 \leq 3,\ x_1, x_2 \geq 0.$$

Solution First we convert the given (primal) problem into its dual. As there are 4 constraints in the primal problem, we have four variables w_1, w_2, w_3, w_4 in its dual. We convert the given problem into its canonical form by rearranging some of the constraints.

Max $\quad Z = 3x_2 + 2x_2$

Subject to,

$$-x_1 - x_2 \leq -1$$
$$x_1 + x_2 \leq 7$$
$$x_1 + 2x_2 \leq 10$$
$$0x_1 + x_2 \leq 3$$
$$x_1, x_2 \geq 0$$

Dual

Max $\quad Z' = -w_1 + 7w_2 + 10w_3 + 3w_4$

Subject to,

$$-w_1 + w_2 + w_3 + 0w_4 \geq 3$$
$$-w_1 + w_2 + 2w_3 + w_4 \geq 2$$
$$w_1, w_2, w_3, w_4 \geq 0$$

We apply the Big-M method to get the solution of the dual problem, as it involves artificial variables.

$$\text{Max} \quad Z' = w_1 - 7w_2 - 10w_3 - 3w_4 + 0S_1 + 0S_2 - MA_1 - MA_2$$

$$\text{Subject to,} \quad -w_1 + w_2 + w_3 + 0w_4 - S_1 + A_1 = 3$$

$$-w_1 + w_2 + 2w_3 + w_4 - S_2 + A_2 = 2$$

$$w_1, w_2, w_3, w_4, S_1, S_2, A_1, A_2 \geq 0$$

Since all $Z_j - C_j \geq 0$ (refer to Table 6.1) the solution is optimum. The optimal solution of the dual problem is,

$$w_1 = w_3 = w_4 = 0,\ w_2 = 3,\ \text{Min } Z' = -21$$

Also, from the optimum simplex table of the dual problem, the optimal solution of the primal problem is given by the value $Z_j - C_j$, corresponding to the column of surplus variables S_1 and S_2.

$$\therefore \quad x_1 = 7,\ x_2 = 0,\ \text{Max } Z = 21$$

Example 6.8 Write down the dual of the following LPP and solve it.

Write down the solution of the primal.

$$\text{Max} \quad Z = 4x_1 + 2x_2$$

$$\text{Subject to,} \quad x_1 + x_2 \geq 3$$

$$x_1 - x_2 \geq 2$$

$$x_1, x_2 \geq 0$$

Solution The dual of the given (primal) problem is as follows. First we convert the given problem into its canonical form by rearranging the constraints.

$$\text{Max} \quad Z' = 4x_1 + 2x_2$$

$$\text{Subject to,} \quad -x_1 - x_2 \leq -3$$

$$-x_1 + x_2 \leq -2$$

$$x_1, x_2 \geq 0$$

Dual

$$\text{Min} \quad Z' = -3w_1 - 2w_2$$

$$\text{Subject to,} \quad -w_1 - w_2 \geq 4$$

$$-w_1 + w_2 \geq 2$$

$$w_1, w_2 \geq 0$$

Introducing the surplus variables $S_1, S_2 \geq 0$ and artificial variables $A_1, A_2 \geq 0$ the problem becomes,

$$\text{Max} \quad Z' = 3w_1 + 2w_2 + 0S_1 + 0S_2 - MA_1 - MA_2$$

$$\text{Subject to,} \quad -w_1 - w_2 - S_1 + A_1 = 4$$

$$-w_1 + w_2 - S_2 + A_2 = 2$$

$$w_1, w_2, S_1, S_2, A_1, A_2 \geq 0$$

Table 6.1

C_B	B	x_B	w_1	w_2	w_3	w_4	S_1	S_2	A_1	A_2	*Min* x_B/w_3
	C_j		1	–7	–10	–3	0	0	$-M$	$-M$	
$-M$	A_1	3	–1	1	1	0	–1	0	1	0	3/1 = 3
← $-M$	A_2	2	–1	1	(2)	1	0	–1	0	1	2/2 = 1
	Z_j	$-5M$	$2M$	$-2M$	$-3M$	$-M$	M	M	$-M$	$-M$	
	$Z_j - C_j$		$2M-1$	$-2M+7$	$-3M+10$ ↑	$-M+3$	M	M	0	0	*Min* x_B/w_2
$-M$	A_1	2	–1/2	1/2	0	–1/2	–1	1/2	1	1	2/1/2 = 4
← –10	w_3	1	–1/2	(1/2)	1	1/2	0	–1/2	0	—	1/1/2 = 2
	Z_j	$-2M-10$	$\frac{1}{2}M+5$	$-\frac{1}{2}M-5$	–10	$\frac{1}{2}M-5$	M	$-\frac{1}{2}M+5$	$-M$	—	
	$Z_j - C_j$		$\frac{M}{2}+4$	$-\frac{M}{2}+2$ ↑	0	$\frac{M}{2}-2$	M	$5-\frac{M}{2}$	0	—	Min x_B/S_2
← $-M$	A_1	1	0	0	–1	–1	–1	(1)	—	—	1/1 = 1
–7	w_2	2	–1	1	2	1	0	–1	—	—	—
	Z_j	$-M-14$	7	–7	$M-14$	$M-7$	M	$-M+7$	—	—	
	$Z_j - C_j$		6	0	$M-4$	$M-4$	M	$7-M$ ↑	—	—	
0	S_2	1	0	0	–1	–1	–1	1			
–7	W_2	3	–1	1	1	0	–1	0			
	Z_j	–21	7	–7	–7	0	7	0			
	$Z_j - C_j$		6	0	3	3	7	0			

	C_j		3	2	0	0	$-M$	$-M$	
C_B	B	x_B	w_1	w_2	S_1	S_2	A_1	A_2	Min x_B/w_2
$-M$	A_1	4	-1	-1	-1	0	1	0	—
$\leftarrow -M$	A_2	2	-1	(1)	0	-1	0	1	$2/1 = 2 \leftarrow$
	Z_j	$-6M$	$2M$	0	M	M	$-M$	$-M$	
	$Z_j - C_j$		$2M - 3$	$-2\uparrow$	M	M	0	0	
$-M$	A_1	6	-2	0	-1	-1	1	—	
2	W_2	6	-1	1	0	-1	0	—	
	Z_j	$-6M + 4$	$2M - 2$	2	M	$M - 2$	$-M$	—	
	$Z_j - C_j$		$2M - 5$	0	M	$M - 2$	0	—	

$\therefore$ All $Z_j - C_j \geq 0$ and artificial variable A_1 is in the basis at positive level. Thus, the dual problem does not possess any optimum basic feasible solution. Consequently, there exists no finite optimum solution to the given LP problem or the solution of the given LPP is unbounded.

Example 6.9 Prove using duality theory that the following LPP has a feasible but not optimal solution.

Min $Z = x_1 - x_2 + x_3$

Subject to,

$$x_1 - x_3 \geq 4$$
$$x_1 - x_2 + 2x_3 \geq 3$$

and $x_1, x_2, x_3 \geq 0$

Solution Given primal LPP is,

Min $Z = x_1 - x_2 + x_3$

Subject to,

$$x_1 + 0x_2 - x_3 \geq 4$$
$$x_1 - x_2 + 2x_3 \geq 3$$
$$x_1, x_2, x_3 \geq 0$$

Dual Since there are two constraints, there are two variables w_1 and w_2 in the dual, given by

Max $Z' = 4w_1 + 3w_2$

Subject to,

$$w_1 + w_2 \leq 1$$
$$0w_1 - w_2 \leq -1$$
$$-w_1 + 2w_2 \leq 1$$
$$w_1, w_2 \geq 0$$

To solve the dual problem,

Max $Z' = 4w_1 + 3w_2$

Subject to,

$$w_1 + w_2 + S_1 = 1$$
$$0w_1 - w_2 - S_2 + A_1 = 1$$
$$-w_1 + 2w_2 + S_3 = 1$$

where, S_1 and S_3 are the slack variables, S_2 the surplus variable and A_1 the artificial variable.

		C_j	4	3	0	0	$-M$	0	
C_B	B	x_B	w_1	w_2	S_1	S_2	A_1	S_3	$Min\ x_B/w_2$
0	S_1	1	1	1	1	0	0	0	1
$-M$	A_1	1	0	1	0	-1	1	0	1
$\leftarrow 0$	S_3	1	-1	(2)	0	0	0	1	$\frac{1}{2}$
	Z_j	$-M$	0	$-M$	0	M	$-M$	0	
	$Z_j - C_j$		-4	$-M-3$ ↑	0	M	0	0	
									$Min\ \frac{x_B}{w_1}$
$\leftarrow 0$	S_1	1/2	(3/2)	0	1	0	0	$-1/2$	1/3
$-M$	A_1	1/2	1/2	0	0	-1	1	$-1/2$	1
3	w_2	1/2	$-1/2$	1	0	0	0	1/2	—
	Z_j	$-\frac{1}{2}M-3/2$	$-\frac{1}{2}M-3/2$	3	0	M	$-M$	$\frac{1}{2}M+3/2$	
	$Z_j - C_j$		$-\frac{M}{2}+\frac{5}{2}$ ↑	0	0	M	0	$\frac{M+3}{2}$	

Since all $Z_j - C_j \geq 0$ and an artificial variable appears in the basis at positive level, the dual problem has no optimal basic feasible solution.

$\therefore$ There exists no finite optimum solution to the given primal LPP (Unbounded solution).

6.5 DUAL SIMPLEX METHOD

The dual simplex method is very similar to the regular simplex method. The only difference lies in the criterion used for selecting a variable to enter and leave the basis. In dual simplex method, we first select the variable to leave the basis and then the variable to enter the basis. This method yields an optimal solution to the given LPP in a finite number of steps, provided no basis is repeated.

The dual simplex method is used to solve the problems which start with dual feasible (i.e., whose primal is optimal but infeasible). In this method the solution starts optimum basis, but remains infeasible until the true optimum is reached, at which the solution becomes feasible. The advantage of this method lies in its avoiding the artificial variables introduced in the constraints along with the surplus variables as all '≥' constraints are converted into '≤' type.

6.5.1 Dual Simplex Algorithm

The iterative procedure for dual simplex method is listed below.

Step 1 Convert the problem to maximization form if it is initially in the minimization form.

Step 2 Convert '≥' type constraints, if any, to '≤' type, by multiplying both sides by –1.

Step 3 Express the problem in standard form by introducing slack variables. Obtain the initial basic solution, display this solution in the simplex table.

Step 4 Test the nature of $Z_j - C_j$ (optimal condition).

Case I If all $Z_j - C_j \geq 0$ and all $x_{Bi} \geq 0$ then the current solution is an optimum feasible solution.

Case II If all $Z_j - C_j \geq 0$ and at least one $x_{Bi} < 0$ then the current solution is not an optimum basic feasible solution. In this case go to the next step.

Case III If any $Z_j - C_j < 0$ then the method fails.

Step 5 In this step we find the leaving variable, which is the basic variable corresponding to the most negative value of x_{Bi}. Let x_k be the leaving variable, i.e., $x_{Bk} = \min \{x_{Bi}, x_{Bi} < 0\}$

To find out the variable entering the basis, we compute the ratio between $Z_j - C_j$ row and the key row *i.e.* compute Max $\{Z_j - C_j/c_{ik}, a_{ik} < 0\}$ (Consider the ratios with negative denominator alone). The entering variable is the one having the maximum ratio. If there is no such ratio with negative denominator, then the problem does not have a feasible solution.

Step 6 Convert the leading element to unity and all the other elements of key column to zero, to get an improved solution.

Step 7 Repeat steps (4) and (5) until either an optimum basic feasible solution is attained or an indication of no feasible solution is obtained.

Example 6.10 Use dual simplex method to solve the following LPP.

$$\text{Max} \quad Z = 3x_1 - x_2$$

$$\text{Subject to,} \quad x_1 + x_2 \geq 1$$
$$2x_1 + 3x_2 \geq 2$$
$$x_1, x_2 \geq 0$$

Solution Convert the given constraints into $\leq$ type.

$$\text{Max} \quad Z = -3x_1 - x_2$$

$$\text{Subject to,} \quad -x_1 - x_2 \leq -1$$
$$-2x_1 - 3x_2 \leq -2$$
$$x_1, x_2 \geq 0$$

Introducing slack variables $S_1, S_2 \leq 0$, we get

$$\text{Max} \quad Z = -3x_1 - x_2 + 0S_1 + 0S_2$$

$$\text{Subject to,} \quad -x_1 - x_2 + S_1 = -1$$
$$-2x_1 - 3x_2 + S_2 = -2$$
$$x_1, x_2, S_1, S_2 \geq 0$$

An initial basic (infeasible) solution of the modified LPP is $S_1 = -1$, $S_2 = -2$

	C_j		−3	−1	0	0
C_B	B	x_B	x_1	x_2	S_1	S_2
0	S_1	−1	−1	−1	1	0
←0	S_2	−2	−2	(−3)	0	1
	Z_j	0	0	0	0	0
	$Z_j - C_j$		3	1↑	0	0

Since all $Z_j - C_j \geq 0$ and all $x_{Bi} < 0$, the current solution is not an optimum basic feasible solution. Since $x_{B2} = -3$, the most negative, the corresponding basic variable S_2 leaves the basis. Also since max $\{Z_j - C_j/a_{ik}, a_{ik} < 0\}$, where x_k is the leaving variable, max $\{3/-2, 1/-3\} = -1/3 = Z_2 - C_2/a_{22}$ the non-basic variable x_2 enters the basis.

Drop S_2 and introduce x_2.

First iteration

		C_j	−3	−1	0	0
C_B	B	x_B	x_1	x_2	S_1	S_2
←0	S_1	−1/3	−1/3	0	1	(−1/3)
−1	x_2	2/3	2/3	1	0	−1/3
	Z_j	−2/3	−2/3	−1	0	1/3
	$Z_j - C_j$		7/3	0	0	1/3
						↑

Since all $Z_j - C_j \geq 0$ and $x_{B1} = -1/3 < 0$, the current solution is not an optimum basic feasible solution.

$\because$ $x_{B1} = -1/3$ the basic variable S_1 leaves the basis. Also since max $\{Z_j - C_j/a_{i1}, a_{i1} < 0\}$ = max $\{(1/3)/(-1/3) \ldots (1/3)/(-1/3)\} = -1$ corresponds to the non-basic variable S_2.

$\therefore$ Drop S_1 and introduce S_2.

Second iteration

		C_j	−3	−1	0	0
C_B	B	x_B	x_1	x_2	S_1	S_2
0	S_2	1	1	0	−3	1
−1	x_2	1	1	1	−1	0
	Z_j	−1	−1	−1	1	0
	$Z_j - C_j$		2	0	1	0

Since all $Z_j - C_j \leq 0$ and also $x_{Bi} \geq 0$, an optimum basic feasible solution has been reached. The optimal solution to the given LPP is $x_1 = 0$; $x_2 = 1$, Maximum $Z = -1$.

Example 6.11 Solve by the dual simplex method the following LPP.

Min $\quad Z = 5x_1 + 6x_2$

Subject to,

$$x_1 + x_2 \geq 2$$
$$4x_1 + x_2 \geq 4$$
$$x_1, x_2 \geq 0$$

Solution The given LPP is Max $Z = -5x_1 - 6x_2$

Subject to,

$$-x_1 - x_2 \leq -2$$
$$-4x_1 - x_2 \leq -4$$

and $\quad x_1, x_2 \geq 0$

By introducing slack variables S_1, S_2 the standard form of LPP becomes,

Max $\quad Z = -5x_1 - 6x_2 + 0S_1 + 0S_2$

Subject to,

$$-x_1 - x_2 + S_1 = -2$$
$$-4x_1 - x_2 + S_2 = -4$$

Initial table

	C_j		−5	−6	0	0
C_B	B	x_B	x_1	x_2	S_1	S_2
0	S_1	−2	−1	−1	1	0
←0	S_2	−4	(−4)	−1	0	1
	Z_j	0	0	0	0	0
	$Z_j - C_j$		5↑	6	0	0

Since all $Z_j - C_j \geq 0$ and $x_{Bi} \leq 0$, the current solution is not an optimum basic feasible solution.

$\therefore$ $x_{B2} = -4$, is most negative, the corresponding basic variable S_2 leaves the basis.

Also, Max $Z_j - C_j/a_{i2}$, $a_{i2} < 0$ = Max {– 5/4, 6/ –1, ...} = –5/4 gives the non-basic variable, x_1 enters into the basis.

First iteration

	C_j		−5	−6	0	0
C_B	B	x_B	x_1	x_2	S_1	S_2
←0	S_1	−1	0	−3/4	1	(−1/4)
−5	x_1	1	1	1/4	0	−1/4
	Z_j	−5	−5	−5/4	0	5/4
	$Z_j - C_j$		0	$\frac{19}{4}$	0	5/4
						↑

Since all $Z_j - C_j \geq 0$ and also $x_{B1} = -1 < 0$, the current basic feasible solution is not optimum. As $x_{B1} = -1 < 0$ therefore, the basic variable S_1 leaves the basis.

Also, since $\text{Max}\left\{\dfrac{Z_j - C_j}{a_{i1}}, a_{i1} < 0\right\} = \text{Max}\left\{\dfrac{19/4}{-3/4}, \dfrac{-5/4}{1/4}\right\} = -5$ corresponds to the non-basic variable S_2.

$\therefore$ Drop S_1 and introduce S_2.

Second iteration

	C_j		−5	−6	0	0
C_B	B	x_B	x_1	x_2	S_1	S_2
0	S_2	4	0	3	−4	1
−5	x_1	2	1	1	−1	0
	Z_j	−10	−5	−5	5	0
	$Z_j - C_j$		0	1	5	0

Since all $Z_j - C_j \geq 0$ and also all $x_{Bi} \geq 0$, the current basic feasible solution is optimum. The optimal solution is given by $x_1 = 2, x_2 = 0$, Max $Z = -10$

i.e., Min $Z = 10$

Example 6.12 Use dual simplex method to solve the LPP.

$$\text{Max} \quad Z = -3x_1 - 2x_2$$

Subject to,

$$x_1 + x_2 \geq 1$$
$$x_1 + x_2 \leq 7$$
$$x_1 + 2x_2 \geq 10$$
$$x_2 \leq 3$$
$$x_1, x_2 \geq 0$$

Solution Interchanging the $\geq$ inequality of the constraints into $\leq$, the given LPP becomes,

$$\text{Max} \quad Z = -3x_1 - 2x_2$$

Subject to,

$$-x_1 - x_2 \leq -1$$
$$x_1 + x_2 \leq 7$$
$$-x_1 - 2x_2 \leq -10$$
$$0x_1 + x_2 \leq 3$$

By introducing the non-negative slack variables S_1, S_2, S_3, S_4, the standard form of the LPP becomes,

$$\text{Max} \quad Z = -3x_1 - 2x_2 + 0S_1 + 0S_2 + 0S_3 + 0S_4$$

Subject to,

$$-x_1 - x_2 + S_1 = -1$$
$$x_1 + x_2 + S_2 = 7$$
$$-x_1 - 2x_2 + S_3 = -10$$
$$0x_1 + x_2 + S_4 = 3$$

The initial solution is given by,

$$S_1 = -1, S_2 = 7, S_3 = -10, S_4 = 3$$

Initial table

	C_j		−3	−2	0	0	0	0
C_B	B	x_B	x_1	x_2	S_1	S_2	S_3	S_4
0	S_1	−1	−1	−1	1	0	0	0
0	S_2	7	1	1	0	1	0	0
←0	S_3	−10	−1	(−2)	0	0	1	0
0	S_4	3	0	1	0	0	0	1
	Z_j	0	0	0	0	0	0	0
	$Z_j - C_j$		3	↑2	0	0	0	0

Since all $Z_j - C_j \geq 0$ and some $x_{Bi} \leq 0$, the current solution is not a basic feasible solution. $\therefore x_{B3} = -10$ being the most negative, the basic variable S_3 leaves the basis.

Also, Max $\{Z_j - C_j/a_{i2}, a_{i2} < 0\}$ = Max $\{3/-1, 2/-2\}$ = −1, the non-basic variable x_2 enters the basis.

First iteration

	C_j		−3	−2	0	0	0	0	
C_B	B	x_B	x_1	x_2	S_1	S_2	S_3	S_4	
0	S_1	4	−1/2	0	1	0	−1/2	0	
0	S_2	2	1/2	0	0	1	1/2	0	
−2	x_2	5	1/2	1	0	0	−1/2	0	
← 0	S_4	−2	(−1/2)	0	0	0	1/2	1	←
	Z_j	−10	−1	−2	0	0	1	0	
	$Z_j - C_j$		2	0	0	0	1	0	
			↑						

Second iteration

Drop S_4 and introduce x_1.

$\because$ $x_{B4} = -2 < 0$, S_4 leaves the basis.

$$\text{Max}\left\{\frac{Z_j - C_j}{a_{1i}} a_{1i} < 0\right\} = \text{Max}\left\{\frac{2}{-1/2}\ldots\right\} = -4$$

Hence, x_1 enters the basis.

	C_j		3	2	0	0	0	0
C_B	B	x_B	x_1	x_2	S_1	S_2	S_3	S_4
0	S_1	2	0	0	1	0	−1	−1
0	S_2	0	0	0	0	1	1	1
−2	x_2	3	0	1	0	0	0	1
−3	x_1	4	1	0	0	0	−1	−2
	Z_j	−18	−3	−2	0	0	3	4
	$Z_j - C_j$		0	0	0	0	3	4

Since all $Z_j - C_j \geq 0$ and all $x_{Bi} \geq 0$, the current solution is an optimum basic feasible solution.

$\therefore$ The optimum solution is, Max $Z = -18$, $x_1 = 4$, $x_2 = 3$.

Example 6.13 Use dual simplex method to solve the LPP.

Max $Z = -2x_1 - x_3$

Subject to,

$$x_1 + x_2 - x_3 \geq 5$$
$$x_1 - 2x_2 + 4x_3 \geq 8$$
$$x_1, x_2, x_3 \geq 0$$

Solution The given problem can be written as

Max $Z = -2x_1 - 0x_2 - x_3$

Subject to,

$$-x_1 - x_2 + x_3 \geq -5$$
$$-x_1 + 2x_2 - 4x_3 \leq -8$$
$$x_1, x_2, x_3 \geq 0$$

Adding the slack variables S_1 and S_2, we get the constraints,

$$-x_1 - x_2 + x_3 + S_1 = -5$$
$$-x_1 + 2x_2 - 4x_3 + S_2 = -8$$

	C_j		-2	0	-1	0	0
C_B	B	x_B	x_1	x_2	x_3	S_1	S_2
0	S_1	–5	–1	–1	1	1	0
←0	S_2	–8	–1	2	(–4)	0	1
	Z_j	0	0	0	0	0	0
	$Z_j - C_j$		2	0	1	0	0
					↑		

Since all $Z_j - C_j \geq 0$ and also some $x_{Bi} \geq 0$, the solution is not optimum. As $x_{B2} = -8$ is most negative, the basic variable S_2 leaves the basis. Also,

$$\text{Max}\left\{\frac{Z_j - C_j}{a_{iK}}, a_{ik} < 0\right\} \text{ gives}$$

$$\text{Max}\left\{\frac{2}{-1}, -, \frac{1}{-4}, - -\right\} = -\frac{1}{4}$$

x_3 enters the basis. Drop S_2 and introduce x_3.

First iteration

	C_j		-2	0	-1	0	0
C_B	B	x_B	x_1	x_2	x_3	S_1	S_2
← 0	S_1	–7	–5/4	(–1/2)	0	1	1/4
–1	x_3	2	1/4	1/2	1	0	–1/4
	Z_j	–2	–1/4	1/2	–1	0	1/4
	$Z_j - C_j$		7/4	1/2↑	0	0	1/4

Drop S_1 and introduce x_2.

Since $x_{B1} = -7 < 0$, S_1 the basic variable leaves the basis.

Therefore, the non-basic variable x_2 enters the basis.

$$\text{Max}\left\{\frac{Z_j - C_j}{a_{iK}}, a_{ik} < 0\right\} \text{ gives}$$

$$\text{Max}\left\{\frac{7/4}{-5/4}, \frac{1/2}{-1/2}, -, -\right\} = -1.$$

Second iteration

	C_j		−2	0	−1	0	0
C_B	B	x_B	x_1	x_2	x_3	S_1	S_2
0	x_2	14	5/2	1	0	−2	−1/2
−1	x_3	9	3/2	0	1	−1	−1/2
	Z_j	−9	−3/2	0	−1	1	1/2
	$Z_j - C_j$		1/2	0	0	1	1

Since all $Z_j - C_j \geq 0$ and all $x_{Bi} \geq 0$, the current basic feasible solution is optimum. The optimal solution is given by $x_1 = 0, x_2 = 14, x_3 = 9$

$$\text{Max } Z = -9$$

EXERCISES

1. Obtain the dual of the following LPP

Max $Z = x_1 - x_2 + 3x_3$

Subject to, $x_1 + x_2 + x_3 \leq 10,$
$2x_1 - x_3 \leq 2,$
$2x_1 - 2x_2 + 3x_3 \leq 6$
$x_1, x_2, x_3 \geq 0.$

[**Ans.** Min $Z' = 10w_1 + 2w_2 + 6w_3$
Subject to, $w_1 + 2w_2 + 2w_3 \geq 1$
$w_1 + 2w_3 \geq -1$
$w_1 - w_2 + 3w_3 \geq 3$]

2. Max $Z = 3x_1 + x_2 + 2x_3 - x_4$

Subject to the constraints,

$2x_1 - x_2 + 3x_3 + x_4 = 1,$
$x_1 + x_2 - x_3 + x_4 = 3$
$x_1, x_2, x_3 \geq 0$

and x_4 is unrestricted.

[**Ans.** Min $Z' = w_1 + 3w$
Subject to, $2w_1 + w_2 \geq 3$
$-w_1 + w_2 \geq 1$
$3w_1 - w_2 \geq 1$]

3. Max $Z = 2x_1 + x_2$

Subject to, $x_1 + 5x_2 \leq 10$
$x_1 + 3x_2 \leq 6$
$x_2 \geq 0$, x_1 is unrestricted.

[**Ans.** Min $Z' = 10w_1 + 6w_2 + 8w_3$
Subject to, $w_1 + w_2 + 2w_3 \geq 2$
$5w_1 + 3w_2 + 2w_3 \geq 1$
$w_1, w_2, w_3 \geq 0$]

4. Max $Z = 2x_1 + 5x_2 + 6x_3$

Subject to, $x_1 + 6x_2 - x_3 \leq 3$
$-2x_1 + x_2 + 4x_3 \leq 4$

$$x_1 - 5x_2 + 3x_3 \le 1$$
$$-3x_1 - 3x_2 + 7x_3 \le 6$$
$$x_1, x_2, x_3 \ge 0$$

Also verify that the dual of the dual problem is the primal problem.

[**Ans.** Min $Z' = 3w_1 + 4w_2 + w_3 + 6w_4$
Subject to, $w_1 - 2w_2 + w_3 - 3w_4 \ge 2$
$6w_1 + w_2 - 5w_3 - 3w_4 \ge 5$
$-w_1 + 4w_2 + 3w_3 + 7w_4 \ge 6$
$w_1, w_2, w_3, w_4 \ge 0$]

5. Max $Z = 3x_1 + 17x_2 + 9x_3$
   Subject to, $x_1 - x_2 + x_3 \ge 3$
   $-3x_1 + 2x_3 \le 1$
   $x_1, x_2, x_3 \ge 0.$

[**Ans.** Min $Z' = -3w_1 + w_2$
Subject to, $w_1 - 3w_2 \ge 3$
$-w_1 + 0w_2 \ge 17$
$w_1 + 2w_2 \ge 9$
$w_1, w_2 \ge 0$]

6. Use the duality theory to solve the following LPP.
   Max $Z = 3x_1 + 4x_2$
   Subject to, $x_1 - x_2 \le 1$
   $x_1 + x_2 \ge 4$
   $x_1 - 3x_2 \le 3$
   $x_1, x_2 \ge 0.$

   [**Ans.** No feasible solution exists for the dual problem, hence the primal has no finite optimum solution.]

7. Use duality to solve the LPP.
   Min $Z = 4x_1 + 2x_2 + 3x_3$
   Subject to, $2x_1 + 4x_3 \ge 5$
   $2x_1 + 3x_2 + x_3 \ge 4$
   $x_1, x_2, x_3 \ge 0.$

$$\left[\textbf{Ans.}\ \text{Primal: Min } Z = \frac{67}{12}, x_1 = 0, x_2 = \frac{11}{12}, x_3 = \frac{5}{4}\ \text{Dual: Min } Z' = \frac{67}{12}, w_1 = \frac{7}{2}, w_2 = \frac{2}{3}\right]$$

8. Use duality to solve the LPP.
   Max $Z = 5x_1 + 12x_2 + 4x_3$
   Subject to, $x_1 + 2x_2 + x_3 \le 5$
   $2x_1 - x_2 + 3x_3 \le 2$
   $x_1, x_2, x_3 \ge 0.$

$$\left[\textbf{Ans.}\ \text{Primal: Max } Z = \frac{141}{5}, x_1 = \frac{9}{5}, x_2 = \frac{8}{5}, x_3 = 0\ \text{Dual: Min } Z' = \frac{141}{5}, w_1 = \frac{29}{5}, w_2 = \frac{-2}{5}\right]$$

9. Use the dual simplex method to solve,
   Max $Z = -3x_1 - x_2$
   Subject to, $x_1 + x_2 \ge 1$
   $x_1 + 3x_2 \ge 2$
   $x_1, x_2 \ge 0.$

[**Ans.** Max $Z = -1$, $x_1 = 0$, $x_2 = 1$]

10. Apply the principle of duality to solve the following LPP.

Max $Z = 3x_1 + 4x_2$

Subject to,
$$x_1 - x_2 \le 1$$
$$x_1 + x_2 \le 4$$
$$x_1 - 3x_2 \le 3$$
$$x_1, x_2 \ge 0.$$

[**Ans.** Primal: unbounded solution]

11. Use the dual simplex method to solve the following LPP.

Min $Z = 10x_1 + 6x_2 + 2x_3$

Subject to,
$$-x_1 + x_2 + x_3 \ge 1$$
$$3x_1 + x_2 - x_3 \ge 2$$
$$x_1, x_2, x_3 \ge 0.$$

$\left[\textbf{Ans. } x_1 = \frac{1}{4}, x_2 = \frac{5}{4}, x_3 = 0, \text{Min } Z = 10\right]$

12. Using the dual simplex method, solve

Min $Z = 2x_1 + 2x_2 + 4x_3$

Subject to,
$$2x_1 + 3x_2 + 5x_3 \ge 2$$
$$3x_1 + x_2 + 7x_3 \le 3$$
$$x_1 + 4x_2 + 6x_3 \le 5$$
$$x_1, x_2, x_3 \ge 0.$$

$\left[\textbf{Ans. } \text{Min } Z = \frac{4}{3}, x_1 = 0, x_2 = \frac{2}{3}, x_3 = 0\right]$

13. Use the dual simplex method to solve

Max $Z = 2x_1 + 3x_2$

Subject to,
$$2x_1 - x_2 - x_3 \ge 3$$
$$x_1 - x_2 + x_3 \ge 2$$
$$x_1, x_2, x_3 \ge 0.$$

$\left[\textbf{Ans. } \text{Max } Z = \frac{13}{3}, x_1 = \frac{5}{3}, x_2 = 0, x_3 = \frac{1}{3}\right]$

14. Use the dual simplex method to solve

Max $Z = -2x_1 - 2x_2 - 4x_3$

Subject to,
$$2x_1 + 3x_2 + 5x_3 \ge 2$$
$$3x_1 + x_2 + 7x_3 \le 3$$
$$x_1 + 4x_2 + 6x_3 \le 5$$
$$x_1, x_2, x_3 \ge 0.$$

$\left[\textbf{Ans. } \text{Max } Z = -\frac{4}{3}, x_1 = 0, x_2 = \frac{2}{3}, x_3 = 0\right]$

15. Show that the following LPP has a feasible solution but no finite optimal solution.

Max $Z = 3x_1 + 2x_2$

Subject to,
$$x_1 - x_2 \le 1$$
$$x_1 + x_2 \ge 3$$
$$x_1, x_2 \ge 0.$$

[**Ans.** Max $Z = -1$, $x_1 = 0$, $x_2 = 1$]

❑❑❑

Chapter

7 Revised Simplex Method

7.1 INTRODUCTION

While working on a computer, it is observed that the simplex method is not very economical as many inessential calculations are carried out and stored in the memory of the computer. A revised simplex method, which is the modification of the original, is more economical on the computer, as it computes and stores only the relevant information needed currently for testing and updating the current solution.

7.2 COMPUTATIONAL PROCEDURE

Step 1 Introduce slack and surplus variables, if needed, and bring the problem in the standard form after converting the objective function into maximization. (if not)

Step 2 Find an initial basic feasible solution with initial basis $B = I_m$ and form the auxiliary matrix $\hat{B}$, such that

$$\hat{B} = \begin{pmatrix} B & 1 \\ -C_B & 1 \end{pmatrix} \text{ and } \hat{B}^{-1} = \begin{pmatrix} B^{-1} & 0 \\ C_{B\,B^{-1}} & 1 \end{pmatrix}$$

Step 3 Considering the objective function $Z = CX$ as an additional constraint, form $\hat{A}$ and $\hat{b}$, such that

$$\hat{A} = \begin{pmatrix} A \\ -C \end{pmatrix} \text{ and } \hat{b} = \begin{pmatrix} b \\ 0 \end{pmatrix}$$

Step 4 Compute the net evaluation

$$Z_j - C_j = \begin{pmatrix} C_{BB^{-1}} & 1 \end{pmatrix} \begin{pmatrix} A \\ -C \end{pmatrix}$$

i.e., by multiplying the successive column of $\hat{A}$ with the last row of $\hat{B}^{-1}$.

(*i*) If all $Z_j - C_j \geq 0$, the current basic solution is an optimum solution.

(*ii*) If at least one $Z_j - C_j < 0$, determine the most negative of them say $Z_k - C_k$, corresponding to the variable X_k enters the basis. Go to step 5.

Step 5 Compute $\hat{X}_K = \hat{B}^{-1}_{\text{curr}}\, \hat{a}_K$

Case I If all $\hat{X}_{ik} \leq 0$, then there exists an unbounded solution to the given LPP.

Case II If at least one $X_{ik} > 0$, consider the current X_m and determine the leaving variable by

computing Min $\left\{ \dfrac{X_{Bi}}{X_{ik}}, X_{ik} > 0 \right\}$. Go to step 6.

Step 6 Write down the results obtained from step (2) to step (5) in the revised simplex table.

Step 7 Convert the leading element unity and all other elements of the key column to zero and improve the current basic feasible solution.

Step 8 Go to step (4) and repeat the procedure until an optimum basic feasible solution is obtained or there is an indication of an unbounded solution.

Example 7.1 Use the revised simplex method to solve the following LPP.

Max $$Z = 6x_1 - 2x_2 + 3x_3$$

Subject to,
$$2x_1 - x_2 + 2x_3 \le 2$$
$$x_1 + 4x_3 \le 4$$
$$x_1, x_2, x_1 \ge 0$$

Solution Convert the given problem into its standard form by adding slack variables $S_1, S_2 \ge 0$

Max $$Z = 6x_1 - 2x_2 + 3x_3 + 0S_1 + 0S_2$$

Subject to,
$$2x_1 - x_2 + 2x_3 + S_1 = 2$$
$$x_1 + 0x_2 + 4x_3 + S_2 = 4$$
$$x_1, x_2, x_3, S_1, S_2 \ge 0$$

$$A = \begin{pmatrix} 2 & -1 & 2 & 1 & 0 \\ 1 & 0 & 4 & 0 & 1 \end{pmatrix} \quad b = \begin{pmatrix} 2 \\ 4 \end{pmatrix}$$

$$C = (6 \ \ -2 \ \ 3 \ \ 0 \ \ 0) \ C_B = (0 \ \ 0)$$

The initial basic feasible solution is $S_1 = 2, S_2 = 4$

$$\hat{A} = \begin{pmatrix} A \\ -C \end{pmatrix} = \begin{pmatrix} 2 & -1 & 2 & 1 & 0 \\ 1 & 0 & 4 & 0 & 1 \\ -6 & +2 & -3 & 0 & 0 \end{pmatrix}$$

$$\hat{B}^{-1}_{\text{curr}} = \begin{pmatrix} B^{-1} & 0 \\ C_{B\,B^{-1}} & 1 \end{pmatrix} = \begin{pmatrix} 1 & 0 & 0 \\ 0 & 1 & 0 \\ 0 & 0 & 1 \end{pmatrix}$$

The net evaluations are given by,

$$Z_j - C_j = (C_{B\,B^{-1}} \ 1) \ \hat{A}$$

$$= (0 \ \ 0 \ \ 1) \begin{pmatrix} 2 & -1 & 2 & 1 & 0 \\ 1 & 0 & 4 & 0 & 1 \\ -6 & 2 & -3 & 0 & 0 \end{pmatrix}$$

$$= (-6 \ \ 2 \ \ -3 \ \ 0 \ \ 0)$$

Since $Z_1 - C_1 = -6$ is most negative, x_1 enters the basis.

$$\hat{X}_1 = \hat{B}^{-1}_{\text{curr}} \ \hat{a}_1 = \begin{pmatrix} 1 & 0 & 0 \\ 0 & 1 & 0 \\ 0 & 0 & 1 \end{pmatrix} \begin{pmatrix} 2 \\ 1 \\ -6 \end{pmatrix} = \begin{pmatrix} 2 \\ 1 \\ -6 \end{pmatrix}$$

$$\hat{X}_B = \hat{B}^{-1}_{\text{curr}} \ \hat{b}_1 = \begin{pmatrix} 1 & 0 & 0 \\ 0 & 1 & 0 \\ 0 & 0 & 1 \end{pmatrix} \begin{pmatrix} 2 \\ 4 \\ 0 \end{pmatrix} = \begin{pmatrix} 2 \\ 4 \\ 0 \end{pmatrix}$$

To find the leaving variable, find Min $\left(\frac{x_B}{x_{i1}}, x_{i1} > 0\right)$

$$= \text{Min}\left(\frac{2}{2}, \frac{4}{1}, -\right) = 1 \text{ gives } S_1\text{, to leave the basis.}$$

The revised simplex table is shown below.

x_B	B	$\hat{B}^{-1}_{\text{curr}}$			$\hat{x}_1$	*Ratio*
2	S_1	1	0	0	(2)	2/2 = 1
4	S_2	0	1	0	1	4/1 = 4
0		0	0	1	– 6 ↑	

First iteration

Convert the leading element to unity and all other elements of the key column to 0. We have,

$$\hat{B}^{-1}_{\text{curr}} = \begin{pmatrix} \frac{1}{2} & 0 & 0 \\ -\frac{1}{2} & 1 & 0 \\ 3 & 0 & 1 \end{pmatrix}$$

$$(Z_j - C_j) = (C_{B\,B}^{-1}\ 1)\,\hat{A}$$

$$= \begin{pmatrix} 3 & 0 & 1 \end{pmatrix} \begin{pmatrix} +2 & -1 & 2 & 1 & 0 \\ 1 & 0 & 4 & 0 & 1 \\ -6 & 2 & -3 & 0 & 0 \end{pmatrix}$$

$$= \begin{pmatrix} 0 & -1 & 3 & 3 & 0 \end{pmatrix}$$

Since $Z_2 - C_2 = -1$ is most negative, x_2 enters the basis.

$$\hat{x}_2 = \hat{B}^{-1}_{\text{curr}}\ \hat{a}_2 = \begin{pmatrix} \frac{1}{2} & 0 & 0 \\ \frac{-1}{2} & 1 & 0 \\ 3 & 0 & 1 \end{pmatrix} \begin{pmatrix} -1 \\ 0 \\ 2 \end{pmatrix} = \begin{pmatrix} -\frac{1}{2} \\ \frac{1}{2} \\ -1 \end{pmatrix}$$

$$\hat{x}_B = \hat{B}^{-1}_{\text{curr}}\ \hat{b} = \begin{pmatrix} \frac{1}{2} & 0 & 0 \\ \frac{-1}{2} & 1 & 0 \\ 3 & 0 & 1 \end{pmatrix} \begin{pmatrix} 2 \\ 4 \\ 0 \end{pmatrix} = \begin{pmatrix} 1 \\ 3 \\ 6 \end{pmatrix}$$

To find the leaving variable, find Min $\left(\frac{\hat{x}_2}{\hat{x}_{i2}}, \hat{x}_{i2} > 0\right)$

$= \text{Min}\left(-\frac{3}{1/2}, -\right) = -6$ gives the basic variable S_2 to leave the basis.

The revised simplex table is

B	x_B	$\hat{B}^{-1}_{\text{curr}}$			$\hat{x}_2$	Ratio
x_B	1	+1/2	0	0	–1/2	—
$\leftarrow S_2$	3	–1/2	1	0	1/2	6
	6	3	0	1	– 1	

Second iteration

Convert the leading element to unity and other elements in the key column as 0.

$$\hat{B}^{-1}_{\text{curr}} = \begin{pmatrix} 0 & 1 & 0 \\ -1 & 2 & 0 \\ 2 & 2 & 1 \end{pmatrix}$$

$$(Z_j - C_j) = (C_B\ B^{-1}\ 1)\ \hat{A} = \begin{pmatrix} 2 & 2 & 1 \end{pmatrix} \begin{pmatrix} 2 & -1 & 2 & 1 & 0 \\ 1 & 0 & 4 & 0 & 1 \\ -6 & 2 & -3 & 0 & 0 \end{pmatrix}$$

$$= \begin{pmatrix} 0 & 0 & 9 & 2 & 2 \end{pmatrix}$$

Since all $Z_j - C_j \geq 0$, the current feasible solution is optimal

$$\hat{x}_B = \hat{B}^{-1}_{\text{curr}}\ \hat{b} = \begin{pmatrix} 0 & 1 & 0 \\ -1 & 2 & 0 \\ 2 & 2 & 1 \end{pmatrix} \begin{pmatrix} 2 \\ 4 \\ 0 \end{pmatrix} = \begin{pmatrix} 4 \\ 6 \\ 12 \end{pmatrix}$$

$\therefore$ The optimal solution is given by,

$\Rightarrow x_1 = 4, x_2 = 6, x_3 = 0$ and

Max $Z = 12$.

Example 7.2 Use the revised simplex method to solve the following LPP.

Max $\quad Z = x_1 + 2x_2$

Subject to,

$$x_1 + x_2 \leq 3$$
$$x_1 + 2x_2 \leq 5$$
$$3x_1 + x_2 \leq 6$$
$$x_1, x_2 \geq 0$$

Solution Introducing the slack variables S_1, S_2, S_3, we convert the given problem into its standard form.

Max $\quad Z = x_1 + 2x_2 + 0S_1 + 0S_2 + 0S_3$

Subj to,

$$x_1 + x_2 + S_1 = 3$$
$$x_1 + 2x_2 + S_2 = 5$$
$$3x_1 + x_2 + S_3 = 6$$
$$x_1, x_2, S_1, S_2, S_3 \geq 0$$

Initial solution is given by, $S_1 = 3, S_2 = 5, S_3 = 6.$

$$A = \begin{pmatrix} 1 & 1 & 1 & 0 & 0 \\ 1 & 2 & 0 & 1 & 0 \\ 3 & 1 & 0 & 0 & 1 \end{pmatrix} \quad b = \begin{pmatrix} 3 \\ 5 \\ 6 \end{pmatrix}$$

$$C = (1 \;\; 2 \;\; 0 \;\; 0 \;\; 0) \quad C_B = (0 \;\; 0 \;\; 0)$$

$$\hat{A} = \begin{pmatrix} A \\ -C \end{pmatrix} = \begin{pmatrix} 1 & 1 & 1 & 0 & 0 \\ 1 & 2 & 0 & 1 & 0 \\ 3 & 1 & 0 & 0 & 1 \\ -1 & -2 & 0 & 0 & 0 \end{pmatrix} \quad \hat{b} = \begin{pmatrix} b \\ 0 \end{pmatrix} = \begin{pmatrix} 3 \\ 5 \\ 6 \\ 0 \end{pmatrix}$$

$$\hat{B}_{\text{curr}}^{-1} = \begin{pmatrix} B^{-1} & 0 \\ C_{B B^{-1}} & 1 \end{pmatrix} = \begin{pmatrix} 1 & 0 & 0 & 0 \\ 0 & 1 & 0 & 0 \\ 0 & 0 & 1 & 0 \\ 0 & 0 & 0 & 1 \end{pmatrix}$$

The net evaluations are given by, $Z_j - C_j = (C_{B B^{-1}} \; 1)\, \hat{A}$

$$= (0 \;\; 0 \;\; 0 \;\; 1) \begin{pmatrix} 1 & 1 & 1 & 0 & 0 \\ 1 & 2 & 0 & 1 & 0 \\ 3 & 1 & 0 & 0 & 1 \\ -1 & -2 & 0 & 0 & 0 \end{pmatrix}$$

$$= (-1 \;\; -2 \;\; 0 \;\; 0 \;\; 0)$$

Since $Z_2 - C_2 = -2$ is most negative, x_2 enters the basis.

$$\hat{x}_2 = \hat{B}_{\text{curr}}^{-1} \; \hat{a}_2 = \begin{pmatrix} 1 & 0 & 0 & 0 \\ 0 & 1 & 0 & 0 \\ 0 & 0 & 1 & 0 \\ 0 & 0 & 0 & 1 \end{pmatrix} \begin{pmatrix} 1 \\ 2 \\ 1 \\ -2 \end{pmatrix} = \begin{pmatrix} 1 \\ 2 \\ 1 \\ -2 \end{pmatrix}$$

$$\hat{x}_B = \hat{B}_{\text{curr}}^{-1} \; \hat{b} = \begin{pmatrix} 1 & 0 & 0 & 0 \\ 0 & 1 & 0 & 0 \\ 0 & 0 & 1 & 0 \\ 0 & 0 & 0 & 1 \end{pmatrix} \begin{pmatrix} 3 \\ 5 \\ 6 \\ 0 \end{pmatrix} = \begin{pmatrix} 3 \\ 5 \\ 6 \\ 0 \end{pmatrix}$$

The revised simplex table is as follows:

B	x_B	$\hat{B}^{-1}_{\text{curr}}$				$\hat{x}_2$	*Ratio*
S_B	3	1	0	0	0	1	3/1 = 3
S_2	5	0	1	0	0	2	5/2 = 2.5
S_3	6	0	0	1	0	1	6/1 = 6
	0	0	0	0	1	–2	—

Thus, S_2 leaves the basis.

First iteration

Drop S_2 and introduce x_2. Convert the leading element into one and remaining elements as zero in the key column. Thus we have,

$$\hat{B}^{-1}_{\text{curr}} = \begin{pmatrix} 1 & \frac{-1}{2} & 0 & 0 \\ 0 & \frac{1}{2} & 0 & 0 \\ 0 & \frac{-1}{2} & 1 & 0 \\ 0 & 1 & 0 & 1 \end{pmatrix}$$

Compute $Z_j - C_j = (C_{B\,B^{-1}}\ 1)\,\hat{A}$

$$= \begin{pmatrix} 0 & 1 & 0 & 1 \end{pmatrix} \begin{pmatrix} 1 & 1 & 1 & 0 & 0 \\ 1 & 2 & 0 & 1 & 0 \\ 3 & 1 & 0 & 0 & 1 \\ -1 & -2 & 0 & 0 & 0 \end{pmatrix}$$

$$= \begin{pmatrix} 0 & 0 & 0 & 1 & 0 \end{pmatrix}$$

Since all $Z_j - C_j \geq 0$, we have reached the optimum solution.

$$\hat{x}_B = \hat{B}^{-1}_{\text{curr}}\ \hat{b} = \begin{bmatrix} 1 & \frac{-1}{2} & 0 & 0 \\ 0 & \frac{1}{2} & 0 & 0 \\ 0 & \frac{-1}{2} & 1 & 0 \\ 0 & 1 & 0 & 1 \end{bmatrix} \begin{bmatrix} 3 \\ 5 \\ 6 \\ 0 \end{bmatrix} = \begin{bmatrix} \frac{1}{2} \\ \frac{5}{2} \\ \frac{+7}{2} \\ 5 \end{bmatrix}$$

The optimum solution is given by,

$$x_1 = 0, x_2 = \frac{5}{2}, \text{ Max } Z = 5.$$

Example 7.3 Use the revised simplex method to solve the following LPP.

Max $Z = x_1 + x_2$

Subject to, $2x_1 + 5x_2 \leq 6$

$x_1 + x_2 \geq 2$

$x_1\, x_2 \geq 6$

Solution By introducing slack, surplus and artificial variables, the standard form of LPP thus takes the following form.

Max $Z = x_1 + x_2 + 0S_1 + 0S_2 - MA_1$

Subject to, $2x_1 + 5x_2 + S_1 = 6$

$x_1 + x_2 - S_2 + A_1 = 2$

$x_1, x_2, S_1, S_2, A_1 \geq 0$

The initial basic feasible solution is given by, $S_1 = 6$, $A_1 = 2$.

$$C = \begin{pmatrix} 1 & 1 & 0 & 0 & -M \end{pmatrix} \; C_B = \begin{pmatrix} 0, & -M \end{pmatrix}$$

$$A = \begin{pmatrix} 2 & 5 & 1 & 0 & 0 \\ 1 & 1 & 0 & -1 & 1 \end{pmatrix}$$

$$\hat{A} = \begin{pmatrix} A \\ -C \end{pmatrix} = \begin{pmatrix} 2 & 5 & 1 & 0 & 0 \\ 1 & 1 & 0 & -1 & 1 \\ -1 & -1 & 0 & 0 & M \end{pmatrix}$$

$$\hat{b} = \begin{pmatrix} b \\ 0 \end{pmatrix} = \begin{pmatrix} 6 \\ 2 \\ 0 \end{pmatrix}, \; \hat{B}_{\text{curr}}^{-1} = \begin{pmatrix} B^{-1} & 0 \\ C_{BB^{-1}} & 1 \end{pmatrix}$$

$$\hat{B}_{\text{curr}}^{-1} = \begin{pmatrix} 1 & 0 & 0 \\ 0 & 1 & 0 \\ 0 & -M & 1 \end{pmatrix}$$

The net evaluation is given by,

$$Z_j - C_j = (C_{B\,B^{-1}}\; 1)\; \hat{A}$$

$$= (-M-1 \quad -M-1 \quad 0 \quad M \quad 0)$$

Since $Z_1 - C_1$ is most negative, x_1 enters the basis

$$\hat{x}_1 = \hat{B}_{\text{curr}}^{-1}\; \hat{a}_1 = \begin{pmatrix} 1 & 0 & 0 \\ 0 & 1 & 0 \\ 0 & -M & 1 \end{pmatrix} \begin{pmatrix} 2 \\ 1 \\ -1 \end{pmatrix} = \begin{pmatrix} 2 \\ 1 \\ -M-1 \end{pmatrix}$$

$$\hat{x}_B = \hat{B}_{\text{curr}}^{-1}\; \hat{b} = \begin{pmatrix} 1 & 0 & 0 \\ 0 & 1 & 0 \\ 0 & -M & 1 \end{pmatrix} \begin{pmatrix} 6 \\ 2 \\ 0 \end{pmatrix} = \begin{pmatrix} 6 \\ 2 \\ -2M \end{pmatrix}$$

The revised simplex table is shown below.

B	x_B	$\hat{B}^{-1}_{curr}$			$\hat{x}_1$	Ratio
S_1	6	1	0	0	2	6/2 = 3
← A_1	2	0	1	0	(1)	2/1 = 2
Z	$-2M$	0	$-M$	1	$-M-1$ ↑	

First iteration

Drop A_1 and introduce x_1. Convert the leading element into one and the remaining elements in the key column as 0.

$$\hat{B}^{-1}_{curr} = \begin{pmatrix} 1 & -2 & 0 \\ 0 & 1 & 0 \\ 0 & 1 & 1 \end{pmatrix}$$

The net evaluation is given by,

$$Z_j - C_j = (0 \;\; 1 \;\; 1) \begin{pmatrix} 2 & 5 & 1 & 0 & 0 \\ 1 & 1 & 0 & -1 & 1 \\ -1 & -1 & 0 & 0 & M \end{pmatrix}$$

$$= (0 \;\; 0 \;\; 0 \;\; -1 \;\; M+1)$$

Since $Z_4 - C_4$ is most negative, S_2 enters the basis.

$$\hat{S}_2 = \hat{B}^{-1}_{curr} \; \hat{a}_4 = \begin{pmatrix} 1 & -2 & 0 \\ 0 & 1 & 0 \\ 0 & 1 & 1 \end{pmatrix} \begin{pmatrix} 0 \\ -1 \\ 0 \end{pmatrix} = \begin{pmatrix} 2 \\ -1 \\ -1 \end{pmatrix}$$

$$\hat{x}_B = \hat{B}^{-1}_{curr} \; \hat{b} = \begin{pmatrix} 1 & -2 & 0 \\ 0 & 1 & 0 \\ 0 & 1 & 1 \end{pmatrix} \begin{pmatrix} 6 \\ 2 \\ 0 \end{pmatrix} = \begin{pmatrix} 2 \\ 2 \\ 2 \end{pmatrix}$$

The revised simplex table is shown below.

B	$\hat{x}_B$	$\hat{B}^{-1}_{curr}$			$\hat{S}_2$	Ratio
← S_1	2	1	−2	0	2	2/2 = 1
x_1	2	0	1	0	−1	—
Z	2	0	1	1	−1↑	

In the above table, S_1 leaves the basis.

Second iteration

Introduce $\hat{S}_2$ and drop S_1. Convert the leading element into one and the remaining elements in the key column as zero.
We have,

$$\hat{B}^{-1}_{\text{curr}} = \begin{pmatrix} \frac{1}{2} & -1 & 0 \\ \frac{1}{2} & 0 & 0 \\ \frac{1}{2} & 0 & 1 \end{pmatrix}$$

The net evaluation is given by,

$$(Z_j - C_j) = (C_{B\,B^{-1}}\ 1)\,\hat{A}$$

$$= \begin{pmatrix} \frac{1}{2} & 0 & 1 \end{pmatrix} \begin{pmatrix} 2 & 5 & 1 & 0 & 0 \\ 1 & 1 & 0 & -1 & 1 \\ -1 & -1 & 0 & 0 & M \end{pmatrix} = \begin{pmatrix} 0 & \frac{3}{2} & \frac{1}{2} & 0 & M \end{pmatrix}$$

Since all $Z_j - C_j \geq 0$, the current feasible solution is optimum

$$\hat{x}_B = \hat{B}^{-1}_{\text{curr}}\ \hat{b} = \begin{pmatrix} \frac{1}{2} & -1 & 0 \\ \frac{1}{2} & 0 & 0 \\ \frac{1}{2} & 0 & 1 \end{pmatrix} \begin{pmatrix} 6 \\ 2 \\ 0 \end{pmatrix} = \begin{pmatrix} 1 \\ 3 \\ 3 \end{pmatrix}$$

The optimal solution is given by,

$$x_1 = 3,\ x_2 = 1 \text{ and Max } Z = 3.$$

Example 7.4 Use the revised simplex method to solve the following LPP.

Min $\quad Z = x_1 + x_2$

Subject to,

$$x_1 + 2x_2 \geq 7$$
$$4x_1 + x_2 \geq 6$$
$$x_1, x_2 \geq 0$$

Solution By introducing the surplus variables S_1, S_2 and artificial variables $A_1, A_2, \geq 0$ and converting the objective function into maximization type, we have,

Max $\quad Z = -x_1 - x_2 + 0S_1 + 0S_2 - MA_1 - MA_2$

Subject to,

$$x_1 + 2x_2 - S_1 + A_1 = 7$$
$$4x_1 + x_2 - S_2 + A_2 = 6$$
$$x_1, x_2, S_1, S_2, A_1, A_2, \geq 0$$

The initial basic feasible solution is given by,

$$A_1 = 7, A_2 = 6.$$

$$A = \begin{pmatrix} 1 & 2 & -1 & 0 & 1 & 0 \\ 4 & 1 & 0 & -1 & 0 & 1 \end{pmatrix}$$

$$b = \begin{pmatrix} 7 \\ 6 \end{pmatrix} \quad C_B = \begin{pmatrix} -M & -M \end{pmatrix} \quad \hat{b} = \begin{pmatrix} b \\ 0 \end{pmatrix} = \begin{pmatrix} 7 \\ 6 \\ 0 \end{pmatrix}$$

$$\hat{B}^{-1}_{\text{curr}} = \begin{pmatrix} B^{-1} & 0 \\ C_{B}B^{-1} & 1 \end{pmatrix} = \begin{pmatrix} 1 & 0 & 0 \\ 0 & 1 & 0 \\ -M & -M & 1 \end{pmatrix}$$

$$\hat{A} = \begin{pmatrix} A \\ -C \end{pmatrix} = \begin{pmatrix} 1 & 2 & -1 & 0 & 1 & 0 \\ 4 & 1 & 0 & -1 & 0 & 1 \\ 1 & 1 & 0 & 0 & M & M \end{pmatrix}$$

The net evaluation is given by,

$$Z_j - C_j = (C_B B^{-1} \; 1)\hat{A} = \begin{pmatrix} -M & -M & 1 \end{pmatrix} \begin{pmatrix} 1 & 2 & -1 & 0 & 1 & 0 \\ 4 & 1 & 0 & -1 & 0 & 1 \\ 1 & 1 & 0 & 0 & M & M \end{pmatrix}$$

$$= (-5M + 1 - 3M + 1 \quad M \quad M \quad 0 \quad 0)$$

Since $Z_1 - C_1$ is most negative, x_1 enters the basis.

$$\hat{x}_1 = \hat{B}^{-1}_{\text{curr}} \; \hat{a}_1 = \begin{pmatrix} 1 & 0 & 0 \\ 0 & 1 & 0 \\ -M & -M & 1 \end{pmatrix} \begin{pmatrix} 1 \\ 4 \\ 1 \end{pmatrix} = \begin{pmatrix} 1 \\ 4 \\ -5M + 1 \end{pmatrix}$$

$$\hat{x}_1 = \hat{B}^{-1}_{\text{curr}} \; \hat{b} = \begin{pmatrix} 1 & 0 & 0 \\ 0 & 1 & 0 \\ -M & -M & 1 \end{pmatrix} \begin{pmatrix} 7 \\ 6 \\ 0 \end{pmatrix} = \begin{pmatrix} 7 \\ 6 \\ -13M \end{pmatrix}$$

The revised simplex table is shown below

B	$\hat{x}_B$		$\hat{B}^{-1}_{\text{curr}}$		$\hat{x}_2$	***Ratio***
A_1	7	1	0	0	1	7/1 = 7
$\leftarrow A_2$	6	0	1	0	4	6/4 = 3/2
	–13M	$-M$	$-M$	1	$-5M + 1$ ↑	

A_2 leaves the basis.

First iteration

Introduce x_1 and drop A_2. Convert the leading element into unity and remaining elements in the key column as 0.

We have,

$$\hat{B}^{-1}_{\text{curr}} = \begin{pmatrix} 1 & \frac{-1}{4} & 0 \\ 0 & \frac{1}{4} & 0 \\ -M & \frac{M-1}{4} & 1 \end{pmatrix}$$

$$(Z_j - C_j) = \begin{pmatrix} -M & \frac{M-1}{4} & 1 \end{pmatrix} \begin{pmatrix} 1 & 2 & -1 & 0 & 1 & 0 \\ 4 & 1 & 0 & -1 & 0 & 1 \\ 1 & 1 & 0 & 0 & -M & -M \end{pmatrix}$$

$$= \begin{pmatrix} 0 & -\frac{7M+3}{4} & 2M & \frac{-M+1}{4} & 0 & 0 \end{pmatrix}$$

Since $Z_2 - C_2$ is most negative, x_2 enters the basis.

$$\hat{x}_2 = \left(\hat{B}_{\text{curr}}^{-1}\right)\hat{a} = \begin{pmatrix} 1 & \frac{-1}{4} & 0 \\ 0 & \frac{1}{4} & 0 \\ -M & \frac{M-1}{4} & 1 \end{pmatrix} \begin{pmatrix} 2 \\ 1 \\ 1 \end{pmatrix} = \begin{pmatrix} \frac{7}{4} \\ \frac{1}{4} \\ \frac{-7M+3}{4} \end{pmatrix}$$

$$\hat{x}_B = \left(\hat{B}_{\text{curr}}^{-1}\right)\hat{b} = \begin{pmatrix} 1 & \frac{-1}{4} & 0 \\ 0 & \frac{1}{4} & 0 \\ -M & \frac{M-1}{4} & 1 \end{pmatrix} \begin{pmatrix} 7 \\ 6 \\ 0 \end{pmatrix} = \begin{pmatrix} \frac{11}{2} \\ \frac{3}{2} \\ \frac{-11M-3}{2} \end{pmatrix}$$

The revised simplex table is shown below

B	$\hat{x}_B$	$\hat{B}_{\text{curr}}^{-1}$			$\hat{x}_2$	*Ratio*
$\leftarrow A_1$	11/2	1	–1/4	0	(7/4)	11/2 × 4/7 = 22/7
x_1	3/2	0	1/4	0	1/4	3/2 × 4 = 6
	$\frac{-11M-3}{2}$	$-M$	$\frac{M-1}{4}$	1	$\frac{-7M+3}{4}$	

A_1 leaves the basis.

Second iteration

Introduce x_2 and drop A_1. Convert the leading element into one and remaining elements in the key column as 0. We have,

$$\hat{B}_{\text{curr}}^{-1} = \begin{pmatrix} \frac{4}{7} & \frac{-1}{7} & 0 \\ \frac{-1}{7} & \frac{2}{7} & 0 \\ \frac{-3}{7} & \frac{-1}{7} & 1 \end{pmatrix}$$

$$Z_j - C_j = \begin{pmatrix} \frac{-3}{7} & \frac{-1}{7} & 1 \end{pmatrix} \hat{A} = \begin{pmatrix} 0 & 0 & \frac{3}{7} & \frac{1}{7} & \frac{-3}{7}+M & M-\frac{1}{7} \end{pmatrix}$$

Since all $Z_j - C_j \geq 0$, the solution is optimum. The optimal feasible solution is $\hat{x}_B = \hat{B}_{\text{curr}}^{-1} \ \hat{b}$

$$\hat{x}_B = \begin{pmatrix} \frac{4}{7} & \frac{-1}{7} & 0 \\ \frac{-1}{7} & \frac{2}{7} & 0 \\ \frac{-3}{7} & \frac{-1}{7} & 1 \end{pmatrix} \begin{pmatrix} 7 \\ 6 \\ 0 \end{pmatrix} = \begin{pmatrix} \frac{22}{7} \\ \frac{5}{7} \\ \frac{-27}{7} \end{pmatrix}$$

$\therefore$ The optimal solution is given by,

$$x_2 = \frac{22}{7}, x_1 = \frac{5}{7} \text{ Max } Z = \frac{-27}{7}$$

$$\therefore \qquad \text{Min } Z = \frac{27}{7},\ x_1 = \frac{5}{7},\ x_2 = \frac{22}{7}.$$

EXERCISES

Use the revised simplex method to solve the following LPP.

1. Max $Z = 3x_1 + 5x_2$
   Subject to, $x_1 \leq 4$
   $x_2 \leq 6$
   $3x_1 + 2x_2 \leq 18$ and $x_1, x_2 \geq 0$. **[Ans.** $x_1 = 2$, $x_2 = 6$, Max $Z = 36$]
2. Max $Z = 30x_1 + 23x_2 + 29x_3$
   Subject to, $6x_1 + 5x_2 + 3x_3 \leq 26$
   $4x_1 + 2x_2 + 5x_3 \leq 7$
   $x_1, x_2, x_3 \geq 0$ **[Ans.** $x_1 = 0$, $x_2 = 7/2$, $x_3 = 0$, Max $Z = 161/2$]
3. Max $Z = x_1 + 2x_2$
   Subject to, $2x_1 + 5x_2 \geq 6$
   $x_1 + x_2 \geq 2$
   $x_1, x_2 \geq 0$ **[Ans.** Min $Z = 8/3$, $x_1 = 4/3$, $x_2 = 2/3$]
4. Max $Z = 3x_1 + 2x_2 + 5x_3$
   Subject to, $x_1 + 2x_2 + x_3 \leq 430$
   $3x_1 + 2x_3 \leq 460$
   $x_1 + 4x_2 \leq 420$
   $x_1, x_2, x_3 \leq 0$ **[Ans.** $x_1 = 0$, $x_2 = 100$, $x_3 = 230$, Max $Z = 1350$]

❑❑❑

Chapter 8

Transportation Problem

8.1 INTRODUCTION

The transportation problem is one of the subclasses of LPPs. Here the objective is to transport various quantities of a single homogeneous commodity that are initially stored at various origins to different destinations in such a way that the transportation cost is minimum. To achieve this, we must know the amount and location of available supplies and the quantities demanded. In addition, we must know the costs that result from transporting one unit of commodity from various origins to various destinations.

8.2 MATHEMATICAL FORMULATION

Consider a transportation problem with m origins (rows) and n destinations (columns). Let C_{ij} be the cost of transporting one unit of the product from the ith origin to jth destination. a_i be the quantity of commodity available at origin i, b_j be the quantity of commodity needed at destination j. x_{ij} is the quantity transported from ith origin to jth destination. The above transportation problem can be stated in the following tabular form.

Destinations

Origin	*1*	*2*	*3*	...	*n*	*Capacity*
1	C_{11} x_{11}	C_{12} x_{12}	C_{13} x_{13}	... ...	C_{1n} x_{1n}	a_1
2	C_{21} x_{21}	C_{22} x_{22}	C_{23} x_{23}	... ...	C_{2n} x_{2n}	a_2
3	C_{31} x_{31}	C_{32} x_{32}	C_{33} x_{33}	... ...	C_{3n} x_{3n}	a_3
m	C_{m1} x_{n1}	C_{m2} x_{m2}	C_{m3} x_{m3}	... ...	C_{mn} x_{mn}	a_m
Demand	b_1	b_2	b_3	...	b_n	$\sum_{i=1}^{m} a_i = \sum_{j=1}^{n} b_j$

The Linear programming model representing the transportation problem is given by,

$$\text{Minimize } Z = \sum_{i=1}^{m} \sum_{j=1}^{n} c_{ij}\, x_{ij}$$

Subject to the constraints,

$$\sum_{j=1}^{n} x_{ij} = a_i \quad i = 1, 2, \ldots n$$

(Row Sum)

$$\sum_{i=1}^{m} x_{ij} = b_j \quad j = 1, 2, \ldots n$$

(Column Sum)

$$x_{ij} \geq 0 \quad \text{for all } i \text{ and } j$$

The given transportation problem is said to be balanced if

$$\sum_{i=1}^{m} a_i = \sum_{j=1}^{n} b_j$$

i.e. if the total supply is equal to the total demand.

8.3 DEFINITIONS

Feasible Solution: Any set of non-negative allocations ($x_{ij} > 0$) which satisfies the row and column sum (rim requirement) is called a 'feasible solution'.

Basic Feasible Solution: A feasible solution is called a 'basic feasible solution' if the number of non-negative allocations is equal to $m + n - 1$, where m is the number of rows and n the number of columns in a transportation table.

Non-degenerate Basic Feasible Solution: Any feasible solution to a transportation problem containing m origins and n destinations is said to be 'non-degenerate' if it contains $m + n - 1$ occupied cells and each allocation is in an independent position.

The allocations are said to be in independent positions, if it is impossible to form a closed path.

A path which is formed by allowing horizontal and vertical lines and all the corner cells of which are occupied is called a 'closed path'.

The allocations in the following tables are not in independent positions.

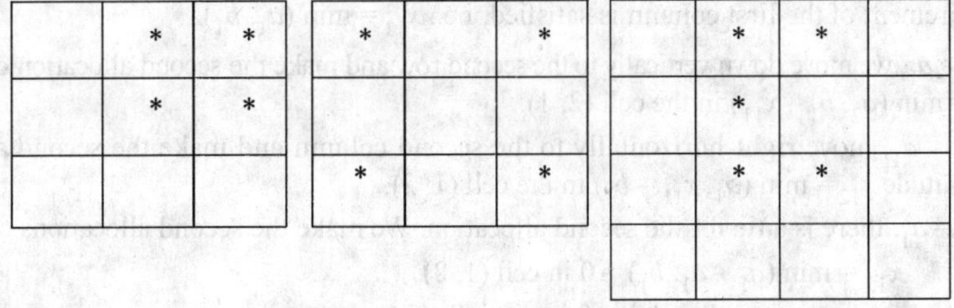

The allocations in the following tables are in independent positions.

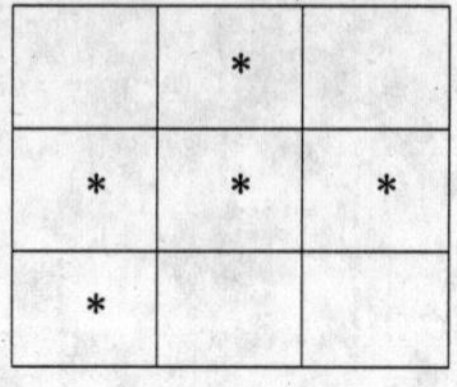

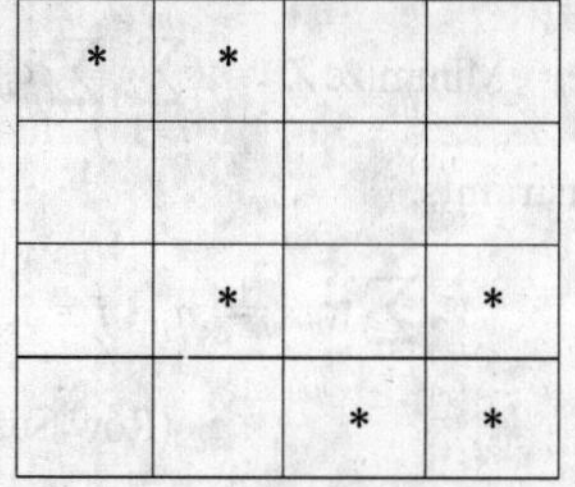

Degenerate Basic Feasible Solution: If a basic feasible solution contains less than $m + n - 1$ non-negative allocations, it is said to be 'degenerate'.

8.4 OPTIMAL SOLUTION

Optimal solution is a feasible solution (not necessarily basic), which minimizes the total cost.

The solution of a transportation problem can be obtained in two stages, namely initial and optimum solution.

Initial solution can be obtained by using any one of the three methods, viz.,

(*i*) North-West Corner Rule (NWCR)
(*ii*) Least Cost Method or Matrix Minima Method
(*iii*) Vogel's Approximation Method (VAM)

VAM is preferred over the other two methods, since the initial basic feasible solution obtained by this method is either optimal or very close to the optimal solution.

The cells in the transportation table can be classified as occupied and unoccupied cells. The allocated cells in the transportation table are called *occupied cells* and the empty ones are called *unoccupied cells*.

The improved solution of the initial basic feasible solution is called 'optimal solution', which is the second stage of solution and can be obtained by MODI (modified distribution method).

8.4.1 North-West Corner Rule

Step 1 Starting with the cell at the upper left corner (north-west) of the transportation matrix, we allocate as much as possible so that either the capacity of the first row is exhausted or the destination requirement of the first column is satisfied, i.e., $x_{11} = \min (a_1, b_1)$.

Step 2 If $b_1 > a_1$, we move down vertically to the second row and make the second allocation of magnitude $x_{22} = \min (a_2, b_1 - x_{11})$ in the cell (2, 1).

If $b_1 < a_1$, move right horizontally to the second column and make the second allocation of magnitude $x_{12} = \min (a_1, x_{11} - b_1)$ in the cell (1, 2).

If $b_1 = a_1$, there is a tie for the second allocation. We make the second allocations of magnitude

$$x_{12} = \min (a_1 - a_1, b_1) = 0 \text{ in cell } (1, 2)$$

or $$x_{21} = \min (a_2, b_1 - b_1) = 0 \text{ in the cell } (2, 1)$$

Step 3 Repeat steps 1 and 2, moving down towards the lower right corner of the transportation table until all the rim requirements are satisfied.

Example 8.1 Obtain the initial basic feasible solution of a transportation problem whose cost and rim requirement table is given below.

Origin/Destination	D_1	D_2	D_3	*Supply*
O_1	2	7	4	5
O_2	3	3	1	8
O_3	5	4	7	7
O_4	1	6	2	14
Demand	7	9	18	34

Solution Since $\Sigma ai = 34 = \Sigma bj$, there exists a feasible solution to the transportation problem. We obtain initial feasible solution as follows.

The first allocation is made in the cell (1, 1), the magnitude being x_{11} = min (5, 7) = 5. The second allocation is made in the cell (2, 1) and the magnitude of the allocation is given by x_{21} = min (8, 7 – 5) = 2.

	D_1	D_2	D_3	*Supply*
O_1	2 (5)	7	4	~~5~~ 0
O_2	3 (2)	3 (6)	1	~~8~~ ~~6~~ 0
O_3	5	4 (3)	7 (4)	~~7~~ ~~4~~ 0
O_4	1	6	2 (14)	~~14~~ 0
Demand	~~7~~ ~~2~~ 0	~~9~~ ~~3~~ 0	~~18~~ ~~14~~ 0	34

The third allocation is made in the cell (2, 2), the magnitude being x_{22} = min (8 – 2, 9) = 6.

The magnitude of fourth allocation is made in the cell (3, 2) given by min (7, 9 – 6) = 3.

The fifth allocation is made in the cell (3, 3) with magnitude x_{33} = min (7 – 3, 14) = 4.

The final allocation is made in the cell (4, 3) with magnitude x_{43} = min (14, 18 – 4) = 14.

Hence we get the initial basic feasible solution to the given T.P. which is given by,

$$x_{11} = 5;\ x_{21} = 2;\ x_{22} = 6;\ x_{32} = 3;\ x_{33} = 4;\ x_{43} = 14$$

$$\text{Total cost} = (5 \times 2) + (2 \times 3) + (6 \times 3) + (3 \times 4) + (4 \times 7) + (14 \times 2)$$

$$= 10 + 6 + 18 + 12 + 28 + 28 = ₹\ 102.$$

Example 8.2 Determine an initial basic feasible solution to the following transportation problem using NWCR.

	D_1	D_2	D_3	D_4	*Supply*
O_1	6	4	1	5	14
O_2	8	9	2	7	16
O_3	4	3	6	2	5
Required	6	10	15	4	35

Solution The problem is a balanced TP as the total supply is equal to the total demand. Using the steps involved in the north-west corner rule, we find the initial basic feasible solution as given in the following table.

	D_1	D_2	D_3	D_4	*Supply*
O_1	6 (6)	4 (8)	1	5	~~14~~ ~~8~~ 0
O_2	8	9 (2)	2 (14)	7	~~16~~ ~~14~~ 0
O_3	4	3	6 (1)	2 (4)	~~5~~ ~~4~~
Demand	~~6~~	~~10~~ ~~2~~ 0	~~15~~ ~~1~~ 0	~~4~~	35

Solution is given by,

$$x_{11} = 6;\ x_{12} = 8;\ x_{22} = 2;\ x_{23} = 14;\ x_{33} = 1;\ x_{34} = 4$$

Total cost $= (6 \times 6) + (8 \times 4) + (2 \times 9) + (14 \times 2) + (1 \times 6) + (4 \times 2)$

$=$ ₹ 128.

8.4.2 Least Cost or Matrix Minima Method

Step 1 Determine the smallest cost in the cost matrix of the transportation table. Let it be C_{ij}. Allocate $x_{ij} = \min(a_i, b_j)$ in the cell (i, j)

Step 2 If $x_{ij} = a_i$, cross off the ith row of the transportation table and decrease b_j by a_i. Then go to step 3.

If $x_{ij} = b_j$, cross off the jth column of the transportation table and decrease a_i by b_j. Go to step 3.

If $x_{ij} = a_i = b_j$, cross off either the ith row or the jth column but not both.

Step 3 Repeat steps 1 and 2 for the resulting reduced transportation table until all the rim requirements are satisfied. Whenever the minimum cost is not unique, make an arbitrary choice among the minima.

Example 8.3 Obtain an initial feasible solution to the following TP using the matrix minima method.

	D_1	D_2	D_3	D_4	*Supply*
O_1	1	2	3	4	6
O_2	4	3	2	0	8
O_3	0	2	2	1	10
Demand	4	6	8	6	24

Solution Since $\Sigma a_i = \Sigma b_j = 24$, there exists a feasible solution to the TP. Using the steps in the least cost method, the first allocation is made in the cell (3, 1) the magnitude being $x_{31} = 4$. It satisfies the demand at the destination D_1 and we delete this column from the table as it is exhausted.

	D_1	D_2	D_3	D_4	*Supply*
O_1	1	2 (6)	3	4	~~6~~ 0
O_2	4	3	2 (2)	0 (6)	~~8~~ ~~2~~
O_3	0 (4)	2	2 (6)	1	~~10~~ ~~6~~
Demand	~~4~~ 0	~~6~~ 0	~~8~~ ~~2~~ 0	~~6~~ 0	24

The second allocation is made in the cell (2, 4) with magnitude $x_{24} = \min(6, 8) = 6$. Since it satisfies the demand at the destination D_4, it is deleted from the table. From the reduced table the third allocation is made in the cell (3, 3) with magnitude $x_{33} = \min(8, 6) = 6$. The next allocation is made in the cell (2, 3) with magnitude x_{23} of $\min(2, 2) = 2$. Finally the allocation is made in the cell (1, 2) with magnitude $x_{12} = \min(6, 6) = 6$. Now all the rim requirements have been satisfied and hence, initial feasible solution is obtained.

The solution is given by,

$$x_{12} = 6,\ x_{23} = 2,\ x_{24} = 6,\ x_{31} = 4,\ x_{33} = 6$$

Since the total number of occupied cells = 5 < $m + n + 1$.

We get a degenerate solution.

$$\text{Total cost} = (6 \times 2) + (2 \times 2) + (6 \times 0) + (4 \times 0) + (6 \times 2)$$

$$= 12 + 4 + 12 = ₹\,28.$$

Example 8.4 Determine an initial basic feasible solution for the following TP, using least cost method.

	D_1	D_2	D_3	D_4	*Supply*
O_1	6	4	1	5	14
O_2	8	9	2	7	16
O_3	4	3	6	2	5
Demand	6	10	15	4	35

Solution Since $\Sigma a_i = \Sigma b_j$, there exists a basic feasible solution. Using the steps in least cost method, we make the first allocation to the cell (1, 3) with magnitude x_{13} = min (14, 15) = 14 (as it is the cell having the least cost).

This allocation exhausts the first row supply. Hence, the first row is deleted. From the reduced table, the next allocation is made in the next least cost cell (2, 3) which is chosen arbitrarily with magnitude x_{23} = min (1, 16) = 1, which exhausts the 3rd column destination.

From the reduced table, the next least cost cell is (3, 4) to which allocation is made with magnitude min (4, 5) = 4. This exhausts the destination D_4 requirement, deleting the fourth column from the table. The next allocation is made in the cell (3, 2) with magnitude x_{32} = Min (1, 10) = 1, which exhausts the 3rd origin capacity. Hence, the 3rd row is exhausted. From the reduced table the next allocation is given to the cell (2,1) with magnitude x_{21} = min (6, 15) = 6. This exhausts the first column requirement. Hence, it is deleted from the table.

Finally the allocation is made to the cell (2, 2) with magnitude x_{22} = min (9, 9) = 9, which satisfies the rim requirement. These allocations are shown in the transportation table as follows:

(I allocation)

	D_1	D_2	D_3	D_4	*Supply*
O_1	6	4	1 (14)	5	~~14~~
O_2	8	9	2	7	16
O_3	4	3	6	2	5
Demand	6	10	~~15~~ 1	4	

(II allocation)

	D_1	D_2	D_3	D_4	*Supply*
O_2	8	9	2 (1)	7	~~16~~ 15
O_3	4	3	6	2	5
Demand	6	10	~~1~~ 0	4	

(III allocation)

	D_1	D_2	D_4	*Supply*
O_2	8	9	7	15
O_3	4	3	2 (4)	~~5~~ 1
Demand	6	10	~~4~~ 0	

(IV allocation)

	D_1	D_2	*Supply*
O_2	8	9	15
O_3	4	3 (1)	~~1~~ 0
Demand	6	~~10~~ 9	

(V, VI allocation)

	D_1	D_2	Supply
O_2	8 ⑥	9 ⑨	15
Demand	6	9	

The following table gives the initial basic feasible solution.

	D_1	D_2	D_3	D_4	Supply
O_1	6	4	1 ⑭	5	14
O_2	8 ⑥	9 ⑨	2 ①	7	16
O_3	4	3 ①	6	2 ④	5
Demand	6	10	15	4	

Solution is given by,

$$x_{13} = 14; \quad x_{21} = 6; \quad x_{22} = 9; \quad x_{23} = 1; \quad x_{32} = 1; \quad x_{34} = 4$$

Transportation cost

$$= (14 \times 1) + (6 \times 8) + (9 \times 9) + (1 \times 2) + (1 \times 3) + (4 \times 2)$$

$$= ₹\,156.$$

8.4.3 Vogel's Approximation Method (VAM)

The steps involved in this method for finding the initial solution are as follows.

Step 1 Find the penalty cost, namely the difference between the smallest and next to smallest costs in each row and column.

Step 2 Among the penalties as found in step (1), choose the maximum penalty. If this maximum penalty is more than one (i.e., if there is a tie), choose any one arbitrarily.

Step 3 In the selected row or column as by step (2), find out the cell having the least cost. Allocate to this cell as much as possible, depending on the capacity and requirements.

Step 4 Delete the row or column that is fully exhausted. Again compute the column and row penalties for the reduced transportation table and then go to step (2). Repeat the procedure until all the rim requirements are satisfied.

Note: If the column is exhausted, then there is a change in row penalty, and vice versa.

Example 8.5 Find the initial basic feasible solution for the following transportation problem by VAM.

	Destination					
		D_1	D_2	D_3	D_4	Supply
Origin	O_1	11	13	17	14	250
	O_2	16	18	14	10	300
	O_3	21	24	13	10	400
	Demand	200	225	275	250	950

Solution Since $\Sigma a_i = \Sigma b_j = 950$, the problem is balanced and there exists a feasible solution to the problem.

First we find the row and column penalty P_I as the difference between the least and next least cost. The maximum penalty is 5. Choose the first column arbitrarily. In this column choose the cell having the least cost (1, 1). Allocate to this cell with minimum magnitude (i.e., (250, 200) = 200). This exhausts the first column. Delete this column. Since the column is deleted, there is a change in row penalty P_{II} and column penalty P_{II} remains the same. Continuing in this manner we get the remaining allocations as given in the table below.

I allocation

	D_1	D_2	D_3	D_4	Supply	P_I
O_1	11 (200)	13	17	14	50 ~~250~~	2
O_2	16	18	14	10	300	4
O_3	21	24	13	10	400	3
Demand	~~200~~ 0	225	275	250		
P_I	5↑	5	3	0		

II allocation

	D_2	D_3	D_4	Supply	P_{II}
O_1	13 (50)	17	14	~~50~~	1
O_2	18	14	10	300	4
O_3	24	13	10	400	3
Demand	~~225~~ 175	275	250		
P_{II}	5↑	1	0		

III allocation

	D_2	D_3	D_4	Supply	P_{III}
O_2	18 (175)	14	10	~~300~~ 125	4
O_3	24	13	10	400	3
Demand	~~175~~ 0	275	250		
P_{III}	6↑	1	0		

IV allocation

	D_3	D_4	Supply	P_{IV}
O_2	14	10 (125)	~~125~~ 0	4 ←
O_3	13	10	400	3
Demand	275	~~250~~ 125		
P_{IV}	1	0		

V allocation

	D_3	D_4	Supply	P_V
O_3	13 (275)	10	~~400~~ 125	3
Demand	~~275~~ 0	125		
P_V	13↑	10		

VI allocation

	D_4	Supply	P_{VI}
O_3	10 (125)	~~125~~ 0	10 ←
Demand	~~125~~ 0		
P_{VI}	10		

Finally, we arrive at the initial basic feasible solution, which is shown in the following table.

	D_1	D_2	D_3	D_4	Supply
O_1	11 (200)	13 (50)	17	14	250
O_2	16	18 (175)	14	10 (125)	300
O_3	21	24	13 (275)	10 (125)	400
Demand	200	225	275	250	

There are 6 positive independent allocations which are equal to $m + n - 1 = 3 + 4 - 1$. This ensures that the solution is a non-degenerate basic feasible solution.

∴ The transportation cost

$$= 200 \times 11 + 50 \times 13 + 175 \times 18 + 125 \times 10 + 275 \times 13 + 125 \times 10$$
$$= ₹\ 12{,}075.$$

Example 8.6 Find the initial solution to the following TP using VAM.

		Destination				
		D_1	D_2	D_3	D_4	Supply
Factory	F_1	3	3	4	1	100
	F_2	4	2	4	2	125
	F_3	1	5	3	2	75
	Demand	120	80	75	25	300

Solution Since $\Sigma a_i = \Sigma b_j$, the problem is a balanced TP. So there exists a feasible solution.

	D_1	D_2	D_3	D_4	*Supply*	P_I	P_{II}	P_{III}	P_{IV}	P_V	P_{VI}
F_1	3 (45)	3	4 (30)	1 (25)	100	2	2 ←	0	1 ←	4	4
F_2	4	2 (80)	4 (45)	2	125	2	2	2 ←	0	4 ←	—
F_3	1 (75)	5	3	2	75	1	—	—	—	—	—
Demand	120	80	75	25							
P_I	2↑	1	1	1							
P_{II}	1	1	0	1							
P_{III}	1	1	0	—							
P_{IV}	1	—	0	—							
P_V	—	—	0	—							
P_{VI}	—	—	4↑	—							

Finally, we have the initial basic feasible solution as given in the following table.

	D_1	D_2	D_3	D_4	*Supply*
F_1	3 (45)	3	4 (30)	1 (25)	100
F_2	4	2 (80)	4 (45)	2	125
F_3	1 (75)	5	3	2	75
Demand	120	80	75	25	

There are 6 independent non-negative allocations equal to $m + n - 1 = 3 + 4 - 1 = 6$. This ensures that the solution is non-degenerate basic feasible.

∴ The transportation cost

$$= 45 \times 3 + 30 \times 4 + 25 \times 1 + 80 \times 2 + 45 \times 4 + 75 \times 1$$

$$= 135 + 120 + 25 + 160 + 180 + 75 = ₹\, 695.$$

8.5 OPTIMALITY TEST

Once the initial basic feasible solution has been computed, the next step in the problem is to determine whether the solution obtained is optimum or not.

Optimality test can be conducted on any initial basic feasible solution of a TP provided such an allocation has exactly $m + n - 1$, non-negative allocations where m is the number of origins and n is the number of destinations. Also these allocations must be in independent positions.

To perform this optimality test, we shall discuss the modified distribution method (MODI). The various steps involved in MODI method for performing the optimality test are given below.

8.5.1 MODI Method

Step 1 Find the initial basic feasible solution of a TP by using any one of the three methods.

Step 2 Find out a set of numbers u_i and v_j for each row and column satisfying $u_i + v_j = c_{ij}$ for each occupied cell. To start with, we assign a number '0' to any row or column having maximum number of allocations. If this maximum number of allocations is more than one, choose any one arbitrarily.

Step 3 For each empty (unoccupied) cell, we find the sum u_i and v_j written in the bottom left corner of that cell.

Step 4 Find out the net evaluation value $\Delta_{ij} = c_{ij} - (u_i + v_j)$ for each *empty cell*, which is written at the bottom right corner of that cell. This step gives the optimality conclusion,

(*i*) If all $\Delta_{ij} > 0$ (i.e., all the net evaluation value), the solution is optimum and a *unique solution* exists.

(*ii*) If $\Delta_{ij} \geq 0$, then the solution is optimum, but an alternate solution exists.

(*iii*) If at least one $\Delta_{ij} < 0$, the solution is not optimum. In this case we go to the next step, to improve the total transportation cost.

Step 5 Select the empty cell having the most negative value of Δ_{ij}. From this cell we draw a closed path by drawing horizontal and vertical lines with the corner cells occupied. Assign sign + and – alternately and find the minimum allocation from the cell having negative sign. This allocation should be added to the allocation having positive sign and subtracted from the allocation having negative sign.

Step 6 The above step yields a better solution by making one (or more) occupied cell as empty and one empty cell as occupied. For this new set of basic feasible allocations repeat from step (2) onwards, till an optimum basic feasible solution is obtained.

Example 8.7 Solve the following transportation problem.

		Destination				
		P	***Q***	***R***	***S***	***Supply***
Source	***A***	21	16	25	13	11
	B	17	18	14	23	13
	C	32	17	18	41	19
	Demand	6	10	12	15	43

Origin/Dest.	*P*	*Q*	*R*	*S*	*Supply*	P_{I}	P_{II}	P_{III}	P_{IV}	P_{V}	P_{VI}
A	21	16	25	13 (11)	11	3	—	—	—	—	—
B	17 (6)	18	14 (3)	23 (4)	13	3	3	3	3 ←		—
C	32	17 (10)	18 (9)	41	19	1	1	1	1	1	17
Demand	6	10	12	15	43						
P_{I}	4	1	4	10↑							
P_{II}	15	1	4	18↑							
P_{III}	15↑	1	↑4	—							
P_{IV}	—	1	↑4								
P_{V}	—	17	18↑	—							
P_{VI}	—	17↑	—	—							

Solution We first find the initial basic feasible solution by using VAM. Since $\Sigma a_i = \Sigma b_j$, the given TP is a balanced one. Therefore, there exists a feasible solution.

Finally, we have the initial basic feasible solution as given in the following table.

		Destination			
		P	***Q***	***R***	***S***
Source	***A***	21	16	25	13 (11)
	B	17 (6)	18	14 (3)	23 (4)
	C	32	17 (10)	18 (9)	41

From this table we see that the number of non-negative independent allocation is $6 = m + n - 1 = 3 + 4 - 1$.

Hence, the solution is non-degenerate basic feasible.

$\therefore$ The initial transportation cost

$$= (11 \times 13) + (3 \times 14) + (4 \times 23) + (6 \times 17) + (10 \times 17) + (9 \times 18) = ₹\,711.$$

To find the optimal solution We apply MODI method in order to determine the optimum solution. We determine a set of numbers u_i and v_j for each row and column, with $u_i + v_j = c_{ij}$ for each occupied cell. To start with, we give $u_2 = 0$ as the 2nd row has the maximum number of allocation.

$$c_{21} = u_2 + v_1 = 17 = 0 + v_1 = 17 \Rightarrow v_1 = 17$$

$$c_{23} = u_2 + v_3 = 14 = 0 + v_3 = 14 \Rightarrow v_3 = 14$$

$$c_{24} = u_2 + v_4 = 23 = 0 + v_4 = 23 \Rightarrow v_4 = 23$$

$$c_{14} = u_1 + v_4 = 13 = u_1 + 23 = 13 \Rightarrow u_1 = -10$$

$$c_{33} = u_3 + v_3 = 18 = u_3 + 14 = 18 \Rightarrow u_3 = 4$$

$$c_{32} = u_3 + v_2 = 17 = 4 + v_2 = 17 \Rightarrow v_2 = 13$$

Now we find the sum u_i and v_j for each empty cell and enter it at the bottom left corner of that cell.

Next we find the net evaluation $\Delta_{ji} = C_{ij} - (u_i + v_j)$ for each unoccupied cell and enter it at the bottom right corner of that cell.

Initial table

	P	**Q**	**R**	**S**	u_i
A	21 7 14	16 3 13	25 4 21	13 (11)	$u_i = -10$
B	17 (6)	18 13 5	14 (3)	23 (4)	$u_2 = 0$
C	32 21 9	17 (10)	18 (9)	41 25 16	$u_3 = 4$
v_j	$v_1 = 17$	$v_2 = 13$	$v_3 = 14$	$v_4 = 23$	

Since all $\Delta_{ij} > 0$, the solution is optimal and unique. The optimum solution is given by,

$$x_{14} = 11, x_{21} = 6, x_{23} = 3, x_{24} = 4, x_{32} = 10, x_{33} = 9$$

The min. transportation cost

$$= 11 \times 13 + 6 \times 17 + 3 \times 14 + 4 \times 23 + 10 \times 17 + 9 \times 18$$

$$= ₹\ 711.$$

Example 8.8 Solve the following transportation problem starting with the initial solution obtained by VAM.

	D_1	D_2	D_3	D_4	*Supply*
O_1	2	2	2	1	3
O_2	10	8	5	4	7
O_3	7	6	6	8	5
Demand	4	3	4	4	15

Solution Since $\Sigma_{ai} = \Sigma_{bj}$, the problem is a balanced TP. Therefore, there exists a feasible solution.

	D_1	D_2	D_3	D_4	*Supply*	P_I	P_{II}	P_{III}	P_{IV}	P_V	P_{VI}
O_1	2 (3)	2	2	1	3	1	—	—	—	—	—
O_2	10	8	5 (3)	4 (4)	7	1	1	3 ←	—	—	—
O_3	7 (1)	6 (3)	6 (1)	8	5	0	0	0	0	0	6 ←
Demand	4	3	4	4	15						
P_I	5↑	4	4	3							
P_{II}	3	2	1	4↑							
P_{III}	3	2	1	—							
P_{IV}	7↑	6	6	—							
P_V	—	6↑	6	—							
P_{VI}	—		6	—							

Finally, the initial basic feasible solution is given as below:

	D_1	D_2	D_3	D_4	*Supply*
O_1	2 (3)	2	2	1	3
O_2	10	8	5 (3)	4 (4)	7
O_3	7 (1)	6 (3)	6 (1)	8	5
Demand	4	3	4	4	15

Since the number of occupied cells = 6 = $m + n - 1$ and are also independent, there exists a non-degenerate basic feasible solution.

The initial transportation cost

$$= (3 \times 2) + (3 \times 5) + (4 \times 4) + (1 \times 7) + (3 \times 6) + (1 \times 6) = ₹\,68.$$

To find the optimal solution Applying the MODI method, we determine a set of numbers u_i and v_j for each row and column, such that $u_i + v_j = c_{ij}$ for each occupied cell. Since the 3rd row has maximum number of allocations, we give number $u_3 = 0$. The remaining numbers can be obtained as given here.

$$c_{31} = u_3 + v_1 = 7 = 0 + v_1 = 7 \Rightarrow v_1 = 7$$
$$c_{32} = u_3 + v_2 = 6 = 0 + v_2 = 6 \Rightarrow v_2 = 6$$
$$c_{33} = u_3 + v_3 = 6 = 0 + v_3 = 6 \Rightarrow v_3 = 6$$
$$c_{23} = u_2 + v_3 = 5 = u_2 + 6 = 5 \Rightarrow u_2 = -1$$
$$c_{24} = u_2 + v_4 = 4 = -1 + v_4 = 4 \Rightarrow v_4 = 5$$
$$c_{11} = u_1 + v_1 = 2 = u_1 + 7 = 2 \Rightarrow u_1 = -5$$

We find the sum of u_i and v_j for each empty cell and enter it at the bottom left corner of the cell. Next we find the net evaluation Δ_{ij} given by,

Initial table

	D_1	D_2	D_3	D_4	u_4
O_1	2 (3)	2; 1, 1	2; 1, 1	1; 0, 1	$u_1 = -5$
O_2	10; 6, 4	8; 5, 3	5 (3)	4 (4)	$u_2 = -1$
O_3	7 (1)	6 (3)	6 (1)	8; 5, 3	$u_3 = 0$
	$v_1 = 7$	$v_2 = 6$	$v_3 = 6$	$v_4 = 5$	

$\Delta_{ij} = C_{ij} - (u_i + v_j)$ for each empty cell and enter it at the bottom right corner of the cell.

Since all $\Delta_{ij} > 0$, the solution is optimum and unique. The solution is given by,

$$x_{11} = 3; \quad x_{23} = 3; \quad x_{24} = 4$$

$$x_{31} = 1; \quad x_{32} = 3; \quad x_{33} = 1$$

The total transportation cost

$$= (3 \times 2) + (3 \times 5) + (4 \times 4) + (1 \times 7) + (3 \times 6) + (1 \times 6) = ₹\ 68$$

Degeneracy in transportation problem In a TP, if the number of non-negative independent allocations is less than $m + n - 1$, where m is the number of origins (rows) and n is the number of destinations (columns), there exists a degeneracy. This may occur either at the initial stage or at subsequent iteration.

To resolve this degeneracy, we adopt the following steps:

1. Among the empty cells, we choose an empty cell having the least cost, which is of an independent position. If such cells are more than one, choose any one arbitrarily.
2. To the cell as chosen in step (1), we allocate a small positive quantity $\varepsilon > 0$.

The cells containing ε are treated like other occupied cells and degeneracy is removed by adding one (more) accordingly. For this modified solution, we adopt the steps involved in MODI method till an optimum solution is obtained.

Example 8.9 Solve the transportation problem for minimization.

		Destinations			
		1	***2***	***3***	***Capacity***
	1	2	2	3	10
Sources	**2**	4	1	2	15
	3	1	3	1	40
	Demand	20	15	30	65

Solution Since $\Sigma a_i = \Sigma b_j$, the problem is a balanced TP. Hence, there exists a feasible solution. We find the initial solution by north-west corner rule as given below.

	1	***2***	***3***	***Capacity***
1	2 (10)	2	3	10
2	4 (10)	1 (15)	2	15
3	1	3 (5)	1 (30)	40
Demand	20	15	30	

Since the number of occupied cells = 5 = $m + n - 1$ and all the allocations are independent, we get an initial basic feasible solution.

The initial transportation cost

$$= 10 \times 2 + 10 \times 4 + 5 \times 1 + 10 \times 3 + 30 \times 1 = ₹\,125.$$

To find the optimal solution (MODI method) We use the above table to apply MODI method. We find out a set of numbers u_i and v_j for which $u_i + v_j = c_{ij}$, only for occupied cells. To start with, as the maximum number of allocations is 2 in more than one row and column, we choose arbitrarily column 1, and assign a number 0 to this column, i.e., $v_1 = 0$. The remaining numbers can be obtained as follows.

$$c_{11} = u_1 + v_1 = 2 = u_1 + 0 = 2 \Rightarrow u_1 = 2$$

$$c_{21} = u_2 + v_1 = 4 \Rightarrow u_2 = 4 - 0 = 4$$

$$c_{22} = u_2 + v_2 = 1 \Rightarrow v_2 = 1 - u_2 = 1 - 4 = -3$$

$$c_{32} = u_3 + v_2 = 3 = u_3 = 3 - v_2 = 3 - (-3) = 6$$

$$c_{33} = u_3 + v_3 = 1 = v_3 = 1 - u_3 = 1 - 6 = -5$$

Initial table

	1	2	3	u_i
1	2 (10)	2 –1 3	3 –3 6	$u_1 = 2$
2	4 (10) –	1 (5) +	2 –1 3	$u_2 = 4$
3	1 6 + –5	3 (10) –	1 (30)	$u_3 = 6$
v_j	$v_1 = 0$	$v_2 = -3$	$v_3 = -5$	

We find the sum of u_i and v_j for each empty cell and write it at the bottom left corner of that cell. Find the net evaluation $\Delta_{ij} = c_{ij} - (u_i + v_j)$ for each empty cell and enter it at the bottom right corner of the cell. The solution is not optimum as the cell (3, 1) has a negative Δ_{ij} value. We improve the allocation by making this cell namely (3, 1) as an allocated cell. We draw a closed path from this cell and assign + and – signs alternately. From the cell having negative sign we find the min. allocation given by min (10, 10) = 10. Hence, we get two occupied cells (2, 1) (3, 2) that become empty and the cell (3, 1) is occupied, resulting in a degenerate solution. (Degeneracy in subsequent iteration).

Number of allocated cell = 4 < $m + n - 1 = 5$.

We get a degeneracy and to resolve it, we add the empty cell (1, 2) and allocate $\varepsilon > 0$. This cell namely (1, 2) is added as it satisfies the two steps for resolving the degeneracy. We assign a number 0 to the first row, namely $u_1 = 0$, we get the remaining numbers as follows.

$$c_{11} = u_1 + v_1 = 2 \Rightarrow v_1 = 2 - u_1 = 2 - 0 = 2$$

$$c_{12} = u_1 + v_2 = 2 \Rightarrow v_2 = 2 - u_1 = 2 - 0 = 2$$

$$c_{31} = u_3 + v_1 = 1 \Rightarrow u_3 = 1 - v_1 = 1 - 2 = -1$$
$$c_{33} = u_3 + v_3 = 1 \Rightarrow v_3 = 1 - u_3 = 1 - (-1) = 2$$
$$c_{22} = u_2 + v_2 = 1 \Rightarrow u_2 = 1 - v_2 = 1 - 2 = -1$$

Next we find the sum of u_i and v_j for the empty cell and enter it at the bottom left corner of that cell and also the net evaluation $\Delta_{ij} = c_{ij} - (u_i + v_j)$ for each empty cell and enter it at the bottom right corner of the cell.

Iteration table

	1	*2*	*3*	u_i
1	2 (10)	2 (ε)	3 2 1	0
2	4 1 3	1 (15)	2 1 1	− 1
3	1 (10)	3 1 2	1 (30)	− 1
v_j	2	2	2	

The modified solution is given in the following table. This solution is also optimal and unique as it satisfies the optimality condition that all $\Delta_{ij} > 0$.

	1	*2*	*3*	*Capacity*
1	2 (10)	2 (ε)	3	10
2	4	1 (15)	2	15
3	1 10	3	1 30	40
Demand	(20)	15	(30)	65

$$x_{11} = 10; \quad x_{22} = 15; \quad x_{33} = 30;$$
$$x_{12} = \varepsilon_j; \quad x_{31} = 10$$
$$\text{Total cost} = (10 \times 2) + (\varepsilon \times 2) + (15 \times 1) + (10 \times 1) + (30 \times 1)$$
$$= 75 + 2\,\varepsilon = ₹\ 75.$$

Example 8.10 Solve the following transportation problem whose cost matrix is given below.

		Destination				
		A	***B***	***C***	***D***	***Capacity***
Origin	**1**	1	5	3	3	34
	2	3	3	1	2	15
	3	0	2	2	3	12
	4	2	7	2	4	19
	Demand	21	25	17	17	80

Solution Since $\Sigma a_i = \Sigma b_j$, the problem is a balanced transportation problem. Hence, there exists a feasible solution. We find the initial solution by north-west corner rule.

		Destination				
		A	***B***	***C***	***D***	***Capacity***
Origin	**1**	1 (21)	5 (13)	3	3	~~34~~ ~~13~~ 0
	2	3	3 (12)	1 (3)	2	~~15~~ ~~3~~ 0
	3	0	2	2 (12)	3	~~12~~ 0
	4	2	7	2 (2)	4 (17)	~~19~~ ~~17~~ 0
	Demand	~~21~~ 0	~~25~~ ~~12~~	~~17~~ ~~14~~ ~~2~~	~~17~~ 0	80

We get the total number of allocated cells = 7 = 4 + 4 – 1. As all the allocations are independent, the solution is a non-degenerate solution.

Total transportation cost

$$= 21 \times 1 + 13 \times 5 + 12 \times 3 + 3 \times 1 + 12 \times 2 + 2 \times 2 + 17 \times 4$$

$$= ₹\, 221.$$

To find the optimal solution (MODI Method) We determine a set of numbers u_i and v_j for each row and each column with $u_i + v_j = c_{ij}$ for each occupied cell. To start with, we give 0 to the third column as it has the maximum number of allocations.

Initial table

	A	B	C	D	u_i
1	1 (21)	5 (13)	3 3 0	3 5 −2	$3 = u_1$
2	3 −1 4	3 (12) −	1 + (3)	2 3 −1	$1 = u_2$
3	0 0 0	+ 2 4 −2	2 − (12)	3 4 −1	$2 = u_3$
4	2 0 2	7 4 3	2 (2)	4 (17)	$2 = u_4$
v_j	$-2 = v_1$	$2 = v_2$	$0 = v_3$	$2 = v_4$	

$$c_{23} = u_2 + v_3 = 1 \Rightarrow u_2 = 1 - 0 = 1$$
$$c_{33} = u_3 + v_3 = 2 \Rightarrow$$
$$u_3 = 2 - v_3 = 2 - 0 = 2$$
$$c_{43} = u_4 + v_3 = 2 \Rightarrow$$
$$u_4 = 2 - 0 = 2$$
$$c_{44} = u_4 + v_4 = 4 \Rightarrow v_4 = 4 - 2 = 2$$
$$c_{22} = u_2 + v_2 = 3 \Rightarrow$$
$$v_2 = 3 - u_2 = 2$$
$$c_{12} = u_1 + v_2 = 5 \Rightarrow$$
$$u_1 = 5 - v_2 = 3$$
$$c_{11} = u_1 + v_1 = 1 \Rightarrow$$
$$v_1 = 1 - u_1 = 1 - 3 = -2$$

We find the sum of u_i and v_j for each empty cell and enter it at the bottom left corner of that cell. We find the net evaluation $\Delta_{ij} = c_{ij} - (u_i + v_j)$ for each empty cell and enter it at the bottom right corner of that cell. The solution is not optimum as some of $\Delta_{ij} < 0$. We choose the most negative Δ_{ij}, i.e., –2. There is a tie between the cells (1, 4) and (3, 2) but we choose the cell (3, 2) as it has the least cost. From this cell we draw a closed path and assign + and – signs alternately and find the minimum allocation from the cell having – sign.

Thus we get, Min (12, 12) = 12. Hence, one empty cell (3, 2) becomes occupied and two occupied cells (2, 2) (3, 3) become empty, resulting in degeneracy (Degeneracy in subsequent iteration). By adding and subtracting this minimum allocation, we get the modified allocation as given in the table below. For these modified allocations, we repeat the steps in MODI method.

I Iteration table

	A	*B*	*C*	*D*
1	1 (21)	5 (13)	3	3
2	3	3	1 (15)	2
3	0	2 (12)	2	3
4	2	7	2 (2)	4 (17)

The number of allocation = 6 < $m + n - 1 = 7$. We add the cell (3, 3) as it is the least cost empty cell, which is of independent position. Give a small quantity $\varepsilon > 0$. This removes degeneracy. The modified allocation is given in the table below.

	A	*B*	*C*	*D*	u_i
1	1 (21)	5 – (13)	3 5 – 2	3 + ε 7 – 4	5
2	3 – 3 6	3 1 2	1 (15)	2 3 – 1	1
3	0 – 2 2	2 + (12)	2 – (ε)	3 4 –1	2
4	2 – 2 4	7 2 5	2 + (2)	4 – (17)	2
v_j	– 4	0	0	2	

The solution is not optimum. The next negative value of $\Delta_{ij} = -\ 4$. (the cell (1, 4)).

The minimum allocation is min. (13, ε, 17) = ε . Proceeding in the same manner we have the 2nd iteration table as given below.

II Iteration table

	A	B	C	D	u_i
1	1; (21)	5; — —; (13–ε)	3; 1 2	3; +; (ε)	0
2	3; 1 2	3; +ε; 5 −2	1; –; (15)	2; 3 −1	0
3	0; −2 2	2; (12 + ε)	2; −2 4	3; 0 3	−3
4	2; 2 0	7; 6 1	2; +; (2 + ε)	4; —; (17 − ε)	1
	1	5	1	3	

As the solution is not optimum, we improve it by using the steps involved in MODI method. The most negative value of $\Delta_{ij} = -2$. Min allocation is min. $(13 - \varepsilon, 15, 17 - \varepsilon) = 13 - \varepsilon$.

III Iteration table

	A	B	C	D	
1	1; (21)	5; 3 2	3; 1 2	3; (13)	0
2	3; 1 2	3; (13 − ε)	1; (2 + ε) –	2; + ε; 3 −1	0
3	0; 0 0	2; (12 + ε)	2; 0 2	3; 2 1	0 – 1
4	2; 2 0	7; 4 3	2; +; (15)	4; –; (4)	1
	1	3	1	3	

Improve the solution by adding and subtracting the new allocation given by min. $(2 + \varepsilon, 4) = (2 + \varepsilon)$

IV Iteration table

	A	B	C	D	u_i
1	1 (21)	5 4 1	3 1 2	3 (13)	3
2	3 0 3	3 (13 − ε)	1 0 1	2 (2 + ε)	2
3	0 −1 1	2 (12 + ε)	2 −1 3	3 1 2	1
4	2 2 0	7 5 2	2 (17 + ε)	4 (2 − ε)	4
v_j	−2	1	−2	0	

Since all $\Delta_{ij} \geq 0$, the solution is optimum (alternate solution exists). The solution is given by,

$$X_{11} = 21; X_{14} = 13; X_{22} = 13 - \varepsilon = 13; X_{24} = 2 + \varepsilon = 2;$$

$$X_{32} = 12 + \varepsilon = 12; X_{43} = 17 + \varepsilon = 17; X_{44} = 2 - \varepsilon = 2$$

Total transportation cost $= 21 \times 1 + 13 \times 3 + (13 - \varepsilon) \times 3 + (2 + \varepsilon) \times 2 + (12 + \varepsilon) \times 2$

$$+ (17 + \varepsilon) \times 2 + (2 - \varepsilon) \times 4 = 169 - \varepsilon = ₹\ 169$$

Example 8.11 A company has three plants *A*, *B* and *C*, 3 warehouses *X*, *Y* and *Z*. The number of units available at the plants is 60, 70, 80 and the demand at *X*, *Y*, *Z* is 50, 80, 80 respectively. The unit cost of the transportation is given in the following table:

	X	Y	Z
A	8	7	3
B	3	8	9
C	11	3	5

Find the allocation so that the total transportation cost is minimum.

Solution

	Warehouses			
	X	**Y**	**Z**	**Capacity**
Plants A	8	7	3	60
B	3	8	9	70
C	11	3	5	80
Demand	50	80	80	210

Since $\Sigma a_i = \Sigma b_j = 210$, the problem is a balanced one. Hence, there exists a feasible solution. Let us find the initial solution by least cost method.

Iteration: 1

	X	Y	Z	Supply
A	8	7	3	60
B	3 (50)	8	9	70
C	11	3	5	80
Demand	50	80	80	210

Here the least cost cell is not unique, i.e., the cells (2, 1) (1, 3) and (3, 2) have the least value 3. So choose the cell arbitrarily. Let us choose the cell (2, 1) and allocate with magnitude min. (70, 50) = 50. This exhausts the first column. So delete this column. The reduced transportation table is given by,

Iteration: 2

	Y	Z	Supply
A	7	3 (60)	60
B	8	9	20
C	3	5	80
Demand	80	80	

Continuing in this manner, we finally arrive at the initial solution, which is shown in the following table:

Iteration: 3

	X	Y	Z	Supply
A	8	7	3 (60)	60
B	3 (50)	8	9 (20)	70
C	11	3 (80)	5 (0)	80
Demand	50	80	80	

Iteration: 4

	Y	Z	Supply
B	8	9	20
C	3 (80)	5	80
Demand	80	20	

The number of allocated cells is $m + n - 1 = 5$,

This solution is non-degenerate.

The solution is given by,

$$X_{13} = 60,\ x_{21} = 50$$

$$X_{23} = 20,\ X_{32} = 80,\ x_{33} = 0.$$

The total transportation cost

$$= (60 \times 3) + (50 \times 3) + (20 \times 9) + (80 \times 3) + (0 \times 5)$$

$$= ₹\,750$$

To find the optimal solution We apply the steps involved in MODI method to the above table. We find a set of numbers u_i and v_j for which $u_i + v_j = c_{ij}$ is satisfied for each of the occupied cells. To start with, we assign a number 0 to the third column (i.e., $v_3 = 0$) as it has the maximum number of allocations. The remaining numbers are obtained as follows.

	X	Y	Z	u_i
	8	7	3	
A	−3 11	1 6	(60)	3
	3	8	9	
B	(50)	7 1	(20)	9
	11	3	5	
C	−1 12	(80)	(0)	5
v_j	−6	−2	0	

Since all $\Delta_{ij} > 0$, we have obtained an optimum solution.

The solution is given by, $X_{13} = 60; X_{21} = 50; X_{23} = 20; X_{32} = 80; X_{33} = 0$

$$\text{Total transportation cost} = (60 \times 3) + (50 \times 3) + (20 \times 9) + (80 \times 3) + (0 \times 5)$$
$$= ₹\,750$$

Unbalanced transportation problem The given TP is said to be unbalanced if $\Sigma a_i \neq \Sigma b_j$, i.e., if the total supply is not equal to the total demand.

There are two possible cases.

Case I $\sum_{i=1}^{m} a_i < \sum_{j=1}^{n} b_j$

If the total supply is less than the total demand, a dummy source (row) is included in the cost matrix with zero cost, the excess demand is entered as a rim requirement for this dummy source (origin). Hence, the unbalanced transportation problem can be converted into a balanced TP.

Case II $\sum_{i=1}^{m} a_i > \sum_{j=1}^{n} b_j$

If the total supply is greater than the total demand, the unbalanced TP can be converted into a balanced TP by adding a dummy destination (column) with zero cost. The excess supply is entered as a rim requirement for the dummy destination.

Example 8.12 Solve the transportation problem when the unit transportation costs, demands and supplies are as given below:

		Destination				
		D_1	D_2	D_3	D_4	Supply
Origins	O_1	6	1	9	3	70
	O_2	11	5	2	8	55
	O_3	10	12	4	7	70
	Demand	85	35	50	45	

Solution Since the total demand $\Sigma b_j = 215$ is greater than the total supply $\Sigma a_i = 195$, the problem is an unbalanced TP.

We convert this into a balanced TP by introducing a dummy origin O_4 with cost zero and giving supply equal to 215 – 195 = 20 units. Hence, we have the converted problem as follows:

		Destination				
		D_1	**D_2**	**D_3**	**D_4**	**Supply**
Origins	**O_1**	6	1	9	3	70
	O_2	11	5	2	8	55
	O_3	10	12	4	7	70
	O_4	0	0	0	0	20
	Demand	85	35	50	45	215

As this problem is balanced, there exists a feasible solution to this problem. Using VAM we get the following initial solution.

	D_1	D_2	D_3	D_4	Supply	P_I	P_{II}	P_{III}	P_{IV}	P_V	P_{VI}	P_{VII}
O_1	6 (65)	1 (5)	9	3	70	2	2	2	—	—	—	—
O_2	11	5 (30)	2 (25)	8	55	3	3	3	3	6 ←	—	—
O_3	10	12	4 (25)	7 (45)	70	3	3	3	3	3	3	4 ←
O_4	0 (20)	0	0	0	20	0	—	—	—	—	—	—
Demand	85	35	50	45								
P_I	6↑	1	2	3								
P_{II}	4↑	4	2	3								
P_{III}	—	4↑	2	4								
P_{IV}	—	7↑	2	1								
P_V	—	—	2	1								
P_{VI}	—	—	4	7↑								
P_{VII}	—	—	4	7								

The initial solution to the problem is given by,

	D_1	D_2	D_3	D_4
O_1	6 (65)	1 (5)	9	3
O_2	11	5 (30)	2 (25)	8
O_3	10	12	4 (25)	7 (45)
O_4	0 (20)	0	0	0

There are 7 independent non-negative allocations equals to $m + n - 1$. Hence, the solution is a non-degenerate one. The total transportation cost

$$= 65 \times 6 + 5 \times 1 + 30 \times 5 + 25 \times 2 + 25 \times 4 + 45 \times 7 + 20 \times 0$$

= ₹ 1,010.

To find the optimal solution We apply the steps in MODI method to the above table.

Initial table

	D_1	D_2	D_3	D_4	u_i
O_1	6 (65) −	1 + (5)	9 0 9	3 3 0	0
O_2	11 10 1	5 − (30)	2 + (25)	8 5 3	4
O_3	+ 10 12 −2	12 7 5	4 − (25)	7 (45)	6
O_4	0 (20) −5	0 5 −4	0 4 −5	0 5 −6	
v_j	6	1	−2	1	

Since all $\Delta_{ij} \geq 0$, the solution is not optimum. We introduce the cell (3, 1) as this cell has the most negative value of Δ_{ij}. We modify the solution by adding and subtracting the minimum allocation given by min (65, 30, 25). While doing this, the occupied cell (3, 3) becomes empty.

I Iteration table

	D_1		D_2		D_3		D_4		u_i
		6		1		9		3	
O_1	40		30		–2	11	3	0	6
		11		5		2		8	
O_2	10	1	5		50		7	1	10
		10		12		4		7	
O_3	25		5	7		2	45		10
		0		0		0		0	
O_4	20		–5	5	–8	8	–3	3	0
v_j		0		– 5		–8		– 3	

As the number of independent allocations are equal to $m + n - 1$, we check the optimality.

Since all $\Delta_{ij} \geq 0$, the solution is optimal and an alternate solution exists as $\Delta_{14} = 0$. Therefore, the optimum allocation is given by,

$$X_{11} = 40, X_{12} = 30, X_{22} = 5, X_{23} = 50, X_{31} = 25, X_{34} = 45, X_{41} = 20.$$

The optimum transportation cost is

$$= 6 \times 40 + 1 \times 30 + 5 \times 5 + 2 \times 50 + 10 \times 25 + 7 \times 45 + 0 \times 20 = ₹\,960.$$

Example 8.13 A product is produced by 4 factories F_1, F_2, F_3 and F_4. Their unit production costs are ₹ 2, 3, 1 and 5 respectively. Production capacity of the factories are 50, 70, 30 and 50 units respectively. The product is supplied to 4 stores S_1, S_2, S_3 and S_4, the requirements of which are 25, 35, 105 and 20 respectively. Unit costs of transportation are given below.

Find the transportation plan such that the total production and transportation cost is minimum.

		Destination			
		S_1	S_2	S_3	S_4
Factory	F_1	2	4	6	11
	F_2	10	8	7	5
	F_3	13	3	9	12
	F_4	4	6	8	3

Solution We form the transportation table, which consists of both production and transportation costs.

	S_1	S_2	S_3	S_4	***Capacity***
F_1	4	6	8	13	50
F_2	13	11	10	8	70
F_3	14	4	10	13	30
F_4	9	11	13	8	50
Demand	25	35	105	20	

Total capacity = 200 units
Total demand = 185 units

Therefore $\Sigma a_i > \Sigma b_j$. Hence the problem is unbalanced. We convert it into a balanced one by adding a dummy store S_5 with cost 0 and the excess supply is given as the rim requirement to this store namely (200–185) units.

	S_1	S_2	S_3	S_4	S_5	*Supply*
F_1	4 (25)	6 (5)	8 (20)	13	0	50
F_2	13	11	10 (50)	8 (20)	0	70
F_3	14	4 (30)	10	13	0	30
F_4	9	11	13 (35)	8	0 (15)	50
Demand	25	35	105	20	15	200

The initial basic feasible solution is obtained by least cost method. We get the solution containing 8 non-negative independent allocations equals to $m + n - 1$. So the solution is a non-degenerate solution.

The total transportation cost

$$= (25 \times 4) + (5 \times 6) + (20 \times 8) + (50 \times 10) + (20 \times 8) + (30 \times 4) + (35 \times 13) + (15 \times 0)$$

= ₹ 1,525

To find the optimal solution We apply MODI method to the above table as it has $m + n - 1$ independent non-negative allocation.

Initial table

	S_1	S_2	S_3	S_4	S_5	u_i
F_1	4 (25)	6 (5)	8 (20)	13; 6 7	0; –5 5	0
F_2	13; 6 7	11; 8 3	10 (50)	8 (20) –	0; –3 3	2
F_3	14; 2 12	4 (30)	10; 6 4	13; 4 9	0; –7 7	–2
F_4	9; 9 0	11; 11 0	13 (35) –	8; 11 –3	0 (15)	5
v_j	4	6	8	6	–5	

The solution is not optimum as the cell (4, 5) is having a negative net evaluation value, i.e., $\Delta_{44} = -3$. We draw a closed path from this cell and have a modified allocation by adding and subtracting the allocation min (35, 20) = 20. This modified allocation is given in the following table.

I Iteration table

	S_1	S_2	S_3	S_4	S_5	u_i
F_1	4 (25)	6 (5)	8 (20)	13 3 0	0 –5 5	0
F_2	13 6 7	11 8 3	10 (70)	8 5 –3	0 –3 3	2
F_3	14 2 12	4 (30)	10	13 1 12	0 –7 7	–2
F_4	9 9 0	11 11 0	13 (15)	8 (20)	0 (15)	5
v_j	4	6	8	6	–5	

Since all the values of $\Delta_{ij} \geq 0$, the solution is optimum but an alternate solution exists.

The optimum solution or the transportation plan is given by,

$X_{11} = 25$ units $\qquad X_{32} = 30$ units

$X_{12} = 5$ units $\qquad X_{43} = 15$ units

$X_{13} = 20$ units $\qquad X_{44} = 20$ units

$X_{23} = 70$ units $\qquad X_{45} = 15$ units

This is the surplus capacity that is not transported, which is manufactured in factory F_4. The optimum production with transportation cost

$$= (25 \times 4) + (5 \times 6) + (20 \times 8) + (70 \times 10) + (30 \times 4) + (20 \times 8) + (15 \times 13) + (15 \times 0) = ₹\ 1{,}465$$

Maximization case in transportation problem Here the objective is to maximize the total profit for which the profit matrix is given. For this, first we have to convert the maximization problem into minimization by subtracting all the elements from the highest element in the given transportation table. This modified minimization problem can be solved in the usual manner.

Example 8.14 There are three factories A, B and C, which supply goods to four dealers D_1, D_2, D_3 and D_4. The production capacities of these factories are 1,000, 700 and 900 units per month respectively. The requirements from the dealers are 900, 800, 500 and 400 units per month respectively. The per unit return (excluding transportation cost) are ₹ 8, ₹ 7 and ₹ 9 at the three factories. The following table gives the unit transportation costs from the factories to the dealers.

	D_1	D_2	D_3	D_4
A	2	2	2	4
B	3	5	3	2
C	4	3	2	1

Determine the optimum solution to maximize the total returns.

Solution Profit = return – transportation cost. With this we form a transportation table with profit.

	D_1	D_2	D_3	D_4
A	8 – 2 = 6	8 – 2 = 6	8 – 2 = 6	8 – 4 = 4
B	7 – 3 = 4	7 – 5 = 2	7 – 3 = 4	7 – 2 = 5
C	9 – 4 = 5	9 – 3 = 6	9 – 2 = 7	9 – 1 = 8

Profit matrix

	D_1	D_2	D_3	D_4	*Capacity*
A	6	6	6	4	1,000
B	4	2	4	5	700
C	5	6	7	8	900
Requirement	900	800	500	400	2,600

The above profit matrix is converted into its equivalent loss matrix by subtracting all the elements from the highest element namely 8. Hence, we have the following loss matrix.

	D_1	D_2	D_3	D_4	*Capacity*
A	2	2	2	4	1,000
B	4	6	4	3	700
C	3	2	1	0	900
Requirement	900	800	500	400	2,600

We use VAM to get the initial basic feasible solution.

	D_1	D_2	D_3	D_4	*Capacity*	P_I	P_{II}	P_{III}	P_{IV}	P_V	P_{Vi}
A	2 (200)	2 (800)	2	4	200 1,000	0	0	0	2	2	2
B	4 (700)	6	4	3	0 700	1	0	2	4 ←	—	—
C	3 (0)	2	1 (500)	0 (400)	900	1	1 ←	1	3 ←	3	—
Demand	900	800	500	400	2,600						
P_I	1	0	1	3↑							
P_{II}	1	0	1	—							
P_{III}	2	4↑	—	—							
P_{IV}	2	—	—	—							
P_V	2	—	—	—							
P_{vi}	2↑										

The initial solution is given in the following table:

	D_1	D_2	D_3	D_4	*Capacity*
A	2 (200)	2 (800)	2	4	1,000
B	4 (700)	6	4	3	700
C	3 (0)	2	1 (500)	0 (400)	900
Demand	900	800	500	400	

Since the number of allocated cells = 5 < $m + n - 1$ = 6, the solution is non-degenerate.

This cell is the least cost cell and of independent position. The initial basic feasible solution is given as follows:

Initial table

	D_1	D_2	D_3	D_4
A	2 (200)	2 (800)	2	4
B	4 (700)	6	2	3
C	3 (0)	2	1 (500)	0 (400)

Number of allocations = 6 = $m + n - 1$ and the 6 allocations are in independent positions. Hence, we can perform the optimality test using MODI method.

	D_1	D_2	D_3	D_4	u_i
A	2 (200)	2 (800)	2 2 0	4 1 3	0
B	4 (700)	6 4 2	2 4 2	3 3 0	2
C	3 1 2	2 1	1 (500)	0 (400)	–1
u_i	2	2	2	1	

Since all the net evaluations Δ_{ji} are non-negative, the initial solution is optimum.

The optimum distribution is,

$$A \to D_1 = 200 \text{ units}$$
$$A \to D_2 = 800 \text{ units}$$
$$A \to D_3 = \varepsilon \text{ units}$$

$B \to D_1 = 700$ units

$C \to D_3 = 500$ units

$C \to D_4 = 400$ units

Total profit or the Max. return $= 200 \times 6 + 6 \times 800 + 4 \times 700 + 7 \times 500 + 8 \times 400 =$ ₹ 15,500.

Example 8.15 Solve the following transportation problem to maximize the profit.

		Destination				
		A	***B***	***C***	***D***	***Supply***
Source	**1**	15	51	42	33	23
	2	80	42	26	81	44
	3	90	40	66	60	33
	Demand	23	31	16	30	100

Solution Since the given problem is to maximize the profit, we convert this into loss matrix and minimize it. For converting it into minimization type, we subtract all the elements from the highest element 90. Hence, we have the following loss matrix.

		Destination				
		A	***B***	***C***	***D***	***Supply***
Source	1	75	39	48	57	23
	2	10	48	64	9	44
	3	0	50	24	30	33
	Demand	23	31	16	30	100

Since $\Sigma a_i = \Sigma b_j$, there exists a feasible solution and is obtained by VAM.

	A	***B***	***C***	***D***	***Supply***	P_{I}	P_{II}	P_{III}	P_{IV}	P_{V}	P_{VI}
1	75	39 (23)	48	57	23	9	18	18	18	39	39
2	10 (6)	48 (8)	64	9 (30)	44	1	1	1	39	48 ←	—
3	0 (17)	50	24 (16)	30	33	24	30 ←	—	—	—	—
Demand	23	31	16	30							
P_{I}	10	9	24↑	21							
P_{II}	10	9	—	21							
P_{III}	65↑	9	—	48							
P_{IV}	—	9	—	48↑							
P_{V}	—	9	—	—							
P_{VI}	—	39↑	—	—							

The initial basic feasible solution is given in the following table.

	A	*B*	*C*	*D*	*Capacity*
1	75	39 (23)	48	57	23
2	10 (6)	48 (8)	64	9 (30)	44
3	0 (17)	50	24 (16)	30	33
Demand	23	31	16	30	

As the number of independent allocated cells = 6 = $m + n - 1$, the solution is non-degenerate.

Optimality Test Using MODI Method:

	A	*B*	*C*	*D*	u_i
1	75 19 56	39 (23)	48 23 25	57 18 39	9
2	10 (6)	48 (8) 14	64 50	9 (30)	0
3	0 (17)	50 38 12	24 (16)	30 –1 31	–10
v_j	10	48	14	9	

Since all the net evaluation $\Delta_{ij} > 0$, the solution is optimum and unique. The optimum solution is given by,

$$x_{12} = 23; x_{21} = 6; x_{22} = 8; x_{24} = 30; x_{31} = 17; x_{33} = 16$$

The optimum profit = (23 × 51) + (6 × 80) + (8 × 42) + (30 × 81) + (90 × 17) + (16 × 66)

= ₹ 7,005

8.6 THE STEPPING-STONE METHOD

This method is an approximation in which initial feasible solution is moved to an optimal solution.Main application of this method is to evaluate the cost effectiveness of shipping goods through routs used in transportation which are not currently being used in the solution.

Following the determination of an initial basic feasible solution to a transportation problem, we next obtain the optimum solution. An optimality test can be performed only on the feasible solution in which

(a) The number of allocations is $m + n - 1$ where m-number of rows, n-Number of columns.

(b) These $m + n - 1$ allocations should be in independent positions.

The technique is similar to that of simplex method by finding the net evaluations for the non-basic variables (empty cells) and then determine the entering and leaving variables. Compute a better basic feasible solution until an optimum solution has been reached.

Stepping-stone method is one of the methods for finalising an optimum solution of a T.P.

The steps involved in this method are given below.

Step 1: Using anyone of the three methods namely WWCR, LCM or VAM, find the initial basic feasible solution.

Step 2: Check the number of occupied cells. If the number of cells are less than $m + n - 1$, then degeneracy exists. To remove degeneracy, add an empty cell with small positive assignment of ($\in = 0$) in suitable independent position, so that the number of occupied cells is exactly equal to $m + n - 1$.

Step 3: Each empty (non-allocated) cell is now examined for a possible decrease in the transportation cost. One unit is allocated to an empty cell. A number of adjacent cells are balanced so that the row and the column constraints are not violated. If the net result of these changes is a decrease in the transportation cost, we exclude as many units as possible in the selected empty cell and the necessary changes has to be carried out with other cells.

Step 4: Repeat step 3, with all the empty cells till no further reduction in the transportation cost is possible. If there is another with zero decrease or increase in the transportation cost, then the problem has multiple solutions.

Example: Using stepping-stone method find the optimum solution of the transportation problem.

Distribution Centres

Sources	D_1	D_2	D_3	D_4	*Supply*
S_1	2	3	11	7	6
S_2	1	0	6	1	1
S_3	5	8	15	9	10
Requirements	7	5	3	2	

Solution: Using VAM initial basic feasible solution is obtained and given in the following table

2 (1)	3 (5)	11	7
1	0	6	1 (1)
5 (6)	8	15 (3)	9 (1)

The solution is non-degenerate since the number of non-zero variables is $m + n - 1 = 3 + 4 - 1 = 6$.

Consider an arbitrary cell (a cell without allocation) (2, 3) and allocate +1 to this cell. In order to keep up the row 3 restrictions, +1 must be allocated to the cell (3, 4) and allocate it to the cell (3, 3) and –1 to the cell (2, 4).

This new allocation is shown in the following table.

2 ①	3 ⑤	11	7
1	0	6 ①	1
5 ⑥	8	15 ②	9 ②

The increase in the transportation cost per unit quantity of reallocation is 6 + 9 – 1 – 15 = – 1.

The total number of occupied cell = 3 + 4 – 1 = 6.

By choosing the empty cell (2, 1)

2 ①	3 ⑤	5	7
1 ①	0	6	1
5 ⑤	8	15 ③	9 ②

The increase in the transportation cost per unit quantity of reallocation is 1 + 15 – 6 – 5 = 5, which can't decrease the transportation cost. So we choose the next empty cell (2, 2) and make the new allocation. The transportation table with the new allocation is given below by choosing all possible empty cells.

2 ②	3 ④	11	7
1	0 ①	6	1
5 ⑤	8	15 ③	9 ②

The increase in transportation cost per unit of reallocation is

$$(1 \times 0) + (1 \times 2) - (1 \times 1) - (3 \times 1) = -2.$$

This procedure is repeated with the remaining empty cells namely (1, 3) (1, 4) (3, 2).

The reallocation tables are given below;

2 ①	3 ④	11 ①	7
1	0	6	1
5 ⑥	8	15 ②	9 ②

The increase in total cost per unit of reallocation is

$$(1 \times 11) + (1 \times 5) - (1 \times 2) - (1 \times 15) = -1.$$

2 ①	3	11	7 ①
1	0	6	1
5 ⑥	8	15 ③	9 ①

The increase in total cost per unit of reallocation is

$$(1 \times 7) + (1 \times 15) - (1 \times 9) - (1 \times 11) = 2.$$

2 ②	3 ④	11	7
1	0	6 ①	1
5 ⑤	8 ①	15 ③	9 ①

The increase in total cost per unit of reallocation is

$$(1 \times 8) + (1 \times 2) - (1 \times 3) - (1 \times 5) = 2.$$

EXERCISES

1. What do you understand by transportation model?
2. Define feasible solution, basic solution, non-degenerate solution and optimal solution in a transportation problem.
3. Explain the following briefly with examples:
   (*i*) North-West Corner Rule
   (*ii*) Least Cost Method
   (*iii*) Vogel's Approximation Method.

4. Explain degeneracy in a TP and how to resolve it.
5. What do you mean by an unbalanced TP? Explain how you would convert an unbalanced TP into a balanced one.
6. Give the mathematical formulation of a TP.
7. Explain an algorithm to solving a transportation problem.
8. Obtain the initial solution for the following TP using (i) NWCR (ii) Least cost method (iii) VAM.

		Destination			
		A	B	C	Supply
Source	1	2	7	4	5
	2	3	3	1	8
	3	5	4	7	7
	4	1	6	2	14
	Demand	7	9	18	34

[Ans.

(*i*) $x_{11} = 5$, $x_{21} = 2$, $x_{22} = 6$, $x_{32} = 3$, $x_{33} = 4$, $x_{43} = 14$ and the transportation cost ₹ 102.

(*ii*) $x_{12} = 2$, $x_{13} = 3$, $x_{23} = 8$, $x_{32} = 7$, $x_{41} = 7$, $x_{43} = 7$ and transportation cost ₹ 83.

(*iii*) $x_{11} = 5$, $x_{23} = 8$, $x_{32} = 7$, $x_{41} = 2$, $x_{42} = 2$, $x_{43} = 10$ and transportation cost ₹ 80.]

9. Solve the following TP where the cell entries denote the unit transportation costs (using least cost method).

		Destination				
		A	B	C	D	Supply
Origin	P	5	4	2	6	20
	Q	8	3	5	7	30
	R	5	9	4	6	50
	Demand	10	40	20	30	100

[Ans. $x_{12} = 10$, $x_{13} = 10$, $x_{22} = 30$, $x_{31} = 10$, $x_{33} = 10$, $x_{34} = 30$. The optimum transportation cost is ₹ 420.]

10. Solve the following transportation problem (least cost method).

		Destination		
	1	2	3	Capacity
1	2	2	3	10
2	4	1	2	15
3	1	3	1	40
Demand	20	15	30	

[Ans. $x_{12} = 10$, $x_{23} = 15$, $x_{31} = 20$, $x_{33} = 15$, $x_{32} = 5$. The transportation cost is ₹ 100.]

11. Find the minimum transportation cost (NWCR & MODI).

	Warehouse					
		D_1	D_2	D_3	D_4	**Supply**
Factory	F_1	19	30	50	10	7
	F_2	70	30	40	60	9
	F_3	40	8	70	20	18
	Demand	5	8	7	14	

[**Ans.** x_{11} = 5, x_{14} = 2, x_{22} = 2, x_{23} = 7, x_{32} = 6, x_{34} = 12 and the minimum transportation cost = ₹ 743.]

12. Solve the following TP using Vogel's method.

	Warehouse							
		A	**B**	**C**	**D**	**E**	**F**	**Availability**
Factory	**1**	9	12	9	6	9	10	5
	2	7	3	7	7	5	5	6
	3	6	5	9	11	3	11	2
	4	6	8	11	2	2	10	9
	Requirement	4	4	6	2	4	2	

[**Ans.** x_{13} = 5, x_{22} = 4, x_{26} = 2, x_{31} = 1, x_{32} = ε, x_{33} = 1, x_{41} = 3, x_{44} = 2, x_{45} = 4 and the min. transportation cost is ₹ 112.]

13. Solve the following TP.

	Destination					
		A	**B**	**C**	**D**	**Supply**
Source	**1**	1	2	3	4	6
	2	4	3	2	0	8
	3	0	2	2	1	10
	Demand	4	6	8	6	

[**Ans.** x_{12} = 6, x_{23} = 2, x_{24} = 6, x_{31} = 4, x_{32} = ε, x_{33} = 6. The min. transportation cost is ₹ 28.]

14. Solve the following TP.

	Destination					
		A	**B**	**C**	**D**	**Supply**
Source	**1**	11	20	7	8	50
	2	21	16	20	12	40
	3	8	12	8	9	70
	Demand	30	25	35	40	

[**Ans.** x_{13} = 35, x_{14} = 15, x_{24} = 10, x_{25} = 30, x_{31} = 30, x_{32} = 25, x_{34} = 15 min. transportation cost = ₹ 1160.]

15. Solve the following TP to maximize the profit.

		Destination				
		A	B	C	D	Supply
Source	1	40	25	22	33	100
	2	44	35	30	30	30
	3	38	38	28	30	70
	Demand	40	20	60	30	

[**Ans.** x_{11} = 20, x_{14} = 30, x_{15} = 50, x_{21} = 20, x_{23} = 10, x_{32} = 20, x_{33} = 50 and the optimum profit is ₹ 5130.]

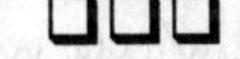

Chapter

9 Transhipment and Assignment Problems

9.1 INTRODUCTION

This chapter deals with a very interesting method called the 'assignment technique', which is applicable to a class of very practical problems generally called 'assignment problems'.

The objective of assignment problems is to assign a number of origins (jobs) to the equal number of destinations (persons) at a minimum cost or maximum profit.

9.2 TRANSHIPMENT PROBLEM

9.2.1 Definition

In a transportation problem, where shipments are allowed only between source-sink pairs, there is a possibility of existing points via which units of a goods/merchandise may be transhipped from a source to a sink. It is a strong assumption that shipments may be allowed between sources and between sinks, and also, inter-linking source-sink. Transportation models which have these additional features are called transhipment problems. Often, we see a gradual shift towards conversion from a transhipment problem to a transportation problem. This conversion procedure is of great significance as it broadens the applicability of algorithm as a solution for transportation problems. This conversion procedure can be well defined with the following example:

9.2.2 Transhipment Problem-to-Transportation Problem

An organic food company manufactures cereals in two cities, Leeds and Kent. The daily cereal production capacity at Leeds and Kent are 160 and 200 packets, respectively. Cereals are shipped by air to consumers in London and New York. The consumers in each city require 140 packets of cereals per day. However, due to the deregulation of air fares, the organic food company believes that it may be cheaper to fly some variety of cereals to Leeds or Dallas, and then do the final packaging to fly the packets of cereals to London and New York (final destinations). The table given below shows the cost of flying one packets (in £) of the cereals between these cities:

From →	*Leeds*	*Kent*	*London*	*Dallas*	*New York*
Leeds	£ 0	—	£ 9	£ 14	£ 29
Kent	—	£ 0	£ 16	£ 13	£ 26
London	—	—	£ 0	£ 7	£ 18
Dallas	—	—	£ 7	£ 0	£ 17
New York	—	—	—	—	£ 0

Now, to minimize the total incurred cost of daily shipments of the cereals to its consumers, we first need to understand terminologies, such as source and sink. Source is a city that can send products, however cannot receive any product from any other city. Whereas, sink is a city that can receive products but cannot send to any other city.

So, in this example we can say, that Leeds and Kent are source, and Leeds and Dallas are transhipment points, and finally, London and New York are sinks (each with a daily requirement of 140 packets of cereals).

So, we see a mismatch in demand and supply with the total supply equals to 156 and the total demand equals to 122.

Now, to solve this imbalance, we need to create a dummy sink, with a demand of 34. We would now have 2 sources, 2 sinks, and 2 transhipment points. As discussed before, transhipment points can act in dual roles, both as sources and sinks. As there are no transportation costs from a transhipment point to itself, the primary objective to reduce costs remain unaffected.

Therefore, we should perform a reformulation and use the transhipment points as an optimal solution for imbalanced demand-supply as well as reduce the transportation problem (costs) to ensure maximization of profits.

9.2.3 Transhipment Model

In a transhipment model, the objects are supplied from various specific sources to various specific destinations. It is also economic if the shipment passes via the transient nodes which are in between the sources and the destinations. It is different from transportation problem where the shipments are directly sent from a specific source to a specific destination, whereas in the transhipment problem the main goal is to reduce the total cost of shipments. Hence, the shipment passes via one or more intermediary nodes before it reaches its desired specific destination. Basically, there are two methods of evaluating transhipment problems as discussed below.

The following is the schematic illustration of the sources and destinations acting as transient nodes of a simple transhipment problem.

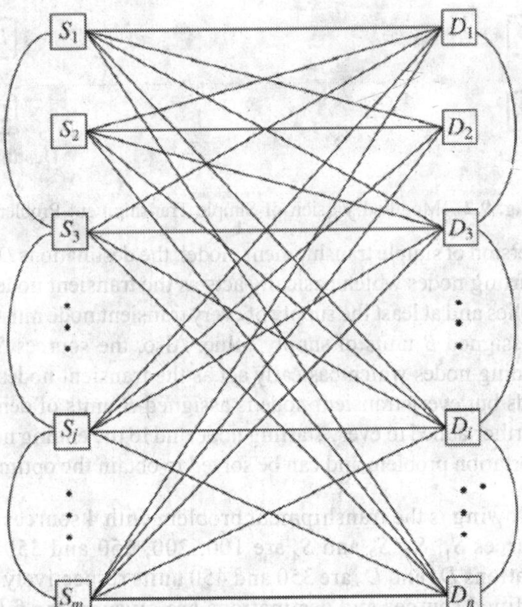

Fig. 9.1 Schematic Diagram of Simple Transhipment Model

The figure shows the shipment of objects from source S_1 to destination D_2. Shipment from source S_1 can pass via S_2 and D_1 before it reaches the desired destination D_2. Because the shipment passes via the particular transient nodes, this arrangement is named as transhipment model. The goal of the transhipment problem is to discover the optimal shipping model so that the total transportation cost is reduced.

Figure 9.2 shows a different approach where the number of first starting nodes and also the number of last ending nodes is the sum of the total number of sources and destinations of the original problem. Let B be the buffer which should be maintained at every transient source and transient destination. Considering it as a balanced problem, buffer B at the least may be equal to the sum of total supplies or the sum of total demands. Therefore, a constant B is further added to all the starting nodes and the ending nodes as shown below:

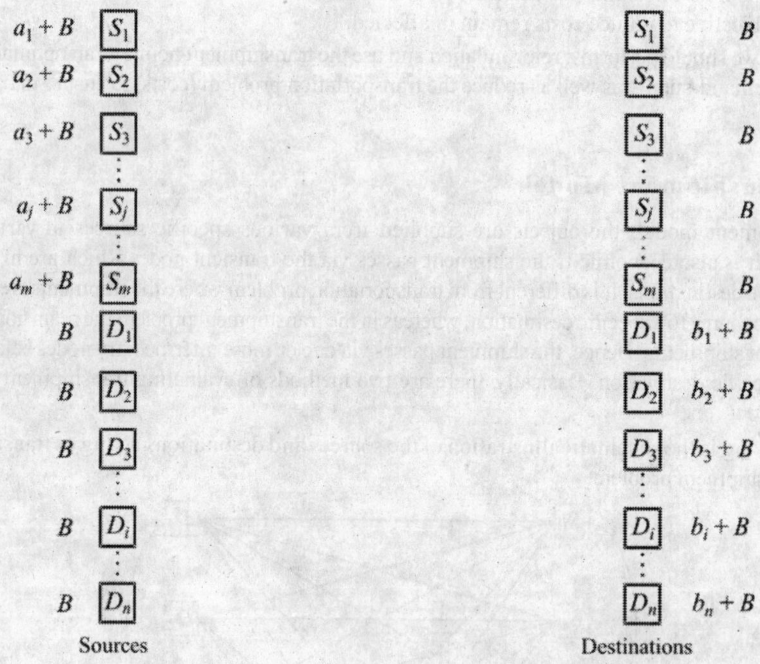

Fig. 9.2 Modified Version of Simple Transhipment Problem

Here in the modified version of simple transhipment model, the destinations $D_1, D_2, D_3, ..., D_i, ..., D_n$ are incorporated as added starting nodes which basically acts as the transient nodes. Hence, these nodes do not have the original supplies and at least the supply of every transient node must be equal to B. Therefore, every transient node is assigned B units of supply value. Also, the sources S_1, S_2, S_3,..., S_j..., S_m are incorporated as added ending nodes which basically act as the transient nodes. These nodes too do not have the original demands but every transient node is assigned B units of demand value. To make it a balanced problem, B is further added to every starting node and to the ending nodes. Hence, the problem resembles a usual transportation problem and can be solved to obtain the optimum shipping plan.

Example 9.1 The following is the transhipment problem with 4 sources and 2 destinations. The supply values of the sources S_1, S_2, S_3 and S_4 are 100, 200, 150 and 350 units respectively. The demand values of destinations D_1 and D_2 are 350 and 450 units respectively. Transportation cost per unit between various defined sources and destinations are given in the following table. Solve the transhipment problem.

Source	Destination					
	S_1	S_2	S_3	S_4	D_1	D_2
S_1	0	4	20	5	25	12
S_2	10	0	6	10	5	20
S_3	15	20	0	8	45	7
S_4	20	25	10	0	30	6
D_1	20	18	60	15	0	10
D_2	10	25	30	23	4	0

Solution: In the above table the number of sources is 4 and the number of destinations is 2. Therefore, the total number of starting nodes and the ending nodes of the transhipment problem will be 4 + 2 = 6. We also have,

$$B = \sum_{i=1}^{n} a_i = \sum_{j=1}^{m} b_i$$

The following is the detailed format of the transhipment problem after including transient nodes for the sources and the destinations. Here the value of B is added to all the rows and columns.

Source	Destination						Supply
	S_1	S_2	S_3	S_4	D_1	D_2	
S_1	0	4	20	5	25	12	100 + 800 = 900
S_2	10	0	6	10	5	20	200 + 800 = 1000
S_3	15	20	0	8	45	7	150 + 800 = 950
S_4	20	25	10	0	30	6	350 + 800 = 1150
D_1	20	18	60	15	0	10	800
D_2	10	25	30	23	4	0	800
	800	800	800	800	350 + 800 = 1150	450 + 800 = 1250	

The optimal solution and the corresponding total cost transportation is ₹ 5600. The allocations defined in the main diagonal cells are ignored. The diagrammatic representation of the optimal shipping pattern of the shipments related to the off-diagonal cells is shown below:

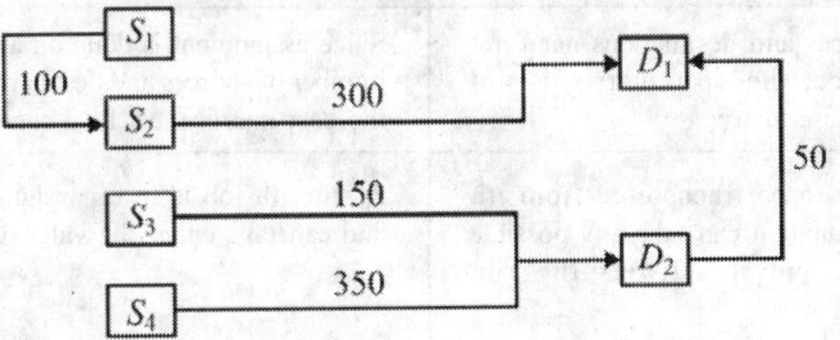

Optimal Shipping Pattern

9.3 ASSIGNMENT PROBLEM

9.3.1 Definition

Suppose there are n jobs to be performed and n persons are available for doing these jobs. Assume that each person can do each job at a time, though with varying degrees of efficiency. Let c_{ij} be the cost if the ith person is assigned to the jth job. The problem is to find an assignment (which job should be assigned to which person, on a one-to-one basis) so that the total cost of performing all the jobs is minimum. Problems of this kind are known as assignment problems.

An assignment problem can be stated in the form of $n \times n$ cost matrix $[c_{ij}]$ of real numbers as given in the following table.

Jobs

$$
\textbf{Persons}\quad
\begin{array}{c}
 \\ 1 \\ 2 \\ 3 \\ \\ i \\ \vdots \\ n
\end{array}
\begin{array}{c}
\begin{array}{ccccccc} 1 & 2 & 3 & \ldots & j & \ldots & n \end{array} \\
\begin{bmatrix}
c_{11} & c_{12} & c_{13} & \ldots & c_{1j} & \ldots & c_{1n} \\
c_{21} & c_{22} & c_{23} & \ldots & c_{2j} & \ldots & c_{2n} \\
c_{31} & c_{32} & c_{33} & \ldots & c_{3j} & \ldots & c_{3n} \\
 & & & & & & \\
c_{i1} & c_{i2} & c_{i3} & \ldots & c_{ij} & \ldots & c_{in} \\
 & \vdots & & & & & \\
c_{n1} & c_{n2} & c_{n3} & \ldots & c_{nj} & \ldots & c_{nn}
\end{bmatrix}
\end{array}
$$

9.3.2 Mathematical Formulation of an Assignment Problem

Mathematically, an assignment problem can be stated as,

$$\text{Minimize } z = \sum_{i=1}^{n} \sum_{j=1}^{n} c_{ij}\, x_{ij}, \text{ where, } i = 1, 2, \ldots n, \text{ and } j = 1, 2, \ldots n$$

Subject to the restrictions,

$$x_{ij} = \begin{cases} 1, \text{ if the } i\text{th person is assigned } j\text{th job} \\ 0, \text{ if not} \end{cases}$$

$$\sum_{j=1}^{n} x_{ij} = 1 \text{ (one job is done by the } i\text{th person)}$$

and $$\sum_{j=1}^{n} x_{ij} = 1 \text{ (only one person should be assigned the } j\text{th job)}$$

where, x_{ij} denotes that the jth job is to be assigned to the ith person.

9.3.3 Difference between Transportation and Assignment Problems

	Transportation Problem	*Assignment Problem*
1.	Number of sources and destinations need not be equal. Hence, the cost matrix is not necessarily a square matrix.	Since assignment is done on a one-to-one basis, the number of sources and destinations are equal. Hence, the cost matrix must be a square matrix.
2.	x_{ij}, the quantity to be transported from ith origin to jth destination can take any possible positive value, and it satisfies the rim requirements.	x_{ij}, the jth job is to be assigned to the ith person and can take either the value 1 or zero.
3.	The capacity and the requirement value is equal to a_i and b_j for the ith source and jth destination ($i = 1, 2, \ldots m$; $j = 1, 2, \ldots n$).	The capacity and the requirement value is exactly one, i.e., for each source of each destination, the capacity and the requirement value is exactly one.
4.	The problem is unbalanced if the total supply and total demand are not equal.	The problem is unbalanced if the cost matrix is not a square matrix.

9.4 HUNGARIAN METHOD PROCEDURE

Solution of an assignment problem can be arrived at, by using the **Hungarian method**. The steps involved in this method are as follows.

Step 1 Prepare a cost matrix. If the cost matrix is not a square matrix then add a dummy row (or column) with zero cost element.

Step 2 Subtract the minimum element in each row from all the elements of the respective rows.

Step 3 Further, modify the resulting matrix by subtracting the minimum element of each column from all the elements of the respective columns. Thus, obtain the modified matrix.

Step 4 Then, draw the minimum number of horizontal and vertical lines to cover all zeros in the resulting matrix. Let the minimum number of lines be N. Now there are two possible cases.

Case I If $N = n$, where n is the order of matrix, then an optimal assignment can be made. So make the assignment to get the required solution.

Case II If $N < n$, then proceed to step 5.

Step 5 Determine the smallest uncovered element in the matrix (element not covered by N lines). Subtract this minimum element from all uncovered elements and add the same element at the intersection of horizontal and vertical lines. Thus, the second modified matrix is obtained.

Step 6 Repeat steps 3 and 4 until we get the case (*i*) of Step 4.

Step 7 (To make zero assignment) Examine the rows successively until a row-wise exactly single zero is found. Circle (O) this zero to make the assignment. Then mark a cross (×) over all zeros if lying in the column of the circled zero, showing that they cannot be considered for future assignment. Continue in this manner until all the zeros have been examined. Repeat the same procedure for columns also.

Step 8 Repeat step 6 successively until one of the following situation arises—

(*i*) If no unmarked zero is left, then the process ends or

(*ii*) If there lie more than one unmarked zero in any column or row, circle one of the unmarked zeros arbitrarily and mark a cross in the cells of remaining zeros in its row or column. Repeat the process until no unmarked zero is left in the matrix.

Step 9 Thus, exactly one marked circled zero in each row and each column of the matrix is obtained. The assignment corresponding to these marked circled zeros will give the optimal assignment.

Example 9.2 Using the following cost matrix, determine (*a*) optimal job assignment (*b*) the cost of assignments.

$$\textbf{Mechanic}\quad \begin{array}{c} \\ A \\ B \\ C \\ D \\ E \end{array} \overset{\textbf{Job}}{\begin{array}{ccccc} 1 & 2 & 3 & 4 & 5 \\ \hline \end{array}}$$

$$\begin{array}{c|ccccc} & 1 & 2 & 3 & 4 & 5 \\ \hline A & 10 & 3 & 3 & 2 & 8 \\ B & 9 & 7 & 8 & 2 & 7 \\ C & 7 & 5 & 6 & 2 & 4 \\ D & 3 & 5 & 8 & 2 & 4 \\ E & 9 & 10 & 9 & 6 & 10 \end{array}$$

Solution Select the smallest element in each row and subtract this smallest element from all the elements in its row.

$$\begin{array}{c|ccccc} & 1 & 2 & 3 & 4 & 5 \\ \hline A & 8 & 1 & 1 & 0 & 6 \\ B & 7 & 5 & 6 & 0 & 5 \\ C & 5 & 3 & 4 & 0 & 2 \\ D & 1 & 3 & 6 & 0 & 2 \\ E & 3 & 4 & 3 & 0 & 4 \end{array}$$

Select the minimum element from each column and subtract from all other elements in its column. With this we get the first modified matrix.

$$\begin{array}{c} \\ A \\ B \\ C \\ D \\ E \end{array} \begin{array}{c} \begin{array}{ccccc} 1 & 2 & 3 & 4 & 5 \end{array} \\ \begin{bmatrix} 7 & 0 & 0 & 0 & 4 \\ 6 & 4 & 5 & 0 & 3 \\ 4 & 2 & 3 & 0 & 0 \\ 0 & 2 & 5 & 0 & 0 \\ 2 & 3 & 2 & 0 & 2 \end{bmatrix} \end{array}$$

In this modified matrix we draw the minimum number of lines to cover all zeros (horizontal or vertical).

$$\begin{array}{c} \\ A \\ B \\ C \\ D \\ E \end{array} \begin{array}{c} \begin{array}{ccccc} 1 & 2 & 3 & 4 & 5 \end{array} \\ \begin{bmatrix} 7 & 0 & 0 & 0 & 4 \\ 6 & 4 & 5 & 0 & 3 \\ 4 & 2 & 3 & 0 & 0 \\ 0 & 2 & 5 & 0 & 0 \\ 2 & 3 & 2 & 0 & 2 \end{bmatrix} \end{array}$$

Number of lines drawn to cover all zeros is $4 = N$.

The order of matrix is $n = 5$

Hence, $N < n$.

Now we get the second modified matrix by subtracting the smallest uncovered element from the remaining uncovered elements and adding it to the element at the point of intersection of lines.

$$\begin{array}{c} \\ A \\ B \\ C \\ D \\ E \end{array} \begin{array}{c} \begin{array}{ccccc} 1 & 2 & 3 & 4 & 5 \end{array} \\ \begin{bmatrix} 9 & \textcircled{0} & \times & 2 & 6 \\ 6 & 2 & 3 & \textcircled{0} & 3 \\ 4 & \times & 1 & \times & \textcircled{0} \\ \textcircled{0} & \times & 3 & \times & \times \\ 2 & 1 & \textcircled{0} & \times & 2 \end{bmatrix} \end{array}$$

Number of lines drawn to cover all zeros = $N = 5$

The order of matrix is $n = 5$.

Hence $N = n$. Now we determine the optimum assignment.

Assignment

$$\begin{array}{c} \\ A \\ B \\ C \\ D \\ E \end{array} \begin{array}{c} \begin{array}{ccccc} 1 & 2 & 3 & 4 & 5 \end{array} \\ \begin{bmatrix} 9 & \boxed{0} & \times & 2 & 6 \\ 6 & 2 & 3 & \boxed{0} & 3 \\ 4 & \times & 1 & \times & \boxed{0} \\ \boxed{0} & \times & 3 & \times & \times \\ 2 & 1 & \boxed{0} & \times & 2 \end{bmatrix} \end{array}$$

First row contains more than one zero. So proceed to the 2nd row. It has exactly one zero. The corresponding cell is $(B, 4)$. Circle this zero thus, making an assignment. Mark (×) for all other zeros in its column. Showing that they cannot be used for making other assignments. Now row 5 has a single zero in the cell $(E, 3)$. Make an assignment in this cell and cross the 2nd zero in the 3rd column.

Now row 1 has a single zero in the column 2, i.e., in the cell $(A, 2)$. Make an assignment in this cell and cross the other zeros in the 2nd column. This leads to a single zero in column 1 of the cell $(D, 1)$, make an assignment in this cell and cross the other zeros in the 4th row. Finally, we have a single zero left in the 3rd row, making an assignment in the cell (C, 5). Thus, we have the following assignment.

Optimal assignment and optimum cost of assignment.

Job	*Mechanic*	*Cost*
1	D	3
2	A	3
3	E	9
4	B	2
5	C	4
		₹ 21

Therefore, $1 \to D, 2 \to A, 3 \to E, 4 \to B, 5 \to C$, with minimum cost equal to ₹ 21.

Example 9.3 A company has 5 jobs to be done on five machines. Any job can be done on any machine. The cost of doing the jobs on different machines are given below. Assign the jobs for different machines so as to minimize the total cost.

Jobs	*Machines*				
	A	*B*	*C*	*D*	*E*
1	13	8	16	18	19
2	9	15	24	9	12
3	12	9	4	4	4
4	6	12	10	8	13
5	15	17	18	12	20

Solution We form the first modified matrix by subtracting the minimum element from all the elements in the respective row, and the same with respective columns.

Step 1

$$\begin{array}{c} \\ 1\\2\\3\\4\\5 \end{array}\begin{array}{c} \begin{array}{ccccc} A & B & C & D & E \end{array} \\ \begin{bmatrix} 5 & 0 & 8 & 10 & 11 \\ 0 & 6 & 15 & 0 & 3 \\ 8 & 5 & 0 & 0 & 0 \\ 0 & 6 & 4 & 2 & 7 \\ 3 & 5 & 6 & 0 & 8 \end{bmatrix} \end{array}$$

Since each column has the minimum element 0, we have the first modified matrix. Now we draw the minimum number of lines to cover all zeros.

Step 2

$$\begin{array}{c} \\ 1\\2\\3\\4\\5 \end{array}\begin{array}{c} \begin{array}{ccccc} A & B & C & D & E \end{array} \\ \begin{bmatrix} 5 & 0 & 8 & 10 & 11 \\ 0 & 6 & 15 & 0 & 3 \\ 8 & 5 & 0 & 0 & 0 \\ 0 & 6 & 4 & 2 & 7 \\ 3 & 5 & 6 & 0 & 8 \end{bmatrix} \end{array}$$

Number of lines drawn to cover zero is $N = 4 <$ the order of matrix $n = 5$.

We find the second modified matrix by subtracting the smallest uncovered element (3) from all the uncovered elements and adding to the element that is the point of intersection of lines.

Step 3

	A	B	C	D	E
1	5	0	5	10	8
2	0	6	12	0	0
3	11	8	0	3	0
4	0	6	1	2	4
5	3	5	3	0	5

Number of lines drawn to cover all zeros = 5,
which is the order of matrix. Hence, we can form an assignment.

Assignment

	A	B	C	D	E
1	5	[0]	5	10	8
2	~~0~~	6	12	~~0~~	[0]
3	11	8	[0]	3	~~0~~
4	[0]	6	1	2	4
5	3	5	3	[0]	5

All the five jobs have been assigned to 5 different machines.

Here the optimal assignment is,

Job	***Machine***
1	B
2	E
3	C
4	A
5	D

Minimum (Total cost) = 8 + 12 + 4 + 6 + 12 = ₹ 42.

Example 9.4 Four different jobs can be done on four different machines and the take-down time costs are prohibitively high for change overs. The matrix below gives the cost in rupees for producing job *i* on the machine *j*.

Jobs	***Machines***			
	M_1	M_2	M_3	M_4
J_1	5	7	11	6
J_2	8	5	9	6
J_3	4	7	10	7
J_4	10	4	8	3

How should the jobs be assigned to the various machines so that the total cost is minimized?

Solution We form a first modified matrix by subtracting the least element in the respective rows and respective columns.

$$\begin{array}{c} \\ J_1 \\ J_2 \\ J_3 \\ J_4 \end{array}\begin{array}{c} \begin{array}{cccc} M_1 & M_2 & M_3 & M_4 \end{array} \\ \begin{bmatrix} 0 & 2 & 6 & 1 \\ 3 & 0 & 4 & 1 \\ 0 & 3 & 6 & 3 \\ 7 & 1 & 5 & 0 \end{bmatrix} \end{array}$$

Since the third column has no zero element, we subtract the smallest element 4 from all the elements.

$$\begin{array}{c} \\ J_1 \\ J_2 \\ J_3 \\ J_4 \end{array}\begin{array}{c} \begin{array}{cccc} M_1 & M_2 & M_3 & M_4 \end{array} \\ \begin{bmatrix} 0 & 2 & 2 & 1 \\ 3 & 0 & 0 & 1 \\ 0 & 3 & 2 & 3 \\ 7 & 1 & 1 & 0 \end{bmatrix} \end{array}$$

Now we draw minimum number of lines to cover all zeros.

$$\begin{array}{c} \\ J_1 \\ J_2 \\ J_3 \\ J_4 \end{array}\begin{array}{c} \begin{array}{cccc} M_1 & M_2 & M_3 & M_4 \end{array} \\ \begin{bmatrix} 0 & 2 & 2 & 1 \\ 3 & 0 & 0 & 1 \\ 0 & 3 & 2 & 3 \\ 7 & 1 & 1 & 0 \end{bmatrix} \end{array}$$

Number of lines drawn to cover all zeros = 3, which is less than the order of matrix = 4.

Hence, we form the 2nd modified matrix, by subtracting the smallest uncovered element from all the uncovered elements and adding to the element that is at the point of intersection of lines.

$$\begin{array}{c} \\ J_1 \\ J_2 \\ J_3 \\ J_4 \end{array}\begin{array}{c} \begin{array}{cccc} M_1 & M_2 & M_3 & M_4 \end{array} \\ \begin{bmatrix} 0 & 1 & 1 & 1 \\ 4 & 0 & 0 & 2 \\ 0 & 2 & 1 & 3 \\ 7 & 0 & 0 & 0 \end{bmatrix} \end{array} \qquad \begin{array}{c} \\ J_1 \\ J_2 \\ J_3 \\ J_4 \end{array}\begin{array}{c} \begin{array}{cccc} M_1 & M_2 & M_3 & M_4 \end{array} \\ \begin{bmatrix} 0 & 0 & 0 & 0 \\ 5 & 0 & 0 & 2 \\ 0 & 1 & 0 & 2 \\ 8 & 0 & 0 & 0 \end{bmatrix} \end{array}$$

$N = 3 < n = 4$ $\qquad$ $N = 4 = n = 4$

Hence, we can make an assignment.

$$\begin{array}{c} \\ J_1 \\ J_2 \\ J_3 \\ J_4 \end{array}\begin{array}{c} \begin{array}{cccc} M_1 & M_2 & M_3 & M_4 \end{array} \\ \begin{bmatrix} \times & \times & \times & \textcircled{0} \\ 5 & \textcircled{0} & \times & 2 \\ \textcircled{0} & 1 & \times & 2 \\ 8 & \times & \textcircled{0} & \times \end{bmatrix} \end{array}$$

Since no rows and no columns have single zero, we have a different assignment (Multiple solution).

Optimal assignment

Job	**Machine**
J_1	M_4
J_2	M_2
J_3	M_1
J_4	M_3

Minimum (Total cost)

$$6 + 5 + 4 + 8 = ₹ 23.$$

Alternate Solution

$$J_1 \to M_1; \quad J_2 \to M_2; \quad J_3 \to M_3; \quad J_4 \to M_4.$$

Minimum (Total cost)

$$5 + 5 + 10 + 3 = ₹ 23.$$

Example 9.5 Solve the following assignment problem in order to minimize the total cost. The cost matrix given below gives the assignment cost when different operators are assigned to various machines.

Operators

Machines	I	II	III	IV	V
A	30	25	33	35	36
B	23	29	38	23	26
C	30	27	22	22	22
D	25	31	29	27	32
E	27	29	30	24	32

Solution We form the first modified matrix by subtracting the least element from all the elements in the respective rows and then in the respective columns.

	I	II	III	IV	V
A	5	0	8	10	11
B	0	6	15	0	3
C	8	5	0	0	0
D	0	6	4	2	7
E	3	5	6	0	8

Since each column has the minimum element 0, the first modified matrix is obtained. We draw the minimum number of lines to cover all zeros.

The number of lines drawn to cover all zeros = 4 < the order of matrix = 5. Hence, we form the second modified matrix by subtracting the smallest uncovered element from the remaining uncovered elements and adding to the element that is at the point of intersection of lines.

	I	II	III	IV	V
A	8	0	8	13	11
B	0	3	12	0	0
C	11	5	0	3	0
D	0	3	1	2	4
E	3	2	3	0	5

$N = 5$, i.e., the number of lines drawn to cover all zeros = order of matrix. Hence, we can make an assignment.

$$\begin{array}{c} \\ A \\ B \\ C \\ D \\ E \end{array} \begin{array}{c} \begin{array}{ccccc} I & II & III & IV & V \end{array} \\ \begin{bmatrix} 5 & \textcircled{0} & 5 & 10 & 8 \\ \not{0} & 6 & 12 & \not{0} & \textcircled{0} \\ 11 & 8 & \textcircled{0} & 3 & \not{0} \\ \textcircled{0} & 6 & 1 & 2 & 4 \\ 3 & 5 & 3 & \textcircled{0} & 5 \end{bmatrix} \end{array}$$

The optimum assignment is

Operators	***Machines***
I	D
II	A
III	C
IV	E
V	B

The optimum cost is given by

$$25 + 25 + 22 + 24 + 26 = ₹\ 122.$$

9.5 UNBALANCED ASSIGNMENT PROBLEM

Any assignment problem is said to be unbalanced if the cost matrix is not a square matrix, i.e., the number of rows and columns are not equal. To make it balanced, we add a dummy row or dummy column with all the entries as zero.

Example 9.6 There are four jobs to be assigned to five machines. Only one job can be assigned to one machine. The amount of time in hours required for the jobs per machine are given in the following matrix.

Jobs	***Machines***				
	A	***B***	***C***	***D***	***E***
1	4	3	6	2	7
2	10	12	11	14	16
3	4	3	2	1	5
4	8	7	6	9	6

Find an optimum assignment of jobs to the machines to minimize the total processing time and also find out for which machine no job is assigned. What is the total processing time to complete all the jobs?

Solution Since the cost matrix is not a square matrix, the problem is unbalanced. We add a dummy job 5 with corresponding entries zero.

Modified Matrix

$$\begin{array}{c} \\ 1 \\ 2 \\ 3 \\ 4 \\ 5 \end{array}\begin{array}{c} \begin{array}{ccccc} A & B & C & D & E \end{array} \\ \begin{bmatrix} 4 & 3 & 6 & 2 & 7 \\ 10 & 12 & 11 & 14 & 16 \\ 4 & 3 & 2 & 1 & 5 \\ 8 & 7 & 6 & 9 & 6 \\ 0 & 0 & 0 & 0 & 0 \end{bmatrix} \end{array}$$

We subtract the smallest element from all the elements in the respective rows.

$$\begin{array}{c} \\ 1 \\ 2 \\ 3 \\ 4 \\ 5 \end{array}\begin{array}{c} \begin{array}{ccccc} A & B & C & D & E \end{array} \\ \begin{bmatrix} 2 & 1 & 4 & 0 & 5 \\ 0 & 2 & 1 & 4 & 6 \\ 3 & 2 & 1 & 0 & 4 \\ 2 & 1 & 0 & 3 & 0 \\ 0 & 0 & 0 & 0 & 0 \end{bmatrix} \end{array}$$

Since each column has minimum element as zero, we draw minimum number of lines to cover all zeros.

$$\begin{array}{c} \\ 1 \\ 2 \\ 3 \\ 4 \\ 5 \end{array}\begin{array}{c} \begin{array}{ccccc} A & B & C & D & E \end{array} \\ \begin{bmatrix} 2 & 1 & 4 & 0 & 5 \\ 0 & 2 & 1 & 4 & 6 \\ 3 & 2 & 1 & 0 & 4 \\ 2 & 1 & 0 & 3 & 0 \\ 0 & 0 & 0 & 0 & 0 \end{bmatrix} \end{array}$$

The number of lines to cover all zeros = 4 < the order of matrix. We form the 2nd modified matrix by subtracting the smallest uncovered element from the remaining uncovered elements and adding to the element at the point of intersection of lines.

$$\begin{array}{c} \\ 1 \\ 2 \\ 3 \\ 4 \\ 5 \end{array}\begin{array}{c} \begin{array}{ccccc} A & B & C & D & E \end{array} \\ \begin{bmatrix} 2 & \boxed{0} & 3 & \xcancel{0} & 4 \\ \boxed{0} & 1 & \xcancel{0} & 4 & 5 \\ 3 & 1 & \xcancel{0} & \boxed{0} & 3 \\ 3 & 1 & \boxed{0} & 4 & \xcancel{0} \\ 1 & \xcancel{0} & \xcancel{0} & 1 & \boxed{0} \end{bmatrix} \end{array}$$

Here the number of lines drawn to cover all zeros = 5 = Order of matrix. Therefore, we can make the assignment.

Optimum assignment

1	B	3
2	A	10
3	D	1
4	C	6
5	E	0

For machine D, no job is assigned.

Optimum (minimum) cost = 3 + 10 + 1 + 6 = ₹ 20.

Example 9.7 A company has 4 machines to do 3 jobs. Each job can be assigned to only one machine. The cost of each job on each machine is given below. Determine the job assignments that will minimize the total cost.

Machine

$$\textbf{Job}\quad \begin{array}{c} \\ A \\ B \\ C \end{array}\begin{array}{c} \begin{array}{cccc} W & X & Y & Z \end{array} \\ \begin{bmatrix} 18 & 24 & 28 & 32 \\ 8 & 13 & 17 & 18 \\ 10 & 15 & 19 & 22 \end{bmatrix} \end{array}$$

Solution Since the cost matrix is not a square matrix, we add a dummy row D with all the elements 0.

$$\begin{array}{c} \\ A \\ B \\ C \\ D \end{array}\begin{array}{c} \begin{array}{cccc} W & X & Y & Z \end{array} \\ \begin{bmatrix} 18 & 24 & 28 & 32 \\ 8 & 13 & 17 & 18 \\ 10 & 15 & 19 & 22 \\ 0 & 0 & 0 & 0 \end{bmatrix} \end{array}$$

Subtract the minimum element in each row from all the elements in its row.

$$\begin{array}{c} \\ A \\ B \\ C \\ D \end{array}\begin{array}{c} \begin{array}{cccc} W & X & Y & Z \end{array} \\ \begin{bmatrix} 0 & 6 & 10 & 14 \\ 0 & 5 & 9 & 10 \\ 0 & 5 & 9 & 12 \\ 0 & 0 & 0 & 0 \end{bmatrix} \end{array}$$

Since each column has a minimum element 0, we draw minimum number of lines to cover all zeros.

$$\begin{array}{c} \\ A \\ B \\ C \\ D \end{array}\begin{array}{c} \begin{array}{cccc} W & X & Y & Z \end{array} \\ \begin{bmatrix} 0 & 6 & 10 & 14 \\ 0 & 5 & 9 & 10 \\ 0 & 5 & 9 & 12 \\ 0 & 0 & 0 & 0 \end{bmatrix} \end{array}$$

∴ The number of lines drawn to cover all zeros = 2 < the order of matrix, we form a second modified matrix. By subtracting the minimum uncovered value from all other uncovered values i.e. 5 and adding 5 to the element at the point of intersection of lines →

$$\begin{array}{c} \\ A \\ B \\ C \\ D \end{array}\begin{array}{c} \begin{array}{cccc} W & X & Y & Z \end{array} \\ \begin{bmatrix} 0 & 1 & 5 & 9 \\ 0 & 0 & 4 & 5 \\ 0 & 0 & 4 & 7 \\ 5 & 0 & 0 & 0 \end{bmatrix} \end{array}$$

Here, $N = 3 < n = 4$.

Again we subtract the smallest uncovered element from all the uncovered elements and add to the element at the point of intersection

$$\begin{array}{c} \\ A \\ B \\ C \\ D \end{array} \begin{array}{c} \begin{array}{cccc} W & X & Y & Z \end{array} \\ \begin{bmatrix} 0 & 1 & 1 & 5 \\ 0 & 0 & 0 & 1 \\ 0 & 0 & 0 & 3 \\ 9 & 4 & 0 & 0 \end{bmatrix} \end{array}$$

Here, $N = 4 = n$. Hence, we make an assignment.

Assignment

$$\begin{array}{c} \\ A \\ B \\ C \\ D \end{array} \begin{array}{c} \begin{array}{cccc} W & X & Y & Z \end{array} \\ \begin{bmatrix} \textcircled{0} & 1 & 1 & 4 \\ \cancel{0} & \textcircled{0} & \cancel{\textcircled{0}} & 1 \\ \cancel{0} & \cancel{0} & \textcircled{0} & \textcircled{3} \\ 9 & 4 & \cancel{0} & \textcircled{0} \end{bmatrix} \end{array} \quad \begin{array}{l} A \to W \\ D \to Z \\ B \to X \\ C \to Y \end{array} \quad \text{or} \quad \begin{array}{c} \\ A \\ B \\ C \\ D \end{array} \begin{array}{c} \begin{array}{cccc} W & X & Y & Z \end{array} \\ \begin{bmatrix} \textcircled{0} & 1 & 1 & 4 \\ \cancel{0} & \cancel{\textcircled{0}} & \textcircled{0} & 1 \\ \cancel{0} & \textcircled{0} & \cancel{0} & 3 \\ 9 & 4 & \cancel{0} & \textcircled{0} \end{bmatrix} \end{array} \quad \begin{array}{l} A \to W \\ D \to Z \\ B \to Y \\ C \to X \end{array}$$

Since D is a dummy job, machine Z is assigned no job.

Therefore, optimum cost = 18 + 13 + 19 = ₹ 50.

9.6 MAXIMIZATION IN ASSIGNMENT PROBLEM

In this, the objective is to maximize the profit. To solve this, we first convert the given profit matrix into the loss matrix by subtracting all the elements from the highest element. For this converted loss matrix we apply the steps in Hungarian method to get the optimum assignment.

Example 9.8 The owner of a small machine shop has four mechanics available to assign jobs for the day. Five jobs are offered with expected profit for each mechanic on each jobs, which are as follows:

		Job				
		A	B	C	D	E
Mechanic	1	62	78	50	111	82
	2	71	84	61	73	59
	3	87	92	111	71	81
	4	48	64	87	77	80

By using the assignment method, find the assignment of mechanics to the job that will result in maximum profit. Which job should be declined ?

Solution The given profit matrix is not a square matrix as the number of jobs is not equal to the number of mechanics. Hence, we introduce a dummy mechanic 5 with all the elements 0.

Job

$$\textbf{Mechanic}\quad \begin{matrix} \\ 1 \\ 2 \\ 3 \\ 4 \\ 5 \end{matrix}\begin{matrix} A & B & C & D & E \\ \left[\begin{matrix} 62 & 78 & 50 & 111 & 82 \\ 71 & 84 & 61 & 73 & 59 \\ 87 & 92 & 111 & 71 & 81 \\ 48 & 64 & 87 & 77 & 80 \\ 0 & 0 & 0 & 0 & 0 \end{matrix}\right] \end{matrix}$$

Now we convert this profit matrix into loss matrix by subtracting all the elements from the highest element 111.

Loss Matrix

$$\begin{matrix} \\ 1 \\ 2 \\ 3 \\ 4 \\ 5 \end{matrix}\begin{matrix} A & B & C & D & E \\ \left[\begin{matrix} 49 & 33 & 61 & 0 & 29 \\ 40 & 27 & 50 & 38 & 52 \\ 24 & 19 & 0 & 40 & 30 \\ 63 & 47 & 24 & 34 & 31 \\ 111 & 111 & 111 & 111 & 111 \end{matrix}\right] \end{matrix}$$

We subtract the smallest element from all the elements in the respective rows.

$$\begin{matrix} \\ 1 \\ 2 \\ 3 \\ 4 \\ 5 \end{matrix}\begin{matrix} A & B & C & D & E \\ \left[\begin{matrix} 49 & 33 & 61 & 0 & 29 \\ 13 & 0 & 23 & 11 & 25 \\ 24 & 19 & 0 & 40 & 30 \\ 39 & 23 & 0 & 10 & 7 \\ 0 & 0 & 0 & 0 & 0 \end{matrix}\right] \end{matrix}$$

Since each column has minimum element as zero, we draw minimum number of lines to cover all zeros.

$$\begin{matrix} \\ 1 \\ 2 \\ 3 \\ 4 \\ 5 \end{matrix}\begin{matrix} A & B & C & D & E \\ \left[\begin{matrix} 49 & 33 & 61 & 0 & 29 \\ 13 & 0 & 23 & 11 & 25 \\ 24 & 19 & 0 & 40 & 30 \\ 39 & 23 & 0 & 10 & 7 \\ 0 & 0 & 0 & 0 & 0 \end{matrix}\right] \end{matrix}$$

Here the number of lines drawn to cover all zeros = $N = 4$, is less than the order of matrix.

We form the 2nd modified matrix by subtracting the smallest uncovered element from the remaining uncovered elements and adding to the element that is at the point of intersection of lines.

$$\begin{array}{c} \\ 1 \\ 2 \\ 3 \\ 4 \\ 5 \end{array}\begin{array}{c} \begin{array}{ccccc} A & B & C & D & E \end{array} \\ \left[\begin{array}{ccccc} 49 & 40 & 68 & 0 & 29 \\ 6 & 0 & 23 & 4 & 18 \\ 17 & 19 & 0 & 33 & 23 \\ 32 & 23 & 0 & 3 & 0 \\ 0 & 7 & 7 & 0 & 0 \end{array}\right] \end{array}$$

Here, $N = 5 = n$ (the order of matrix).

We make the assignment.

$$\begin{array}{c} \\ 1 \\ 2 \\ 3 \\ 4 \\ 5 \end{array}\begin{array}{c} \begin{array}{ccccc} A & B & C & D & E \end{array} \\ \left[\begin{array}{ccccc} 49 & 40 & 68 & \boxed{0} & 29 \\ 6 & \boxed{0} & 23 & 5 & 18 \\ 17 & 19 & \boxed{0} & 33 & 23 \\ 32 & 23 & \times & 3 & \boxed{0} \\ \boxed{0} & 7 & 7 & \times & \times \end{array}\right] \end{array}$$

The optimum assignment is

Job	*Mechanic*
A	5
B	2
C	3
D	1
E	4

Since the 5th mechanic is a dummy, job *A* is assigned to the 5th mechanic, this job is declined. The maximum profit is given by, 84 + 111 + 111 + 80 = ₹ 386.

Example 9.9 A marketing manager has 5 salesmen and there are 5 sales districts. Considering the capabilities of the salesmen and the nature of districts, the estimates made by the marketing manager for the sales per month (in 1,000 rupees) for each salesman in each district would be as follows:

$$\begin{array}{c} \\ 1 \\ 2 \\ 3 \\ 4 \\ 5 \end{array}\begin{array}{c} \begin{array}{ccccc} A & B & C & D & E \end{array} \\ \left[\begin{array}{ccccc} 32 & 38 & 40 & 28 & 40 \\ 40 & 24 & 28 & 21 & 36 \\ 41 & 27 & 33 & 30 & 37 \\ 22 & 38 & 41 & 36 & 36 \\ 29 & 33 & 40 & 35 & 39 \end{array}\right] \end{array}$$

Find the assignment of salesmen to the districts that will result in the maximum sales.

Solution We are given the profit matrix. To maximize the profit, first we convert it into a loss matrix, which can be minimized. To convert it into loss matrix, we subtract all the elements from the highest element 41. Subtract the smallest element from all the elements in the respective rows and columns, to get the first modified matrix.

Loss Matrix

$$\begin{array}{cc} & \begin{array}{ccccc} A & B & C & D & E \end{array} \\ \begin{array}{c} 1\\2\\3\\4\\5 \end{array} & \begin{bmatrix} 9 & 3 & 1 & 13 & 1 \\ 1 & 17 & 13 & 20 & 5 \\ 0 & 14 & 8 & 11 & 4 \\ 19 & 3 & 0 & 5 & 5 \\ 12 & 8 & 1 & 6 & 2 \end{bmatrix} \end{array}$$

$$\begin{array}{cc} & \begin{array}{ccccc} A & B & C & D & E \end{array} \\ \begin{array}{c} 1\\2\\3\\4\\5 \end{array} & \begin{bmatrix} 8 & 2 & 0 & 12 & 0 \\ 0 & 16 & 12 & 19 & 4 \\ 0 & 14 & 8 & 11 & 4 \\ 19 & 3 & 0 & 5 & 5 \\ 11 & 7 & 0 & 5 & 1 \end{bmatrix} \end{array}$$

Subtracting minimum element i.e. 2, 5 from each element in 2nd and 4th column respectively.

$$\begin{array}{cc} & \begin{array}{ccccc} A & B & C & D & E \end{array} \\ \begin{array}{c} 1\\2\\3\\4\\5 \end{array} & \begin{bmatrix} 8 & 0 & 0 & 7 & 0 \\ 0 & 14 & 12 & 14 & 4 \\ 0 & 12 & 8 & 6 & 4 \\ 19 & 1 & 0 & 0 & 5 \\ 11 & 5 & 0 & 0 & 1 \end{bmatrix} \end{array}$$

We now draw minimum number of lines to cover all zeros.

$$\begin{array}{cc} & \begin{array}{ccccc} A & B & C & D & E \end{array} \\ \begin{array}{c} 1\\2\\3\\4\\5 \end{array} & \begin{bmatrix} 8 & 0 & 0 & 7 & 0 \\ 0 & 14 & 12 & 4 & 4 \\ 0 & 12 & 8 & 6 & 4 \\ 9 & 1 & 0 & 0 & 5 \\ 11 & 5 & 0 & 0 & 1 \end{bmatrix} \end{array}$$

$N = 4 < n = 5$.

We subtract the smallest uncovered element from the remaining uncovered elements and add to the elements at the point of intersection of lines, to get the second modified matrix.

$$\begin{array}{cc} & \begin{array}{ccccc} A & B & C & D & E \end{array} \\ \begin{array}{c} 1\\2\\3\\4\\5 \end{array} & \begin{bmatrix} 12 & 0 & 0 & 7 & 0 \\ 0 & 10 & 8 & 0 & 0 \\ 0 & 8 & 4 & 2 & 0 \\ 13 & 1 & 0 & 0 & 5 \\ 15 & 5 & 0 & 0 & 1 \end{bmatrix} \end{array}$$

$N = 5 = n = 5$. Hence we make the assignment.

Assignment

$$\begin{array}{c} \\ 1 \\ 2 \\ 3 \\ 4 \\ 5 \end{array}\begin{array}{c} \begin{array}{ccccc} A & B & C & D & E \end{array} \\ \begin{bmatrix} 12 & \textcircled{0} & 1 & 8 & \cancel{0} \\ \textcircled{0} & 10 & 9 & 1 & \cancel{0} \\ \cancel{0} & 8 & 5 & 3 & \textcircled{0} \\ 12 & \cancel{0} & \textcircled{0} & \cancel{0} & 4 \\ 14 & 4 & \cancel{0} & \textcircled{0} & \cancel{0} \end{bmatrix} \end{array}$$

Since no row or column has single zero, we get a multiple solution.

(*i*) The optimum assignment is:

$1 \to B, 2 \to A, 3 \to E, 4 \to C, 5 \to D.$

With maximum profit (38 + 40 + 37 + 41 + 35) = ₹ 191

(*ii*) The optimum assignment is:

$1 \to B, 2 \to A, 3 \to E, 4 \to D, 5 \to C.$

Maximum profit (38 + 40 + 37 + 36 + 40) = ₹ 191

9.6.1 The Travelling Salesman Problem

Assuming a salesman has to visit n cities. He wishes to start from a particular city, visit each city once and then return to his starting point. His objective is to select the sequence in which the cities are visited in such a way that his total travelling time is minimized.

To visit 2 cities (A and B), there is no choice. To visit 3 cities we have 2 possible routes. For 4 cities we have 3 possible routes. In general, to visit n cities there are $(n - 1)$ possible routes.

9.6.2 Mathematical Formulation

Let C_{ij} be the distance or time or cost of going from city i to city j. Let the decision variable X_{ij} be 1, if the salesman travels from city i to city j, otherwise let it be 0.

The objective is to minimize the travelling time.

$$Z = \sum_{i=1}^{n} \sum_{j=1}^{n} C_{ij} X_{ij}$$

Subject to the constraints,

$$\sum_{j=1}^{n} X_{ij} = 1, i = 2 \ldots n.$$

$$\sum_{i=1}^{n} X_{ij} = 1, j = 2 \ldots n.$$

and subject to the additional constraint that X_{ij} is so chosen that, no city is visited twice before all the cities are visited.

In particular, going from i directly to i is not permitted. This means $C_{ij} = \infty$, when $i = j$.

In the travelling salesman problem, we cannot choose the element along the diagonal and this can be avoided by filling the diagonal with infinitely large elements.

The travelling salesman problem is very similar to the assignment problem except that in the former case, there is an additional restriction, that X_{ij} is so chosen that no city is visited twice before the tour of all the cities is completed.

Example 9.10 A travelling salesman has to visit 5 cities. He wishes to start from a particular city, visit each city once and then return to his starting point. Cost of going from one city to another is shown below. You are required to find the least cost route.

To City

From City
$$\begin{array}{c} \\ A \\ B \\ C \\ D \\ E \end{array}\begin{array}{c} \begin{array}{ccccc} A & B & C & D & E \end{array} \\ \begin{bmatrix} \infty & 4 & 10 & 14 & 2 \\ 12 & \infty & 6 & 10 & 4 \\ 16 & 14 & \infty & 8 & 14 \\ 24 & 8 & 12 & \infty & 10 \\ 2 & 6 & 4 & 16 & \infty \end{bmatrix} \end{array}$$

Solution Treat the problem as an assignment problem and solve it using the same procedures. If the optimal solution of the assignment problem satisfies the additional constraint, then it is also an optimal solution of the given travelling salesman problem. If the solution to the assignment problem does not satisfy the additional restriction, then after solving the problem by assignment technique, we use the method of enumeration.

First we solve this problem as an assignment problem.

Subtract the minimum element in each row from all the elements in its row.

$$\begin{array}{c} \\ A \\ B \\ C \\ D \\ E \end{array}\begin{array}{c} \begin{array}{ccccc} A & B & C & D & E \end{array} \\ \begin{bmatrix} \infty & 2 & 8 & 12 & 0 \\ 8 & \infty & 2 & 6 & 0 \\ 8 & 6 & \infty & 0 & 6 \\ 16 & 0 & 4 & \infty & 2 \\ 0 & 4 & 2 & 14 & \infty \end{bmatrix} \end{array}$$

Subtract the minimum element in each column from all the elements in its column.

$$\begin{array}{c} \\ A \\ B \\ C \\ D \\ E \end{array}\begin{array}{c} \begin{array}{ccccc} A & B & C & D & E \end{array} \\ \begin{bmatrix} \infty & 2 & 8 & 12 & 0 \\ 8 & \infty & 2 & 6 & 0 \\ 8 & 6 & \infty & 0 & 6 \\ 16 & 0 & 4 & \infty & 2 \\ 0 & 4 & 2 & 14 & \infty \end{bmatrix} \end{array}$$

We have the first modified matrix. Draw minimum number of lines to cover all zeros.

$$\begin{array}{c} \\ A \\ B \\ C \\ D \\ E \end{array}\begin{array}{c} \begin{array}{ccccc} A & B & C & D & E \end{array} \\ \begin{bmatrix} \infty & 0 & 6 & 12 & 0 \\ 6 & \infty & 0 & 6 & 0 \\ 6 & 4 & \infty & 0 & 6 \\ 16 & 0 & 4 & \infty & 4 \\ 0 & 4 & 2 & 16 & \infty \end{bmatrix} \end{array}$$

$N = 4 < n = 5$. Subtract the smallest uncovered element from all the uncovered elements and add to the element that is at the point of intersection of lines. Hence, we get the 2nd modified matrix.

$$\begin{array}{c} \\ A \\ B \\ C \\ D \\ E \end{array}\begin{array}{c} \begin{array}{ccccc} A & B & C & D & E \end{array} \\ \begin{bmatrix} \infty & 0 & 6 & 12 & 0 \\ 8 & \infty & 0 & 6 & 0 \\ 8 & 4 & \infty & 0 & 6 \\ 18 & 0 & 4 & \infty & 4 \\ 0 & 4 & 0 & 14 & \infty \end{bmatrix} \end{array}$$

$N = 5$, $n = 5$. We make an assignment.

Assignment

$$\begin{array}{c} \\ A \\ B \\ C \\ D \\ E \end{array}\begin{array}{c} \begin{array}{ccccc} A & B & C & D & E \end{array} \\ \begin{bmatrix} \infty & \cancel{0} & 6 & 12 & \textcircled{0} \\ 6 & \infty & \textcircled{0} & 6 & \cancel{0} \\ 6 & 4 & \infty & \textcircled{0} & 6 \\ 16 & \textcircled{0} & 4 & \infty & 4 \\ \textcircled{0} & 4 & 2 & 16 & \infty \end{bmatrix} \end{array} \begin{array}{l} \\ A \rightarrow E \quad 2 \\ B \rightarrow C \quad 6 \\ C \rightarrow D \quad 8 \\ D \rightarrow B \quad 8 \\ E \rightarrow A \quad 2 \end{array}$$

The salesman should go from A to E and then come back to A without covering B, C, D. But this is contradicting the constraint that no city is visited twice before all the cities are visited.

If since all the cities have been visited and no city is visited twice before completing the tour of all the cities, we have an optimal solution for the travelling salesman.

The least cost route is A → E.

Example 9.11 A machine operator processes five types of items on his machine each week and must choose a sequence for them. The set-up cost per change depends on the items presently on the machine and the set-up to be made, according to the following table.

To Item

$$\textbf{From Item} \quad \begin{array}{c} \\ A \\ B \\ C \\ D \\ E \end{array}\begin{array}{c} \begin{array}{ccccc} A & B & C & D & E \end{array} \\ \begin{bmatrix} \infty & 4 & 7 & 3 & 4 \\ 4 & \infty & 6 & 3 & 4 \\ 7 & 6 & \infty & 7 & 5 \\ 3 & 3 & 7 & \infty & 7 \\ 4 & 4 & 5 & 7 & \infty \end{bmatrix} \end{array}$$

If he processes each type of item only once in each week, how should he sequence the items on his machine in order to minimize the total set-up cost?

Solution Reduce the cost matrix and make assignments in rows and columns having single row.

Modify the matrix by subtracting the least element from all the elements in its row and also in its column.

$$\begin{array}{c} \\ A \\ B \\ C \\ D \\ E \end{array}\begin{array}{c} \begin{array}{ccccc} A & B & C & D & E \end{array} \\ \begin{bmatrix} \infty & 1 & 4 & 0 & 1 \\ 1 & \infty & 3 & 0 & 1 \\ 2 & 1 & \infty & 2 & 0 \\ 0 & 0 & 4 & \infty & 4 \\ 0 & 0 & 1 & 3 & \infty \end{bmatrix} \end{array}$$

$$\begin{array}{c} \\ A \\ B \\ C \\ D \\ E \end{array}\begin{array}{c} \begin{array}{ccccc} A & B & C & D & E \end{array} \\ \begin{bmatrix} \infty & 1 & 3 & 0 & 1 \\ 1 & \infty & 2 & 0 & 1 \\ 2 & 1 & \infty & 2 & 0 \\ 0 & 0 & 3 & \infty & 4 \\ 0 & 0 & 0 & 3 & \infty \end{bmatrix} \end{array}$$

Here, $N = 4 < n = 5$, i.e., $N < n$.

Subtract the smallest uncovered element from all the uncovered elements and add to the element that is at the point of intersection of lines and get the reduced 2nd modified matrix.

$$\begin{array}{c} \\ A \\ B \\ C \\ D \\ E \end{array}\begin{array}{c} \begin{array}{ccccc} A & B & C & D & E \end{array} \\ \begin{bmatrix} \infty & 0 & 2 & 0 & 1 \\ 0 & \infty & 1 & 0 & 1 \\ 1 & 0 & \infty & 1 & 0 \\ 0 & 0 & 3 & \infty & 5 \\ 0 & 0 & 0 & 4 & \infty \end{bmatrix} \end{array}$$

$N = 5 = n = 5$. We make the assignment.

Assignment

$$\begin{array}{c} \\ A \\ B \\ C \\ D \\ E \end{array}\begin{array}{c} \begin{array}{ccccc} A & B & C & D & E \end{array} \\ \begin{bmatrix} \infty & \textcircled{0} & 2 & \times & 1 \\ \times & \infty & 1 & \textcircled{0} & 1 \\ 1 & \textcircled{0} & \infty & 1 & \times \\ \textcircled{0} & \times & 3 & \infty & 5 \\ \times & \times & \textcircled{0} & 4 & \infty \end{bmatrix} \end{array}\begin{array}{l} \\ A \to B \\ B \to D \\ C \to B \\ D \to A \\ E \to C \end{array}$$

We get the solution $A \to B \to D \to A$.

This schedule does not provide the required solution as each item is not processed only once in a week.

EXERCISES

1. Describe the assignment problem, giving a suitable example.
2. Explain the differences between a transportation problem and an assignment problem.
3. Give a mathematical formulation of the assignment problem.
4. Describe the algorithm for the solution of the assignment problem.
5. How can you maximize an objective function in the assignment problem?
6. Explain the nature of *i* in travelling salesman problem and give its mathematical formulation.
7. Solve the following assignment problem.

(a)
$$\begin{array}{c} \\ I \\ II \\ III \\ IV \end{array}\begin{array}{c} \begin{array}{cccc} A & B & C & D \end{array} \\ \begin{bmatrix} 1 & 4 & 6 & 3 \\ 9 & 7 & 10 & 9 \\ 4 & 5 & 11 & 7 \\ 8 & 7 & 8 & 5 \end{bmatrix} \end{array}$$

(b) **Men**
$$\textbf{Job}\ \begin{array}{c} \\ I \\ II \\ III \\ IV \end{array}\begin{array}{c} \begin{array}{cccc} A & B & C & D \end{array} \\ \begin{bmatrix} 10 & 25 & 15 & 20 \\ 15 & 30 & 5 & 15 \\ 35 & 20 & 12 & 24 \\ 17 & 25 & 24 & 20 \end{bmatrix} \end{array}$$

[**Ans.** (*a*) $I \to A$, $II \to C$, $III \to B$, $IV \to D$, Min cost = ₹ 21.
(*b*) $I \to A$, $II \to C$, $III \to B$, $IV \to D$, Min time = 55 hours]

8. **Men**

$$\textbf{Tasks}\ \begin{array}{c} \\ I \\ II \\ III \\ IV \\ V \end{array}\begin{array}{c} \begin{array}{ccccc} A & B & C & D & E \end{array} \\ \begin{bmatrix} 1 & 3 & 2 & 8 & 8 \\ 2 & 4 & 3 & 1 & 5 \\ 5 & 6 & 3 & 4 & 6 \\ 3 & 1 & 4 & 2 & 2 \\ 1 & 5 & 6 & 5 & 4 \end{bmatrix} \end{array}$$

[**Ans.** (a) $A \to I$, $B \to IV$, $C \to III$, $D \to II$, $E \to V$]

9. There are five jobs to be assigned, one each to 5 machines and the associated cost matrix is as follows.

Machine

$$\textbf{Job}\ \begin{array}{c} \\ A \\ B \\ C \\ D \\ E \end{array}\begin{array}{c} \begin{array}{ccccc} 1 & 2 & 3 & 4 & 5 \end{array} \\ \begin{bmatrix} 11 & 17 & 8 & 16 & 20 \\ 9 & 7 & 12 & 6 & 15 \\ 13 & 16 & 15 & 12 & 16 \\ 21 & 24 & 17 & 28 & 26 \\ 14 & 10 & 12 & 11 & 15 \end{bmatrix} \end{array}$$

Find the optimum assignment schedule

[**Ans.** $A \to 1$, $B \to 4$, $C \to 5$, $D \to 3$, $E \to 2$, Min. cost = ₹ 60]

10. A salesman has to visit five cities *A*, *B*, *C*, *D* and *E*. The distance (in hundred miles) between the five cities is as follows.

To

$$\textbf{From}\ \begin{array}{c} \\ A \\ B \\ C \\ D \\ E \end{array}\begin{array}{c} \begin{array}{ccccc} A & B & C & D & E \end{array} \\ \begin{bmatrix} - & 7 & 6 & 8 & 4 \\ 7 & - & 8 & 5 & 6 \\ 6 & 8 & - & 9 & 7 \\ 8 & 5 & 9 & - & 8 \\ 4 & 6 & 7 & 8 & - \end{bmatrix} \end{array}\ 0$$

If the salesman starts from city *A* and has to come back to his starting point, which route should he select so that the total distance travelled is minimum?

[**Ans.** $A \to E \to B \to D \to C \to A$, Min. distance = 30 hundred miles]

11. Determine the optimum assignment schedule for the following assignment problem. The cost matrix is given below.

Machine

Job	1	2	3	4	5	6
A	11	17	8	16	20	15
B	9	7	12	6	15	13
C	13	16	15	12	16	8
D	21	24	17	28	2	15
E	14	10	12	11	15	6

If the job *C* cannot be assigned to machine 6, will the optimum solution change?

[**Ans.** $A \rightarrow 3$, $B \rightarrow 4$, $C \rightarrow 1$, $D \rightarrow 6$, $E \rightarrow 2$. Min. cost = ₹ 52]

12. Solve the travelling salesman problem using the given data.

$C_{12} = 20$, $C_{13} = 4$, $C_{14} = 10$, $C_{23} = 5$, $C_{34} = 6$, $C_{25} = 10$, $C_{35} = 6$, $C_{45} = 20$, where $C_{ij} = C_{ji}$. There is no route between *i* and *j* if a value for C_{ij} is not shown.

[**Ans.** $1 \rightarrow 4 \rightarrow 5 \rightarrow 2 \rightarrow 3 \rightarrow 1$, Total cost = ₹ 49]

13. What is transhipment problem?
14. Differentiate between source, sink and transhipment.
15. A logistics specialist for Richthofen Inc. must distribute case of parts from 3 factories to 3 assembly plants. The monthly supplies and demands, along with the per-case transportation costs are:

Destination Assembly Plant

		Source			
		1	2	3	Supply
	A	5	9	16	200
Factory	B	1	2	6	400
	C	2	8	7	200
Demand		120	620	60	

Using the optimal solution, how many case of parts should be shipped form factory *C* to assembly plant 1? What is the cost of shipping these units from factory *B* to assembly plant 1?

16. A large book publisher has five manuscripts that must be edited as soon as possible. Five editors are available for doing the work, however their working times on the various manuscripts will differ based on their backgrounds and interests. The publisher wants to use an assignment method to determine who does what manuscript. Estimates of editing times (in hours) for each manuscript by each editor is.

Ms	*A*	*B*	*C*	*D*	*E*
1	12	18	10	16	13
2	9	10	14	13	9
3	17	14	9	18	12
4	15	7	11	9	18
5	12	18	22	11	27

What is that total minimum editing time?

Which of the following assumptions is not an assumption of the transportation model?

(*a*) Shipping costs are constant.

(*b*) There is only one transportation route between source and destination.

(*c*) There is only one transportation mode between source and destination.

(*d*) Actual supply and actual demand must be equal.

17. Answer whether the following is True or False:
    (*a*) In a transportation problem, items are allocated from sources to destinations at a maximum cost.
    (*b*) The linear programming model for a transportation problem has constraints for supply at each source and demand at each destination.
    (*c*) In a balanced transportation model where supply equals demand, all constraints are equalities.
    (*d*) The transhipment model is an extension of the transportation model in which intermediate transhipment points are added between the source and destinations.
    (*e*) In a transhipment problem, items may be transported from one transhipment point to another.

Chapter 10

Goal Programming

Goal programming is an offshoot of multi-objective optimization. This is interconnected to the branch of multi-criteria decision analysis (MCDA), which is also known as multi-criteria decision making (MCDM). Thus, we can say that goal programming is an optimization programme, which is used to handle multiple and conflicting objective measures. These measures are given a goal or target value which they are supposed to be achieved. Often, it is thought to be an extension of the concept of linear programming, which is used to minimize the unwanted deviations from the set of target values.

Table 10.1 Difference between goal programming and linear programming

Goal Programming	*Linear Programming*
1. Has to handle multiple objective functions and attain optimization in multi-criteria decision making.	1. Has a single objective function to be optimized, like profit maximization and cost minimization.
2. Effective analysis for a decision-maker in a complex system of competing objectives.	2. Effective only when decision-maker is looking for single objective.
3. Goal programming problems use ordinal ranking of goals, which is decided on the basis of ordinal ranking of goals.	3. Linear programming problems are solved on the basis of cardinal value (exact amount).
4. Ordinal value, which calculates goal programming is based on their significance or impact on the organization.	4. Cardinal value, which is the basis of calculation is expressed in exact amount, i.e., profit or loss.

10.1 CONCEPT OF GOAL PROGRAMMING

Goal programming, as a concept, was first used by Charnes, Cooper and Ferguson in 1955. However, it was only in 1961 that the actual name appeared in a text introduced by Charnes and Cooper. In this text, they suggested the usage of a method that could be used for solving the multi-criteria dilemma faced due to the constraints of linear programming. Critical works on goal programming by Lee (1972) and Ignizio (1976) followed. This led to wide-scale usage of goal programming in planning, resource allocation, policy analysis and functional management issues. The first application of goal programming was done on an engineering application for design and placement of the antennas. This was during the second stage of Saturn V, which was used to launch the Apollo space capsule (this had landed the first men on the moon).

One of the landmark books on goal programming was written by Ijiri (1965) where he developed the concept of pre-emptive priority factors, assigning different priority levels to disproportionate goals and variant weights for the goals at the identical priority level. In goal programming, there is an achievement function that minimizes the deviations from the entrenched goal targets within a set of constraints. These are also known as slack variables (in the simplex algorithm of linear programming), and are used as dummy variables.

10.1.1 Terms: Objectives, Goals and Constraints

Objectives are referred to the optimization of the measure of performance of a decision, such as profit maximization or cost minimization.

Goals state a target value, i.e., the minimum acceptable level of performance of any decision taken by the decision-maker.

Constraints are similar to goals, in terms of their mathematical formulation. However, while goals are implied as the right-hand side value to achieve a certain target value, it is desirable for the constraints to achieve the right-hand side value.

10.1.2 Goal Programming Model Formulation

Single goal with Multiple Subgoals

An objective is the desired level of result by a decision-maker. This desired level of result (goal) may be underachieved, completely achieved, or overachieved within the given decision-making environment. The target level of any goal is determined by the relative managerial effort that is applied to an activity. In mathematical terms, one unit of applied effort towards activity x_j might contribute the amount a_{ij} towards the ith goal. If this applied effort achieves its target value, the *ith* constraint would be denoted as:

$$\sum_{j=1}^{n} a_{ij} x_j = b_i$$

However, one of the key features of goal programming is its flexibility and non-binding implications to mathematical interpretation. Thus, to allow underachievement or overachievement in the goal, we may denote:

$d_i^- =$ negative deviation from i^{th} goal, i.e., below the target value.
$d_i^+ =$ positive deviation from i^{th} goal, i.e., above the target value.

In the light of these notations, the ith goal can be further written as:

$$\sum_{j=1}^{n} a_{ij} x_j + d_i^- - d_i^+ = b_i$$

$$\begin{bmatrix}\text{Value of the}\\ \text{objective}\end{bmatrix} + \begin{bmatrix}\text{Amount}\\ \text{below the}\\ \text{goal}\end{bmatrix} + \begin{bmatrix}\text{Amount}\\ \text{above the}\\ \text{goal}\end{bmatrix} = \text{Goal}$$

Here, i is equal to 1, 2,..., m.

It is important to note that it is not possible to achieve amount below the goal or above the goal simultaneously. In such a case, deviational variables of both the target values or goals $\left(d_i^- \text{ or } d_i^+\right)$ may be zero in the solution $\left(d_i^- \times d_i^+ = 0\right)$. Taking this at its optimal value, one may assume it to be of a positive value in the solution or must be kept at zero. The only significant point to be taken care of is that the goal deviational variables must be non-negative.

Note: Slack and surplus variables in the linear programming model are equivalent to the deviational variables in goal programming.

The surplus variable in linear programming and the deviational variable in goal programming, that is denoted as d_i^+, is done away from the objective function when there is a situation of overachievement. Similarly, in case of underachievement, d_i^- (known as slack variable or deviational variable) is removed from the objective function of goal programming. But, there is an exceptional situation in which both d_i^- and d_i^+ are included in the objective function. This happens only when there is an exact attainment of the goal and it is ranked as per the pre-emptive priority factor.

Example 10.1 A packaged food manufacture produces two kinds of products, chips and soda. The unit profit from a packet of chips is ₹ 80, and of a bottle of soda is ₹ 40. The goal of the plant manager is to earn a total profit of exactly ₹ 640 in the next week.

Model Formulation

We may interpret the profit goal in terms of subgoals, which are sales volume of chips and soda. Thereby, a goal programming model may be formulated as:

$$\text{Minimize, } z = d_i^- + d_i^+,$$

$$\text{subject to } 80x_1 + 40x_2 + d_i^- - d_i^+ = 640$$

$$x_1, x_2, d_i^-, d_i^+ \geq 0$$

where,

x_1 = number of packet of chips sold

x_2 = number of bottles of soda sold

d_i^- = underachievement of the profit goal of ₹ 640

d_i^+ = overachievement of the profit goal of ₹ 640

If the profit goal is not fully achieved, the slack in the profit goal will be expressed by d_i^- (negative deviational variable). Contrary to this situation, if the solution shows a profit in excess of ₹ 640, then both d_i^+ and d_i^- will be zero. Here it must be noted that d_i^- and d_i^+ are complementary to each other. So, if the profit goal of ₹ 640 is exactly achieved, both d_i^- and d_i^+ will be zero.

In the above example 10.1, there are an infinite number of combinations of x_1 and x_2 that would achieve the goal. The solution would be of any linear combination of x_1 and x_2 between the two points ($x_1 = 8$, $x_2 = 0$) or ($x_1 = 0$, $x_2 = 16$). This straight line is exactly the iso-profit function line when the total profit is ₹ 640.

Equally Ranked Multiple goals

This model given below can be extended to handle cases of multiple goals. Let us suppose that there are no model constraints.

Taking the same example as example 10.1:

Example 10.2 Let us consider that the package food manufacturer now desires to achieve a weekly profit as close as to ₹ 640 as possible. He wants to achieve sales volume for chips and soda close to six and four respectively. We can formulate this effort as a goal programming model.

Model Formulation

$$\text{Minimize, } z = d_1^- + d_2^+ + d_3^- + d_i^+$$

$$\text{Subject to, } 80x_1 + 40x_2 + d_i^- - d_i^+ = 640$$

$$x_1 + d_2^- = 6$$

$$x_2 + d_3^- = 4$$

$$x_1, x_2, d_1^-, d_1^+ d_2^-, d_3^- \geq 0$$

The above equation expresses the profit goal and the sales goals.

Here, d_2^- and d_3^- represent the underachievements of sales volume for chips and soda. It should be noted that d_2^+ and d_3^+ are not included in the second and third constraints, since the sales goal are given as the maximum sales volume. The solution to this problem can be formulated by a simple examination of the problem: if $x_2 = 6$ and $x_2 = 4$, then all targets will be completely achieved.

Therefore, $d_1^- = d_2^- = d_3^- = d_1^+ = 0$

Ranking and Weighting of Unequal Multiple Goals

In general terms, goal programming model is a linear representation in which the optimum attainment of objectives is sought within the given decision environment. It is this decision environment which determines the basic component of the model, like constraints, decision variables and the objective function. Since multiple and conflicting goals are usually not of equal importance, negative or positive deviations are not added. To achieve the goals as per the pre-emptive priority factor, p_1, p_2... and so on are assigned to deviational variables in the formulation of the objective function to be minimized. The p_s does not assume any numerical value, so they are simply a convenient way of indicating that one goal is comparatively more important than another. The relationship between various priority factors is based on priority ranking, such as $p_1 >> p_2 >> ... p_k >> p_{k+1}$ ..., where >> 'denotes more important than'.

This further means, $p_j >> p_{j+1}$ ($j = 1, 2, ..., k$) where n is a large number. The priority ranking of any target value or goal cannot be improved by multiplying by n. Thus, it is important to note that the deviational variables at a similar priority level must have the same unit of measurability. This can be well illustrated in the following example:

Example 10.3 An office furniture manufacturer produces two types of products: desks and chairs. For manufacturing a chair or a desk, the manufacturer requires one hour of production capacity in the plant (maximum production capacity is 50 hours per week). However, due to limited sales capacity, the maximum number of desks and chairs which could be sold are six and eight per week, respectively. The gross margin from the sale of a desk is ₹ 90 and ₹ 60 for a chair.

The manufacturer desires to determine the number of units of each desk and chair, which should be produced per week in consideration of the following set of goals:

Goal 1: Available production capacity should be utilized as much as possible but should not exceed 50 hours per week.

Goal 2: Sales of both the products (desks and chairs) produced per week should be as much as possible.

Goal 3: Overtime should not exceed 20 per cent of the available time.

Model Formulation

We can formulate this problem according to a goal programming model so that the manufacturer may achieve his goals.

Suppose x_1 and x_2 = number of units of desk and chair produced. The first goal pertains to production capacity attainment with a target set at 50 hours per week. This constraint can be expressed as:

$$x_1 + x_2 + d_1^- + d_1^+ = 50$$

here, d_1^- = underutilization of production capacity

d_1^+ = overutilization of production capacity.

If this goal is not achieved, then d_1^- would take on a positive value and d_1^+ would be zero.

The second goal pertains to maximization of sales volume with a target of 6 units of desks and 8 units of chairs per week. The sales constraints can be expressed as:

$$x_1 + d_2^- = 6 \qquad x_2 + d_3^- = 8$$

Thus, it is important to note that the sales goals are the maximum possible sales volume, d_2^+ and d_3^+ will not appear as these constraints. So, here the overachievement of sales goals is ruled out.

The third goal looks for the minimization of overtime hours as minimum as possible. The constraint is denoted as:

$$d_1^+ + d_4^- - d_4^+ = 0.2\,(50) = 10$$

here,

d_4^- = overtime less than 20 per cent of goal constraint

d_4^+ = overtime more than 20 per cent of goal constraint

d_1^+ = overtime beyond 50 hours

Now, we an formulate a model to express the above given problem as a goal programming model.

Minimize (total deviation) $Z = d_1^+ + d_2^- + d_3^- + d_4^+$ subject to the above mentioned constraints,

(*i*) Production capacity constraint

$$x_1 + x_2 + d_1^- - d_1^+ = 50$$

(*ii*) Sales constraints

$$x_1 + d_2^- = 6$$
$$x_2 + d_3^- = 8$$

(*iii*) Overtime constraint

$$d_1^+ + d_4^- - d_4^+ = 10, \text{ and}$$
$$x_1, x_2, d_1^-, d_2^-, d_3^-, d_4^-, d_4^+ \geq 0.$$

10.2 GOAL PROGRAMMING ALGORITHM

The procedure, which is also known as algorithm, is used to formulate a goal programming model is summarized below:

1. Identification of the goals and constraints based on the availability of resources or constraints that may act as hindrances in way of achievement of the targets.
2. Prioritize the significance of each goal in such a way that goals with priority level p_1 are most important, followed by p_2 (next most important) and so on.
3. Define the decision variables.
4. Formulate the constraints in the same manner as linear programming model.
5. Develop an equation constraint-wise by adding deviational variables $\left(d_i^- + d_i^+\right)$. These variables indicate the possible deviations (below or above the target value or goal value).
6. Write the objective function in terms of minimizing a prioritized function of the deviational variables.

Goal programming approach for solving decision-making problems can be divided as:

(*i*) General goal programming model

(*ii*) Modified simplex method of goal programming

(*iii*) Alternative simplex method for goal programming

10.2.1 General Model

Assuming *m* goals, the general goal programming model may be stated as:

Minimize,
$$Z = \sum_{i=1}^{m} w_i\, P_i\left(d_i^- + d_i^+\right)$$

This is subject to the linear constraints, and can be expressed as:

$$\sum_{j=1}^{m} a_{ij}\, x_j + d_i^- - d_i^+ = b_i; i = 1, 2, \ldots, m$$

and, $x_j, d_i^-, d_i^+ \geq 0$, for all i and j

$$d_i^- \times d_i^+ = 0$$

where, Z is the sum of the deviations from all desired goals. The w_i is the non-negative constants used for representing the relative weight to be assigned or allocated to the deviational variables d_i^-, d_i^+ within a certain priority level. The p_i are the priority levels that are assigned to each relevant deviational variables according to the priority rankings, such as $p_1 > p_2, \ldots, > p_n$. The a_{ij} are constraints that are attached to each variable (utilized and crucial for decision making), and b_i are the right handed side target values (goals) of each constraint. Keeping these in view, two goal programming models may be formulated as follows:

(*i*) system constraints (indirectly related to goals)

(*ii*) goal constraints (directly related to target values)

Example 10.4 A carpenter produces two products, desks and chairs. Each product must be processed through two departments. Department *A* delivers 30 hours of production capacity per day, and department *B* delivers 60 hours. Each unit of a desk requires 2 hours in department *A* and 6 hours in department *B*. Each unit of chair requires 3 hours in department *A* and 4 hours in department *B*. Management has prioritized the following target values and expects to achieve the following daily product mix:

p_1 : Minimize the underachievement of total production of desks and chairs for 10 units.

p_2 : Minimize the underachievement of production for 7 units of chairs.

p_3 : Minimize the underachievement of production for 8 units of desks.

We can formulate this problem as per the goal programming model and after that look to solve it using the graphical method.

Model Formulation: Let us suppose,

x_1 and x_2 = number of units of products, *i.e.*, desks and chairs manufactured.

d_i^- and d_i^+ = underachievement and overachivement associated with goal *i*, respectively.

Thereby, we have the goal programming model stated as follows:

Minimize,

$$Z = p_1\, d_1^- + p_2\, d_3^- + p_3\, d_2^-$$

As this is subject to the constraints, we may say—

$$2x_1 + 3x_2 \leq 30$$
$$6x_1 + 4x_2 \leq 60$$
$$x_1 + x_2 + d_1^- - d_1^+ = 10$$
$$x_1 + d_2^- - d_2^+ = 8$$
$$x_1 + d_3^- - d_3^+ = 7$$
$$x_1, x_2, d_i^-, d_i^+ \leq 0, \text{ for all } i$$

10.2.2 The Algorithm

In order to solve and formulate example 10.4, we will use the graphical solution method. This requires algorithmic calculations. You may follow the given points:

(*i*) Graph all the system constraints and identify all the feasible solutions space. However, if there are no existing system constraints, then the feasible solution space is the first quadrant. Further, if there are no feasible solution space exists, there is no solution.

(*ii*) Graph the straight lines corresponding to the goal constraints, labelling the deviational variables.

(*iii*) Select the point or points, which are best suited to satisfy the highest priority goal. This may be done through the feasible solutions space that is identified in step *1*.

(*iv*) Consider the remaining goals in a sequential manner. Identify a point that would satisfy them to a great extent. Ensure that a goal set on the lower priority is not achieved at the cost of reducing the degree of achievement of higher priority target values.

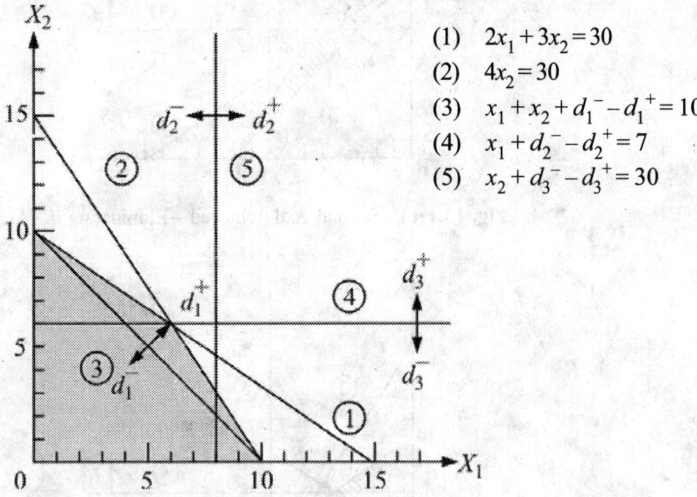

Fig. 10.1 (*a*) Systems and Goal constraints

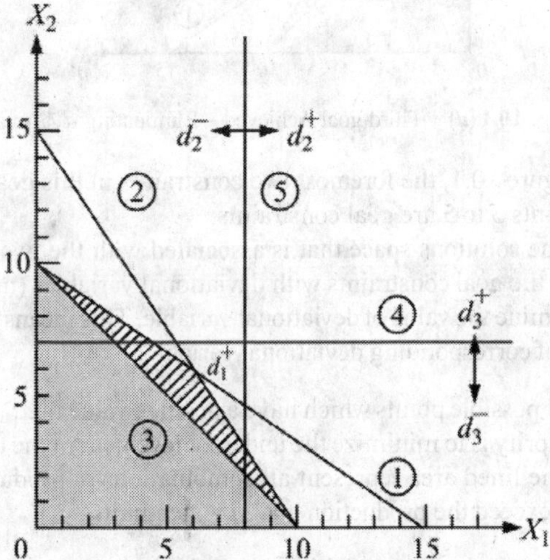

Fig. 10.1 (*b*) First goal Achieved—Eliminating d_1^- Area

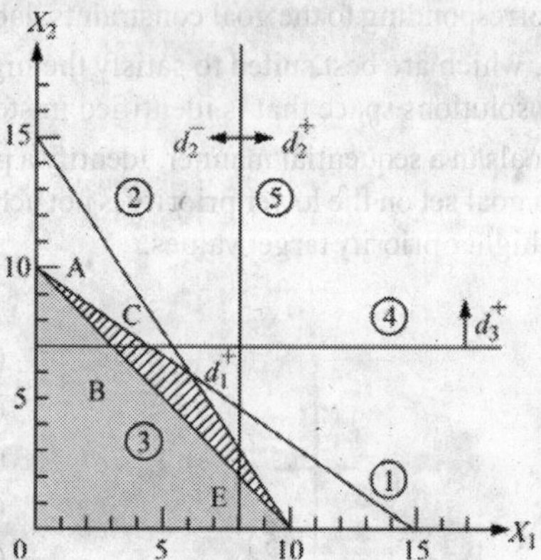

Fig. 10.1 (c) Second goal Achieved—Eliminating d_2^- Area

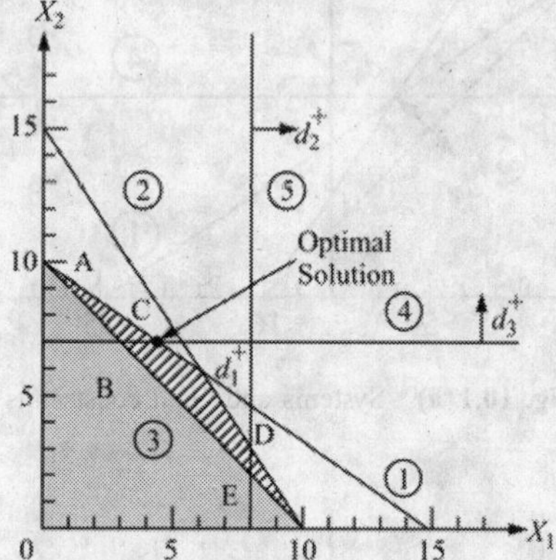

Fig. 10.1 (d) Third goal Achieved—Eliminating d_3^- Area

Graphical Solution: In Figure 10.1, the foremost two constraints in this goal programming model are system constraints. Constraints 3 to 5 are goal constraints.

Figure 10.1(*a*) represents the solutions space that is associated with the two system constraints, while the lines are associated with the goal constraints with deviational variables (marked). The distance from the goal constraint line determine the value of deviational variable. This means, farther a point from a goal constraint, larger the value of corresponding deviational variable.

Figure 10.1(*b*) illustrates all possible points which have a positive value of d_1^- and have been eliminated. In this graph, the highest priority is to minimize the underachievement of the total production goal of ten units, represented as d_1^-. The lined area represent all combinations of products, *i.e.,* desks and chairs, which can be produced and exceed the production goal, *i.e.,* ten units.

In **Figure 10.1(*c*)** due significance is given to achieve second priority goal, where all points with positive values for d_3^- are eliminated. The points which lie below the second goal constraint line are eliminated. These points represent combinations of products (desks and chairs) which fall short of the production goal of seven units for chairs.

The third priority is established on the lined ABC point, which represents underachievement of the third goal (identify a point that would satisfy to a great extent).

Figure 10.1(*d*) wants to minimize d_2^- which represents the underachievement of the production goal of eight units of desks. This one point, known as **optimal solution,** occurs at corner point *C*, where d_3^- is contracted to as small as possible. At points *D* or *E*, positive values for d_3^- could be given and d_2^- would become zero. Here we see that point *C* occurs at the intersection point of constraints numbers 1 and 4. We can solve these equations, assuming $x_1 = 4.5$ and $x_2 = 7$. Thus, we find that the carpenter should produce 4.5 units of desks and seven units of chairs. Substituting $x_1 = 4.5$ and $x_2 = 7$ in the above-mentioned constraints, we may calculate:

(*a*) Department *A* utilized its maximum capacity of 30 hours.

(*b*) Department *B* has unutilized time, better known as slack, of 5 hours.

Thus, we can conclude that there is an overachievement of the total production goal equal to 11.5 (4.5 + 17 – 10) units. The production goal of seven units of chairs has been completely achieved, however, there has been an underachievement in meeting the production goal for desks, with the carpenter making only 3.5 (8 – 4.5) units.

10.2.3 Modified Simplex Method of Goal Programming

The simplex method for a goal programming problem solution is somewhat similar to that of a linear programming problem. The salient features of this method for goal programming problem are:

(*i*) The z_j and $c_j - z_j$ values are calculated separately for each of the ranked goal $p_1, p_2, \ldots$. Different goals are measured in different units. On the basis of the priority, the first priority goal (p_1) is shown at the bottom and the least prioritized goal is shown at the top.

The criterion for optimality z_j or $c_j - z_j$ becomes a matrix $k \times n$ size. Here, k represents the number of pre-emptive priority levels, and n is the number of variables including decision and deviational variables.

(*ii*) Firstly, we need to examine $c_j - z_j$ values in the p_1 row. Optimal solution can be obtained, only if all $c_j - z_j \leq 0$ at the highest priority levels in the same column. If $c_j - z_j > 0$ at a certain priority level does not have any negative entry and in any similar column there is no higher unachieved priority levels, then the current optimal solution is not achieved.

(*iii*) The solution is optimal, if the target value of each goal in X_B- column is zero.

(*iv*) In order to determine the variable, which is needed to enter into the solution mix, we must start by examining $(c_j - z_j)$ row of highest priority (marked as p_1). After this, we need to select the largest negative value, else should more to the next higher priority (p_2) and select the largest negative value.

(*v*) To compute the 'minimum ratio' apply the usual procedure so that you are able to choose a variable to leave the current solution mix.

(*vi*) We need to ignore, if any negative value in the $(c_j - z_j)$ row has positive $(c_j - z_j)$ value under any lower priority rows. With the entry of this variable in the current solution mix, deviations from the highest priority goal would be increased.

Example 10.5 Using the modified simplex method to solve the following goal programming problem:

Minimize,
$$Z = p_1 d_1^- + p_2\left(2d_2^- + d_3^-\right) + p_3 d_1^+$$

Depending on the constraints,

$$x_1 + x_2 + d_1^- - d_1^+ = 400$$
$$x_1 + d_2^- = 240$$
$$x_2 + d_3^- = 300, \text{ and}$$
$$x_1, x_2, d_1^-, d_1^+, d_2^-, d_3^- \geq 0$$

Solution:

Table 10.2 Initial solution

C_B	*Variables in basics B*	*Solution values* $b(=x_B)$	x_1	x_2	d_1^-	d_2^-	d_3^-	d_1^+	*Minimum Ratio* x_B/x_1
p_1	d_1^-	400	1	1	1	0	0	–1	400/1
$2p_2$	d_2^-	240	(1)	0	0	1	0	0	240/1
p_2	d_3^-	300	0	1	0	0	1	0	—
$c_j - z_j$	p_3	0	0	0	—	—	—	1	
	p_2	780	–2	–1	—	—	—	0	
	p_1	400	–1	–1	—	—	—	1	

The initial modified simplex table for the problem is shown in Table 10.2. The initial table for the goal programming problem is formulated with the basic assumption that it is same as any linear programming problem. The c_j value in liner programming and goal programming are same, keeping the pre-emptive factors and difference weights corresponding.

In the Table 10.2, the criterion for optimality is 3 × 6 matrix as there are three priority levels and six variables in the model. Two are for decision and four are deviational. By using the standard simplex method for the computation of z - value, we can get the z - value, in goal programming as:

$z = p_1 \times 400 + 2p_2 \times 240 + p_2 \times 300 = 400p_1 + 780p_2.$

The values of the various priority levels, $p_1 = 400$, $p_2 = 780$ and $p_3 = 0$ in the X_B- column (represent the unachieved portion of each goal).

Now let us compute, the $c_j - z_j$ values as given in Table 10.2. As already confirmed, c_j values represent the priority factors which affect the deviational variables and z_j values represent the sum of the product of entries in C_B- column with columns of coefficient matrix. So, we can say that the $c_j - z_j$ values for each of the column is computed as follows:

$$c_1 - z_1 = 0 - (p_1 \times 1 + 2p_2 \times 1 + p_2 \times 0) = -p_1 - 2p_2$$
$$c_2 - z_2 = 0 - (p_1 \times 1 + 2p_2 \times 0 + p_2 \times 1) = -p_1 - p_2$$
$$c_6 - z_6 = p_3 - (p_1 \times -1) = p_3 + p_1$$

10.2.4 Alternative Simplex Method for Goal Programming

The alternative simplex method for goal programming can be explained through the following two steps:

Step 1: Formulation of initial solution trade

Step 2: Modify the initial solution

Now to explain it in detail,

Step 1: Formulation of Initial Solution Trade

The general formulation and calculation of an alternative simplex method for goal programming problem, can be done with some minimal alternations and modifications to the critical solution table. Firstly, the goal constraint needs to be reformulated in terms of their basic variables (d_i^+):

$$d_i^+ = -b_i + \sum_{j=1}^{n} a_{ij}\, x_j + d_i^- ; i \text{ here } i \text{ denotes } 1, 2, ..., m.$$

If any of the goal constraint does not possess a d_i^+ variable then, we may artificially induce a zero priority for formulating an initial solution table. The variables with zero value are non-basic variables.

Table 10.3 Initial table for a generalized goal programming model

	(1)	(2)	(3)	(4)	(5)
				$x_1, x_2, ..., x_n$	$d_1^-, d_2^-, ..., d_m^-$
(1)	Weighted priority	Z	$\sum_{j=1}^{m} [w_i - b_i]$	0, 0, ..., 0	$w_1, w_2, ..., w_m$
(2)	$w_1 p_1$	d_1^+	$-b_1$	$a_{11}, a_{12}, ..., a_{1n}$	1 0 ... 0
(3)	$w_2 p_2$ ...	d_2^+ ...	$-b_2$ ...	$a_{21}, a_{22}, ..., a_{2n}$	0 1 ... 0
	$w_m p_m$	d_m^+	$-b_m$	⋮	⋮
				$a_{m1}, a_{m2}, ..., a_{mn}$	0 0 ... 1

In the above Table 10.3,

(*i*) Row 1 lables the decision variables x_i and negative deviational variable d_i^-. Row 2 contains a value called 'total absolute deviation'.

(*ii*) The right-handed values, (b_i), are located in third column.

(*iii*) The decision-variable coefficients (a_{ij}) are located in the fourth column.

(*iv*) The fifth column has an identity matrix placed in it, which represents the inclusion of negative deviational variables (d_i^-). Owing to the fact that all deviational variables are not included, all problem formulations are equal to zero.

(*v*) Second column lists the artificial deviational variables alongwith the first column, which lists the appropriate priority factors p_i and weights w_i for each positive deviational variable.

Step 2: Modify the Initial Solution

First determine which variable is to be used to exit the solution basis. This can be accomplished by selecting the one with the highest ranked priority. We need to choose the variables with greatest mathematical weight, if two or more variables have the same priority ranking. However, as we look towards the calculation for an optimal solution, we need to choose a pivot row. This pivot row (positive coefficients) is divided into pivot column. Thus, the element found at the intersection of pivot row and pivot column is known as pivot element. Then, new alternative element corresponds by taking the reciprocal of pivot element. It can be formulated as:

$$\text{New Element} = \text{Old Element} - \frac{\text{Product of Two Corner Elements}}{\text{Pivot Element}}$$

We can find the total absolute deviation by the following formula:

$$Z = \sum_{i=1}^{m} [w_i \cdot b_i]$$

Select the column with the smallest resulting ratio when the negative coefficients in the pivot row are divided into their positive elements in the second row charging the resulting sign, to determine which variable is to enter the solution basis.

Thus, only when the basic variables are all positive and objective functions have a negative sign, the solution is optimal.

10.3 CONCLUSION

Goal programming can be easily thought to be an extension or a further generalization of linear programming. This chapter would help you to handle multiple and conflicting objective measures which will assist in decision making. Each of these measures are further evaluated for target value to be achieved. Unwanted deviations from this set of target values which could then be minimized in an achievement function. The major strength of goal programming is its simplicity and ease of use. Goal programming as a concept, help you to handle relatively large number of variables and constraints effectively which could not be done in linear programming. The techniques and models discussed, here will make you a rational decision-maker.

EXERCISES

1. Explain the meaning of 'satisficing', and reasons for using the term in conjunction with goal programming.
2. If you were the owner of company *A* and using goal programming to help in your decision making, what would be your goals? Please mention the kind of constraints which you would like to include in your model?
3. Mention the importance of ranking goals in goal programming? What impact does it have on the solution of the problem.
4. Differentiate between goal programming and linear programming.
5. Mr Shah is the president and owner of Shah Prints, a company which prints two types of newspapers. The demand for newspaper *A* is upto 600 papers per week, demand for newspaper *B* is limited to 400 papers per week.

   Shah prints have a weekly operating power of 1500 hours. Newspaper *A* takes 2 hours to produce and newspapor *B* takes 3 hours. Each newspaper sold yields a profit of ₹ 10, and profit for a larger subscription model is ₹ 20.

   Mr. Shah has listed down the following goals in order of significance:

   (*i*) Attain a profit of ₹ 15,000 approximately each week.

   (*ii*) Ensure the firm's production capacity is not underutilized.

   (*iii*) Sell maximum number of newspaper *A* and newspaper *B*, as demand indicates.

   Explain with illustrations as a goal programming problem.
6. Miss Margaret Hall, Principal of Carmel Convent for girls, is concerned about 20 students taking a training programme and how they are spending their leisure time. Miss Hall has recognized the total needed hours per week is 170. She charted out a time-table as follows:

   X_1 = number of hours of sleep needed per week

   X_2 = number of hours for personal work

   X_3 = number of class and study hours

   X_4 = number of hours for social time.

   She assumes that the students must study 40 hours a week to have sufficient time to absorb subject-matter. This is the principal's major goal. Miss Margaret feels that students need at most 7 hours of sleep per night and she marked this goal at number 2. Further, she believes that goal 3 is to provide a minimum 20 hours of social time per week.

   (*a*) Formulate this as a goal programming problem.

   (*b*) Solve the problem using computer software.
7. What is goal programming?
8. Discuss the significance of goal programming in multiple choices for decision-making process.

Chapter

11 Integer Programming Problems

11.1 INTRODUCTION

A linear programming problem in which all or some of the decision variables are constrained to assume non-negative integer values is called an *Integer Programming Problem* (IPP).

In a linear programming problem, if all the variables are required to take integral values then it is called the *Pure (all) Integer Programming Problem* (Pure IPP).

If only some of the variables in the optimal solution of a LPP are restricted to assume non-negative integer values, while the remaining variables are free to take any non-negative values, then it is called a *Mixed Integer Programming Problem* (Mixed IPP).

Further, if all the variables in the optimal solution are allowed to take values 0 or 1, then the problem is called the *0–1 Programming Problem* or *Standard Discrete Programming Problem.*

The general integer programming problem is given by,

Max $Z = CX$

Subject to the constraints, $A\ x \leq b$

$x \geq 0$ and some or all variables are integers.

11.2 IMPORTANCE OF INTEGER PROGRAMMING PROBLEMS

In LPP, all the decision variables are allowed to take any non-negative real values as it is quite possible and appropriate to have fractional values in many situations. There are several frequently occurring circumstances in business and industry that lead to planning models involving integer-valued variables. For example, in production, manufacturing is frequently scheduled in terms of batches, lots or runs. In allocation of goods, a shipment must involve a discrete number of trucks or aircrafts. In such cases, the fractional values of variables like 13/3 may be meaningless in the context of the actual decision problem.

This is the main reason why integer programming is so important for marginal decisions.

11.3 APPLICATIONS OF INTEGER PROGRAMMING

Integer programming is applied in business and industry. All assignments and transportation problems are integer programming problems, as in the assignment and travelling salesmen problem, all the decision variables are either zero or one.

i.e., $x_{ij} = 0$ or 1

Other examples are capital budgeting and production scheduling problems. In fact, any situation involving decisions of the type 'either to do a job or not' can be viewed as an IPP. In all such situations,

$x_{ij} = 1$, if the jth activity is performed,

$= 0$ if the jth activity is not performed.

In addition, allocation problems involving the allocation of men or machines give rise to IPP, since such commodities can be assigned only in integers and not in fractions.

Note: If the non-integer variable is rounded off, it violates the feasibility and there is no guarantee that the rounded off solution will be optimal. Due to these difficulties, there is a need for developing a systematic and efficient procedure for obtaining the exact optimal integer solution to such problems.

11.4 METHODS OF INTEGER PROGRAMMING PROBLEM

There are two methods used to solve IPP, namely,

(*i*) Gomory's Cutting-Plane Method

(*ii*) Branch and Bound Method (Search Method).

11.4.1 Cutting-Plane Method

A systematic procedure for solving pure IPP was first developed by R.E. Gomory, in 1956, which he later used to deal with the more complicated case of mixed integer programming problem. This method consists of first solving the IPP as an ordinary LPP by ignoring the restriction of integer values and then introducing a new constraint to the problem such that the new set of feasible solutions includes all the original feasible integer solutions, but does not include the optimum non-integer solution initially found. This new constraint is called 'Fractional cut' or 'Gomorian constraint'. Then the revised problem is solved using the simplex method, till an optimum integer solution is obtained.

11.4.2 Search Method

This is an enumeration method in which all the feasible integer points are enumerated. The widely used search method is the Branch and Bound method. It was developed in 1960, by A.H. Land and A.G. Doig. This method is applicable to both pure and mixed IPP. It first divides the feasible region into smaller subsets that eliminate parts containing no feasible integer solution.

11.4.3 Gomory's Fractional Cut Algorithm or Cutting Plane Method for Pure (All) IPP

Step 1 Convert the minimization IPP into an equivalent maximization IPP. Ignore the integrality condition.

Step 2 Introduce slack and/or surplus variables, if necessary, to convert the given LPP in its standard form and obtain the optimum solution of the given LPP by using simplex method.

Step 3 Test the integrality of the optimum solution.

(*i*) If all $x_{Bi} \geq 0$ and are integers, an optimum integer solution is obtained.

(*ii*) If all $x_{Bi} \geq 0$ and at least one x_{Bi} is not an integer, then go to the next step.

Step 4 Rewrite each x_{Bi} as $x_{Bi} = [x_{Bi}] + f_i$ where x_{Bi} is the integral part of x_{Bi} and f_i is the posit fractional part of x_{Bi} $0 \leq f_i < 1$.

Choose the largest fraction of x_{Bi}'s, i.e., Choose max (f_i), if there is a tie, select arbitrarily. Let max $(f_i) = f_K$, corresponding to x_{BK} (the Kth row is called the 'source row').

Step 5 Express each negative fraction, if any, in the source row of the optimum simplex table as the sum of a negative integer and a non-negative fraction.

Step 6 Find the fractional cut constraint (Gomorian Constraint)

From the source row $\sum_{j=1}^{n} a_{k_j} x_j = x_{Bi}$

i.e., $\sum_{j=1}^{n} ([a_{kj}] + f_{kj})\, x_j = [x_{BK}] + f_K$

in the form $\sum_{j=1}^{n} f_{kj} x_j \geq f_K - \sum_{j=1}^{n} f_{kj}\, x_j \leq -f_K$

or, $-\sum_{j=1}^{n} f_{kj} x_j + G_1 = -f_K$

where, G_1 is the Gomorian slack.

Step 7 Add the fractional cut constraint obtained in step (6) at the bottom of the simplex table obtained in step (2). Find the new feasible optimum solution using dual simplex method.

Step 8 Go to step (3) and repeat the procedure until an optimum integer solution is obtained.

Example 11.1 Find the optimum integer solution to the following LPP.

Max $Z = x_1 + x_2$

Subject to constraints, $3x_1 + 2x_2 \leq 5$

$x_2 \leq 2$

$x_1, x_2 \geq 0$ and are integers.

Solution Introducing the non-negative slack variable $S_1, S_2 \geq 0$, the standard form of the LPP becomes,

Max $Z = x_1 + x_2 + 0S_1 + 0S_2$

Subject to, $3x_1 + 2x_2 + S_1 = 5$

$0x_1 + x_2 + S_2 = 2$

$x_1, x_2, S_1, S_2 \geq 0$

Ignoring the integrality condition, solve the problem by simplex method. The initial basic feasible solution is given by,

$S_1 = 5$ and $S_2 = 2$.

Since all $Z_j - C_j \geq 0$ an optimum solution is obtained, given by

Max $Z = 7/3, x_1 = 1/3, x_2 = 2.$

To obtain an optimum integer solution, we have to add a fractional cut constraint in the optimum simplex table.

Since $x_B = 1/3$, the source row is the first row.

Expressing the negative fraction –2/3 as a sum of negative integer and positive fraction, we get

$-2/3 = -1 + 1/3$

	C_j		1	1	0	0	
C_B	B	x_B	x_1	x_2	S_1	S_2	$Min \frac{x_B}{x_1}$
0	S_1	5	(3)	2	1	0	5/3 ←
0	S_2	2	0	1	0	1	—
	Z_j	0	0	0	0	0	
	$Z_j - C_j$		–1↑	–1	0	0	$Min \frac{x_B}{x_2}$
1	x_1	5/3	1	2/3	1/3	0	5/3 × 3/2 = 5/2
← 0	S_2	2	0	(1)	0	1	2/1 = 2
	Z_j	5/3	1	2/3	1/3	0	
	$Z_j - C_j$		0	–1/3↑	1/3	0	
1	x_1	1/3	1	0	1/3	–2/3	
1	x_2	2	0	1	0	1	
	Z_j	7/3	1	1	1/3	1/3	
	$Z_j - C_j$		0	0	1/3	1/3	

Since x_1 is the source row, we have,

$$1/3 = x_1 + 1/3\ S_1 - 2/3\ S_2$$

i.e.,

$$1/3 = x_1 + 1/3S_1 + (-1 + 1/3)\ S_2$$

The fractional cut (Gomorian) constraint is given by

$$1/3S_1 + 1/3S_2 \geq 1/3$$

$$\Rightarrow \quad -1/3S_1 - 1/3S_2 \leq -1/3$$

$$\Rightarrow \quad -1/3S_1 - 1/3\ S_2 + G_1 = -1/3$$

where, G_1 is the Gomorian slack. Add this fractional cut constraint at the bottom of the above optimal simplex table.

	C_j		1	1	0	0	
C_B	B	x_B	x_1	x_2	S_1	S_2	G_1
1	x_1	1/3	1	0	1/3	–2/3	0
1	x_2	2	0	1	0	1	0
← 0	G_1	–1/3	0	0	(–1/3)	–1/3	1
	Z_j	7/3	1	1	1/3	1/3	0
	$Z_j - C_j$		0	0	1/3↑	1/3	0

We apply dual simplex method. Since $G_1 = -1/3$, G_1 leaves the basis. To find the entering variable we find,

$$\text{Max}\left\{\frac{Z_j - C_j}{a_{ik}}, a_{ik} < 0\right\} = \text{Max}\left\{\frac{1/3}{-1/3}, \frac{1/3}{-1/3}\right\}$$

$$\text{Max}\ \{-1, -1\} = -1$$

We choose S_1 as the entering variable arbitrarily.

	C_j		1	1	0	0	
C_B	B	x_B	x_1	x_2	S_1	S_2	G_1
1	x_1	0	1	0	0	–1	1
1	x_2	2	0	1	0	1	1
0	S_1	1	0	0	1	1	–3
	Z_j	2	1	1	0	0	1
	$Z_j - C_j$		0	0	0	0	1

Since all $Z_j - C_j \geq 0$ and all $x_{Bi} \geq 0$, we obtain an optimal feasible integer solution.

∴ The optimum integer solution is,

Max $Z = 2, x_1 = 0, x_2 = 2$.

Example 11.2 Find an optimum integer solution to the following LPP.

Max $Z = x_1 + 2x_2$

Subject to the contraints, $2x_2 \leq 7$

$x_1 + x_2 \leq 7$

$2x_1 \leq 11$

$x_1, x_2 \geq 0$ and x_1, x_2 are integers.

Solution Introducing slack variables $S_1, S_2, S_3 \geq 0$, we get,

Max $Z = x_1 + 2x_2 + 0S_1 + 0S_2 + 0S_3$

Subject to, $2x_2 + S_1 = 7$

$x_1 + x_2 + S_2 = 7$

$2x_1 + S_3 = 11$

Ignoring the integer condition, we get the optimum solution of the given LPP, with initial basic feasible solution as, $S_1 = 7, S_2 = 7, S_3 = 11$.

	C_j		1	2	0	0	0	
C_B	B	x_B	x_1	x_2	S_1	S_2	S_3	$Min \frac{x_B}{x_2}$
←0	S_1	7	0	(2)	1	0	0	7/2 = 3.5
0	S_2	7	1	1	0	1	0	7/1 = 7
0	S_3	11	2	0	0	0	1	—
	Z_j	0	0	0	0	0	0	
	$Z_j - C_j$		–1	–2↑	0	0	0	$Min \frac{x_B}{x_1}$
2	x_2	7/2	0	1	1/2	0	0	—
←0	S_2	7/2	(1)	0	–1/2	1	0	7/2 = 3.5
0	S_3	11	2	0	0	0	1	11/2 = 5.5
	Z_j	7	0	2	1	0	0	
	$Z_j - C_j$		–1↑	0	1	0	0	
2	x_2	7/2	0	1	1/2	0	0	
1	x_1	7/2	1	0	–1/2	1	0	
0	S_3	4	0	0	1	–2	1	
	Z_j	21/2	1	2	1/2	1	0	
	$Z_j - C_j$		0	0	1/2	1	0	

Since all $Z_j - C_j \geq 0$, an optimum solution is obtained which is given by,

$$\text{Max } Z = \frac{21}{2}, x_1 = \frac{7}{2}, x_2 = \frac{7}{2}$$

Since the optimum solution obtained above is not an integer, we now select a constraint corresponding to

$$\text{Max } \{f_i\} = \text{Max } \{f_1, f_2, f_3\}$$

$$x_1 = 7/2 = 3 + 1/2$$

$$x_2 = 7/2 = 3 + 1/2$$

$$S_3 = 4 = 4 + 0$$

$$\therefore \quad \text{Max } \{f_i\} = \text{Max } \left(\frac{1}{2}, \frac{1}{2}, 0\right) = 1/2$$

Since the max fraction is same for both x_1 and x_2 rows, we choose x_1 row as the source row arbitrariiy. From this row we have,

$$7/2 = x_1 + 0x_2 - 1/2\, S_1 + 1S_2 + 0S_3.$$

On expressing the negative fraction as a sum of negative integer and a positive fraction, we have,

$$3 + 1/2 = x_1 + 0x_2 + (-1 + 1/2)\, S_1 + 1S_2 + 0S_3$$

$\therefore$ The Gomorian constraint is given by,

$$1/2\, S_1 \geq 1/2$$

i.e.,

$$-1/2\, S_1 \leq -1/2 \Rightarrow -1/2\, S_1 + G_1 = -1/2$$

where, G_1 is the Gomorian slack. Adding this new constraint at the bottom of the above optimal simplex table, we get a new table.

		C_j	1	2	0	0	0	0
C_B	B	x_B	x_1	x_2	S_1	S_2	S_3	G_1
2	x_2	7/2	0	1	1/2	0	0	0
1	x_1	7/2	1	0	–1/2	1	0	0
0	S_3	4	0	0	1	–2	1	0
←0	G_1	–1/2	0	0	(–1/2)	0	0	1
	Z_j	21/2	1	2	1/2	1	0	0
	$Z_j - C_j$		0	0	1/2	1	0	0
					↑			

We apply dual simplex method. Since $G_1 = -1/2$, G_1 leaves the basis. Entering variable is given by,

$$\text{Max}\left\{\frac{Z_j - C_j}{a_{k_j}}, a_{k_j} < 0\right\} = \text{Max}\left\{\frac{1/2}{-1/2}\right\}$$

gives the non-basic variable S_1 to enter into the basis. Drop G_1 and introduce S_1.

	C_j		1	2	0	0	0	0
C_B	B	x_B	x_1	x_2	S_1	S_2	S_3	G_1
2	x_2	3	0	1	0	0	0	1
1	x_1	4	1	0	0	1	0	-1
0	S_3	3	0	0	0	–2	1	2
0	S_1	1	0	0	1	0	0	–2
	Z_j	10	1	2	0	1	0	1
	$Z_j - C_j$		0	0	0	1	0	1

Since all $Z_j - C_j \geq 0$, an optimum solution has been obtained in integers. Hence, the integer optimum solution is given by,

$$\text{Max } Z = 10, x_1 = 4, x_2 = 3.$$

Example 11.3 Solve the following integer programming problem.

Max $$Z = 2x_1 + 20x_2 - 10x_3$$

Subject to, $$2x_1 + 20x_2 + 4x_3 \leq 15$$

$$6x_1 + 20x_2 + 4x_3 = 20$$

$$x_1, x_2, x_3 \geq 0 \text{ and are integers.}$$

Solution Introducing slack variable $S_1 \geq 0$ and an artificial variable $A_1 \geq 0$, the initial basic feasible solution is $S_1 = 15, A_1 = 20$. Ignoring the integer condition, solve the problem by simplex method.

Max $$Z = 2x_1 + 20x_2 - 10x_3 + 0S_1 - MA_1$$

Subject to, $$2x_1 + 20x_2 + 4x_3 + S_1 = 15$$

$$6x_1 + 20x_2 + 4x_3 + A_1 = 20$$

$$x_1, x_2, x_3, S_1, A_1 \geq 0$$

	C_j		2	20	–10	0	$-M$	
C_B	B	x_B	x_1	x_2	x_3	S_1	A_1	Min $\frac{x_B}{x_2}$
←0	S_1	15	2	(20)	4	1	0	15/20 = 3/4
$-M$	A_1	20	6	20	4	0	1	20/20 = 1
	Z_j	$-20M$	$-6M$	$-20M$	$-4M$	0	$-M$	
	$Z_j - C_j$		$-6M - 2$	$-20M - 20$ ↑	$-4M + 10$	0	0	

	C_j		2	20	−10	0	−M	
C_B	B	x_B	x_1	x_2	x_3	S_1	A_1	Min x_B/x_1
20	x_2	3/4	1/10	1	$\frac{1}{5}$	1/20	0	$\frac{3}{4} \times 10 = \frac{15}{2} = 7.5$
← −M	A_1	5	4	0	0	−1	1	$\frac{5}{4} = 1.25$
	Z_j	15 − 5M	2 − 4M	20	4	1 + M	−M	
	$Z_j - C_j$		−4 — ↑	0	14	M + 1	0	
20	x_2	5/8	0	1	1/5	3/40	—	
2	x_1	5/4	1	0	0	−1/4	—	
	Z_j	15	2	20	4	1	—	
	$Z_j - C_j$		0	0	14	1		

Since all $Z_j - C_j \geq 0$, the solution is optimum but the variables are non-integer.

∴ The non-integer optimum solution is given by,

$$x_1 = 5/4, x_2 = 5/8, x_3 = 0, \text{Max } Z = 15$$

To obtain an integer optimum solution, we proceed as follows.

$$\text{Max } \{f_1, f_2\} = \text{Max } \{5/8, 1/4\} = 5/8$$

∴ The source row is the first row, namely, x_2 row. From this source row we have,

$$5/8 = 0x_1 + 1x_2 + (1/5)x_3 + (3/40)S_1.$$

The fractional cut constraint is given by,

$$(1/5)x_3 + (3/40)S_1 \geq 5/8$$

$$(-1/5)x_3 - (3/40)S_1 \leq -5/8 \Rightarrow (-1/5)x_3 - (3/40)S_1 + G_1 = 5/8$$

where, G_1 is the Gomorian slack.

Adding this additional constraint in the optimum simplex table, the new table is given below.

	C_j		2	20	−10	0	0
C_B	B	x_B	x_1	x_2	x_3	S_1	G_1
20	x_2	5/8	0	1	1/5	3/40	0
2	x_1	5/4	1	0	0	−1/4	0
←0	G_1	−5/8	0	0	−1/5	(−3/40)	1
	Z_j	15	2	20	4	1	0
	$Z_j - C_j$		0	0	14	1 ↑	0

We apply dual simplex method. Since $G_1 = -5/8$, G_1 leaves the basis.

Also, $$\text{Max}\left\{\frac{Z_j - C_j}{a_i k}, a_i k < 0\right\} = \text{Max}\left\{\frac{14}{-1/5} \frac{1}{-3/40}\right\} = \text{Max } -\frac{40}{3}$$

gives the non-basic variable S_1, this enters the basis.

		C_j	2	20	–10	0	0
C_B	B	x_B	x_1	x_2	x_3	S_1	G_1
20	x_2	0	0	1	0	0	+ 1
2	x_1	10/3	1	0	2/3	0	–10/3
0	S_1	25/3	0	0	8/3	1	–40/3
	Z_j	20/3	2	20	4/3	0	40/3
	$Z_j - C_j$		0	0	34/3	0	40/3

Again since the solution is non-integer, we add one more fractional cut constraint.

$$\text{Max}\{f_i\} = \text{Max}\ \{0, 1/3, 1/3\}$$

Since the max fraction is same for both the rows x_1 and S_1, we choose S_1 arbitrarily.

$\therefore$ From the source row we have,

$$25/3 = 0x_1 + 0x_2 + (8/3)x_3 + 1S_1 - (40/3)G_1$$

Expressing the negative fraction as the sum of negative integer and positive fraction we have,

$$(8 + 1/3) = 0x_1 + 0x_2 + (2 + 2/3)x_3 + 1S_1 + (-14 + 2/3)G_1$$

The corresponding fractional cut is given by,

$$-2/3x_3 - 2/3\ G_1 + G_2 = -1/3.$$

Add this second Gomorian constraint at the bottom of the above simplex table and apply dual simplex method.

		C_j	2	20	–10	0	0	0
C_B	B	x_B	x_1	x_2	x_3	S_1	G_1	G_2
20	x_2	0	0	1	0	0	1	0
2	x_1	10/3	1	0	2/3	0	–10/3	0
0	S_1	25/3	0	0	8/3	1	–40/3	0
← 0	G_2	–1/3	0	0	(–2/3)	0	–2/3	1
	Z_j	20/3	2	20	4/3	0	40/3	0
	$Z_j - C_j$		0	0	34/3↑	0	40/3	0

Since $G_2 = -1/3$, G_2 leaves the basis. Also,

$$\text{Max}\left(\frac{Z_j - C_j}{a_ik}, a_ik < 0\right) = \text{Max}\left(\frac{34/3}{-2/3}\ \frac{40/3}{-2/3}\right) = -17$$

gives the non-basic variable x_3 which enters the basis. Using dual simplex method, introduce x_3 and drop G_2.

		C_j	2	20	–10	0	0	0
C_B	B	x_B	x_1	x_2	x_3	S_1	G_1	G_2
20	x_2	0	0	1	0	0	1	0
2	x_1	3	1	0	0	0	– 4	1
0	S_1	7	0	0	0	1	16	4
–10	x_3	1/2	0	0	1	0	1	–3/2
	Z_j	1	2	20	–10	0	2	17
	$Z_j - C_j$		0	0	0	0	2	17

Since the solution is still a non-integer, a third fractional cut is required. It is given from the source row (x_3 row) as,

$$-1/2 = -1/2\ G_2 + G_3$$

Insert this additional constraint at the bottom of the table, the modified simplex table is shown below.

	C_j		2	20	−10	0	0	0	0
C_B	B	x_B	x_1	x_2	x_3	S_1	G_1	G_2	G_3
20	x_2	0	0	1	0	0	1	0	0
2	x_1	3	1	0	0	0	−4	1	0
0	S_1	7	0	0	0	1	−16	4	0
−10	x_3	1/2	0	0	1	0	1	3/2	0
←0	G_3	−1/2	0	0	0	0	0	−1/2	1
	Z_j	1	2	20	−10	0	2	17	0
	$Z_j - C_j$		0	0	0	0	2	17↑	0

Using dual simplex method, we drop G_3 and introduce G_2.

	C_j		2	20	−10	0	0	0	0
C_B	B	x_B	x_1	x_2	x_3	S_1	G_1	G_2	G_3
20	x_2	0	0	1	0	0	0	0	0
2	x_1	2	1	0	0	0	−4	0	2
0	S_1	3	0	0	0	1	−16	0	8
−10	x_3	2	0	0	1	0	−1	0	−3
0	G_2	1	0	0	0	0	6	1	−2
	Z_j	−16	2	20	−10	0	2	0	34
	$Z_j - C_j$		0	0	0	0	2	0	34

Since all $Z_j - C_j \geq 0$ and also the variables are integers, the optimum integer solution is obtained and given by, $x_1 = 2$, $x_2 = 0$, $x_3 = 2$ and Max $Z = 16$.

Example 11.4 Solve the integer programming problem.

Max $$Z = 7x_1 + 9x_2$$

Subject to, $$-x_1 + 3x_2 \leq 6$$

$$7x_1 + x_2 \leq 35$$

$$x_1, x_2 \geq 0 \text{ are integers.}$$

Solution Introducing slack variables $S_1, S_2 \geq 0$, we get the standard form of LPP as,

Max $$Z = 7x_1 + 9x_2 + 0S_1 + 0S_2$$

Subject to, $$-x_1 + 3x_2 + S_1 = 6$$

$$7x_1 + x_2 + S_2 = 35$$

Now ignoring the integer conditions, solve the given LPP by simplex method.

	C_j		7	9	0	0	
C_B	B	x_B	x_1	x_2	S_1	S_2	$Min \frac{x_B}{x_2}$
←0	S_1	6	–1	(3)	1	0	6/3 = 2
0	S_2	35	7	1	0	1	35/1 = 35
	Z_j	0	0	0	0	0	$Min \frac{x_B}{x_1}$
	$Z_j - C_j$		–7	–9↑	0	0	
9	x_2	2	(–1/3)	1	1/3	0	–
←0	S_2	33	22/3	0	–1/3	1	$33 \times \frac{3}{22} = \frac{9}{2}$
	Z_j	18	–3	9	3	0	
	$Z_j - C_j$		–10↑	0	3	0	
9	x_2	9/2	0	1	7/22	1/22	
7	x_1	7/2	1	0	–1/22	3/22	
	Z_j	63	7	9	28/11	15/11	
	$Z_j - C_j$		0	0	28/11	15/11	

Since all $Z_j - C_j \geq 0$, optimum solution is obtained as $x_1 = \frac{9}{2}$

$$x_2 = \frac{7}{2} \text{ and Max } Z = 63.$$

Since the optimum solution obtained above is not an integer solution, we select a constraint corresponding to,

$$\text{Max } \{f_i\} = \text{Max } \{f_1, f_2\}$$

$$= \text{Max } \left\{\frac{1}{2}, \frac{1}{2}\right\} \left[x_{B1} = \frac{7}{2} = [3] + \frac{1}{2},\ x_{B2} = \frac{9}{2} = [4] + \frac{1}{2} \right]$$

Since both the equations have the same value of f_i, either one of the two equations can be used. Let us consider the x_2 row as source row.

From x_2 row we have,

$$\frac{7}{2} = 0x_1 + x_2 + \frac{7}{22} S_1 + \frac{1}{22} S_2$$

There is no negative fraction.

The Gomorian constraint is given by,

$$\frac{7}{22} S_1 + \frac{1}{22} S_2 \geq \frac{1}{2}$$

i.e.,
$$-\frac{7}{22} S_1 - \frac{1}{22} S_2 \leq -\frac{1}{2}$$

⇒
$$-\frac{7}{22} S_1 - \frac{1}{22} S_2 + G_1 = -\frac{1}{2}$$

where, G_1 is the Gomorian slack. Adding this new constraint at the bottom of the above optimal simplex table, we have the new table.

	C_j		7	9	0	0	0
C_B	B	x_B	x_1	x_2	S_1	S_2	G_1
9	x_2	9/2	0	1	7/22	1/22	0
7	x_1	7/2	1	0	–1/22	3/22	0
0	G_1	–1/2	0	0	–7/22	–1/22	1
	Z_j	63	9	7	28/11	15/11	0
	$Z_j - C_j$		0	0	28/11↑	15/11	0

We apply dual simplex method, since $G_1 = -1/2$, G_1 leaves the basis. Also,

$$\text{Max}\left\{\frac{Z_j - C_j}{a_{ik}}, a_{ik} < 0\right\} = \text{Max}\left\{\frac{\frac{28}{11}}{-\frac{7}{22}}, \frac{\frac{15}{11}}{-\frac{1}{22}}\right\}$$

$$= \text{MAX}(-8, -30) = -8$$

gives the non-basic variable S_1 to enter into the basis.

Applying dual simplex method, drop G_1 and introduce S_1.

	C_j		7	9	0	0	0
C_B	B	x_B	x_1	x_2	S_1	S_2	G_1
9	x_2	3	0	1	0	0	1
7	x_1	32/7	1	0	0	1/7	–1/7
0	S_1	11/7	0	0	1	+1/7	–22/7
	Z_j	59	7	9	0	1	8
	$Z_j - C_j$		0	0	0	1	8

The optimal solution obtained by dual simplex method as above is still a non-integer. Thus a new Gomory's constraint is to be reconsidered.

$$\text{Max}\ \{f_i\} = \text{Max}\left\{-, \frac{4}{7}, \frac{4}{7}\right\} = \frac{4}{7}$$

Choose the x_1 row as source row arbitrarily as both the fraction values are the same. From the source row we have,

$$\frac{4}{7} = 1x_1 + 0x_2 + 0S_1 + \frac{1}{7}S_2 + \frac{6}{7}G_1$$

There is no negative fraction in the source row.

The Gomory's constraint is given by,

$$\frac{1}{7}S_2 + \frac{6}{7}G_1 \geq \frac{4}{7} \quad \text{i.e.,} \quad \frac{1}{7}S_2 - \frac{6}{7}G_1 + G_2 = -\frac{4}{7}$$

where, G_2 is the Gomorian slack. Adding this constraint in the above simplex table we get a modified table.

	C_j		7	9	0	0	0	0
C_B	B	x_B	x_1	x_2	S_1	S_2	G_1	G_2
9	x_2	3	0	1	0	0	1	0
7	x_1	32/7	1	0	0	1/7	–1/7	0
0	S_1	11/7	0	0	1	1/7	–22/7	0
0	G_2	–4/7	0	0	0	–1/7	–6/7	1
	Z_j	59	7	9	0	1	8	0
	$Z_j - C_j$		0	0	0	1↑	8	0

We again apply the dual simplex method.

Since $G_2 = -\frac{4}{7}$, G_2 leaves the basis. Also,

$$\text{Max}\left\{\frac{Z_j - C_j}{a_{ik}}, a_{ik} < 0\right\} = \text{Max}\left\{\frac{1}{-1/7}, \frac{8}{-6/7}\right\}$$

$$= \text{Max}\,(-7, -28/3) = -7$$

gives the non-basic variable S_2 to enter into the basis.

	C_j		7	9	0	0	0	0
C_B	B	x_B	x_1	x_2	S_1	S_2	G_1	G_2
9	x_2	3	0	1	0	0	1	0
7	x_1	4	1	0	0	0	–1	1
0	S_1	1	0	0	1	0	–4	1
0	S_2	4	0	0	0	1	6	–7
	Z_j	55	7	9	0	0	2	7
	$Z_j - C_j$		0	0	0	0	2	7

Since all $Z_j - C_j \geq 0$ and also the solution is an integer, we obtain an optimum integer solution given by, $x_1 = 4$, $x_2 = 3$ and Max $Z = 55$.

EXERCISES

Find the optimum integer solution of the following pure integer programming problems.

1. Max $Z = 4x_1 + 3x_2$

   Subject to, $x_1 + 2x_2 \leq 4$

   $2x_1 + x_2 \leq 6$

   $x_1, x_2 \geq 0$ and are integers. **[Ans.** Max $Z = 12$, $x_1 = 3$, $x_2 = 0$]

2. Max $Z = 3x_1 + 4x_2$

   Subject to, $3x_1 + 2x_2 \leq 8$

   $x_1 + 4x_2 \geq 10$

   $x_1, x_2 \geq 0$ and are integers. **[Ans.** Max $Z = 16$, $x_1 = 0$, $x_2 = 4$]

3. Max $Z = 3x_1 - 2x_2 + 5x_3$

 Subject to, $4x_1 + 5x_2 + 5x_3 \le 30$

 $5x_1 + 2x_2 + 7x_3 \le 28$

 $x_1, x_2, x_3 \ge 0$ and are integers. [**Ans.** Max $Z = 20$, $x_1 = x_2 = 0$, $x_3 = 4$]

4. Min $Z = -2x_1 - 3x_2$

 Subject to, $2x_1 + 2x_2 + \le 7$

 $x_1 \le 2$

 $x_2 \le 2$

 $x_1, x_2 \ge 0$ and are integers. [**Ans.** Min $Z = -8$, $x_1 = 1$, $x_2 = 2$]

11.5 MIXED INTEGER PROGRAMMING PROBLEM

In mixed IPP only some of the variables are restricted to integer values, while the other variables may take integer or other real values.

Mixed integer cutting plane procedure The iterative procedure for the solution of mixed integer programming problem is as follows.

Step 1 Reformulate the given LPP into a standard maximization form and then determine an optimum solution using simplex method.

Step 2 Test the integrality of the optimum solution.

(*i*) If all $x_{Bi} \ge 0$ $(i = 1, 2, \ldots m)$ and are integers, then the current solution is an optimum one.

(*ii*) If all $x_{Bi} \ge 0$ $(i = 1, 2, \ldots m)$ but the integer restricted variables are not integers, then go to the next step.

Step 3 Choose the largest fraction among those x_{Bi}, which are restricted to integers. Let it be $x_{Bk} = f_k$ (assume)

Step 4 Find the fractional cut constraints from the source row, namely K^{th} row.

From the source row,

$$\sum_{j=1}^{n} a_{kj}\, k_j = x_{Bk}$$

i.e,

$$\sum_{j=1}^{n} \left(\left[a_{kj} \right] + f_{ki} \right) r_j = [x_{BK}] + f_k$$

in the form

$$\sum_{j=1}^{n} f_{ki}\, x_j \ge f_k$$

i.e.,

$$\sum_{j \in j^+} f_{kj}\, x_j + \left(\frac{f_k}{f_{k-1}} \right) \sum_{j \in j^-} f_{kj}\, x_j \ge +f_k$$

$$-\sum_{j \in j^+} f_{kj}\, x_j - \left(\frac{f_k}{f_{k-1}} \right) \sum_{j \in j^-} f_{kj}\, x_j \le -f_k$$

$$-\sum_{j \in j^+} f_{kj}\, x_j - \left(\frac{f_k}{f_{k-1}} \right) \sum_{j \in j^-} f_{kj}\, x_j + G_k = -f_k$$

where, G_k is Gomorian slack

$$\begin{matrix} j^+ = \\ j^{-1} = \end{matrix} \begin{bmatrix} j / f_{kj} \ge 0 \\ j / f_{kj} < 0 \end{bmatrix}$$

Step 5 Add this cutting plane generated in step 4 at the bottom of the optimum simplex table obtained in step 1. Find the new optimum solution using dual simplex method.

Step 6 Go to step 2 and repeat the procedure until all $x_{Bi} \geq 0$ $(i = 1, 2,... m)$ and all restricted variables are integers.

Example 11.5

Max $$Z = x_1 + x_2$$

Subject to,
$$3x_1 + 2x_2 \leq 5$$
$$x_2 \leq 2$$
$$x_1 + x_2 \geq 0 \text{ and } x_1 \text{ is an integer.}$$

Solution Introducing slack variables $S_1, S_2 \geq 0$ the standard form of LPP is,

Max $$Z = x_1 + x_2 + 0S_1 + 0S_2$$

Subject to,
$$3x_1 + 2x_2 + S_1 = 5$$
$$x_2 + S_2 = 2$$
$$x_1, x_2, S_1, S_2 \geq 0$$

Initial basic feasible solution,
$$S_1 = 5, S_2 = 2$$

Ignore the integer condition and solve the problem using simplex method, to obtain optimum solution.

	C_j		1	1	0	0	
C_B	B	x_B	x_1	x_2	S_1	S_2	$Min \frac{x_B}{x_1}$
←0	S_1	5	(3)	2	1	0	5/3
0	S_2	2	0	1	0	1	—
	Z_j	0	0	0	0	0	
	$Z_j - C_j$		−1↑	−1	0	0	$Min \frac{x_B}{x_2}$
1	x_1	5/3	1	2/3	1/3	0	5/2
←0	S_2	2	0	(1)	0	1	2/1 = 2
	Z_j	5/3	1	2/3	1/3	0	
	$Z_j - C_j$		0	−1/3↑	1/3	0	
1	x_1	1/3	1	0	1/3	−2/3	
1	x_2	2	0	1	0	1	
	Z_j	7/3	1	1	1/3	1/3	
	$Z_j - C_j$		0	0	1/3	1/3	

Since all $Z_j - C_j \geq 0$, the current basic feasible solution is optimum. But x_1 is non-integer. From the source row (first row) we have,
$$1/3 = x_1 + 0\, x_2 + 1/3\, S_1 - 2/3\, S_2$$

The Gomorian constraint is given by,

$$\frac{1}{3}S_1 + \left(\frac{\frac{1}{3}}{\frac{1}{3}-1}\right)\left(\frac{-2}{3}\right)S_2 \geq \frac{1}{3}$$

$$\frac{1}{3}S_1 + \frac{1}{3}S_2 \geq \frac{1}{3} \quad \Rightarrow \quad -\frac{1}{3}S_1 - \frac{1}{3}S_2 \leq -\frac{1}{3}$$

$$\frac{-1}{3}S_1 - \frac{1}{3}S_2 + G_1 = -\frac{1}{3}$$

where, G_1 is the Gomorian slack.

Adding this Gomorian constraint at the bottom of the above simplex table, we have,

	C_j		1	1	0	0	0
C_B	B	x_B	x_1	x_2	S_1	S_2	G_1
1	x_1	1/3	1	0	1/3	–2/3	0
1	x_2	2	0	1	0	1	0
0	G_1	–1/3	0	0	(–1/3)	–1/3	1
	Z_j	7/3	1	1	1/3	1/3	0
	$Z_j - C_j$		0	0	1/3↑	1/3	0

Using the dual simplex method, since $G_1 = -1/3 < 0$, G_1 leaves the basis. Also,

$$\text{Max}\left\{\frac{Z_j - C_j}{a_{ik}},\ a_{ik} < 0\right\}$$

$$\text{Max}\left\{\frac{\frac{1}{3}}{\frac{-1}{3}}, \frac{\frac{1}{3}}{\frac{-1}{3}}\right\} = \text{Max}\ \{-1, -1\} = -1$$

As this corresponds to both S_1 and S_2, we choose S_1 arbitrarily as the entering variable.

Drop G_1 and introduce S_1.

	C_j		1	1	0	0	0
C_B	B	x_B	x_1	x_2	S_1	S_2	G_1
1	x_1	0	1	0	0	– 1	1
1	x_2	2	0	1	0	1	0
0	S_1	1	0	0	1	1	– 3
	Z_j	2	1	1	0	0	1
	$Z_j - C_j$		0	0	0	0	1

Since all $Z_j - C_j \geq 0$ and all $x_{Bi} \geq 0$, the current solution is feasible and optimal.

The required optimal integer solution is given by,

$$x_1 = 0, x_2 = 2 \text{ and Max } Z = 2.$$

Example 11.6

Max $Z = 4x_1 + 6x_2 + 2x_3$

Subject to,

$$4x_1 - 4x_2 \le 5,$$
$$-x_1 + 6x_2 \le 5,$$
$$-x_1 + x_2 + x_3 \le 5$$
$$x_1, x_2, x_3 \ge 0 \text{ and } x_1, x_3 \text{ are integers.}$$

Solution Introducing slack variables $S_1, S_2, S_3 \ge 0$ the standard form of LPP is,

Max $Z = 4x_1 + 6x_2 + 2x_3 + 0S_1 + 0S_2 + 0S_3$

Subject to,

$$4x_1 - 4x_2 + S_1 = 5$$
$$-x_1 + 6x_2 + S_2 = 5$$
$$-x_1 + x_2 + x_3 + S_3 = 5$$

The initial basic feasible solution is given by $S_1 = 5$, $S_2 = 5$ and $S_3 = 5$. Ignoring the integer condition, the optimum solution of given LPP is obtained by the simplex method.

Since all $Z_j - C_j \ge 0$, the solution is optimum. But the integer constrained variables x_1 and x_3 are non-integer.

$$x_1 = 5/2 = 2 + 1/2$$
$$x_3 = 25/4 = 6 + 1/4$$

Max $(f_1 f_3)$ = Max (1/2, 1/4) = 1/2

From the first row we have,

$$(2 + 1/2) = x_1 + 0x_2 + 0x_3 + (3/10)\, S_1 + (1/5)\, S_2$$

	C_j		4	6	2	0	0	0	
C_B	B	x_B	x_1	x_2	x_3	S_1	S_2	S_3	*Min* x_B/x_2
0	S_1	5	4	–4	0	1	0	0	—
←0	S_2	5	–1	(6)	0	0	1	0	5/6
0	S_3	5	–1	1	1	0	0	1	5/1
	Z_j	0	0	0	0	0	0	0	
	$Z_j - C_j$		–4	–6↑	–2	0	0	0	*Min* x_B/x_1
0	S_1	25/3	(10/3)	0	0	1	2/3	0	25/10 = 5/2
6	x_2	5/6	–1/6	1	0	0	1/6	0	—
0	S_3	25/6	–5/6	0	1	0	–1/6	1	—
	Z_j	5	–1	6	0	0	1	0	
	$Z_j - C_j$		–5↑	0	–2	0	1	0	*Min* x_B/x_3
4	x_1	5/2	1	0	0	3/10	1/5	0	—
6	x_2	5/4	0	1	0	1/20	1/5	0	—
←0	S_3	25/4	0	0	(1)	1/4	0	1	25/4
	Z_j	35/2	4	6	0	3/2	2	0	
	$Z_j - C_j$		0	0	–2↑	3/2	2	0	
4	x_1	5/2	1	0	0	3/10	1/5	0	
6	x_2	5/4	0	1	0	1/20	1/5	0	
2	x_3	25/4	0	0	1	1/4	0	1	
	Z_j	35/2	4	6	2	3/2	2	0	
	$Z_j - C_j$		0	0	0	3/2	2	0	

The Gomorian constraint is given by,

$$3/10\ S_1 + 1/5\ S_2 \geq 1/2$$
$$-3/10\ S_1 - 1/5\ S_2 \leq -1/2$$

i.e., $-3/10\ S_1 - 1/5\ S_2 + G_1 = -1/2$, where G_1 is the Gomorian slack. Introduce this new constraint at the bottom of the above simplex table.

Using dual simplex method, since $G_1 = -1/2 < 0$,

G_1 leaves the basis. Also,

$$\text{Max}\left\{\frac{Z_j - C_j}{a_{ik}}, a_{ik} < 0\right\} = \text{Max}\left\{\frac{2}{\frac{-3}{10}}, \frac{2}{\frac{-1}{5}}\right\} = \text{Max}\left\{\frac{-20}{3}, -10\right\} = \frac{-20}{3}$$

	C_j		4	6	2	0	0	0
C_B	B	x_B	x_1	x_2	x_3	S_1	S_2	G_1
4	x_1	5/2	1	0	0	3/10	1/5	0
6	x_2	5/4	0	1	0	1/20	1/5	0
2	x_3	25/4	0	0	1	1/4	0	0
←0	G_1	–1/2	0	0	0	(–3/10)	–1/5	1
	Z_j	30	4	6	2	2	2	0
	$Z_j - C_j$		0	0	0	2↑	2	0

corresponding to S_1.Therefore, the non-basic variable S_1 enters the basics. Drop G_1 and introduce S_1.

	C_j		4	6	2	0	0	0	
C_B	B	x_B	x_1	x_2	x_3	S_1	S_2	S_3	G_1
4	x_1	2	1	0	0	0	0	0	1
6	x_2	7/6	0	1	0	0	1/6	0	1/6
2	x_3	35/6	0	0	1	0	–1/6	1	5/6
0	S_1	5/3	0	0	0	1	2/3	0	–10/3
	Z_j	80/3	4	6	2	0	2/3	2	20/3
	$Z_j - C_j$		0	0	0	0	2/3	2	20/3

Since all $Z_j - C_j \geq 0$, the solution is optimum and also the integer restricted variable $x_3 = 35/6$ is not an integer, therefore, we add another Gomorian constraint

$$x_3 = 35/6 = 5 + 5/6$$

The source row is the third row.

From this row we have,

$$5 + \frac{5}{6} = 0x_1 + 0x_2 + x_3 + 0S_1 - \frac{1}{6}S_2 + S_3 + \frac{5}{6}G_1$$

The Gomorian constraint is given by,

$$\left(\frac{\frac{5}{6}}{\frac{5}{6}-1}\right)\left(\frac{-1}{6}\right)S_2 + \frac{5}{6}G_1 \geq \frac{5}{6}$$

$$\Rightarrow \qquad \frac{5}{6}S_2 + \frac{5}{6}G_1 \geq \frac{5}{6}$$

$$\Rightarrow \qquad \frac{-5}{6}S_2 - \frac{5}{6}G_1 + G_2 \leq \frac{-5}{6}$$

where, G_2 is the Gomorian slack.

Add this second cutting plane constraint at the bottom of the above optimum simplex table.

	C_j		4	6	2	0	0	0	0	0
C_B	B	x_B	x_1	x_2	x_3	S_3	S_1	S_2	G_1	G_2
4	x_1	2	1	0	0	0	0	0	1	0
6	x_2	7/6	0	1	0	0	0	1/6	1/6	0
2	x_3	35/6	0	0	1	1	0	–1/6	5/6	0
0	S_1	5/3	0	0	0	0	1	2/3	–10/3	0
← 0	G_2	–5/6	0	0	0	0	0	–5/6	–5/6	1
	Z_j	80/3	4	6	2	2	2/3	2/3	20/3	0
	$Z_j - C_j$		0	0	0	2	2/3	↑2/3	20/3	0

Use dual simplex method. ($\because G_2 = -5/6 < 0$)

G_2 leaves the basics.

$$\text{Also,} \quad \text{Max}\left\{\frac{Z_j - C_j}{a_{ik}}\, a_{ik} < 0\right\} = \text{Max}\left\{\frac{\frac{2}{3}}{\frac{-5}{6}}, \frac{\frac{20}{3}}{\frac{-5}{6}}\right\} = \text{Max}\left\{\frac{-4}{5}, -8\right\} = -\frac{4}{5},$$

which corresponds to S_2.

Drop G_2 and introduce S_2.

Since all $Z_j - C_j \geq 0$ and also all the restricted variables x_1 and x_3 are integers, an optimum integer solution is obtained.

The optimum integer solution is,

$x_1 = 2, x_2 = 1, x_3 = 6$ and Max $Z = 26$

	C_j		4	6	2	0	0	0	0	0
C_B	B	x_B	x_1	x_2	x_3	S_1	S_2	S_3	G_1	G_2
4	x_1	2	1	0	0	0	0	0	1	0
6	x_2	1	0	1	0	0	0	0	0	1/5
2	x_3	6	0	0	1	0	0	1	1	–1/5
0	S_1	1	0	0	0	1	0	0	–4	4/5
0	S_2	1	0	0	0	0	1	0	1	–6/5
	Z_j	26	4	6	2	0	0	2	6	4/5
	$Z_j - C_j$		0	0	0	0	0	2	6	4/5

EXERCISES

Solve the following mixed integer programming problems using Gomory's cutting plane method.

1. Max $Z = 7x_1 + 9x_2$

   Subject to, $-x_1 + 3x_2 \le 6$

   $7x_1 + x_2 \le 35$

   $x_1, x_2 \ge 0$ and x_1 is an integer.

   [**Ans.** $x_1 = 3, x_2 = 2$, Max $Z = 5$ or $x_1 = 4, x_2 = 1$, Max $Z = 5$]

2. Max $Z = 3x_1 + x_2 + 3x_3$

   Subject to, $-x_1 + 2x_2 + x_3 \le 4$

   $4x_2 - 3x_3 \le 2$

   $x_1 - 3x_2 + 2x_3 \le 3$

   $x_1, x_2, x_3 \ge 0$, where x_1 and x_3 are integers.

   [**Ans.** $x_1 = 5, x_2 = 11/4, x_3 = 3$, Max $Z = 107/4$]

3. Max $Z = x_1 + x_2$

   Subject to, $2x_1 + 5x_2 \le 16$

   $6x_1 + 5x_2 \le 30$

   $x_1, x_2 \ge 0$ and x_1 is an integer. [**Ans.** $x_1 = 4, x_2 = 6/5$, Max $Z = 26/5$]

4. Min $Z = 10x_1 + 9x_2$

   Subject to, $x_1 \le 8$

   $x_2 \le 10$

   $5x_1 + 3x_2 \ge 45$

   $x_1, x_2 \ge 0$ and x_1 is an integer. [**Ans.** $x_1 = 8, x_2 = 5/3$, Min $Z = 95$]

11.6 BRANCH AND BOUND METHOD

This method is applicable to both, pure as well as mixed IPP. Some times a few or all the variables of an IPP are constrained by their upper or lower bounds. The most general method for the solution of such constrained optimization problems is called 'Branch and Bound method'.

This method first divides the feasible region into smaller subsets and then examines each of them successively, until a feasible solution that gives an optimal value of objective function is obtained.

Let the given IPP be,

Max $Z = Cx$

Subject to, $Ax \le b$

$x \ge 0$ where x integers.

In this method, we first solve the problem by ignoring the integrality condition.

(*i*) If the solution is in integers, the current solution is optimum for the given IPP.

(*ii*) If the solution is not in integers, say one of the variable x_r is not an integer, then $x_r^* < x_r < x^*_{r+1}$ where x^*_r, x^*_{r+1} are consecutive non-negative integers.

Hence, any feasible integer value of x_r must satisfy one of the two conditions.

$$x_r \le x_r^* \text{ or } x_r \ge x^*_{r+1}.$$

These two conditions are mutually exclusive (both cannot be true simultaneously). By adding these two conditions separately to the given LPP, we form different sub-problems.

Sub-problem 1	**Sub-problem 2**
Max $Z = Cx$	Max $Z = Cx$
Subject to, $Ax \le b$	Subject to, $Ax \le b$
$x_r \le x^*_r$	$x_r \ge x^*_{r+1}$
$x \ge 0.$	$x \ge 0.$

Thus, we have branched or partitioned the original problem into two sub-problems. Each of these sub-problems is then solved separately as LPP.

If any sub-problem yields an optimum integer solution, it is not further branched. But if any sub-problem yields a non-integer solution, it is further branched into two sub-problems. This branching process is continued until each problem terminates with either an integer optimal solution or there is an evidence that it cannot yield a better solution. The integer-valued solution among all the sub-problems, which gives the most optimal value of the objective function is then selected as the optimum solution.

Note: For minimization problem, the procedure is same except that upper bounds are used. The sub-problem is said to be fathomed and is dropped from further consideration if it yields a value of the objective function lower than that of the best available integer solution and it is useless to explore the problem any further.

Example 11.7 Use branch and bound technique to solve the following:

Max $Z = x_1 + 4x_2$

Subject to,
$$2x_1 + 4x_2 \le 7$$
$$5x_1 + 3x_2 \le 15$$
$$x_1, x_2 \ge 0 \text{ and are integers.}$$

Solution Ignoring the integrality condition we solve the LPP,

Max $Z = x_1 + 4x_2$

Subject to,
$$2x_1 + 4x_2 \le 7$$
$$5x_1 + 3x_2 \le 15$$
$$x_1, x_2 \ge 0$$

Introducing slack variables $S_1, S_2 \ge 0$, the standard form of LPP becomes,

Max $Z = x_1 + 4x_2 + 0S_1 + 0S_2$

Subject to,
$$2x_1 + 4x_2 + S_1 = 7$$
$$5x_1 + 3x_2 + S_2 = 15$$

	C_j		1	4	0	0	
C_B	B	x_B	x_1	x_2	S_1	S_2	*Min* x_B/x_2
←0	S_1	7	2	(4)	1	0	7/4
0	S_2	15	5	3	0	1	15/3 = 5
	Z_j	0	0	0	0	0	
	$Z_j - C_j$		–1	–4↑	0	0	
4	x_2	7/4	$\frac{1}{2}$	1	1/4	0	
0	S_2	$\frac{39}{4}$	$\frac{7}{2}$	0	–3/4	1	
	Z_j	7	2	4	1	0	
	$Z_j - C_j$		1	0	1	0	

Since all $Z_j - C_j \geq 0$, an optimum solution is obtained.

$x_1 = 0, x_2 = 7/4$ and Max $Z = 7$

Since $x_2 = \frac{7}{4}$, this problem should be branched into two sub-problems.

For $x_2 = \frac{7}{4}, 1 < x_2 < 2 = x_2 \leq 1,\ x_2 \geq 2$

Applying these two conditions separately in the given LPP we get two sub-problems.

Sub-problem (1)

Max $Z = x_1 + 4x_2$

Subject to, $2x_1 + 4x_2 \leq 7$

$5x_1 + 3x_2 \leq 15$

$x_2 \leq 1$

$x_1, x_2 \geq 0$

Sub-problem (2)

Max $Z = x_1 + 4x_2$

Subject to, $2x_1 + 4x_2 \leq 7$

$5x_1 + 3x_2 \leq 15$

$x_2 \geq 2$

$x_1, x_2 \geq 0$

Sub-Problem (1)

	C_j		1	4	0	0	0	
C_B	B	x_B	x_1	x_2	S_1	S_2	S_3	$Min \frac{x_B}{x_2}$
0	S_1	7	2	4	1	0	0	7/4
0	S_2	15	5	3	0	1	0	15/3
←0	S_3	1	0	(1)	0	0	1	1/1
	Z_j	0	0	0	0	0	0	
	$Z_j - C_j$		–1	–4↑	0	0	0	$Min \frac{x_B}{x_1}$
←0	S_1	3	(2)	0	1	0	–4↑	3/2
0	S_2	12	5	0	0	1	–3	12/5
0	x_2	1	0	1	0	0	1	
	Z_j	4	0	4	0	0	4	
	$Z_j - C_j$		–1↑	0	0	0	4	

	C_j		1	4	0	0	0
C_B	B	x_B	x_1	x_2	S_1	S_2	S_3
1	x_1	3/2	1	0	1/2	0	–2
0	S_2	9/2	0	0	–5/2	1	7
4	x_2	1	0	1	0	0	1
	Z_j	11/2	1	4	1/2	0	2
	$Z_j - C_j$		0	0	1/2	0	2

Since all $Z_j - C_j \geq 0$, the solution is optimum, given by $x_1 = 3/2$

$x_2 = 1$, and Max $Z = 11/2$

Since $x_1 = 3/2$ is not an integer, this sub-problem is branched again.

Sub-Problem (2)

Max $Z = x_1 + 4x_2$

Subject to,
$$2x_1 + 4x_2 \le 7$$
$$5x_1 + 3x_2 \le 15$$
$$x_2 \ge 2$$
$$x_1, x_2 \ge 0.$$

	C_j		1	4	0	0	0	$-M$	
C_B	B	x_B	x_1	x_2	S_1	S_2	S_3	A_1	$Min\ x_B/x_2$
←0	S_1	7	2	(4)	1	0	0	0	7/4
0	S_2	15	5	3	0	1	0	0	15/3
$-M$	A_1	2	0	1	0	0	−1	1	2/1
	Z_j	$-2M$	0	$-M$	0	0	M	$-M$	
	$Z_j - C_j$		−1	$-M-4$	0	0	M	0	
4	x_2	7/4	1/2	1	1/4	0	0	0	
0	S_2	39/4	7/2	0	−3/4	1	0	0	
$-M$	A_1	1/4	−1/2	0	−1/4	0	−1	1	
	Z_j	$7-\frac{5M}{4}$	$2+\frac{M}{2}$	4	$1+\frac{M}{4}$	0	M	$-M$	
	$Z_j - C_j$		$\frac{M}{2}+1$	0	$\frac{M}{4}+1$	0	M	0	

Since all $Z_j - C_j \ge 0$, but an artificial variable A_1 is in the basis at positive level, there exists no feasible solution. Hence, this sub-problem is dropped.

In sub-problem (1) Since, $x_1 = 3/2$

we have, $1 \le x_1 \le 2$

$\Rightarrow x_1 \le 1, \quad x_1 \ge 2$

Applying these two conditions separately in the sub-problem (1), we get two sub-problems.

Sub-problem (3)

Max $Z = x_1 + 4x_2$

Subject to, $2x_1 + 4x_2 \le 7$
$$5x_1 + 3x_2 \le 15$$
$$x_2 \le 1$$
$$x_1 \le 1$$
$$x_1, x_2 \ge 0.$$

Sub-problem (4)

Max $Z = x_1 + 4x_2$

Subject to, $2x_1 + 4x_2 \le 7$
$$5x_1 + 3x_2 \le 15$$
$$x_2 \le 1$$
$$x_1 \ge 2$$
$$x_1, x_2 \ge 0$$

Sub-Problem (3)

Since all $Z_j - C_j \ge 0$, an optimum solution is obtained. It is given by, $x_1 = 1, x_2 = 1$ and Max $Z = 5$. Since this solution is integer-valued this sub-problem cannot be branched further. The lower bound of the objective function is 5.

C_B	B	x_B	x_1	x_2	S_1	S_2	S_3	S_4	$Min \frac{x_B}{x_2}$
C_j			1	4	0	0	0	0	
0	S_1	7	2	4	1	0	0	0	7/4
0	S_2	15	5	3	0	1	0	0	15/3
←0	S_3	1	0	(1)	0	0	1	0	1/1
0	S_4	1	1	0	0	0	0	1	—
	Z_j	0	0	0	0	0	0	0	
	$Z_j - C_j$		–1	–4↑	0	0	0	0	$Min \frac{x_B}{x_1}$
0	S_1	3	2	0	1	0	–4	0	3/2
0	S_2	12	5	0	0	1	–3	0	12/5
4	x_2	1	0	1	0	0	1	0	—
←0	S_4	1	(1)	0	0	0	0	1	1/1
	Z_j	4	0	4	0	0	4	0	
	$Z_j - C_j$		–1↑	0	0	0	4	0	

C_B	B	x_B	x_1	x_2	S_1	S_2	S_3	S_4
C_j			1	4	0	0	0	0
0	S_1	1	0	0	1	0	–4	–2
0	S_2	7	0	0	0	1	–3	–5
4	x_2	1	0	1	0	0	1	0
1	x_1	1	1	0	0	0	0	1
	Z_j	5	1	4	0	0	4	1
	$Z_j - C_j$		0	0	0	0	4	1

Sub-Problem (4)

Max $Z = x_1 + 4x_2$

Subject to,

$$2x_1 + 4x_2 \leq 7$$
$$5x_1 + 3x_2 \leq 15$$
$$x_2 \leq 1$$
$$x_1 \geq 2$$
$$x_1, x_2 \geq 0$$

Since all $Z_j - C_j \geq 0$, the solution is optimum and is given by,

Max $Z = 5$ and $x_1 = 2, \quad x_2 = 3/4$

	C_B	x_B	B	x_1	x_2	S_1	S_2	S_3	S_4	A_1	$Min\ \frac{x_B}{x_1}$
			C_j	1	4	0	0	0	0	$-M$	
	0	7	S_1	2	4	1	0	0	0	0	7/2
	0	15	S_2	5	3	0	1	0	0	0	15/5
	0	1	S_3	0	1	0	0	1	0	0	—
←	$-M$	2	A_1	(1)	0	0	0	0	–1	1	2/1
		$-2M$	Z_j	$-M$	0	0	0	0	M	$-M$	
		—	$Z_j - C_j$	$-M-1$	–4	0	0	0	M	0	

C_B	B	x_B	x_1	x_2	S_1	S_2	S_3	S_4	A_1	$Min\ x_B/x_2$
	C_j		1	4	0	0	0	0	$-M$	
←0	S_1	3	0	(4)	1	0	0	2	–2	3/4
0	S_2	5	0	3	0	1	0	5	–5	5/3
0	S_3	1	0	1	0	0	1	0	0	1/1
1	x_1	2	1	0	0	0	0	–1	1	—
	Z_j	2	1	0	0	0	0	–2	1	
	$Z_j - C_j$		0	–4	0	0	0	–2	$1 + M$	
4	x_2	3/4	0	1	1/4	0	0	1/2	—	
0	S_2	11/4	0	0	–3/4	1	0	7/2	—	
0	S_3	1/4	0	0	–1/4	0	1	–1/2	—	
1	x_1	2	1	0	0	0	0	–1	—	
	Z_j	5	1	4	1	0	0	1	—	
	$Z_j - C_j$		0	0	1	0	0	1	—	

Since $x_2 = 3/4$ is not an integer, this sub-problem is branched further.

In sub-problem (4) since $x_2 = 3/4$, $0 \le x_2 \le 1$

$$\Rightarrow x_2 \le 0, \quad \text{or} \quad x_2 \ge 1$$

Applying these two conditions in the sub-problem (4)

We get two sub-problems.

Sub-problem (5)

Max $Z = x_1 + 4x_2$

Subject to, $2x_1 + 4x_2 \le 7$

$$5x_1 + 3x_2 \le 15$$
$$x_2 \le 1$$
$$x_1 \ge 2$$
$$x_2 \le 0$$
$$x_1, x_2 \ge 0$$

Sub-problem (6)

Max $Z = x_1 + 4x_2$

Subject to, $2x_1 + 4x_2 \le 7$

$$5x_1 + 3x_2 \le 15$$
$$x_2 \le 1$$
$$x_1 \ge 2$$
$$x_2 \ge 1$$
$$x_1, x_2 \ge 0.$$

Sub-Problem (5)

	C_B	B	x_B	x_1	x_2	S_1	S_2	S_3	S_4	A_1	S_5	$Min\ x_B/x_1$
		C_j		1	4	0	0	0	0	$-M$	0	
	0	S_1	7	2	4	1	0	0	0	0	0	7/2
	0	S_2	15	5	3	0	1	0	0	0	0	15/5
	0	S_3	1	0	1	0	0	1	0	0	0	—
←	$-M$	A_1	2	(1)	0	0	0	0	–1	1	0	2/1
	0	S_5	0	0	1	0	0	0	0	0	1	—
		Z_j	$-2M$	$-M$	0	0	0	0	M	$-M$	0	
		$Z_j - C_j$		$-M$–1	–4	0	0	0	M	0	0	$Min\ x_B/x_2$
	0	S_1	3	0	4	1	0	0	2	—	0	3/4
	0	S_2	5	0	3	0	1	0	(5)	—	0	5/3
	0	S_3	1	0	1	0	0	1	0	—	0	1/1
1	x_1	2	1	0	0	0	0	–1	—	0	—	
←	0	S_5	0	0	(1)	0	0	0	0	—	1	0/1
		Z_j	2	1	0	0	0	0	–2	—	0	
		$Z_j - C_j$		0	–4↑	0	0	0	–2	—	0	$Min\ x_B/S_4$
	0	S_1	3	0	0	1	0	0	2	—	0	3/2
←	0	S_2	5	0	0	0	1	0	5	—	0	1
	0	S_3	1	0	0	0	0	1	0	—	–1	—
	1	x_1	2	1	0	0	0	0	–1	—	0	—
	4	x_2	0	0	1	0	0	0	0	—	1	—
		Z_j	2	1	4	0	0	0	–1	—	0	
		$Z_j - C_j$		0	0	0	0	0	–1↑	—	0	
	0	S_1	1	0	0	1	–2/5	0	0	—	0	
	0	S_4	1	0	0	0	1/5	0	1	—	0	
	0	S_3	1	0	0	0	0	1	0	—	0	
	1	x_1	3	1	0	0	1/5	(1)	0	—	0	
	4	x_2	0	0	1	0	0	0	0	—	1	
		Z_j	3	1	4	0	3/5	0	0	—	4	
		$Z_j - C_j$		0	0	0	3/5	0	0	—	4	

Since all $Z_j - C_j \geq 0$, the solution is optimum and is given by $x_1 = 3$, $x_2 = 0$ and Max $Z = 3$. This sub-problem yields an optimum integer solution. Hence, this sub-problem is dropped.

Sub-Problem (6)

Max $Z = x_1 + 4x_2$

Subject to,

$$2x_1 + 4x_2 \leq 7$$
$$5x_1 + 3x_2 \leq 15$$
$$x_2 \leq 1$$
$$x_1 \geq 2$$
$$x_2 \geq 1$$
$$x_1, x_2 \geq 0$$

This sub-problem has no feasible solution. Hence, this sub-problem is also fathomed.

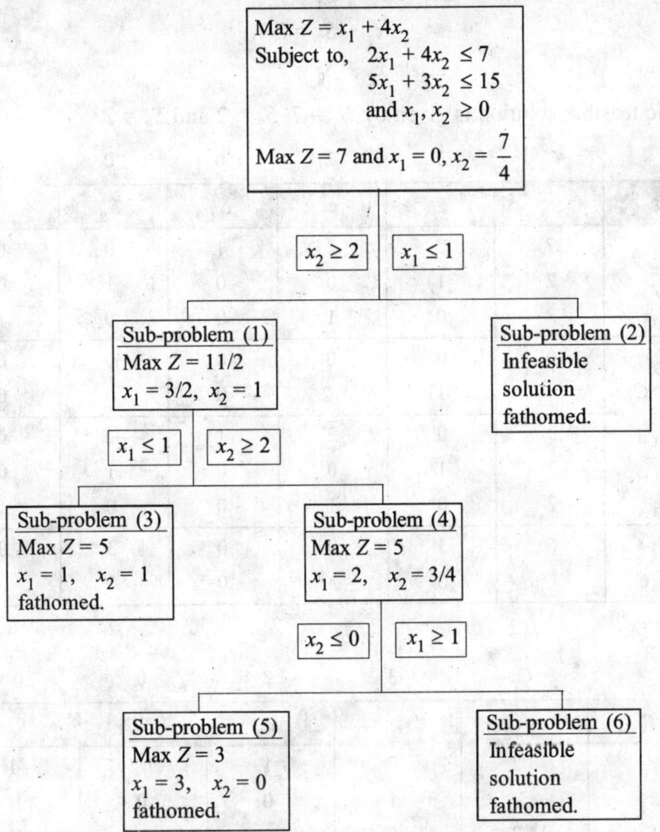

Among the available integer-valued solutions, the best integer solution is given by sub-problem (3).

$\therefore$ The optimum integer solution is,

$$x_1 = 1 \text{ and } x_2 = 1, \text{ Max } Z = 5.$$

The best available integer optimal solution is,

$$x_1 = 1 \text{ and } x_2 = 1, \text{ Max } Z = 5.$$

Example 11.8 Use branch and bound technique to,

$$\text{Maximize } Z = 3x_1 + 2x_2$$

Subject to,

$$2x_1 + 2x_2 \le 7$$
$$x_1 \le 2$$
$$x_2 \le 2, \text{ where } x_1\ x_2 \ge 0 \text{ and are integers.}$$

Solution Ignoring the integrality condition, we solve the given LPP by introducing slack variables $S_1, S_2, S_3 \ge 0$.

The standard form of LPP is given by,

Max $Z = 3x_1 + 2x_2 + 0S_1 + 0S_2 + 0S_3$

Subject to,
$$2x_1 + 2x_2 + S_1 = 7$$
$$x_1 + S_2 = 2$$
$$x_2 + S_3 = 2$$

The initial basic feasible solution is given by, $S_1 = 7$, $S_2 = 2$ and $S_3 = 2$.

		C_j	3	2	0	0	0	
C_B	B	x_B	x_1	x_2	S_1	S_2	S_3	$Min\ x_B/x_1$
0	S_1	7	2	2	1	0	0	7/2
← 0	S_2	2	(1)	0	0	1	0	2/1
0	S_3	2	0	1	0	0	1	—
	Z_j	0	0	0	0	0	0	
	$Z_j - C_j$		–3↑	–2	0	0	0	$Min\ x_B/x_2$
← 0	S_1	3	0	(2)	1	–2	0	3/2
3	x_1	2	1	0	0	1	0	—
0	S_3	2	0	1	0	0	1	2/1
	Z_j	6	3	0	0	3	0	
	$Z_j - C_j$		0	–2↑	0	3	0	

		C_j	3	2	0	0	0
C_B	B	x_B	x_1	x_2	S_1	S_2	S_3
2	x_2	3/2	0	1	1/2	–1	0
3	x_1	2	1	0	0	1	0
0	S_3	1/2	0	0	–1/2	1	1
	Z_j	9	3	2	1	1	0
	$Z_j - C_j$		0	0	1	1	0

Since all $Z_j - C_j \geq 0$, solution is optimal. Since $x_2 = 3/2$ is a non-integer, this problem should be branched into two sub-problems.

For $\quad x_2 = 3/2, 1 < x_2 < 2$

$\Rightarrow \quad x_2 \geq 2, x_2 \leq 1.$

Applying these two conditions separately in the given LPP.

We have two sub-problems.

Sub-problem (1)

Max $Z = 3x_1 + 2x_2$

Subject to, $2x_1 + 2x_2 \leq 7$
$$x_1 \leq 2$$
$$x_2 \leq 2$$
$$x_2 \leq 1$$

Sub-problem (2)

Max $Z = 3x_1 + 2x_2$

Subject to, $2x_1 + 2x_2 \leq 7$
$$x_1 \leq 2$$
$$x_2 \geq 2$$
$$x_2 \geq 2$$

Sub-Problem (1)

C_B	B	x_B	x_1	x_2	S_1	S_2	S_3	S_4	$Min\ x_B/x_1$
	C_j		3	2	0	0	0	0	
0	S_1	7	2	2	1	0	0	0	7/2
← 0	S_2	2	(1)	0	0	1	0	0	2/1
0	S_3	2	0	1	0	0	1	0	—
0	S_4	1	0	1	0	0	0	1	—
	Z_j	0	0	0	0	0	0	0	
	$Z_j - C_j$		–3↑	–2	0	0	0	0	

Since all $Z_j - C_j \geq 0$, the solution is optimum and is given by $x_1 = 2$, $x_2 = 1$, and Max $Z = 8$. Since x_1 and x_2 are integers, this sub-problem cannot be branched further.

Sub-Problem (2)

Max $Z = 3x_1 + 2x_2 + 0S_1 + 0S_2 + 0S_3 + 0S_4 - MA_1$

Subject to,

$$2x_1 + 2x_2 + S_1 = 7$$
$$x_1 + S_2 = 2$$
$$x_2 + S_3 = 2$$
$$x_2 + S_4 + A_1 = 2$$
$$x_1, x_2, S_1, S_2, S_3, S_4, A_1 \geq 0$$

C_B	B	x_B	x_1	x_2	S_1	S_2	S_3	S_4	$Min\ x_B/x_2$
	C_j		3	2	0	0	0	0	
0	S_1	7	2	2	1	–2	0	0	3/2 = 1.5
3	x_1	2	1	0	0	1	0	0	—
0	S_3	2	0	1	0	0	1	0	2/1 = 2
← 0	S_4	2	0	(1)	0	0	0	1	1/1 = 1
	Z_j	6	3	0	0	3	0	0	
	$Z_j - C_j$		0	–2↑	0	3	0	0	
0	S_1	1	0	0	1	–2	0	–2	
3	x_1	2	1	0	0	1	0	0	
0	S_3	1	0	0	0	0	1	–1	
2	x_2	1	0	1	0	0	0	1	
	Z_j	8	3	2	0	3	0	2	
	$Z_j - C_j$		0	0	0	3	0	2	

	C_j		3	2	0	0	0	0	$-M$	
C_B	B	x_B	x_1	x_2	S_1	S_2	S_3	S_4	A_1	$Min\ x_B/x_2$
0	S_1	7	2	2	1	0	0	0	0	7/2
0	S_2	2	1	0	0	1	0	0	0	—
0	S_3	2	0	(1)	0	0	1	0	0	2/1 = 2
← $-M$	A_1	2	0	1	0	0	0	–1	1	2/1 = 2
	Z_j	$-2M$	0	$-M$	0	0	0	M	$-M$	
	$Z_j - C_j$		–3	$-M-2$	0	0	0	M	0	$Min\ x_B/x_1$
← 0	S_1	3	(2)	0	1	0	0	2	—	3/2
0	S_2	2	1	0	0	1	0	0	—	2/1
0	S_3	0	0	0	0	0	1	1	—	—
2	x_2	2	0	1	0	0	0	–1	—	—
	Z_j	4	0	2	0	0	0	–2	—	
	$Z_j - C_j$		–3↑	0	0	0	0	–2		
3	x_1	3/2	1	0	1/2	0	0	1	—	
0	S_2	1/2	0	0	–1/2	1	0	–1	—	
0	S_3	0	0	0	0	0	1	1	—	
2	x_2	2	0	1	0	0	0	–1	—	
	Z_j	17/2	3	2	3/2	0	0	1	—	
	$Z_j - C_j$		0	0	3/2	0	0	1		

Since all $Z_j - C_j \geq 0$, the solution is optimum and is given by $x_1 = 3/2$ and $x_2 = 2$. Since $x_1 = 3/2$ is not an integer, this problem should be further branched into two sub-problems.

For $\quad x_1 = 3/2,\ 1 < x_1 < 2 \Rightarrow x_1 \leq 1, x_1 \geq 1.$

Applying these two conditions separately in the sub-problem (2), we obtain another two sub-problems.

Sub-problem (3)

Max $Z = 3x_1 + 2x_2$

Subject to, $2x_1 + 2x_2 \leq 7$

$x_1 \leq 2$

$x_2 \leq 2$

$x_2 \geq 1$

$x_1 \leq 1$

Sub-problem (4)

Max $Z = 3x_1 + 2x_2$

Subject to, $2x_1 + 2x_2 \leq 7$

$x_1 \leq 2$

$x_2 \leq 2$

$x_2 \geq 2$

$x_1 \geq 1$

Sub-Problem (3)

		C_j	3	2	0	0	0	0	$-M$	0	
C_B	B	x_B	x_1	x_2	S_1	S_2	S_3	S_4	A_1	S_5	$Min\ x_B/x_2$
0	S_1	7	2	2	1	0	0	0	0	0	7/2
0	S_2	2	1	0	0	1	0	0	0	0	—
0	S_3	2	0	1	0	0	1	0	0	0	2/1 = 2
$\leftarrow -M$	A_1	2	0	(1)	0	0	0	–1	1	0	2/1 = 2
0	S_5	1	1	0	0	0	0	0	0	1	—
	Z_j	$-2M$	0	$-M$	0	0	0	M	$-M$	0	
	$Z_j - C_j$		–3	$-M$–2 ↑	0	0	0	M	0	0	$Min\ x_B/x_1$
0	S_1	3	2	0	1	0	0	2	—	0	3/2
0	S_2	2	1	0	0	1	0	0	—	0	2/1
0	S_3	0	0	0	0	0	1	1	—	0	—
2	x_2	2	0	1	0	0	0	–1	—	0	—
$\leftarrow 0$	S_5	1	(1)	0	0	0	0	0	—	1	1/1
	Z_j	4	0	2	0	0	0	–2	—	0	
	$Z_j - C_j$		–3↑	0	0	0	0	–2	—	0	$Min\ x_B/S_1$
0	S_1	1	0	0	1	0	0	2		–2	1/2
0	S_2	1	0	0	0	1	0	(1)	—	0	—
$\leftarrow 0$	S_3	0	0	0	0	0	1	1	—	0	0
2	x_2	2	0	1	0	0	0	–1	—	0	—
3	x_1	1	1	0	0	0	0	0	—	1	—
	Z_j	7	3	2	0	0	0	–2↑	—	3	

		C_j	3	2	0	0	0	0	$-M$	0
C_B	B	x_B	x_1	x_2	S_1	S_2	S_3	S_4	A_1	S_5
0	S_1	1	0	0	1	0	–2	0	—	–2
0	S_2	1	0	0	0	1	0	0	—	0
0	S_4	0	0	0	0	0	1	1	—	0
2	x_2	2	0	1	0	0	1	0	—	0
3	x_1	1	1	0	0	0	0	0	—	1
	Z_j	7	3	2	0	0	2	0	—	3
	$Z_j - C_j$		0	0	0	0	2	0	—	3

Since all $Z_j - C_j \geq 0$, the solution is optimum and also since $x_1 = 1$, $x_2 = 2$ are integers, Max $Z = 7$, this sub-problem cannot be branched further.

Sub-Problem (4)

	C_j		3	2	0	0	0	0	M	0	$-M$	
C_B	B	x_B	x_1	x_2	S_1	S_2	S_3	S_4	A_1	S_5	A_2	$Min \frac{x_B}{x_1}$
0	S_1	7	2	2	1	0	0	0	0	0	0	7/2
0	S_2	2	1	0	0	1	0	0	0	0	0	2/1
0	S_3	2	0	1	0	0	1	0	0	0	0	—
$-M$	A_1	2	0	1	0	0	0	-1	1	0	0	—
$-M$	A_2	1	(1)	0	0	0	0	0	0	-1	1	1/1
	Z_j	$-3M$	$-M$	$-M$	0	0	0	M	$-M$	M	$-M$	
	$Z_j - C_j$		$-M-3\uparrow$	$-M-2$	0	0	0	M	0	M	0	$Min\ x_B/x_2$
0	S_1	5	0	2	1	0	0	0	0	2	—	5/2
0	S_2	1	0	0	0	1	0	0	0	1	—	—
0	S_3	2	0	1	0	0	1	0	0	0	—	2/1 = 2
$\leftarrow -M$	A_1	2	0	(1)	0	0	0	-1	1	0	—	2/1 = 2
3	x_1	1	1	0	0	0	0	0	0	-1	—	—
	Z_j	$-2M+3$	3	$-M$	0	0	0	M	$-M$	-3		
	$Z_j - C_j$		0	$-M-2$	0	0	0	M	0	-3		
				$\uparrow$								

Since all $Z_j - C_j \geq 0$ and an optimum integer solution is obtained, this sub-problem cannot be branched further. The solution is given by $x_1 = 2$, $x_2 = 2$ and Max $Z = 10$. Among the available integer solutions, the best integer solution is given by sub-problem (4).

The optimum integer solution is given by Max $Z = 10$, $x_1 = 2$ and $x_2 = 2$.

	C_j		3	2	0	0	0	0	0	
C_B	B	x_B	x_1	x_2	S_1	S_2	S_3	S_4	S_5	$Min\ x_B/S_5$
$\leftarrow 0$	S_1	1	0	0	1	0	0	2	2	1/2
0	S_2	1	0	0	0	1	0	0	1	1/1
0	S_3	0	0	0	0	0	1	1	0	—
2	x_2	2	0	1	0	0	0	-1	0	—
3	x_1	1	1	0	0	0	0	0	-1	—
	Z_j	7	3	2	0	0	0	-2	-3	$Min\ x_B/S_4$
	$Z_j - C_j$		0	0	0	0	0	-2	$-3\uparrow$	
0	S_5	1/2	0	0	1/2	0	0	1	1	$\frac{1/2}{1}$
0	S_2	1/2	0	0	$-1/2$	1	0	-1	0	—
$\leftarrow 0$	S_3	0	0	0	0	0	1	1	0	0
2	x_2	2	0	1	0	0	0	(-1)	0	—
3	x_1	2	1	0	0	1	0	0	0	—
	Z_j	10	3	2	0	3	0	(-2)	0	
	$Z_j - C_j$		0	0	0	3	0	$-2\uparrow$	0	
0	S_5	1/2	0	0	1/2	0	-1	0	1	

(Contd...)

0	S_2	1/2	0	0	–1/2	1	1	0	0	
0	S_4	0	0	0	0	0	1	1	0	
2	x_2	2	0	1	0	0	1	0	0	
3	x_1	2	1	0	0	1	0	0	0	
	Z_j	10	3	2	0	3	2	0	0	
	$Z_j - C_j$		0	0	0	3	2	0	0	

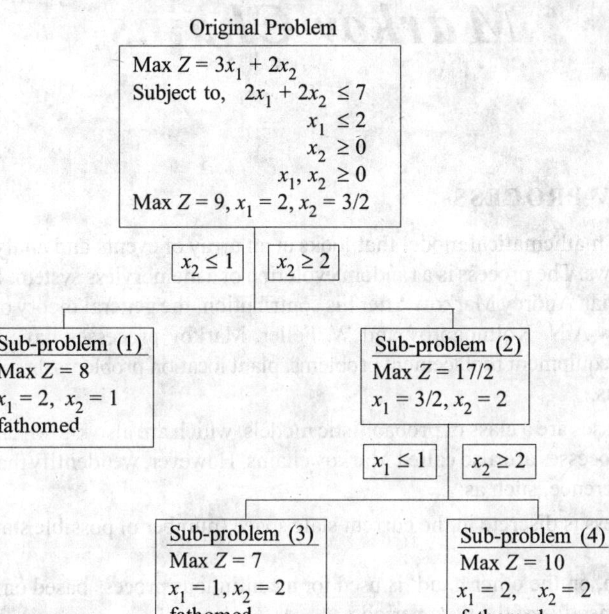

The best available solution is, Max $Z = 10$, $x_1 = 2$ and $x_2 = 2$.

EXERCISES

Use branch and bound method to solve the following problems:

1. Max $Z = 3x_1 + 4x_2$
   Subject to, $7x_1 + 16x_2 \le 52$
   $3x_1 - 2x_2 \le 18$
   $x_1, x_2 \ge 0$ and are integers. [**Ans.** Max $Z = 19$, $x_1 = 5$, $x_2 = 1$]
2. Max $Z = 2x_1 + 2x_2$
   Subject to, $5x_1 + 3x_2 \le 8$
   $x_1 + 2x_2 \le 4$
   $x_1, x_2 \ge 0$ and are integers. [**Ans.** Max $Z = 4$, $x_1 = 1$, $x_2 = 1$ or $x_1 = 0$, $x_2 = 2$]
3. Max $Z = 2x_1 + 20x_2 - 10x_3$
   Subject to, $2x_1 + 20x_2 + 4x_3 \le 15$
   $6x_1 + 20x_2 + 4x_3 = 20$
   $x_1, x_2, x_3 \ge 0$ and are integers. [**Ans.** Max $Z = -16$, $x_1 = 2$, $x_2 = 0$, $x_3 = 2$]
4. Max $Z = 3x_1 + 4x_2$
   Subject to, $3x_1 - x_2 + x_3 = 12$
   $3x_1 + 11x_2 + x_4 = 66$
   $x_j \ge 0$ and integers for $j = 1, 2, 3, 4$ [**Ans.** Max $Z = 31$, $x_1 = 5$, $x_2 = 4$]

❑❑❑

Chapter

12

Markov Processes and Markov Chains

12.1 MARKOV PROCESS

Markov process is a mathematical model that looks at an array of events and analyzes the tendencies of each event as it follows. The process is a random evolution of a memoryless system. It was named after the Russian mathematician Andrey Markov. After his contribution, the general theory of Markov process was further developed by A.N. Kolmogorov and W. Feller. Markov processes have been used to analyse inventory problems, equipment replacement problems, plant location problems, brand-switching problems and dynamic systems.

Markovian processes are a class of probabilistic models, which are also known as stochastic processes. At times, Markov processes are also called Markov chains. However, we identify that the two are separate concepts with a difference, such as:

- Markov process is discrete in the current state space (number of possible states) and in time (only one at a time).
- Markov chain, on the other hand, is used for a continuous process based on a finite countable set of states irrespective of the time period.

12.1.1 Formal Definition

- Markov process is a stochastic process where the state *t* is $x(t)$, for *t* is greater than zero, and history of state is $x(s)$, for *s* is lesser than *t*;
$$P_r\,[x(t+h] = y|x(s)=x(s),\ \forall s \le t]$$
$$= P_r\,[X(t+h)=y|\ X(t)=x(t)]$$
- Markov chain is a sequence of indiscriminate variables $x_1, x_2, x_3 \ldots x_n$, that may be represented as,
$$P_r\,(x_{n+1} = x, x_1 = x_1, x_2 = x_2 \ldots, x_n = x_n)$$
$$= P_r\,(x_{n+1} = x; x_n = x_n).$$
- These processes start independently in any one of the states, which successively moves to all other states. Each move taken in a process is called a step. For example, in a state process if the current step is *s*, then probable step would be denoted as P_{ij}. The probable step is not affected by the previous state, *i.e.*, in which state the chain was prior to the current state. These probabilities are called transition probabilities.
- Markov chain process, Markov chain or Markov process can be used in the following systems:
  (*i*) To understand the market place for a product viś-a-viś its competitive brands
  (*ii*) Billing, credit and collection procedures

12.1.2 Characteristics of Markov Process

Important characteristics of Markov process are as follows:

1. The basic characteristic of a Markov process is that the probabilities of going to each of the states of the system depend only on the current state and not on the manner in which the current state was reached. This means that the next state of the system is dependant on the current state and is completely independent of the previous states of the system.
2. The other important characteristic of a Markov process is that there are initial conditions which take on less and less importance as the process operates eventually washing out when the process reaches the steady state.
3. We assume that the process is discrete in state space and also in time.
4. In a simple Markov process, we assume that the switching behavior is represented by a transition matrix that is permanent. The state probabilities for a particular time period is called transient probabilities. The transition probabilities are the same at any point of time for a set of states, $s = \{s_1, s_2, s_3 ..., s_n\}$.

12.2 MARKOV CHAINS

A **Markov chain** is a graphical representation of the many possibilities and probabilities that may randomly impact the state in the next change. For example, if there is a toothpaste brand T in the market, then the probability of the random events changing the customer's state would be implied as per the Markov chain. Based on this Markov chain of random events, the customer may change his toothpaste to brand S.

We will explain Markov chain separately for better understanding of the concept.

A Markov chain is a sequence of random events whose probabilities at the current state is dependent on the interlinked probability at the prior state. This shows us that controlling factor in a Markov chain is the conditional probability or transitional probability. This conditional probability is meant for the system that has to complete a transition to the next state, depending on the sequence of events in the current state of system.

What makes the Markov chain models interestingly important is the fact that it makes it possible to predict or forecast how a Markov chain would behave. This helps in calculation and computation of the various probabilities and help derivation of the expected values which assist to quantify that behaviour.

Markov chains are mainly considered in:

(*i*) Continuous time

(*ii*) Discrete time

Formula for continuous time

$$t \in R^+ = [0, \infty].$$

Formula for discrete time

$$n \in Z^+ = \{0, 1, 2, ...\}$$

In both these formulae, we see that the letters *n*, *m*, *k* are denoted as integers, whereas, *t* and *s* refer to real numbers. Thereby, we can write $(x_t)_t \geq 0$ for a discrete process of Markov chain.

Properties of Markov Chains

(*i*) **Reducibility** → If a process is started at a state, there is zero probability of transition to next state.	(*i*) The probability of a possible jump from state *i* to state *j* in *n* time steps is:
(*ii*) **Periodicity** → A state in a process that is periodic returns to the same state everytime.	(*ii*) $P_{ij} = Pr(x_n = j \mid x_o = i)$
(*iii*) **Recurrence** → If a state in the process is transient, then there is zero possibility of returning to the same state.	(*iii*) For a single step transition: $P_{ij} = Pr(x_1 = j \mid x_o = i)$
(*iv*) **Ergodicity** → A state is supposed to be ergodic if it is in the positive reccurence state and periodic in nature	(*iv*) For a time-homogeneous Markov chain: $P_{ij}^{(n)} = Pr(x_{n+k} = j \mid x_k = i)$

Note: *S* is the state space of the Markov chain, (*n*) is an index. So, we can say $P_{ij}^{(n)} = \sum_{r \in S} p_{ir}^{(k)} p_{rj}^{(n-k)}$

Diagrammatic Representation

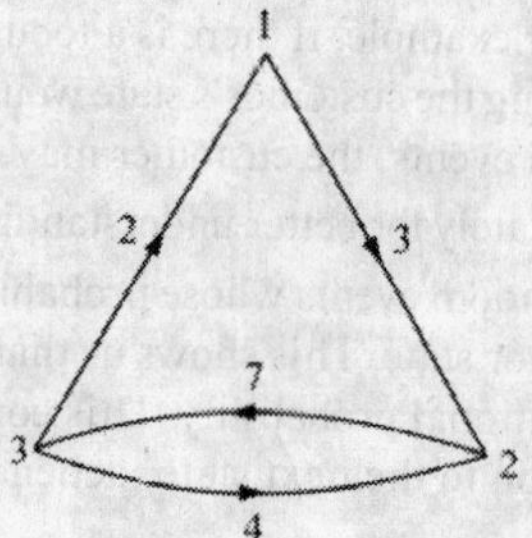

Fig. 12.1 *Continuous time*

In Fig. 12.1, we see a Markov chain in continuous time. In state 3, we have taken two independent exponential times, represented as $T_1 \sim E(2)$ and $T_2 \sim E(4)$. If T_1 is the smaller one then, you go to 1 after time T_1, and if T_2 is the smaller one then, you go to 2 after time T_2. Thus, we can simply calculate it as the time spent in 3 is exponential of parameter 2 + 4 = 6 and the conditional probability of 3 Transiting to 1 is 2/(2 + 4) = 1/3.

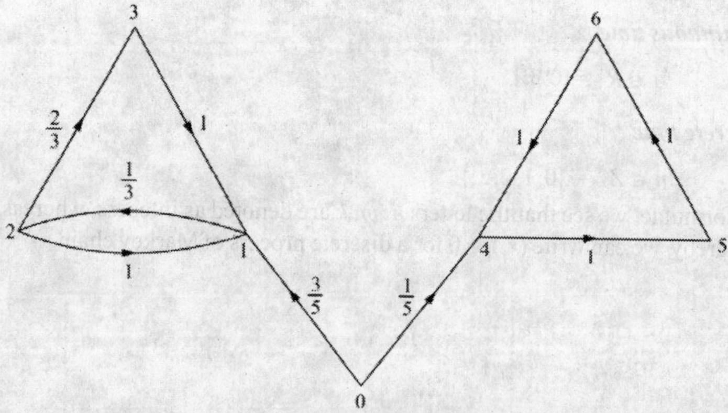

Fig. 12.2 *Discrete time*

In Figure 12.2, the various states are interlinked yet, partitioned into communicating sections, such as {0}, {1, 2, 3} and {4, 5, 6}. Two of these sections are closed which means that there would be no major changes. The closed sections are in recurrent state, *i.e.*, returning to the same state again and again section {0} is transient but section {4, 5, 6} is periodic. However, it is section {1, 2, 3} which is recurrent.

We can say that the following are the deductions of the discrete time diagram:

(*i*) Starting from 0, the transitional probability to 6 is 1/4.

(*ii*) Starting from 1, the transitional probability to 3 is 1.

(*iii*) Starting form 1, to transient to 3 we need three steps on an average.

(*iv*) Starting from 1, the proportional time to be spent in the long-run at 2 is 3/8.

Markov chains can be best represented in two types of chains:

(*a*) Absorbing chains

(*b*) Ergodic chains

We have explained both these types in detail, for the understanding of the reader. The explanation will further help in better application of the theorem.

12.2.1 Absorbing Chains

Calculation of the long-run System State

Markov chains are often best understood through special types of Markov chains. One such special Markov chain study is an Absorbing chain.

A Markov chain is understood to be an absorbing chain, when it meets the following criteria.

(*a*) At least one state in the chain process is absorbing, or

(*b*) All non-absorbing states in the chain process is connected or communicates with atleast one absorbing state.

Absorbing Markov chains are also known as Markov chains with a finite state space. In the finite state space, the distribution of probability for transition can be represented by a matrix, popularly known as transition matrix.

This can best be explained by an example and a diagram (Fig. 12.3).

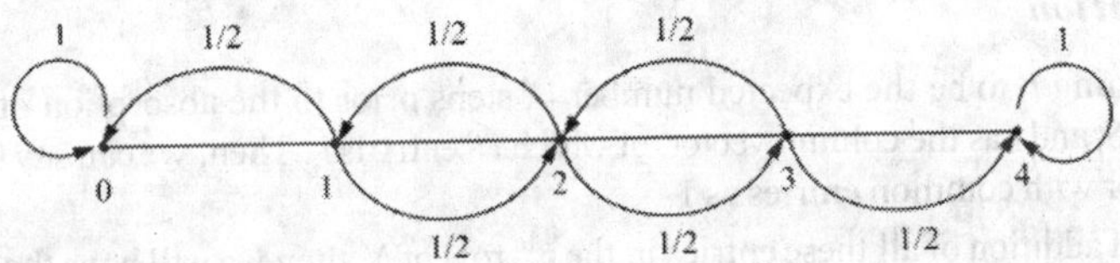

Fig. 12.3 A toddler's first walk

Example 12.1 A toddler takes his first step and there are four corners in the room (see Fig. 12.3). If the toddler is in any of the corners 1, 2, or 3, then there is an equal probability that he would take to the left or right. If the toddler continues to walk without stumbling until he has reached corner 4 (placed at the right and extreme of the bar). There is also an alternative probability that he may simply take a small circular walk and sit down at the starting point 0.

We can depict it in a Markov chain with the set of states 0, 1, 2, 3, and 4.

Here we see that states 0 and 4 are absorbing states. The transition matrix of a toddler's first walk will look like this:

$$P = \begin{array}{c} \\ 0 \\ 1 \\ 2 \\ 3 \\ 4 \end{array} \begin{array}{c} \begin{array}{ccccc} 0 & 1 & 2 & 3 & 4 \end{array} \\ \begin{bmatrix} 1 & 0 & 0 & 0 & 0 \\ 1/2 & 0 & 1/2 & 0 & 0 \\ 0 & 1/2 & 0 & 1/2 & 0 \\ 0 & 0 & 1/2 & 0 & 1/2 \\ 0 & 0 & 0 & 0 & 1 \end{bmatrix} \end{array}$$

We would like to let you first know, that in an absorbing Markov chain, if there is a state which is not absorbing, then we call it to be transient. In this example, we can say that the states 1, 2, and 3 are static or in transient state. Yet, it is important in the chain, as it is the interconnecting link which will help to reach the absorbing states *i.e.* 0 and 4. Whenever, a process reaches any one of the absorbing states (0 or 4) then, it is known to be absorbed.

Probability of Absorption

Theorem: The probability that in an absorbing Markov chain, the process will be absorbed is 1 *i.e.* $Q^n \to 0$ as $n \to \infty$.

Proof: Any Markov chain would be known and understood to be in absorbing state, only if each of the non-absorbing state (s_n) shows probability to reach an absorbing state. There will be same minimum number of steps which would be required for cach non-absorbing state to reach an absorbing state. The minimum number of steps may be depicted as m_n. The probability (p_n) would actually start from s_n and the non-absorbing state would fail top reach the absorbing state in m_n steps. In this case, $p_n < 1$. In a different scenario, if we take m_i to be the largest step of m_n (minimum number of steps) and take p_i as the largest of p_n (the probabilities), we will see that there is a conditional probability that m_i steps might not reach an absorbing state and be less than or equal to p_i. As $p_n < 1$, the probabilities show a tendency towards 0. As we see that there is a probability of remaining unabsorbed in twice, the minimum number of steps (n) is decreasing, then these possibilities might also tend to 0. So, we can say $\lim\limits_{n} \to \infty\, Q^n = 0$.

Time to Absorption

Theorem: Assuming t_i to be the expected number of steps prior to the absorption of the chain let the chain start at state S_i and t as the column vector, of which i^{th} entry is t_i. Then, we can say that, $t = N_c$, where c is a column vector with common entries as 1.

Proof: In case of addition of all these entries in the ith row of N, then we will have the expected number of times when any of the transient states (starting at S_i) would be expected to be absorbed. Thus, we may say that t_i is the total sum of the entries in the ith row of N.

Absorption Probabilities

Theorem: Let's take B as the matrix for the entries (b_{ij}). This b_{ij} is the probability for any absorbing state S_j. To be absorbed in the state S_j, a system must start from a transient state S_i. Then, we can say that B is an t – by – r matrix, and

$B = NR$, where N is the fundamental matrix and R is the canonical form.

Proof:

$$B_{ij} = \sum_n \sum_j q_{ik}^{(n)}\ p_{kj} = \sum_n \sum_j q_{ik}^{(n)}\ r_{kj}$$

$$= \sum_n n_{ik}\ r_{kj} = (NR)_{ij}$$

12.2.2 Fundamental Matrix

Theorem: An absorbing Markov chain can be explained by the transition matrix $I - Q$ with an inverse N. Here, we can say $N = 1 + Q + Q^2 + \ldots$ matrix N is the number of times the state in state S_j is expected to start in state S_i, so that the starting state is computed if, $i = j$.

Proof: Assuming $(I - Q)x = 0$; and $x = Q_x$, we can say that $x = Q^n \hat{x}$. As $Q^n \to 0$, we can say $Q^n \hat{x} \to 0$, so $x = 0$. Thus, $(I - Q)^{-1} = N$ exists.

$$(I - Q)(I - Q + Q^2 + \ldots + Q^n) = I - Q^{n+1}$$

We may multiply both the sides by N which would give,

$I + Q + Q^2 + \ldots + Q^n = N(I - Q^{n+1})$; if we let n take an infinite value, we have $P(x^{(k)} = 1) = q_{ij}^{(k)}$, and $P(x^{(k)} = 0 = 1 - q_{ij}^{(k)})$ here it is important to say that $q_{ij}^{(k)}$ is the ij^{th} entry of Q^k. The value of k in the equation is 0 since $Q^0 = I$. Thus, $x^{(k)|}$ is a $0 - 1$ random variable, is represented as $E(x^{(k)}) = q_{ij}^{(k)}$ and the equation further says j:

$$E(x^{(0)} + x^{(1)} + \ldots + x^{(n)}) = q_{ij}^{(0)} + q_{ij}^{(1)} + \ldots + q_{ij}^{(n)}$$

getting n take on to infinity, we see an equation that says;

$$E(x^{(0)} + x^{(1)} + \ldots) = q_{ij}^{(0)} + q_{ij}^{(1)} + \ldots = n_{ij}.$$

Thus, we can finally derive that for an absorbing Markov chain P, the matrix $N = (I - Q)^{-1}$ is supposed to be the fundamental matrix of P.

Example 12.2 This can be further well-explained with the toddler's first walk example (see Fig. 12.3), where the transition matrix in canonical form would be:

$$P = \begin{array}{c} \\ 1 \\ 2 \\ 3 \\ 0 \\ 4 \end{array}\begin{array}{c} \begin{array}{ccccc} 1 & 2 & 3 & 0 & 4 \end{array} \\ \left[\begin{array}{ccc|cc} 0 & 1/2 & 0 & 1/2 & 0 \\ 1/2 & 0 & 1/2 & 0 & 0 \\ 0 & 1/2 & 0 & 0 & 1/2 \\ \hline 0 & 0 & 0 & 1 & 0 \\ 0 & 0 & 0 & 0 & 1 \end{array}\right] \end{array}$$

The matrix Q, further reads as:

$$Q = \begin{bmatrix} 0 & 1/2 & 0 \\ 1/2 & 0 & 1/2 \\ 0 & 1/2 & 0 \end{bmatrix}, \text{ and } I - Q = \begin{bmatrix} 1 & -1/2 & 0 \\ -1/2 & 1 & -1/2 \\ 0 & -1/2 & 1 \end{bmatrix}$$

In the final computation process, we find $(I - Q)^{-1}$ can be calculated as follows:

$$N = (I - Q)^{-1} = \begin{array}{c} \\ 1 \\ 2 \\ 3 \end{array}\begin{array}{c} \begin{array}{ccc} 1 & 2 & 3 \end{array} \\ \begin{bmatrix} 3/2 & 1 & 1/2 \\ 1 & 2 & 1 \\ 1/2 & 1 & 3/2 \end{bmatrix} \end{array}$$

Thus, we can conclude that based on the computation of this fundamental matrix, we may say that if we start in state 2, then the expected number of times the states 1, 2 and 3 would be absorbed are 1, 2 and 1.

12.2.3 Ergodic Chains

A Markov chain is known as an ergodic chain only when there is a possibility to go from one state to another state (in one or more steps). While absorbing, Markov chains are easily organizable with its characteristic reducibility, ergodic Markov chains are known to be irreducible.

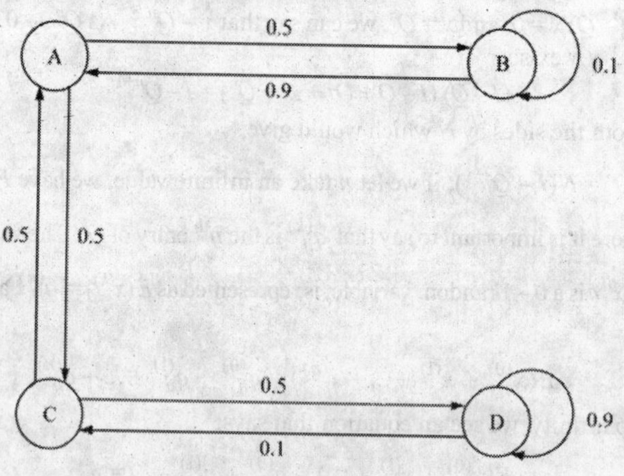

Fig. 12.4

Though ergodic chains share the common properties of a Markov chain, yet there is a characterized way of easy recognition with steady-state possibilities. See Fig. 12.4, for a diagrammatic representation of an ergodic chain. In a finite ergodic chain, with sufficient transition numbers there is a probability of being in any independent state from any of the starting states.

12.3 STATE AND TRANSITION PROBABILITIES

Calculation of the State of the System at any Time Period

The probabilities that are collected are placed in a matrix. Such a matrix is used for predicting the possible changes from one state to another and is known as matrix of transition probabilities.

The transitional probabilities are best represented by the transition diagram. Here is an example:

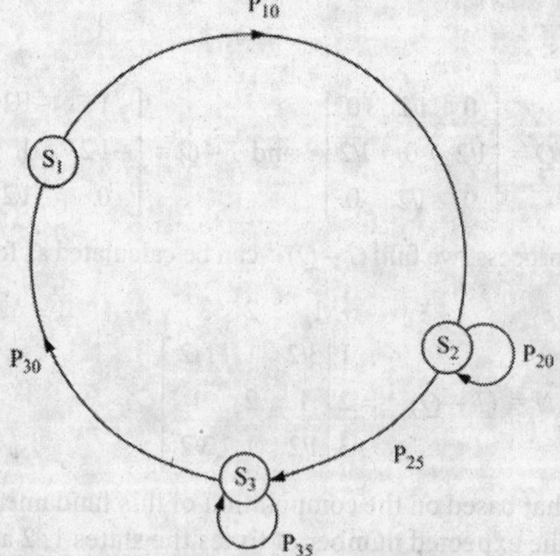

Fig. 12.5

The matrix of transition probabilities of the above diagram is:

$$P = \text{Initial state} \begin{matrix} \\ S_1 \\ S_2 \\ S_3 \end{matrix} \overset{\text{Succeding state}}{\begin{matrix} S_1 & S_2 & S_3 \\ \end{matrix}} \begin{bmatrix} 0 & P_{10} & 0 \\ 0 & P_{20} & P_{25} \\ P_{30} & 0 & P_{35} \end{bmatrix}$$

A zero element in the transition matrix indicates that the transition is impossible.

$$P\begin{bmatrix} \text{State 2} & & \text{State 1} \\ \text{on day} & + & \text{on day} \\ 2 & & 1 \end{bmatrix} = (0.7)(0.7) + (0.4)(0.3) = (0.49) + (0.12) = 0.61, \text{ and}$$

$$\because \quad P\begin{bmatrix} \text{State 2} & & \text{State 1} \\ \text{on day} & - & \text{on day} \\ 3 & & 1 \end{bmatrix} = P\begin{bmatrix} \text{State 2} & & \text{State 1} \\ \text{on day} & - & \text{on day} \\ 3 & & 2 \end{bmatrix} \times$$

$$P\begin{bmatrix} \text{State 2} & & \text{State 1} \\ \text{on day} & - & \text{on day} \\ 3 & & 1 \end{bmatrix} = P\begin{bmatrix} \text{State 2} & & \text{State 1} \\ \text{on day} & - & \text{on day} \\ 3 & & 2 \end{bmatrix} \times$$

$$P\left[\begin{array}{c|c} \text{State 2} & \text{State 1} \\ \text{on day} & \text{on day} \\ 2 & 1 \end{array}\right] = (0.3)(0.7) + (0.6)(0.3) = (0.21) + (0.18) = 0.39$$

Putting all these values in our equation for $P\left[\begin{array}{c|c} \text{State 1} & \text{State 1} \\ \text{on day} & \text{on day} \\ 4 & 1 \end{array}\right]$ developed as per tree 1 and tree 2, we may state the required probability to be equal to:

$$P\left[\begin{array}{c|c} \text{State 1} & \text{State 1} \\ \text{on day} & \text{on day} \\ 4 & 1 \end{array}\right] = (0.7)(0.61) + (0.4)(0.39) = (0.427) + (0.156) = 0.583$$

In the current state, these trees can also be used to evaluate and determine how probably is that the given system will be in any particular state at any time period. P is a stochastic matrix.

12.3.1 Probability Tree Diagram

A Markov process can be illustrated as follows:

Suppose there is a two state Markov process whose probabilities of change are as given below:

If the system starts initially in state 1 then the probability that the system will be in state 1 on the fourth day, which is equal to $(0.343 + 0.084 + 0.084 + 0.072 = 0.583)$, as per the probability tree shown here and this can be calculated as mentioned below:

Taking:

$$\begin{bmatrix} \text{State 1} & \text{State 1} \\ \text{on day} & \text{on day} \\ 4 & 1 \end{bmatrix}$$ = probability that the system will be in state 1 on day 4, given that it was state 1 on day 1.

And keeping in view:

$$P\begin{bmatrix} \text{State 1} & \text{State 1} \\ \text{on day 4} & \text{on day 3} \end{bmatrix} = 0.7, \text{ and}$$

$$P\begin{bmatrix} \text{State 1} & \text{State 2} \\ \text{on day 4} & \text{on day 3} \end{bmatrix} = 0.4$$

We have:

$$P\begin{bmatrix} \text{State 1} & \text{State 1} \\ \text{on day 4} & \text{on day 1} \end{bmatrix} = (0.7)\begin{bmatrix} \text{State 1} & \text{State 1} \\ \text{on day 3} & \text{on day 1} \end{bmatrix} + 0.4\begin{bmatrix} \text{State 2} & \text{State 1} \\ \text{on day 3} & \text{on day 1} \end{bmatrix}$$

Now, we will try to diagramically illustrate a limited number of transitions of a Markov chain.

Probability Tree One

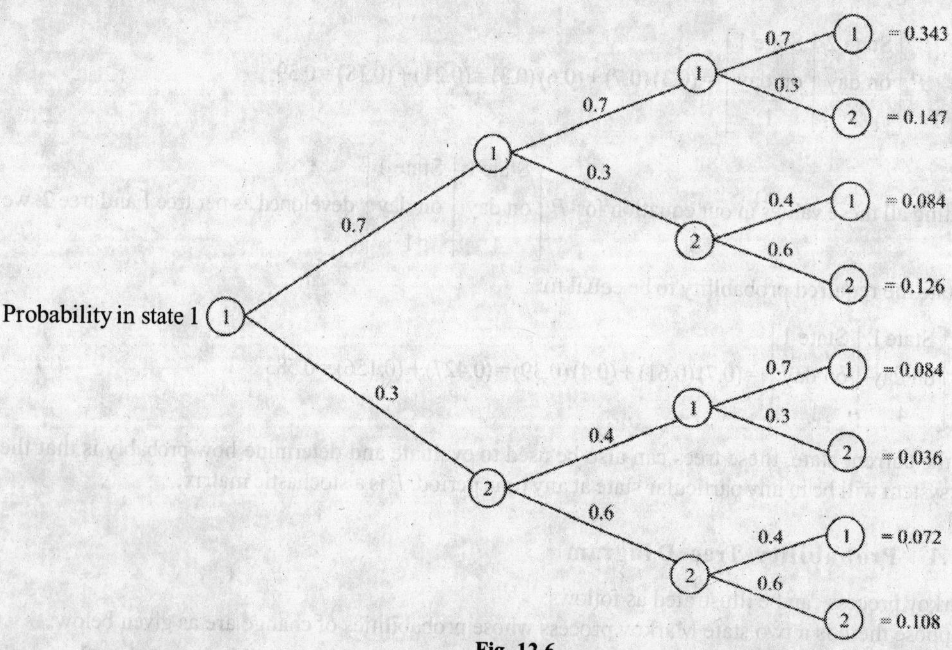

Fig. 12.6

Probability Tree Two

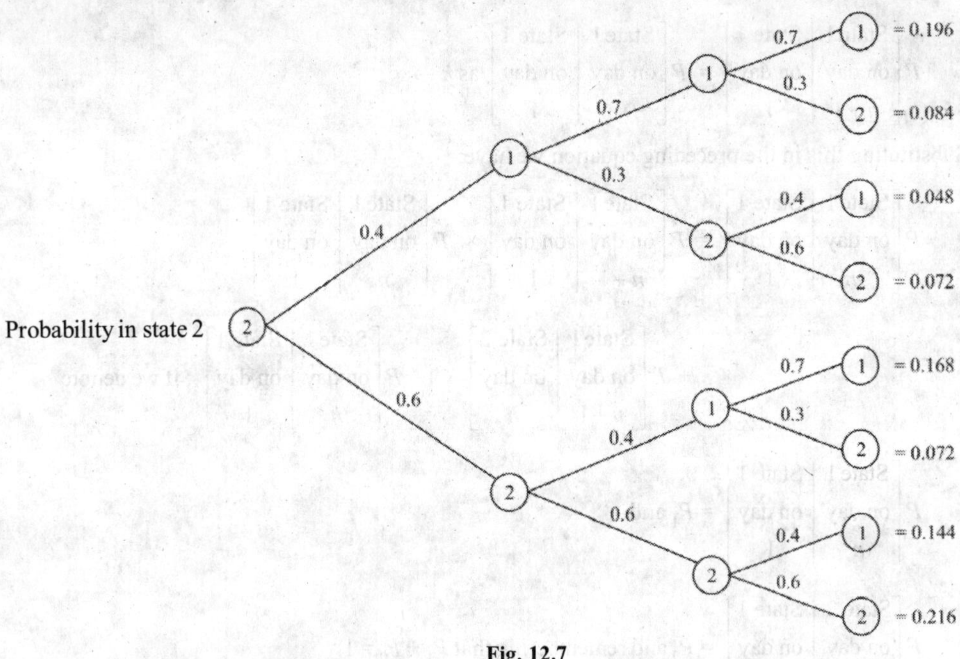

Fig. 12.7

$$\because \quad P\left[\begin{array}{c|c} \text{State 1} & \text{State 1} \\ \text{on day 3} & \text{on day 1} \end{array}\right]$$

$$= P\left[\begin{array}{c|c} \text{State 1} & \text{State 1} \\ \text{on day 3} & \text{on day 2} \end{array}\right] \times P\left[\begin{array}{c|c} \text{State 1} & \text{State 1} \\ \text{on day 2} & \text{on day 1} \end{array}\right] + P\left[\begin{array}{c|c} \text{State 1} & \text{State 2} \\ \text{on day 3} & \text{on day 2} \end{array}\right]$$

12.3.2 Calculation of Steady-State Probabilities

The steady-state probabilities are often significant for decision-making purposes. Such probabilities are the state probabilities when the system reaches the steady-state or when the system attains the equilibrium. As such they are also know as probabilities of the state of the system in a long-run position.

We can calculate such probabilities as stated below:

As the day number (n) increases to a very large number, the state probabilities for day n and for day $n + 1$ becomes more or less identical. As n approaches to infinity, separability of being in state 1 after n periods should be the same as the probability of being in state 1 after $n + 1$ periods.

Thereby, we can say:

$$P\left[\begin{array}{c|c} \text{State 1} & \text{State 1} \\ \text{on day} & \text{on day} \\ n+1 & 1 \end{array}\right] = P\left[\begin{array}{c|c} \text{State 1} & \text{State 1} \\ \text{on day} & \text{on day} \\ n+1 & n \end{array}\right] \times \left[\begin{array}{c|c} \text{State 1} & \text{State 1} \\ \text{on day} & \text{on day} \\ n & 1 \end{array}\right] +$$

$$P\left[\begin{array}{c|c} \text{State 1} & \text{State 2} \\ \text{on day} & \text{on day} \\ n+1 & n \end{array}\right] \times P\left[\begin{array}{c|c} \text{State 2} & \text{State 1} \\ \text{on day} & \text{on day} \\ n & 1 \end{array}\right]$$

and in addition, we reason that;

$$P\begin{bmatrix} \text{State 1} & \text{State 1} \\ \text{on day} & \text{on day} \\ n+1 & 1 \end{bmatrix} = P\begin{bmatrix} \text{State 1} & \text{State 1} \\ \text{on day} & \text{on day} \\ n & 1 \end{bmatrix} \text{ as } n \to \infty$$

Substituting this in the preceding equation we have;

$$P\begin{bmatrix} \text{State 1} & \text{State 1} \\ \text{on day} & \text{on day} \\ n & 1 \end{bmatrix} = P\begin{bmatrix} \text{State 1} & \text{State 1} \\ \text{on day} & \text{on day} \\ n+1 & 1 \end{bmatrix} \times P\begin{bmatrix} \text{State 1} & \text{State 1} \\ \text{on day} & \text{on day} \\ n & 1 \end{bmatrix}$$

$$+ P\begin{bmatrix} \text{State 1} & \text{State 2} \\ \text{on day} & \text{on day} \\ n+1 & n \end{bmatrix} \times 1 - P\begin{bmatrix} \text{State 1} & \text{State 1} \\ \text{on day} & \text{on day} \\ n & 1 \end{bmatrix}^{*} \text{; if we denote}$$

$$P\begin{bmatrix} \text{State 1} & \text{State 1} \\ \text{on day} & \text{on day} \\ n & 1 \end{bmatrix} = P_1 \text{ and}$$

$$P\begin{bmatrix} \text{State 2} & \text{State 1} \\ \text{on day} & \text{on day} \\ n & 1 \end{bmatrix} = P_2 \text{ and remembering that } P_1 + P_2 = 1.$$

So we can write:

$$P_1 = \left\{ P\left(\begin{matrix} \text{state 1} \\ \text{on day } n+1 \end{matrix} \middle| \begin{matrix} \text{state 1} \\ \text{on day } n \end{matrix} \right) (P_1) \right\}$$

$$+ \left\{ P\left(\begin{matrix} \text{state 1} \\ \text{on day } n+1 \end{matrix} \middle| \begin{matrix} \text{state 1} \\ \text{on day } n \end{matrix} \right) (1 - P_1) \right\} \text{ and } P_2 = 1 - P_1$$

This is how steady-state probabilities (P_1 and P_2)** can be worked out in a Markov process with two states only. We can illustrate the same by an example:

* Since $P\begin{bmatrix} \text{State 1} & \text{State 1} \\ \text{on day} & \text{on day} \\ n & 1 \end{bmatrix} = P\begin{bmatrix} \text{State 2} & \text{State 1} \\ \text{on day} & \text{on day} \\ n & 1 \end{bmatrix} = 1$

Hence $P\begin{bmatrix} \text{State 2} & \text{State 1} \\ \text{on day} & \text{on day} \\ n & 1 \end{bmatrix} = 1 - P\begin{bmatrix} \text{State 1} & \text{State 1} \\ \text{on day} & \text{on day} \\ n & 1 \end{bmatrix}$

** If we start in state 2 initially (instead of starting in state1) then the steady-state probabilities will be stated as under:

$$P_1 = \left\{ \begin{matrix} \text{state 1} \\ \text{on day } n \end{matrix} \middle| \begin{matrix} \text{state 2} \\ \text{on day 1} \end{matrix} \right\}$$

$$P_2 = \left\{ \begin{matrix} \text{state 2} \\ \text{on day } n \end{matrix} \middle| \begin{matrix} \text{state 2} \\ \text{on day 1} \end{matrix} \right\}$$

Example 12.3 Calculate the steady-state probabilities from the following transition probability matrix meant for time period of one year concerning a certain system.

But the value of P_1 and P_2 will remain the same as we have worked out above.

From	To	
	State 1	*State 2*
State 1	0.8	0.2
State 2	0.4	0.6

Solution Presuming that we start in state 1 initially, we can write

$$P_1 = \left\{P\left(\begin{array}{c|c}\text{state 1} & \text{state 1}\\ \text{on day } n+1 & \text{on day } n\end{array}\right)(P_1)\right\}$$

$$+\left\{P\left(\begin{array}{c|c}\text{state 1} & \text{state 2}\\ \text{on day } n+1 & \text{on day } n\end{array}\right)(1-P_1)\right\}$$

or, $$P_1 = (0.8)(P_1) + (0.4)(1-P_1)$$

or, $$P_1 = 0.8P_1 + 0.4 - 0.4P_1$$

or, $$0.6P_1 = 0.4$$

$\therefore$ $$P_1 = \frac{4}{6} = \frac{2}{3}$$

Since $$P_1 + P_2 = 1$$

$\therefore$ $$P_2 = 1 - \frac{2}{3} = \frac{1}{3}$$

Thus the steady-state probability of the system being in state 1 on any n day ($n \to \infty$) is 2/3 and that it would be in state 2 is 1/3.

Alternatively, we may work out the steady-state probabilities (presuming that we start in state 2 initially) as follows:

$$P_1 = \left\{P\left(\begin{array}{c|c}\text{state 1} & \text{state 1}\\ \text{on day } n+1 & \text{on day } n\end{array}\right)(P_1)\right\} + \left\{P\left(\begin{array}{c|c}\text{state 1} & \text{state 2}\\ \text{on day } n+1 & \text{on day } n\end{array}\right)(1-P_1)\right\}$$

or, $$P_1 = (0.8)(P_1) + (0.4)(1-P_1)$$

or, $$P_1 = \frac{2}{3}$$

Hence $$P_2 = 1 - \frac{2}{3} = \frac{1}{3}$$

Steady-state probabilities in case of systems involving more than two states can be worked out by applying the same approach as we have used so far. The only complication is that instead of having just one equation, there will be two or more simultaneous linear equations* which when solved will produce the concerning steady-state probabilities. We can illustrate the same by an example:

Example 12.4 Calculate the steady-state probabilities from the information given below presuming the system is in state 1 at the start:

---

* The number of these equations to be solved will be equal to one less than the number of states of the given system.

Transition Probability Matrix

From \ To	A (State 1)	B (State 2)	C (State 3)
A (State 1)	0.8	0.2	0.0
B (State 2)	0.2	0.0	0.8
C (State 3)	0.2	0.2	0.6

Solution

Let P_1 represent $P\left(\begin{array}{c|c}\text{state 1} & \text{state 1}\\ \text{on day } n & \text{on day 1}\end{array}\right)$, the steady-state probability of the system being a state 1 on day n

P_2 represent $P\left(\begin{array}{c|c}\text{state 2} & \text{state 1}\\ \text{on day } n & \text{on day 1}\end{array}\right)$, the steady-state probability of the system being a state 2 on day n

P_3 represent $P\left(\begin{array}{c|c}\text{state 3} & \text{state 1}\\ \text{on day } n & \text{on day 1}\end{array}\right)$, the steady-state probability of the system being in state 3 on day n.

and remember that

$$P_1 + P_2 + P_3 = 1$$

we may state

$$P_3 = (1 - P_1 - P_2)$$

and now using the information given in transition probabilities matrix we have

$$P_1 = (0.8)(P_1) + (0.2)(P_2) + (0.2)(P_3) \text{ as } n \to \propto \quad ...(i)$$

$$P_2 = (0.2)(P_1) + (0.0)(P_2) + (0.2)(P_3) \text{ as } n \to \propto \quad ...(ii)$$

$$P_3 = (0.0)(P_1) + (0.8)(P_2) + (0.6)(P_3) \text{ as } n \to \propto \quad ...(iii)$$

and now we have to find values of P_1, P_2 and P_3 which can be worked out as under:

Equation (*i*) can be written as under:

$$P_1 = 0.8P_1 + 0.2P_2 + 0.2(1 - P_1 - P_2) \quad ...(iv)$$

and Equation (*ii*) can be written as under:

$$P_2 = 0.2P_1 + 0.2(1 - P_1 - P_2) \quad ...(v)$$

Solving the equations (*iv*) and (*v*) for P_1 and P_2 we obtain

$$P_1 = \frac{1}{2} \text{ and } P_2 = \frac{1}{6}$$

$$\because \quad P_3 = 1 - P_1 - P_2 \; \therefore \; P_3 = 1 - \frac{1}{2} - \frac{1}{6} = \frac{1}{3}$$

Hence the required steady state probabilities are $P_1 = 1/2$, $P_2 = 1/2$, $P_2 = 1/6$ and $P_3 = 1/3$ for the given system concerning which the given transition probability matrix remains stable over time.

12.3.3 Applications of Markov Processes in Decision Problems

Various decisions problems can be solved by formulating a Markov process model of the situation and then computing the steady-state probabilities and finally, using this information for decision purpose. Short-term forecasts are also possible with this approach. We illustrate the same by some examples:

Example 12.5 Suppose the marketing division of a tale powder manufacturing company has worked out the following transition probability matrices concerning the behaviour of the customers before and after an advertising campaign:

Transition probability matrix
(Before advertising campaign)

From \ To	*Our brand (State 1)*	*Any other (State 2)*
Our brand (state 1)	0.8	0.2
Any other (state 2)	0.4	0.6

Transition probability matrix
(After advertising campaign)

From \ To	*Our brand (State 1)*	*Any other (State 2)*
Our brand (state 1)	0.9	0.1
Any other (state 2)	0.5	0.5

If the advertising campaign costs ₹ 20,000 per year, would it be worth while for the company to undertake the campaign? You may suppose there are 60,000 buyers of tale powder in the market and for each customer, the average annual profit the company makes is ₹ 2.50.

Solution To solve this problem applying Markovian analysis let us first workout the steady-state probabilities that a customer will be buying out product when there is no advertising campaign for the same. The same can be worked out as under:

Steady state probabilities when there is no advertising:

$$P_1 = (0.8)(P_1) + (0.4)(1 - P_1)$$

or, $$P_1 = 0.8P_1 + 0.4 - 0.4P_1$$

or, $$P_1 = \frac{4}{6} = \frac{2}{3}$$

Hence, $$P_2 = 1 - \frac{2}{3} = \frac{1}{3}$$

Accordingly, we expect that in the long run out of 60,000 buyers × (2/3) = 40,000 will buy our brand of tale power.

Steady-state probabilities when there is advertising campaign:

$$P_1 = (0.9)(P_1) + (0.5)(1 - P_1)$$

$$P_1 = 0.9P_1 + 0.5 - 0.5P_1$$

$$P_1 = \frac{5}{6}$$

Hence, $$P_2 = 1 - \frac{5}{6} = \frac{1}{6}$$

Accordingly, we expect that in the long run out of 60,000 buyers 60,000 × 5/6 = 50,000 will buy our brand of tale powder.

The above analysis shows that as a result of advertising campaign we shall be able to attract 50,000 – 40,000 = 10,000 additional customers and thereby will make an additional profit of

10,000 × ₹2.50 = ₹25,000 per year. But the advertising campaign costs only ₹20,000 per year, and hence there will be a net profit of ₹5,000 from advertising campaign. As such the company should undertake the advertising campaign.

Example 12.6 Kothari Car Rental Company rents cars from three centres, *viz.*, *X*, *Y* and *Z*. Customers return cars to each of the centres according to the following probabilities.

From \ *To*	*X* (*State 1*)	*Y* (*State 2*)	*Z* (*State 3*)
X (state 1)	0.0	0.4	0.6
Y (state 2)	0.8	0.0	0.2
Z (state 3)	0.8	0.2	0.0

Kothari Company is planning to build a maintenance facility at one of the three centres. Which centre would you recommend for this purpose? State, why so?

Solution First of all we should work out the steady-state probabilities concerning the given system and the same has been done as follows:

$$P_1 = (0.0)(P_1) + (0.8)(P_2) + (0.8)(1 - P_1 - P_2) \text{ as } n \to \alpha$$

$$P_2 = (0.4)(P_1) + (0.0)(P_2) + (0.2)(1 - P_1 - P_2) \text{ as } n \to \alpha$$

Solving the above two equations for P_1 and P_2 we have

$$P_1 = \frac{4}{9} = 0.4445 = 44.45\%$$

$$P_2 = \frac{13}{54} = 0.2407 = 24.07\%$$

Since $P_1 + P_2 + P_3 = 1$

Hence, $P_3 = 1 - P_1 - P_2$

$$= 1 - \frac{4}{9} - \frac{13}{54}$$

$$= \frac{54 - 24 - 13}{54} = \frac{17}{54} = 0.3148 = 31.48\%$$

The above analysis shows that the maintenance facility be developed at centre *X* (representing state 1 of the system) for in the long run 44.45 per cent cars are expected to reach this centre where as percentage of cars reaching centres *Y* and *Z* are 24.07 per cent and 31.48 per cent respectively.

Transient-state Probabilities

Sometimes the decision-maker is concerned with the short-run (or what is described as transient) behaviour of the process instead with its long-run behaviour. In such a situation, we should calculate the transient-state probabilities, and not the steady-state probabilities. Once the transient-state probabilities, as required in a given problem, are worked out either through the use of probability tree diagram or using the matrix multiplication then a decision can easily be taken easing it on such probabilities. We take an example to illustrate the same.

Example 12.7 The transition probability matrix for a day period concerning a machine system is as under:

From \ To	Working (State 1)	Not working (State 2)
Working (state 1)	0.7	0.3
Not working (state 2)	0.4	0.6

Suppose that when the machine is in state 1 for a day, a profit of ₹ 200 is gained and if the machine is in state 2 for a day, a loss of ₹ 100 is incurred. The decision maker wants to know the expected profit for a four-days period. Workout such profit presuming that the machine is in state 1 on day 1.

Solution The expected profit may be calculated by evaluating all branches of the probability tree (that we had drawn earlier) weighted by the appropriate profit for each branch. But here we use an alternative approach based on the use of matrix algebra* for the sake of convenience in finding out the transient-state probabilities for each day of a four-day period, and then they may be multiplied by the profit pay-offs and then summing the products we may obtain the expected profit over the four-day period. The same has been done as under:

Taking the initial state of the system on day 1 as that of state 1, the transient-state probability vector for day 1 is:

$$\pi'(1) = (10)$$

For day 2 we shall write the transient-state probabilities as:

$$\pi'(2) = \pi'(1).P$$

$$= (10)\begin{bmatrix} 0.7 & 0.3 \\ 0.4 & 0.6 \end{bmatrix} = (0.7 + 0.3 + 0)$$

$$= (0.7 \quad 0.3)$$

For day 3 we shall write the transient-state probabilities as:

$$\pi'(3) = \pi'(2).P$$

$$= (0.7 \quad 0.3)\begin{bmatrix} 0.7 & 0.3 \\ 0.4 & 0.6 \end{bmatrix} = (0.49 + 0.12 \quad 0.21 + 0.18)$$

$$= (0.61 \quad 0.39)$$

For day 4 we shall write the transient-state probabilities as:

$$\pi'(4) = \pi'(3).P$$

$$= (0.61 \ 0.39)\begin{bmatrix} 0.7 & 0.3 \\ 0.4 & 0.6 \end{bmatrix}$$

$$= (0.427 + 0.156 \quad 0.183 + 0.234) = (0.583 \quad 0.417)$$

Now the expected profit for four-day period can be worked out as shown on page 227 in the table of expected profit. Expected profit for a four-days (1 – 4) period is ₹ 467.90 or an average daily profit of ₹ 116.98 given that the machine is in state 1 on day 1.

---

* For this purpose, we shall denote $\pi(n)$ as the vector transient-state probabilities at period n, given that the initial state probabilities at time zero are $p(0)'$. The individual transient-state probabilities $\pi_1(n)$ and $\pi_2(n)$ are the two components of the vector $\pi(n)$. For any general period n, $\pi'(n) = \pi'(n-1)$. P where P is the transition probability matrix.

Table showing expected profit for day *n*

Day number	*Transient state probability vector*	*Expected profit for day n* $EP(n) = \pi'(n)\,[200 - 100]$ ₹
1	(1 0)	(200 – 0) = 200
2	(0.7 0.3)	(140 – 30) = 110
3	(0.61 0.39)	(122 – 39) = 83
4	(0.583 0.417)	(116.6 – 41.7) = 74.9
		Total = 467.9

12.3.4 Multi-Period Transition Probabilities

When Markov process occuss without any discrete break, then it is known as Markov chain. One of the purposes of Markov chain is to predict the future.

12.3.5 Steps of Computation

Determine Retention Probabilities

To determine the retention probabilitics, wc may divide the total number of customers[1] subjects who/ which were retained for the given time period. This would then be reviewed by the number of customers at the beginning of the period.

Determine Gains and Losses Probabilities

Very often, manufactures brands complain that customers/subjects switch over to the competitor's brand. This switching nature causes an unbalance. So, we may use a matrix of transition that would show the gains and losses among the brands. This matrix can be calculated by dividing the number of customers (gained or lost) of each business entity/brand by the total actual number of customers served by each business entity/brand.

Develop Matrix of Transition Probabilities

You may develop a matrix of transition probabilities by following this simple step — take the retention probabilities as the value for the main diagonal. The matrix rows depict the retention and loss of customers, subjects and the columns show the retention and gain of customers/subjects.

This can be shown as a transition diagram:

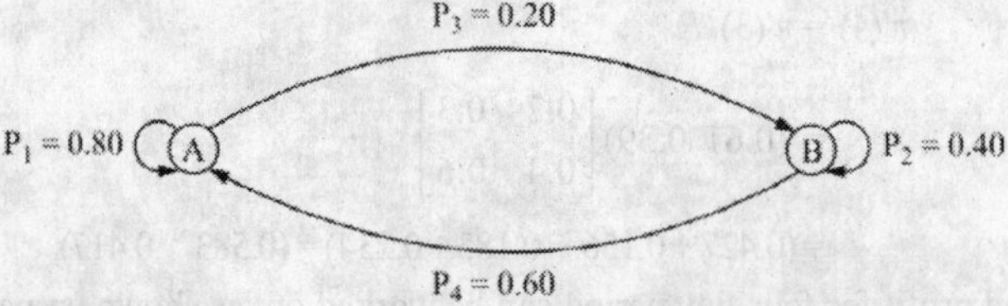

Fig. 12.8

Here, we use this diagram to predict the probability of the customers/subject in the next shopping step. We understand that it depends on the product that the customer/subject currently have so, we can say that it is a conditional probability that the customer/subject may shift to a different or competitor's brand. The example has two brands: Brand *A* and Brand *B*.

$$P = \text{present shopped brand } (n=0) \begin{array}{c} \\ A \\ B \end{array} \overset{\begin{array}{cc} A & B \end{array}}{\begin{bmatrix} 0.80 & 0.20 \\ 0.60 & 0.40 \end{bmatrix}} \begin{array}{l} \text{Retention} \\ \text{and gains} \\ \downarrow \end{array}$$

Retention and losses $\longrightarrow$

Now, we can state that the conditional transition matrix is as follows:

(*i*) $P(A_0|A_1) = P_1 = 0.80$, which means that the customer is currently using brand A's product at $n = 0$, and there is a probability that the customer will again buy brand A at $n = 1$ is 0.80. This shows retention for brand A's product.

(*ii*) $P(B_0|A_1) = P_4 = 0.60$, which means that the customers who are currently using B's product at $n = 0$, will probably purchase A's brand at $n = 1$ is 0.60. This indicates loss for Brand B.

(*iii*) $P(A_0|B_1) = P_3 = 0.20$, this indicates that customers who are currently using brand A's product at $n = 0$, most probably may purchase brand B at $n = 1$ at next shopping step is 0.20. This shows a loss for brand A.

(*iv*) $P(B_0|B_1) = P_2 = 0.40$, this shows a probability amongst customers, who are currently using brand B at $n = 0$, may continue to use it at next purchase for $n = 1$. This implies retention for brand B's product.

Purchase next time $n = 1$	*Purschase next time* $n = 2$	*Joint probabilities*

Current purchase situation, Brand A

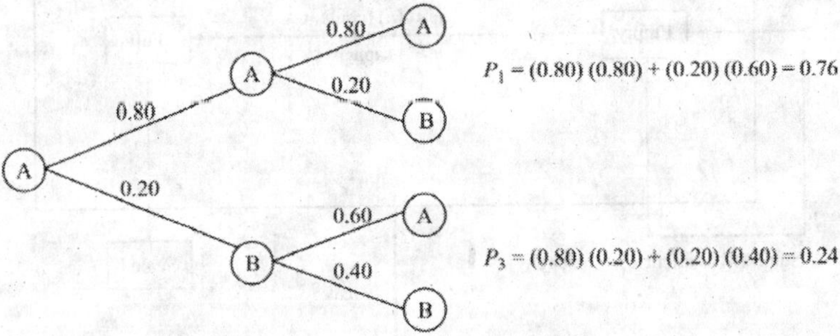

Current purchase situation, Brand B

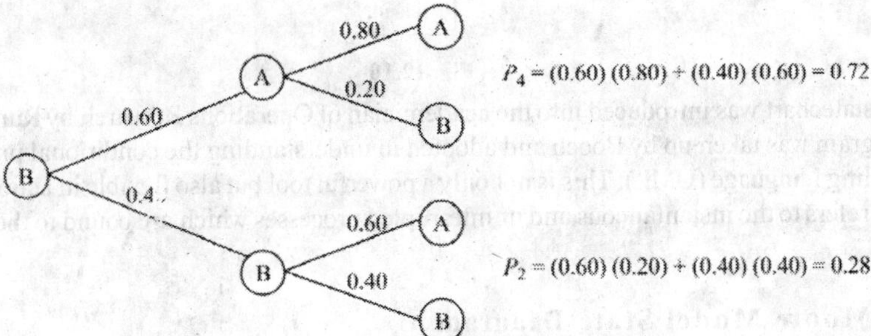

Fig. 12.9

Thus, we can conclude that if the present purchasing state is at $n = 0$, then two periods later (*i.e.* $n = 2$), the probability of the purchasing state is $P_1 = 0.76$ and $P_3 = 0.24$, which shows that the probability of retention of brand *A*'s market. Share is 76 per cent and brand *B*'s market share is 24 per cent. Similarly, from the customers view point the present state is for $P_1 = 0.80$, and next state is $P_3 = 0.20$. This shows that the retention probability of any customers using brand *A*'s product is 80 per cent and loss probability of brand *A* is 20 per cent.

12.3.6 State-Transition Diagrams

This is a diagram that consists of circles. These circles represent the states and the directed line segments represent transitions between each state.

Each transition may be associated with one or more outputs. It is a finite state machine.

State-transition diagrams have been actively in usage for object-oriented modelling since early times. The primary idea is to define a 'finite state machine' which has a discrete number of states. The 'finite state machine' faces various events shows a probability that the machine may transit into the next state. It also gives a well-defined and formal meaning of behaviours. The most popular variety of state transition diagram is Harel statechart shown in Fig. 12.10.

12.3.6.1 Harel Statechart

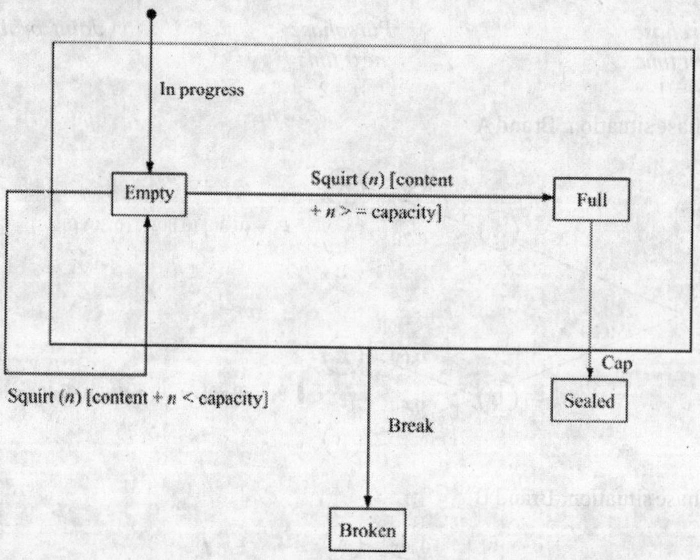

Fig. 12.10

The Harel statechart was introduced into the academician of Operations Research by Rumbaugh. This transition diagram was taken up by Booch and adopted in understanding the conditional probabilities of Unified Modeling Language (UML). This is not only a powerful tool but also flexible in action. An *action*, in this contet, refers to the instantaneous and uninterrupted processes which are bound to the entry or exit of a state.

12.3.6.2 Moore Model State Diagram

This is an alternative state transition diagram. The Moore model state diagram is most notably promoted by Shlaer/Mellor. Shlaer/Mellor are of the opinion that the Moore model state diagram is simple and has no super states. The transition diagram allows processes to occur naturally when in a state as shown in Fig. 12.11

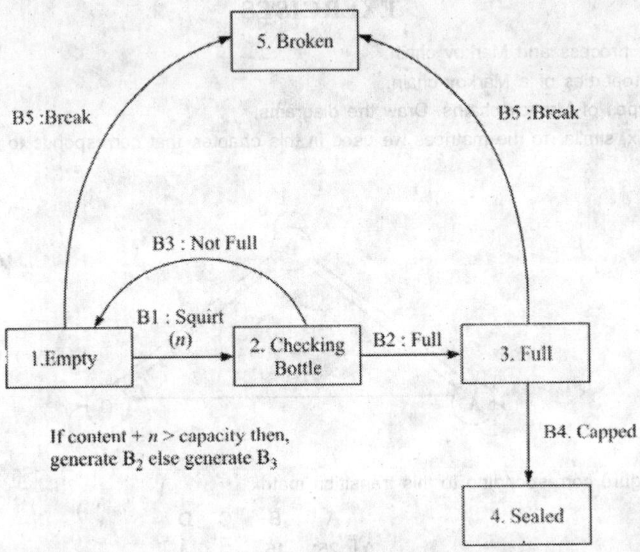

Fig. 12.11

State-transition diagrams are generally used to describe the behaviour of a single object or subject or customer in a given state. However as we often, deal in human elements, which are unshakable, we use interaction diagrams or activity diagrams.

12.3.6.3 Interaction Diagram

Interaction diagrams are the models which are used to describe or define how a group of objects collaborate in a certain behaviour in a single use case. Interaction diagrams are of two types:

(*a*) Sequence diagram
(*b*) Collaboration diagram.

12.3.6.4 Activity Diagram

Activity diagrams are more definite and are focused on the range of activities, corresponding processes and sequence of events. The representation of an activity diagram is like a flowchart. Thus, a process that has three lines of activity would initiate four parallel lines of activity. This would state the activity and synchronize so that the process is completed.

This is used to describe a behaviour in a 'multi-use case' and its interactions.

12.4 CONCLUSION

In this chapter, we have tried to define and explain Markov process and Markov chain. Though the terms are often used interchangeably, we have put in great efforts to show the distinguishing factors and impact on decision making. The examples are kept to basic day-to-day operations for the readers to understand and apply. We have tried to touch upon the various aspects of transitional probability. The chapter is introductory and basic in approach and has multiple numbers of figures diagrams, and examples. The theorems are backed by proof which gives a reader wholesome knowledge about Markov process and Markov chains. The toddler's first walk has been a stalmart example cited for understanding Markov chains.

EXERCISES

1. Define Markov process and Markov chain.
2. Discuss the properties of a Markov chain.
3. Mention the types of Markov chains. Draw the diagrams.
4. Set up a matrix, similar to the matrices we used in this chapter, that corresponds to this diagram:

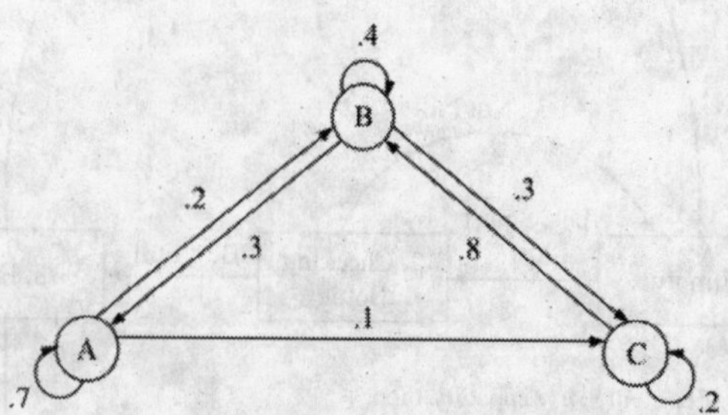

(*a*) Draw a figure corresponding to this transition matrix:

$$\begin{array}{c} \\ A \\ B \\ C \\ D \end{array} \begin{array}{c} \begin{array}{cccc} A & B & C & D \end{array} \\ \begin{bmatrix} .25 & .15 & .2 & .4 \\ 0 & .5 & .5 & 0 \\ 0 & 0 & 1 & 0 \\ .3 & .4 & .1 & .2 \end{bmatrix} \end{array}$$

(*b*) Look closely at *C* is your figure. What do you notice that is strange about the way information flows near *C*? What effect do you think this might have on the long-range distribution of matter in this system?

5. Which of the following are transition matrices? Explain.

(*a*) $\begin{bmatrix} .4 & .3 & .3 \\ .2 & .4 & .4 \\ .6 & .1 & .3 \end{bmatrix}$

(*b*) $\begin{bmatrix} .2 & .3 & .5 \\ .6 & .1 & .2 \\ .7 & .1 & .3 \end{bmatrix}$

(*c*) $\begin{bmatrix} .25 & .15 & .3 & .4 \\ .5 & 0 & .15 & .3 \\ .15 & .35 & .4 & .2 \\ .1 & .5 & .2 & .2 \end{bmatrix}$

6. Which of these situation can be modelled by a homogeneous Markov Chain? If they cannot be modelled by a Markov chain, explain the reason behind it.

(*a*) The figure represents the probability that a delivery truck that is currently in region *i*(*A*, *B*, or *C*) will be in region *j*(*A*, *B*, or *C*) for the next time period.

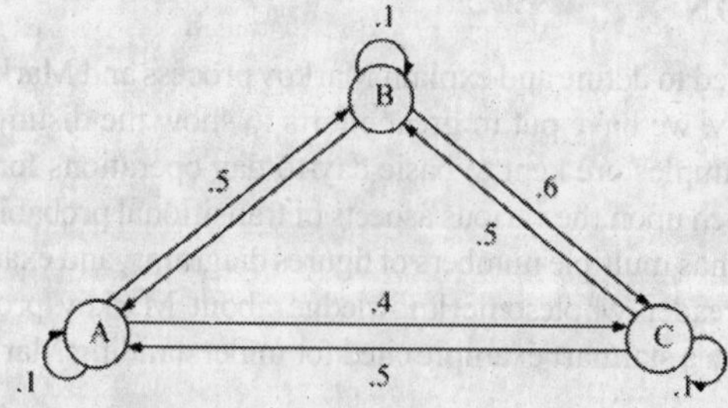

(*b*) The figure represents the probability that a person eating meal *i*(*H*, *S*, or *P*) for lunch today will eat meal *j*(*H*, *S*, or *P*) for lunch tomorrow. The letter *H* stands for hamburger, *S* stands for salad, and *P* stands for Pizza.

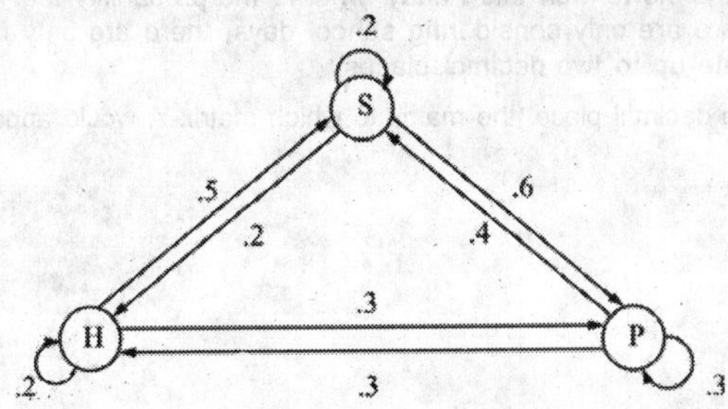

7. Look at the question in problem 4. Write a sample transition matrix for the problem or problem that can be modeled using a Markov chain. Assume *S* is the transition matrix

$$\begin{array}{c} \\ A \\ B \\ C \end{array}\begin{array}{c} \begin{array}{ccc} A & B & C \end{array} \\ \begin{bmatrix} .2 & .3 & .5 \\ .4 & .4 & .2 \\ .4 & .6 & 0 \end{bmatrix} \end{array}$$

(*a*) What is the probability of going form state *A* to state *B* in one step?

(*b*) What is the probability of going from state *B* to state *C* in exactly two steps?

(*c*) What is the probability of going from state *C* to state *A* in exactly three steps?

(*d*) Give the transition matrix, *S* for two steps (S_2 would give the probabilities of going from state *i* to stage *j* in exactly 2 steps).

(*e*) Give the transition matrix for three steps.

(*f*) Give the transition matrix for four steps.

(*g*) To what matrix do these transition matrices appear to converge after a large number of steps? Your solution should be accurate to two decimal places.

8. A math teacher, not wanting to be predictable, decided to assign homework based on probabilities. On the first day of class, she drew this figure on the board to tell the students whether to expect a full assignment, a partial assignment or no assignment on next day.

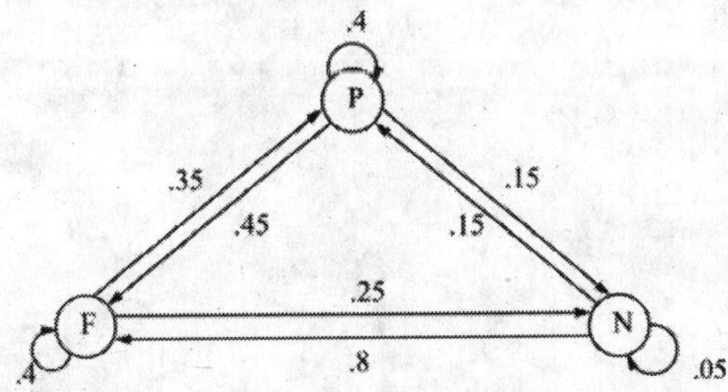

(*a*) Construct and label the transition matrix that corresponds to this drawing. Label it *A*.

(*b*) If students have a full assignment today, what is the probability that they will have a full assignment again tomorrow?

(*c*) If students have no assignment today, what is the probability that they will have no assignment again tomorrow?

(*d*) Today is Wednesday and students have a partial assignment. What is the probability that they will have no homework on Friday?

(*e*) Matrix A is the transition matrix for one day. Find the transition matrix for two days (for example, if today is Monday, what are the chances of getting each kind of assignment on Wednesday?

(*f*) Find the transition matrix for three days.

(*g*) If you have no homework on this Friday, what is the probability that you will have no homework next Friday (since we are only considering school days, there are only five days in a week)? Give your answer accurate up to two decimal places.

(h) Find, up to two decimal place, the matrix to which matrix *A* would appear to converge after many days.

Chapter

13

Dynamic Programming

13.1 INTRODUCTION

Many decision-making problems involve a process that takes place in such a way that at each stage, the process is dependent on the strategy chosen. Such type of a problem is called Dynamic Programming Problem (D.P.P.) Thus, D.P.P. is concerned with the theory of multistage decision process. Mathematically, a D.P.P. is a decision-making problem in *n* variables, the problem being sub-divided into *n* subproblems (segments), each subproblem being a decision-making problem in one variable only. The solution to a D.P.P. is achieved sequentially, starting from one (initial) stage and moving to the next, till the final stage is reached.

13.2 DECISION TREE AND BELLMAN'S PRINCIPLE OF OPTIMALITY

A multistage decision system in which each decision and state variables can take only finite number of values which can be represented graphically by a **decision tree**.

Stage 1

Stage 2

Stage 3

Circles represent nodes corresponding to stages, and lines between circles denote arcs, corresponding to decisions. The dynamic programming technique deals with such situations by dividing the given problem into sub-problems or stages.

Bellman's principle of optimality states that 'An optimal policy (a set of decisions) has the property that whatever the initial state and decisions are, the remaining decisions must constitute an optimal policy with regard to the state resulting from the first decision.'

The problem that does not satisfy the principle of optimality cannot be solved by the dynamic programming method.

13.2.1 Characteristics of DPP

The basic features which characterize the dynamic programming problem are as follows:

(*i*) The problem can be divided into stages, with a policy decision required at each stage.
(*ii*) Every stage consists of a number of states associated with it. The states are the different possible conditions in which the system may find itself at that stage of the problem.
(*iii*) Decision at each stage converts the current stage into the state associated with the next stage.
(*iv*) The state of the system at a given stage is described by a set of variables called 'state variables'.
(*v*) When the current state is known, an optimal policy for the remaining stages is independent of the policy of the previous ones.
(*vi*) The solution procedure begins by finding the optimal policy for each state, from the first to the last stage.
(*vii*) A recursive relationship occurs, which identifies the optimal policy for each state with n stages remaining, given the optimal policy for each state with $(n-1)$ stages left.
(*viii*) Using recursive equation approach, each time the solution procedure moves backwards for obtaining the optimum policy of each state for the particular stage, till it attains the optimum policy beginning at the initial stage.

***Note*:** A stage may be defined as the portion of the problem that possesses a set of mutually exclusive alternatives from which the best alternative is to be selected.

13.3 DYNAMIC PROGRAMMING ALGORITHM

The solution of a multistage problem by dynamic programming involves the following steps:

Step 1 Identify the decision variables and specify the objective function to be optimized under certain limitations, if any.

Step 2 Decompose the given problem into a number of smaller subproblems. Identify the state variable at each stage.

Step 3 Write down the general recursive relationship for computing the optimal policy. Decide whether forward or backward method is to be followed to solve the problem.

Step 4 Construct appropriate stages to show the required values of the return function at each stage.

Step 5 Determine the overall optimal policy or decisions and its value at each stage. There may be more than one such optimal policies.

Remarks

1. Generally the solution of a recursive equation involves two types of computations depending upon whether the system is continuous or discrete. In the first case, the optimal decision at each stage is obtained by using the usual classical method of optimization. In the second case, a tabular computational scheme is followed.
2. The D.P.P. is solved by using the recursive equation, starting from the first to the last stage, i.e., obtaining the sequence $f_1, f_2, f_3 \dots f_n$ of the optimal solution. This computation is called the 'forward computational procedure'. If the recursive equations are formulated to obtain a sequence $f_n, f_{n-1}, \dots f_1$, then the computation is known as the 'backward computational procedure'.

13.3.1 Applications of Dynamic Programming

Dynamic programming has more applications in small scale systems. Following are a few of the fields in which D.P. has been successfully applied.

(*i*) *Production:* This technique has been used in production, scheduling and employment, proving successful in the face of widely fluctuating demand requirements.

(*ii*) *Inventory control:* It is used to determine the optimum inventory level and for formulating the inventory recording rules, indicating when to replenish an item and by what amount.

(*iii*) *Allocation of resources:* It has been employed for allocating the scarce resources to different alternative uses, such as allocating salesmen to different sales zones and for capital budgeting procedures.

(*iv*) Spare part level determination to guarantee high efficiency utilization of expensive equipments.

(*v*) It is used to determine the best combination of advertising media (T.V., Radio, Newspaper) within a certain constraint to maximize the expected sales.

(*vi*) It is helpful in systematic planning or search to discover the whereabouts of a valuable resource.

(*vii*) It is used in cargo loading problems.

(*viii*) It is used in optimal sub-dividing problems.

(*ix*) It is used to solve the shortest path or stagecoach problems.

(*x*) It is used in capital budgeting problems, for maximizing profits over the long term.

Difference between Linear and Dynamic Programming

Dynamic Programming	*Linear Programming*
(*i*) It is a multistage decision-making process that spans time intervals. However, the intervals may consist only of stages in which the problem is solved.	(*i*) It gives a solution that will pertain only to one time period within given capacity, quantity and cost constraints.
(*ii*) It is similar to calculus.	(*ii*) It is similar to solving sets of simultaneous linear equations.
(*iii*) It permits one to determine the optimal decisions for future time periods, regardless of any earlier decisions.	(*iii*) It requires constant updating of values obtained, in order to reflect the current constraints necessary for an optimal answer.
(*iv*) It uses whatever mathematics is deemed to be appropriate for the solution of the problem.	(*iv*) In this case, certain rules must always be followed in the iterative G.P. process.
(*v*) Computation technique is not easy.	(*v*) Computation technique is easier.

Example 13.1 Use the principle of optimality to find the maximum value of $Z = b_1 x_1 + b_2 x_2 + \ldots + b_n x_n$

when,
$$x_1 + x_2 + x_3 + \ldots + x_n = C$$
$$x_1, x_2, \ldots x_n \geq 0$$

Solution The problem can be considered to divide the positive quantity C in n parts $x_1, x_2 \ldots x_n$ so that $b_1 x_1 + b_2 x_2 + \ldots + b_n x_n$ is maximum.

Let $f_n(c) = b_1 x_1 + b_2 x_2 + \ldots + b_n x_n$.

Recursive equation

If Z_i be the ith part ($i = 1, 2 \ldots n$) of the quantity, then the recursive equations of the problem are,

$$f_1(x_1) = \text{Max}\ b_1 Z_1 = b_1 x_1$$
$$Z_1 = x_1$$

and
$$f_i(x_i) = \text{Max}\ [b_i Z_i + f_{i-1}(x_i - Z_i)]$$
$$0 \leq Z_i \leq x_i\ [\text{where } i = 1, 2 \ldots n]$$

Solution of Recursive Equations

For one stage problem $i = 1$,

$$f_1(x_1) = b_1 x_1$$

This gives, $f_1(C) = b_1 C$ which is trivially true.

For two stage problem, where $i = 1, 2$

$$f_2(x_2) = \text{Max}\ [b_2 Z_2 + f_1(x_2 - Z_2)]$$
$$0 \leq Z_2 \leq x_2$$
$$f_2(C) = \text{Max}\ [b_2 Z_2 + f_1(C - Z)]$$
$$0 \leq Z_2 \leq C$$

for $x_2 = C_1, Z_2 = Z$

$$= \text{Max}\ [b_2 Z + b_1(C - Z)]$$
$$0 \leq Z \leq C$$
$$= \text{Max}\ [(b_2 - b_1) Z + b_1 C]$$
$$0 \leq Z \leq C$$

If $b_2 - b_1$ is positive then this is maximum for $Z = C$, otherwise, it will be minimum.

Thus $f_2(C) = b_2 C$

Similarly for three stage problem ($i = 1, 2, 3$)

$$f_3(x_3) = \text{Max}\ [b_3 Z_3 + f_2(x_3 - Z_3)]$$
$$0 \leq Z_3 \leq x_3$$
$$f_3(C) = \text{Max}\ [b_3 Z + f_2(C - Z)]$$
$$0 \leq Z \leq C$$
$$= \text{Max}\ [b_3 Z + b_2(C - Z)]$$
$$0 \leq Z \leq C$$
$$= \text{Max}\ [(b_3 - b_2) C + b_2 C]$$
$$0 \leq Z \leq C$$

Again if $b_3 - b_2$ is positive, then it gives maximum value for $Z = C$ otherwise, it gives the minimum value.

Thus, $f_3(C) = b_3 C$

From the results of the three stages 1, 2, 3, it can be easily shown by induction method that,

$$f_n(C) = b_n C$$

Hence, the optimal policy will be,

$(0, 0, 0 \ldots x_n = C)$ with $f_n(C) = b_n C$

Example 13.2 Use dynamic programming to show that,

$$Z = p_1 \log p_1 + p_2 \log p_2 + ... + p_n \log p_n$$

Subject to the constraints, $p_1 + p_2 + ... + p_n = 1$ and

$P_j \geq 0\ (j = 1, 2 ... n)$ is minimum. Where, $p_1 = p_2 = ... p_n = \dfrac{1}{n}$

Solution The problem here is to divide unity into n parts so as to minimize the quantity

$$Z = \Sigma\, p_i \log p_i$$

Let $f_n(1)$ denotes the minimum attainable sum of

$$p_i \log p_i (i = 1, 2 ... n)$$

For $n = 1$ (**Stage 1**)

$$f_1(1) = \underset{0 < x \leq 1}{\text{Min}}\ (p_1 \log p_1) = 1 \log 1$$

as unity is divided only into $p_1 = 1$ part

For $n = 2$, the unity is divided into two parts p_1 and p_2 such that $p_1 + p_2 = 1$

If $p_1 = x, p_2 = 1 - x$, then

$$f_2(1) = \underset{0 \leq x \leq 1}{\text{Min}}\ (p_1 \log p_1 + p_2 \log p_2)$$

$$= \underset{0 \leq x \leq 1}{\text{Min}}\ [x \log x + (1 - x) \log (1 - x)]$$

$$= \underset{0 < x \leq 1}{\text{Min}}\ [x \log x + f_1 (1 - x)]$$

In general, for an n stage problem, the recursive equation is,

$$f_n(1) = \underset{0 \leq x \leq 1}{\text{Min}}\ (p_1 \log p_1 + p_2 \log p_2 + ... + p_n \log p_n)$$

$$= \underset{0 \leq x \leq 1}{\text{Min}}\ [x \log x + f_1 (1 - x)]$$

We can solve this recursive equation,

For $n = 2$, (**Stage 2**)

The function $x \log x + (1 - x) \log (1 - x)$ attains its minimum value at

$$x = \frac{1}{2}, \text{ satisfying the condition } 0 < x \leq 1$$

$$f_2(1) = \frac{1}{2} \log \frac{1}{2} + \left(1 - \frac{1}{2}\right) \log \left(1 - \frac{1}{2}\right) = 2\left(\frac{1}{2} \log \frac{1}{2}\right)$$

Similarly for stage 3, the minimum value of the recursive equation is obtained as,

$$f_3(1) = \underset{0 \leq x \leq 1}{\text{Min}}\ [x \log x + f_2 (1 - x)]$$

$$= \underset{0 \leq x \leq 1}{\text{Min}} \left[x \log x + 2\left(\frac{1 - x}{2}\right) \log \left(\frac{1 - x}{2}\right) \right]$$

Now, since the minimum value of

$$x \log x + 2\left(\frac{1-x}{2}\right)\log\left(\frac{1-x}{2}\right) \text{ is attained at } x = \frac{1}{3}, \text{ satisfying } 0 < x \leq 1$$

we have, $$f_3(1) = \frac{1}{3}\log\frac{1}{3} + 2\left(\frac{1}{3}\log\frac{1}{3}\right) = 3\left(\frac{1}{3}\log\frac{1}{3}\right)$$

$\therefore$ optimal policy is $P_1 = P_2 = P_3 = \frac{1}{3}$

In general, for n stage problem, we assume the optimal policy to be,

$$P_1 = P_2 = \ldots P_n = \frac{1}{n} \text{ and } f_n(1) = n\left[\frac{1}{n}\log\frac{1}{n}\right]$$

This can be shown easily using mathematical induction.

For $n = m + 1$, the recursive equation is,

$$f_{m+1}(1) = \underset{0 \leq x \leq 1}{\text{Min}}\ [x \log x + f_m(1-x)]$$

$$= \underset{0 \leq x \leq 1}{\text{Min}}\left[x \log x + m\left(\frac{1-x}{m}\right)\log\left(\frac{1-x}{m}\right)\right]$$

$$= \frac{1}{m+1}\log\frac{1}{m+1} + m\left(\frac{1}{m+1}\log\frac{1}{m+1}\right)$$

$$= (m+1)\left(\frac{1}{m+1}\log\frac{1}{m+1}\right)$$

Since, minimum $x \log x + \frac{1-x}{x}\log\frac{1-x}{m}$ is attained at $x = \frac{1}{m+1}$.

Hence, the required optimum policy is $\left(\frac{1}{n}, \frac{1}{n}, \ldots \frac{1}{n}\right)$ with $f_n(1) = n\left(\frac{1}{n}\log\frac{1}{n}\right)$.

Example 13.3 Minimize $Z = Y_1^2 + Y_2^2 + Y_3^2$

Subject to, $Y_1 + Y_2 + Y_3 \geq 15$,

$Y_1, Y_2, Y_3 \geq 0$.

Solution Since the decision variables are Y_1, Y_2, Y_3, the given problem is a three stage problem defined as follows:

$$S_3 = Y_1 + Y_2 + Y_3 \geq 15$$
$$S_2 = Y_1 + Y_2 = S_3 - Y_3$$
$$S_1 = Y_1 = S_2 - Y_2$$

and $$f_3(S_3) = \underset{Y_3}{\text{Min}}\ (Y_3^2 + F_2(S_2))$$

$$f_2(S_2) = \underset{Y_2}{\text{Min}}\left[Y_2^2 + F_1(S_1)\right]$$

$$f_1(S_1) = Y_1^2 = (S_2 - Y_2)^2$$

Thus,
$$f_2(S_2) = \underset{Y_2}{\text{Min}}\left[Y_2^2 + (S_2 - Y_2)^2\right]$$

$Y_2^2 + (S_2 - Y_2)^2$ is minimum, if its derivative, w.r.t., Y_2 is zero.

$$2Y_2 - 2(S_2 - Y_2) = 0$$

Which gives
$$Y_2 = \frac{S_2}{2}$$

Hence,
$$f_2(S_2) = \frac{S_2^2}{2}$$

Now,
$$f_3(S_3) = \underset{Y_3}{\text{Min}}\left[Y_3^2 + f_2(S_2)\right]$$

$$= \underset{Y_3}{\text{Min}}\left[Y_3^2 + \frac{1}{2}(S_3 - Y_3)^2\right]$$

or
$$f_3(15) = \underset{Y_3 \le 15}{\text{Min}}\left[Y_3^2 + \frac{1}{2}(15 - Y_3)^2\right] \qquad [\therefore S_3 (Y_1 + Y_2 + Y_3) \ge 15]$$

Since the minimum value of the function,

$$Y_3^2 + \frac{1}{2}(15 - Y_3)^2 \text{ occurs for } Y_3 = 5$$

$\Rightarrow$
$$f_3(15) = 5^2 + \frac{1}{2}(15 - 5)^2 = 75$$

Thus,
$$S_3 = 15 \Rightarrow Y_3^* = 5$$

$$S_2 = S_3 - Y_3 = 15 - 5 = 10 \Rightarrow Y_2^* = \frac{S_2}{2} = 5$$

$$S_1 = S_2 - Y_2 = 10 - 5 = 5$$

$\Rightarrow$
$$Y_1^* = S_1 = 5$$

Hence, the optimal policy is

$$(5, 5, 5) \text{ with } f_3^*(Y_3) = 75.$$

Example 13.4 Use dynamic programming to solve

Maximum $Z = Y_1 \,.\, Y_2 \,.\, Y_3$

Subject to constraints,

$$Y_1 + Y_2 + Y_3 = 5$$

and
$$Y_1, Y_2, Y_3 \ge 0$$

Solution Since there are 3 decision variables, the given problem is a 3 stage problem, with the state variables S_1, S_2, S_3 defined as,

$$S_3 = Y_1 + Y_2 + Y_3 = 5$$
$$S_2 = Y_1 + Y_2 + = S_3 - Y_3$$
$$S_1 = Y_1 = S_2 - Y_2$$

The recursive equations are,

$$f_1(S_1) = \underset{0 \le Y_1 \le x_1}{\text{Max}} (Y_1) = S_1 = (S_2 - Y_2)$$
$$f_2(S_2) = \text{Max}(Y_1 \cdot Y_2) = \underset{0 \le Y_2 \le x_2}{\text{Max}} (Y_2 \cdot f_1(S_1))$$
$$0 \le Y_2 \le x_2$$
$$f_3(S_3) = \underset{0 \le Y_3 \le x_3}{\text{Max}} (Y_1 \cdot Y_2 \cdot Y_3)$$
$$= \underset{0 \le Y_3 \le x_3}{\text{Max}} (Y_3 \cdot f_2(S_2))$$

To solve the recursive equation,

$$f_1(S_1) = S_2 - Y_2 = S_1$$
$$f_2(S_2) = \underset{0 \le Y_2 \le x_2}{\text{Max}} (Y_2 f_1(S_1))$$
$$= \underset{0 \le Y_2 \le x_2}{\text{Max}} (Y_2 \cdot f_1(S_2 - Y_2)) \qquad (\because S_1 = S_2 - Y_2)$$
$$= \underset{0 \le Y_2 \le x_2}{\text{Max}} (Y_2 (S_2 - Y_2))$$

The function $Y_2(S_2 - Y_2)$ will attain its maximum at $Y_2 = \dfrac{S_2}{2}$

$$\therefore \qquad f_2(Y_2) = \underset{0 \le Y_2 \le x_2}{\text{Max}} (Y_2 (S_2 - Y_2))$$
$$= \frac{S_2}{2}\left(S_2 - \frac{S_2}{2}\right) = \left(\frac{S_2}{2}\right)^2$$
$$f_3(S_3) = \underset{0 \le Y_3 \le x_3}{\text{Max}} (Y_3 . f_2(S_2))$$
$$= \underset{0 \le Y_3 \le x_3}{\text{Max}} (Y_3 . f_2(S_3 - Y_3)) \qquad (\because S_2 = S_3 - Y_3)$$
$$= \underset{0 \le Y_3 \le x_3}{\text{Max}} \left(Y_3 \left(\frac{S_3 - Y_3}{2} \right)^2 \right)$$

The function $Y_3\left(\dfrac{S_3 - Y_3}{2}\right)^2$ will attain its maximum when $Y_3 = \dfrac{S_3}{3}$

$$\therefore \qquad f_3(S_3) = \frac{S_3}{3}\left(\frac{S_3 - \frac{S_3}{3}}{2}\right)^2 = \left(\frac{S_3}{3}\right)^3$$

But $$S_3 = 5 \Rightarrow Y_3 = \frac{S_3}{3} = \frac{5}{3}$$

$$S_2 = S_3 - Y_3 = 5 - \frac{5}{3} = \frac{10}{3} \Rightarrow Y_2 = \frac{Y_2}{2} = \frac{10}{3 \times 2} = \frac{5}{3}$$

$$S_1 = S_2 - Y_2 = \frac{10}{3} - \frac{5}{3} = \frac{5}{3}$$

$$Y_1 = S_1 = \frac{5}{3}$$

and $$f_3(S_3) = f_3(5) = \left(\frac{5}{3}\right)^3 = \frac{125}{27} = \text{Max } Z.$$

$\therefore$ The optimal policy is $\left(\frac{5}{3}, \frac{5}{3}, \frac{5}{3}\right)$ and Max $Z = \frac{125}{27}$.

Example 13.5 A student has to take examinations in three courses *X*, *Y* and *Z*. He has three days available for study. He feels it would be best to devote a whole day to study the same course, so that he may study a course for one day, two days, three days or not at all. The estimate of grades he may get by studying in this manner are as follows:

Study days/Course	*x*	*y*	*z*
0	1	2	1
1	2	2	2
2	2	4	4
3	4	5	4

How should he plan to study so that he maximizes the sum of his grades?

Solution Let n_1, n_2 and n_3 be the number of days he should study the courses *x*, *y* and *z* respectively. If $f_1(n_1), f_2(n_2), f_3(n_3)$ be the grades earned by such a study then the problem becomes,

Max $Z = f_1(n_1) + f_2(n_2) + f_3(n_3)$

Subject to, $n_1 + n_2 + n_3 \leq 3$ and integers.

Here n_j are the decision variables and $t_j(n_j)$ are the corresponding return functions for $j = 1, 2, 3$. Now, introducing state variables S_j as follows:

$$S_3 = n_1 + n_2 + n_3 \leq 3$$
$$S_2 = n_1 + n_2 = S_3 - n_3$$
$$S_1 = n_1 = S_2 - n_2$$

Thus, state transformation function is defined as,

$$S_{j-1} = T_j(S_j, n_j) \text{ where, } j = 2, 3$$

Recursive equations applicable here are,

$$F_j(S_j) = \underset{n_j}{\text{Max}} [f_j(n_j) + F_{j-1}(S_j - 1)] \text{ where, } j = 2, 3$$

or $$F_1(S_1) = f_1(n_1)$$

where, $$F_3(S_3) = \underset{n_1, n_2, n_3}{\text{Max}} [f_1(n_1) + f_2(n_2) + f_3(n_3)]$$

for any feasible value of S_3. Then the required solution would become,

$$\underset{S_2}{\text{Max}}\, f_3(S_3)$$

Recursive operations leading to the answer are tabulated as follows:

S_2 \ n_2	$f_2(n_2)$				$F_1(S_1) = f_1(n_1)$				$f_2(n_2) + F_1(S_1)$				$F_2(S_2)$
	0	1	2	3	0	1	2	3	0*	1	2	3	
0	2	–	–	–	1	–	–	–	3	–	–	–	3
1	[2]	2	–	–	[2]	1	–	–	[4]	3	–	–	[4]
2	2	2	4	–	2	2	1	–	4	4	5	–	5
3	2	2	4	5	4	2	2	1	6	4	6	6	6
	$f_3(n_3)$				$F_2(S_2) = f_2(n_2)$				$f_3(n_3) + F_2(S_2)$				$F_3(S_3)$
S_2 \ n_2	0	1	2	3	0	1	2	3	0	1	2*	3	
0	1	–	–	–	3	–	–	–	4	–	–	–	4
1	1	2	–	–	4	3	–	–	5	5	–	–	5
2	1	2	4	–	5	4	3	–	6	6	7	–	7
3	1	2	[4]	4	6	5	[4]	3	7	7	[8]	7	[8]

Stage returns $f_j(n_j)$

j \ n_j	0	1*	2	3
1	1	[2]	2	4
2	2	2	4	5
3	1	2	4	4

Stage transformation S_{j-1}

$j = 2, 3$

S_j \ n_j	0	1	2	3
0	0	–	–	–
1	1	0	–	–
2	2	1	0	–
3	3	2	1	0

Proceeding backwards through enclosed type numbers, the optimal policy is obtained as $n_3 = 2$, $n_2 = 0$, $n_1 = 1$, keeping in view $n_1 + n_2 + n_3 \leq 3$.

The required maximum return is 8.

***Example 13.6* (Product allocation problem)** The owner of a chain of four grocery stores has purchased six crates of fresh strawberries. The estimated probability distribution of potential sales of the strawberries before spoilage differ among the four stores. The following table gives the estimated total expected profit at each store when various number of crates are allocated to it. For administrative reasons, the owner does not wish to split crates between stores. However, he is willing to distribute zero crates to any of his stores. Find the allocation of six crates to four stores so as to maximize the expected profit.

Number of Crates	Stores			
	1	2	3	4
0	0	0	0	0
1	4	2	6	2
2	6	4	8	3
3	7	6	8	4
4	7	8	8	4
5	7	9	8	4
6	7	10	8	4

Solution Let the four stores be considered as four stages in a dynamic programming formulation. The decision variables x_j ($j = 1, 2, 3, 4$) denote the number of crates allocated as the jth stage from the previous one.

Now let $P_j(x_j)$ be the expected profit from allocation of x_j crates to store j. The problem can be formulated as LPP,

Max $Z = P_1(x_1) + P_2(x_2) + P_3(x_3) + P_4(x_4)$

Subject to, $$x_1 + x_2 + x_3 + x_4 = 6$$
$$x_1, x_2, x_3, x_4 \geq 0$$

Let there be S crates available for j remaining stores and x_j be the initial allocation. Define $f_j(x_j)$ as the value of the optimal allocation for stores 1 through 4 both inclusive.

Thus, for stage $j = 1$

$$f_1(S_1, x_1) = P_1(x_1)$$

If $f_j(S, x_j)$ be the profit associated with the optimum solution.

$f_j{}^*(S)$ where, $$j = 1, 2, 3, 4$$

Then, $$f_1{}^*(S) = \text{Max } P_1(x_1)$$
$$0 \leq x_1 \leq S$$

Thus the recurrence relation is,

$$f_j(S, x_j) = P_j(x_j) + f_{j+1}(S - x_j)$$

where, $$j = 1, 2, 3, 4$$

and, $$f_j(S) = \text{Max } [P_j(x_j) + f_{j+1}(S - x_j)]$$
$$0 \leq x_1 \leq S$$

The solution to this problem starts with $f_4{}^*(S)$ and is completed when $f_1{}^*(S)$ is obtained. The computations for one stage problem $j = 1$, are as follows:

S	$f_4{}^*(S)$	$x_4{}^*$
0	0	0
1	2	1
2	3	2
3	4	3
4	4	3, 4
5	4	3, 4, 5
6	4	3, 4, 5, 6

For $j = 2$, we have a two stage problem. The computations are as follows:

$$f_3(S_1, x_3) = P_3(x_3) + f_3^*(S - x_3)$$

S \ x_3	0	1	2	3	4	5	6	$f_3^*(S)$	x_3^*
	00 + 0							0	0
1	0 + 2	6 + 0						6	1
2	0 + 3	6 + 2	8 + 0					8	1, 2
3	0 + 4	6 + 3	8 + 2	8 + 0				10	2
4	0 + 4	6 + 4	8 + 3	8 + 2	8 + 0			11	2
5	0 + 4	6 + 4	8 + 4	8 + 3	8 + 2	8 + 0		12	2
6	0 + 4	6 + 4	8 + 4	8 + 4	8 + 3	8 + 2	8 + 0	12	2, 3

For $j = 3$, we have three stage problem,

$$f_2(S, x_2) = P_2(x_2) + f_3^*(S - x_2)$$

S \ x_2	0	1	2	3	4	5	6	$f_2^*(S)$	x_2^*
0	0 + 6							0	0
1	0 + 6	2 + 0						6	0
2	0 + 8	2 + 6	4 + 0					8	0, 1
3	0 + 10	2 + 8	4 + 6	6 + 0				10	0, 1, 2
4	0 + 11	2 + 10	4 + 8	6 + 6	8 + 0			12	1, 2, 3
5	0 + 12	2 + 11	4 + 10	6 + 8	8 + 6	9 + 0		14	2, 3, 4
6	0 + 12	2 + 12	4 + 11	6 + 8	8 + 8	9 + 6	10 + 0	16	3, 4

For $j = 4$, we have the required four stage problem,

$$f_1(S, x_1) = P_1(x_1) + f_2^*(S - x_1)$$

S \ x_1	0	1	2	3	4	5	6	$f_2^*(S)$	x_2^*
6	0 + 16	4 + 14	6 + 12	7 + 10	7 + 8	7 + 6	7 + 0	18	1, 2

From the above computation, it is observed that the maximum profit of ₹ 18 can be obtained by choosing the following eight alternative solutions.

Store 1	*Store 2*	*Store 3*	*Store 4*
1	2	2	1
1	3	1	1
1	3	2	0
1	4	1	0
2	1	2	1
2	2	1	1
2	2	2	0
2	3	1	0

13.3.2 Solution of LPP by Dynamic Programming

Consider the general LPP.

$$\text{Max } Z = C_1 x_1 + C_2 + x_2 + \ldots + C_n x_n$$

Subject to the constraints,

$$a_{i1} x_1 + a_{i2} x_2 + \ldots + a_{in} x_n \le b_i \text{ where, } i = 1, 2 \ldots m$$

and, $x_j \ge 0$ where $j = 1, 2 \ldots n$.

The problem can be formulated as a dynamic programming problem as follows.

Let the general LPP be considered as a multistage problem with each activity j ($j = 1, 2 \ldots m$) as an individual stage. Then this is a n stage problem and the decision variables are the level of activities $x_j (\ge 0)$ at stage j. As x_j is continuous, each activity has an infinite number of alternatives within the feasible region.

We know that allocation problems are a particular type of LPP. These problems require the allocation of available resources to the activities. Each constraint represents the limitation of different resources and $b_1, b_2 \ldots b_m$ are the amounts of available resources. Since there are m resources, states must be represented by an m-dimensional vector, given by $(\beta_1, \beta_2 \ldots \beta_m)$.

Let $f_n(\beta_1, \beta_2 \ldots \beta_m)$ be the maximum value of the general LPP defined for stages $x_1, x_2 \ldots x_n$ for states $(b_1, b_2 \ldots b_m)$ using forward recursive equation, that is,

$$f_j(\beta_1\, \beta_2 \ldots \beta_m) = \max_{0 \le x_j \le \beta} (C_j x_j + f_{j-1}(\beta_1 - a_{1j} x_2, \beta_2 - a_{2j} x_j \ldots \beta_m - a_{mj} x_j)$$

The maximum value of β that x_j can assume is, $\beta = \text{Min}\left\{\frac{b_1}{a_{1j}}, \frac{b_2}{a_{2j}} \ldots \frac{b_m}{a_{mj}}\right\}$ because the minimum value satisfies the set of constraints simultaneously.

Example 13.7 Use dynamic programming to solve the following LPP,

$$\text{Max } Z = 3x_1 + 5x_2$$

Subject to the constraints,

$$x_1 \le 4$$
$$x_2 \le 6,$$
$$3x_1 + 2x_2 \le 18$$
$$x_1, x_2 \ge 0$$

Solution The problem consists of three resources and two decision variables. Hence the problem has two stages and three state variables.

Let B_{1j}, B_{2j}, B_{3j} be the state of the system at stage j and f_j (B_{1j}, B_{2j}, B_{3j}) be the optimal (maximum) value of the objective function for state $j = 1, 2$ given the state (B_{1j}, B_{2j}, B_{3j}). Using backward computation procedure, we have

$$f_2(B_{12}, B_{22}, B_{23}) = \text{Max } [5x_2]$$
$$0 \le x_2 \le P_{22}$$
$$0 \le 2x_2 \le P_{32}$$
$$= 5 \text{ Max } (x_2)$$
$$0 \le x_2 \le \beta_{22}$$
$$0 \le x_2 \le \frac{\beta_{32}}{2}$$

Since Max x_2, which satisfies $0 \le x_2 \le \beta_{22}$,

$$0 \le x_2 \le \frac{\beta_{32}}{2} \text{ is the minimum of } \left(\beta_{22}, \frac{\beta_{32}}{2}\right)$$

i.e.,
$$\text{Max}\,(x_2) = x_2^* = \text{Min}\left(\beta_{22}, \frac{\beta_{32}}{2}\right) \quad (1)$$

$$\therefore \quad f_2(\beta_{12}, \beta_{22}, \beta_{32}) = 5\,\text{Min}\left(\beta_{22}, \frac{\beta_{32}}{2}\right) \quad (2)$$

Also,

$$f_1(\beta_{11}, \beta_{21}, \beta_{31}) = \text{Max}\,[3x_1 + f_2(\beta_{11} - x_1, \beta_{21} - 0, \beta_{31} - 3x_1)]$$
$$0 \le x_1 \le \beta_{11}$$
$$0 \le 3x_1 \le \beta_{31}$$

From $f_2(\beta_{11} - x_1, \beta_{21} - 0, \beta_{31} - 3x_1) = 5\,\text{Min}\left(\beta_{21}, \dfrac{\beta_{31} - 3x_1}{2}\right)$

$$\therefore \quad f_1(\beta_{11}, \beta_{21}, \beta_{31}) = \text{Max}\left[3x_1 + 5\,\text{Min}\left(\beta_{21}, \frac{\beta_{31} - 3x_1}{2}\right)\right]$$
$$0 \le x_1 \le \beta_{11}$$
$$0 \le 3x_1 \le \frac{\beta_{31}}{3}$$

Since it is a two-stage problem, at the first stage

$$\beta_{11} = 4, \beta_{21} = 6, \beta_{31} = 18$$

$$\therefore \quad f_1(\beta_{11}, \beta_{21}, \beta_{31}) = \text{Max}\left\{3x_1 + 5\,\text{Min}\left(6, \frac{18 - 3x_1}{2}\right)\right\}$$
$$0 \le x_1 \le 4$$
$$0 \le x_1 \le 6$$
$$= \text{Max}\left\{3x_1 + 5\,\text{Min}\left(6, \frac{18 - 3x_1}{2}\right)\right\}$$
$$0 \le x_1 \le 4$$

Now,
$$\text{Min}\left(6, \frac{18 - 3x_1}{2}\right) = \begin{cases} 6 & \text{if } 0 \le x_1 \le 2 \\ \dfrac{18 - 3x_1}{2} & \text{if } 2 \le x_1 \le 4 \end{cases} \quad (3)$$
$$0 \le x_1 \le 4$$

From (3)

$$f_1(\beta_{11}, \beta_{21}, \beta_{31}) = \text{Max}\begin{cases} 3x_1 + 5(6) & \text{if } 0 \le x_1 \le 2 \\ 3x_1 + 5\left(\dfrac{18 - 3x_1}{2}\right) & \text{if } 2 \le x_1 \le 4 \end{cases}$$

Since, Max of $3x_1 + 30$, $0 \le x_1 \le 2$ occurs at $x_1 = 2$ and

Max of $\dfrac{90 - 9x_1}{2}$, $2 \le x_1 \le 4$ also occurs at $x_1 = 2$

$\therefore \quad f_1(\beta_{11}, \beta_{21}, \beta_{31}) = 3 \times 2 + 30 = 36$

Now, $\quad x_2 = \text{Min}\left\{\beta_{21}, \frac{\beta_{31} - 3x_1}{2}\right\}$

$$= \text{Min}\left\{6, \frac{18 - 3x_1}{2}\right\} = \text{Min}(6, 6) = 6$$

The optimal solution is, Max $Z = 36$, $x_1 = 2$, $x_2 = 6$.

Example 13.8 Use dynamic programming to solve the LPP

Max $Z = x_1 + 9x_2$

Subject to the constraints, $\quad 2x_1 + x_2 \leq 25$

$$x_2 \leq 11$$

$$x_1, x_2 \geq 0$$

Solution The problem has two resources and two decision variables. The states of the equivalent dynamic programming are $\beta_{1j}, \beta_{2j}, j = 1, 2$.

$$f_2(\beta_{12}, \beta_{22}) = \text{Max}(9x_2)$$

$$0 < x_2 \leq 25$$

$$0 \leq x_2 \leq 11$$

i.e., $\quad f_2(\beta_{12}, \beta_{22}) = 9\,\text{Max}(x_2)$

$$= 9\,\text{Max}(25, 11)$$

Since the Max of x_2 satisfying the conditions of $x_2 \leq 25$, $x_2 \leq 11$, is the Min of (25, 11)

$\therefore \quad x_2^* = 11$

Now, $\quad f_1(\beta_{11}, \beta_{21}) = \text{Max}\,[x_1 + f_2(\beta_{11} - 2x_1, \beta_{21} - 0)]$

$$0 \leq x_1 \leq \frac{25}{2}$$

At this last stage, substitute $\beta_{11} = 25$, $\beta_{21} = 11$

$$f_1(25, 11) = \text{Max}\,[x_1 + 9\,\text{Min}(25 - 2x_1, 11)]$$

$$\text{Min}(25 - 2x_1, 11) = \{11, 0 \leq x_1 \leq 7\}$$

$$25 - 2x_1, 7 \leq x_1 \leq \frac{25}{2}$$

$\therefore \quad x_1 + 9\,\text{Min}(25 - 2x_1, 11) = x_1 + 99, 0 \leq x_1 \leq 7$

$$225 - 17x_1, 7 \leq x_1 \leq \frac{25}{2}$$

Since the maximum of both $(x_1 + 99, 225 - 17x_1)$ occurs at $x_1 = 7$

$$f_1(25, 11) = 7 + 9\,\text{Min}(11, 11)$$

$$= 106 \text{ at } x_1^* = 7$$

$$x_1^* = \text{Min}(25–2x_1^*, 11) = \text{Min}(11, 11) = 11$$

Hence the optimum solution is,

$$x_1^* = 7, x_2^* = 11 \text{ and Max } Z = 106$$

Salesmen Allocation Problem

This problem deals with allocation in the case when a company has salesmen for marketing in different zones. The amount of sales depends upon the number of salesmen is each zone. The objective is to determine the optimum allocation of salesmen, in order to maximize the profit or total sales.

Example 13.9 A company has six salesmen and three market areas (*A*, *B* and *C*). It is asked to determine the number of salesmen to allocate to each market area, to maximize profit. The following table gives the profit from each market area as a function of the number of salesmen allocated. Use dynamic programming to determine the optimal solution.

No. of Salesmen

	0	*1*	*2*	*3*	*4*	*5*	*6*
Area *A*	38	41	48	58	66	72	83
Area *B*	40	42	50	60	66	75	82
Area *C*	60	64	68	78	90	102	109

Solution 1. The problem is of allocating salesmen to three marketing areas *A*, *B* and *C* in such a way that the total profits of the company are maximized. In this problem, the three areas are the stages and the number of salesmen are the state variables. The profit return corresponding to the different number of salesmen allocated to area *A* is shown in Table 13.1 below.

Table 13.1(*a*) Stage 1: Area *A*

No. of Salesmen	0	1	2	3	4	5	6
Profits	38	41	48	58	66	72	83

2. Consider the combination of area *A* and area *B* as stage 2. Enter the profit values of area *A* row-wise and area *B* column-wise, as shown in Table 13.1(b). Compute the combined profit values for all the possible combinations. For a particular number of salesmen, the profit values for different combinations can be read along the diagonal. Mark the maximum values along each diagonal by putting ∗ above the values.

Table 13.1(*b*) Stage 2: Area *B*

Area B / ***Area A***	***Salesmen***	***0***	***1***	***2***	***3***	***4***	***5***	***6***
Salesmen	Profit	40	42	50	60	66	75	82
0	38	78*	80	88*	98*	104	113*	120
1	41	81*	83	91	101	107	116	
2	48	88*	90	98	108	114		
3	58	98*	100	108	118			
4	66	106*	108	116				
5	72	112	114					
6	83	123*						

The optimum returns for the various combinations from Table 13.1(b) are,

No. of salesmen	0	1	2	3	4	5	6
Profit (A and B)	78	81	88	98	106	113	123

3. Now consider the combined area profit values for areas A and B. Enter these values in the row and enter the area C values in the column. Compute all the possible combinations and put these values in Table 13.1(c).

Table 13.1(c) Stage 3: Area C

Area B / *Area A and B*	*Salesmen*	*0*	*1*	*2*	*3*	*4*	*5*	*6*
Salesmen	Profit	60	64	68	78	90	102	109
0	78	138*	142*	146	156	168*	180*	187*
1	81	141	145	149	159	171	183	
2	88	148*	152	156	166	178		
3	98	158*	162	166	176			
4	106	166	170	174				
5	113	173	177					
6	123	183						

4. In the third stage, the maximum profit value of ₹ 187 is in the last diagonal. Corresponding to this value, the number of salesmen is 6 from area C and zero from the combined area A and B. Moving back to stage 2, corresponding to zero salesman, the profits for the areas A and B are ₹ 38 and ₹ 40 respectively.

Result

The optimal solution is,

Area	*Salesmen*	*Profit ₹*
A	0	38
B	0	40
C	6	109
Total	6	187

Example 13.10 A soft drink distributor takes the contract for the sale of soft drinks at a cricket stadium during a one-day match. He has five sales boys to assign to three areas of the stadium. The table shows the estimated sales that can be made with different assignments.

No. of persons assigned	*East stand*	*North stand*	*Club stand*
1	15	45	30
2	30	90	60
3	60	135	90
4	120	180	120
5	150	180	150

Using dynamic programming, determine how he should assign the boys in order to maximize his sales.

Solution

1. Since there are three areas, the problem has three stages and the state variables are five sales boys. The sales return corresponding to the various number of sales boys allocated to the east stand is shown in Table 13.1(*d*) below.

Table 13.1(*d*) Stage 1: East stand

No. of boys	0	1	2	3	4	5
Estimated sales	0	15	30	60	120	150

2. Consider the combination of east stand and north stand as stage 2. Enter the corresponding sales return in Table 13.2 and compute the combined sales revenue for all the possible combinations. Mark the maximum values along the diagonal.

Table 13.2 Stage 2 : North stand

North stand / *East stand*	*Salesmen*	*0*	*1*	*2*	*3*	*4*	*5*
No. of boys	Estimated sales	0	45	90	135	180	180
0	0	0	45*	90*	135*	180*	180
1	15	15	60	105	150	195*	
2	30	30	75	120	165		
3	60	60	105	150			
4	120	120	165				
5	150	150					

The optimum returns for the various combinations from Table 13.2 are,

No of boys	0	1	2	3	4	5
Estimated sales	0	45	90	135	180	195

3. Now consider the stand and north stand areas and enter these values row-wise. Enter the club stand values in the column. Compute all the possible combinations and put these values in Table 13.3.

Table 13.3 Stage 3: Club stand

Club stand / *East + North stand*	*No. of boys*	*0*	*1*	*2*	*3*	*4*	*5*
No. of boys	Estimated sales	0	30	60	90	120	150
0	0	0	30	60	90	120	150
1	45	45*	75	105	135	165	
2	90	90*	120	150	180		
3	135	135*	165	195			
4	180	180*	210*				
5	195	195					

4. In the third stage, the optimum expected sales value of ₹ 210 is in the last diagonal. Corresponding to this value, the number of boys in the club stand is 1 and his estimated sales is ₹ 30. The number of boys from the combined north and east stand is 4 and the corresponding sales values from stage 2 is ₹ 180. The number of boys in the east stand is 0 and the north stand is 4. The corresponding estimated sales are ₹ 0 and ₹ 180, respectively.

Result

The optimal solution is:

Area	*No. of boys assigned*	*Estimated sales in rupees*
East stand	0	0
North stand	4	180
Club stand	1	30
Total	5	210

Example 13.11 A student has to take examinations in three courses *A*, *B* and *C*. He has three days available for study. He feels it would be the best to devote a whole day to the study of the same course, so that he may study a course for one day, two days, three days or not at all. The estimates of grades he may get by study are as follows.

Study days \ *Course*	*A*	*B*	*C*
0	0	1	0
1	1	1	1
2	1	3	3
3	3	4	3

How should he plan to study so that he maximizes the sum of his grades? Use dynamic programming technique.

Solution

1. Since there are three courses, the problem has three stages and the stage variables are three days. The estimation of grades from course *A* is shown in Table 13.4 below.

Table 13.4 Stage 1: Course *A*

No. of study days	0	1	2	3
Estimated grades	0	1	1	3

2. Consider the combination of course *A* and *B* as stage 2. Enter the corresponding grades-return in table 2 and compute the combined grade values for all possible combinations. Mark the maximum values along the diagonal.

Table 13.5 Stage 2: Course *B*

Course B / *Course A*	*No. of days*	*0*	*1*	*2*	*3*
No. of days	Estimated grades	1	1	3	4
0	0	1*	1	3*	4*
1	1	2*	2	4*	
2	1	2	2		
3	3	4*			

The optimum returns for the various combinations from Table 13.5 are,

No. of days	0	1	2	3
Estimated grades	1	2	3	4

3. Now consider the combined course *A* and *B* and enter these values row-wise. Enter course *C* values in the column. Compute all the possible combinations and put these values in Table 13.6.

Table 13.6 Stage 3: Course *C*

Course B / *Course A*	*No. of days*	*0*	*1*	*2*	*3*
No. of days	Estimated grades	0	1	3	3
0	1	1*	2*	4*	4
1	2	2*	3	5*	
2	3	3	4		
3	4	4			

4. In the third stage, the optimum return is five in the last diagonal. The number of days corresponding to this grade in course *C* is two and the combined courses *A* and *B* is one. Moving back to Table 13.5, the number of days corresponding to course *A* and course *B* is one and zero respectively.

Result

The optimal solution is,

Course	*No. of study days*	*Estimated grades*
A	1	1
B	0	1
C	2	3
Total	3	5

Optimal Routing Problem

In this type of problem, a company has to transport goods from one city to another. The cost of transportation between the different cities will be given in a network. The objective is to determine the optimal route connecting the starting city to the destination city. In some problems, the distance between different cities will be given. Here the objective is to determine the shortest distance between the two cities.

Example 13.12 A salesman has to reach city No. 10 from city 1 by car. Though his starting and destination points are fixed, he has considerable choice as to which cities to travel through '*n*' routes. The cost c_{ij} (in appropriate units) on the car travel from city *i* to *j* is given as follows.

From city \ To	2	3	4
1	2	4	3

From city \ To	5	6	7
2	7	4	6
3	3	2	4
4	4	1	5

From city \ To	8	9
5	1	4
6	6	3
7	3	3

From city \ To	10
8	3
9	4

Find the route for which the total travelling cost is minimum?

Solution

1. Construct a network diagram. The nodes in the diagram represent the cities and the line connecting two cities represents the cost of travelling. The problem can be divided into four stages, i.e., $N = 4$. Let S represent the state. By backward pass approach, $f_N(S)$ = Minimum cost policy, when he is in state S with N more stages to go to reach his destination.

i.e.,
$$f_N(S) = \underset{S}{\text{Min}}\left[r(d_n) + f_{N-1}, \{T(S, d_n)\}\right].$$

2. Consider stage 1

$$f_1(S) = \underset{S}{\text{Min}}\left[r(d_1) + 0\right]$$

$$\delta = (8, 9)$$

$f_1(8)$ = 3, the salesman takes the path 8–10.

$f_1(9)$ = 4, the salesman takes the path 9–10.

The smallest of these values $f_1(S)$ is to be selected.

i.e., $f_1(8)$ = 3, route 8–10.

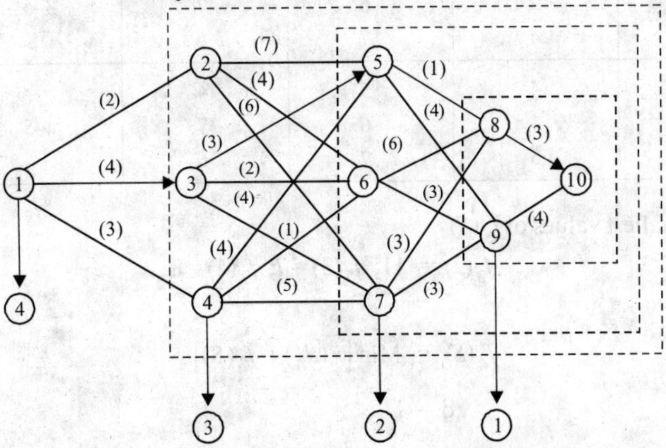

3. Consider stage 2.

$$f_2(S) = \text{Min}\,[r(d_2) + f_1(S)]$$
$$\delta = 5, 6, 7.$$

State (S) (1)	Decision (d_n) (2)	Immediate return (3)	Resulting state T (S, d_n) (4)	Optimal policy from resulting state (5)	Resulting function f (n) (6)	Optimal cost policy (7) = (3) + (5)
5	5–8	1	8	3	5–8	4*
	5–9	4	9	4		8
6	6–8	6	8	3	6–9	9
	6–9	3	9	4		7*
7	7–8	3	8	3	7–8	6*
	7–9	3	9	4		7

Select the smallest values of $f_2(S)$.

$$f_2(5) = 4;\ f_2(6) = 7;\ f_2(7) = 6$$

4. Consider stage 3.

$$f_3(S) = \underset{S}{\text{Min}}\left[r(d_3) + f_2(S)\right]$$
$$S = 2, 3, 4.$$

State (S) (1)	Decision (d_n) (2)	Immediate return (3)	Resulting state T (S, d_n) (4)	Optimal policy from resulting state (5)	Resulting function f (n) (6)	Optimal cost policy (7) = (3) + (5)
2	2–5	7	5	4	2–5	11*
	2–6	4	6	7		11*
	2–7	6	7	6		12
3	3–5	3	5	4	3–5	7*
	3–6	2	6	7		9
	3–7	4	7	6		10
4	4–5	4	5	4	4–5	8*
	4–6	1	6	7		8*
	4–7	5	7	6		11

Select the smallest values of $f_3(S)$

$$f_3(2) = 11;\ f_3(3) = 7;\ f_3(4) = 8.$$

5. Consider stage 4.

$$f_4(S) = \underset{S}{\text{Min}}\left[r(d_4) + f_3(S)\right]$$
$$\delta = 1$$

State (S) (1)	Decision (d_n) (2)	Immediate return (3)	Resulting state T (S, d_n) (4)	Optimal policy from resulting state (5)	Resulting function f (n) (6)	Optimal cost policy (7) = (3) + (5)
	1–2	2	2	11		13
1	1–3	4	3	7	–	11*
	1–4	3	4	8		11

From the table, it is observed that the optimal routes are 1–3–5–8–10 and 1–4–5–8–10. The associated total travelling cost is ₹ 11.

Cargo Loading Problem

In this type of problem, there are *N* items available with weights w_j (j = 1, 2, ... *N*) per unit and their expected revenues are P_j per unit. A vessel or a parcel van is to be loaded with these items in such a way that the total weight and the value of the cargo is maximized.

Example 13.13 Shankar Roadlines has 4 types of packages *A*, *B*, *C* and *D* to be carried to their parcel van. The bulk density of each package is different. As per the company's rules, the packages fall under different categories of freight classification and, therefore, the revenue per unit of each package also varies. Data regarding the weights and the expected revenue for each package is available:

Type of package	*Weight per unit*	*Expected revenue per unit (₹/unit)*
A	2,000	200
B	4,000	425
C	5,000	550
D	3,000	350

Determine the number of units of each package that would maximize the revenue, given that the capacity of the van is limited to 10,000 kg.

Solution

1. Since there are four types of packages, therefore, it is a four-stage problem. Formulation of the problem is as follows.

   Let y_1, y_2, y_3 and y_4 be the number of units of packages of type *A*, *B*, *C* and *D* respectively. Since the total weight is limited to 10,000 kg, the constraint equation becomes,

   $$2{,}000\, y_1 + 4{,}000\, y_2 + 5{,}000\, y_3 + 3{,}000\, y_4 \leq 10{,}000.$$

   The objective function is,

   Max $Z = 200\, y_1 + 425\, y_2 + 550\, y_3 + 350\, y_4$ and $y_1, y_2, y_3, y_4 \geq 0$ and are integers.

2. Define the static variables. Each unit of package *A* is 2,000 kg. Since the total weight is 10,000 kg. The number of units of package *A* can go up to five. Similarly, define the state variables for other packages.

   $$S_1 = 0, 1, 2, 3, 4, 5$$
   $$S_2 = 0, 1, 2$$
   $$S_3 = 0, 1, 2$$
   $$S_4 = 0, 1, 2, 3$$

3. By backward pass approach, consider stage 1.

$$f_1(S_4) = \text{Max}\,[r(d_n) + 0].$$

Enter the possible weights row-wise. The state variables and their expected revenues are entered column-wise. Compute the expected revenues for all possible combinations and mark the maximum values in Table 1. Enter the resulting function state variable corresponding to the maximum revenue.

Table 1: Stage 1: Package D, each of 3,000 kg

S	***0***	***1***	***2***	***3***	***Resulting function stage***	***Optimum revenue***
Possible weights / ***Revenue***	***0***	***350***	***700***	***1050***		
0	0	–	–	–	0	0
2000	0	–	–	–	0	0
3000	0	350*	–	–	1	350*
4000	0	350* + 0	–	–	1	350*
5000	0	350* + 0	–	–	1	350*
6000	0	350	700*	–	2	700*
7000	0	350	700* + 0	–	2	700*
8000	0	350	700*	–	2	700*
9000	0	350	700	1050*	3	1050*
10000	0	350	700	1050* + 0	3	1050*

4. Consider stage 2. Enter the computed optimal value in table 2 row-wise and the package C revenues column-wise. Compute the expected revenues for all possible combinations and then mark the maximum values in Table 2.

Table 2: Stage 2: Package C, each of 5,000 kg

S	***0***	***1***	***2***	***Resulting function stage***	***Optimum revenue***
Possible weights / ***Revenue***	***0***	***550***	***1100***		
2000	0*	–	–	0	0*
3000	350*	–	–	0	350*
4000	350*	–	–	0	350*
5000	350*	550*	–	1	550*
6000	700*	550	–	0	700*
7000	700*	550	–	0	700*
8000	700	550 + 350*	–	1	900*
9000	1050*	550 + 350	–	0	1050*
10000	1050	550 + 350	1100*	2	1100*

5. Consider stage 3 and compute the optimum expected revenues. Enter these values in Table 3.

Table 3: Stage 3: Package *B*, each of 4000 kg

S	0	1	2	Resulting function stage	Optimum revenue
Possible weights \ Revenue	0	425	850		
2000	0*	–	–	0	0*
3000	350*	–	–	0	350*
4000	350	425*	–	1	425*
5000	550*	425	–	0	550*
6000	700*	425	–	0	700*
7000	700	425+350*	–	1	775*
8000	900*	425+350	850	0	900*
9000	1050*	425+550	850	0	1050*
10000	1100	425+700*	850	1	1125*

6. Consider stage 4 and compute all the possible combinations and their expected revenues. Enter these values in Table 4.

Table 4: Stage 4: Package *A*, each of 2,000 kg

S	0	1	2	3	4	5	Resulting function stage	Optimum revenue
Possible weights \ Revenue	0	200	400	600	800	1000		
2000	0	200*	–	–	–	–	1	200*
3000	350*	200	–	–	–	–	0	350*
4000	425*	200	400	–	–	–	0	425*
5000	550*	200 + 350*	400	–	–	–	0	550*
6000	700*	200 + 425	400 + 0	600	–	–	0	700*
7000	775*	200 + 550	400 + 350	600	–	–	0	775*
8000	900*	200 + 700	400 + 425	600 + 0	800	–	0	900*
9000	1050*	200 + 425 + 350	400 + 550	600 + 350	800	–	0	1050*
10000	1125*	200 + 550 + 350	400 + 700	600 + 425	800	1000	0	1125*

Here the objective is to maximize the revenue. Therefore, from last stage the optimal revenue is ₹ 1,125. The value is in state 0, hence package *A* is not loaded in the parcel van. Moving back to the stage 3, the maximum value is in stage 1. Corresponding to this, one unit (4,000 kg) of package *B* is loaded and its revenue is ₹ 425. To find the balance ₹ 700, go back to stage 2, where this value is in state 0. It means that the package *C* is not loaded. Move to stage 1, where this value (₹ 700) is in state 2. Therefore, 2 units (2 × 3000 kg) of package *D* are loaded in the parcel van.

The optimal solution is,

Package	*No. of units*	*Total weight (kg)*	*Expected revenues (₹)*
A	0	0	0
B	1	4000	425
C	0	0	0
D	2	6000	700
Total		10,000	1,125

Selection of Advertising Media

In this type of problem, a company uses different advertising media to increase the total sales. The objective is to select the best media and the frequency of advertising in each, in order to increase the sales of product.

Example 13.14 A cosmetics manufacturing company is interested in selecting the advertising media for its product and the frequency of advertising in each media. The data collected over the past two years regarding the frequency of advertising in three types of media i.e. of newspaper, radio and television and the related sales of the product gives the following.

Expected sales in thousand rupees

Frequency/Week	*Television*	*Radio*	*Newspaper*
1	220	150	100
2	275	250	175
3	325	300	225
4	350	320	250

The cost of advertising in newspaper is ₹ 500 per appearance, and on radio and television ₹ 1,000 and ₹ 2,000 per appearance, respectively. The advertising budget provides ₹ 4,500 per week. The problem is of determining the optimal combination of advertising media and frequency. Using the dynamic programming techniques, solve the above problem.

Solution

1. Since there are three kinds of media for advertising, it is a three-stage problem.

   Formulation of the problem:

   Let y_1, y_2 and y_3 be the number of appearances of advertising in television, radio and newspaper respectively. Since the total budget is limited to ₹ 4,500, the constraint equation becomes,

$$500y_1 + 1000y_2 + 2000y_3 \leq 4{,}500$$

2. Define the state variables. The cost of advertising in television is ₹ 2,000 per appearance. Since the total budget is ₹ 4,500, the number of appearance per week can go up to two. Similarly, define the state variables for other advertising media.

$$S_1 = 0, 1, 2$$

$$S_2 = 0, 1, 2, 3, 4$$

$$S_3 = 0, 1, 2, 3, 4.$$

3. By forward pass approach, consider stage 1.

$$F_1(S_1) = \text{Max}\,[r(d_n) + 0]$$

Enter the possible advertising amount row-wise. The state variables and their expected sales column-wise. Compute the expected sales for all possible combinations. It is not possible to advertise in this media for the cost of ₹ 500, 1,000 and 1,500, since the cost of one appearance per week is ₹ 2,000. Enter the resulting function state variable corresponding to the maximum sales in Table 1.

Table 1: Stage 1: Media for Advertising: Television: ₹ 2000 per appearance

S / ***Sales*** / ***Possible adv. cost***	***0*** / ***0***	***1*** / ***550***	***2*** / ***1100***	***Frequency***	***Optional expected sales***
0	0	–	–	0	0
500	0	–	–	0	0
1000	0	–	–	0	0
1500	0	–	–	0	0
2000	0	220*	–	1	220*
2500	0	220 + 0*	–	1	220*
3000	0	220*	–	1	220*
3500	0	220*	–	1	220*
4000	0	220	275*	2	275*
4500	0	220	275 + 0*	2	275*

4. Consider stage 2. Enter the computed optimal value in table 2 row-wise and the expected sales column-wise. Compute the expected sales revenue for all possible combinations and then mark the maximum values in Table 2.

Table 2: Stage 2: Media: Radio: ₹ 1000 per appearence

S / ***Sales*** / ***Possible adv. cost***	***0*** / ***0***	***1*** / ***150***	***2*** / ***250***	***3*** / ***300***	***4*** / ***320***	***Frequency***	***Optional expected sales***
500	0*	–	–	–	–	0	0*
1000	0	150*	–	–	–	1	150*
1500	0	150 + 0*	–	–	–	1	150*
2000	220	150 + 0	250*	–	–	2	250*
2500	220	150	250 + 0*	–	–	2	250*
3000	220	150 + 220*	250	300	–	1	370*
3500	220	150 + 220*	250	300	–	1	370*
4000	275	150 + 220	250 + 220*	300	320	2	470*
4500	275	150 + 220	250 + 220*	300 + 0	320 + 0	2	470*

The above table shows that the maximum sales is ₹ 4,70,000. The above amount is achieved by means of advertising two times on the radio and once on television. The corresponding advertising expenses are ₹ 4,000 and ₹ 4,500.

5. Consider stage 3 and compute the optimum expected sales revenue, then enter these values in Table 3.

Table 3: Stage 3: Media: Newspaper: ₹ 500 per appearance

S	***0***	***1***	***2***	***3***	***4***		
Sales / ***Possible adv. cost***	***0***	***100***	***175***	***225***	***250***	***Frequency***	***Optional revenue sales***
500	0	100*	–	–	–	1	100
1000	150	100 + 0	175*	–	–	2	175
1500	150	100 + 150*	175 + 0	225	–	1	250
2000	250	100 + 150	175 + 150*	225 + 0	250	2	325
2500	250	100 + 250	175 + 150	225 + 150*	250	3	375
3000	370	100 + 250	175 + 250*	225 + 150	250 + 150	2	425
3500	370	100 + 370	175 + 250	225 + 250*	250 + 150	3	475
4000	470	100 + 370	175 + 370*	225 + 250	250 + 250	2	545
4500	470	100 + 470	175 + 370	225 + 370*	250 + 250	3	595

From the above table, the optimum solution is ₹ 5,95,000.

Media of advertising	***No. of times per week***	***Expected sales***
Television	1 time	2,20,000
Radio	1 time	1,50,000
Newspaper	3 times	2,25,000
Total Sales		₹ 5,95,000

Capital Budgeting Problem

A capital budgeting problem is the one in which a given amount of capital is allotted to a set of decisions by selecting the most promising alternative for each selected decision such that the total revenue of the organization is maximized. This is clearly explained in the following problem.

Example 13.15 A manufacturing company has three sections producing automobile parts, bicycle parts and machine tool parts respectively. The management has allotted ₹ 20,000 for expanding the production facilities. In the auto-parts and bicycle parts sections, the production can be increased either by adding new machines or by replacing some old inefficient machines with automatic machines. The machine tool parts section was started only a few years back and thus the additional amount can be invested only by adding new machines to the section. The cost of adding and replacing the machines, along with the associated expected returns in the different sections is given in the table below. Select a set of expansion plans, which may yield the maximum return.

Alternatives	Auto-parts section		Bicycle parts section		Machine tool parts section	
	Cost (₹)	Return (₹)	Cost (₹)	Return (₹)	Cost (₹)	Return (₹)
1. No Expansion	0	0	0	0	0	0
2. Add New Machines	4,000	8,000	8,000	12,000	2,000	8,000
3. Replace Old Machines	6,000	10,000	12,000	18,000	–	–

Solution

1. Since there are three different sections, it is a three-stage problem. At each stage, a certain number of alternatives are possible for expansion of the department. Consider the auto-parts section as stage 1. Since the total allotment is of ₹ 20,000, stage 1 may vary from 0 to ₹ 20,000.

   The three alternatives are,

$$S_1 = 1, 2, 3$$
$$S_2 = 1, 2, 3$$
$$S_3 = 1, 2$$

Table 1

State / Possible Allocations	1 Cost 0	1 Return 0	2 Cost 4	2 Return 8	3 Cost 6	3 Return 10	Optimal decision	Optimal return
0	0*		–		–		1	0*
2	0*		–		–		1	0*
4	0		8*		–		2	8*
6	0		8		10*		3	10*
8	0		8		10*		3	10*
10	0		8		10*		3	10*
12	0		8		10*		3	10*
14	0		8		10*		3	10*
16	0		8		10*		3	10*
18	0		8		10*		3	10*
20	0		8		10*		3	10*

2. From the above table, we observed that the third alternative is selected because it gives a return of ₹ 10,000 after investing ₹ 6,000.

3. Now move to the second stage. Here also three alternatives are available for expansion of the department. Consider bicycle parts section as stage 2 and enter the given values in Table 2. Compare the various possible alternatives and select the maximum values and the corresponding decision values.

Table 2: State 2: Bicycle Parts Section

State / Possible Allocations	1		2		3		Optimal decision	Optimal return
	Cost 0	Return 8	Cost 12	Return 12	Cost 18	Return		
0	0 + 0 = 0*		–		–		1	0*
2	0 + 0 = 0*		–		–		1	0*
4	0 + 8 = 8*		–		–		1	8*
6	0 + 10 = 10*		–		–		1	10*
8	0 + 10 = 10		12 + 0 = 12*		–		2	12*
10	0 + 10 = 10		12 + 0 = 12*		–		2	12*
12	0 + 10 = 10		12 + 8 = 20*		18 + 0 = 18		2	20*
14	0 + 10 = 10		12 + 10 = 22*		18 + 0 = 18		2	22*
16	0 + 10 = 10		12 + 10 = 22		18 + 8 = 26*		3	26*
18	0 + 10 = 10		12 + 10 = 22		18 + 10 = 28*		3	28*
20	0 + 10 = 10		12 + 10 = 22		18 + 10 = 28*		3	28*

4. Now consider the third stage.

Table 3: Stage 3: Machine Tool Parts Section

State / Possible Allocations	1		2		Optimal decision	Optimal return
	Cost 0	Return 0	Cost 2	Return 8		
0	0 + 0 = 0*		–		1	0*
2	0 + 0 = 0		8 + 0 = 8*		2	8*
4	0 + 8 = 8*		8 + 0 = 8*		1, 2	8*
6	0 + 10 = 10		8 + 8 = 16*		2	16*
8	0 + 12 = 12		8 + 10 = 18*		2	18*
10	0 + 12 = 12		8 + 12 = 20*		2	20*
12	0 + 20 = 20*		8 + 12 = 20*		1, 2	20*
14	0 + 22 = 22		8 + 20 = 28*		2	28*
16	0 + 26 = 26		8 + 12 + 10 = 30*		2	30*
18	0 + 28 = 28		8 + 18 + 8 = 34*		2	34*
20	0 + 28 = 28		8 + 18 + 10 = 36*		2	36*

5. As per Table 3, the optimal decision for stage 3 is the second alternative, which gives a total return of ₹ 36,000. Now go back to stage 2; the corresponding alternative is the third one. From stage 1 also it is the third alternative. The optimal solution is,

Result

Sl. No.	*Alternatives*	*Capital allotted (₹)*	*Optimal return (₹)*
1.	Replace old machines with automatic machines in auto-parts section	6,000	10,000
2.	Replace old machines with automatic machines in bicycle parts section	12,000	18,000
3.	Add new machines to the machine tool parts section	2,000	8,000
		20,000	36,000

EXERCISES

1. Using dynamic programming, solve the following problem

   Max $Z = y_1^2 + y_2^2 + y_3^2$

   Subject to, $y_1 y_2 y_3 \leq 4$, where $y_1 y_2 y_3 \geq 0$ **[Ans.** $y_1 = 4$, $y_2 = 1$, $y_3 = 1$, Max $Z = 18$]

2. Using dynamic programming, solve

   Min XYZ

   Subject to, $X + Y + Z = 5$, $X, Y, Z \geq 0$ **[Ans.** $X = 0$, $Y = 0$, $Z = 5$, Min $Z = 0$]

3. A student has to take examinations in three courses *A*, *B* and *C*. He has three days available for studying. He feels it would be best to devote a whole day to the study of the same course, so that he may study a course for one day, two days, three days or not at all. The estimates of the grades he may get by studying are as follows:

Course/Study days	***A***	***B***	***C***
0	0	1	0
1	1	1	1
2	1	3	3
3	3	4	3

   How should he plan to study so that he maximizes the sum of his grades?

   [Ans. $X \to 1$, $Y \to 0$, $Z \to 2$ and Max return is 5]

4. Solve the following LPPby dynamic programming

   (i) Max $Z = 3x + 2y$

   Subject to,
   $$x + y \leq 300$$
   $$2x + 3y \leq 800$$
   $$x, y \geq 0$$
   [Ans. $x = 100$, $y = 200$, Max $Z = 700$]

   (ii) Max $Z = 3x_1 + x_2$

   Subject to,
   $$2x_1 + x_2 \leq 6$$
   $$x_1 \leq 2$$
   $$x_2 \leq 4$$
   $$x_1, x_2 \geq 0$$
   [Ans. $x_1 = 2$, $x_2 = 2$, Max $Z = 8$]

❑❑❑

Chapter 14

Sequencing Problems

14.1 INTRODUCTION

In this chapter, we determine an appropriate order (sequence) for a series of jobs to be done on a finite number of service facilities in some pre-assigned order, so as to optimize the total cost (time) involved.

14.1.1 Definition

Sequencing gives us an idea of the order in which things happen or come in event. Suppose there are n jobs (1, 2 ... n), each of which has to be processed one at a time at m machines (A, B, C ...). The order of processing each job through each machine is given. The problem is to find a sequence among $(n!)^m$ number of all possible sequences for processing the jobs so that the total elapsed time for all the jobs will be minimum.

14.1.2 Terminology and Notations

The following are the terminologies and notations used in this chapter.

Number of machines It means the service facilities through which a job must pass before it is completed.

Processing order It refers to the order in which various machines are required for completing the job.

Processing time It means the time required by each job to complete a prescribed procedure on each machine.

Idle time on a machine This is the time for which a machine remains idle during the total elapsed time. During the time, the machine awaits completion of manual work. The notation x_{ij} is used to denote the idle time of a machine j between the end of the $(i-1)$th job and the start of the ith job.

Total elapsed time This is the time between starting the first job and completing the last job, which also includes the idle time, if it occurs.

No passing rule It means, passing is not allowed, i.e., maintaining the same order of jobs over each machine. If each of N-jobs is to be processed through 2 machines M_1 and M_2 in the order M_1 M_2, then this rule will mean that each job will go to machine M_1 first and then to M_2. If a job is finished on M_1, it goes directly to machine M_2 if it is free, otherwise it starts a waiting line or joins the end of the waiting line, if one already exists. Jobs that form a waiting line are processed on machine M_2 when it becomes free.

14.1.3 Principal Assumptions

(*i*) No machine can process more than one operation at a time.

(*ii*) Each operation once started must be performed till completion.

(*iii*) Each operation must be completed before starting any other operation.

(*iv*) Time intervals for processing are independent of the order in which operations are performed.

(*v*) There is only one machine of each type.

(*vi*) A job is processed as soon as possible, subject to the ordering requirements.

(*vii*) All jobs are known and are ready for processing, before the period under consideration begins.

(*viii*) The time required to transfer the jobs between machines is negligible.

14.2 TYPE I: PROBLEMS WITH *n* JOBS THROUGH TWO MACHINES

The algorithm, which is used to optimize the total elapsed time for processing n jobs through two machines is called 'Johnson's algorithm' and has the following steps.

Consider n jobs (1, 2, 3 ...n) processing on two machines A and B in the order AB. The processing periods (time) are $A_1\ A_2 \ldots A_n$ and $B_1\ B_2 \ldots B_n$ as given in the following table.

Machine/Job	*1*	*2*	*3*	...	*n*
A	A_1	A_2	A_3	...	A_n
B	B_1	B_2	B_3	...	B_n

The problem is to sequence the jobs so as to minimize the total elapsed time.

The solution procedure adopted by Johnson is given below.

Step 1 Select the least processing time occurring in the list $A_1\ A_2 \ldots A_n$ and $B_1\ B_2 \ldots B_n$. Let this minimum processing time occurs for a job K.

Step 2 If the shortest processing is for machine A, process the Kth job first and place it in the beginning of the sequence. If it is for machine B, process the Kth job last and place it at the end of the sequence.

Step 3 When there is a tie in selecting the minimum processing time, then there may be three solutions.

(*i*) If the equal minimum values occur only for machine A, select the job with larger processing time in B to be placed first in the job sequence.

(*ii*) If the equal minimum values occur only for machine B, select the job with larger processing time in A to be placed last in the job sequence.

(*iii*) If there are equal minimum values, one for each machine, then place the job in machine A first and the one in machine B last.

Step 4 Delete the jobs already sequenced. If all the jobs have been sequenced, go to the next step. Otherwise, repeat steps 1 to 3.

Step 5 In this step, determine the overall or total elapsed time and also the idle time on machines A and B as follows.

Total elapsed time = The time between starting the first job in the optimal sequence on machine A and completing the last job in the optimal sequence on machine B.

Idle time on A = (Time when the last job in the optimal sequence is completed on machine B) – (Time when the last job in the optimal sequence is completed on machine A)

Idle time on B = [when the first job in the optimal sequence starts on machine B + $\sum_{K=2}^{n}$ [time k^{th} job starts on machine B – time $(K-1)$th job finished on machine B]

Example 14.1 There are five jobs, each of which must go through the two machines A and B in the order AB. Processing times are given below.

Job	*1*	*2*	*3*	*4*	*5*
Machine A	5	1	9	3	10
Machine B	2	6	7	8	4

Determine a sequence for the five jobs that will minimize the total elapsed time.

Solution The shortest processing time in the given problem is 1 on machine A. So perform job 2 in the beginning, as shown below.

2				

The reduced list of processing time becomes

Job	*1*	*3*	*4*	*5*
Machine A Machine B	5 2	9 7	3 8	10 4

Again the shortest processing time in the reduced list is 2 for job 1 on machine B. So place job 1 as the last.

2				1

Continuing in the same manner the next reduced list is obtained as

Job	*3*	*4*	*5*
Machine A Machine B	9 7	3 8	10 4

Leading to the sequence

2	4			1

and the list

Job	*3*	*5*
Machine A Machine B	9 7	10 4

gives rise to the sequence

2	4		5	1

Finally, the optimal sequence n is obtained as

2	4	3	5	1

Flow of jobs through machines A and B using the optimal sequence is,

$$2 \rightarrow 4 \rightarrow 3 \rightarrow 5 \rightarrow 1.$$

Computation of the total elapsed time and the machine's idle time in hours.

Job	Machine A		Machine B		Idle time	
	In	Out	In	Out	A	B
2	0	1	1	7	0	1
4	1	4	7	15	0	0
3	4	13	15	22	0	0
5	13	23	23	27	0	1
1	23	28	28	30	30 – 28 = 2	1 3

From the above table we find that the total elapsed time is 30 hours and the idle time on machine *A* is 2 hours and on machine *B* is 3 hours.

Example 14.2 Find the sequence that minimizes the total elapsed time (in hours) required to complete the following tasks on two machines.

Task	A	B	C	D	E	F	G	H	I
Machine *I*	2	5	4	9	6	8	7	5	4
Machine *II*	6	8	7	4	3	9	3	8	11

Solution The shortest processing time is 2 hours on machine I for job *A*. Hence, process this job first.

A								

Deleting these jobs, we get the reduced list of processing time.

Task	B	C	D	E	F	G	H	I
Machine *I*	5	4	9	6	8	7	5	4
Machine *II*	8	7	4	3	9	3	8	11

The next minimum processing time is same for jobs *E* and *G* on machine *II*. The corresponding processing time on machine *I* for this job is 6 and 7. The longest processing time is 7 hours. So sequence job *G* at the end and *E* next to it.

A							E	G

Deleting the jobs that are sequenced, the reduced processing list is,

Job	B	C	D	F	H	I
Machine *I*	5	4	9	8	5	4
Machine *II*	8	7	4	9	8	11

The minimum processing time is 4 hours for job *C*, *I* and *D*. For job *C* and *I* it is on machine *I* and for job *D* it is on machine *II*. There is a tie in sequencing jobs *C* and *I*. To break this, we consider the corresponding time on machine *II*, the longest time is 11 (eleven) hours. Hence, sequence job *I* in the beginning followed by job *C*. For job *D*, as it is on machine *II*, sequences it last.

A	*I*	*C*				*D*	*E*	*G*

Deleting the jobs that are sequenced, the reduced processing list is,

Job	*B*	*F*	*H*
Machine *I*	5	8	5
Machine *II*	8	9	8

The next minimum processing time is 5 hours on machine *I* for jobs *B* and *H*, which is again a tie. To break this, we consider the corresponding longest time on the other machine (*II*) and sequence job *B* or *H* first. Finally, job *F* is sequenced.

The optimal sequence for this job is,

A	*I*	*C*	*B*	*H*	*F*	*D*	*E*	*G*

The total elapsed time and idle time for both the machines are calculated from the following table.

Job	*Machine A*		*Machine B*		*Idle time*	
	In	*Out*	*In*	*Out*	M_1	M_2
A	0	2	2	8	0	2
I	2	6	8	19	0	0
C	6	10	19	26	0	0
B	10	15	26	34	0	0
H	15	20	34	42	0	0
F	20	28	42	51	0	0
D	28	37	51	55	0	0
E	37	43	55	58	0	0
G	43	50	58	61	61 – 50	0
					11 hours	2 hours

Total elapsed time = 61 hours.

Idle time for Machine *I* = 11 hours; Idle time for Machine *II* = 2 hours.

Example 14.3 A company has six jobs, *A* to *F*. All the jobs have to go through two machine *M*I and *MII*. The time required for the jobs on each machine in hours is given below. Find the optimum sequence that minimizes the total elapsed time.

Job	*A*	*B*	*C*	*D*	*E*	*F*
Machine *I*	1	4	6	3	5	2
Machine *II*	3	6	8	8	1	5

Solution The minimum processing time is 1 hour on machine *I* for job *A* and on machine *II* for job *E*. So process job *A* first and sequence it in the beginning and process job *E* last.

A						*E*

Deleting these jobs, the reduced processing time list is,

	B	*C*	*D*	*F*
Machine *I*	4	6	3	2
Machine *II*	6	8	8	5

The next minimum processing time is on machine *I* for job *F*, so sequence this job in the beginning.

A						*E*

Continuing this way, we get the optimum sequence as follows.

A	*F*	*D*	*B*	*C*	*E*

The total elapsed time and idle time for each machine can be obtained as follows.

Job	*Machine A*		*Machine B*		*Idle time*	
	In	*Out*	*In*	*Out*	M_1	M_2
A	0	1	1	4	–	1
F	1	3	4	9	–	
D	3	6	9	17	–	–
B	6	10	17	23	–	–
C	10	16	23	31	–	–
E	16	21	31	32	–	–
					32 – 21 = 11	1

Total elapsed time = 32 hours.

Idle time for Machine *I* = 11 hours: Idle time for Machine *II* = 1 hour.

14.3 TYPE II: PROCESSING *n* JOBS THROUGH THREE MACHINES *A*, *B*, *C*

Consider *n* jobs (1, 2 ... *n*) processing on three machines *A*, *B*, *C* in the order *ABC*. The optimal sequence can be obtained by converting the problem into a two-machine problem. From this, we get the optimum sequence using Johnson's algorithm.

The following steps are used to convert the given problem into a two-machine problem.

Step 1 Find the minimum processing time for the jobs on the first and last machine and the maximum processing time for the second machine.

$$\text{i.e., find } \underset{i}{\text{Min}}\,(A_i, C_i)\ i = 1, 2 \ldots n$$

$$\text{and } \underset{i}{\text{Max}}\,(B_i)$$

Step 2 Check the following inequality

$$\underset{i}{\text{Min}}\, A_i \geq \underset{i}{\text{Max}}\, B_i$$

or

$$\underset{i}{\text{Min}}\, C_i \geq \underset{i}{\text{Max}}\, B_i$$

Step 3 If none of the inequalities in step 2 are satisfied, this method cannot be applied.

Step 4 If at least one of the inequalities in step 2 is satisfied, we define two machines G and H, such that the processing time on G and H are given by,

$$G_i = A_i + B_i \qquad i = 1, 2 \ldots n$$

$$H_i = B_i + C_i \qquad i = 1, 2 \ldots n$$

Step 5 For the converted machines G and H, we obtain the optimum sequence using two-machine algorithm.

Example 14.4 A machine operator has to perform three operations, turning, threading and knurling, on a number of different jobs. The time required to perform these operations (in minutes) on each job is known. Determine the order in which the jobs should be processed in order to minimize the total time required to turn out all the jobs. Also find the minimum elapsed time.

Job	*1*	*2*	*3*	*4*	*5*	*6*
Turning	3	12	5	2	9	11
Threading	8	6	4	6	3	1
Knurling	13	14	9	12	8	13

Solution Let us consider the three machines as A, B and C.

$$A = \text{Turning};\ B = \text{Threading};\ C = \text{Knurling}$$

Step 1 $\underset{i}{\text{Min}}\ (A_i\ C_i) = (2, 8)$

$\underset{i}{\text{Max}}\ (B_i) = 8$

Step 2 $\underset{i}{\text{Min}}\ A_i = 2 \not\geq \underset{i}{\text{Max}} B_i = 8$

$\underset{i}{\text{Min}}\ C_i = 8 \geq \underset{i}{\text{Max}} B_i$ is satisfied.

We define two machines G and H

Such that, $G_i = A_i + B_i$

$H_i = B_i + C_i$

Job	*1*	*2*	*3*	*4*	*5*	*6*
G	11	18	9	8	12	12
H	21	20	13	18	11	14

We adopt Johnson's algorithm steps to get the optimum sequence.

4	3	1	6	2	5

To find the min. total elapsed time and idle time for machines *A*, *B* and *C*,

Job	Machine A		Machine B		Machine C		Idle time		
	In	Out	In	Out	In	Out	A	B	C
4	0	2	2	8	8	20	–	2	8
3	2	7	8	12	20	29	–	–	–
1	7	10	12	20	29	42	–	–	–
6	10	21	21	22	42	55	–	1	–
2	21	33	33	39	55	69	–	11	–
5	33	42	42	45	69	77	–	3	–
							77 – 42	(77 – 45)+ 17	–
							35	49	8

Total elapsed time = 77 minutes

Idle time for machine *A* = 35 minutes; Idle time for machine *B* = 49 minutes;

Idle time for machine *C* = 8 minutes.

Example 14.5 We have five jobs, each of which must go through the machines *A*, *B* and *C* in the order *ABC*. Determine the sequence that will minimize the total elapsed time.

Job No.	1	2	3	4	5
Machine *A*	5	7	6	9	5
Machine *B*	2	1	4	5	3
Machine *C*	3	7	5	6	7

Solution The optimum sequence can be obtained by converting the problem into that of two-machines, by using the following steps.

Step 1 Find $\underset{i}{\text{Min}}\ (A_i\ C_i)\ i = 1, 2 \ldots 5$

$$= (5, 3).$$

Step 2

$$\underset{i}{\text{Max}}\ (B_i) = 5$$

$$\underset{i}{\text{Min}}\ A_i = 5 = \underset{i}{\text{Max}}\ B_i = 5$$

$$\therefore \quad \underset{i}{\text{Min}}\ A_i \geq \underset{i}{\text{Max}}\ B_i \text{ is satisfied.}$$

We convert the problem into a two-machine problem by defining two machines *G* and *H*, such that the processing time on *G* and *H* are given by,

$$G_i = A_i + B_i$$

$$i = 1, 2, \ldots 5$$

$$H_i = B_i + C_i$$

Job	1	2	3	4	5
G	7	8	10	14	8
H	5	8	9	11	10

We obtain the optimum sequence by using the steps in Johnson's algorithm.

5	2	4	3	1

To find the total elapsed time and idle time on three machines.

Job	Machine A		Machine B		Machine C		Idle time		
	In	Out	In	Out	In	Out	A	B	C
5	0	5	5	8	8	15	–	5	8
2	5	12	12	13	15	22	–	4	–
4	12	21	21	26	26	32	–	8	4
3	21	27	27	31	32	37	–	1	–
1	27	32	32	34	37	40	–	1	–
							40 – 32	40 – 34	–
								= 6 + 19	–
							8	25	12

Total elapsed time = 40 hours.

Idle time for machine $A = 8$ hours; Idle time for machine $B = 25$ hours; Idle time for machine $C = 12$ hours.

Example 14.6 A readymade garments manufacturer has to process 7 items through two stages of production, namely, cutting and sewing. The time taken for each of these at the different stages are given below in appropriate units.

Item		1	2	3	4	5	6	7
Process	*Cutting*	5	7	3	4	6	7	12
Time	*Sewing*	2	6	7	5	9	5	8

(*a*) Find an order in which these items are to be processed through these stages, so as to minimize the total processing time.

(*b*) Suppose a third stage of production is added, namely, pressing and packing with the processing time as follows.

Item	1	2	3	4	5	6	7
Processing time (Pressing and packing)	10	12	11	13	12	10	11

Find an order in which these seven items are to be processed so as to minimize the time taken to process all the items through all the three stages.

Solution

1. We consider the two stages of cutting and sewing by the machines A and B. The optimum sequence for these 7 items can be given as follows using the steps involved in Johnson's algorithm.

3	4	5	7	2	6	1

Job	*Machine A*		*Machine B*		*Idle time*	
	In	*Out*	*In*	*Out*	*A*	*B*
3	0	3	3	10	–	3
4	3	7	10	15	–	–
5	7	13	15	24	–	–
7	13	25	25	33	–	1
2	25	32	33	39	–	–
6	32	39	39	44	–	–
1	39	44	44	46	–	–
					46 – 44 = 2	4

Total elapsed time = 46 hours.

Idle time for machine A = 2 hours; Idle time for machine B = 4 hours.

2. To get the optimum sequence for including the third stage, namely, pressing and packing, we use the optimum sequence for three-machine problem by considering the stage pressing and packing for machine C. We convert the problem into a two-machine problem using the following steps.

$$\min_i (A_i, C_i) = (3, 10) \qquad i = 1, 2 \ldots 7$$
$$\max_i (B_i) = 9$$

Since min $C_i = 10 > \text{Max } B_i = 9$ is satisfied, we convert it into a two-machine problem with machines G and H such that,

$$G_i = A_i + B_i, H_i = B_i + C_i$$
$$i = 1, 2 \ldots 7$$

Item	*1*	*2*	*3*	*4*	*5*	*6*	*7*
Machine G	7	13	10	9	15	12	20
Machine H	12	18	18	18	21	15	19

1	4	3	6	2	5	7

To compute the total elapsed time.

Job	*Machine A*		*Machine B*		*Machine C*		*Idle time*		
	In	*Out*	*In*	*Out*	*In*	*Out*	*A*	*B*	*C*
1	0	5	5	7	7	17	–	5	7
4	5	9	9	14	17	30	–	2	–
3	9	12	14	21	30	41	–	–	–
6	12	19	21	26	41	51	–	–	–
2	19	26	26	32	51	63	–	–	–
5	26	32	32	41	63	75	–	–	–
7	32	44	44	51	75	86	–	2	–
							86 – 43 = 43	86 – 51 = 35	– –
							43	44	7

Total elapsed time = 86 hours

Idle time for machine $A = 43$ hours; Idle time for machine $B = 44$ hours; Idle time for machine $C = 7$ hours.

14.4 TYPE III: PROBLEMS WITH *n* JOBS AND *k* MACHINES

Consider n jobs (1, 2 ... n) processing through k machines M_1 M_2 ... M_k in the same order. The iterative procedure of obtaining an optimal sequence is as follows.

Step 1 Find Min. M_i and Min. M_{ik} and Max. of each of $M_{i2}, M_{i3} ... M_{ik-1}$ for $i = 1, 2 ... n$.

Step 2 Check whether

$$\underset{i}{\text{Min}}\ M_{i_1} \geq \underset{i}{\text{Max}}\ M_{ij}, \text{ for } j = 2, 3 \ldots k-1 \text{ or}$$
$$\underset{i}{\text{Min}}\ M_{i_k} \geq \underset{i}{\text{Max}}\ M_{ij}, \text{ for } j = 2, 3 \ldots k-1.$$

Step 3 If the inequalities in step 2 are not satisfied, the method fails, otherwise, go to the next step.

Step 4 In addition to step 2, if $M_{i2} + M_{i3} + \ldots M_{ik-1} = C$, where C is a positive fixed constant for all, $i = 1, 2 \ldots n$

Then determine the optimal sequence for n jobs, where the two machines are M_l and M_k in the order $M_l\ M_k$, by using the optimum sequence algorithm.

Step 5 If the condition $M_{i2} + M_{i3} + \ldots M_{ik-1} \neq C$ for all $i = 1, 2 \ldots n$, we define two machines G and H such that,

$$G_i = M_{i1} + M_{i2} + \ldots + M_{ik-1}$$
$$H_i = M_{i2} + M_{i3} + \ldots + M_{ik} \quad i = 1, 2, \ldots, n.$$

Determine the optimal sequence of performance of all jobs on G and H using the optimum sequence algorithm for two machines.

Example 14.7 Four jobs 1, 2, 3 and 4 are to be processed on each of the five machines A, B, C, D and E in the order $A\ B\ C\ D\ E$. Find the total minimum elapsed time if no passing of jobs is permitted. Also find the idle time for each machine.

Machines	***Jobs***			
	1	***2***	***3***	***4***
A	7	6	5	8
B	5	6	4	3
C	2	4	5	3
D	3	5	6	2
E	9	10	8	6

Solution Since the problem is to be sequenced on five machines, we convert the problem into a two-machine problem by adopting the following steps.

Step 1 Find $\text{Min}(A_i, E_i) = (5, 6)$

$$i = 1, 2, 3, 4$$
$$\text{Max}\,(B_i, C_i, D_i) = (6, 5, 6)$$

Step 2 The inequality

$$\underset{i}{\text{Min}}\ E_i = 6 \geq \underset{i}{\text{Max}}(B_i, C_i, D_i)$$

is satisfied. Therefore, we can convert the problem into a two-machine problem.

Step 3 Since $B_i + C_i + D_i \neq C$, where C is a fixed constant, we define two machines G and H such that,

$$G_i = A_i + B_i + C_i + D_i$$
$$H_i = B_i + C_i + D_i + E_i \qquad i = 1, 2, 3, 4.$$

Job	1	2	3	4
G	17	21	20	16
H	19	25	23	14

1	3	2	4

Job	Machine A		Machine B		Machine C		Machine D		Machine E	
	In	Out	In	Out	In	Out	In	Out	In	Out
1	0	7	7	12	12	14	14	17	17	26
3	7	12	12	16	14	19	19	25	26	34
2	12	18	18	24	24	28	28	33	34	44
4	18	26	26	29	29	32	33	35	44	50

	Idle time			
A	B	C	D	E
–	7	12	14	17
–	–	–	2	–
–	2	5	3	–
–	2	1	–	–
50 – 26	50 – 29 = 21	50 – 32 = 18	50 – 35 = 15	–
24	32	36	34	17

Total elapsed time = 50 hours.

Idle time for machine A = 24 hours; Idle time for machine B = 32 hours; Idle time for machine C = 36 hours; Idle time for machine D = 34 hours; Idle time for machine E = 17 hours.

Example 14.8 When passing is not allowed, solve the following problem giving an optimal solution.

Job	Machine			
	M_1	M_2	M_3	M_4
A	24	7	7	29
B	16	9	5	15
C	22	8	6	14
D	21	6	8	32

Solution The given problem lists four jobs on four machines. The optimum sequence can be obtained by converting it into a two-machine problem. The following steps are adopted to find the optimum sequence.

Step 1 $\underset{i}{\text{Min}}\,(M_{i1}, M_{i4}) = (16, 14)$
$\underset{i}{\text{Max}}\,(M_{i2}, M_{i3}) = (9, 8)$

Step 2 Both the inequalities

$$\underset{i}{\text{Min}}\, M_{i1} = 16 \geq \underset{i}{\text{Max}}(M_{i2}, M_{i3})$$
$$(9, 8)$$

and, $$\underset{i}{\text{Min}}\,(M_{i4}) = 14 \geq \underset{i}{\text{Max}}\,(M_{i2}, M_{i3}) \text{ are satisfied.}$$
$$(9, 8)$$

Step 3 In addition we also have $M_{i2} + M_{i3} = 14$ for $i = 2, 3$. We have two machines M_1 and M_4 in the order $M_1\, M_4$

Total elapsed time = 125 hours.

Job	*A*	*B*	*C*	*D*
M_1	24	16	22	21
M_4	29	15	14	32

D	*A*	*B*	*C*

Job	*Machine* M_1		*Machine* M_2		*Machine* M_3		*Machine* M_4	
	In	*Out*	*In*	*Out*	*In*	*Out*	*In*	*Out*
D	0	21	21	27	27	35	35	67
A	21	45	45	52	52	59	67	96
B	45	61	61	70	70	75	96	111
C	61	83	83	91	91	97	111	125

Idle time			
M_1	M_2	M_3	M_4
–	21	27	35
–	18	17	–
–	9	11	–
42	13	16	–
–	125 – 91 = 34	125 – 97 = 28	–
125 – 83 = 42	95	99	35

Idle time for machine $M_1 = 42$ hours; Idle time for machine $M_2 = 95$ hours; Idle time for machine $M_3 = 99$ hours; Idle time for machine $M_4 = 35$ hours.

Example 14.9 Find an optimal sequence for processing nine jobs through the machines A, B, C in the order ABC. Processing times are given below in hours. Find the total elapsed time for the optimal sequences.

Jobs	*1*	*2*	*3*	*4*	*5*	*6*	*7*	*8*	*9*
Machine A	4	9	5	10	6	12	8	3	8
Machine B	6	4	8	9	4	6	2	6	4
Machine C	10	12	9	11	14	15	10	14	12

Solution The optimal sequence can be obtained by converting the problem into a two-machine problem, using the following steps.

Step 1 Find

$$\underset{i}{\text{Min}}\,(A_i, C_i) = (3,9) \quad i = 1, 2, \ldots 9$$

$$\underset{i}{\text{Max}}\,(B_i) = 9$$

Step 2 The inequality $\underset{i}{\text{Min}}\, C_i = 9 \geq \underset{i}{\text{Max}}\, B_i = 9$ is satisfied. Hence we convert the given problem into a two-machine problem.

Step 3 Define two machines G and H, such that the processing time on G and H are given by,

$$G_i = A_i + B_i$$

$$i = 1,\ 2, \ldots 9$$

$$H_i = B_i + C_i$$

Job	*1*	*2*	*3*	*4*	*5*	*6*	*7*	*8*	*9*
Machine G	10	13	13	19	10	18	10	9	12
Machine H	16	16	17	20	18	21	12	20	16

8	1	5	7	9	3	2	6	4

Total elapsed time can be calculated from the following table:

Job	*Machine A*		*Machine B*		*Machine C*		*Idle time*		
	In	*Out*	*In*	*Out*	*In*	*Out*	*A*	*B*	*C*
8	0	3	3	9	9	23	–	3	9
1	3	7	9	15	23	33	–	–	–
5	7	13	15	19	33	47	–	–	–
7	13	21	21	23	47	57	–	2	–
9	21	29	29	33	57	69	–	6	–
3	29	34	34	42	69	78	–	1	–
2	34	43	43	47	78	90	–	1	–
6	43	55	55	61	90	105	–	8	–
4	55	65	65	74	105	116	–	4	–
							116 – 65	(116–74) 42	
							51	67	9

Total elapsed time = 116 hours.

Idle time for machine A = 51 hours; Idle time for machine B = 67 hours; Idle time for machine C = 9 hours.

14.5 TYPE IV: PROBLEMS WITH 2 JOBS THROUGH *K* MACHINES

Consider two jobs, each of which is to be processed on *K* machines $M_1, M_2 \dots M_K$ in two different orders. The ordering of each of the two jobs through *K* machines is known in advance. Such ordering may not be the same for both the jobs. The exact or expected processing times on all the given machines are known.

Each machine can perform only one job at a time. The objective is to determine the optimal sequence of processing the jobs so as to minimize the total elapsed time.

The optimal sequence in this case can be obtained by making use of the graph.

The procedure is given in the following steps.

Step 1 First draw a set of axes, where the horizontal axis represents processing time on job 1 and the vertical axis represents processing time on job 2.

Step 2 Mark the processing time for job 1 and job 2 on the horizontal and vertical lines respectively, according to the given order of machines.

Step 3 Construct various blocks starting from the origin (starting point), by pairing the same machines until the end point.

Step 4 Draw the line starting from the origin to the end point by moving horizontally, vertically and diagonally along a line which makes an angle of 45° with the horizontal line (base). The horizontal segment of this line indicates that the first job is under process while second job is idle. Similarly, the vertical line indicates that the second job is under process while first job is idle. The diagonal segment of the line shows that the jobs are under process simultaneously.

Step 5 An optimum path is the one that minimizes the idle time for both the jobs. Thus, we must choose the path on which diagonal movement is maximum.

Step 6 The total elapsed time is obtained by adding the idle time for either job to the processing time for that job.

Example 14.10 Use graphical method to minimize the time needed to process the following jobs on the machines shown below, i.e., for each machine find the job that should be done first. Also calculate the total time needed to complete both the jobs.

Job 1	Sequence of machine Time	*A* 2	*B* 3	*C* 4	*D* 6	*E* 2
Job 2	Sequence of machine Time	*C* 4	*A* 5	*D* 3	*E* 2	*B* 6

Solution The given information is shown in the figure. The shaded blocks represent the overlaps that are to be avoided.

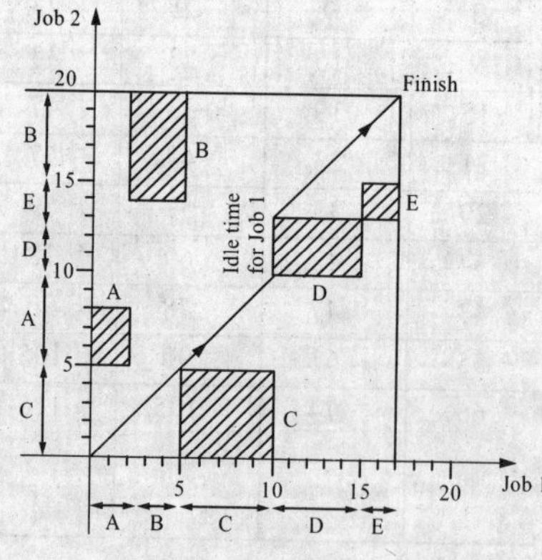

Fig. 14.1

An optimal path is one that minimizes the idle time for job 1 (horizontal movement). Similarly, an optimal path is one that minimizes the idle time for job 2 (vertical movement).

For the elapsed time, we add the idle time for either of the job to the processing time for that job.

In this problem, the idle time for the chosen path is seen to be 3 hours for job 1 and zero for job 2.

Thus, the total elapsed time = 17 + 3 = 20 hours.

Example 14.11 Use the graphical method to minimize the time needed to process the following jobs on the machines shown, that is, for each machine find the job that should be done first. Also calculate the total elapsed time to complete both the jobs.

Job 1	Sequence of machine	*A*	*B*	*C*	*D*	*E*
	Time	3	4	2	6	2
Job 2	Sequence of machine	*B*	*C*	*A*	*D*	*E*
	Time	5	4	3	2	6

Solution The given information is shown in the following figure. The shaded blocks represent the overlaps that are to be avoided.

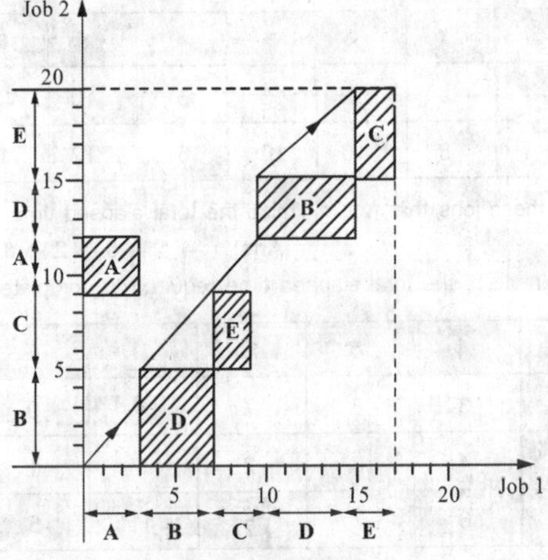

Fig. 14.2

An optimal path is one that minimizes the idle time for job 1 (horizontal movement). Similarly, an optimal path is one that minimizes the idle time for job 2 (vertical movement).

For the elapsed time, we add the idle time for either of the job to the processing time for that job.

In this problem the idle time for the chosen path is 5 hours for job 1 and 2 hours for job 2. Therefore, the total elapsed time is obtained as follows.

Processing time of job 1 + idle time for job 1 = 17 + (2 + 3) = 22 hours

Processing time of job 2 + idle time for job 2 = 20 + 2 = 22 hours.

EXERCISES

1. What is no passing rule in a sequencing algorithm?
2. Explain the principle assumptions made while dealing with a sequencing problem.
3. Describe the method of processing *n* jobs through two machines.
4. What is sequencing problem?
5. Explain the method of processing *m* jobs through three machines *A*, *B* and *C* in the order *ABC*.
6. Explain how to process *n* jobs through *m* machines.
7. Explain the graphical method to solve two jobs on machines with given technological ordering for each job. What are the limitations of the method?
8. Six jobs go first through machine *I* and then through machine *II*. The order of completion of jobs have no significance. The following gives the machine times in hours, for six jobs and the two machines.

Job	**1**	**2**	**3**	**4**	**5**	**6**
Machine *I*	5	9	4	7	8	6
Machine *II*	7	4	8	3	9	5

Find the sequence of jobs that minimizes the total elapsed time to complete the jobs.

[**Ans.** 3 → 1 → 5 → 6 → 2 → 4. Min. time = 42 hours]

9. We have seven jobs, each of which has to go through the machines M_1 and M_2 in the order M_1 M_2. Processing time (in hours) are given as:

Job	**1**	**2**	**3**	**4**	**5**	**6**	**7**
Machine *I*	3	12	15	6	10	11	9
Machine *II*	8	10	10	6	12	1	3

Determine a sequence of these jobs that will minimize the total elapsed time.

[**Ans:** 1 → 4 → 5 → 2 → 3 → 7 → 6. Total time = 67 hours]

10. Find the sequence that minimizes the total elapsed time required to complete the following tasks.

Tasks	**A**	**B**	**C**	**D**	**E**	**F**	**G**
Time on I machine	3	8	7	4	9	8	7
Time on II machine	4	3	2	5	1	4	3
Time on III machine	6	7	5	11	5	6	12

[**Ans.** $A \to D \to G \to F \to B \to C \to E$ or $A \to D \to G \to B \to F \to C \to E$.
Total elapsed time = 59 hours]

11. Find the sequence for the following eight jobs that will minimize the total elapsed time for the completion of all the jobs. Each job is processed in the same order.

Time for machines	**Jobs**							
	1	**2**	**3**	**4**	**5**	**6**	**7**	**8**
A	4	6	7	4	5	3	6	2
B	8	10	7	8	11	8	9	13
C	5	6	2	3	4	9	15	11

The entries give the time in hours on the machine.

[**Ans.** 4 → 5 → 3 → 1 → 2 → 8 → 7 → 6. Min. time is = 81 hrs.]

12. Solve the following sequencing problem, when passing is not allowed.

Items	Machines				
	A	B	C	D	E
I	9	7	5	4	11
II	8	8	6	7	12
III	7	6	7	8	10
IV	10	5	5	4	8

[**Ans.** I → III → II → IV. Min. time is 66 hours]

13. We have 4 jobs, each of which has to go through the machines M_j, j = 1, 2 ... 6 in the order M_1 M_2 ... M_6. Processing time (in hours) is given below.

	M_1	M_2	M_3	M_4	M_5	M_6
Job *A*	18	8	7	2	10	25
Job *B*	17	6	9	6	8	19
Job C	11	5	8	5	7	15
Job *D*	20	4	3	4	8	12

Determine a sequence of these four jobs that minimizes the total elapsed time.

[**Ans.** *C* → *A* → *B* → *D*. Total elapsed time = 112 hours]

14. When passing is not allowed, solve the following problem giving an optimal solution.

Jobs	Machines				
	M_1	M_2	M_3	M_4	M_5
A	9	7	4	5	11
B	8	8	6	7	12
C	7	6	7	8	10
D	10	5	5	4	8

[**Ans.** *A* → *C* → *B* → *D*. Min. time = 67 hours]

15. Two jobs are to be processed on four machines *A*, *B*, *C* and *D*. The technological order for these machines is as follows.

Job 1	*A*	*B*	*C*	*D*
Job 2	*D*	*B*	*A*	*C*

Processing periods (time) are given in the following table.

	Machines			
	A	*B*	*C*	*D*
Job 1	4	6	7	3
Job 2	4	7	5	8

Find the optimal sequence of jobs on each of the machines.

[**Ans.** Total elapsed time = 24 hours]

16. A machine shop has four machines *A*, *B*, *C* and *D*. Two jobs must be processed through each of these machines. The time taken (in hours) on each of the machines and the necessary sequence of jobs are given below.

Job 1	Sequence of machine Time	*A* 2	*B* 4	*C* 5	*D* 1
Job 2	Sequence Time	*D* 6	*B* 4	*A* 2	*C* 3

Use graphical method to obtain the total elapsed time.

[**Ans.** Total elapsed time = 15 hours]

Chapter

15

Network Scheduling by PERT/CPM

15.1 INTRODUCTION

Network scheduling is a technique used for planning and scheduling large projects, in the fields of construction, maintenance, fabrication and purchasing of computer systems, etc. It is a method of minimizing the trouble spots such as production, delays and interruptions, by determining critical factors and co-ordinating various parts of the overall job.

There are two basic planning and controlling techniques that utilize a network to complete a predetermined project or schedule. These are Programme Evaluation Review Technique (PERT) and Critical Path Method (CPM).

A project is defined as a combination of interrelated activities, all of which must be executed in a certain order for its completion.

The work involved in a project can be divided into three phases, corresponding to the management functions of planning, scheduling and controlling.

Planning: This phase involves setting the objectives of the project as well as the assumptions to be made. It also involves the listing of tasks or jobs that must be performed in order to complete a project under consideration. In this phase, in addition to the estimates of costs and duration of the various activities, the manpower, machines and materials required for the project are also determined.

Scheduling: This consists of laying the activities according to their order of precedence and determining the following:

(*i*) The start and finish times for each activity.
(*ii*) The critical path on which the activities require special attention.
(*iii*) The slack and float for the non-critical paths.

Controlling: This phase is exercised after the planning and scheduling. It involves the following:

(*i*) Making periodical progress reports
(*ii*) Reviewing the progress
(*iii*) Analyzing the status of the project
(*iv*) Making management decisions regarding updating, crashing and resource allocation, etc.

15.2 BASIC TERMS

To understand the network techniques, one should be familiar with a few basic terms of which both CPM and PERT are special applications.

Network: It is the graphic representation of logically and sequentially connected arrows and nodes, representing activities and events in a project. Networks are also called *arrow diagrams*.

Activity: An activity represents some action and is a time consuming effort necessary to complete a particular part of the overall project. Thus, each and every activity has a point of time where it begins and a point where it ends.

It is represented in the network by an arrow,

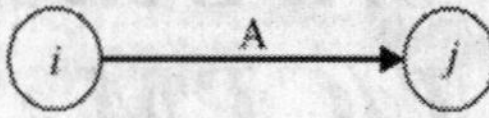

Here *A* is called the *activity*.

Event The beginning and end points of an activity are called *events or nodes*. Event is a point in time and does not consume any resources. It is represented by a numbered circle. The head event called the *jth event* always has a number higher than the tail event, which is also called the *ith event*.

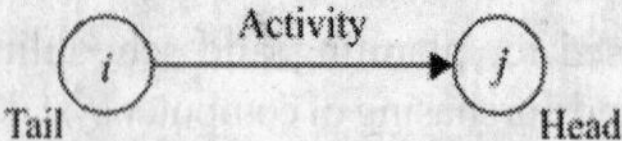

Merge and burst events It is not necessary for an event to be the ending event of only one activity as it can be the ending event of two or more activities. Such an event is defined as a *merge event*.

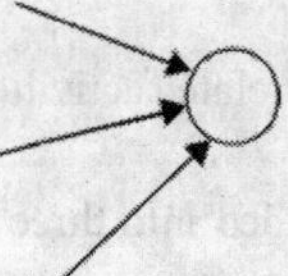

If the event happens to be the beginning event of two or more activities, it is defined as a *burst event*.

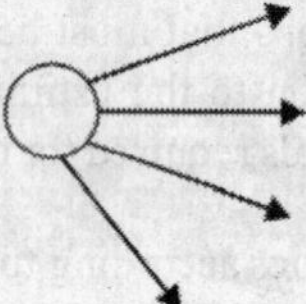

Preceding, succeeding and concurrent activities Activities that must be accomplished before a given event can occur, are termed as *preceding activities*.

Activities that cannot be accomplished until an event has occurred, are termed as *succeeding activities*.

Activities that can be accomplished concurrently i.e., activities taking place at the same time or in the same location, are known as *concurrent activities*.

This classification is relative, which means that one activity can be preceding to a certain event, and the same activity can be succeeding to some other event or it may be a concurrent activity with one or more activities.

Dummy activity Certain activities, which neither consume time nor resources but are used simply to represent a connection or a link between the events are known as *dummies*. It is shown in the network by a dotted line. The purpose of introducing dummy activity is:

(*i*) to maintain uniqueness in the numbering system, as every activity may have a distinct set of events by which the activity can be identified.

(*ii*) to maintain a proper logic in the network.

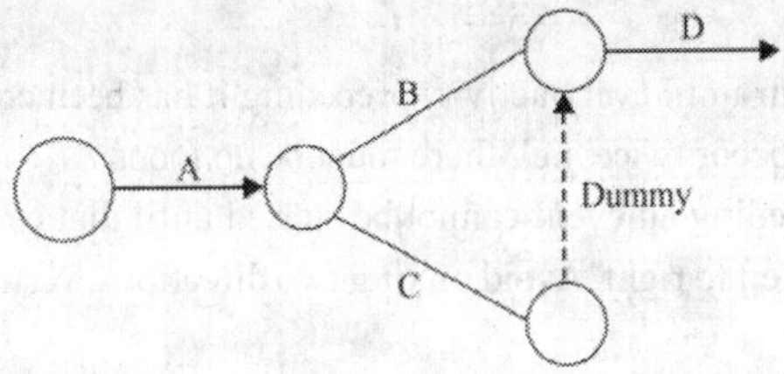

15.3 COMMON ERRORS

Following are the three common errors in a network construction:

***Looping* (*cycling*)** In a network diagram, a looping error is also known as *cycling error*. Drawing an endless loop in a network is known as *error of looping*. A loop can be formed, if an activity is represented as going back in time.

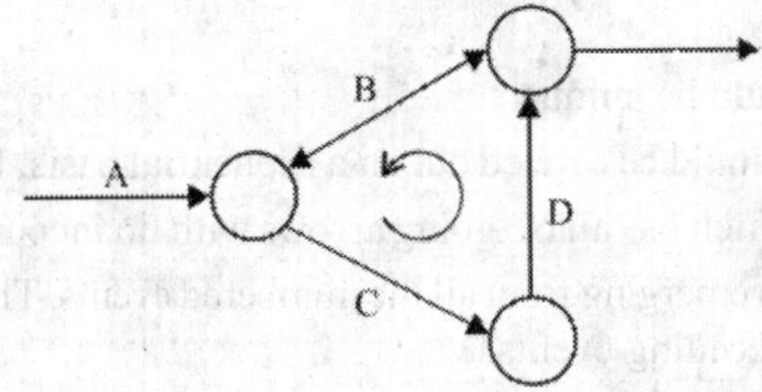

Dangling To disconnect an activity before the completion of all the activities in a network diagram, is known as *dangling*.

Redundancy If a dummy activity is the only activity emanating from an event and can be eliminated, it is known as *redundancy*.

15.4 RULES OF NETWORK CONSTRUCTION

There are a number of rules in connection with the handling of events and activities of a project network that should be followed.

(*i*) Try to avoid the arrows that cross each other.
(*ii*) Use straight arrows.
(*iii*) No event can occur until every activity preceding it has been completed.
(*iv*) An event cannot occur twice, i.e., there must be no loops.
(*v*) An activity succeeding an event cannot be started until that event has occurred.
(*vi*) Use arrows from left to right. Avoid mixing two directions, vertical and standing arrows may be used, if necessary.
(*vii*) Dummies should be introduced only, if it is extremely necessary.
(*viii*) The network has only one entry point called the *start event* and one point of emergence called the *end or terminal event*.

15.5 NUMBERING THE EVENTS (FULKERSON'S RULE)

After the network is drawn in a logical sequence, every event is assigned a unique number. The number sequence must be such so as to reflect the flow of the network. In numbering the events, the following rules should be observed.

(*i*) Event numbers should be unique.
(*ii*) Event numbering should be carried out on a sequential basis, from left to right.
(*iii*) The initial event, which has all outgoing arrows with no incoming arrow is numbered as 1.
(*iv*) Delete all the arrows emerging from all the numbered events. This will create at least one new start event, out of the preceding events.
(*v*) Number all new start events 2, 3 and so on. Repeat this process until the terminal event without any successor activity is reached. Number the terminal node suitably.

Note: The head of an arrow should always bear a number higher than the one assigned to the tail of the arrow.

15.5.1 Construction of Network

Example 15.1 Construct a network for the project whose activities and precedence relationships are as given below:

Activities	*A*	*B*	*C*	*D*	*E*	*F*	*G*	*H*	*I*
Immediate Predecessor	–	*A*	*A*	–	*D*	*B, C, E*	*F*	*D*	*G, H*

Solution From the given constraints, it is clear that *A* and *D* are the starting activities and *I* the terminal activity. *B* and *C* are starting with the same event and are both the predecessors of the activity *F*. Also, *E* has to be the predecessor of both *F* and *H*. Hence, we have to introduce a dummy activity.

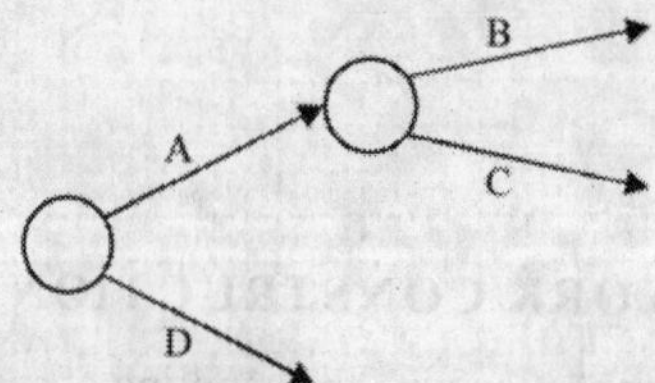

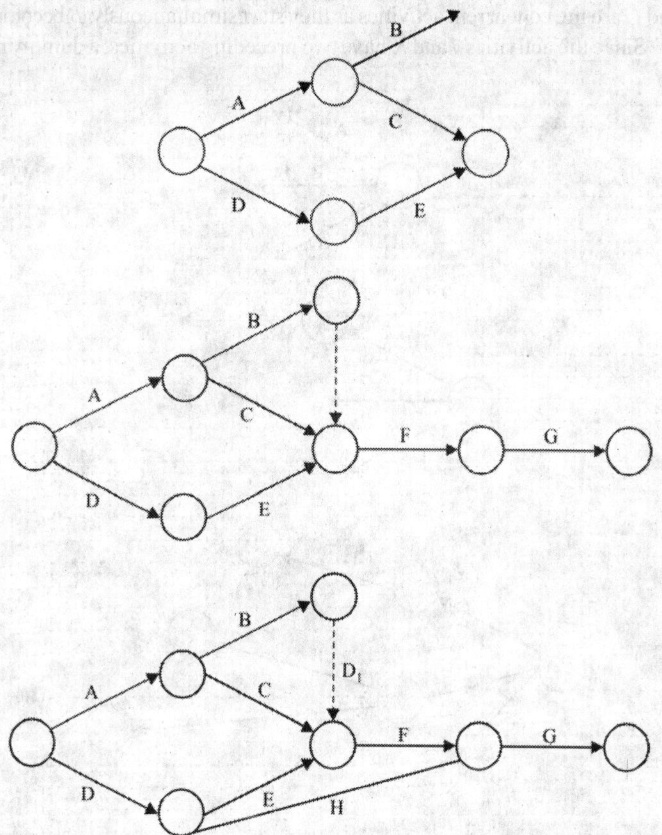

D_1 is the dummy activity.

Finally, we have the following network.

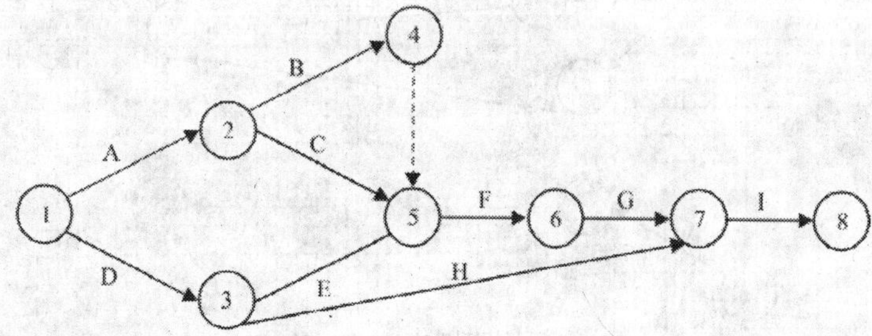

Example 15.2 Construct a network for each of the projects whose activities and their precedence relationships are given below.

Activity	*A*	*B*	*C*	*D*	*E*	*F*	*G*	*H*	*I*	*J*	*K*
Predecessor	–	–	–	*A*	*B*	*B*	*C*	*D*	*E*	*H, I*	*F, G*

Solution *A*, *B* and *C* are the concurrent activities as they start simultaneously. *B* becomes the predecessor of activities *E* and *F*. Since the activities *J* and *K* have two preceding activities, a dummy may be introduced (if possible).

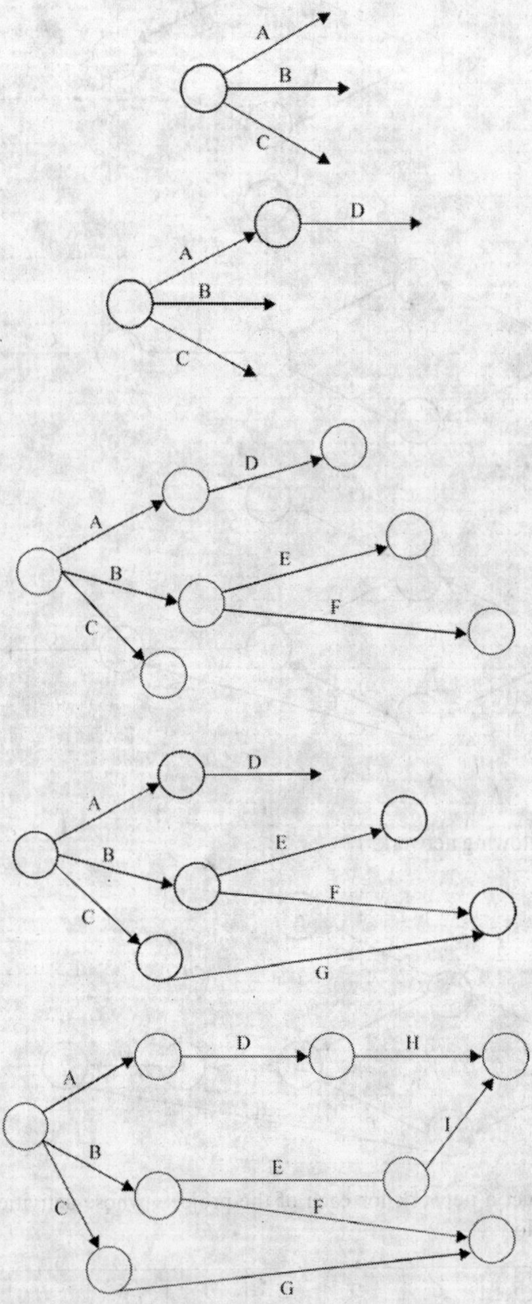

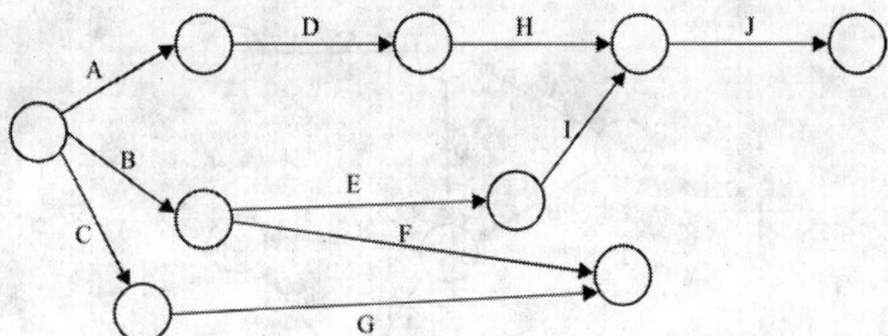

Finally we have,

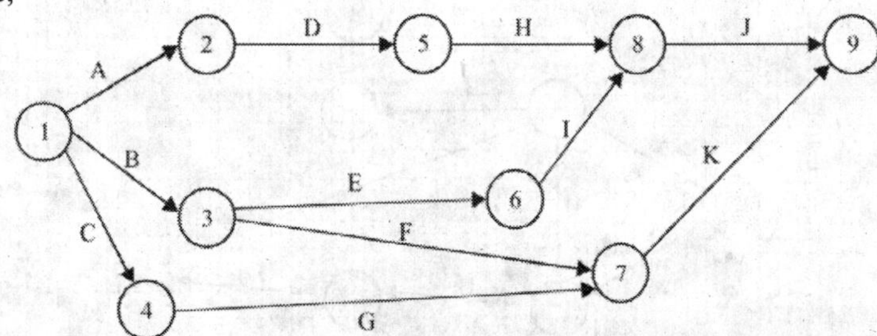

Example 15.3 $A < C, D, I; B < G, F; D < G, F; F < H, K; G, H < J; I, J, K < E$

Solution Given $A < C$, which means that C cannot be started until A is completed. That is, A is the preceding activity to C. The above constraints can be given in the following table.

Activity	*A*	*B*	*C*	*D*	*E*	*F*	*G*	*H*	*I*	*J*	*K*
Predecessor	–	–	*A*	*A*	*I, J, K*	*B, D*	*B, D*	*F*	*A*	*G, H*	*F*

A and *B* are the starting activities, and *E* is the terminal activity.

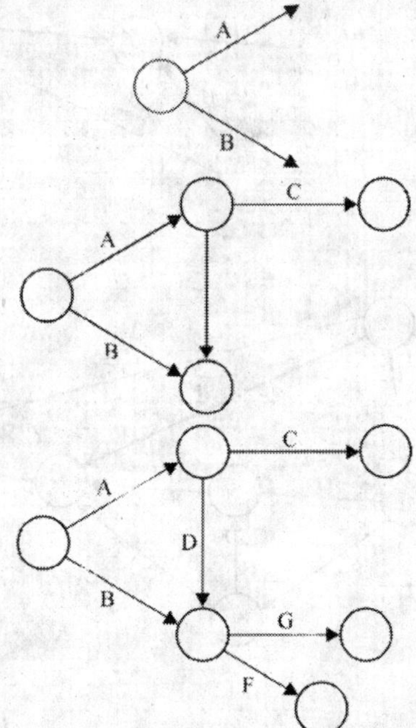

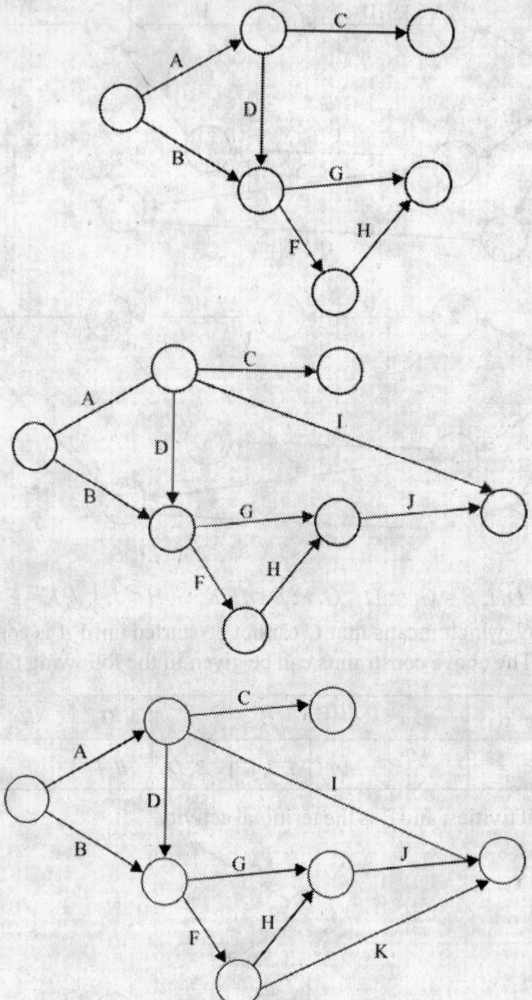

Finally, we have,

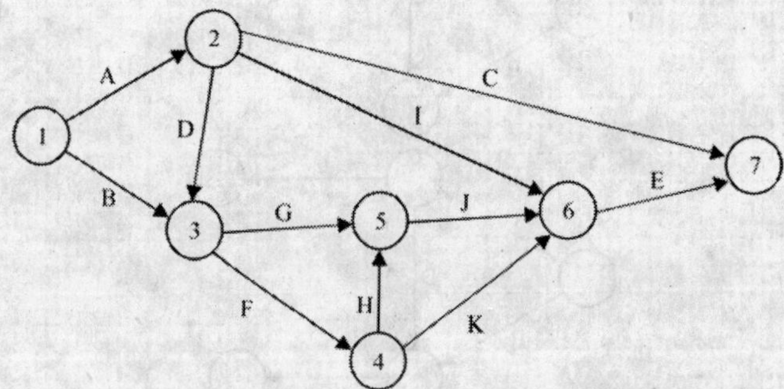

Example 15.4

Activities	A	B	C	D	E	F	G	H	I
Immediate Predecessor	–	–	A, B	B	B	A, B	F, D	F, D	C, G

Solution A and B are concurrent activities as they start simultaneously. I is the terminal activity. Since the activities C and F are coming from both activities A and B, we need to introduce a dummy activity.

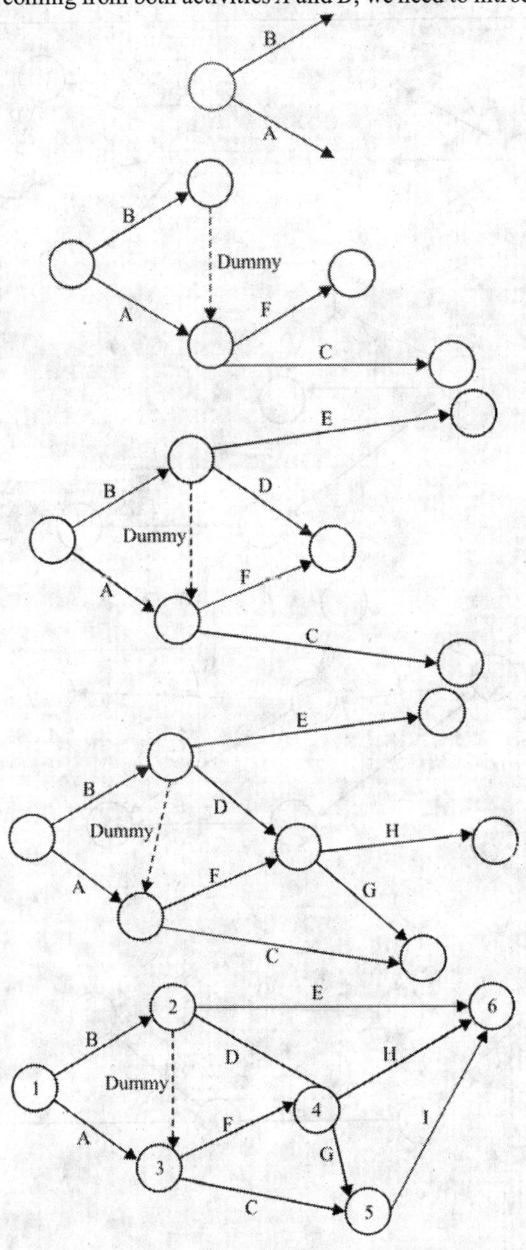

Example 15.5 A, B and C can start simultaneously

$$A < D, I; B < G, F; D < G, F; C < E; E < H, K; F < H, K; G, H < J.$$

Solution The above constraints can be formatted into a table.

Activity	*A*	*B*	*C*	*D*	*E*	*F*	*G*	*H*	*I*	*J*	*K*
Predecessor Activity	–	–	–	*A*	*C*	*B, D*	*B, D*	*E, F*	*A*	*G,*	*E, F*

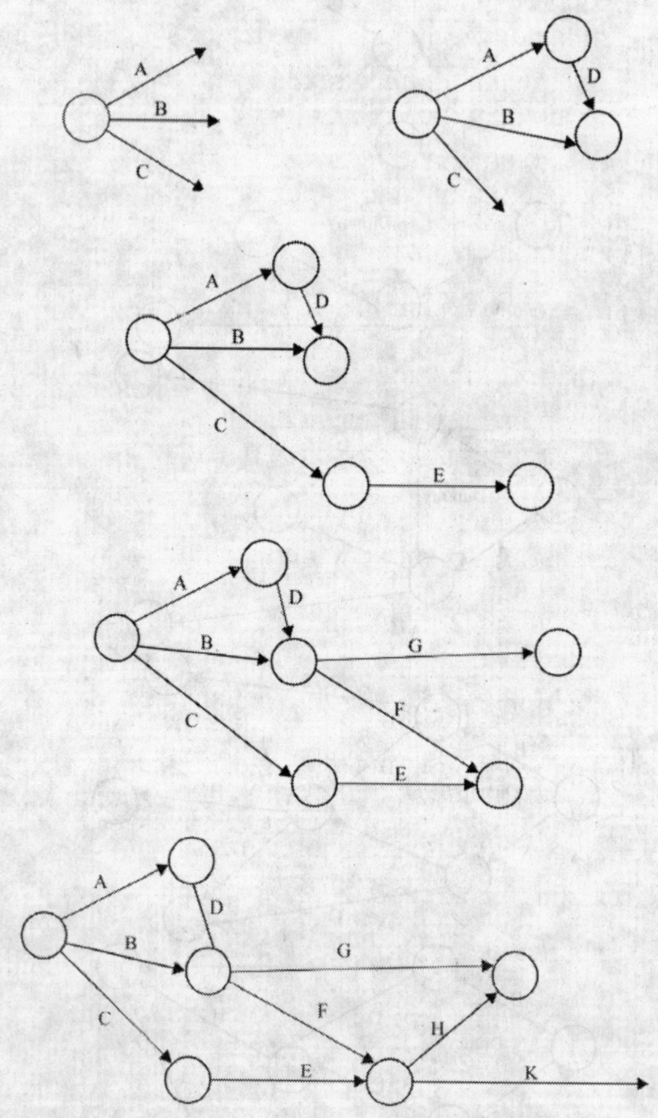

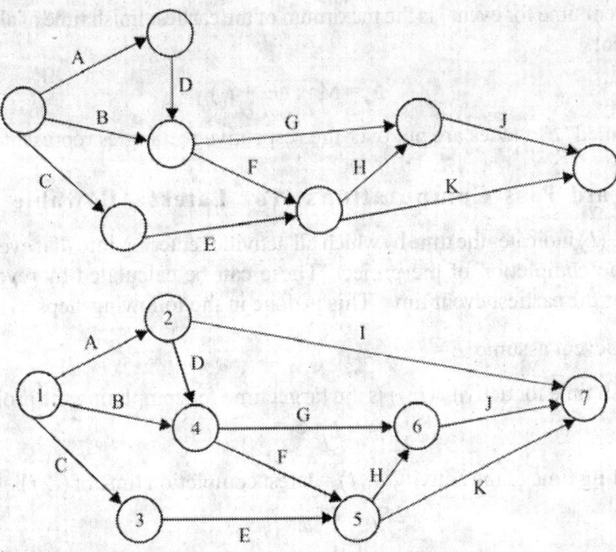

15.6 TIME ANALYSIS

Once the network of a project is constructed, the time analysis of the network becomes essential for planning various activities of the project. Activity time is a forecast of the time for an activity which is expected to take from its starting point to its completion (under normal conditions).

We shall use the following notation for basic scheduling computations.

(i, j) = Activity (i, j) with tail event i and head event j

T_{ij} = Estimated completion time of activity (i, j)

ES_{ij} = Earliest starting time of activity (i, j)

EF_{ij} = Earliest finishing time of activity (i, j)

LS_{ij} = Latest starting time of activity (i, j)

LF_{ij} = Latest finishing time of activity (i, j).

The basic scheduling computation can be put under the following three groups.

15.6.1 Forward Pass Computations (For Earliest Event Time)

Before starting computations, the occurrence time of the initial network event is fixed. The forward pass computation yields the earliest start and the earliest finish time for each activity (i, j) and indirectly the earliest occurrence time for each event namely E_i. This consists of the following three steps:

Step 1 The computations begin from the start node and move towards the end node. Let zero be the starting time for the project.

Step 2 Earliest starting time $(ES)_{ij} = E_i$ is the earliest possible time when an activity can begin, assuming that all of the predecessors are also started at their earliest starting time. Earliest finish time of activity (i, j) is the earliest starting time + the activity time.

$$(EF)_{ij} = (ES)_{ij} + t_{ij}$$

Step 3 Earliest event time for event j is the maximum of the earliest finish time of all the activities, ending at that event.

$$E_j = \underset{i}{\text{Max}}\,(E_i + t_{ij})$$

The computed 'E' values are put over the respective rectangles representing each event.

15.6.2 Backward Pass Computations (For Latest Allowable Time)

The latest event time (L) indicates the time by which all activities entering into that event must be completed without delaying the completion of the project. These can be calculated by reversing the method of calculations used for the earliest event time. This is done in the following steps.

Step 1 For ending event assume, $E = L$.

Step 2 Latest finish time for activity (i, j) is the target time for completing the project,

$$(LF_{ij}) = L_j$$

Step 3 Latest starting time of the activity (i, j) = latest completion time of (i, j) – the activity time

$$LS_{ij} = LF_{ij} - t_{ij}$$
$$= L_j - t_{ij}$$

Step 4 Latest event time for event i is the minimum of the latest start time of all activities originating from the event.

$$L_i = \underset{j}{\text{Min}}\,(L_j - t_{ij})$$

The computed 'L' values are put over the respective triangles representing each event.

15.6.3 Determination of Floats and Slack Times

Float is defined as the difference between the latest and the earliest activity time.

Slack is defined as the difference between the latest and the earliest event time.

Hence, the basic difference between the slack and float is that slack is used for events only; whereas float is used for activities.

There are mainly three kinds of floats as given below.

Total float It refers to the amount of time by which the completion of an activity could be delayed beyond the earliest expected completion time, without affecting the overall project duration time.

Mathematically, the total float of an activity (i, j) is the difference between the latest start time and the earliest start time of that activity.

Hence, the total float for an activity (i, j) denoted by $(TF)_{ij}$ is calculated by the formula,

$(TF)_{ij}$ = (Latest start – Earliest start) for activity (i, j)

$$\text{i.e., } (TF)_{ij} = (LS)_{ij} - (ES)_{ij}$$
$$\text{or } (TF)_{ij} = (L_j - E_i) - t_{ij}$$

where, E_i and L_j are the earliest time and latest time for the tail event i and head event j and t_{ij} is the normal time for the activity (i, j). This is the most important type of float as it concerns the overall project duration.

Free float The time by which the completion of an activity can be delayed beyond the earliest finish time, without affecting the earliest start of a subsequent succeeding activity.

Mathematically, the free float for activity (i, j) denoted by $(FF)_{ij}$ can be calculated by the formula,

$$FF_{ij} = (E_j - E_i) - t_{ij}$$

$$(FF)_{ij} = \text{Total float} - \text{Head event slack}$$

Head event slack $= L_j - E_j$

This float is concerned with the commencement of the subsequent activity.

The free float can take values from zero up to total float, but it cannot exceed total float. This float is very useful for rescheduling an activity with minimum disruption in earlier plans.

Independent float The amount of time by which the start of an activity can be delayed, without affecting the earliest start time of any immediately following activities, assuming that the preceding activity has finished at its latest finish time.

Mathematically, independent float of an activity (i, j) denoted by $(IF)_{ij}$ can be calculated by the formula,

$$IF_{ij} = (E_j - L_i) - t_{ij}$$

or

$$(IF)_{ij} = \text{Free Float} - \text{Tail event slack}$$

where tail event slack is given by,

$$\text{Tail event slack} = L_i - E_i$$

The negative independent float is always taken as zero. This float is concerned with prior and subsequent activities.

$$IF_{ij} \le FF_{ij} \le TF_{ij}$$

Notes: (*i*) If the total float TF_{ij} for any activity (i, j) is zero, then such an activity is called *critical activity*.

(*ii*) The float can be used to reduce project duration. While doing this, the float of not only that activity, but that of other activities will also change.

Critical activity An activity is said to be critical, if a delay in its start cause a further delay in the completion of the entire project.

Critical path The sequence of critical activities in a network which determines the duration of a project is called the critical path. It is the longest path in the network, from the starting event to the ending event and defines the minimum time required to complete the project. In the network it is denoted by a double line and identifies all the critical activities of the project. Hence, for the activities (i, j) to lie on the critical path, following conditions must be satisfied.

(*a*) $ES_i = LF_i$

(*b*) $ES_j = LF_j$

(*c*) $ES_j - ES_i = LF_j - LF_i = t_{ij}$

ES_i and ES_j are the earliest start and finish time of the events *i* and *j*.

LF_i and LF_j are the latest start and finish time of the events *i* and *j*.

15.7 CRITICAL PATH METHOD (CPM)

The critical path method (CPM) is a step-by-step procedure for scheduling the activities in a project. It is an important tool related to effective project management. The iterative procedure of determining the critical path is as follows:

Step 1 List all the jobs and then draw an arrow (network) diagram. Each job is indicated by an arrow with the direction of the arrow showing the sequence of jobs. The length of the arrows has no significance. The arrows are placed based on the predecessor, successor and concurrent relation within the job.

Step 2 Indicate the normal time (t_{ij}) for each activity (i, j) above the arrow, which is deterministic.

Step 3 Calculate the earliest start time and the earliest finish time for each event and write the earliest time E_i for each event i in the ☐. Also calculate the latest finish and latest start time. From this we calculate the latest time L_j for each event j and put it in the Δ.

Step 4 Tabulate the various times, namely, normal time, earliest time and latest time on the arrow diagram.

Step 5 Determine the total float for each activity by taking the difference between the earliest start and the latest start time.

Step 6 Identify the critical activities and connect them with the beginning and the ending events in the network diagram by double line arrows. This gives the critical path.

Step 7 Calculate the total project duration.

Note: The earliest start and finish time of an activity, as well as the latest start and finish time of an activity are shown in the table. These are calculated by using the following hints.

To find the earliest time, we consider the tail event of the activity. Let the starting time of the project namely $ES_i = 0$. Add the normal time with the starting time, to get the earliest finish time. The earliest starting time for the tail event of the next activity is given by the maximum of the earliest finish time for the head event of the previous activity.

Similarly, to get the latest time, we consider the head event of the activity.

The latest finish time of the head event of the final activity is given by the target time of the project. The latest start time can be obtained by subtracting the normal time of that activity. The latest finish time for the head event of the next activity is given by the minimum of the latest start time for the tail event of the previous activity.

Example 15.6 A project schedule has the following characteristics.

Activity	*1–2*	*1–3*	*2–4*	*3–4*	*3–5*	*4–9*	*5–6*	*5–7*	*6–8*	*7–8*	*8–10*	*9–10*
Time (days)	4	1	1	1	6	5	4	8	1	2	5	7

From the above information, you are required to:

1. Construct a network diagram.
2. Compute the earliest event time and latest event time.
3. Determine the critical path and total project duration.
4. Compute total and free float for each activity.

Solution First we construct the network with the given constraints (here we get it by just connecting the event numbers).

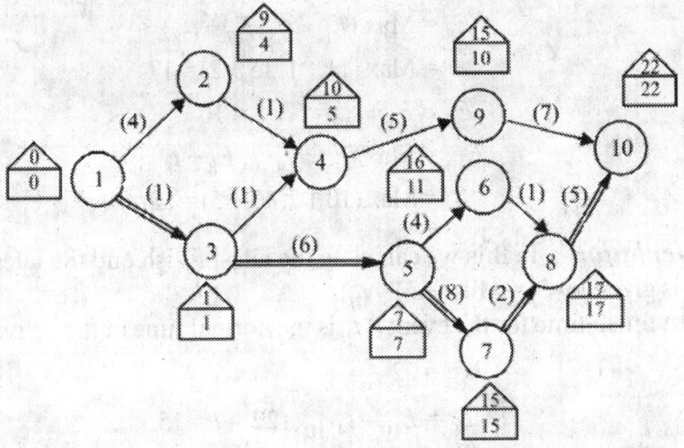

The following table gives the critical path as well as total and free floats calculation.

Activity	Normal time	Earliest		Latest		TF	FF
		Start	Finish	Start	Finish		
1 – 2	4	0	4	5	9	5	5 – 5 = 0
1 – 3	1	0	1	0	1	(0)	0
2 – 4	1	4	5	9	10	5	0
3 – 4	1	1	2	9	10	8	3
3 – 5	6	1	7	1	7	(0)	0
4 – 9	5	5	10	10	15	5	0
5 – 6	4	7	11	12	16	5	0
5 – 7	8	7	15	7	15	(0)	0
6 – 8	1	11	12	16	17	5	0
7 – 8	2	15	17	15	17	(0)	0
8 –10	5	17	22	17	22	(0)	0
9 – 10	7	10	17	15	22	5	5

The earliest and latest calculations are shown below.

Forward pass calculation In this we estimate the earliest start (Es_i) and finish times (Es_j). The earliest time for the event i is given by,

$$E_i = \operatorname*{Max}_{i} (ES_i + t_{ij})$$
$$ES_1 = 0 = E_1 = 0$$
$$E_2 = ES_2 = ES_1 + t_{12} = 0 + 4 = 4$$
$$E_3 = ES_3 = ES_1 + t_{13} = 0 + 1 = 1$$
$$E_4 = ES_4 = \text{Max}\,(ES_3 + t_{34}, ES_2 + t_{24})$$
$$= \text{Max}\,(1 + 1, 4 + 1) = 5$$
$$E_5 = (E_3 + t_{35}) = 1 + 6 = 7$$
$$E_6 = E_5 + t_{56} = 7 + 4 = 11$$
$$E_7 = E_5 + t_{57} = 7 + 8 = 15$$

$$E_8 = \text{Max}(E_6 + t_{68}, E_7 + t_{78})$$
$$= \text{Max}(11+1, 15+2) = 17$$
$$E_9 = E_4 + t_{49} = 5 + 5 = 10$$
$$E_{10} = \text{Max}(E_9 + t_{9,10}, E_8 + t_{8,10})$$
$$= \text{Max}(10+7, 17+5) = 22.$$

Backward pass calculation In this we calculate the latest finish and the latest start time. The latest time L for an event i is given by $L_i = \underset{j}{\text{Min}}\ (LF_j - t_{ij})$,
where, LF_j is the latest finish time for the event j, t_{ij} is the normal time of the activity.

$$L_{10} = 22$$
$$L_9 = L_{10} - t_{9,10} = 22 - 7 = 15$$
$$L_8 = L_{10} - t_{8,10} = 22 - 5 = 17$$
$$L_7 = L_8 - t_{7,8} = 17 - 2 = 15$$
$$L_6 = L_8 - t_{6,8} = 17 - 1 = 16$$
$$L_5 = \text{Min}(L_6 - t_{5,6}, L_7 - t_{5,7})$$
$$= \text{Min}(16-4, 15-8) = 7$$
$$L_4 = L_9 - t_{4,9} = 15 - 5 = 10$$
$$L_3 = \text{Min}(L_4 - t_{3,4}, L_5 - t_{3,5})$$
$$= \text{Min}(10-1, 7-6) = 1$$
$$L_2 = L_4 - t_{2,4} = 10 - 1 = 9$$
$$L_1 = \text{Min}(L_2 - t_{12}, L_3 - t_{13}) = \text{Min}(9-4, 1-1) = 0.$$

These calculations are shown in the above table.

To find the TF (Total Float) Considering the activity 1 – 2, *TF* of (1 – 2) = Latest start–Earliest start
$= 5 - 0 = 5$

Similarly *TF* (2 – 4) = *LS* – *ES*
$= 9 - 4 = 5$

Free float = *TF* – Head event slack.
Consider the activity 1 – 2
FF of (1 – 2) = *TF* of (1 – 2) – Slack for the head event 2
$= 5 - (9 - 4)$ (from the figure for event 2)
$= 5 - 5 = 0$
FF of (2 – 4) = *TF* of (2 – 4) – Slack for the head event 4
$= 5 - (10 - 5) = 5 - 5 = 0$
Like this we calculate the *TF* and *FF* for the remaining activities.
From the above table we observe that the activities 1 – 3, 3 – 5, 5 – 7, 7 – 9, 8 – 10 are the critical activities as their total float is 0.
Hence, we have the following critical path.
1 – 3 – 5 – 7 – 8 – 10, with the total project duration of 22 days.

Example 15.7 A small maintenance project consists of the following jobs, whose precedence relationships are given below.

Job	*1–2*	*1–3*	*2–3*	*2–5*	*3–4*	*3–6*	*4–5*	*4–6*	*5–6*	*6–7*
Duration (days)	15	15	3	5	8	12	1	14	3	14

1. Draw an arrow diagram representing the project.
2. Find the total float for each activity.
3. Find the critical path and the total project duration.

Solution

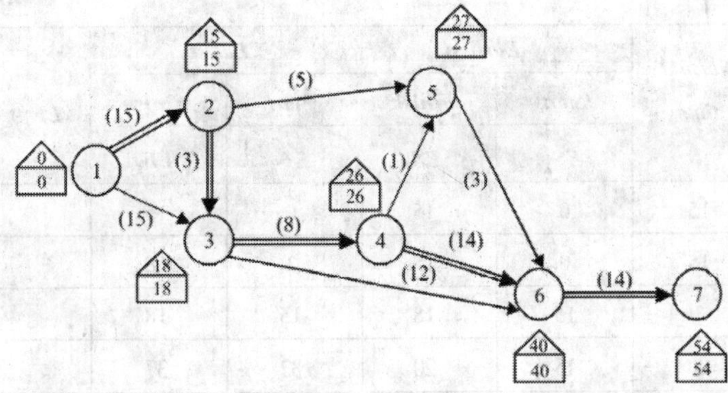

Forward pass calculation In this we estimate the earliest start and the earliest finish time ES_j given by,

$ES_j = \underset{i}{\text{Max}}\ (ES_i + t_{ij})$ where, ES_i is the earliest start time and t_{ij} is the normal time for the activity (i, j).

$$\begin{aligned}
ES_1 &= 0 \\
ES_2 &= ES_1 + t_{15} = 0 + 15 = 15 \\
ES_3 &= \text{Max}\ (ES_2 + t_{23}, ES_1 + t_{13}) \\
&= \text{Max}\ (15 + 3, 0 + 15) = 18 \\
ES_4 &= ES_3 + t_{34} = 18 + 8 = 26 \\
ES_5 &= \text{Max}\ (ES_2 + t_{25}, ES_4 + t_{45}) \\
&= \text{Max}\ (15 + 5, 26 + 1) = 27 \\
ES_6 &= \text{Max}\ (ES_3 + t_{36}, ES_4 + t_{46}, ES_5 + t_{56}) \\
&= \text{Max}\ (18 + 12, 26 + 14, 27 + 3) \\
&= 40 \\
ES_7 &= ES_6 + t_{67} = 40 + 14 = 54.
\end{aligned}$$

Backward pass calculation In this we calculate the latest finish and latest start time LF_i, given by $LF_i = \underset{i}{\text{Min}}\ (LF_j - t_{ij})$ where, LF_j is the latest finish time for the event j

$$\begin{aligned}
LF_7 &= 54 \\
LF_6 &= LF_7 - t_{67} = 54 - 14 = 40
\end{aligned}$$

$$LF_5 = LS_6 - t_{56} = 40 - 3 = 37$$

$$LF_4 = \text{Min}\,(LS_5 - t_{45}, LS_6 - t_{46})$$
$$= \text{Min}\,(37 - 1, 40 - 14) = 26$$

$$LF_3 = \text{Min}\,(LF_4 - t_{34}, LF_6 - t_{36})$$
$$= \text{Min}\,(26 - 8, 40 - 12) = 18$$

$$LF_2 = \text{Min}\,(LF_5 - t_{25}, LF_3 - t_{23})$$
$$= \text{Min}\,(37 - 5, 18 - 3) = 15$$

$$LF_1 = \text{Min}\,(LF_3 - t_{13}, LF_2 - t_{12})$$
$$= \text{Min}\,(18 - 15, 15 - 15) = 0$$

The following table gives the calculations for critical path and total float.

Activity	***Normal time***	***Earliest***		***Latest***		***Total float***
		Start	***Finish***	***Start***	***Finish***	$LF_j - ES_j$ or $LF_i - ES_i$
		ES_i	ES_j	LF_i	LF_j	
1 – 2	15	0	15	0	15	⓪
1 – 3	15	0	15	3	18	3
2 – 3	3	15	18	15	18	⓪
2 – 5	5	15	20	32	37	17
3 – 4	8	18	26	18	26	⓪
3 – 6	12	18	30	28	40	10
4 – 5	1	26	27	36	37	10
4 – 6	14	26	40	26	40	⓪
5 – 6	3	27	30	37	40	10
6 – 7	14	40	54	40	54	⓪

From the above table, we observe that the activities 1—2, 2—3, 3—4, 4—6, 6—7 are the critical activities and the critical path is given by, 1—2—3—4—6—7.

The total time taken for project completion is 54 days.

Example 15.8 The following table shows the jobs of a project with their duration in days. Draw the network and determine the critical path. Also calculate all the floats.

Jobs	***1–2***	***1–3***	***1–4***	***2–5***	***3–7***	***4–6***	***5–7***	***5–8***	***6–7***	***6–9***	***7–10***	***8–10***	***9–10***	***10–11***	***11–12***
Duration	10	8	9	8	16	7	7	7	8	5	12	10	15	8	5

Solution First we construct the network as shown below:

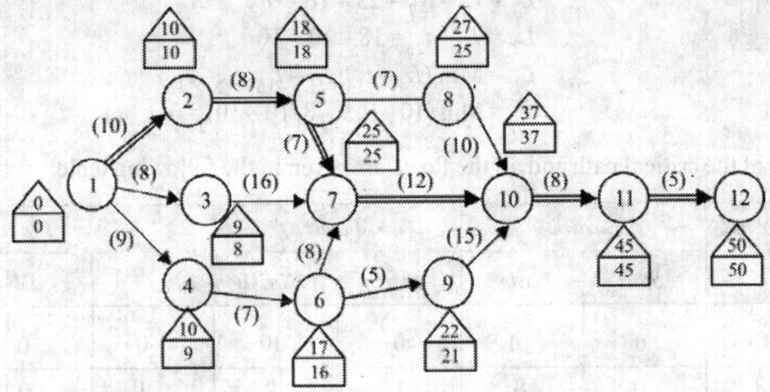

Forward pass calculation In this we calculate the earliest start and the earliest finish time for the activity and the earliest time for each event.

$$ES_1 = 0$$
$$ES_2 = ES_1 + t_{12} = 0 + 10 = 10$$
$$ES_3 = ES_1 + t_{13} = 0 + 8 = 8$$
$$E_4 = E_1 + t_{14}$$
$$= 0 + 9 = 9$$
$$E_5 = E_2 + t_{25} = 10 + 8 = 18$$
$$E_6 = E_4 + t_{46} = 9 + 7 = 16$$
$$E_7 = \text{Max}\,(E_3 + t_{37}, E_5 + t_{57}, E_6 + t_{67})$$
$$= \text{Max}\,(8 + 16, 16 + 8, 18 + 7) = 25$$
$$E_8 = E_5 + t_{58} = 18 + 7 = 25$$
$$E_9 - E_6 + t_{69} - 16 + 5 - 21$$
$$E_{10} = \text{Max}\,(E_7 + t_{7,10}, E_8 + t_{8,10}, E_9 + t_{9,10}$$
$$= \text{Max}\,(25 + 12, 25 + 10, 21 + 15) = 37$$
$$E_{11} = E_{10} + t_{10,11} = 37 + 8 = 45$$
$$E_{12} = E_{11} + t_{11,12} = 45 + 5 = 50$$

Backward pass calculation In this we calculate the latest finish and the latest start time LF_i, given by,

$$LF_i = \underset{i}{\text{Min}}\,(LF_j - t_{ij})$$
$$L_{12} = E_{12} = 50 \text{ (the target completion time)}$$
$$L_{11} = L_{12} - t_{11,12} = 50 - 5 = 45$$
$$L_{10} = L_{11} - t_{10,11} = 45 - 8 = 37$$
$$L_9 = L_{10} - t_{9.10} = 37 - 15 = 22$$
$$L_8 = L_{10} - t_{8.10} = 37 - 10 = 27$$
$$L_7 = L_{10} - t_{7.10} = 37 - 12 = 25$$
$$L_6 = \text{Min}\,(L_9 - t_{69}, L_7 - t_7 - t_{67})$$
$$= \text{Min}\,(22 - 5, 25 - 8) = 17$$
$$L_5 = \text{Min}\,(L_8 - t_{58}, L_7 - t_{57})$$
$$= \text{Min}\,(27 - 7, 25 - 7) = 18$$

$$L_4 = L_6 - t_{46} = 17 - 7 = 10$$
$$L_3 = L_7 - t_{37} = 25 - 16 = 9$$
$$L_2 = L_5 - t_{25} = 18 - 10 = 10$$
$$L_1 = \text{Min}\,(L_4 - t_{14}, L_3 - t_{13}, L_2 - t_{12})$$
$$= \text{Min}\,(10 - 9, 9 - 8, 10 - 10) = 0.$$

Computations of the critical path and all the floats are given in the following table:

Activity	Normal time	Earliest		Latest		Floats		
		Start	Finish	Start	Finish	TF	FF	IF
1–2	10	0	10	0	10	⓪	0	0
1–3	8	0	8	1	9	1	0	0
1–4	9	0	9	1	10	1	0	0
2–5	8	10	18	10	18	⓪	0	0
3–7	16	8	24	9	25	1	1	0
4–6	7	9	16	10	17	1	0	–1=0
5–7	7	18	25	18	25	⓪	0	0
5–8	7	18	25	20	27	2	0	0
6–7	8	16	24	17	25	1	1	0
6–9	5	16	21	17	22	1	0	–1=0
7–10	12	25	37	25	37	⓪	0	0
8–10	10	25	35	27	37	2	2	0
9–10	15	21	36	22	37	1	1	0
10–11	8	37	45	37	45	⓪	0	0
11–12	5	45	50	45	50	⓪	0	0

TF = Total float = $LS - ES$ or $LF - EF$

FF = Free float = TF – Head event slack = $TF - (L_j - E_j)$

IF = Independent float = FF – Tail event slack = $FF - (L_i - E_i)$

From the above calculation, we observe that the activity 1–2, 2–5, 5–7, 7–10, 10–11, 11–12 are the critical activities as their total float is 0. Hence, we have the critical path 1–2–5–7–10–11–12, with the total project duration as 50 days.

Example 15.9 A project consists of a series of tasks labelled $A, B \ldots H, I$ with the following constraints, $A < D, E; B, D < F; C < G; B < H; F, G < I; W < X, Y$ means X and Y cannot start until W is completed. You are required to construct a network using this notation. Also find the minimum time of completion of the project when the time of completion of each task is given as follows:

Task	A	B	C	D	E	F	G	H	I
Time (days)	23	8	20	16	24	18	19	4	10

Solution The constraints can be given as in the following table:

Activity	*A*	*B*	*C*	*D*	*E*	*F*	*G*	*H*	*I*
Preceding Activity	–	–	–	*A*	*A*	*B*, *D*	*C*	*B*	*F*, *G*

To determine the minimum time of completion of the project, we compute ES_{ij} and LF_{ij} for each of the tasks (i, j) of the project. The critical path calculations are as follows.

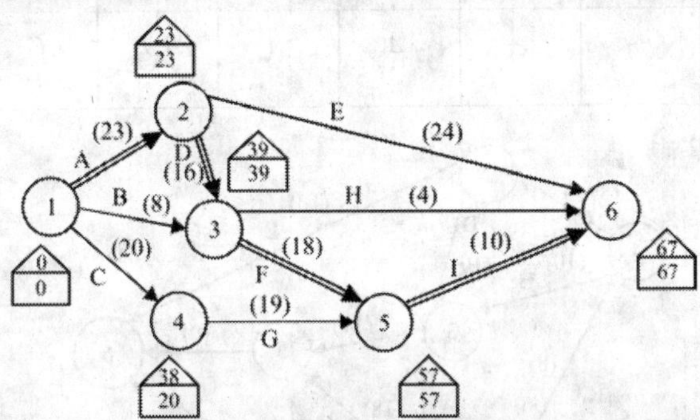

Task	*Normal time* t_{ij}	*Earliest*		*Latest*		*Total floats*
		Start	*Finish*	*Start*	*Finish*	
A 1–2	23	0	23	0	23	(0)
B 1–3	8	0	8	31	39	8
C 1–4	20	0	20	18	38	18
D 2–3	16	23	39	23	39	(0)
E 2–6	24	23	47	43	67	20
F 3–5	18	39	57	39	57	(0)
H 3–6	4	39	43	63	67	24
G 4–5	19	20	39	38	57	18
I 5–6	10	57	67	57	67	(0)

The above table shows that the critical activities are 1–2, 2–3, 3–5, 5–6 as their total float is zero. Hence, we have the critical path, 1–2–3–5–6, with the total project duration (the least possible time to complete the entire project) as 67 days.

Example 15.10 Tasks *A*, *B*, ... *H*, *I* constitute a project. The notation $X < Y$ means that the task *X* must be completed before *Y* is started. With the notation,

$$A < D, A < E, B < F, D < F, C < G, C < H, F < I, G < I$$

Draw a graph to represent the sequence of tasks and find the minimum time of completion of the project, when the time (in days) of completion of each task is as follows.

The above constraints can be given as in the following table:

Task	*A*	*B*	*C*	*D*	*E*	*F*	*G*	*H*	*I*
Time (days)	8	10	8	10	16	17	18	14	9

Solution The above constraints are given in the following table:

Activity	*A*	*B*	*C*	*D*	*E*	*F*	*G*	*H*	*I*
Preceding Activity	–	–	–	*A*	*A*	*B*, *D*	*C*	*C*	*F*, *G*

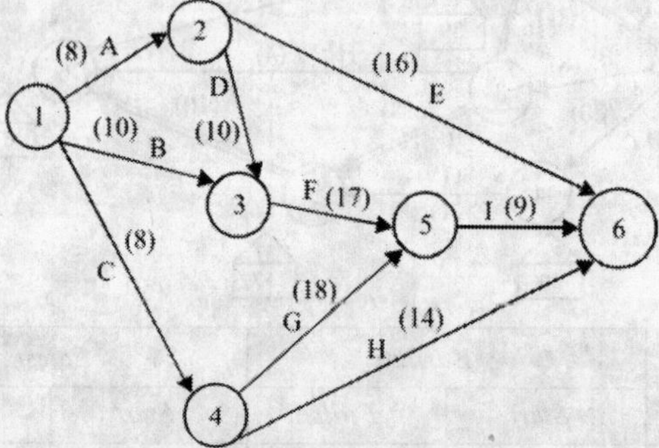

Time calculation Using forward and backward pass calculation, we first estimate the earliest and the latest time for each event.

$$ES_1 = E_1 = 0$$
$$E_2 = E_1 + t_{12} = 0 + 8 = 8$$
$$E_3 = \text{Max}\,(E_1 + E_{13}, E_2 + t_{23})$$
$$= \text{Max}\,(0 + 10, 8 + 10) = 18$$
$$E_4 = E_1 + t_{14} = 0 + 8 = 8$$
$$E_5 = \text{Max}\,(E_3 + t_{35}, E_4 + t_{45})$$
$$= \text{Max}\,(18 + 17, 8 + 18) = 35$$
$$E_6 = \text{Max}\,(E_2 + t_{26}, E_4 + t_{46}, E_5 + t_{56})$$
$$= \text{Max}\,(8 + 16, 8 + 14, 35 + 9) = 44$$

The value of the latest time can now be obtained.

$L_6 = E_6 = 44$ (Target completion time for the project)

$$L_5 = L_6 - t_{56} = 44 - 9 = 35$$
$$L_4 = \text{Min}\,(L_6 - t_{46}, L_5 - t_{45})$$
$$= \text{Min}\,(44 - 14, 35 - 18) = 17$$
$$L_3 = L_5 - t_{35} = 35 - 17 = 18$$
$$L_2 = \text{Min}\,(L_6 - t_{26}, L_3 - t_{23})$$
$$= \text{Min}\,(44 - 16, 18 - 10 = 8$$
$$L_1 = \text{Min}\,(L_4 - t_{14}, L_3 - t_{13}, L_2 - t_{12})$$
$$= \text{Min}\,(17 - 8, 18 - 10, 8 - 8) = 0.$$

To evaluate the critical events, all these calculations are put in the following table.

Task	Normal Time/days	Earliest		Latest		Floats		
		Start	Finish	Start	Finish	TF	FF	IF
A 1–2	8	0	8	0	8	(0)	0 – 0 = 0	0 – 0 = 0
B 1–3	10	0	10	8	18	8	8 – 0 = 8	8 – 0 = 8
C 1–4	8	0	8	9	17	9	9 – 9 = 0	0 – 0 = 0
D 2–3	10	8	18	8	18	(0)	0 – 0 = 0	0 – 0 = 0
E 2–6	16	8	24	28	44	20	20 – 0 = 20	20 – 0 = 20
F 3–5	17	18	35	18	35	(0)	0 – 0 = 0	0 – 0 = 0
G 4–5	18	8	26	17	35	9	9 – 0 = 9	9 – 9 = 0
H 4–6	14	8	22	30	44	22	22 – 0 = 22	22 – 9 = 13
I 5–6	9	35	44	35	44	(0)	0 – 0 = 0	0 – 0 = 0

The above table shows that the critical events are the tasks 1 – 2, 2 – 3, 3 – 5, 5 – 6 as their total float is zero.

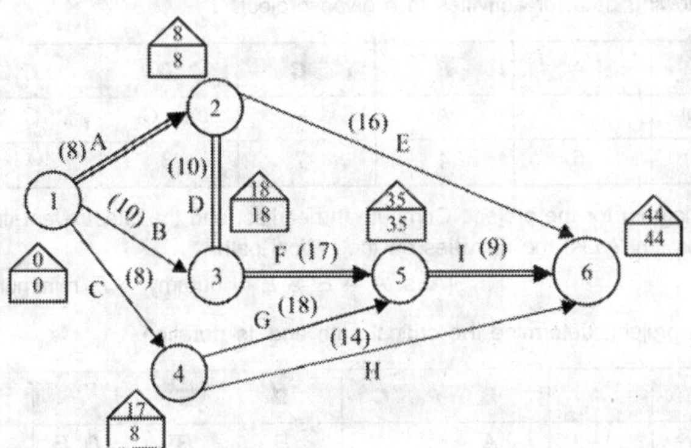

The critical path is given by 1–2–3–5–6 or *A–D–F–I*, with the total project duration as 44 days.

EXERCISES

1. The following table gives the activities and duration of a construction project.

Activity	1–2	1–3	2–3	2–4	3–4	4–5
Duration (days)	20	25	10	12	6	10

(*i*) Draw the network for the project

(*ii*) Find the critical path. **[Ans.** CPM: 1–2–3–4–5]

2. A small project consists of 11 activities *A*, *B*, *C* ... *K*. According to the precedence relationship *A* and *B* can start simultaneously, given *A* < *C*, *D*, *I*; *B* < *G*, *F*; *D* < *G*, *F*; *F* < *H*, *K*; *G*, *H* < *J*; *I*, *J*, *K* < *E*. The duration of the activities are as follows.

Activity	A	B	C	D	E	F	G	H	I	J	K
Duration (days)	5	3	10	2	8	4	5	6	12	8	9

Draw the network of the project. Summarise the CPM calculations in a tabular form computing the total and free floats of activities as well as determine the critical path. [**Ans.** Critical path *A–D–F–H–J–E* Project duration 33 days]

3. Draw the network and determine the critical path for the given data. Also calculate all the floats involved in CPM.

Jobs	1–2	1–3	2–4	3–4	3–5	4–5	4–6	5–6
Duration	6	5	10	3	4	6	2	9

[**Ans.** Critical path 1–2–4–5–6 Project duration 31 days]

4. A small maintenance project consists of the following 12 jobs.

Jobs	1–2	2–3	2–4	3–4	3–5	4–6	5–8	6–7	6–10	7–9	8–9	9–10
Duration (days)	2	7	3	3	5	3	5	8	4	4	1	7

Draw the arrow network of the project. Summarise CPM calculations in a tabular form, calculating the three types of floats and hence determine the critical path. [**Ans.** Critical path 1–2–3–4–5–6–7–9–10]

5. Consider the following data for activities in a given project.

Activity	A	B	C	D	E	F
Predecessor	–	*A*	–	*B*, *C*	*C*	*D*, *E*
Time (days)	5	4	7	3	4	2

Draw an arrow diagram for the project. Compute the earliest and the latest event times. What is the minimum project completion time? List the activities on the critical path.

[**Ans.** $A \rightarrow B \rightarrow E \rightarrow$ dummy $\rightarrow F$; minimum completion time 15 days]

6. For the following project, determine the critical path and its duration.

Activity	A	B	C	D	E	F	G	H
Predecessors	–	*A*	*A*	*B*	*B*	*D*, *E*	*D*	*C*, *F*, *G*
Time (days)	2	4	8	3	2	3	4	8

[**Ans.** 1–2–3–4–6–7; Project duration 21 days]

7. A project has the following time schedule.

Activity	1–2	1–3	1–4	2–5	3–6	3–7	4–6	5–8	6–9	7–8	8–9
Duration (months)	2	2	1	4	8	5	3	1	5	4	3

Construct the network and compute,

(*i*) Total float for each activity.

(*ii*) Critical path and its duration. [**Ans.** 1–3–6–9; Project duration 15 months]

15.8 PROGRAMME EVALUATION AND REVIEW TECHNIQUE (PERT)

The network methods discussed so far may be termed as deterministic, since estimated activity times are assumed to be known with certainty. However, in the research project or design of a gear box or a new machine, various activities are based on judgement. It is difficult to obtain a reliable time estimate due to the changing technology since time values are subject to chance variations. For such cases, where the activities are non-deterministic in nature, PERT was developed. Hence, PERT is a probabilistic method, where the activity times are represented by a probability distribution. This distribution of activity times is based on three different time estimates made for each activity, which are as follows:

(*i*) Optimistic time estimate (*ii*) Most likely time estimate
(*iii*) Pessimistic time estimate

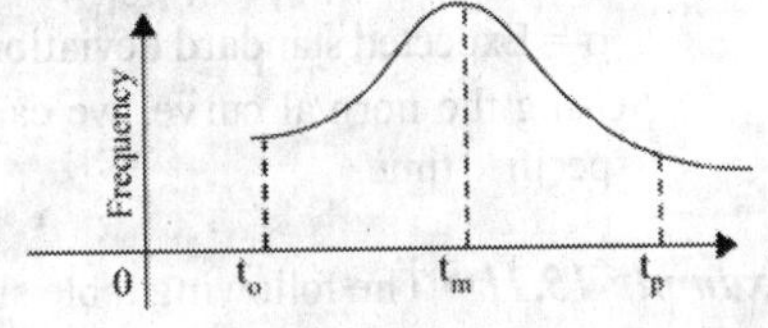

Time distribution curve

Optimistic time estimate It is the smallest time taken to complete the activity, if everything goes well. There is very little chance that an activity can be completed in a time less than the optimistic time. It is denoted by t_o or *a*.

Most likely time estimate It refers to the estimate of the normal time the activity would take. This assumes normal delays. It is the mode of the probability distribution. It is denoted by t_m or *m*.

Pessimistic time estimate It is the longest time that an activity would take, if everything goes wrong. It is denoted by t_p or *b*. These three time values are shown in the following figure.

From these three time estimates, we have to calculate the expected time of an activity. It is given by the weighted average of the three time estimates,

$$\boxed{t_e = \frac{t_o + 4t_m + t_p}{6}}$$

[β distribution with weights of 1, 4 and 1, for t_o, t_m and t_p estimates respectively.]

Variance of the activity is given by,

$$\sigma^2 = \left[\frac{t_p - t_o}{6}\right]^2$$

The expected length (duration), denoted by T_c of the entire project is the length of the critical path, i.e., the sum of the t_c's of all the activities along the critical path.

The main objective of the analysis through PERT is to find the completion date for a particular event within the specified date T_s, given by $P(Z \le D)$ where,

$$D = \frac{\text{Due date} - \text{Expected date of completion}}{\sqrt{\text{Project variance}}}$$

Here, *Z* stands for standard normal variable.

15.8.1 PERT Procedure

Step 1 Draw the project network.

Step 2 Compute the expected duration of each activity using the formula,

$$t_e = \frac{t_o + 4t_m + t_p}{6}$$

Also calculate the expected variance $\sigma^2 = \left(\frac{t_p - t_o}{6}\right)^2$ of each activity.

Step 3 Compute the earliest start, earliest finish, latest start, latest finish time and total float of each activity.

Step 4 Find the critical path and identify the critical activities.

Step 5 Compute the project length variance σ^2, which is the sum of the variance of all the critical activities and hence, find the standard deviation of the project length σ.

Step 6 Calculate the standard normal variable $Z = \dfrac{T_s - T_e}{\sigma}$, where T_s is the scheduled time to complete the project.

T_e = Normal expected project length duration.

σ = Expected standard deviation of the project length.

Using the normal curve, we can estimate the probability of completing the project within a specified time.

Example 15.11 The following table shows the jobs of a network along with their time estimates.

Job	*1–2*	*1–6*	*2–3*	*2–4*	*3–5*	*4–5*	*6–7*	*5–8*	*7–8*
a (days)	1	2	2	2	7	5	5	3	8
m (days)	7	5	14	5	10	5	8	3	17
b (days)	13	14	26	8	19	17	29	9	32

Draw the project network and find the probability of the project completing in 40 days.

Solution First we calculate the expected time and standard deviation for each activity.

Activity	$t_e = \dfrac{t_o + 4t_m + t_p}{6}$	$\sigma^2 = \left(\dfrac{t_p - t_o}{6}\right)^2$
1–2	$\dfrac{1+(4\times7)+13}{6} = 7$	$\left(\dfrac{13-1}{6}\right)^2 = 4$
1–6	$\dfrac{2+(4\times5)+14}{6} = 6$	$\left(\dfrac{14-2}{6}\right)^2 = 4$
2–3	$\dfrac{2+(4\times14)+26}{6} = 14$	$\left(\dfrac{26-2}{6}\right)^2 = 16$
2–4	$\dfrac{2+(5\times4)+8}{6} = 5$	$\left(\dfrac{8-2}{6}\right)^2 = 1$
3–5	$\dfrac{7+(4\times10)+19}{6} = 11$	$\left(\dfrac{19-7}{6}\right)^2 = 4$
4–5	$\dfrac{5+(5\times4)+17}{6} = 7$	$\left(\dfrac{17-5}{6}\right)^2 = 4$
6–7	$\dfrac{5+(8\times4)+29}{6} = 11$	$\left(\dfrac{29-5}{6}\right)^2 = 16$
5–8	$\dfrac{3+(3\times4)+9}{6} = 4$	$\left(\dfrac{9-3}{6}\right) = 1$
7–8	$\dfrac{8+(4\times17)+32}{6} = 18$	$\left(\dfrac{32-8}{6}\right)^2 = 16$

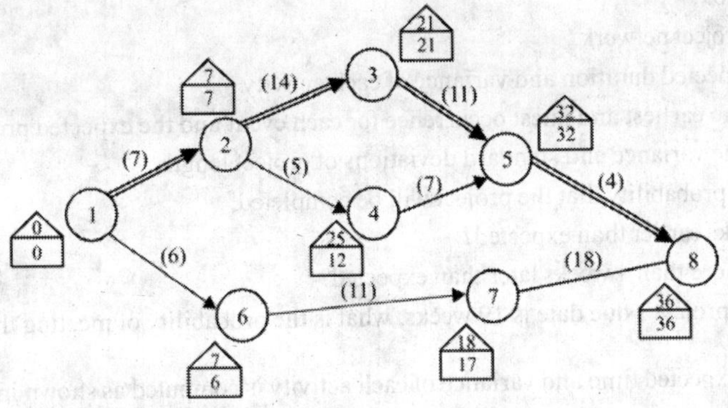

Expected project duration = 36 days

Critical path 1–2–3–5–8

Project length variance, $\sigma^2 = 4 + 16 + 4 + 1 = 25$

Std. Deviation $\sigma = 5$

The probability that the project will be completed in 40 days is giv

$$P(Z \le D)$$

$$D = \frac{T_s - T_e}{\sigma} = \frac{40 - 36}{5} = \frac{4}{5} = 0.8$$

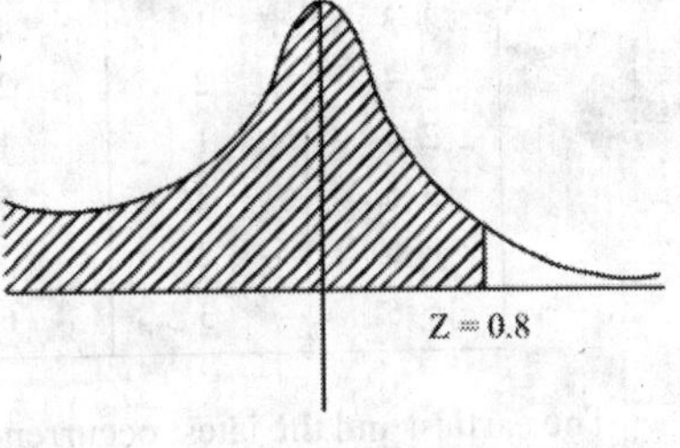

Area under the normal curve for the region $Z \le 0.8$

$$P(Z \le 0.8)$$

$$= 0.5 + \phi(0.8)$$

$$= 0.5 + 0.2881 = 0.7881$$

$$= 78.81\%$$

$[\phi(8) = 0.2881$ (from table)$]$

Conclusion If the project is performed 100 times, under the same conditions, there will be 78.81 occasions for this job to be completed in 40 days.

Example 15.12 A small project is composed of seven activities, whose time estimates are listed in the table as follows:

Activity	*Estimated duration (weeks)*		
	Optimistic (a)	*Most likely (m)*	*Pessimistic (b)*
1–2	1	1	7
1–3	1	4	7
2–4	2	2	8
2–5	1	1	1
3–5	2	5	14
4–6	2	5	8
5–6	3	6	15

You are required to:

1. Draw the project network.
2. Find the expected duration and variance of each activity.
3. Calculate the earliest and latest occurrence for each event and the expected project length.
4. Calculate the variance and standard deviations of project length.
5. What is the probability that the project will be completed,
   (*i*) 4 weeks earlier than expected?
   (*ii*) Not more than 4 weeks later than expected?
   (*iii*) If the project's due date is 19 weeks, what is the probability of meeting the due date?

Solution The expected time and variance of each activity is computed as shown in the table below:

Activity	*a*	*m*	*b*	$t_e = \dfrac{a+4m+b}{6}$	$\sigma^2 = \left(\dfrac{b-a}{6}\right)^2$
1–2	1	1	7	2	1
1–3	1	4	7	4	1
2–4	2	2	8	3	1
2–5	1	1	1	1	0
3–5	2	5	14	6	4
4–6	2	5	8	5	1
5–6	3	6	15	7	4

The earliest and the latest occurrence time for each is calculated as below:

$$E_1 = 0;$$
$$E_2 = 0+2+2$$
$$E_3 = 0+4=4$$
$$E_4 = 0+3=3$$
$$E_5 = \text{Max}\,(2+1, 4+6) = 10$$
$$E_6 = \text{Max}\,(10+7, 3+5) = 17.$$

To determine the latest expected time, we start with E_6 being the last event and move backwards subtracting t_e from each activity. Hence, we have,

$$L_6 = E_6 = 17$$
$$L_5 = L_6 - 7 = 17 - 7 = 10$$
$$L_4 = 17 - 5 = 12$$
$$L_3 = 10 - 6 = 4$$
$$L_2 = 10 - 1 = 9$$
$$L_1 = \text{Min}\,(9-2, 4-4, 12-3) = 0$$

Using the above information we get the following network, where the critical path is shown by the double-line arrows.

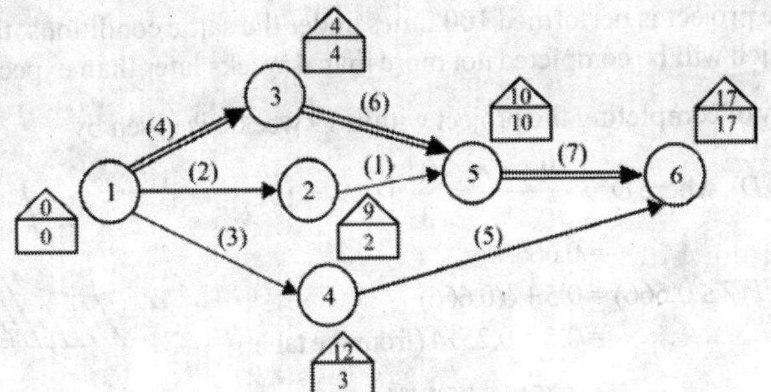

We observe the critical path of the above network as $1 \to 3 \to 5 \to 6$.

The expected project duration is 17 weeks, i.e., $T_e = 17$ weeks.

The variance of the project length is given by,

$$\sigma^2 = 1 + 4 + 4 = 9.$$

(*i*) The probability of completing the project within 4 weeks earlier than expected is given by,

$$P(Z \le D), \text{ where } D = \frac{T_s - T_e}{\sigma}$$

$$D = \frac{\text{Due date} - \text{Expected date of completion}}{\sqrt{\text{Project variance}}}$$

$$D = \frac{17 - 4 - 17}{3} = \frac{-21 + 17}{3} = \frac{-4}{3}$$

$$= -1.33$$

-1.33

$$\therefore \quad P(Z \le -1.33) = 0.5 - \phi(1.33)$$

$$= 0.5 - 0.4082 \text{ (from the table)}$$

$$= .0918 = 9.18\%.$$

Conclusion If the project is performed 100 times under the same conditions, then there will be 9 occasions for this job to be completed in 4 weeks earlier than expected.

(*ii*) The probability of completing the project not more than 4 weeks later than expected is given by,

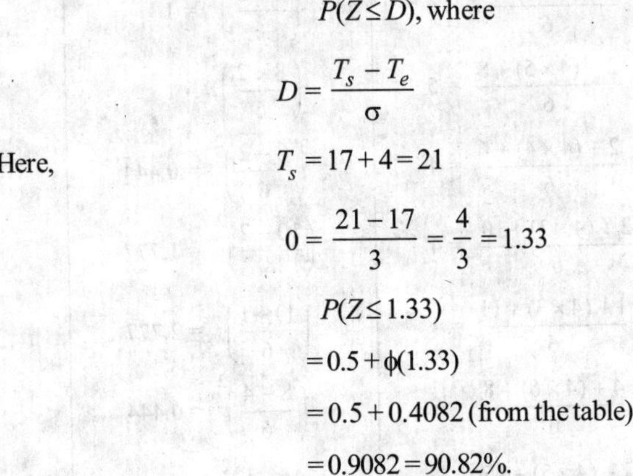

$$P(Z \le D), \text{ where}$$

$$D = \frac{T_s - T_e}{\sigma}$$

Here, $\quad T_s = 17 + 4 = 21$

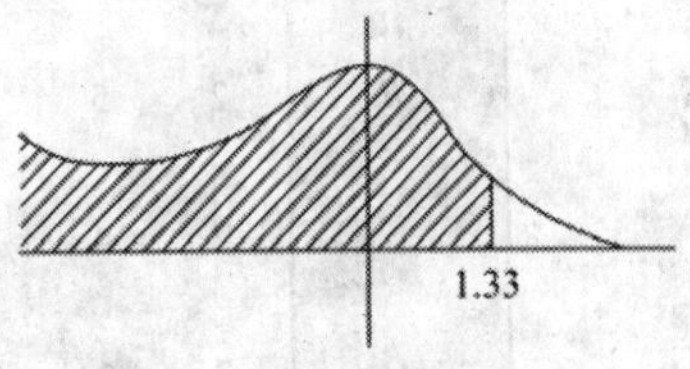

$$0 = \frac{21 - 17}{3} = \frac{4}{3} = 1.33$$

$$P(Z \le 1.33)$$

$$= 0.5 + \phi(1.33)$$

$$= 0.5 + 0.4082 \text{ (from the table)}$$

$$= 0.9082 = 90.82\%.$$

Conclusion If the project is performed 100 times under the same conditions, then there will be 90.82 occasions when this job will be completed not more than 4 weeks later than expected.

(*iii*) The probability of completing the project within 19 weeks, is given by,

$$P(Z \le D), \text{ where } D = \frac{19-17}{3} = \frac{2}{3} \quad [\because T_s = 19]$$
$$= 0.666.$$
$$\text{i.e., } P(Z \le 0.666) = 0.5 + \phi(0.666)$$
$$= 0.5 + 0.2514 \text{ (from the table)}$$
$$= 0.7514 = 75.14\%.$$

Z = 0.660

Conclusion If the project is performed 100 times, under the same conditions, then there will be 75.14 occasions for this job to be completed in 19 weeks.

Example 15.13 Consider the following project.

Activity	*Time estimate in weeks*			*Predecessor*
	t_o	t_m	t_p	
A	3	6	9	None
B	2	5	8	None
C	2	4	6	*A*
D	2	3	10	*B*
E	1	3	11	*B*
F	4	6	8	*C, D*
G	1	5	15	*E*

Find the path and standard deviation. Also find the probability of completing the project by 18 weeks.

Solution First we calculate the expected time and variance of each activity as in the following table.

Activity	t_o	t_m	t_p	$t_e = \dfrac{t_o + 4t_m + t_p}{6}$	$\sigma^2 = \left(\dfrac{t_p - t_o}{6}\right)^2$
A	3	6	9	$\frac{3+(4\times 6)+9}{6} = 6$	$\left(\frac{9-3}{6}\right)^2 = 1$
B	2	5	8	$\frac{2+(4\times 5)+8}{6} = 5$	$\left(\frac{8-2}{6}\right)^2 = 1$
C	2	4	6	$\frac{2+(4\times 4)+6}{6} = 4$	$\left(\frac{6-2}{6}\right)^2 = 0.444$
D	2	3	10	$\frac{2+(4\times 3)+10}{6} = 4$	$\left(\frac{10-2}{6}\right)^2 = 1.777$
E	1	3	11	$\frac{1+(4\times 3)+11}{6} = 4$	$\left(\frac{11-1}{6}\right)^2 = 2.777$
F	4	6	8	$\frac{4+(4\times 6)+8}{6} = 6$	$\left(\frac{8-4}{6}\right)^2 = 0.444$
G	1	5	15	$\frac{1+(4\times 5)+15}{6} = 6$	$\left(\frac{15-1}{6}\right)^2 = 5.444$

We construct the network with the help of the predecessor relation given in the data.

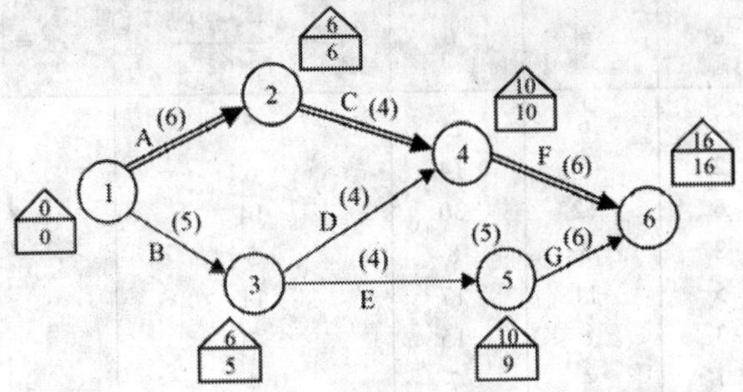

Critical path is 1–2–4–6 or *A*–*C*–*F*.

The project length = 18 weeks.

Project length variance, $\sigma^2 = 1 + 0.444 + 0.444 = 1.888$

Standard deviation, $\sigma = 1.374$

The probability of completing the project in 18 weeks is given by,

$P(Z \leq D)$, where $D = \dfrac{T_s - T_e}{\sigma}$

$T_s = 18; T_e = 16; \sigma = 1.374$

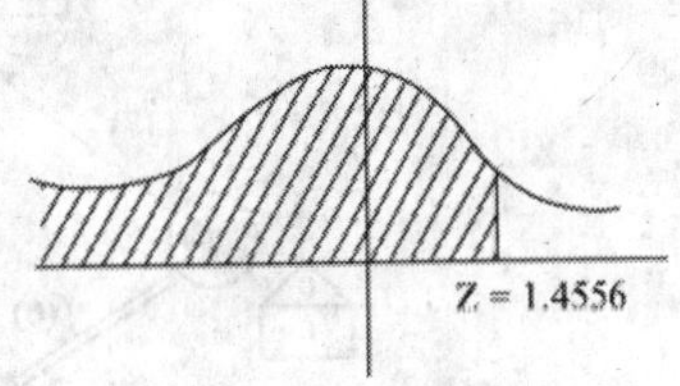

$$D = \frac{18 - 16}{1.374} = 1.4556$$

$$P(Z \leq D) = P(Z \leq 1.4556) = 0.5 + \phi(1.4456)$$

$$= 0.5 + 0.4265 = 0.9265 = 92.65\%.$$

Conclusion If the project is performed 100 times under the same conditions, then there will be 92.65 occasions when this job will be completed by 18 weeks.

Example 15.14 The following table shows the jobs of a network along with their time estimates. The time estimates are in days.

Job	*1–2*	*1–6*	*2–3*	*2–4*	*3–5*	*4–5*	*5–8*	*6–7*	*7–8*
a	3	2	6	2	5	3	1	3	4
m	6	5	12	5	11	6	4	9	19
b	15	14	30	8	17	15	7	27	28

(*i*) Draw the project network.

(*ii*) Find the critical path.

(*iii*) Find the probability of the project being completed in 31 days.

Solution First we calculate the expected time and variance for each activity as shown in the table below.

Activity	*a*	*m*	*b*	$t_e = \frac{a+4m+b}{6}$	$\sigma^2 = \left[\frac{(b-a)}{6}\right]^2$
1–2	3	6	15	7	4
1–6	2	5	14	6	4
2–3	6	12	30	14	16
2–4	2	5	8	5	1
3–5	5	11	17	11	4
4–5	3	6	15	7	4
5–8	1	4	7	4	1
6–7	3	9	27	11	16
7–8	4	19	28	27	16

(*i*) ***Project network***

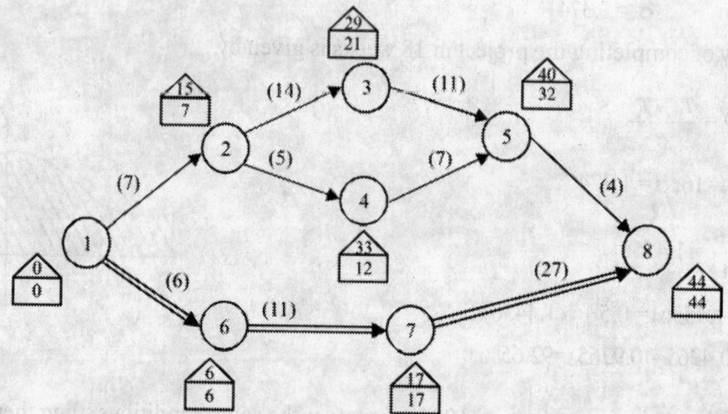

(*ii*) The critical path is given by, 1–6–7–8 and the project length is given by 44 days.

The project length variance, $\sigma^2 = 4 + 16 + 16 = 36$

Standard deviation, $\sigma = \sqrt{36} = 6.$

(*iii*) The probability of completing the project within 31 days is given by,

$$P(Z \le D), \text{ where } D = \frac{T_s - T_e}{\sigma}$$

$$= \frac{31 - 44}{6} = -2.1666$$

i.e., $P(Z \le -2.1666) = 0.5 - \phi(2.166)$

$= 0.5 - 0.4886$

$= 0.0114$

$= 1.14\%.$

Z = −2.1660

Conclusion If the project is performed 100 times, under the same conditions, then there will be 1.14 occasions when this job will be completed in 31 days.

Example 15.15 Using the data given in example 15.14, find the probability of completing the jobs on the critical path in 41 days.

Solution Refer to example 15.14 to find the critical path, project length and project length variance.

The probability of completing the project within 41 days is given by,

$$P(Z \leq D), \text{ where } D = \frac{T_s - T_e}{\sigma}$$

$$= \frac{41-44}{6} = \frac{-3}{6} = -0.5$$

$$P(Z \leq -0.5) = 0.5 - \phi(0.5)$$

$$= 0.5 - 0.1915 \text{ (from the table)}$$

$$= 0.3085 = 30.85\%.$$

–0.5

Conclusion If the project in performed 100 times under the same conditions, then there will be 30.85 occasions when the project will be completed in 41 days.

Example 15.16 Assuming that the expected times are normally distributed, find the probability of meeting the scheduled time as given for the network.

Activity (i – j)	Days		
	Optimistic a	Most likely m	Pessimistic b
1–2	2	5	14
1–3	9	12	15
2–4	5	14	17
3–4	2	5	12
4–5	6	6	12
3–5	8	17	20

Scheduled project completion time is 30 days. Also find the date on which the project manager can complete the project with a probability of 0.90.

Solution The expected time t_e and variance for each activity is calculated in the following table:

Activity	$t_e = \frac{(a+4m+b)}{6}$	$\sigma^2 = \left(\frac{b-a}{6}\right)^2$
1–2	6	4
1–3	12	1
2–4	13	4
3–4	5	1
3–5	16	4
4–5	7	1

To determine the critical path, the earliest expected time and the latest allowable time, we draw the project network.

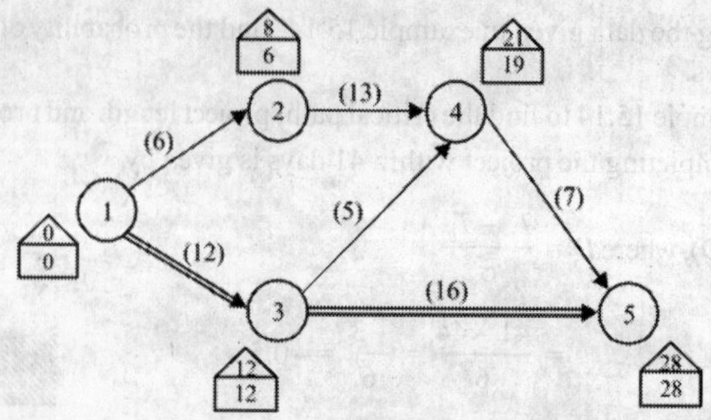

The critical path is given by, 1–3–5 and the project duration is given by 28 days. Project length variance, $\sigma^2 = 1 + 4 = 5$. Standard deviation, $\sigma = 2.236$.

The probability of completing the project within 30 days is given by,

$$P(Z \leq D), \text{ where } D = \frac{T_s - T_e}{\sigma} = \frac{30 - 28}{2.236} = 0.8944$$

$$P(Z \leq 0.8944) = 0.5 + 0.8944$$
$$= 0.5 + 0.3133 \text{ (From table)}$$
$$= 0.8133$$
$$= 81.33\%.$$

Conclusion If the project is performed 100 times under the same conditions, then there will be 81.33 occasions when the project will be completed in 30 days.

If the probability for the completion of the project is 0.90 then the corresponding value of $Z = 1.29$.

$$Z = \frac{T_s - T_e}{S.D} = 1.29$$

i.e., $$\frac{T_s - 28}{2.236} = 1.29.$$

$\therefore$ $$T_s = (1.29)(2.236) + 28$$

$\therefore$ $$T_s = 30.88 \text{ weeks.}$$

EXERCISES

1. The data for a small PERT project is as given below, where *a* represents optimistic time, *m* the most likely time and *b* the pessimistic time. Estimates (in days) of the activities *A*, *B* ... *J*, *K* are given in the table.

Activity	*A*	*B*	*C*	*D*	*E*	*F*	*G*	*H*	*I*	*J*	*K*
a	3	2	6	2	5	3	3	1	4	1	2
m	6	5	12	5	11	6	9	4	19	2	4
b	5	14	30	8	17	15	27	7	28	9	12

A, *B* and *C* can start simultaneously; *A* < *D*, *I*; *B* < *G*, *F*; *D* < *G*, *F*; *C* < *E*; *E* < *H*, *K*; *F* < *H*, *K*; *G*, *H* < *J*.

(*i*) Draw the arrow network of the project.

(*ii*) Calculate the earliest and the latest expected times to each event and find the critical path.

(*iii*) What is the probability that the project will be completed 2 days later than expected?

[**Ans.** Critical path *A–D–F–H–J*; Required probability 62.93%]

2. The three estimates for the activities of a project are given below:

Activity	Estimate duration (days)		
	a	m	b
1–2	5	6	7
1–3	1	1	7
1–4	2	4	12
2–5	3	6	15
3–5	1	1	1
4–6	2	2	8
5–6	1	4	7

Draw the project network. Find out the critical path and duration of the project. What is the probability that the project will be completed at least 5 days earlier than expected?

What is the probability that the project will be completed by 22 days?

[**Ans.** Critical path 1–2–5– 6; Project duration 17 days. Required probability = 1.36%; Probability that the project will be completed in 22 days = 98.64%]

3. Consider the network shown in the figure below. The estimate t_o, t_m and t_p are shown in this order for each of the activities, on top of the arcs denoting the respective activities.

Find the probability of completing the project in 25 days.

[**Ans.** 85.99%]

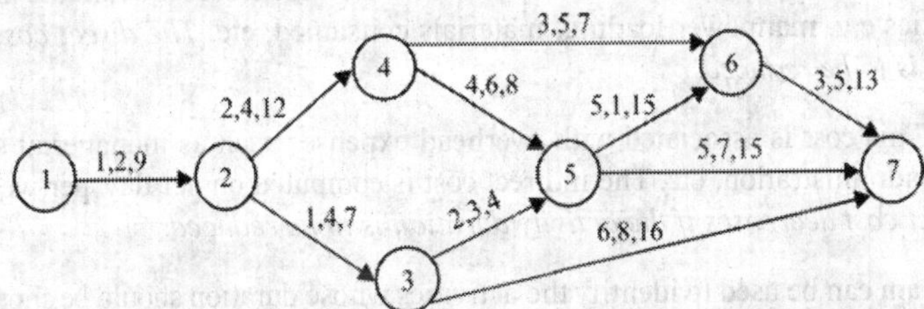

4. A project is represented by the network shown below and has the following table:

Task	A	B	C	D	E	F	G	H	I
Least time	5	18	26	16	15	6	7	7	3
Greatest time	10	22	40	20	25	12	12	9	5
Most likely time	8	20	33	18	20	9	10	8	4

Determine the following:

(*i*) Expected time of tasks and their variance.

(*ii*) The earliest and the latest expected time to reach each mode.

(*iii*) The critical path.

(*iv*) The probability of completing the project within 41.5 weeks.

[**Ans.** Critical path 1 → 4 → 7; Project duration = 42.8 weeks; Probability of completing the project within 41.5 weeks = 0.30]

5. Consider a project having the following activities and their time estimates.

Draw an arrow diagram for the project. Identify the critical path and compute the expected completion time. What is the probability that the project will require at least 75 days?

Activity	Predecessor	t_o	t_m	t_p
			days	
A	–	2	4	6
B	A	8	12	16
C	A	14	16	30
D	B	4	10	16
E	C, B	6	12	18
F	E	6	8	22
G	D	18	18	30
H	F, G	8	14	32

[**Ans.** $A \rightarrow D \rightarrow G \rightarrow H$; Expected completion time = 62 days;
Probability of requiring at least 75 days = 0.9944]

15.9 COST CONSIDERATION IN PERT/CPM

15.9.1 Project Cost

In order to include the cost factors in project scheduling, we must first define the cost duration relationships for various activities in the project. The total cost of any project comprises of direct and indirect costs.

Direct cost This cost is directly dependent upon the amount of resources available in the execution of individual activities e.g. manpower loading, materials consumed, etc. *The direct cost increases if the activity duration is to be reduced.*

Indirect cost This cost is associated with overhead expenses such as managerial services, indirect supplies, general administration, etc. The indirect cost is computed on per day, per week, or per month basis. *The indirect cost decreases if the activity duration is to be reduced.*

Network diagram can be used to identify the activities whose duration should be shortened, so that the completion time of the project can be shortened in the most economic manner. The process of reducing the activity duration by putting on extra effort is called *crashing the activity.*

The crash time (T_C) represents the minimum activity duration time that is possible and any attempts to further crash would only raise the activity cost without reducing the time. The activity cost corresponding to the crash time is called the *crash cost* (C_C), which is the minimum direct cost required to achieve the crash performance time.

The *normal cost* (C_N) is equal to the absolute minimum of the direct cost required to perform an activity. Normal cost is the cost associated when the project is completed with normal time. The corresponding time duration taken by an activity is known as the *normal time* (T_N).

15.9.2 Cost Slope

The cost slope, indicating the increase in cost per unit reduction in time is defined as,

$$\text{Cost slope} = \frac{\text{Crash cost} - \text{Normal cost}}{\text{Normal time} - \text{Crash time}} = \frac{C_C - C_N}{T_N - T_C}$$

i.e., it represents the rate of increase in the cost of performing the activity per unit reduction in time and is called *cost/time trade off.* It varies from activity to activity. The total project cost is the sum total of the project's direct and indirect costs.

15.9.3 Time-Cost Optimization Algorithm

Following are the steps involved in project crashing.

Step 1 Find the normal critical path and identify the critical activities.

$$\text{Cost slope} = \frac{\text{Crash cost} - \text{Normal cost}}{\text{Normal time} - \text{Crash time}}$$

Step 2 Calculate the cost slope for the different activities by using the above formula.

Step 3 Rank the activities. The activity whose cost slope in minimum is to be ranked 1, the next minimum as rank 2 and so on, i.e., the ranking takes place in ascending order of cost slope.

Step 4 By crashing the activities on the critical path, other paths also become critical and are called *parallel paths.*

In such cases, the project duration can be reduced by crashing activities simultaneously on the parallel critical path.

Step 5 Find the total cost of the project at each step.

Step 6 Continue the process until all the critical activities are fully crashed or no further crashing is possible.

In the case of indirect cost, the process of crashing is repeated until the total cost is minimum, beyond which it may increase.

This minimum cost is called the *optimum project cost* and the corresponding time, the *optimum project time.*

Example 15.17 Determine the optimum project duration and cost for the following data.

Activity	*Normal*		*Crash*	
	Time (days)	*Cost (₹)*	*Time (days)*	*Cost (₹)*
1–2	8	100	6	200
1–3	4	150	2	350
2–4	2	50	1	90
2–5	10	100	5	400
3–4	5	100	1	200
4–5	3	80	1	100

Indirect cost is ₹ 70 per day.

Solution Since the overhead of the project is given, the cost is indirect. Hence, the project duration can be reduced with the total cost.

Making use of the normal time, we have the following network.

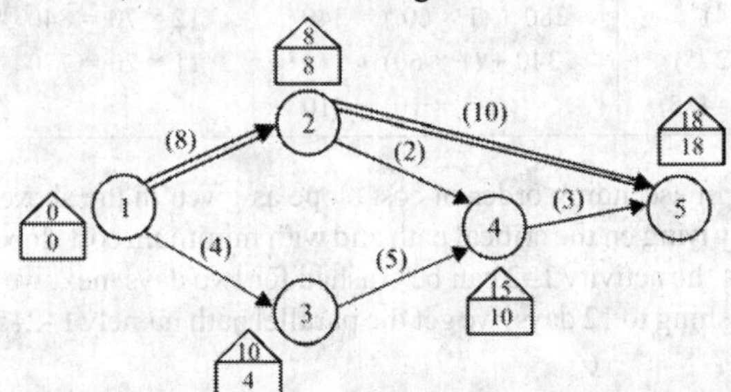

Critical path 1–2–5

Project normal duration = 18 days

Cost of the project = Normal cost of all the activities + Indirect cost

$= 580 + (70 \times 18) = ₹\,1{,}840.$

We can reduce the project duration from 18 days, by crashing the activity on the critical path.

The cost slope and the number of days to be crashed are given in Table (A).

Table (A)

Activity	*Cost slope* = $\dfrac{C_C - C_N}{T_N - T_C}$	
	$\dfrac{200-100}{8-6} =$	
1–2	100(2) (VI)	
1–3	50(2) (IV)	The number given in the bracket corresponds to the days allowed for crashing and is the difference between T_N and T_C
2–4	40(1) (III)	
2–5	60(5) (V)	
3–4	25(4) (II)	
4–5	10(2) (I)	

From the network, the other paths are given by,

1 – 2 – 5 | ~~18~~ ~~17~~ ~~16~~ ~~15~~ ~~14~~ ~~13~~ ~~12~~ ~~11~~

1 – 2 – 4 – 5 | ~~13~~ ~~12~~ 11

1 – 3 – 4 – 5 | ~~12~~ 11

We form a table (B) to calculate the optimum project duration and its cost.

Table (B)

Normal duration	*Crash activity*	*Crash cost*	*Indirect cost*	*Total cost*
18	–	–	18 × 70 = 1260	1260 + 580 = 1840
17	1–2 (1)	1 × 50 = 50	17 × 70 = 1190	1820
16	1–2 (2)	50 + (1 × 50) = 100	16 × 70 = 1120	1800
15	2–5 (1)	100 + (60 × 1) = 160	15 × 70 = 1050	1790
14	2–5 (2)	160 + (1 × 60) = 220	14 × 70 = 980	1780
13	2–5 (3)	220 + (1 × 60) = 280	13 × 70 = 910	1770
12	2–5 (4)	280 + (1 × 60) = 340	12 × 70 = 840	1760
11	2–5 (1–2–5) 4–5 (1–3–4–5)	340 + (1 × 60) + (1 × 10) = 410	11 × 70 = 770	1760

We rank the activities in ascending order of cost slope as given in the above table. First we crash the activity 1–2. It is the activity lying on the critical path and with minimum cost slope. This crashing is shown in the other paths also. As the activity 1–2 can be crashed for two days, next we have the activity 2–5 on the critical path. After crashing to 12 days, we get the parallel path namely 1–2–5 and 1–3–4–5.

As there is no common activity between these 2 paths, we crash the activity 2–5 on the path 1–2–5 and 4–5 on the path 1–3–4–5 as it is the activity having the minimum rank. No more crashing is possible as all the activities in the path 1–2–5 are in crash time, even though there are activities available in other parallel paths.

Hence, the optimum project duration is 11 days with total cost of ₹ 1,760.

Example 15.18 The following table gives the activities of a construction project along with other relevant information.

(*i*) What is the normal project length and the minimum project length?

(*ii*) Determine the minimum crashing costs of schedule, ranging from normal length down to and including the minimum length schedule.

Activity i–j	*Normal duration (days)*	*Crash duration (days)*	*Cost of crashing (₹ per day)*
1–2	9	6	20
1–3	8	5	25
1–4	15	10	30
2–4	5	3	10
3–4	10	6	15
4–5	2	1	40

(*iii*) What is the optimal length schedule duration of each job for your solution? Overhead of the project is ₹ 60 per day.

Solution Since the overhead cost is given, the cost is indirect. The project duration can be reduced by reducing the total cost associated with it.

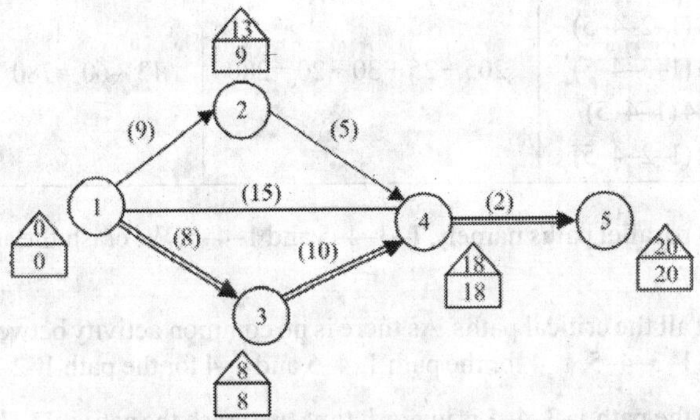

The critical path comprises the activities 1–3, 3–4 and 4–5 with the normal duration as 20 days.

The total cost associated with the project is 20 × 60 = ₹ 1,200.

Activity	*Cost of crashing*
1–2	20 (3) III
1–3	25 (3) IV
1–4	30 (5) V
2–4	10 (2) I
3–4	15 (4) II
4–5	40 (1) VI

The cost slope is given in the data. We reduce the project duration by crashing the activities lying on the critical path.

The critical activity 3–4 has the minimum cost slope. It is ranked I, so this activity is crashed first for 4 days.

The other paths of the network are:

1 – 3 – 4 – 5| ~~20~~ ~~19~~ ~~18~~ ~~17~~ ~~16~~ ~~15~~ ~~14~~ 13

1 – 4 – 5| ~~17~~ ~~16~~ ~~15~~ ~~14~~ 13

1 – 2 – 4 – 5| ~~16~~ ~~15~~ ~~14~~ 13

Normal duration	***Crash activity***	***Crash cost***	***Overhead cost***	***Total cost***
20	–	–	20 × 60 = 1200	1200
19	3–4 (1)	1 × 15 = 15	19 × 60 = 1140	1155
18	3–4 (2)	15 + (1 × 15) = 30	18 × 60 = 1080	1110
17	3–4 (3)	30 + (1 × 15) = 45	17 × 60 = 1020	1065
16	4–5 (1 3 4 5 1 4 5)	45 + (1 × 40) = 85	16 × 60 = 960	1045
15	3–4 (1–3–4–5) 1–4 (1–4–5) 2–4 (1–2–4–5)	85 + 15 + 30 + 10 = 140	15 × 60 = 900	1040
14	1–3 (1–3–4–5) 1–4 (1–4–5) 2–4 (1–2–4–5)	140 + 25 + 30+ 10 = 205	14 × 60 = 840	1045
13	1–3 (1–3–4–5) 1–4 (1–4–5) 1–2 (1–2–4–5)	205 + 25 + 30 + 20 = 280	13 × 60 = 780	1060

After 17 days, we get parallel paths namely, 1–3–4–5 and 1–4–5. We crash the activity 4–5 for one day at the rate of ₹ 40 per day.

After 16 days, we get all the critical paths. As there is no common activity between them, we crash the activity 3–4 for the path 1–3–4–5, 1–4 for the path 1–4–5 and 2–4 for the path 1–2–4–5.

As the activity 3–4 in the path 1–3–4–5 is in crash time, we crash the activity 1–3 for 1 day at the rate of ₹ 25 per day. The optimum duration is 15 days as it gives the minimum cost of ₹ 1,040.

To find the minimum duration we crash further.

Normal duration	***Crash activity***	***Crash cost***	***Overhead cost***	***Total cost***
12	1–3 (1–3–4–5) 1–4 (1–4–5) 1–2 (1–2–4–5)	280 + 25 + 30 +20 = 355	12 × 60 = 720	1075

The minimum duration is 12 days and no more crashing is possible as all the activities in the path 1–3–4–5 are in crash time.

Optimum duration = 15 days with total cost associated as ₹ 1,040

Minimum duration = 12 days with total cost associated as ₹ 1,075.

***Note*:** From the above problem, we observe that the optimum duration and minimum duration are not the same.

Optimum duration refers to the duration that yields the minimum total cost, whereas minimum duration is the one in which no more crashing is possible beyond that duration.

Example 15.19 The table below provides costs and estimates for a seven-activity project.

Activity	*Time estimate (weeks)*		*Direct cost estimate (₹ 1,000)*	
	Normal	*Crash*	*Normal*	*Crash*
A 1–2	2	1	10	15
B 1–3	8	5	15	21
C 2–4	4	3	20	24
D 3–4	1	1	7	7
E 3–5	2	1	8	15
F 4–6	5	3	10	16
G 5–6	6	2	12	36

(*i*) Draw the project network corresponding to normal time.

(*ii*) Determine the critical path, normal duration and cost of the project.

(*iii*) Crash the activities so that the project completion time reduces to 9 weeks.

Solution As the problem involves *direct cost*, we expect that the project duration can be reduced with an increase in total cost. First we draw the network.

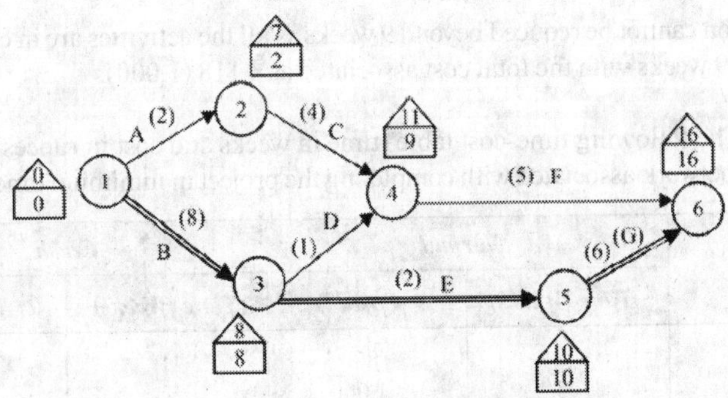

Critical path 1–3–5–6; Normal duration = 16 weeks

Total cost = ₹ 82,000

The calculations for cost slope and crashing number of days are shown in the table below:

Activity	Slope (₹ 1000)
1–2	5 (1) IV
1–3	2 (3) I
2–4	4 (1) III
3–4	0
3–5	7 (1) VI
4–6	3 (2) II
5–6	6 (4) V

The different paths of the network are,

1–3–5–6 | ~~16~~ ~~13~~ ~~11~~ 9

1–3–4–6 | ~~14~~ ~~11~~ 9

1–2–4–6 | ~~11~~ 9

First crashing We crash the activity 1–3, as it is the critical activity with minimum rank. We crash it for 3 weeks at the rate of ₹ 2 (1000) per day.

Project duration reduced to 16 – 3 = 13 weeks

Total cost = 82 + (3 × 2) – 88 (₹ 1,000)

Second crashing Next, we crash the activity 5–6 for 2 weeks at the rate of ₹ 6 (1,000) per week, as this activity has the next minimum rank.

Project duration reduced to 13 – 2 = 11 weeks

Total cost = 88 + (2 × 6) = 100 (₹ 1,000).

Third crashing After 11 days, we get all the paths that are critical. As there is no activity in common, we crash the activity 5–6 for 2 weeks in the path 1–3–5–6 and crash the activity 4–6 for 2 weeks, which is common to the paths 1–3–4–6 and 1–2–4–6.

Project duration reduces to 11–2 = 9 weeks.

Total cost = 100 + 2 × 6 + 2 × 3 = 118 (₹ 1,000).

The project duration cannot be reduced beyond 9 weeks as all the activities are in crash time. Hence, the optimum duration is 9 weeks with the total cost associated as ₹ 118 (1,000).

Example 15.20 The following time-cost table (time in weeks and cost in rupees) applies to a project. Use it to arrive at the network associated with completing the project in minimum time with minimum cost.

Activity	Normal		Crash	
	Time (Weeks)	Cost (₹)	Time (Weeks)	Cost (₹)
1–2	2	800	1	1,400
1–3	5	1,000	2	2,000
1–4	5	1,000	3	1,800
2–4	1	500	1	500
2–5	5	1,500	3	2,100
3–4	4	2,000	3	3,000
3–5	6	1,200	4	1,600
4–5	5	900	3	1,600

Solution As the direct cost is given, we reduce the project duration by an increase in total cost. First we construct the network.

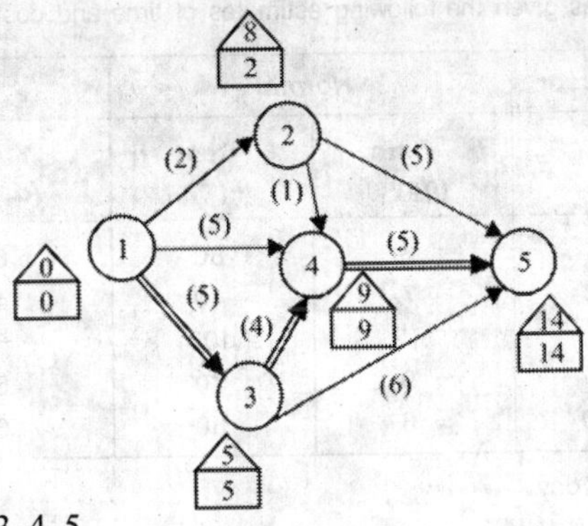

Critical path is given by, 1–3–4–5

Project duration = 5 + 4 + 5 = 14 weeks

Total cost associated = ₹ 8,900

We calculate the cost slope for each activity as given in the following table:

Activity	*Cost slope* = $\dfrac{C_C - C_N}{T_N - T_C}$
1–2	600 (1) VI
1–3	333.333 (3) III
1–4	400 (2) V
2–4	–
2–5	300 (2) II
3–4	1,000 (1) VII
3–5	200 (2) I
4–5	350 (2) IV

The project duration is reduced by crashing the activities. First, the activity that lies on the critical path and ranks the minimum is crashed.

First crashing We crash the activity 1–3 for 3 weeks at the rate of ₹ 333.33 per week. Project duration reduced to 14 – 3 = 11 weeks.

Total cost = 8,900 + 3 (333.33)

= ₹ 9,899.99

= ₹ 9,900

Second crashing Next, crash the activity 4–5 as this activity lies on the critical path with next minimum rank. Crash 4–5 for 2 weeks at the rate of ₹ 350 per week. Project duration is reduced to 11 – 2 = 9 weeks.

Total cost = 9,900 + (2 × 350) = ₹ 10,600

Third crashing Next, we crash the activity 3–4 for one week, at the rate of ₹ 1,000 per week. Project duration reduced to 9 – 1 = 8 weeks.

Total cost = 10,600 + 1,000 = ₹ 11,600

As all the activities on the path 1–3–4–5 are in crash time, no more crashing is possible beyond this.

∴ Optimum and minimum project duration is given by 8 weeks with total cost as ₹ 11,600.

EXERCISES

1. A maintenance foreman has given the following estimates of time and cost of jobs in a maintenance project.

Job	Predecessor	Normal		Crash	
		Time (days)	Cost (₹)	Time (days)	Cost (₹)
A	–	8	80	6	100
B	A	7	40	4	94
C	A	12	100	5	184
D	A	9	70	5	102
E	B, C, D	6	50	6	50

Overhead cost is ₹ 25 per day.

Find,

(*i*) The normal duration and associated cost of the project.

(*ii*) The optimum duration and associated cost of the project.

[**Ans.** Critical path 1–2–5–6; Normal duration = 26 days Cost = ₹ 990; Optimum duration = 17 days; Cost = ₹ 937]

2. Determine the least cost schedule for the following projcct, using CPM technique.

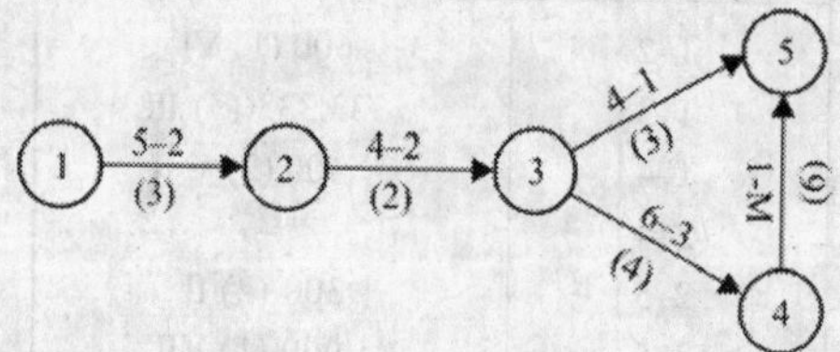

Overhead cost per day is ₹ 6. The numbers above and below the activities have the usual meaning.

[**Ans.** Optimum duration = 9 days; Least cost = ₹ 88]

3. Find the optimum schedule for the given project. The overhead cost is ₹ 75 per day.

Activity	Predecessor	Duration (days)		Increase in cost for crashing by one day (₹)
		Normal time	Crash time	
A	–	3	2	150
B	–	4	3	100
C	A	5	4	200
D	A	7	5	300
E	B, C	3	3	0
F	B, C, D	6	2	75

(a) Draw the project, using normal duration.

(b) Find the path and the project duration for the above case.

(c) Find the optimal schedule and optimal project duration.

[**Ans.** CPM *A–D–F*; Project duration = 16 days; Optimum duration 12 days; Least cost = ₹ 1,200]

4. The following table gives the activities in a construction project along with other relevant information.

Activity	*Normal time (days)*	*Crash time (days)*	*Normal cost (₹)*	*Crash cost (₹)*
1–2	20	17	600	720
1–3	25	25	200	200
2–3	10	8	300	440
2–4	12	6	400	700
3–4	5	2	300	420
4–5	10	5	300	600
4–6	5	3	600	900
5–7	10	5	500	800
6–7	8	3	400	700

(a) Draw the activity network of the project.

(b) Find the free and total float for each activity.

(c) Using the above information, crash the activity step-by-step, until all the paths are critical.

[Ans. Critical path 1–2–3–4–5–7;
Normal duration 55 days with cost ₹ 3,600;
Reduced duration = 37 days with total cost ₹ 4,860]

SUMMARY

Network Scheduling

Network It is the graphic representation of logically and sequentially connected arrows and nodes representing activities and events in a project.

Activity An activity represents some action and is a time consuming effort, necessary to complete a particular part of the overall project.

Event The beginning and end points of an activity are called events or nodes.

Dummy activity Certain activities, which neither consume time nor resources but are used simply to represent a connection or a link between the events, are known as dummies.

Time analysis We shall use the following notation for basic scheduling computations.

(i, j) = Activity (i, j) with tail event i and head event j

T_{ij} = Estimated completion time of activity (i, j)

ES_{ij} = Earliest starting time of activity (i, j)

EF_{ij} = Earliest finishing time of activity (i, j)

LS_{ij} = Latest starting time of activity (i, j)

LF_{ij} = Latest finishing time of activity (i, j).

Forward pass computations (for earliest event time)

Step 1 The computations begin from the start node and move towards the end node. Let zero be the starting time for the project.

Step 2 Earliest starting time $(ES_{ij}) = E_i$, is the earliest possible time when an activity can begin assuming that all the predecessors also started at their earliest starting time. Earliest finishing time of activity (i, j) is the earliest starting time + the activity time.

$$(EF)_{ij} = (ES)_{ij} + t$$

Step 3 Earliest event time for event j is the maximum of the earliest finish time of all the activities ending at that event.

$$E_j = \underset{i}{\text{Max}}\,(E_i + t_{ij})$$

Backward Pass Computations (for latest allowable time)

Step 1 For ending event assume $E = L$

Step 2 Latest finish time for activity (i, j) is the target time for completing the project.

$$(LF_{ij}) = L_j$$

Step 3 Latest starting time of the activity (i, j)

= Latest completion time of (ij) – the activity time

$= LS_{ij} = LF_{ij} - t_{ij} = L_j - t_{ij}$

Step 4 Latest event time for event i is the minimum of the latest start time of all activities originating from the event.

$$L_i = \underset{j}{\text{Max}}\,(E_j + t_{ij})$$

Float is defined as the difference between the latest and the earliest activity time.

Slack is defined as the difference between the latest and the earliest event time.

Total float:

$$(TF)_{ij} = (\text{Latest start} - \text{Earliest start}) \text{ for activity } (i, j)$$

i.e., $(TF)_{ij} = (LS)_{ij} - (ES)_{ij}$

or, $(TF)_{ij} = (L_j - E_i) - t_{ij}$

Free float:

$$FF_{ij} = (E_j - E_i) - t_{ij}$$

$$FF_{ij} = \text{Total float} - \text{head event slack.}$$

Independent float: $IF_{ij} = (E_j - L_i) - t_{ij}$

or, IF_{ij} = Free float – tail event slack.

Critical activity An activity is said to be critical if a delay in its start will cause a further delay in the completion of the entire project.

Critical path The sequence of critical activities in a network is called the critical path.

PERT

Optimistic time estimate (t_o) It is the smallest time taken to complete the activity if everything goes well.

Most likely time estimate (t_m) It refers to the estimate of the normal time the activity would take.

Pessimistic time estimate (t_p) It is the longest time that an activity would take if everything goes wrong.

PERT Procedure

Step 1 Draw the project network.

Step 2 Compute the expected duration of each activity using the formula,

$$t_e = \frac{t_o + 4t_m + t_p}{6}$$

Also calculate the expected variance $\sigma^2 = \left(\frac{t_p - t_o}{6}\right)^2$ of each activity.

Step 3 Compute the earliest start, earliest finish, latest start, latest finish and total float of each activity.

Step 4 Find the critical path and identify the critical activities.

Step 5 Compute the project length variance σ^2, which is the sum of the variance of all the critical activities and hence, find the standard deviation of the project length σ.

Step 6 Calculate the standard normal variable $Z = \frac{T_s - T_e}{\sigma}$, where T_s is the scheduled time to complete the project.

❑❑❑

Chapter

16

Inventory Control

16.1 INTRODUCTION

Inventory is defined as any idle resource of an enterprise. It is a physical stock of goods kept for future use. In a factory, the inventory may be in the form of raw materials, parts, semi-finished goods, etc. An inventory may also include furniture, machinery, etc.

16.2 REASONS FOR MAINTAINING INVENTORIES

The need of the management to make decisions regarding an inventory arises because of the various alternative courses of action available with the enterprise. It is essential for an enterprise to have an inventory, due to the following reasons.

(*i*) It helps in smooth and efficient running of the business.
(*ii*) It provides adequate services to the customers.
(*iii*) It reduces the possibility of duplication of orders.
(*iv*) It helps in maintaining a balance in the economy by absorbing some of the fluctuations, when the demand of an item fluctuates or is seasonal in nature.
(*v*) It helps in minimizing the losses due to deterioration, obsolescence, damage, etc.
(*vi*) It acts as a buffer stock when raw materials are received late and shop rejections are too many.
(*vii*) Takes advantages of price discounts by bulk purchasing.

Though inventories are essential and provide an alternative to production/purchase in the future, they also lock up the capital of the enterprise. These include the expenses of stores, equipment, personnel, insurance, etc. Therefore, excessive inventories are undesirable. Larger inventories do not necessarily lead to a high volume of output; instead, they might hamper the production.

Our problem is to strike a balance between the advantages of having inventories and the cost of carrying them, to arrive at an optimal level of inventories, minimizing the total inventory cost. This calls for controlling the inventories in the most profitable way. The basic objective of inventory control is to release the capital for more productive use.

16.3 TYPES OF INVENTORY

There are five types of inventories, namely,

(*i*) Transportation inventories
(*ii*) Buffer inventories
(*iii*) Anticipation inventories
(*iv*) De-coupling inventories
(*v*) Lot-size inventories.

(*i*) ***Transportation inventories*** They arise due to the transportation of inventory items to the various distribution centres and customers from the various production centres. The amount of transportation inventory depends on the time consumed in transportation and the nature of the demand.

(*ii*) ***Buffer inventories*** These are maintained to meet the uncertainties of demand and supply.

(*iii*) ***Anticipation inventories*** These are built in advance by anticipating or foreseeing the future demand. For example, production of crackers before the Diwali festival; electric fans or coolers before the onset of the summer season.

(*iv*) ***Decoupling inventories*** The inventories used to reduce the interdependence of the various stages of a production system are known as decoupling inventories.

(*v*) ***Lot-size inventories*** Generally, the rate of consumption is different from the rate of production or purchasing. Therefore, the items are produced in larger quantities, which result in lot-size, also known as cycle inventories.

16.4 INVENTORY COSTS

There are four categories of inventory cost associated with maintaining the inventories. These are:

(*i*) item (production or purchase) cost (*ii*) ordering or set-up cost
(*iii*) carrying or holding cost (*iv*) shortage or stock out cost

(*i*) ***Item cost*** It refers to the cost associated with an item, whether it is manufactured or purchased. The purchase price will be considered when discounts are allowed for any purchase above a certain quantity.

(*ii*) ***Set-up cost*** **(C_3)** These costs include the fixed cost associated with obtaining the goods through placing of an order and purchasing , manufacturing or setting up a machinery before starting the production. They include the costs of—purchase, requisition, follow-up, receiving the goods, quality control, etc. These are also called order costs or replenishment costs, usually denoted by C_3, per production run (cycle). They are assumed to be independent of the quantity ordered or produced.

(*iii*) ***Carrying or holding cost*** **(C_1)** The cost associated with carrying or holding the goods in stock is known as *holding or carrying cost*, which is denoted by C_1, per unit of goods for a unit of time. Holding cost is assumed to vary directly with the size of inventory as well as the time for which the item is held in stock. The following components constitute the holding cost.

(*a*) Invested capital cost: This is the interest charged over the capital invested.
(*b*) Record keeping and administrative cost.
(*c*) Handling cost: These include the costs associated with the movement of stock such as cost of labour, etc.
(*d*) Storage costs.
(*e*) Depreciation costs.
(*f*) Taxes and insurance, etc.

If P is the purchase price of an item, I is the stock holding cost per unit time as a fraction of stock value, then the holding cost $C_1 = IP$.

(*iv*) ***Shortage cost or stock out cost*** **(C_2)** The penalty costs that are incurred as a result of running out of stock (i.e., shortage) are known as *shortage or stock out costs*. These are denoted by C_2 per unit of goods for a specified period.

If the unfilled demand for the goods can be satisfied at a latter date (backlog case), these costs are assumed to vary directly with the shortage quantity and the delaying time. If the unfilled demand is lost (no backlog case), shortage cost becomes proportional to the shortage quantity.

16.5 VARIABLES IN THE INVENTORY PROBLEM

The variables involved in the inventory model are of two types:

(*i*) Controlled variables and (*ii*) Uncontrolled variables

Controlled variables These include three basic questions, namely,

(*i*) How much quantity of an item should be ordered?
(*ii*) When should the order be placed? That is, the frequency or timing of acquisition.
(*iii*) The completion stage of stocked items.

Uncontrolled variables These include holding, shortage and set-up costs.

Note: Total inventory cost
= Purchase cost of inventory items + Ordering cost + Carrying cost + Shortage cost.

16.6 OTHER FACTORS INVOLVED IN INVENTORY ANALYSIS

16.6.1 Demand

Demand refers to the number of items required per period. It may be known exactly in terms of probabilities or may be completely unknown.

The demand pattern of items may be either deterministic or probabilistic. Problems in which the demand is known and fixed are called *deterministic problem.* Whereas, those problems in which the demand is assumed to be a random variable are called *stochastic* or *probabilistic problems.*

In case of deterministic demands, it is assumed that the quantities needed over subsequent periods of time are known exactly. However, the known demand may be fixed or variable with time. Such demands are respectively called *static* or *dynamic demands*.

Probabilistic demand occurs when the demand over a certain period of time is not known with certainty; but it is described by a known probability distribution. A probabilistic demand may be either stationary or non-stationary over a period of time.

16.6.2 Lead Time

The time gap between the placing of an order and the actual arrival of the inventory is known as *lead time*. If the lead time is known and is not equal to zero; and if the demand is deterministic, all that one requires to do is to order in advance, by the time equal to the lead time. If the lead time is zero, there is no need to order in advance.

In case the lead time is a variable, which is known only probabilistically, then the question of when to order is more difficult. The amount and timing of replenishment is found by considering the *expected costs* of holding and shortage, over the lead time required.

16.6.3 Amount Delivered (Supply of Goods)

The supply of goods may be instantaneous or spread over a period of time. If a quantity q is ordered, purchased or produced, the amount delivered may vary around q, with a known probability density function.

16.6.4 Order Cycle

The time period between the placement of two successive orders is referred to as *an order cycle*. It may be created on the basis of the following two types of inventory review systems.

(*i*) ***Continuous review*** The record of the inventory level is checked continuously until a certain lower limit (known as recorder level) is reached before a new order is placed. This is often known as a *two-bin system*.

(*ii*) ***Periodic review*** In this, the inventory levels are reviewed at equal time intervals and orders are placed at such intervals. The quantity ordered each time depends on the available inventory level at the time of review.

16.6.5 Time Horizon

The time period over which the inventory level will be controlled is known as *time horizon*.

16.6.6 Recorder Level

The level between the maximum and the minimum stock at which the purchasing (manufacturing) activities for replenishment must begin, is known as *recorder level*.

The inventory model can be classified into two categories.

(*i*) Deterministic inventory model
(*ii*) Probabilistic inventory model

16.7 DETERMINISTIC INVENTORY MODEL

In this model, the demand is assumed to be fixed and completely predetermined, i.e., *static demand*. Such models are referred to as economic lot size models.

There are four types of models under this category, namely,

(*i*) Purchasing model with no shortages
(*ii*) Manufacturing model with no shortages
(*iii*) Purchasing model with shortages
(*iv*) Manufacturing model with shortages.

16.7.1 EOQ Models without Shortages

Model I : Purchasing model with no shortages (a) *The Economic lot size system with uniform demand.*

In this model, we have to derive an economic lot size formula for the optimum production quantity q per cycle of a single product, so as to minimize the total average variable cost per unit time.

The assumptions for this model are as follows.

(*i*) Demand rate is uniform.
(*ii*) Lead time is zero.
(*iii*) Production rate is infinite, i.e., production is instantaneous.
(*iv*) Shortages are not allowed.
(*v*) Holding cost is rupees C_1 per quantity unit, per unit time.
(*vi*) Set-up cost is rupees C_3, per time set-up.

Let each production cycle be made at fixed intervals t and, therefore, the quantity q already present in the beginning is $q = Rt$ where, R is the demand rate.

Since the stock is small time dt is Rdt, the stock in total time t will be,

$$= \int_0^t Rtdt = \frac{1}{2}Rt^2 = \frac{1}{2}qt \qquad [\because Rt = q]$$

$$= \text{Area of the inventory } \Delta POA.$$

The graphical solution of this inventory is shown below.

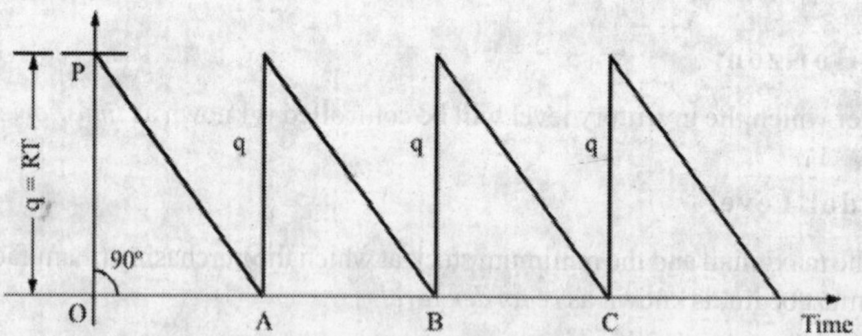

The rate of replenishment = slope of line $OP = \tan 90° = \infty$

Thus, cost of the holding inventory per production run.

$$= C_1 \times \text{Area of } \Delta OPA = C_1\left(\frac{Rt^2}{2}\right)$$

The set-up cost per production = C_3 per production, per time interval.

The cost equation is given by the average total cost,

$$= C(t) = \frac{1}{t}\left[\frac{C_1Rt^2}{2} + C_3\right]$$

$$= \frac{C_1Rt}{2} + \frac{C_3}{t}$$

We want to find the minimum average total cost, by using the property of minimum, we have

$$\frac{dC(t)}{dt} = 0 \Rightarrow \frac{C_1R}{2} - \frac{C_3}{t^2} = 0$$

which gives,

$$t = \sqrt{\frac{2C_3}{C_1R}}$$

$$\frac{d^2C(t)}{dt^2} = 0 + \frac{2C_3}{t^3} > 0$$

Hence, $C(t)$ is minimum for optimum time interval,

$$t^* = \sqrt{\frac{2C_3}{C_1R}}$$

The optimum quantity to be produced (ordered) at each interval t^* is,

$$q^* = Rt^* = R\sqrt{\frac{2C_3}{C_1 R}} = \sqrt{\frac{2C_3 R}{C_1}}$$

$$q^* = \sqrt{\frac{2C_3 R}{C_1}}$$

$$q^* = \sqrt{\frac{2C_3 R}{C_1}}$$

This is called the optimal lot size formula.

$$\text{Min. Cost} = C^* = C_{\min} = \tfrac{1}{2} RC_1\sqrt{\frac{2C_3}{C_1 R}} + C_3\sqrt{\frac{C_1 R}{2C_3}}$$

$$= \sqrt{\frac{C_1 C_3 R}{2}} + \sqrt{\frac{C_1 C_3 R}{2}}$$

$$\boldsymbol{C^* = \sqrt{2C_1 C_3 R}}$$

Characteristics of Model 1

1. Optimum number of orders placed per year.

$$n^* = R/q^* = \sqrt{\frac{RC_1}{2C_3}}$$

2. Optimum length of time between orders.

$$t^* = \sqrt{\frac{2C_3}{RC_1}}$$

3. Minimum total annual inventory cost.

$$C^* = \sqrt{2C_1 C_3 R}$$

4. Optimal lot size formula.

$$q^* = \sqrt{\frac{2C_3 R}{C_1}}$$

Model I (b) *EOQ problem with no shortages and several production runs of unequal length.*

In this problem, all the assumptions are the same as in Model I (a) except that the demand is uniform and the production runs differ in units. By replacing R by $R = D/T$ where, D is the total demand to be satisfied during the period T in the above formula, we get the following optimum quantities.

$$q^* = \sqrt{\frac{2C_3 D/T}{C_1}}$$

$$t^* = \sqrt{\frac{2C_3}{C_1\ D/T}}$$

$$C^* = \sqrt{2C_1 C_3\ D/T}$$

Model II: Manufacturing model with no shortages

Let,

C_1 = holding cost per item, per unit time

C_2 = 0 i.e., shortages are not permitted

C_3 = set-up cost per production cycle

R = number of items required per unit time, i.e., demand rate ($K > R$) is the production rate, which is finite and greater than R

t = interval between production cycles

q = Rt the number of items produced per production run.

In this model each production cycle consists of two parts t_1 and t_2 where,

(*i*) t_1 is the period during which the stock is growing at the rate $(K - R)$ items per unit time.

(*ii*) t_2 is the period during which there is no replenishment (supply or production) but there is only a constant demand at the rate R. Further, we assume that q is the stock available at the end of time t_1, which is expected to be consumed during the remaining period t_2 at the consumption rate R.

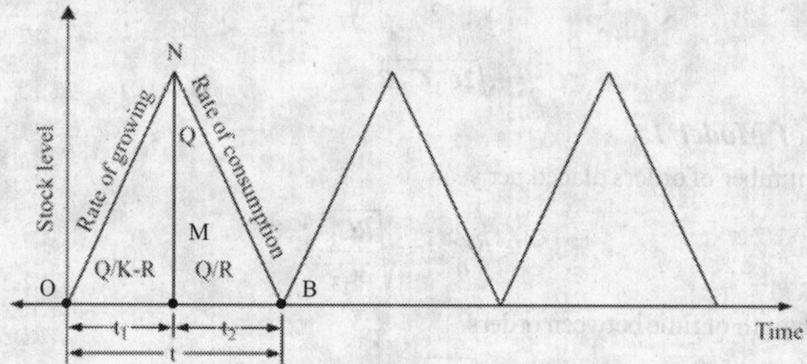

From the graph we have,

$$t_1 = \frac{Q}{K - R}$$

Since the total quantity produced during the production period t_1 is q and the quantity which is consumed during the period t_1 is Rt_1, the remaining quantity that is stored during t_1 is given by,

$$Q = q - Rt_1$$

$$\therefore \quad Q = q - RQ/(K - R)$$

$$q = Q + RQ/(K - R)$$

which gives,

$$Q = \frac{K - R}{K} q$$

Now holding cost for time period t

$$= (\Delta ONB) \times C_1$$

$$= \frac{1}{2} \times MN \times OB \times C_1 = \frac{1}{2} Q \,.\, t \,.\, C_1$$

Set-up cost for the period $t = C_3$.

$\therefore$ total average cost is given by the cost equation,

$$C(q) = \frac{\frac{1}{2}QtC_1}{t} + \frac{C_3}{t}$$

$$= \frac{1}{2}\frac{K-R}{K}qC_1 + \frac{C_3}{t}$$

$$= \frac{1}{2}\frac{K-R}{K}qC_1 + \frac{C_3R}{q}$$

For optimum value of q, we have,

$$\frac{dC}{dq} = \frac{1}{2}\left(1-\frac{R}{K}\right)C_1 - \frac{C_3R}{q^2} = 0$$

which gives, $$q = \sqrt{\frac{2C_3}{C_1}\frac{RK}{K-R}}$$

Also, $$\frac{d^2C}{dq^2} = 0 + \frac{2C_3R}{q} > 0$$

we have,

$$q^* = \sqrt{\frac{2C_3}{C_1}\frac{RK}{K-R}} \text{ (optimal lot size formula)}$$

$$t^* = \frac{q^*}{R} = \sqrt{\frac{2C_3K}{C_1R(K-R)}} \text{ (optimal time interval)}$$

$$C^* = C_{\min} = \sqrt{2C_1\left(1-\frac{R}{K}\right)C_3R}$$

Characteristics of Model II

(*i*) Optimum number of production run per year.

$$n^* = R/q^* = \sqrt{\frac{C_1R}{2C_3}}\sqrt{\frac{K-R}{K}}$$

(*ii*) Optimum length of each lot size production run.

$$t^* = \sqrt{\frac{2C_3}{C_1R}}\sqrt{\frac{K}{K-R}}$$

(*iii*) Optimum lot run size.

$$q^* = \sqrt{\frac{2C_3R}{C_1}}\sqrt{\frac{K}{K-R}}$$

(*iv*) Total minimum production inventory cost.

$$TC^* = \sqrt{2RC_3C_1}\sqrt{\frac{K-R}{K}}$$

Note: (*i*) If $K = R$, then $C^* = 0$, i.e., there will be no holding cost and set-up cost.

(*ii*) If $K = \infty$, i.e., the production rate is finite, then this model reduces to model I.

Example 16.1 The annual demand of an item is 3,200 units. The unit cost is ₹ 6 and inventory carrying charges are 25 per cent per annum. If the cost of one procurement is ₹ 150, determine the:

(*i*) EOQ (*ii*) Number of orders per year
(*iii*) Time between two consecutive orders (*iv*) The optimal cost

Solution Given, $R = 3{,}200$ units

$$C_1 = C \times I \quad C = 6, \qquad I = \frac{25}{100} = \frac{1}{4}$$

$$C_3 = ₹\,150 \qquad C_1 = 6 \times \frac{1}{4} = \frac{3}{2}$$

(*i*) The optimum lot size, $q^* = \sqrt{\frac{2C_3R}{C_1}} = \sqrt{\frac{2 \times 3{,}200 \times 150}{3/2}} = 800$ unit.

(*ii*) Number of orders $= N = \frac{R}{q^*} = \frac{3{,}200}{800} = 4$

(*iii*) Time between two consecutive orders $= t^* = 1/N^* = 1/4$ year or 3 months.

(*iv*) The optimal cost $= 6 \times 3{,}200 + \sqrt{2C_1C_3R}$

$$= 6 \times 3{,}200 + \sqrt{2 \times \frac{3}{2} \times 150 \times 3{,}200}$$

$$= ₹\,20{,}400.$$

Example 16.2 A company purchases 9,000 parts of a machine for its annual requirements, ordering one month's usage at a time. Each part costs ₹ 20. The ordering cost per order is ₹ 15 and the carrying charges are 15 per cent of the average inventory per year. You have been asked to suggest a more economical purchasing policy for the company. What advice would you offer and how much would it save the company per year?

Solution Given, $R = 9{,}000$ parts per year

$C_1 = 15\%$ of the average inventory per year
$= 20 \times 15/100 = ₹\,3$ for each part, per year
$C_3 = ₹\,15$ per order

$$q^* = \sqrt{\frac{2C_3R}{C_1}} = \sqrt{\frac{2 \times 15 \times 9000}{3}} = 300 \text{ units}$$

$$t^* = \frac{q^*}{R} = \frac{300}{9000} = \frac{1}{30} \text{ year} = \frac{365}{30} = 12 \text{ days}$$

$$C^* = C_{\min} = \sqrt{2C_1C_3R} = \sqrt{2 \times 3 \times 15 \times 9000} = ₹\,900$$

If the company follows the policy of ordering every month, then the annual ordering cost becomes $= 12 \times 15 = ₹\,180$.

Lot size of the inventory for each month, $q = \frac{9000}{12} = 750$ parts

$$\text{Average inventory at any time, } \frac{q}{2} = \frac{750}{2} = 375 \text{ parts}$$

$$\text{Storage cost at any time} = 375 \times C_1 = 375 \times 3 = ₹\,1{,}125$$

$$\text{Total cost} = 1{,}125 + 180 = ₹\,1{,}305.$$

If the company purchases 300 parts at time intervals of 12 days instead of ordering 750 parts each month, there will be a net saving of 1305 – 900 = ₹ 405 per year.

Example 16.3 The demand rate of a particular item is 12,000 units per year. The set-up cost per run is ₹ 350 and the holding cost is ₹ 0.20 per unit, per month. If no shortages are allowed and the replacement is instantaneous, determine (*i*) The optimum run size, (*ii*) The optimum scheduling period (*iii*) Minimum total expected annual cost.

Solution Demand rate, $R = 12{,}000$ per year

Holding cost, $C_1 = ₹\,0.2$ per unit per month

$= ₹\,2.4$ per unit per year

Set-up cost, $C_3 = ₹\,350$ per run

(*i*) $$\text{Optimum lot size} = q^* = \sqrt{\frac{2RC_3}{C_1}} = \sqrt{\frac{2 \times 12000 \times 350}{2.4}} = 1{,}870 \text{ units}$$

(*ii*) Optimum scheduling period, (i.e. time between 2 consecutive orders)

$$t^* = \frac{Q^*}{R} = \frac{1870}{1{,}2000} \text{ year}$$

$$= \frac{1870 \times 12}{12000} \text{ months} = 1.87 \text{ months}$$

(*iii*) Minimum total expected annual cost, $= \sqrt{2RC_1C_3}$

$$= \sqrt{2 \times 2.4 \times 350 \times 1{,}2000}$$

$$= ₹\,4{,}490 \text{ per year.}$$

Example 16.4 The annual requirement for a product is 3,000 units. The ordering cost is ₹ 100 per order. The cost per unit is ₹ 10. The carrying cost per unit, per year is 30 per cent of the unit cost. (*i*) Find the EOQ. By using better organizational methods, the ordering cost per order can be brought down to ₹ 80 per order, but the same quantity as determined above has to be ordered. (*ii*) If a new EOQ is found by using the ordering cost as ₹ 80, what would be the further savings in cost?

Solution Given, $R = 3{,}000$ units per year

$C_1 = C \times I = 10 \times 30/100 = ₹\,3$ per unit, per year

$C_3 = ₹\,100$ per order

(*i*) $$\text{Optimal lot size } q^* = \sqrt{\frac{2C_3R}{C_1}} = \sqrt{\frac{2 \times 100 \times 3{,}000}{3}} = 447 \text{ units}$$

$$\text{No. of orders} = \frac{3{,}000}{447} \simeq 7$$

$$C = \text{Total inventory cost} = \sqrt{2RC_1C_3}$$

$$= \sqrt{2 \times 3{,}000 \times 3 \times 100} = ₹\,1{,}341.6 \text{ per year.}$$

(*ii*) $C_3 = 80$

$$C = \sqrt{2 \times 3{,}000 \times 3 \times 80} = 1200$$

(*iii*) $R = 3{,}000$ units per year

$C_1 = ₹\,3$ per unit year

$C_3 = ₹\,80$ per order

$$\text{Optimal size, } q^* = \sqrt{\frac{2RC_3}{C_1}} = \sqrt{\frac{2 \times 3000 \times 80}{3}} = 400 \text{ units per order.}$$

No. of orders = 8

$$\text{Total inventory cost} = \frac{R}{q^*} \times C_3 + \frac{q^*}{2} \times C_1$$

$$= \frac{3000}{400} \times 80 + \frac{400}{2} \times 3 = 600 + \frac{400}{2} \times 3$$

$$= ₹\,1200$$

Net change in the total cost or saving in cost = $a - b$ = 1,342 – 1,200 = 142 = 1.42%

Example 16.5 A company has to supply an item 1,000 times per month at a uniform rate and each time a production run is started it costs ₹ 200. Cost of storing is ₹ 20 per item, per month. The number of items to be produced per run has to be ascertained. Determine the total set-up cost and average inventory cost if the run size is 500, 600, 700 and 800. Find the optimal production run size using the EOQ formula.

Solution Given,

The demand $R = 1{,}000$ per month

Set-up cost, $C_3 = ₹\,200$ per order

Carrying cost, $C_1 = ₹\,20$ per item, per month

Run size	***Set-up cost (₹)***	***Average inventory cost (₹)***	***Total cost (₹)***
500	$\frac{1000}{500} \times 200 = 400$	$\frac{500}{2} \times 20 = 5{,}000$	5,400
600	$\frac{1000}{600} \times 200 = 333.3$	$\frac{600}{2} \times 20 = 6{,}000$	6,333.3
700	$\frac{1000}{700} \times 200 = 285.7$	$\frac{700}{2} \times 20 = 7{,}000$	7,285.7
800	$\frac{1000}{800} \times 200 = 250$	$\frac{800}{2} \times 20 = 8{,}000$	8,250

From the above table, we conclude that the total cost increases when the batch size increases.

$$\text{EOQ } q^* = \sqrt{\frac{2RC_3}{C_1}} = \sqrt{\frac{2 \times 1{,}000 \times 200}{20}} = 141 \text{ units.}$$

Example 16.6 The following table gives the annual demand and unit price of four items.

Item	*A*	*B*	*C*	*D*
Annual demand (units)	800	400	392	13800
Unit price (₹)	0.02	1.00	8.00	0.20

Order cost is ₹ 5 per order and holding cost is 10 per cent of the unit price.

(*i*) Determine the EOQ in units
(*ii*) Calculate total variable cost
(*iii*) Compute EOQ in ₹
(*iv*) Compute EOQ in years of supply
(*v*) Determine the number of orders per year.

Solution

Item *A*:

Given,

$$R = 800 \text{ units per year}$$
$$C_3 = ₹\,5 \text{ per order}$$
$$C_1 = 10/100 \times 0.02 = 0.002$$

$$\text{EOQ} = \sqrt{\frac{2RC_3}{C_1}} = \sqrt{\frac{2 \times 800 \times 5}{0.002}} = 2{,}000 \text{ units}$$

$$\text{Total variable cost} = \sqrt{2C_1C_3R} = \sqrt{2 \times 0.002 \times 5 \times 800} = ₹\,4$$

$$\text{EOQ in ₹} = 2000 \times 0.02 = ₹\,40$$

$$\text{EOQ in years supply} = \frac{2000}{800} = 2.5 \text{ years}$$

$$\text{Number of orders per year} = \frac{R}{q^*} = \frac{800}{2000} = \frac{1}{2.5} = 0.4$$

Item *B*:

$$R = 400 \text{ units per year}$$
$$C_3 = ₹\,5 \text{ per order}$$
$$C_1 = 10/100 \times 1 = 1/10 = ₹\,0.1$$

$$\text{EOQ} = \sqrt{\frac{2RC_3}{C_1}} = \sqrt{\frac{2 \times 400 \times 5}{0.1}} = 200 \text{ units}$$

$$\text{Total variable cost} = \sqrt{2 \times C_3 \times C_1 \times R}$$
$$= \sqrt{2 \times 400 \times 5 \times 0.1} = ₹\,20$$

$$\text{EOQ in ₹} = 200 \times 1 = ₹\,200$$

$$\text{EOQ in years supply} = \frac{200}{400} = 0.5 \text{ year}$$

$$\text{Number of orders per year} = \frac{200}{400} = \frac{1}{2}$$

Item *C*:

$$R = 392 \text{ units per year}$$

$$C_3 = ₹\,5 \text{ per order}$$

$$C_1 = 10/100 \times 8 = 0.8$$

$$\text{EOQ} = \sqrt{\frac{2RC_3}{C_1}} = \sqrt{\frac{2 \times 392 \times 5}{0.8}} = 70 \text{ units}$$

$$\text{Total variable cost} = \sqrt{2RC_1C_3}$$

$$= \sqrt{2 \times 392 \times 0.8 \times 5} = ₹\,56$$

$$\text{EOQ in ₹} = 70 \times 8 = ₹\,560$$

$$\text{EOQ in years of supply} = \frac{70}{392} = 0.18 \text{ year}$$

$$\text{Number of orders per year} = \frac{392}{70} = 5.6$$

Similarly, we can calculate for item *D*. Thus, we arrive at the following answers: (*i*) 2,627 units (*ii*) ₹ 52.54 (*iii*) ₹ 525.40 (*iv*) 0.19 year (*v*) 5.26.

Example 16.7 The demand rate for an item in a company is 18,000 units per year. The company can produce at the rate of 3,000 units per month. The set-up cost is ₹ 500 per order and the holding cost is ₹ 0.15 per unit, per month. Calculate,

(*i*) Optimum manufacturing quantity
(*ii*) The maximum inventory
(*iii*) Time between orders
(*iv*) The number of orders per year
(*v*) The time of manufacture
(*vi*) The optimum annual cost, if the cost of an item is ₹ 2 per unit.

Solution Given,

Item cost, $C = ₹\,2$ per unit
Set-up cost, $C_3 = ₹\,500$ per order
Carrying cost, $C_1 = ₹\,0.15$ per unit, per month
Demand rate, $R = 18{,}000$ units per year
$= 1{,}500$ units per month
Production rate, $K = 3{,}000$ units per month

(*i*) Optimum manufacturing quantity,

$$q^* = \sqrt{\frac{2RC_3}{C_1}}\sqrt{\frac{K}{K-R}}$$

$$= \sqrt{\frac{2 \times 1,500 \times 500}{0.15}} \sqrt{\frac{3,000}{3,000 - 1,500}} = 4,470 \text{ units}$$

(*ii*) Maximum inventory

$$= \frac{q}{K}(K - R)$$

$$= \frac{4470}{3000}(3,000 - 1,500) = 2,235 \text{ units}$$

(*iii*) Times between orders

$$= \frac{q^*}{R} = \frac{4,470}{1,500} = 3 \text{ months (approximately)}$$

(*iv*) Number of orders per year,

$$\frac{12}{3} = 4$$

(*v*) Times between orders

$$= \frac{q^*}{K} = \frac{4,470}{3,000} = 1.5 \text{ months}$$

(*vi*) The optimum annual cost/Total expected system cost

= item cost + ordering cost + holding cost

$$= 18,000 \times 2 + \frac{18,000}{4,470} \times 500 + \frac{2,235}{36,000}(36,000 - 18,000) \times 1.8$$

$= ₹40,025.$

Example 16.8 A contractor has to supply 10,000 bearings per day to an automobile manufacturer. He finds that when he starts production run, he can produce 25,000 bearings per day. The holding cost of a bearing in stock is ₹ 0.02 per year. Set-up cost of a production is ₹ 18. How frequently should the production run be made?

Solution: Given,

Demand rate, $R = 10,000$ units per day

Production rate, $K = 25,000$ units per day

Set-up cost, $C_3 = ₹\,18$ per order

Carrying or holding cost, $C_1 = ₹\,0.02$ per unit, per year

$= ₹\,0.000055$ per unit, per day

Optimum order quantity, $$q^* = \sqrt{\frac{2C_3R}{C_1}} \sqrt{\frac{K}{K - R}}$$

$$= \sqrt{\frac{2 \times 18 \times 10,000}{0.000055}} \sqrt{\frac{25,000}{25,000 - 10,000}}$$

$= 1,04,447$ bearings

$$\text{Time between orders} = \frac{q^*}{R} = \frac{10,4447}{10,000}$$
$$= 10.4 \text{ days}$$

$$\text{Time of manufacture} = \frac{q^*}{K} = \frac{10,4447}{25,000} = 4 \text{ days (approx.)}.$$

$\therefore$ The manufacturing or production cycle starts at an interval of 10.4 days and production continues for 4 days.

In each cycle, a batch of 1,04,447 bearings is produced.

Example 16.9 An item is produced at the rate of 50 units per day. The demand occurs at the rate of 25 items per day. If the set-up cost is ₹ 100 per run and the holdings cost is ₹ 0.01 per unit of item, per day, find the economic Lot size for one run, assuming that shortages are not permitted. Also find the time of the cycle and minimum cost for one run.

Solution Given,

Demand rate, $R = 25$ items per day

Production rate, $K = 50$ items per day

Set-up cost, $C_3 =$ ₹ 100 per run

Holding cost, $C_1 =$ ₹ 0.01 per unit, per day

(*i*) Economic lot size,
$$q^* = \sqrt{\frac{2C_3R}{C_1}}\sqrt{\frac{K}{K-R}}$$
$$= \sqrt{\frac{2 \times 100 \times 25}{0.01}}\sqrt{\frac{50}{50-25}} = 1,000 \text{ units}$$

(*ii*)
$$t^* = \frac{q^*}{R} = \frac{1,000}{25} = 40 \text{ days}$$

Minimum daily cost is given by,

$$C_1^* = \sqrt{2C_1\,C_3R}\sqrt{\frac{K-R}{K}}$$
$$= \sqrt{2 \times 0.01 \times 100 \times 25}\sqrt{\frac{50-25}{50}} = ₹\,5$$

$\therefore$ Minimum cost per run = 5 × 40 = ₹ 200.

Example 16.10 A company has a demand of 12,000 units per year for an item and it can produce 2,000 such items per month. The cost of one set-up is ₹ 400 and the holding cost per unit per month is ₹ 0.15. Find the optimum lot size, maximum inventory manufacturing time and total time.

Solution Given,

$R = 12,000$ units per year

$K = 2,000$ units per month

$= 2,000 \times 12 = 24,000$ units per year

Set-up cost, $C_3 =$ ₹ 400 per run

Holding cost, $C_1 =$ ₹ 0.15 per unit, per month

$= 0.15 \times 12 =$ ₹ 1.8 per unit, per year

$\therefore$ optimum lot size, $$q^* = \sqrt{\frac{2C_3R}{C_1}}\sqrt{\frac{K}{K-R}}$$

$$= \sqrt{\frac{2 \times 400 \times 12000}{1.8}}\sqrt{\frac{24000}{24000-12000}}$$

$$= 3{,}266 \text{ units (approximately)}$$

$$\text{Maximum inventory} = \frac{K-R}{K}q^* = \frac{24000-12000}{24000}(3266)$$

$$= 1{,}633 \text{ units}$$

$$\text{Manufacturing times} = \frac{q^*}{K} = \frac{3266}{24000} = 0.136 \text{ years}$$

$$\text{Total time, } t^* = \frac{q^*}{R} = \frac{3266}{12000} = 0.272 \text{ years.}$$

EXERCISES

1. The annual requirement for a particular raw material is 2,000 units, costing ₹ 1 each to manufacture. The ordering cost is ₹ 10 per order and the carrying cost is 16 per cent per annum of the average inventory value. Find the EOQ and the total inventory cost per annum. **[Ans.** q^* = 500 units, C_{min} = ₹ 80]
2. The production for a particular item is instantaneous. The storage cost of one item is ₹ 1 per month and the set-up cost is ₹ 25 per run. If the demand is 200 units per month, find the optimum quantity to be produced per set-up and hence, find the total cost of storage and set-up per month. **[Ans.** q^* = 100 units; t^* = 15 days; C^* = ₹ 100; Total costs of storage and set-up = 25 + 1 × 100 = ₹ 125]
3. XYZ company buys in lots of 2,000 units, which is the only supply for 3 months. The cost per unit is ₹ 125 and the order cost is ₹ 250. The inventory carrying charge is 20 per cent of unit value. How much money can be saved by using economic order quantity? **[Ans.** ₹ 1,600]
4. The annual demand for a product is 1,00,000 units. The rate of production is 2,00,000 units per year. The set-up cost per production run is ₹ 5,000 and the variable product cost of each items is ₹ 10. The annual holdings cost per unit is 20 per cent of its value. Find the optimum production lot size and the length of the production run. **[Ans.** q^* = 3,162 units; t^* = 115 days]
5. A contractor has to supply 20,000 units per day. He can produce 30,000 units per day. The cost of holding a unit in stock is ₹ 3 per year and the set-up cost per run is ₹ 50. How frequently should the production run be made and of what size should it be? **[Ans.** q^* = 1,414 units; t = 1.68 hours]
6. An item is produced at the rate of 128 units per day. The annual demand is 6,440 units. The set-up cost for each production run is ₹ 24 and inventory carrying charges cost ₹ 3 per unit, per year. There are 250 working days available for production each year. Develop an inventory policy for this item. **[Ans.** q^* = 358 units; t^* = 14 days; Manufacturing time = 2.8 days; C^* = ₹ 858.65]
7. A stockist has to supply 400 units of a product to his customer every Monday. He gets the product at ₹ 50 per unit from the manufacturers. The cost of ordering and transportation from the manufacturers is ₹ 75 per order. The cost of carrying inventory per year is 7.5 per cent of the cost of product. Find (*i*) the economic lot size (*ii*) the total optimal cost (including the capital cost). **[Ans.** q^* = 912 units per order; C^* = 20,065.80 per week]
8. A certain item costs ₹ 250 per tonne. The monthly requirement is 10 tonnes and each time the stock is replenished, there is a set-up cost of ₹ 1,000. The cost of carrying inventory has been estimated at 12 per cent of the value of the stock per year. What is the optimal order quantity and how frequently should orders be placed? **[Ans.** q^* = 89.44 units; t^* = 9 months]

16.7.2 EOQ Models with Shortages

Model III: Purchasing model with shortages

Case I This is an extension of model I, allowing shortages. The assumptions are,

(*i*) C_1 is the holding cost per unit quantity, per unit time

(*ii*) C_2 is the shortage cost per quantity, per unit time

(*iii*) R is the demand rate.

(*iv*) t_p is the scheduling time period, which is constant.

(*v*) q_p is the fixed lot size, $q_p = Rt_p$.

(*vi*) Z is the order level to which the inventory is raised in the beginning of each scheduling period. Shortages if any, have to be taken care of. Here, Z is a variable.

(*vii*) Production rate is infinite.

(*viii*) Lead time is zero.

In this model we can easily observe that the inventory carrying cost C_1 as well as shortage cost C_2 will be involved only when $0 \le Z \le q_p$.

In the following figure, the dotted area (ΔDBC) represents the failure to meet the demand and the shaded area (ΔAOB) shows the inventory.

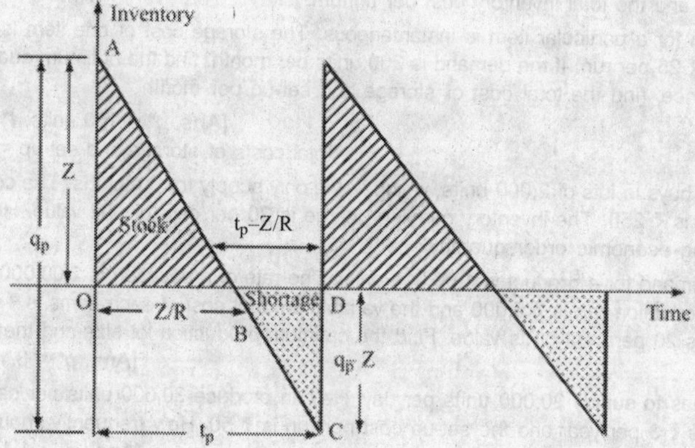

Since q_p is the lot size sufficient to meet the demand for time t_p but ($<q_p$) amount of stock is planned in order to meet the demand for time Z/R, where R is the demand rate. Shortage of amount ($q_p - Z$) will arise for the entire remaining period $t_p - Z/R$.

Holding cost per unit time becomes

$$= C_1 (\Delta OAB)/t_p$$

$$= \frac{C_1}{t_p}\left[\frac{1}{2} Z \cdot \frac{Z}{R}\right]$$

$$= \frac{1}{2}\frac{Z^2 C_1}{Rt_p} = \frac{1}{2}\frac{Z^2 C_1}{q_p}$$

Shortage cost per unit time is

$$= C_2\,(\Delta BDC)/t_p = C_2(\tfrac{1}{2}\,BD\cdot DC)/t_p$$

$$= \frac{C_2}{2t_p}[(t_p - Z/R)(q_p - Z)] = \frac{C_2}{2Rt_p}(Rt_p - Z)(q_p - Z)$$

$$= \frac{1}{2}\frac{C_2}{q_p}(q_p - Z)^2$$

The cost equation for this model is,

$$\boxed{C(Z) = \frac{1}{2}\frac{z^2C_1}{q_p} + \frac{1}{2}\frac{C_2}{q_p}(q_p - Z)^2}$$

$\therefore$ the set-up cost C_3 and period t_p are constant. The average set-up cost C_3/t_p being constant, is not to be considered in the cost equation.

To obtain the optimum order level Z, we differentiate $C(Z)$ with reference to z and equate it to zero, we get,

$$\frac{dC}{dZ} = \frac{1}{2}\frac{C_1}{q_p}(2Z) + \frac{1}{2}\frac{C_2}{q_p}2\,(q_p - Z)(-1) = 0$$

$$\Rightarrow \qquad Z = \frac{C_2}{C_1 + C_2}q_p$$

or,

$$\boxed{Z = \frac{C_2}{C_1 + C_2}Rt_p}$$

Condition for minimum cost is also satisfied because,

$$\frac{d^2C}{dZ^2} = \frac{C_1}{q_p} + \frac{C_2}{q_p} > 0$$

By substituting this value of Z in the cost equation and on simplification we get,

$$C_{\min} = \frac{1}{2}\frac{C_1 + C_2}{C_1 + C_2}Rt_p$$

Case II All the assumptions in this case are same as in case I, except that the scheduling period is not constant here. Hence, we have to consider the average set-up cost C_3/t in the cost equation, so that comparisons can be made between different values of t.

The cost equation becomes,

$$C(t, Z) = \frac{1}{t}\left[\frac{C_1Z^2}{2R} + \frac{C_2}{2R}(Rt - Z)^2 + C_3\right]$$

To minimize the cost $C(t, Z)$, which is the function of two independent variables t and Z.

For this we have,

$$\frac{\partial C}{\partial z} = 0, \quad \frac{\partial C}{\partial t} = 0$$

$$\frac{\partial C}{\partial z} = 0 \quad \text{gives,} \quad \boxed{Z = \frac{C_2Rt}{C_1 + C_2}}$$

$$\frac{\partial C}{\partial t} = 0 \text{ gives,}$$

$$\boxed{t^* = \sqrt{\frac{2C_3}{RC_1}\left(\frac{C_1 + C_2}{C_2}\right)}} \text{ (optimum period)}$$

optimal order quantity q is given by,

$$q^* = Rt^* = R\sqrt{\frac{2C_3}{RC_1}\left(\frac{C_1 + C_2}{C_2}\right)}$$

$$\boxed{q^* = \sqrt{\frac{2C_3}{C_1}\left(\frac{C_1 + C_2}{C_2}\right)}}$$

$$\boxed{C_{\min} = C^* = \sqrt{2C_1C_3R}\sqrt{\frac{C_2}{C_1 + C_2}}}$$

Model IV: Manufacturing model with shortages

Case I In this model the assumptions are,

(*i*) R is the uniform demand rate.

(*ii*) Lead time is zero.

(*iii*) Production rate is finite (K units per unit time).

(*iv*) Inventory carrying cost is, ₹$C_1 = K > R$ (*IP*) per quantity unit, per unit time.

(*v*) Shortages are not allowed or back-logged and the corresponding cost is ₹ 12 per quantity, per unit time.

(*vi*) Set-up cost is ₹ C_3 per set-up.

To obtain the optimum order level Z, we differentiate $C(Z)$ with reference to Z and equate it to zero, we get,

$$\frac{dC}{dZ} = \frac{1}{2}\frac{C_1}{q_p}(2Z) + \frac{1}{2}\frac{C_2}{q_p}2(q_p - Z)(-1) = 0$$

$$\Rightarrow \quad Z = \frac{C_2}{C_1 + C_2}q_p$$

or

$$\boxed{Z = \frac{C_2}{C_1 + C_2}Rt_p}$$

Condition for minimum cost is also satisfied because,

$$\frac{d^2C}{dz^2} = \frac{C_1}{q_p} + \frac{C_2}{q_p} > 0$$

By substituting this value of z in the cost equation and on simplification,

we get,

$$C_{\min} = \frac{1}{2}\frac{C_1 + C_2}{C_1 + C_2}Rt_p$$

Case II All the assumptions in this case are same as in case I, except that the scheduling period is not constant here. Hence, we have to consider the average set-up cost C_3/t in the cost equation, so that comparisons can be made between different values of t.

The cost equation becomes,

$$C(t, z) = \frac{1}{t}\left[\frac{C_1 Z^2}{2R} + \frac{C_2}{2R}(Rt - Z)^2 + C_3\right]$$

To minimize the cost $C(t, Z)$, which is the function of two independent variables t and Z.

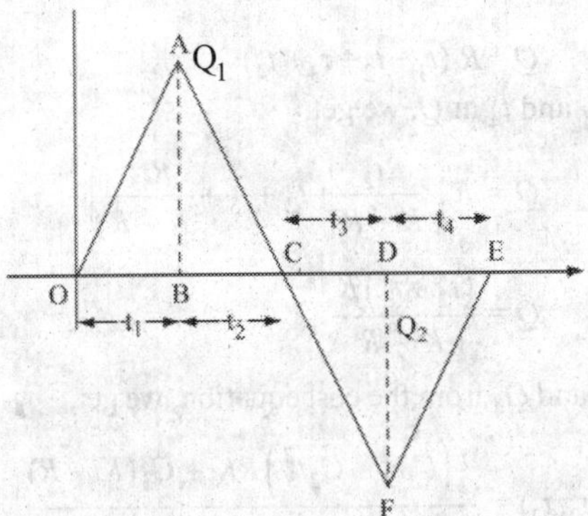

The above figure shows that there is an inventory cycle. Stocks start at zero and increase for a period t_1. They decline for a period t_2, until they again reach zero at the point where a backlog piles up for the time t_3. At the end of t_3, production starts and backlog is diminished for the time t_4 when it reaches zero. The cycle then repeats itself after total time $(t_1 + t_2 + t_3 + t_4)$.

$$\text{Now, holding cost} = C_1 \times \Delta OAC = C_1 \cdot \frac{1}{2} Q_1 (t_1 + t_2).$$

$$\text{Shortage cost} = C_2 \times \Delta EFC = C_2 \cdot \frac{1}{2} Q_2 (t_3 + t_4)$$

The set-up cost per set-up is equal to C_3,

$$C = \frac{1}{2}\left(\frac{C_1 Q_1 (t_1 + t_2) + C_2 Q_2 (t_3 + t_4) + C_3}{t_1 + t_2 + t_3 + t_4}\right)$$

Here, C is a function of variables $(Q_1, Q_2, t_1, t_2, t_3, t_4)$. There are four relationships and this permits us to eliminate two variables.

The inventory is zero at O and during the period t_1 an amount kt_1 is produced, but because orders are being filled up at a rate, the net increase Q_1 in the inventory during time t_1 is given by,

$$Q_1 = Kt_1 - Rt_1 = t_1 (K - R)$$

Now, after time t_1 the production is stopped and the stock Q_1 is used up during t_2. As the rate of use is R we have,

$$Q_1 = Rt_2$$

$$Q_1 = t_1 (K - R) \Rightarrow Rt_2 = t_1 (K - R)$$

$$t_1 = \frac{Rt_2}{K - R}$$

During period t_4, shortages accumulate at a rate R.

$$\therefore \quad Q_2 = Rt_3$$

During period t_4, production rate is K and demand rate is R so that the net rate of reduction of shortage becomes $K - R$, and thus, we have $Q_2 = t_4 (K - R)$

$$Q_2 = t_4 (K - R)$$

$$t_4 = \frac{Q_2}{K - R} = \frac{Rt_3}{K - R}$$

Finally, because the total cycle $(t_1 + t_2 + t_3 + t_4)$ and production q is just sufficient to meet the demand at the rate R_1, we have,

$$Q = R\,(t_1 + t_2 + t_3 + t_4)$$

Substituting the values of t_1 and t_4 in Q, we get,

$$Q = R\left(\frac{Rt_2}{K - R} + t_2 + t_3 + \frac{Rt_3}{K - R}\right).$$

$$Q = \frac{(t_2 + t_3)K}{K - R}.$$

Now, eliminating t_1, t_4, Q_1, and Q_4 from the cost equation, we get,

$$C(t_2, t_3) = \frac{\frac{1}{2}\left(C_1 t_2^2 + C_2 t_3^2\right)RK + C_3(K - R)}{K\left(t_2 + t_3\right)}$$

To find the best values $t_2{}^*$ and $t_3{}^*$ of t_2 and t_3, differentiate the above equation partially, with respect to t_2 and t_3 and set the results equal to zero. We get,

$$t_2{}^* = \sqrt{\frac{2\,C_3 C_2 (1 - R/K)}{R\,(C_1 + C_2)\,C_1}}$$

$$t_3{}^* = \sqrt{\frac{2\,C_3 C_1 (1 - R/K)}{R\,(C_1 + C_2)\,C_2}}$$

Using this result we obtain the optimum order quantity.

$$\boxed{q^* = \sqrt{\frac{2RC_3}{C_1 C_2}}(C_1 + C_2)\sqrt{\frac{K}{K - R}}}$$

$$Q_2^* = \sqrt{\frac{2RC_1\,C_3}{(C_1 + C_2)\,C_2}}\sqrt{\frac{K - R}{K}}$$

Finally the minimum cost is given by,

$$\boxed{C^* = \sqrt{\frac{2RC_1\,C_3}{C_1 + C_2}}\sqrt{\frac{K - R}{K}}}.$$

Example 16.11 The demand of an item is uniform, at a rate of 25 units per month. The fixed cost is ₹ 15 each time a production run is made. The production cost is ₹ 1 per item and the inventory carrying cost is ₹ 0.30 per item, per month. If the shortage cost is ₹ 1.50 per item per month, determine the frequency and size of the production run that is to be made.

Solution Given,

$$C_1 = ₹0.30 \text{ per item, per month}$$
$$C_2 = ₹1.50 \text{ per item, per month}$$
$$C_3 = ₹15 \text{ per item, per month}$$
$$R = 25 \text{ units per month.}$$

The optimum value of q is given by,

$$q^* = \sqrt{\frac{2RC_3}{C_1}}\sqrt{\frac{C_1 + C_2}{C_2}}$$

$$= \sqrt{\frac{2 \times 15 \times 25}{0.3}}\sqrt{\frac{0.3 + 1.5}{1.5}} = 54 \text{ items}$$

$$t^* = \frac{q^*}{R} = \frac{54}{25} \text{ months} = 2.16 \text{ month}$$

Example 16.12 The demand for an item is 18,000 units per year. The holding cost is ₹ 1.20 per unit time and the cost of shortage is ₹ 5. The production cost is ₹ 400. Assuming that the replacement rate is instantaneous, determine the optimum order quantity.

Solution Given,

$$R = 18{,}000 \text{ units per year}$$
$$\text{Holding cost, } C_1 = ₹1.20 \text{ per unit}$$
$$\text{Shortage cost, } C_2 = ₹5$$
$$\text{Set-up cost, } C_3 = ₹400 \text{ per run}$$

The optimum order quantity,

$$q^* = \sqrt{\frac{2\,R\,C_3}{C_1}}\sqrt{\frac{C_1 + C_2}{C_2}}$$

$$= \sqrt{\frac{2 \times 18{,}000 \times 400}{1.2}}\sqrt{\frac{1.2 + 5}{5}}$$

$$= 3{,}857 \text{ units.}$$

$$t^* = \frac{q^*}{R} = \frac{3{,}857}{18{,}000} = 0.214 \text{ year.}$$

$$N^* = \frac{R}{q^*} = 4.67 \text{ orders per year.}$$

Example 16.13 The demand for an item is deterministic and constant over time and is equal to 600 units per year. The per unit cost of the item is ₹ 50, while the cost of placing an order is ₹ 5. The inventory carrying cost is 20 per cent of the cost of inventory per annum and the cost of shortage is ₹ 1 per unit, per month. Find the optimal ordering quantity when stock-outs are permitted. If stock-outs are not permitted, what would be the loss to the company?

Solution Given,

$$R = 600 \text{ units}$$
$$C_1 = 0.20 \times 50 = ₹10$$
$$C_3 = ₹5 \text{ per order}$$
$$C_2 = ₹1 \text{ per unit, per month or } ₹12 \text{ per year, per unit}$$

(*i*) When stock-outs are permitted, the optimal ordering quantity is given by,

$$q^* = \sqrt{\frac{2\,R\,C_3}{C_1}}\sqrt{\frac{C_1+C_2}{C_2}}$$

$$= \sqrt{\frac{2\times 600\times 5}{10}}\sqrt{\frac{10+12}{12}} = 33 \text{ units}$$

(*ii*) Maximum number of back orders,

$$Z^* = q^*\left(\frac{C_1}{C_1+C_2}\right) = 33\left(\frac{10}{10+12}\right) = 15 \text{ units}$$

(*iii*) Total expected yearly cost (with shortage allowed) is,

$$C(q^*) = \sqrt{2\,R\,C_1\,C_3}\sqrt{\frac{C_2}{C_1+C_2}}$$

$$= \sqrt{2\times 600\times 10\times 5}\sqrt{\frac{12}{10+12}} = 181.3$$

$$= ₹\,181$$

If stock outs or back ordering are not permitted, the optimal order quantity is,

$$q^* = \sqrt{\frac{2\,R\,C_3}{C_1}} = 24.5 \text{ units}$$

The total relevant cost is given by,

$$C(q^*) = \sqrt{2\,C_1 C_3\,R} = ₹245$$

Thus, the additional cost when back ordering is not allowed is (245–181) = ₹ 64.

Example 16.14 The demand for an item in a company is 18,000 units per year. The company can produce the items at a rate of 3,000 per month. The cost of one set-up is ₹ 500 and the holding cost of 1 unit per month is ₹ 0.15. The shortage cost of one unit is ₹ 20 per year. Determine the optimum manufacturing quantity and the number of shortages. Also determine the manufacturing time and the time between set-ups.

Solution

$$C_1 = ₹\,0.15 \text{ per month}$$
$$C_2 = ₹\,20 \text{ per year}$$
$$= \frac{20}{12} = ₹\,1.66 \text{ per month}$$
$$C_3 = ₹\,500$$
$$K = 3{,}000 \text{ units per month}$$
$$R = 18{,}000 \text{ units per year}$$
$$= \frac{18{,}000}{12} = 1500 \text{ units per month}$$

$$q^* = \sqrt{\frac{2RC_3}{C_1}\left(\frac{C_1+C_2}{C_2}\right)}\sqrt{\frac{K}{K-R}}$$

$$= \sqrt{\frac{2 \times 1500 \times 500}{0.15}\left(\frac{0.15+1.66}{1.66}\right)} \sqrt{\frac{3000}{3000-1500}}$$

$$= 3301.51 \times 1.414$$

$$= 4668 \text{ units (approximately).}$$

Number of shortages,

$$Q_2^* = q^* \left(\frac{C_1}{C_1 + C_2}\right)\left(\frac{K-R}{K}\right)$$

$$= 4668 \left(\frac{0.15}{0.15+1.66}\right)\left(\frac{3000-1500}{3000}\right)$$

$$= 4668 \times 0.083 \times 0.5$$

$$= 194 \text{ units (approximately).}$$

Manufacturing time,

$$= \frac{q^*}{K} = \frac{4668}{3000} = 1.5 \text{ months}$$

Time between set-ups,

$$= \frac{q^*}{R} = \frac{4668}{1500} = 3 \text{ months.}$$

Example 16.15 The demand for an item is 12,000 per year and shortage is allowed. If the unit cost is ₹ 15 and the holding cost is ₹ 20 per year per unit, determine the optimum total yearly cost. The cost of placing one order is ₹ 6,000 and the cost of one shortage is ₹ 100 per year.

Solution Given,

$R = 12{,}000$ units per year

Holding cost, C_1 = ₹ 20 per unit, per year

Set-up cost, C_3 = ₹ 6,000 per order

Shortage cost, C_2 = ₹ 100 per year

Total annual cost = (Number of orders per year × total cost per period),

$$q^* = \sqrt{\frac{2RC_3}{C_1}} \sqrt{\frac{C_1 + C_2}{C_2}}$$

$$= \sqrt{\frac{2 \times 12{,}000 \times 6{,}000}{20}} \sqrt{\frac{20+100}{100}} = 2{,}939 \text{ units.}$$

Number of orders per year,

$$= \frac{R}{q^*} = \frac{12{,}000}{2{,}939}$$

$$= 4.08$$

Number of shortages,

$$Z^* = q^* \left(\frac{C_1}{C_1 + C_2}\right)$$

$$= 2939\left(\frac{20}{20+100}\right) = 489 \text{ units.}$$

Total yearly cost is given by,

$$= C \times R^* + \sqrt{2RC_1C_3} \cdot \sqrt{\frac{C_2}{C_1 + C_2}}$$

$$= 15 \times 12000 + \sqrt{2 \times 12{,}000 \times 20 \times 6{,}000} \sqrt{\frac{100}{120}}$$

$$= ₹2{,}28{,}989.8.$$

EXERCISES

1. A manufacturer has to supply his customer with 24,000 units of his product per year. The demand is fixed and known. The customer has no storage space and so the manufacturer has to ship the supply on a daily basis. On failure to supply, the manufacturer is liable to pay a penalty of ₹ 0.20 per unit, per month. The inventory holding cost amount is ₹ 0.01 per unit, per month, and the set-up cost is ₹ 350 per production run. Find the optimum lot size for the manufacturer. **[Ans.** 4,744 units per run]

2. The demand for a product is 25 units per month and the items are withdrawn uniformly. The set-up cost each time a product is run is ₹ 15. The inventory holding cost is ₹ 0.30 per item, per month.

   (*i*) Determine how often to make the production run, if shortages are not allowed.
   (*ii*) Determine how often to make the production run, if shortages cost ₹ 1.50 per item, per month.

   [Ans. (*i*) q^* = 50 units; (*ii*) q^* = 54.7 units]

3. The demand for a certain item is 16 units per period. Unsatisfied demand causes a shortage cost of ₹ 0.75 per unit, per short period. The cost of inventory purchasing action is ₹ 15 per purchase and the holding cost is 15 per cent of the average inventory valuation per period. Item cost is ₹ 8,000 per unit. Find the minimum cost purchase quantity. **[Ans.** q^* = 32 units; TC = ₹ 15 approximately]

4. A manufacturing company has to supply 3,000 units per year, to a customer who does not have enough space for storing the material. A penalty of ₹ 40 will be levied when the supplier fails to supply the material. The inventory carrying cost in ₹ 20 per unit, per month and the ordering cost is ₹ 400 per run. Calculate the expected number of shortages at the end of each scheduling. **[Ans.** 41 units per period]

5. A particular item has a demand of 9,000 units per year. The cost of one procurement is ₹ 100 and the holding cost is ₹ 240 per unit, per year. The replacement is instantaneous and shortage is given as ₹ 5 per unit, per year. Determine,

   (*i*) the economic lot size
   (*ii*) the number of orders per year
   (*iii*) the time between orders
   (*iv*) the total cost per year, if the cost of one unit is ₹ 1.

   [Ans. (*i*) q^* = 1,053 units per run; (*ii*) Number of orders per year = 56; (*iii*) 0.117 year; (*iv*) ₹ 10,712]

6. A company has a demand of 12,000 units per year for an item and it can produce 2,000 such items per month. The cost of one set-up is ₹ 400 and the holding cost per unit per month is ₹ 0.15. The shortage cost of one unit is ₹ 20 per year. Determine the optimum lot size and the total cost per year, assuming the cost of 1 unit as ₹ 4. **[Ans.** q^* = 3,413 units; TC = ₹ 51, 336]

7. The demand of an item is uniform at a rate of 20 units per month. The fixed cost is ₹ 10 each time a production run is made. The production cost is ₹ 1 per item and the inventory carrying cost is ₹ 0.25 per item, per month. If the shortage cost is ₹ 1.25 per item, per month, determine the frequency and size of the production run that is to be made. **[Ans.** q^* = 44 items; t^* = 2.2 months]

16.8 INVENTORY MODELS WITH PROBABILISTIC DEMAND

In this model, we consider the situations where demand is not known exactly but the probability distribution of demand is known. The control variable in such cases is assumed to be either the scheduling period or the order level or both. The optimum order level can be derived by minimizing the total expected cost, rather than the actual cost involved. Expected cost is obtained by multiplying the actual costs for a particular situation with the probability of occurrence of that situation.

Model V (a)

Instantaneous demand, no set-up cost, stock in discrete units.

The assumptions in this model are,

(*i*) There is a constant interval between orders. (It may also be considered as unity).

(*ii*) Z is the stock (in discrete) units for time t.

(*iii*) d is the estimated demand with probability $p(d)$.

(*iv*) C_1 is the holding cost per item, per t time unit.

(*v*) C_2 is the shortage cost per item, per t time unit.

(*vi*) Lead time is zero, to determine the optimum order level Z.

Solution In this model, it is assumed that with instantaneous demand, the total demand is filled at the beginning of each period. Thus, depending on the amount d demanded, the inventory position just before the demand occurs may either be in surplus or shortage.

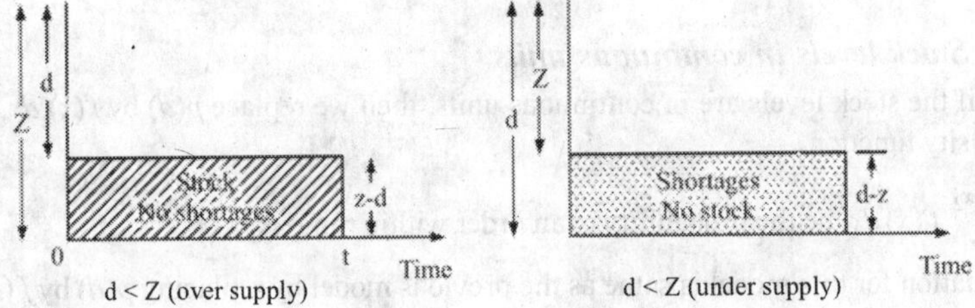

Case 1 When demand d exceeds the stock Z, i.e., $d > Z$ the holding cost becomes

$$= \begin{cases} (Z-d)\,C_1 & \text{for } d \le Z \\ C_1 = 0 & \text{for } d > Z \text{ (no stock)} \end{cases}$$

Case 2 When $d \le Z$, then shortage cost

$$= C_2 = 0$$
$$= (d-Z)\,C_2 \text{ for } d > Z$$

The total expected cost,

$$C(Z) = \underbrace{\sum_{d=0}^{Z}(Z-d)C_1 p(d) + \sum_{d=Z+1}^{\infty}(C_1 = 0)\,p(d)}_{\text{Holding Cost}}$$

$$+ \underbrace{\sum_{d=0}^{Z}(C_2 = 0)\;p(d) + \sum_{d=Z+1}^{\infty}(d-Z)C_2\,p(d)}_{\text{Shortage Cost}}$$

For $C(Z)$ to be minimum,

$$\Delta C(Z-1) < 0 < \Delta C(Z)$$

$$\Delta C(Z) = C_1 \sum_{d=0}^{Z}[(Z+1) - d - (Z-d)]\;p(d) + C_2 \sum_{d=Z+1}^{\infty}[(d-Z+1)-(d-Z)]\;p(d)$$

$$= C_1 \sum_{d=0}^{Z} p(d) + C_2 \sum_{d=Z+1}^{\infty} p(d)$$

$$= C_1 \sum_{d=0}^{Z} p(d) + C_2 \sum_{d=0}^{\infty} p(d) - \sum_{d=0}^{Z} p(d)$$

$$= (C_1 + C_2) \sum_{d=Z+1}^{Z} p(d) - C_2 \quad \because \sum_{d=0}^{Z} p(d) = 1$$

For minimum $\Delta C(Z) > 0$,

$$\therefore \qquad (C_1 + C_2) \sum_{d=0}^{Z} p(d) - C_2 > 0$$

$$\sum_{d=0}^{\infty} p(d) > \frac{C_2}{C_1 + C_2}$$

$\therefore$ The required relationship is,

$$\sum_{d=0}^{Z-1} p(d) < \frac{C_2}{C_1 + C_2} < \sum_{d=0}^{Z} p(d)$$

Model V (b): Stock levels in continuous units

In this model, if the stock levels are in continuous units, then we replace $p(d)$ by $f(x)\,dx$, where, $f(x)$ is probability density function.

Proof Let $\int_{x_1}^{x_2} f(x)\,dx$ be the probability of an order within range x_1 to x_2.

The cost equation for this model is same as the previous model by replacing $p(d)$ by $f(x)\,dx$

$$C(Z) = C_1 \int_0^Z (Z - x)\, f(x)\, dx + C_2 \int_Z^{\infty} (x - Z)\, f(x)\, dx$$

The optimal value of Z is obtained by equating to the first derivative of,

$$\frac{dC(Z)}{dZ} = C_1 \int_0^Z [(1-0)\, f(x)\, dx] + C_1 \left[(Z-x) f(x) \frac{dx}{dZ} \right]_{x=0}^{Z}$$

$$+ C_2 \int_0^{\infty} (0-1)\, f(x)\, dx + C_2 \left((x-Z) f(x) \frac{dx}{dZ} \right)_0^{\infty}$$

$$= C_1 \int_0^Z f(x)\, dx - C_2 \int_Z^{\infty} f(x)\, dx$$

$$= C_1 \int_0^{\infty} f(x)\, dx - C_2 \left[\int_Z^{\infty} f(x) dx - \int_0^Z f(x) dx \right] \qquad \left[\because \int_Z^{\infty} f(x) dx = 1 \right]$$

$$= (C_1 + C_2) \int_0^Z f(x)\, dx - C_2$$

$$\frac{d\,C(Z)}{dZ} = 0 \Rightarrow \quad (C_1 + C_2) \int_0^Z f(x)\, dx = C_2 \Rightarrow \int_0^Z f(x)\, dx = \frac{C_2}{C_1 + C_2}$$

Also, $$\frac{d^2C(Z)}{dZ^2} = (C_1 + C_2)\left(f(x)\frac{dx}{dZ}\right)_0^Z = (C_1 + C_2)f(Z) > 0$$

($\because f(Z) > 0$, C_1 and C_2 are not zero)

Thus, we can get the optimum value of Z by satisfying,

$$\int_0^Z f(x)dx = \frac{C_2}{C_1 + C_2}$$

Example 16.16 A newspaper boy buys papers for 30 paise each and sells them for 70 paise. He cannot return unsold newspapers. Daily demand has the following distribution.

No. of customers	***23***	***24***	***25***	***26***	***27***	***28***	***29***	***30***	***31***	***32***
Probability	.01	.03	0.06	0.10	0.20	0.25	0.15	0.10	0.05	0.05

If each day's demand is independent of the previous day's, how many papers should he order each day?

Solution

$C_1 = 0.30$ $\qquad C_2 = 0.70 - 0.30 = 0.40$

	23	***24***	***25***	***26***	***27***	***28***	***29***	***30***	***31***	***32***
P (*d*)	0.01	0.03	0.06	0.10	0.20	0.25	0.15	0.10	0.05	0.05
Σ *P* (*d*)	0.01	0.04	0.10	0.20	0.40	0.65	0.80	0.90	0.95	1.00

Now, $$\frac{C_2}{C_1 + C_2} = \frac{40}{30 + 40} = 0.5714.$$

Here, $0.40 < 0.5714 < 0.65$

∴ Number of papers to be ordered each day = 28.

Example 16.17 The cost of holding an item in stock is ₹ 2 per unit and the shortage cost is ₹ 8. If ₹ 2 is the purchasing cost per unit, determine the optimal order level of inventory, following probability distribution.

D	***0***	***1***	***2***	***3***	***4***	***5***
P_D	0.05	0.25	0.20	0.15	0.20	0.15

Solution

Given, $C_1 = ₹ 2$

$C_2 = ₹ 8$

Purchasing cost is ₹ 2

D	***0***	***1***	***2***	***3***	***4***	***5***
P_D	0.05	0.25	0.20	0.15	0.20	0.15
ΣP_D	0.05	0.30	0.50	0.65	0.85	1.00

$$\frac{C_2}{C_1 + C_2} = \frac{8}{10} = 0.8$$

$$0.65 < \frac{C_2}{C_1 + C_2} < 0.85.$$

$\therefore$ Optimal order level of inventory = 4.

Example 16.18 The probability distribution of the monthly sales of a certain item is as follows.

Monthly sales	*0*	*1*	*2*	*3*	*4*	*5*	*6*
Probability	0.02	0.05	0.30	0.27	0.20	0.10	0.06

The cost of carrying inventory is ₹ 10 per unit, per month. The current policy is to maintain a stock of four items at the beginning of each month. Assuming that the cost of shortage is proportional to both time and quantity, obtain the imputed cost of shortage of one item for one unit.

Solution

Monthly sales	*0*	*1*	*2*	*3*	*4*	*5*	*6*
Probability	0.02	0.05	0.30	0.27	0.20	0.10	0.06
Cumulative	0.02	0.07	0.37	0.64	0.84	0.94	1.00

We know,
$$\sum_{d=0}^{Z-1} p(d) < \frac{C_2}{C_1+C_2} < \sum_{d=0}^{Z} p(d)$$

here,
$$Z=4 \Rightarrow \sum_{d=0}^{3} p(d) < \frac{C_2}{C_1+C_2} < \sum_{d=0}^{4} p(d)$$

$$\Rightarrow \quad 0.64 < \frac{C_2}{C_1+C_2} < 0.84$$

$$0.64 < \frac{C_2}{10+C_2} < 0.84$$

$$0.64 < \frac{C_2}{10+C_2} \Rightarrow C_2 = 17.7$$

From,
$$\frac{C_2}{C_1+C_2} < 0.84$$

$$C_2 = 52.5$$

Shortage cost, $17.7 < C_2 <$ ₹ 52.5

Example 16.19 The demand for a certain product has a rectangular distribution between 4,000 and 5,000. Find the optimal order quantity, if the storage cost is ₹ 1 per unit and shortage cost is ₹ 7 per unit.

Solution

Given, $C_1 = ₹\,1; C_2 = ₹\,7$

$$\int_0^Q f(x)dx = \frac{C_2}{C_1 + C_2}$$

Since the distribution is rectangular, the probability density function is given by, $\frac{1}{b-a}$

Hence, $$\int_{4,000}^{Q} \frac{1}{5,000-4,000}dx = \frac{7}{8}$$

$\Rightarrow$ $$\int_{4000}^{Q} \frac{1}{1,000}dx = \frac{7}{8}$$

$$\frac{1}{1,000}(x)_{4000}^{Q} = \frac{7}{8}$$

$$\frac{1}{1,000}(Q-4,000) = \frac{7}{8}$$

$$Q-4,000 = \frac{7,000}{8}$$

$$Q = \frac{7,000}{8} + 4,000 = \frac{39,000}{8} = 4,875$$

$$Q = 4,875 \text{ units.}$$

Example 16.20 An ice-cream company sells one of its ice-creams by weight. If the product is not sold on the day it is prepared, it can be sold for a loss of 50 paise per pound. But there is an unlimited market for one day old ice-creams. On the other hand, the company makes a profit of ₹ 3.20 on every pound of ice-cream sold on the day it is prepared. If daily orders form a distribution with $f(x) = 0.02 - 0.0002x: 0 \le x \le 100$, how many pounds of ice-creams should the company prepare every day?

Solution

Given, $C_1 = ₹0.50; C_2 = ₹3.20$

Let Q be the amount of ice-cream prepared every day.

Now, $$\int_0^Q f(x)dx = \frac{C_1}{C_1 + C_2}$$

$$\int_0^Q (0.02 - 0.0002x)dx = \frac{3.2}{3.2+0.5}$$

$$\left(0.02x - \frac{0.0002x^2}{2}\right)_0^Q = 0.865$$

$$0.0002Q^2 - 0.04Q + 1.730 = 0$$

On solving, $Q = 136.7$ and 63.5

But, $Q = 136.7$ is not possible $(\because x \le 100)$

Hence, $Q = 63.5$ pounds is the optimum quantity that should be prepared daily.

Example 16.21 Let the probability density of the demand of a certain item during a day be,

$$f(x) = \begin{cases} 0.10 \le x \le 10 \\ 0 \quad x > 10 \end{cases}$$

The demand is assumed to occur in a uniform pattern during the whole day. Assume that the unit carrying cost of the item in inventory is ₹ 0.5 per day and unit shortage cost is ₹ 4.5 per day. If the purchasing cost per unit is ₹ 0.5, determine the optimum level of inventory.

Solution Given, C_1 = ₹ 0.50, C_2 = ₹ 4.5, C_3 = ₹ 0.5

Let Q be the amount of the item in demand.

$$\int_0^Q f(x)dx = \frac{C_2}{C_1 + C_2}$$

$$\int_0^Q 0.1\, dx = \frac{4.5}{4.5 + 0.5}$$

$$\left((0.1)\, x\right)_0^Q = 0.9$$

$$0.1\, Q = 0.9$$

$$\Rightarrow \qquad Q = 9 \text{ units.}$$

EXERCISES

1. A newspaper boy buys papers for ₹ 1.40 and sells them for ₹ 2.45 each. He cannot claim refund for unsold newspapers. Daily demand has the following distribution.

Customers	25	26	27	28	29	30	31	32	33	34	35	36
Probability	0.03	0.05	0.05	0.10	0.15	0.15	0.12	0.10	0.10	0.07	0.06	0.02

If each day's demand is independent of the previous day's demand, how many papers should he order each day. **[Ans.** 30 newspapers]

2. A contractor of second-hand motor trucks maintains a stock of trucks every month. Demand for the trucks occurs at a relatively constant rate but not in a constant size. The demand is shown in the following probability distribution.

Demand	0	1	2	3	4	5	6 or more
Probability	0.40	0.24	0.20	0.10	0.05	0.01	0.00

The holding cost of an old truck in stock for one month is ₹ 100 and the penalty for a truck not supplied on demand is ₹ 1,000. Determine the optimal size of the conractor's stock? **[Ans.** 3 trucks]

3. A ship-building company has launched a program for the construction of a new class of ships. Certain spare parts, like prime movers, each costing ₹ 2 lakhs have to be purchased. If these units are not available when needed, a very serious loss is incurred, which is in the order of ₹ 1 crore in each instance. Requirements of spares with the correspounding probabilities are given below.

No. of spares	0	1	2	3	4	5
Probability of requirement	0.876	0.062	0.041	0.015	0.005	0.001

How many spare parts should the company buy in order to optimize the inventory decision? **[Ans.** 3 spare parts]

4. A bakery sells cakes by kg weight. It makes a profit of ₹ 5 per kg, on each kg sold on the day it is baked. It disposes off all the cakes not sold on the day they are baked and incurs a loss of ₹ 1.20 per kg. If the demand is known to be rectangular between 2,000 and 3,000 kg, determine the optimal order quantity baked.

[**Ans.** 2,807 kg]

5. A T.V. dealer finds that the cost of holding a television in stock for a week is ₹ 20. Customers who cannot obtain a new television immediately tend to go to other dealers and he estimates that for every customer who does not get immediate delivery, he loses ₹ 200 on an average. For one particular model of television, the probabilities for a demand of 0, 1, 2, 3, 4 and 5 television, in a week are 0.05, 0.10, 0.20, 0.30, 0.20 and 0.15 respectively. How many T.V. sets should the dealer order? [**Ans.** 4 per week]

16.9 RE-ORDER LEVEL AND OPTIMUM BUFFER STOCK

Lead time is defined as the time interval between the placing of the orders and the actual receipt of goods.

Lead time demand is lead time multiplied by demand rate.

Buffer stock refers to the extra inventory maintained in addition to the inventory required, corresponding to normal consumption levels.

Safety stock is maintained as a protection against stock-out. The greater the safety stock maintained, less is the risk of stock-outs.

When the buffer stock is maintained at a very low level, the inventory holding cost will be low, but the shortages will occur very frequently and the cost of shortages will be very high. On the other hand, if the buffer stock is maintained at a high level, shortages would be rare resulting in low shortage cost, but inventory cost would be high. Thus, the objective of maintaining a buffer stock is to maintain a balance between the cost of shortages and inventory cost. To determine the buffer stock, we approximate the estimated maximum lead time and normal lead time.

L_d = Difference between maximum and normal lead times

R = Consumption rate during lead time

$$B - L_d \times R$$

Buffer stock = (Maximum lead time – normal lead time) × consumption rate during lead time.

If we do not maintain a buffer stock, then the total requirements for inventory during the lead time will become L_dR. This implies that as soon as the stock reaches a level L_dR, we place an order for q units. This point is called *re-order point* or *re-order level*, given by,

$$ROL = L_dR$$

Hence, re-order level is that level of an inventory at which the order is placed. However, due to uncertainty in demand, this policy of ROL results in shortages. In order to avoid shortages, we have to maintain a buffer stock B and the

$$ROL = B + L_dR$$

Important Formulae

1. EOQ $q^* = \sqrt{\dfrac{2RC_3}{C_1}}$
2. Optimum buffer (safety) stock, B = (Max. lead time – Min. lead time) × R
3. Re-order level (ROL) = Buffer stock + Normal lead time consumption
4. Maximum inventory = $B + q^*$
5. Average inventory = $B + 1/2\, q^*$
6. Minimum inventory = B

Example 16.22 Consider the inventory system with the following data in usual notation.

$$R = 1{,}000 \text{ units per year}, I = 0.30, P = ₹\,0.50 \text{ per unit}$$
$$C_3 = ₹\,10, L = 2 \text{ years (Lead time)}$$

Determine (*i*) Optimum order quantity
(*ii*) Re-order point
(*iii*) Minimum average cost

Solution

Given,
$$R = 1{,}000 \text{ units per year}$$
$$C_3 = ₹\,10$$
$$C_1 = C \times P = 0.3 \times 0.50 = 0.15 \text{ per annum}$$

(*i*) Optimum order quantity, $q^* = \sqrt{\dfrac{2C_3R}{C_1}}$

$$= \sqrt{\frac{2 \times 10 \times 1000}{0.15}} = 365 \text{ units}$$

$$t^* = \frac{q^*}{R} = \frac{365}{1000} = 0.36 \text{ year.}$$

(*ii*) Since the lead time is 2 years and optimum time is 0.36 year, re-ordering occurs when the level of inventory is sufficient to satisfy the demand for (2 – 0.36) years. Thus, the optimum quantity q^* = 365 units is ordered when the order of inventory reaches 1.64 × 1000 units. Therefore, re-order point is given at 1,640 units.

(*iii*) Minimum average inventory is given by,

$$C_{\min} = \sqrt{2C_1C_3R}$$
$$= \sqrt{2 \times 0.15 \times 10 \times 1000} = ₹\,54.8.$$

Example 16.23 A company uses 50,000 units of an item annually, each costing ₹ 1.20. Each order costs ₹ 45 and inventory carrying charges are 15 per cent of the annual average inventory value.

(*i*) Find EOQ.

(*ii*) If the company operates 250 days a year, the procurement time is 10 days and safety stock is 500 units. Find the re-order level as well as the maximum, minimum, and average inventory values.

Solution

Given,
$$R = 50{,}000 \text{ units}$$
$$C = ₹\,1.20$$
$$C_3 = ₹\,45 \text{ per order}$$
$$C_1 = CI = 1.20 \times \frac{15}{100} = 0.18$$

(*i*)
$$\text{EOQ} = \sqrt{\frac{2C_3R}{C_1}} = \sqrt{\frac{2 \times 50000 \times 45}{0.18}}$$
$$= 5{,}000 \text{ units}$$

(*ii*) Number of days the company operates in a year = 250 days

$$\text{Lead time} = 10 \text{ days}$$
$$\text{Safety stock} = 500 \text{ units}$$
$$\text{Re-order level} = \text{Lead time demand} + \text{Safety stock}$$
$$= 10 \times \frac{50000}{250} + 500$$
$$= 2{,}500 \text{ units}$$
$$\text{Maximum inventory} = \text{EOQ} + \text{Safety stock}$$
$$= 5000 + 500 = 5{,}500 \text{ units}$$
$$\text{Minimum inventory} = \text{Safety stock}$$
$$= 500 \text{ units}$$
$$\text{Average inventory} = q/2 + \text{Safety stock}$$
$$= 2500 + 500 = 3{,}000 \text{ units.}$$

Example 16.24 The annual consumption of an item is 2,000 units. The ordering cost is ₹ 100 per order. The carrying cost is ₹ 0.80 per unit, per year. Assuming working days as 200, lead time as 20 days, and safety stock as 100 units, calculate (*i*) EOQ (*ii*) The number of orders per year (*iii*) Re-order level (*iv*) the total annual ordering and carrying costs.

Solution Given,

$$R = 2{,}000 \text{ items per year}$$
$$C_1 = ₹\,0.80 \text{ per unit, per year}$$
$$C_3 = ₹\,100 \text{ per order}$$
$$\text{Lead time} = 20 \text{ days.}$$
$$\text{Safety stock} = 100 \text{ units}$$

(*i*) $$\text{EOQ}\, q^* = \sqrt{\frac{2C_3R}{C_1}} = \sqrt{\frac{2 \times 100 \times 2000}{0.8}} = 707 \text{ units}$$

(*ii*) $$\text{Number of orders per year} = \frac{R}{q^*} = \frac{2000}{707} = 2.82 \text{ years.}$$

(*iii*) $$\text{Re-order level} = \text{Lead time demand} + \text{Safety stock}$$
$$\text{Re-order level} = 20 \times \frac{2000}{200} \text{ units} + 100 \text{ units} = 300 \text{ units}$$

(*iv*) $$\text{Total annual cost} = \sqrt{2C_1C_3R}$$
$$= \sqrt{2 \times 0.8 \times 100 \times 2000} = ₹\,565.68.$$

Example 16.25 For a fixed order quantity, determine (*i*) EOQ (*ii*) Optimum buffer stock (*iii*) Re-order level for an item, (*iv*) Maximum inventory level with the following data:

Annual consumption, $R = 10{,}000$ units

Cost of one unit = ₹ 1

$C_3 = ₹\,12$ per production run

$C_1 = ₹\,0.24$ per unit.

Past lead time: 15 days; 25 days; 13 days; 14 days; 30 days; 17 days.

Solution

(*i*) $$\text{EOQ} = \sqrt{\frac{2C_3R}{C_1}} = \sqrt{2\times\frac{12\times 10000}{0.24}} = 1{,}000 \text{ units}$$

(*ii*) Optimum buffer stock = (Maximum lead time – Normal lead time) × Monthly consumption

$$= \left(\frac{30-15}{30}\right)\times\frac{10000}{12} = 416.66 \text{ units}$$

$$= 420 \text{ units (approximately)}$$

(*iii*) Normal lead time consumption = Normal lead time × Monthly consumption

$$= \frac{15}{30}\times\frac{10000}{12} = 417 \text{ units}$$

$$\text{ROL} = \text{Safety stock} + \text{Normal lead time consumption}$$

$$= 420 + 417 = 837 \text{ units}$$

(*iv*) Maximum inventory level

$$= \text{Safety stock} + \text{EOQ}$$

$$= 420 + 1000 = 1{,}420 \text{ units}$$

Minimum inventory = 420 units

Since inventory would fluctuate from a maximum of 1,420 units to a minimum of 420 units, the average inventory

$$= 1/2(\text{Safety stock} + \text{Maximum inventory})$$

$$= 1/2\,(420 + 1420)$$

$$= 920 \text{ units.}$$

Example 16.26 The following table gives the distributions for lead time and daily demand during the lead time.

	Lead time (Days)	***3***	***4***	***5***	***6***	***7***	***8***	***9***	***10***
Lead Time	Frequency	2	3	4	4	2	2	2	1
Demand	Demand	0	1	2	3	4	5	6	7
	Frequency	2	4	5	5	4	2	1	2

Determine the buffer stock.

Solution

$$\text{Average lead time} = \frac{\Sigma Lf}{\Sigma f}$$

$$= \frac{6+12+20+24+14+16+18+10}{20}$$

$$= 6 \text{ days.}$$

$$\text{Average demand} = \frac{\Sigma fR}{\Sigma f} = \frac{0+4+10+15+16+10+6+14}{25}$$

$$= 3 \text{ units}$$

$\therefore$ Average lead time demand = Average lead time × Average demand

$= 6 \times 3 = 18$ units.

Maximum lead time = 10 days

Maximum demand = 7 per day.

$\therefore$ Maximum lead time demand = $10 \times 7 = 70$ units

Buffer stock = Maximum lead time demand – Average lead time demand

$= 70 - 18 = 52$ units.

Example 16.27 Demand for a product during an order period is assumed to be normally distributed with a mean of 1,000 units and a S.D. of 40 units. What per cent service can a company expect to provide,

(*i*) if it satisfies the average demand only.
(*ii*) if it satisfies a safety stock of 60 units.

Solution

(*i*) If the company provides only average demand, the service level = 50%
(*ii*) Safety stock = 60 units

The standard normal variable Z is given by the formula,

$$Z = \frac{\text{Safety stock} - 0}{\text{S.D.}} = \frac{60 - 0}{40} = 1.5$$

Area under the normal curve for Z to be 1.5 is, 0.4332

$\therefore$ Service level $= 0.5 + 0.4332 = 0.9332 = 93.32\%$.

EXERCISES

1. A particular item has an annual demand of 9,000 units. The carrying cost is ₹ 2 per unit, per year. The ordering cost is ₹ 90.
(*i*) Find EOQ (*ii*) Determine the number of orders to be placed per annum (*iii*) if the lead time is 2 months and safety stock is 1,000 units, what is the re-order level.
[Ans. (*i*) q^* = 900 units; (*ii*) 10 orders; (*iii*) ROL = 2,500 units]
2. A company annually uses 48,000 units of raw material, costing ₹ 1.20 per unit. Placing each order costs ₹ 45 and inventory carrying costs are 15 per cent per year of the average inventory values. Find (*i*) EOQ (*ii*) Suppose that the company follows the EOQ policy and operates 300 days a year with the procurement time as 12 days and the safety stock as 500 units. Find ROL as well as maximum, minimum and average inventories.
[Ans. q^* = 4,899 units; ROL = 2,420 units; Maximum inventory = 5,399 units; Minimum inventory = 500 units; Average = 2,949 units]
3. In an inventory model, where shortages are not allowed and the production rate is infinite; and R = 600 units per year, I = 0.20, C_3 = ₹ 80, C = ₹ 3 and lead time is 1 year. (*i*) Find the optimal order quantity (*ii*) Re-order point (*iii*) Minimum yearly cost.
[Ans. (*i*) q^* = 4,000 units; (*ii*) ROL = 200 units; (*iii*) t_{min} = ₹ 240]
4. Calculate the various parameters for putting an item with the following data, on an EOQ system.
Annual consumption is 12,000 units at the cost of ₹ 7.50 per unit. Set-up cost is ₹ 6 and the average inventory holding cost is ₹ 0.12 per unit. Normal lead time is 15 days and maximum lead time is 20 days.
[Ans. ROL = 367 units; Buffer stock = 200 units]
5. The following information is provided to you:
Annual demand = 2,400 units
Unit price = ₹ 2.40
Ordering cost = ₹ 4

Storage cost = ₹ 2 per year. Interest rate is 10 per cent per annum. Lead time = 15 days. You are required to calculate EOQ, re-order level and annual total cost. How much does the total annual cost vary if the unit price is changed to ₹ 5? **[Hint**: R = 2,400 units per year]

C_3 = ₹ 4; C = ₹ 2.40; I = 2% + 10% = 12%

[Ans. (*i*) q^* = 258 units (*ii*) ROL = 100 units (*iii*) Total inventory cost = Minimum variable cost + cost of 2,400 units = ₹ 5,834.36 (*iv*) When C equals ₹ 5, total inventory cost = ₹ 12,107.33. [Increase in cost = ₹ 6,273.04]

16.10 EOQ PROBLEMS WITH PRICE BREAKS

In this type of problem, we consider the class of inventory in which cost is a variable factor because when items are purchased in bulk, some discount price is usually offered by the supplier. Such discounts are referred to as *quantity discounts or price breaks*.

If the discount is available, then total cost per unit of inventory system and items would be,

$$TC = RK_1 + \frac{R}{q}C_3 + \frac{1}{2}qK_1 \times I$$

where, K_1 is the cost of manufacturing or purchasing per unit and I denotes the holding cost per unit.

$$\frac{dTC}{dq} = 0 \Rightarrow q = \sqrt{2C_3R/K_1I}$$

$$\frac{d^2TC}{dq^2} > 0 \text{ at } q = \sqrt{2C_3\ R/K_1I}$$

∴ The optimum value of qw, i.e., $q^* = \sqrt{\dfrac{2C_3R}{K_1\,I}}$

Now we proceed to consider EOQ problems where the purchase cost is subject to price breaks.

16.10.1 Case I: EOQ Problems with One Price Break

The procedure for obtaining EOQ for a single discount is given as follows.

Order quantity	*Purchase cost per unit*
$O \le q_1 < b$	K_{11}
$b \le q_2$	K_{12}

where, b is the quantity at and beyond which the quantity discount applies and $K_{12} < K_{11}$.

Step 1 Compute q_2^*, i.e., optimum order quantity for the lowest price (highest discount) and compare it with quantity b.

If $q_2^* \ge b$, then place the orders for quantities of size q_2^* and obtain the discount. Otherwise, go to the next step.

Step 2 If $q_2^* < b$, we cannot place an order at the reduced price K_{12}. Therefore, in order to maintain the optimum order quantity we need only to compare the total inventory cost for $q = q_1^*$ (for price K_{11}) with $q = b$.

The values of $TC\,(q_1^*)$ and $TC\,(b)$ may be determined as follows.

$$TC(q_1^*) = RK_{11} + \frac{R}{q_1^*}C_3 + \frac{1}{2}q_1^* \times K_{11} \times I$$

$$TC(b) = RK_{12} + \frac{R}{b} C_3 + \frac{1}{2} b \times K_{12} \times I$$

If $TC(q_1^*) > TC(b)$, then $q_1^* = b$, otherwise $q^* = q_1^*$.

Example 16.28 Find the optimum order quantity for a product, the price break for which is as follows:

Quantity	*Unit cost (₹)*
$0 \le q_1 \le 500$	10.00
$500 \le q_2$	9.25

The monthly demand for the product is 200 units, the cost of storage is 2 per cent of the unit cost and the cost of ordering is ₹ 350.

Solution Given,

$$C_3 = ₹\,350$$
$$R = 200 \text{ units per month}$$
$$I = 2/100 = 0.02$$
$$K_{11} = ₹\,10, K_{12} = ₹\,9.25.$$

Step 1 The highest discount available is 9.25.

So we compute, $q_2^* = \sqrt{\dfrac{2RC_3}{K_{12}\, I}}$

$$= \sqrt{\frac{2 \times 350 \times 200}{9.25 \times 0.02}} = 870 \text{ units}$$

Now, $q_2^* = 870$ units and $b = 500$.

We have $q_2^* > b$, $\therefore$ the optimum purchase quantity is given by $q^* = q_2^* = 870$ units.

Example 16.29 Find the optimum order quantity for a product, the price breaks of which are as follows.

Quantity	*Unit cost (₹)*
$0 \le q_1 \le 800$	₹ 1.00
$800 \le q_2$	₹ 0.98

The yearly demand for the product is 1,600 units, cost of placing an order is ₹ 5 and the cost of storage is 10 per cent per year.

Solution

Given,

$$R = 1{,}600 \text{ units per year}$$
$$C_3 = ₹\,5 \text{ per order}$$
$$I = 10\% = ₹\,0.10.$$
$$K_{11} = ₹\,1, K_{12} = ₹\,0.98$$

Step 1 The highest discount available is ₹ 0.98 = K_{12}. So we compute q_2 at K_{12},

$$q_2^* = \sqrt{\frac{2 \times R \times C_3}{K_{12} \times I}} = \sqrt{\frac{2 \times 1600 \times 5}{0.98 \times 0.1}}$$

$$= 404 \text{ units}$$

Now $q_2^* = 404$ units, $b = 800$ units. We get the case $q_2^* < b$.

Step 2 Considering, K_{11} = ₹ 1, we find the optimum order quantity,

$$q_1^* = \sqrt{\frac{2RC_3}{K_{11} \times I}}$$

$$= \sqrt{\frac{2 \times 5 \times 1600}{1 \times 0.1}} = 400 \text{ units}$$

Given,

$R = 1600$ units per year

C_3 = ₹ 5 per order

I = ₹ 0.1, K_{11} = ₹ 1.00, K_{12} = ₹ 0.98

Since, $q_1^* = 400$ and $b = 800$, we get $q_1^* < b$. We compare the optimum cost of procuring the least quantity, which will entitle us to a price break.

$$TC(q_1^*) = 1600 \times 1 + \frac{1600}{400} \times 5 + \frac{1}{2} \times 400 \times 1 \times 0.10$$

$$= ₹\,1{,}640$$

$$TC(b) = 1600 \times 0.98 + \frac{1600}{800} \times 5 + \frac{1}{2} \times 800 \times 0.98 \times 0.10$$

$$= ₹\,1{,}617.20$$

$$TC(q_1^*) > TC(b)$$

∴ Optimum purchase quantity is given by, $q^* = b = 800$ units.

Example 16.30 The annual demand of a product is 10,000 units. Each unit costs ₹ 100 for orders placed in quantities below 200 units but for orders of 200 or above the price is ₹ 95. The annual inventory holding cost is 10 per cent of the value of the item and the ordering cost is ₹ 5 per order. Find the economic lot size?

Solution

Quantity	*Unit cost (₹)*
$0 \le q_1 \le 200$	100
$q_2 \ge 200$	95

Given,

$R = 10{,}000$ units per year

C_3 = ₹ 5 per order

I = ₹ 0.1, K_{11} = ₹ 100, K_{12} = ₹ 95

Step 1 Compute the optimal order quantity for the lowest price (highest discount),

$$q_3{}^* = \sqrt{\frac{2RC_3}{I \times K_{12}}} = \sqrt{\frac{2 \times 10000 \times 5}{0.1 \times 95}}$$

$$= 102.59 = 103 \text{ units (approximately)}$$

Now, $q_2{}^* = 103, b = 200$ indicates that $q_2{}^* < b$.

Step 2 Considering, $K_{11} = ₹\,100$, the optimum order quantity $q_1{}^*$ is obtained as follows.

$$q_1{}^* = \sqrt{\frac{2 \times 10000 \times 5}{0.1 \times 100}}$$

Since, $q_1{}^* = 100, b = 200$ indicates $q_1{}^* < b$

we compare the optimum cost,

$$TC(q_1{}^*) = 10000 \times 100 + \frac{10000}{100} \times 5 + \frac{1}{2} \times 100 \times 100 \times 0.1$$

$$= ₹\,10{,}01{,}000$$

$$TC(b) = 10000 \times 95 + \frac{10000}{200} \times 5 + \frac{1}{2} \times 200 \times 95 \times 0.1$$

$$= 9{,}51{,}200$$

Since $TC\,(1q_1{}^*) > TC(b)$, optimum purchase quantity, $q^* = 200$ units.

EXERCISES

1. Find the optimal economic order quantity for a product having the following characteristics:

   Annual demand = 2,400 units

   Ordering cost = ₹ 100

   Cost of storage = 24 per cent of unit cost.

Price break	
Quantity	**Unit cost (₹)**
$0 \le q \le 500$	10.00
$q \ge 500$	9.00

[**Ans.** 472 units]

2. Find the optimum order quantity for a product, the price breaks for which are given below.

Quantity	Unit cost (₹)
$0 \le q \le 500$	15.00
$q \ge 500$	14.00

   Monthly demand for the product is 250 units, the cost of storage is 2 per cent of the unit cost and cost of ordering is ₹ 300. [**Ans.** q^* = 707 units]

3. A sports company manufactures 2,000 bats annually. A fixed cost of ₹ 50 is incurred each time an order is placed. Inventory carrying charge is estimated at 20 per cent. Supplier offers 10 per cent discount per bat of ₹ 100, for orders placed at a time for more than or equal to 150 bats. What should be the economic lot size? [**Ans.** q^* = 150 bats]

16.10.2 Case II: EOQ Problems with Two Price Breaks

When there are two price breaks, the situations is illustrated as follows.

Order quantity	*Unit price (₹)*
$0 \le q_1 \le b_1$	K_{11}
$b_1 \le q_2 \le b_2$	K_{12}
$b_2 \le q_3$	K_{13}

where, b_1, and b_2 are the quantities that determine the price breaks.

The procedure for finding the optimum order quantity is given in the following steps.

Step 1 Compute the optional order quantity for the lowest price (highest discount) q_3* and compare it with b_2.

Step 2 If $q_3^* \ge b_2$, the optimum order quantity is q_3. If $q_3^* < b_2$, go to the next step.

Step 3 Compute q_2^*. Since $q_3^* < b_2$, $q_2^* < b_2$ because $q_1^* < q_2^* < ... < q_n^*$
Thus, either $q_2^* < b_1$ or $b_1 \le q_2^* < b_2$

Step 4 If $q_3^* < b_2$ and $b_1 \le q_2^* < b_2$, then follow the same procedure as in the case of one price break is to be followed, i.e., Compare $Tc(q_2^*)$ and $Tc(b)$ and then determine the optimum quantity.

Step 5 If $q_2^* < b_2$ and $q_2^* < b_1$, then compute q_1^*, which will now satisfy the inequality $q_1 < b_1$. Compare $Tc(q_1^*)$ with $Tc(b_1)$ and $Tc(b_2)$ so as to get the optimum purchase quantity.

Example 16.31 Find the optimal order quantity for a product, the price breaks for which are as follows.

Order quantity	*Unit price (₹)*
$0 \le q_1 \le 500$	10.00
$500 \le q_2 \le 750$	9.25
$750 \le q_3$	8.75

The monthly demand for the product is 200 units, cost storage is 2 per cent of the unit cost and the cost of ordering is ₹350.

Solution Given,

$$C_3 = ₹\,350, I = ₹\,0.02, R = 200 \text{ units per month}$$

$$q_3^* = \sqrt{\frac{2RC_3}{K_{13} \times I}} = \sqrt{\frac{2 \times 200 \times 350}{(8.75)\,(0.02)}} = 894 \text{ units}$$

Since, $q_3^* = 894 > b_2 = 750$

The optimum order quantity is given by, $q = q_3^* = 894$ units.

Example 16.32 Find the optimum order quantity for a product, the price breaks for which are as follows.

Order quantity	*Unit price (₹)*
$0 \le q_1 \le 100$	₹ 20 per unit
$100 \le q_2 < 200$	₹ 18 per unit
$200 \le q_3$	₹ 16 per unit

The monthly demand for the product is 400 units. The storage cost is 20 per cent of the unit cost of the product and the cost of ordering is ₹ 25.

Solution Given,

$$R = 400 \text{ units}$$
$$I = ₹0.20$$
$$C_3 = ₹25$$

$$\text{calculate, } q_3^* = \sqrt{\frac{2RC_3}{K_{13} \times I}} = \sqrt{\frac{2 \times 400 \times 25}{16 \times 0.2}}$$
$$= 79 \text{ units}$$
$$\because \; q_3^* = 79 < b_2 = 200$$

next we compute q_2.

$$q_2^* = \sqrt{\frac{2RC_3}{K_{12} \times I}} = \sqrt{\frac{2 \times 400 \times 25}{18 \times 0.2}} = 75 \text{ units.}$$

Again, since $q_2^* < b_2$ and $q_2^* < b_1 = 100$, we calculate q_1^*.

$$q_1^* = \sqrt{\frac{2RC_3}{K_{11} \times I}} = \sqrt{\frac{2 \times 400 \times 25}{20 \times 0.2}} = 70 \text{ units}$$

Compare $TC(q_1^*)$ with $TC(b_1)$ and $TC(b_2)$ in order to find the optimum order quantity.

$$TC(q_1^*) = 400 \times 20 + \frac{400}{70} \times 25 + \frac{1}{2} \times 70 \times 20 \times 0.2$$
$$= ₹8{,}282.86$$

$$TC(b_1) = 400 \times 18 + \frac{400}{100} \times 25 + \frac{1}{2} \times 100 \times 18 \times 0.2$$
$$= ₹7{,}480$$

$$TC(q_2) = 400 \times 16 + \frac{400}{200} \times 25 + \frac{1}{2} \times 200 \times 16 \times 0.2$$
$$= ₹6{,}770$$

Since $TC(b_1) > TC(b_1) > TC(b_2)$, the optimum order quantity is given by, $q^* = b_2 = 200$ units.

Example 16.33 Find the optimal order quantity for a product, the price breaks for which are as follows.

Order quantity	***Unit price (₹)***
$0 \le q_1 \le 500$	100.00
$500 \le q_2 < 750$	92.50
$750 \le q_3$	87.50

The monthly demand of the product is 200 units, the holding cost is 2 per cent of the unit cost and the ordering cost is ₹ 1,000.

Solution Given,

$$R = 200 \text{ units per month}$$
$$I = 0.02$$
$$C_3 = ₹1{,}000$$

$$K_{11} = ₹\,100, K_{12} = ₹\,92.50, K_{13} = 87.50$$

We calculate, $q_3{}^* = \sqrt{\dfrac{2RC_3}{K_{13} \times I}}$

$$= \sqrt{\frac{2 \times 200 \times 1000}{87.5 \times 0.02}} = 478 \text{ units}$$

Since, $q_3{}^* = 478 < b_2 = 750$, we next calculate

$$q_2{}^* = \sqrt{\frac{2RC_3}{K_{12} \times I}} = \sqrt{\frac{2 \times 200 \times 1000}{92.5 \times 0.02}}$$

$$= 465 \text{ units}$$

Also, since $q_2{}^* < b_2 = 750$ and $q_2{}^* < b_1 = 500$

We calculate, $q_1{}^* = \sqrt{\dfrac{2RC_3}{K_{11} \times I}} = \sqrt{\dfrac{2 \times 200 \times 1000}{100 \times 0.02}}$

$$= 447 \text{ units}$$

Next we compare $TC(q_1{}^*)$ with $TC(b_1)$ and $TC(b_2)$ to get the optimum order quantity.

$$TC(q_1{}^*)\, RK_{11} + \frac{R}{q_1{}^*}C_3 + \frac{1}{2}q_1{}^* \times K_{11} \times I$$

$$= 200 \times 100 + \frac{200}{447} \times 1000 + \frac{1}{2} \times 447 \times 0.02$$

$$= ₹\,20{,}894$$

$$TC(b_1) = RK_{12} + \frac{R}{b_1}C_3 + \frac{1}{2}b_1 \times K_{12} \times I$$

$$= 200 \times 925 + \frac{200}{500} \times 1000 + \frac{1}{2} \times 500 \times 925 \times 0.02$$

$$= ₹\,19{,}362.50$$

$$TC(b_2) = RK_{13} + \frac{R}{b_2}C_3 + \frac{1}{2}b_2 \times K_{13} \times I$$

$$= 200 \times 87.5 + \frac{200}{750} \times 1000 + \frac{1}{2} \times 750 \times 87.5 \times 0.02$$

$$= ₹\,18{,}422.90$$

Since, $TC(q_1{}^*) > TC(b_1) > TC(b_2)$ the optimal order quantity is $q = b_2 = 750$ units. The optimal order quantity corresponds to the lowest total inventory cost.

Example 16.34 A shop-keeper has a uniform demand of an item at the rate of 50 items per month. He buys from a supplier at a cost of ₹ 6 per item and the cost of ordering is ₹ 10 for each order. If the stock holding costs are 20 per cent per year of stock value, how frequently should he replenish his stocks.

Suppose the supplier offers a 5 per cent discount on orders between 200 and 999 items and a 10 per cent discount on orders exceeding or equal to 1,000 items, can the shop-keeper reduce his costs by taking advantage of either of these discounts?

Solution Given,

$$R = 600 \text{ items per year}$$
$$C_3 = ₹\,10 \text{ per order}$$
$$C_1 = ₹\,1.20\ (6 \times 0.2) \text{ per year.}$$

$$q^* = \sqrt{\frac{2C_3R}{C_1}} = \sqrt{\frac{2 \times 600 \times 10}{1.2}} = 100 \text{ items}$$

$$t^* = \frac{q^*}{R} = \frac{100}{600} = \frac{1}{6} \text{ year}$$
$$= 2 \text{ months}$$

The total annual cost includes the fixed, set-up and holding costs.

Fixed cost = ₹ 3,600 (i.e., 6 × 600).

In total, 100 items are ordered each time. This means that a total of 6 orders are placed in a year. Hence, the replenishment cost is ₹ 60.

Average inventory cost throughout the year

∴ Average inventory holding cost = 50 × 0.2 × 6 = ₹ 60

Hence, the total cost = ₹ 3600 + 60 + 60 = ₹ 3,720.

In the case of discounts we have the following formulation:

Quantity	*Unit cost (₹)*
$0 \le q_1 < 200$	6.00
$200 \le q_2 < 1000$	5.70 (5% discount)
$1000 \le q_3$	5.40 (10% discount)

$$\therefore \quad q_3^* = \sqrt{\frac{2C_3R}{K_{13}\,I}} = \sqrt{\frac{2 \times 10 \times 600}{5.4 \times 0.20}} = 105.4 \text{ units}$$

$$\because \quad q_3^* < b_2 = 1000, \text{ we next compute } q_2^*,$$

$$\therefore \quad q_2^* = \sqrt{\frac{2C_3R}{K_{12}\,I}} = \sqrt{\frac{2 \times 10 \times 600}{5.7 \times 0.2}} = 102.6 \text{ units}$$

Again, since $q_2^* < b_1$ we compute,

$$q_1^* = \sqrt{\frac{2C_3R}{K_{11}\,I}} = \sqrt{\frac{2 \times 10 \times 600}{6 \times 0.2}} = 100 \text{ units}$$

To find the optimum order quantity, we compare $TC(q_1)$ with $TC(b_1)$ and $TC(b_2)$.

$$TC(q_1) = \left(10 \times \frac{600}{100}\right) + (600 \times 6) + \left(0.2 \times 6 \times \frac{100}{2}\right)$$
$$= ₹\,3,720$$

$$TC(b_1) = \left(10 \times \frac{600}{200}\right) + (600 \times 5.7) + \left(0.2 \times \frac{5.7 \times 200}{2}\right)$$
$$= ₹\,3,564$$

$$TC(b_2) = \left(10 \times \frac{600}{1000}\right) + (600 \times 5.4) + \left(\frac{0.2 \times 5.4 \times 1000}{2}\right)$$
$$= ₹\,3,786$$

$$\because \quad TC(b_1) < TC(q_1) < TC(b_2).$$

Hence, the optimum purchase quantity is $q^* = b_1 = 200$ units. The shopkeeper should accept the offer at 5 per cent discount, since by doing this he is able to save ₹ 3720 – 3564 = ₹ 156 during the year.

EXERCISES

1. Find the optimal order quantity for a product, the price breaks for which are as follows.

Quantity	Unit cost (₹)
$0 \le q_1 < 50$	₹ 10
$50 \le q_2 < 100$	₹ 9
$100 \le q_3$	₹ 8

The monthly demand for the product is 200 units, the cost of storage is 25 per cent of the unit cost and ordering cost is ₹ 20 per order.

[Ans. $q^* = b_2 = 100$ units**]**

2. The consumption of an item is known to be fixed at 4,800 units per year. The cost of processing an order of this item is ₹ 400 and the inventory carrying charges work out to 24 per cent per annum of the cost of the item. The cost of the item depends on the purchase lot size as per schedule given below. Determine the optimum ordering policy.

Quantity	Unit cost (₹)
up to 999	20.00
1000–1499	18.50
1500 and above	17.00

[Ans. $q^* = 1,000$ units**]**

3. Determine a decision rule using the basic purchasing EOQ model for an annual demand of 20,000 units, having ordering cost of ₹ 200 per order and carrying cost of 10 per cent per year. The basic price is ₹ 8 per unit. This price is in effect of all orders of less than 5,000 units. Orders for 5,000 or more but less than 10,000 units may be purchased for ₹ 7.50 per unit. Orders for 10,000 or more units may be purchased for ₹ 7.25 per unit.

[Ans. $q^* = 10,000$ units**]**

16.10.3 Case III: EOQ Problems with *n* Price Breaks

When there are *n* price breaks, the situation may be illustrated as follows.

Quantity	Unit cost (₹)
$0 \le q_1 < b_1$	K_{11}
$b_1 \le q_2 < b_2$	K_{12}
$\vdots$	$\vdots$
$b_n - 1 \le q_n$	K_{ln}

where, b_1, b_2, b_{n-1} are those quantities that determine the price breaks.

The procedure for obtaining the optimum order quantity in this case will be as follows:

Step 1 Compute optimal order quantity for the lowest price. q_n^*. If $q_n^* \ge b_{n-1}$, the optimum order quantity is reached, i.e., q_n^*.

Step 2 If $q_n^* < b_{n-1}$, compute q_{n-1}. If $q_{n-1}^* \ge b_{n-2}$, proceed as in the case of one price break. The optimum order quantity is determined by comparing $TC(q_{n-1}^*)$ with $TC(b_{n-1})$.

Step 3 If $q_n^* < b_{n-2}$, compute q_{n-2}. If $q_{n-2}^* \ge b_{n-3}$, proceed as in the case of two price breaks, i.e., the optimum order quantity is determined by comparing $TC(q_{n-2}^*)$ with $TC(b_{n-2})$ and $TC(b_{n-1})$.

Step 4 If $q_{n-2}^* < b_{n-2}$, compute q_{n-3}^*. If $q_{n-3}^* \geq b_{n-4}$, then compare $TC(q_{n-3}^*)$ with $TC(b_{n-3})$, $TC(b_{n-2})$ and $TC(b_{n-1})$.

Step 5 Compute in this way unit $q_{n-j}^* \geq (b_{n-j} + 1)$ $0 \leq j \leq n-1$. Then compare $TC(q_{n-j}^*)$ with $TC(b_{n-j-2})$, until $q_{n-j}^* \geq b_{n-j+1}$ $TC(b_{n-1})$.

Example 16.35 Find the optimum order quantity for a product, the price breaks for which are as follows.

Quantity	*Unit cost (₹)*
0–499	25
500–1499	24.80
1500–2999	24.60
Over 3000	24.40

Ordering cost is ₹ 180 per order, carrying cost is ₹ 0.10. Demand is 500 units per year. Also find the minimum inventory cost.

Solution Given,

$$R = 500 \text{ units per year}$$
$$C_3 = ₹\,180 \text{ per order}$$
$$I = ₹\,0.10.$$
$$K_{11} = 25, K_{12} = 24.80, K_{13} = 24.60, K_{14} = 24.40$$
$$b_1 = 500, b_2 = 1{,}500, b_3 = 3{,}000.$$

$$q_4^* = \sqrt{\frac{2RC_3}{K_{14} \times I}} = \sqrt{\frac{2 \times 500 \times 180}{0.1 \times 24.4}} = 272 \text{ units}$$

As, $$q_4^* = 272 < b_3 = 3{,}000$$

Next we compute q_3^*.

$$q_3^* = \sqrt{\frac{2RC_3}{IK_{13}}} = \sqrt{\frac{2 \times 500 \times 180}{0.1 \times 24.60}} = 270 \text{ units}$$

$\because$ $$q_3^* = 270 < b_2 = 1{,}500$$

Next we calculate, $$q_2^* = \sqrt{\frac{2RC_3}{IK_{12}}} = \sqrt{\frac{2 \times 500 \times 180}{0.1 \times 24.8}} = 269 \text{ units}$$

Now we compute, $$q_1^* = \sqrt{\frac{2RC_3}{IK_{11}}} = \sqrt{\frac{2 \times 500 \times 180}{0.1 \times 25}} = 268 \text{ units}$$

Now, $$TC(q_1^*) = RK_{11} + \frac{R}{q_1^*} \times C_3 + \frac{q_1^*}{2}(I \times K_{11})$$
$$= ₹\,13{,}170.82$$

$$TC(b_1) = RK_{12} + \frac{R}{b_1} \times C_3 + \frac{b_1}{2}(I \times K_{12})$$
$$= ₹\,13{,}200$$

$$TC(b_2) = RK_{13} + \frac{R}{b_2} \times C_3 + \frac{b_2}{2}(I \times K_{13})$$
$$= ₹\,14{,}205$$

$\because \quad TC(q_1^*) > TC(b_1) > TC(b_2), q^* = 268$ units

is the optimum order quantity.

Minimum inventory cost = ₹ 13,170.82

SUMMARY

Inventory Costs

Item cost It refers to the cost associated with an item, whether it is manufactured or purchased.

Carrying or holding cost **(C_1)** The cost associated with carrying or holding the goods in stock is known as holding or carrying cost.

Shortage cost or stock out cost **(C_2)** The penalty costs that are incurred as a result of running out of stock (i.e., shortage) are known as shortage or stock-out costs.

Set-up cost **(C_3)** These costs include the fixed costs associated with obtaining the goods through placing an order, purchasing, manufacturing or setting up a machinery before starting the production.

Order cycle

The time period between the placement of two successive orders is referred to as an order cycle.

Characteristics of Model I: Purchasing Model with no Shortages

(*i*) Optimum number of orders placed per year $n^* = \dfrac{R}{q^*} = \sqrt{\dfrac{RC_1}{2C_3}}$

(*ii*) Optimum length of time between orders $t^* = \sqrt{\dfrac{2C_3}{RC_1}}$

(*iii*) Minimum total annual inventory cost $c^* = \sqrt{2C_1C_3R}$

(*iv*) Optimum lot size $q^* = \sqrt{\dfrac{2C_3R}{C_1}}$

Model II: Manufacturing Models with No Shortages

R = number of items required per unit time

t = interval between production cycles

$q = Rt$, the number of items produced per production run.

Characteristics of Model II:

(*i*) Optimum number of production run per year.

$$n^* = \frac{R}{q^*} = \sqrt{\frac{C_1R}{2C_3}}\sqrt{\frac{K-R}{K}}$$

(*ii*) Optimum length of each lot size production run.

$$t^* = \sqrt{\frac{2C_3}{C_1R}}\sqrt{\frac{K}{K-R}}$$

(*iii*) Optimum lot size.

$$q^* = \sqrt{\frac{2C_3R}{C_1}}\sqrt{\frac{K}{K-R}}$$

(*iv*) Total minimum production inventory cost.

$$T_C{}^* = \sqrt{2RC_3C_1}\sqrt{\frac{K-R}{K}}$$

Model III: Purchasing Model with Shortages

(*i*) Optimum period. $t^* = \sqrt{\frac{2C_3}{RC_1}\left(\frac{C_1+C_2}{C_2}\right)}$

(*ii*) Optimal order quantity. $q^* = \sqrt{\frac{2C_3}{C_1}\left(\frac{C_1+C_2}{C_2}\right)}$

(*iii*) $C_{\min} = C^* = \sqrt{2C_1C_3R}\sqrt{\frac{C_2}{C_1+C_2}}$

Model IV: Manufacturing Model with Shortages

$$C(t_2, t_3) = \frac{\frac{1}{2}\left(C_1t_2^2 + C_2t_3^2\right)RK + C_3(K-R)}{K(t_2+t_3)}$$

$$t_2{}^* = \sqrt{\frac{2C_3C_2(1-R/K)}{R(C_1+C_2)C_1}}$$

$$t_3{}^* = \sqrt{\frac{2C_3C_1(1-R/K)}{R(C_1+C_2)C_2}}$$

$$q^* = \sqrt{\frac{2RC_3}{C_1C_2}(C_1+C_2)}\sqrt{\frac{K}{K-R}}$$

$$Q_2{}^* = \sqrt{\frac{2RC_1C_3}{(C_1+C_2)C_2}}\sqrt{\frac{K-R}{K}}$$

$$C^* = \sqrt{\frac{2RC_1C_3}{C_1+C_2}}\sqrt{\frac{K-R}{K}}$$

Inventory Models with Probabilistic Demand

Model V (a): Stock levels in discrete units

Z is the stock (indiscrete) units for time t.

$$\sum_{d=0}^{z-1} p(d) < \frac{C_2}{C_1+C_2} < \sum_{d=0}^{z} p(d)$$

Model V (b): Stock levels in continuous units

$$\int_0^z f(x)dx = \frac{C_2}{C_1+C_2}.$$

Re-Order Level and Optimum Buffer Stock

Lead time is defined as the time interval between the placing of the orders and the actual receipt of goods.

Buffer stock refers to the extra inventory maintained in addition to the required inventory corresponding to normal consumption levels.

Safety stock is maintained as a protection against stock-out. The greater the safety stock maintained, lesser the risk of stock-outs.

(*i*) EOQ $q^* = \sqrt{\frac{2RC_3}{C_1}}$

(*ii*) Optimum buffer (safety) stock
$B = (\text{Max. Lead time} - \text{Min. Lead time}) \times R$

(*iii*) Re-order level (ROL) = Buffer stock + Normal lead time consumption

(*iv*) Maximum inventory $= B + q^*$

(*v*) Average inventory $= B + \frac{q^*}{2}$

(*vi*) Minimum inventory $= B$

EOQ Problems with Price Breaks

(*i*) If the price discount is available, then the total cost to per unit of inventory system and items would be,

$$T_C = RK_1 + \frac{R}{q}C_3 + \frac{1}{2}qK_1 \times I$$

where, K_1 is the cost of manufacturing or purchasing per unit and I denotes the holding cost per unit.

(*ii*) The optimum value of quantity $q^* = \sqrt{\frac{2C_3R}{K_1, I}}$

Case I: EOQ problems with one price break.

Step 1 Compute q^*_2

Step 2 If $q^*_2 < b$, we cannot place an order at the reduced price.

Case II: EOQ problem with two price breaks.

Step 1 Compute q^*_3 and compare it with b_2.

Step 2 If $q^*_3 \geq b_2$, the optimum order quantity is q_3. If $q^*_3 < b_2$ go to the next step.

Step 3 Compute q^*_2, Since $q^*_3 < b_2, q^*_2 < b_2$ because $q^*_1 < q^*_2 < ... < q^*_n$. Thus, either $q^*_2 < b_1$ or $b_1 \leq q^*_2 < b_2$.

Step 4 Compare $T_C(q^*_2)$ and $T_C(b)$ and then determine the optimum quantity.

Step 5 Compare $T_C(q^*_1)$ with $T_C(b_1)$ and (b_2), so as to get the optimum purchase quantity.

Case III: EOQ problem with *n* price breaks.

Step 1 Compute q^*_n. If $q^*_n \geq b_{n-1}$.

Step 2 If $q^*_n < b_{n-1}$, compute q_{n-1}. If $q^*_{n-1} \ge b_{n-2}$, proceed as in the case of one price break. T_c order quantity is determined by comparing $T_C(q^*_{n-1})$ and $T_C(b_{n-1})$.

Step 3 If $q^*_n < b_{n-2}$ compute q_{n-2}. If $q_{n-2} \ge b_{n-3}$, proceed as in the case of two price breaks.

Step 4 If $q^*_{n-2} < b_{n-2}$, compute q^*_{n-3}. If $q^*_{n-3} \ge b_{n-4}$, then compare $T_C(q^*_{n3})$ with $T_C(b_{n-3})$, $T_C(b_{n-2})$ and $T_C(b_{n-1})$.

Step 5 Compute in this way unit $q^*_{n-j} \ge (b_{n-j+1})$, $0 \le j \le n-1$, then compare $T_C(q^*_{n-j})$ with $T_C(b_{n-j-2})$ until $q^*_{n-j} \ge (b_{n-j+1})\, T_c(b_{n-1})$.

□□□

Chapter

17 Replacement Models

17.1 INTRODUCTION

The replacement problems are concerned with the situations that arise when some items such as machines, electric light bulbs, etc., need replacement due to their decreased efficiency, failure or breakdown. This decreased efficiency or complete breakdown may be either gradual or sudden.

Following are some of the situations that demand the replacement of certain items.

(*i*) The old item has become inefficient or requires expensive maintenance.
(*ii*) The old item has failed due to an accident or otherwise and does not work at all or it is expected to fail shortly.
(*iii*) A better design of equipment has been developed, making the older design obsolescent.

The problem of replacement is to decide the best policy in determining a time at which the replacement is most economical, instead of continuing at an increased cost. The main objective of replacement is to direct the organization in maximizing its profit (or minimizing the cost).

The replacement situations may be divided into four categories.

(*i*) Replacement of capital equipment that suffers heavy depreciation in the course of time, e.g., machines tools, buses in a transport organization, planes, etc.
(*ii*) Group replacement of items that fail completely, e.g., light bulbs, radio tubes, etc.
(*iii*) Problems of mortality and staffing.
(*iv*) Miscellaneous problems.

17.2 REPLACEMENT OF ITEMS THAT DETERIORATE WITH TIME

Generally, the cost of maintenance and repair of certain items increases with time and at one stage, these costs become so high that it is more economical to replace the item by a new one. At this point a replacement is justified.

17.2.1 Case I: Value of Money Does Not Change with Time

The aim is to determine the optimum replacement age of an equipment or item, whose running or maintenance cost increases with time and the value of money remains the same during that period.

C: Capital cost of equipment

S: Scrap value or resale value of an equipment

N: Number of years the equipment would be in use

$F(t)$: Maintenance cost function

$A(n)$: Average total annual cost.

When time 't' is a continuous variable:

If the equipment is used for n years then the total cost incurred during this period is given by,

$$TC = \text{Capital cost} - \text{Scrap value} + \text{Maintenance cost}$$

$$= C - S + \int^{n} f(t)\,dt$$

Average annual total cost, $A(N) = \frac{1}{N} TC = \frac{C-S}{N} + \frac{1}{N}\int_{o}^{n} f(t)\,dt$.

For minimum cost, we have, $\frac{d}{dn}(A(N)) = 0$

$$-\frac{C-S}{N^2} - \frac{1}{N^2}\int_{o}^{n} f(t)dt + \frac{1}{n} f(n) = 0$$

or
$$f(n) = \frac{C-S}{N} + \frac{1}{N}\int_{o}^{n} f(t)dt = A(N)$$

Clearly, $\frac{d^2}{dN^2} A(N) \geq 0$ at $f(N) = A(N)$.

This suggests that the equipment should be replaced when the maintenance cost equals the average annual total cost.

For discrete value of t,

n is optimal at the average annual cost.

This suggests the optimal replacement policy. According to which,

$$F(n) = \frac{1}{n}\left[c - s(t) + \sum_{o}^{n} f(t) \right]$$

(*i*) Replace the equipment at the end of N years, if the maintenance cost in the $(N+1)^{th}$ year, is more than the average total cost in the Nth year.

(*ii*) Do not replace the equipment, if the current year's maintenance cost is less than the previous year's total cost.

Example 17.1 The cost of a machine is ₹ 61,000 and its scrap value is ₹ 1,000. The maintenance costs found from the past experiences are as follows:

Year	*1*	*2*	*3*	*4*	*5*	*6*	*7*	*8*
Maintenance Cost in Rupees	1000	2500	4000	6000	9000	12000	16000	20000

When should the machine be replaced?

Solution We are given the running cost $f(n)$, the scrap value S = ₹ 1,000 and the cost of the machine C = ₹ 61,000. In order to determine the optimal time n when the machine should be replaced, we calculate an average. Total cost per year during the life of the machine is shown in the following table.

Year 1	*Running cost* 2	*Cumulative running cost* $\sum f(n)$ 3	*Depreciation cost* $C-S$ 4	*Total cost* TC 5 = 3 + 4	*Average cost* $A(n)$ 6 = 5/1
1	1000	1000	60000	61000	61000
2	2500	3500	60000	63500	31750
3	4000	7500	60000	67500	22500
4	6000	13500	60000	73500	18375
5	9000	22500	60000	82500	16500
6	12000	34500	60000	94500	15750
7	16000	50500	60000	110500	15785.71
8	20000	70500	60000	130500	16312.50

From the table, it is noted that the average total cost per year $A(n)$ is minimum in the 6th year (₹ 15,750). Hence, the machine should be replaced after every 6 years.

Example 17.2 A machine costs ₹ 10,000. Its operating cost and resale values are given below:

Year	*1*	*2*	*3*	*4*	*5*	*6*	*7*	*8*
Operating cost	1000	1200	1400	1700	2000	2500	3000	3500
Resale value	6000	4000	3200	2600	2500	2400	2000	1600

Determine at what time it should be replaced.

Solution Given, the cost of the equipment (C) = ₹ 10,000.

To determine the optimal time, n, when the equipment should be replaced, we calculate an average total cost per year as shown in the following table.

Year 1	$f(n)$ 2	$\Sigma f(n)$ 3	S 4	$C-S$ 5	$TC = C-S+\Sigma f(n)$ 6 = 3 + 5	$A(n) = TC/n$ 7 = 6/1
1	1000	1000	6000	4000	5000	5000
2	1200	2200	4000	6000	8200	4100
3	1400	3600	3200	6800	10400	3466.70
4	1700	5300	2600	7400	12700	3175
5	2000	7300	2500	7500	14800	2940
6	2500	9800	2400	7600	17400	2900
7	3000	12800	2000	8000	20800	2971.4
8	3500	16300	1600	8400	24700	3089.7

From the table it is clear that the average annual cost is minimum at the end of the 6th year (₹ 2,900). We conclude that the equipment should be replaced at the end of the 6th year.

Example 17.3 A machine owner finds from his past records that the costs per year of maintaining a machine, whose purchase price is ₹ 6,000 are as given below.

Year	*1*	*2*	*3*	*4*	*5*	*6*	*7*	*8*
Maintenance cost	1000	1200	1400	1800	2300	2800	3400	4000
Resale price	3000	1500	750	375	200	200	200	200

Determine at what age a replacement is due.

Solution Given, $C = 6{,}000$. The following table gives the average total cost per year.

Year *1*	*f(n)* *2*	$\sum f(n)$ *3*	*C – S* *4*	*Total cost* $TC = C - S + \sum f(n)$ *5*	*Average cost* *A(n)* *6 = 5/1*
1	1000	1000	3000	4000	4000
2	1200	2200	4500	6700	3350
3	1400	3600	5250	8850	2950
4	1800	5400	5625	11025	2756.25
5	2300	7700	5800	13500	2700
6	2800	10500	5800	16300	2716.66
7	3400	13900	5800	19700	2814.28
8	4000	17900	5800	23700	2962.50

We note that the minimum average annual cost $A(n)$ is at the end of the 5th year. Hence, the optimum replacement is due after every 5 years.

Example 17.4

(*i*) Machine *A* costs ₹ 9,000. Annual operating cost is ₹ 200 for the first year and then increases by ₹ 2,000 every year. Determine the best age to replace the machine. If the optimum replacement policy is followed, what will be the average yearly cost of owning and operating the machine?

(*ii*) Machine *B* costs ₹ 10,000. Annual operating cost is ₹ 400 for the first year and then increases by ₹ 800 every year. You now have a machine of type *A*, which is one year old. Should you replace it with *B*, if so, when?

Solution We prepare a table, to find the average cost per year for machine *A*.

Year *1*	*Running cost (₹)* *2*	*Total running cost (₹)* *3*	*Depreciation value C – S (₹)* *4*	$TC = C - S + \sum f(n)$ (₹) $5 = 3 + 4$	*A(n) (₹)* *6 = 5/1*
1	200	200	9000	9200	9200
2	2200	2400	9000	11400	5700
3	4200	6600	9000	15600	5200
4	6200	12800	9000	21800	5450

Since the average annual cost is minimum at the end of 3rd year, the optimum time of replacement is 3 years. The average yearly cost of owning and operating the machine is ₹ 5,200.

Next, we find the average yearly cost for the machine *B* in the following table.

Year	f(n)	$\Sigma f(n)$	C – S	TC = $C-S+\Sigma f(n)$	A(n)
1	2	3	4	5 = 3 + 4	6 = 5/1
1	400	400	10000	10400	10400
2	1200	1600	10000	11600	5800
3	2000	3600	10000	13600	4533.33
4	2800	6400	10000	16400	4100
5	3600	10000	10000	20000	4000
6	4400	14400	10000	24400	4066.66

Conclusion Since the minimum average cost is ₹ 4,000 for machine *B* and less than the average cost of ₹ 5,200 for machine *A*, so *A* can be replaced by *B*.

Machine *B* can be purchased when the *cost for the next year of running machine A, exceeds the average yearly cost for machine B.*

The total yearly cost for machine *A* is as follows:

for, 1st year $=11400-9200=2200<4000$

2nd year $=15600-11400=4200>4000$

3rd year $=21800-15600=6200>4000$

Hence, we observe that the cost ₹ 2,200 for one year old machine A will not exceed the lowest average cost ₹ 4,000 for *B*, until the second year.

Therefore, machine *A* should be replaced with machine *B* after two years, before it reaches the normal replacement age of three years.

Example 17.5 A truck owner finds from his past records that the maintenance costs per year of a truck, whose purchase price is ₹ 8,000 are as given in the table that follows.

Year	1	2	3	4	5	6	7	8
Maintenance cost	1000	1300	1700	2200	2900	3800	4800	6000
Resale price	4000	2000	1200	600	500	400	400	400

Determine the time at which it is profitable to replace the truck.

Solution Given, $C=$ ₹ 8,000

The maintenance cost and resale price are given in the data. The table below shows the optimum period to replace the truck for which the average annual cost is minimum.

Year	f(n)	$\Sigma f(n)$	C – S	TC = $C-S+\Sigma f(n)$	A(n)
1	2	3	4	5	6 = 5/1
1	1000	1000	4000	5000	5000
2	1300	2300	6000	8300	4150
3	1700	4000	6800	10800	3600
4	2200	6200	7400	13600	3400
5	2900	9100	7500	16600	3320
6	3800	12900	7600	20500	3416.66
7	4800	17700	7600	25300	3614.28
8	6000	23700	7600	31300	3912.5

We note that the minimum average annual cost is at the end of the 5th year, therefore, it is profitable to replace the truck at the end of the 5th year.

17.2.2 Case II: Value of Money Changes with Time

When the time value of money is taken into consideration, we shall assume that (*i*) the equipment in question has no salvage value i.e. the estimate value that an asset will realize upon its sale at the end of its useful life. (*ii*) the maintenance costs are incurred in the beginning of various time periods.

Money value Since money has a value over time, we often say money is worth 10 per cent per year. This can be explained in the following two ways.

(*i*) In one way, spending ₹ 100 today would be equivalent to spending ₹ 110 in a year's time or spending ₹ 110 after a year from now, would be equivalent to spending ₹ 100 today, which would be worth ₹ 110 next year.

(*ii*) Alternatively, if we borrow ₹ 100 at a 10 per cent rate of interest per year and spend this amount today, then we have to pay ₹ 110 after one year.

Hence, we conclude, one rupee after a year from now is equivalent to $(1.1)^{-1}$ rupee today.

Present worth factor (PWF) If r is the rate of interest, then $(1+r)^{-n}$ is called the *present worth factor* or the present value of one rupee spent in n years time from now. The expression $(1+r)^{-n}$ is known as the payment *compound amount factor* (caf) of one rupee spent in n years duration.

Discount rate The present worth factor of unit amount to be spent after one year is given by, $V = (1+r)^{-1}$, when r is called the rate of interest and V is called discount rate.

Example 17.6 The cost pattern for two machines A and B, when money value is not considered, is given in the table below.

Year	*Cost at the beginning of year (₹)*	
	Machine A	*Machine B*
1	900	1400
2	600	100
3	700	700

Find the cost pattern for each machine when money is worth 10 per cent per year and hence, find which machine is less costly.

Solution The total outlay for the three years for machine $A = 900 + 600 + 700 =$ ₹ 2,200.

Also, for machine $B = 1400 + 100 + 700 =$ ₹ 2,200.

We find that the total outlay for both machines is the same for 3 years, therefore, both the machines appear to be equally good in this case.

When money carries a rate of 10 per cent per year, the discount cost pattern for each machine for three years is shown in the following table.

Year	*Discounted cost (10% rate)*	
	Machine A	*Machine B*
1	900	1400.00
2	$600 \times \frac{100}{110} = 545.45$	$100 \times \frac{100}{110} = 90.90$
3	$700 \times \left(\frac{100}{110}\right)^2 = 578.52$	$700 \times \left(\frac{100}{110}\right)^2 = 578.52$
Total outlay	₹ 2,023.97	₹ 2,069.43

The outlay of machine A is less than that of machine B. Hence, machine A will be preferred.

Example 17.7 A manual stamping machine currently valued at ₹ 10,000 is expected to last 2 years and costs ₹ 4,000 per year to operate. Another machine, which can be purchased for ₹ 30,000 will last for 4 years and be operated at an annual cost of ₹ 3,000. If money carries the rate of interest at 10 per cent per annum, determine which stamping machine should be purchased.

Solution The present worth factor is given by,

$$V = (1+r)^{-1} = \left(1 + \frac{10}{100}\right)^{-1} = \left(\frac{110}{100}\right)^{-1} = 0.9091.$$

The two given stampers have different expected lives. So we shall consider a span of next 4 years.

The present worth of investments on the manual stampers for the next four years is,

$$10000\,(1 + V^2) + 4000\,(V + V^2 + V^3 + V^4)$$

$$10000\,(1 + (0.9091)^2) + 4000\,[0.9091 + (0.9091)^2 + (0.9091)^3 + (0.9091)^4]$$

$$= 18264.6281 + 12679 = 30943.6281.$$

The present worth of investments on the automatic stamper for the next four years is,

$$= 30000 + 3000\,(V + V^2 + V^3 + V^4)$$

$$= 30000 + 9509 = ₹39{,}509$$

Since the present worth of future costs for the automatic stamper is greater than that of the manual stamper, the latter will be more profitable and hence, it should be purchased.

17.3 TO FIND THE OPTIMAL REPLACEMENT POLICY

Let the initial cost of the equipment be C and let R_n be the operation in year n. Let r be the rate of interest in such a way that $V = (1+r)^{-1}$ is the discount rate. We find the weighted average cost of all the previous n years with weights 1, V, V^2 ... V^{n-1}, respectively.

The expression for weighted average cost is given by,

$$W(n) = \frac{C + R_0 + VR_1 + V^2 R_2 + \ldots + V^{n-1} R_{n-1}}{1 + V + V^2 + \ldots + V^{n-1}}$$

The optimal replacement policy of the equipment after n period is,

(*i*) Do not replace the equipment if the next period's cost is *less than* the weighted average of previous costs.

(*ii*) Replace the equipments if the next period's cost is *greater than* the weighted average of previous costs.

Selection of the best equipment To find an economically best item amongst the available equipments, we have the following procedure.

Step 1 Considering the case of 2 equipments A and B. We first find the replacement age for both the equipments by making use of,

$$R_{n-1} < W(n) < R_n.$$

Let n_1, n_2 be the replacement ages for the equipments A and B.

Step 2 Next, we find the weighted average cost for each equipment. Substitute $n = n_1$ for equipment A and $n = n_2$ for equipment B.

Step 3 (*i*) If $W(n_1) < W(n_2)$, choose equipment A

(*ii*) If $W(n_1) > W(n_2)$, choose equipment B.

(*iii*) If $W(n_1) = W(n_2)$, both equipment are equally good.

Note: If the salvage is not negligible, the expression for weighted average cost is given by,

$$W(n)=\frac{C+\sum_{n=1} R_n V^{n-1}-S_n V^n}{\sum_{n=1} V^{n-1}}$$

Example 17.8 A machine costs ₹ 15,000. The running cost for the different years are given below.

Year	1	2	3	4	5	6	7
Running	2500	3000	4000	5000	6500	8000	10000

Find the optimum replacement period if the capital is worth 10 per cent per annum and has no salvage value.

Solution Since the money is worth 10 per cent per year, the discount rate will be,

$$V=(1+r)^{-1}=\left(1+\frac{10}{100}\right)^{-1}=0.9091$$

We form Table 17.1 to find out the weighted average cost.

$$W(n)=\frac{C+\sum_{n=1} R_n V^{n-1}-S_n V^n}{\sum_{n=1} V^{n-1}}$$

Table 17.1

Year (n) 1	Running cost R_{n-1} 2	V_{n-1} $(0.9091)^{n-1}$ 3	ΣV^{n-1} 4	$R_{n-1}V^{n-1}$ 5	$\Sigma R_n V^{n-1}$ 6	$C+\Sigma R_n V^{n-1}$ 7	$W(n)=$ $8=\frac{7}{4}$ 3/4
1	2500	1	1	2500	2500	17500	17500
2	3000	0.9091	1.9091	2727.3	5227.30	20227.30	10595.2
3	4000	0.8265	2.7356	3306	8533.30	23533.30	8602.60
4	5000	0.75134	3.486	3756.68	12289.98	27289.98	7826.34
5	6500	0.6830	4.169	4439.76	16729.74	31729.74	7610.87
6	8000	0.6209	4.7899	4967.61	21697.35	36697.35	7661.40
7	10000	0.5645	5.3544	5645	27342.42	42342.43	7907.96

From Table 17.1, we observe that the weighted average cost is minimum at the end of 5th year.

$$R_4 < W(5) < R_6$$
$$6500 < 7610.87 < 8000$$

Hence, the optimum replacement period is every 5th year.

Example 17.9 A manufacturer is offered two machines *A* and *B*. *A* is priced at ₹ 50,000 and running costs are estimated at ₹ 8,000 for each of the first five years, increasing by ₹ 2,000 per year in the sixth and subsequent years. Machine *B* of the same capacity costs ₹ 25,000, but will have running costs of ₹ 12,000 per year for six years, increasing by ₹ 2,000 per year thereafter. If money is worth 10 per cent per year, which machine should be purchased?

Solution Since the money is worth 10 per cent per year, the discount rate for both the machines is given by,

$$V = \left(1 + \frac{10}{100}\right)^{-1} = 0.9091$$

Computation of the weighted average cost and the optimum replacement period for both the machines are shown in Table 17.2 and Table 17.3 respectively.

From Table 17.2, we observe that for machine A, $16000 < 17520.45 < 18000$.

As the weighted average cost is minimum at the end of 9th year, the optimum replacement period is 9 years.

$$n_1 = 9 \text{ years}$$
$$W(n_1) = 17520.45$$
$$C = ₹25,000$$

Table 17.2 *C = Ccst = 50,000*

		Machine A					
Year n 1	R_{n-1} 2	V^{n-1} $(0.9091)^{n-1}$ 3	$V^{n-1} R^{n-1}$ 4	$\Sigma V^{n-1} R^{n-1}$ 5	ΣV^{n-1} 6	50000 + $Cw + \Sigma V^{n-1} R_{n-1}$ 7	$W(n)$ 8 = 7/6
1	8000	1	8000	8000	1	58000	58000.0
2	8000	0.9091	7272.8	15272.8	1.9091	65272.8	34190
3	8000	0.8265	6611.70	21884.50	2.7356	71884.50	26277.4
4	8000	0.7513	6010.69	27895.19	3.4869	77895.19	22339.38
5	8000	0.6830	5464.32	33359.51	4.1699	83359.51	19990.76
6	10000	0.6209	6209	39568.51	4.7908	89568.51	18695.9
7	12000	0.5645	6774	46342.59	5.3553	96342.5	17990
8	14000	0.5132	7184.7	53527.3	5.8685	103527.30	17641
9	16000	0.4665	7464.8	60992.1	6.335	110992.1	17520.45
10	18000	0.4241	7633.7	68625.8	6.7591	118625.81	17550.53

From Table 17.3, we observe that,

Table 17.3 *C = cost = 25000*

		Machine B					
Year n 1	R_{n-1} 2	V^{n-1} $(0.9091)^{n-1}$ 3	$V^{n-1} R_{n-1}$ 4	$\Sigma V^{n-1} R_{n-1}$ 5	25000 + $C + \Sigma R_{n-1} V^{n-1}$ 6	ΣV^{n-1} 7	$\omega(n)$ 8 = 6/7
1	12000	1	12000	12000	37000	1	37000
2	12000	0.9091	10909.2	22909.2	47909.2	1.9091	25095.2
3	12000	0.8264	9916.8	32826	57826	2.7353	21140.64
4	12000	0.7513	9015.6	41841.6	66841.6	3.4868	19169.89
5	12000	0.6830	8196	50037.6	75037.6	4.1698	17995.49
6	12000	0.6209	7450.8	57488.4	82488.4	4.7907	17218.44
7	14000	0.5645	7903	65391.4	90391.4	5.3532	16885.48
8	16000	0.5132	8211.2	73602.6	98602.6	5.8684	16802.29
9	18000	0.4665	8397	81999.6	106999.6	6.3349	16890.5
10	20000	0.4241	8482	90481.6	115481.6	6.7590	17085.6

$$16000 < 16802.29 < 18000.$$

Hence, the optimum replacement period for machine B is 8 years, i.e., $n_2 = 8$.

$$W(n_2) = 16802.29.$$

On comparing the weighted average costs for both the machines, we have,

$$W(n_1) > W(n_2)$$

i.e., $$17520.45 > 16802.29.$$

Hence, it is advisable to purchase machine B.

Example 17.10 The cost of a new machine is ₹ 5,000. The maintenance cost of the nth year is given by, $C_n = 500(n-1), n = 1, 2 ...$

Suppose money is worth 5 per cent per year, after how many years will it be economical to replace the machine?

Solution The present worth of the money to be spent in a year is,

$$V = (1+4) - 1$$

$$V = \left(1 + \frac{5}{100}\right)^{-1} = 0.9523$$

The optimum replacement time is determined in the table shown below.

Table 17.4

Year 1	R_{n-1} 2	V^{n-1} 3	$R_{n-1}V^{n-1}$ 4	$\Sigma R_n V^{n-1}$ 5	$C + \Sigma p_v V^{n-1}$ 6	ΣV^{n-1} 7	$W(n)$ 8=6/7
1	0	1	0	0	5000	1	5000
2	500	0.9523	476.15	476.15	5476.15	1.9523	2805
3	1000	0.9069	906.875	1383.02	6383.025	2.8592	2232
4	1500	0.8636	1295.43	2678.44	7678.44	3.7228	2062.5
5	2000	0.8224	1644.8	4323.28	9323.28	4.5452	2051.2
6	2500	0.7832	1957.98	6281.26	11281.26	5.3284	2117

Since the weighted average cost is minimum at the end of 5th year, also $R_4 < W(5) < R_0$, it is economical to replace the machine with a new one at the end of 5 years.

Example 17.11 A machine costs ₹ 6,000. The running cost and the salvage value at the end of the year is given in the table below.

Year	1	2	3	4	5	6	7
Running cost	1200	1400	1600	1800	2000	2400	3000
Salvage value	4000	2666	2000	1500	1000	600	600

If the interest rate is 10 per cent per year, when should the machine be replaced?

Solution

$$C = 6000, V = (1+r)^{-1} = \left(1 + \frac{10}{100}\right)^{-1} = 0.9091$$

Table 17.5

Year 1	R_n 2	V^{n-1} 3	R_nV^{n-1} 4	ΣR_nV^{n-1} 5	S_n 6	S_nV^n 7	ΣV^{n-1} 8	$C - S_nV^n + \Sigma R_nV^{n-1}$ 9	$W(n)$ 10 = 9/8
1	1200	1	1200	1200	4000	3636.4	1	3563.6	3563.6
2	1400	0.9091	1272.74	2472.74	2666	2203.34	1.9091	6269.4	3283.95
3	1600	0.8265	1322.34	3795.08	2000	1502.67	2.7356	6970.8	2548.21
4	1800	0.7513	1352.4	5147.48	1500	1024.56	3.4869	8801.3	2524.10
5	2000	0.6830	1366.01	6513.49	1000	620.95	4.1699	10571.01	2535.07
6	2400	0.6209	1490.196	8003.686	600	338.70	4.7908	12343.4	2576.47
7	3000	0.5644	1693.38	9697.066	600	307.916	5.3552	14067.62	2626.908

Since salvage value is considered, the expression for,

$$w(n) = \frac{C + \sum R_n V^{n-1} - S_n V^n}{\sum V^{n-1}}$$

From Table 17.5 we observe that the weighted average cost is minimum at the end of the 4th year. Hence, the optimum replacement is due every 4 years.

17.4 REPLACEMENT OF EQUIPMENT THAT FAILS SUDDENLY

It is difficult to predict that a particular equipment will fail at a particular time. This difficulty can be overcome by determining the probability distribution of failures. Assuming that the failures occur only at the end of a period, say t, the objective is to find the value of t, which minimizes the total cost involved for the replacement.

We shall consider the following two types of replacement policies.

(i) ***Individual replacement policy*** Under this policy, an item is replaced immediately after it fails.

(ii) ***Group replacement policy*** Under this policy, we take decisions as to when all the items must be replaced, irrespective of the fact that items have failed or not, with a provision that if any item fails before the optimal time, it may be individually replaced.

Hence, we have the following optimal policy.

Let all the items in a system be replaced after a time interval 't' with provisions that individual replacement can be made if and when any item fails during this time period.

Group replacement must be made at the end of tth period if the cost of individual replacements for the tth period is greater than the average cost per period, through the end of t periods.

Group replacement is not possible at the end of period t if the cost of individual replacement at the $t-1$ end period is less than the average cost per period, through the end of t period.

Example 17.12 The following mortality rates have been observed for a certain type of light bulbs.

Week	1	2	3	4	5
Per cent failing by the end of week	10	25	50	80	100

There are 1,000 bulbs in use and it costs ₹ 2 to replace an individual bulb, which has burnt out. If all the bulbs were replaced simultaneously, it would cost 50 paise per bulb. It is proposed to replace all bulbs at fixed intervals, whether or not they have burnt out and to continue replacing burnt out bulbs as they fail. At what intervals should all the bulbs be replaced?

Solution

Step 1 Let P_i be the probability that a bulb, which was new when placed in position for use, fails during the ith week of its life.

$$P_1 = 0.1$$
$$P_2 = 0.25 - 0.1 = 0.15$$
$$P_3 = 0.5 - 0.25 = 0.25$$
$$P_4 = 0.8 - 0.5 = 0.3$$
$$P_5 = 1 - 0.8 = 0.2$$

Since the sum of probabilities is 1, all the probabilities beyond P_5 will be taken as zero.

Step 2 Let N_i be the number of replacements at the end of the ith week.

$$N_0 = \text{Number of items in the beginning}$$
$$= 1000$$
$$N_1 = N_0 P_1 = 1000 \times 0.1 = 100$$
$$N_2 = N_0 P_2 + N_1 P_1 = 150 + 10 = 160$$
$$N_3 = N_0 P_3 + N_1 P_2 + N_2 P_1$$
$$= 1000\,(0.25) + (100)\,(0.15) + 160\,(0.1) = 281$$
$$N_4 = N_0 P_4 + N_1 P_3 + N_2 P_2 + N_3 P_1$$
$$= 1000\,(0.3) + 100\,(0.25) + 160\,(0.15) + 281\,(0.1)$$
$$= 378.7 = 379$$
$$N_5 = N_0 P_5 + N_1 P_4 + N_2 P_3 + N_3 P_2 + N_4 P_1$$
$$= 1000\,(0.2) + 100\,(0.3) + 160\,(0.25) + 281\,(0.15) + 379\,(0.1)$$
$$= 350.05 = 350$$

From the above calculations, we observe that the expected number of bulbs failing each week increases till the 4th week and then starts decreasing. Thus, N_i will oscillate till the system acquires a steady state.

Step 3 We calculate the expected life of each bulb,

$$= \sum_{i=1}^{5} i\, P_i$$
$$= 1 \times 0.1 + 2 \times 0.15 + 3 \times (0.25) + 4(0.3) + 5 \times 0.2$$
$$= 3.35$$

Average number of failures per week,

$$= \frac{1000}{3.35} = 298.50$$
$$= 299 \quad \text{(approximately)}$$

Step 4 The cost of individual replacement

$$= 299 \times 2 = ₹\,598$$

Now, since the replacement of all the 1,000 bulbs simultaneously costs 50 paise per bulb and the replacement of an individual bulb on failure costs ₹ 2, the average cost for different group replacement policies is given below.

End of week	*Individual replacement*	*Total cost (₹) (Individual + group)*	*Average cost*
1	100	100 × 2 + 1000 × 0.5 = 700	700
2	100 + 160 = 260	260 × 2 + 1000 × 0.5 = 1020	510
3	260 + 281 = 541	541 × 2 + 1000 × 0.5 = 1582	527.33
4	541 + 379 = 920	920 × 2 + 1000 × 0.5 = 2340	585
5	920 + 350 = 1270	1270 × 2 + 1000 × 0.5 = 3040	608

Since the average cost is minimum in the 2nd week, the optimal replacement period to have a group replacement is after every 2nd week.

Since the average cost is less than ₹ 598 for individual replacement, the group replacement policy is preferable.

Example 17.13 The probability P_n of failure just before age n is shown below. If individual replacement costs ₹ 12.50 and group replacement costs ₹ 3 per item. Find the optimal replacement policy.

n	*1*	*2*	*3*	*4*	*5*
P_n	0.1	0.2	0.25	0.3	0.15

Solution

Step 1 Let P_i, be the probability of failure during the ith period,

$$P_1 = 0.1$$
$$P_2 = 0.2$$
$$P_3 = 0.25$$
$$P_4 = 0.3$$
$$P_5 = 0.15$$

As the sum of probabilities is 1, the probabilities beyond P_5 will be zero.

$$N_0 = 1000$$
$$N_1 = N_0 P_1 = 1000 \times 0.1 = 100$$
$$N_2 = N_0 P_2 + N_1 P_1$$
$$= 1000 \times 0.2 + 100 \times 0.1 = 210$$
$$N_3 = N_0 P_3 + N_1 P_2 + N_2 P_1$$
$$= 1000\,(0.25) + 100\,(0.2) + (210)\,(0.1) = 291$$
$$N_4 = N_0 P_4 + N_1 P_3 + N_2 P_2 + N_3 P_1$$
$$= 1000\,(0.3) + 100\,(0.25) + 210\,(0.2) + 291\,(0.1)$$
$$= 396.1 = 396$$

$$N_5 = N_0 P_5 + N_1 P_4 + N_2 P_3 + N_3 P_2 + N_4 P_1$$
$$= 1000\,(0.15) + 100\,(0.3) + 210\,(0.25) + 291\,(0.2) + 396\,(0.1)$$
$$= 330.3 = 330$$

Step 2 To start with, we assume that we have 1,000 items. Let N_i be the number of replacements during the *i*th period.

From the above calculations, we observe that the expected number of items failing in each period increases till the 4th period and then starts decreasing. Thus, N_i will oscillate till the system acquires a steady state.

Step 3 In this step, we find the expected life of each item given by,

$$= \sum_{i=1}^{5} i\, p_i$$
$$= 1 \times 0.1 + 2 \times 0.2 + 3 \times 0.25 + 4 \times 0.3 + 5 \times 0.15$$
$$= 3.2$$

Average number of failures per period,

$$\frac{1000}{3.2} = 312.5 \approx 313$$
$$313 \times 12.50 = ₹3{,}912.50$$

The cost of individual replacement

$$= 313 \times 12.50 = ₹3{,}912.50$$

The replacement of all the 1,000 items simultaneously costs ₹ 3 per item and the replacement of an individual item on failure costs ₹ 12.50 per item, the average costs for different group replacement policies are given below.

End of period	*Individual replacement*	*Total cost (₹) (Individual + group)*	*Average cost*
1	100	100 × 12.50 + 1000 × 3 = 4,250	4250
2	100 + 210 = 310	310 × 12.50 + 1000 × 3 = 6,875	3437.50
3	310 + 291 = 601	601 × 12.50 + 1000 × 3 = 10,512.5	3504.166

Since, the average cost is minimum at the end of the 2nd period, we replace all the items simultaneonsly after every 2nd period. Also, the average cost of group replacement policy is less than that of individual replacement of ₹ 3,912.50. Hence, we prefer group replacement policy.

Example 17.14 Let $p(t)$ be the probability that a machine in a group of 30 machines would breakdown in a period t. The cost of repairing a machine is ₹ 200. Preventive maintenance is performed by servicing all the 30 machines at the end of T units of time. Preventive maintenance cost is ₹ 15 per machine. Find optimal T, which will minimize the expected total cost per period of servicing, given that,

$$p(t) = \begin{cases} 0.03, \text{ for } t = 1 \\ p(t-1) + 0.01, \text{ for } t = 2, 3, 10 \\ 0.13, \text{ for } t = 11, 12, 13 \end{cases}$$

Solution

Step 1 The probability of a machine breaking down in period t is given below.

t	*1*	*2*	*3*	*4*	*5*	*6*	*7*	*8*	*9*	*10*	*11*	*12*
$p(t)$	0.03	0.04	0.05	0.06	0.07	0.08	0.09	0.10	0.11	0.12	0.13	0

Since the sum of all probabilities can never be greater than one, we have, $p_{12} = p_{13} = ... = 0$ each.

Step 2 Let N_i be the expected number of replacements during the ith period.

$$N_0 = 30$$
$$N_1 = N_0P_1 = 30 \times 0.03 = 0.9 = 1$$
$$N_2 = N_0P_2 + N_1P_1 = 30 \times 0.04 + 1 \times 0.03$$
$$= 1.23 = 1$$
$$N_3 = N_0P_3 + N_1P_2 + N_2P_1 = 30 \times 0.05 + 1 \times 0.04 + 1 \times 0.03$$
$$= 1.57 = 2$$
$$N_4 = N_0P_{4+} + N_1P_3 + N_2P_2 + N_3P_1 = 1.95 = 2$$

Similarly, $N_5 = 2, N_6 = 3, N_7 = 3,$
$N_8 = 4, N_9 = 4, N_{10} = 5,$
$N_{11} = 6.$

From the above calculations, we observe that the value of N_i is increasing and decreasing. Thus, N_i will oscillate till the system acquires a steady state.

Step 3 Hence, we find in this step the expected life of each machine,

$$= \sum_{i=1}^{11} i\,P_i = 1 \times 0.03 + 2 \times 0.04 + 3 \times 0.05 + ... + 11 \times 0.13 = 6.41$$

We have the average number of machines to be replaced $= \dfrac{30}{6.41} = 5$ (approximately)

$\therefore$ Cost of individual replacement = 5 × 200 = ₹ 1,000

Group replacement cost is calculated in the following table.

End of period	*Individual replacement*	*Total cost (₹) (Individual + group)*	*Average cost*
1	1 × 200 = 200	(30 × 15) + 200 = 650	650
2	(1 + 1) × 200 = 400	400 + (30 × 15) = 850	425
3	(2 + 2) × 200 = 800	800 + (30 × 15) = 1,250	417
4	(4 + 2) × 200 = 1,200	1200 + (30 × 15) = 1,650	412.50
5	(6 + 2) × 200 = 1,600	1600 + (30 × 15) = 2,050	410
6	(8 + 3) × 200 = 2,200	2200 + (30 × 15) = 2,650	441.66 = 442

Since the minimum cost occurs in the 5th period, it is optimal to replace the machine after every 5th period.

$$T = 5\text{th period.}$$

EXERCISES

1. The following table gives the running costs per year and resale price of a certain equipment, whose purchase price is ₹ 5,000.

Year	1	2	3	4	5	6	7	8
Running cost	1500	1600	1800	2100	2500	2900	3400	4400
Resale value	3500	2500	1700	1200	800	500	500	500

In what year is the replacement due? **[Ans.** End of the 4th year]

2. The following table gives the running cost per year and resale price of a certain machine, whose purchase price is ₹ 50,000.

Year	1	2	3	4	5	6	7	8
Running cost (in 1000)	15	16	18	21	25	29	43	40
Resale value (in 1000)	35	25	17	12	8	5	5	5

In what year is the replacement due? **[Ans.** End of the 7th year]

3. The cost of a machine is ₹ 61,000 and its scrap value is ₹ 1,000. The maintenance costs found from the past experiences are as follows:

Year	1	2	3	4	5	6	7	8
Maintenance cost in rupees	1000	2500	4000	6000	9000	12000	16000	20000

When should the machine be replaced? **[Ans.** End of the 6th year]

4. Let $V = 0.9$ and initial price is ₹ 5,000. Running cost varies as follows:

Year	1	2	3	4	5	6	7
Running cost	400	500	700	1000	1300	1700	2100

What would be the optimum replacement interval? **[Ans.** End of the 6th year]

5. A truck is priced at ₹ 60,000 and running costs are estimated at ₹ 6,000 for each of the first four years, increasing by ₹ 2,000 per year in the fifth and subsequent years. If the money is worth 10 per cent per year, when should the truck be replaced. Assume that the truck will eventually be sold for scrap at a negligible price. **[Ans.** After 9 years]

6. The following mortality rates have been observed for a certain type of light bulb.

Week	1	2	3	4	5	6
Per cent failing by the end of week	0.09	0.25	0.49	0.85	0.97	1.00

There are 1,000 bulbs and it costs ₹ 3 to replace an individual bulb, but if all the bulbs are replaced in the same operation it would be done for ₹ 0.70 a bulb. If group replacement policy is followed, (*a*) What is the best interval between the group replacements?

(*b*) At what group replacement cost per bulb would a policy of strictly individual replacement become preferable to the adopted policy?

$$\left[\textbf{Hint: } \text{Rs. } 897 < \frac{1000x + 3(90+108)}{2}\right]$$

[**Ans.** (*a*) Optimal replacement period is after every 2nd week.
(*b*) Let *x* be the group replacement price per bulb, $x >$ ₹ 1.02]

7. A computer contains 10,000 resistors. When any one of the resistor fails, it is replaced. The cost of replacing a single resistor is ₹ 1 only. If all resistors are replaced at the same time, the cost per resistor would be reduced to 35 paise. The per cent surviving by the end of month *t* is as follows.

Month	*1*	*2*	*3*	*4*	*5*	*6*	*7*
% Surviving by the end of month	100	97	90	70	30	15	0

What is the optimum plan?

[**Ans.** Group replacement optimal interval is 3rd month; Group replacement policy is preferable]

8. The following failure rates have been observed for a certain type of light bulb.

Month	*1*	*2*	*3*	*4*	*5*	*6*	*7*
Probability failure to date	0.05	0.15	0.25	0.46	0.68	0.88	1.00

The replacement of an individual bulb on failure costs ₹ 1.25. The cost of group replacement is 80 paise per bulb. Determine the better one among the individual and group replacement policies.

[**Ans.** End of 3rd week, group replacement is preferable]

9. There are 1,000 bulbs in the system. Survival rate is given below.

Week	*0*	*1*	*2*	*3*	*4*
Bulbs in operation at the end of the week	1000	850	500	200	00

The group replacement of 100 bulbs costs ₹ 1 and individual replacement costs ₹ 0.50 per bulb. Suggest a suitable replacement policy.

[**Ans.** Group replacement policy]

SUMMARY

Replacement of Items that Deteriorate with Time

Case I: Value of money does not change with time.

C : Capital cost of equipment

S : Scrap value or resale value of an equipment

N : Number of years the equipment would be in use

$F(t)$: Maintenance cost function

$A(n)$: Average total annual cost

$$T_C = \text{Capital cost} - \text{Scrap value} + \text{Maintenance cost}$$

$$= C - S + \int_0^n F(t)dt.$$

Average annual total cost $A(n) = \frac{1}{n} T_C = \frac{C-S}{n} + \frac{1}{n}\int_0^n F(t)dt$

Case II: Value of money changes with time.

***Present worth factor* (PWF)** If r is the rate of interest then $(1+r)^{-n}$ is called the present worth factor or present value of one rupee spent in n years from now. The expression $(1+r)^{-n}$ is known as the *payment compound amount factor* (CAF) of one rupee spent in the n years duration.

Discount rate The present worth factor of unit amount to be spent after one year is given by $V = (1+r)^{-1}$, where r is called the *rate of interest* and V is called the *discount rate*.

To Find the Optimal Replacement Policy

The expression for weighted average cost is given by,

$$W(n) = \frac{C + R_0 + VR_1 + V^2 R_2 + ... + V^{n-1} R_{n-1}}{1 + V + V^2 + ... + V^{n-1}}$$

Selection of Best Equipment

Step 1 Considering the case of 2 equipment A and B, we first find the replacement age for both the equipment by making use of

$$R_{n-1} < W(n) < R_n.$$

Let n_1, n_2 be the replacement ages for the equipment A and B respectively.

Step 2 Next, we find the weighted average cost for each equipment. Substitute $n = n_1$ for equipment A and $n = n_2$ for equipment B.

Step 3 (*i*) If $W(n_1) < W(n_2)$, choose equipment A.

(*ii*) If $W(n_1) > W(n_2)$, choose equipment B.

(*iii*) If $W(n_1) = W(n_2)$, both equipments are equally good.

Replacement of Equipment that Fails Suddenly

(i) Individual replacement policy Under this policy, an item is replaced immediately after it fails.

(ii) Group replacement policy

Group replacement must be made at the end of tth period, if the cost of individual replacements for the tth period is greater than the average cost per period, through the end of t period.

Group replacement is not possible at the end of period t, if the cost of individual replacement at the $t-1$ end period is less than the average cost per period, through the end of t period.

Chapter

18

Queueing Theory

18.1 INTRODUCTION

A flow of customers from finite/infinite population towards the service facility forms a *queue* (waiting line), on account of a lack of capability to serve them all at a time. In the absence of a perfect balance between the service facilities and the customers, waiting time is required either for the service facilities or for the customer's arrival.

The arriving unit that requires some services to be performed is called *customer*. The customer may be persons, machines, vehicles, etc. Queue (waiting line) stands for the number of customers waiting to be serviced. This does not include the customers being serviced. The process or system that provides services to the customers is termed as service channel or service facility.

18.2 QUEUEING SYSTEM

A queueing system can be completely described by:

(*i*) the input (arrival pattern)
(*ii*) the service mechanism (service pattern)
(*iii*) the queue discipline
(*iv*) customer's behaviour

18.2.1 The Input (Arrival Pattern)

Input describes the way in which the customers arrive and join the system. Generally, customers arrive in a more or less random fashion, which is not possible to predict. Thus, the arrival pattern can be described in terms of probabilities, and consequently, the probability distribution for inter-arrival times (the time between two successive arrivals) must be defined. We deal with those queueing systems in which the customers arrive in Poisson fashion. The mean arrival rate is denoted by λ.

18.2.2 The Service Mechanism

This means, the arrangement of service facility to serve customers. If there is an infinite number of servers, then all the customers are served instantaneously on arrival, and there will be no queue.

If the number of servers is finite then the customers are served according to a specific order, with service time as a constant or random variable. Distribution of service time that is important in practice is the *negative exponential distribution*. The mean service rate is denoted by m.

18.2.3 The Queue Discipline

It is a rule according to which the customers are selected for service when a queue has been formed. The most common disciplines are:

- First come first served (FCFS)
- First in first out (FIFO)
- Last in first out (LIFO)
- Selection for service in random order (SIRO).

There are various other disciplines according to which a customer is served in preference over the others. Under priority discipline, the service is of two types, namely pre emptive and non-pre emptive. In pre-emptive system, the high priority customers are given service over the low priority customers; in non-pre-emptive system, a customer of low priority is serviced before a customer of high priority. In the case of parallel channels 'fastest server rule' is adopted.

18.2.4 Customer's Behaviour

The customers generally behave in the following four ways:

***(i)* Balking** A customer who leaves the queue because the queue is too long and he has no time to wait or does not have sufficient waiting space.

***(ii)* Reneging** This occurs when a waiting customer leaves the queue due to impatience.

***(iii)* Priorities** In certain applications some customers are served before others, regardless of their arrival. These customers have priority over others.

***(iv)* Jockeying** Customers may jockey from one waiting line to another. This is most common in a supermarket.

Transient and steady states A system is said to be in a *transient state* when its operating characteristics are dependent on time.

A steady state system is the one in which the behaviour of the system is independent of time. Let $P_n(t)$ denote the probability that there are n customers in the system, at time t. Then in steady state,

$$\lim_{t\to\infty} p_n(t) = p_n \quad \text{(independent of } t\text{)}$$

$$\Rightarrow \quad \frac{dp_n(t)}{dt} = \frac{dp_n}{dt}$$

$$\Rightarrow \quad \lim_{t\to\infty} p_n'(t) = 0$$

Traffic intensity (or utilization factor) An important measure of a simple queue is its traffic intensity given by,

$$\text{Traffic intensity } \rho = \frac{\text{Mean arrival rate}}{\text{Mean service rate}} = \frac{\lambda}{\mu}$$

The unit of traffic intensity is *Erlang*.

18.3 KENDALL'S NOTATION FOR REPRESENTING QUEUEING MODELS

Generally, queueing model may be completely specified in the following symbol form $(a/b/c):(d/e)$ where,

a = probability law for the arrival (inter-arrival) time
b = probability law according to which the customers are being served
c = number of channels (or service stations)
d = capacity of the system, i.e., the maximum number allowed in the system (in service and waiting)
e = queue discipline

18.4 CLASSIFICATION OF QUEUEING MODELS

The queueing models are classified as follows:

Model I: (M/M/1): (∞ /FCFS): This denotes Poisson arrival (exponential inter-arrival), Poisson departure (exponential service time), Single server, Infinite capacity and First come first served service discipline. The letter *M* is used due to Markovian property of exponential process.

Model II: (M/M/1): (N/FCFS): In this model, the capacity of the system is limited (finite), say *N*. Obviously, the number of arrivals will not exceed the number *N* in any case.

Model III: Multiservice Model (M/M/S):(∞/FCFS): This model takes the number of service channels as *S*.

Model IV: (M/M/S): (N/FCFS): This model is essentially the same as model II, except the maximum number of customers in the system is limited to *N*, where, $(N > S)$.

18.4.1 Model I: (M/M/I) (∞/FCFS) (Birth and Death Model)

To obtain the steady state equations: The probability that there will be n units $(n > 0)$ in the system at time $(t + \Delta t)$, may be expressed as the sum of three independent compound probabilities by using the fundamental properties of probability, Poisson arrivals and exponential service times.

The following are the three cases:

Time (t) *No. of units*	*Arrival*	*Service*	*Time (t + Δt)* *No. of units*
$n-1$	0	0	n
$n-1$	1	0	n
$n+1$	0	1	n

Now, by adding the above three independent compound probabilities, we obtain the probability of n units in the system at time $(t + \Delta t)$.

$$P_n(t+\Delta t) = P_n(t)(1-(\lambda+\mu)\Delta t) + P_{n-1}(t)\,\lambda\,\Delta t + P_{n+1}(t)\mu\Delta t + 0(\Delta t)$$

$$\frac{P_n(t+\Delta t)-P_n(t)}{\Delta t} = -(\lambda+\mu)P_n(t) + \lambda P_{n-1}(t) + \mu P_{n+1}(t) + \frac{0(\Delta t)}{\Delta t}$$

$$\underset{\Delta t\to 0}{Lt}\frac{P_n(t+\Delta t)-P_n(t)}{\Delta t} = \underset{\Delta t\to 0}{Lt}\left[-(\lambda+\mu)P_n(t)+\lambda P_{n-1}(t)+\mu P_{n+1}(t)+\frac{0\Delta(t)}{\Delta t}\right]$$

$$\frac{dP_n(t)}{dt} = -(\lambda+\mu)P_n(t) + \lambda P_{n-1}(t) + \mu P_{n+1}(t)$$

where, $n > 0$ $\left(\because \underset{\Delta t\to 0}{Lt}\frac{0\Delta(t)}{\Delta t} = 0\right)$

In the steady state,

$$P_n(t) \to 0, P_n(t) = P_n$$

$$\boxed{0 = -(\lambda+\mu)P_n + \lambda P_{n-1} + \mu P_{n+1}} \quad (1)$$

In a similar fashion, the probability that there will be n units (i.e., $n = 0$) in the system at time $(t + \Delta t)$, will be the sum of the following two independent probabilities.

(*i*) Probability (that there is no unit in the system at time *t* and no arrival in time Δt)

$$= P_0(t)(1 - \lambda\Delta t)$$

(*ii*) Probability (that there is one unit in the system at time *t*, one unit serviced in Δt and no arrival in Δt)

$$= P_i(t)\mu\Delta t(1 - \lambda\Delta t)$$

$$= P_i(t)\mu\Delta t - 0(\Delta t)$$

Adding these two probabilities,

$$P_0(t - \Delta t) = P_0(t)(1 - \lambda\Delta t) + P_1(t)\mu\Delta t + 0(\Delta t)$$

$$\frac{P_0(t+\Delta t) - P_0(t)}{\Delta t} = -\lambda P_0(t) + \mu P_1(t) + \frac{0(\Delta t)}{\Delta t}$$

$$\underset{\Delta t \to 0}{Lt} \frac{P_0(t+\Delta t) - P_0(t)}{\Delta t} = -\lambda P_0(t) + \mu P_1(t) \quad \text{for } n = 0$$

$$\frac{dP_0(t)}{d(t)} = -\lambda P_0(t) + \mu P_1(t)$$

Under steady state, we have,

$$\boxed{0 = -\lambda P_0 + \mu P_1} \qquad (2)$$

Equations (1) and (2) are called *steady state difference equations* for this model.

From (2), $$P_1 = \frac{\lambda}{\mu} P_0$$

From (1), $$P_2 = \frac{\lambda}{\mu} P_1 = \left(\frac{\lambda}{\mu}\right)^2 P_0$$

Generally, $$P_n = \left(\frac{\lambda}{\mu}\right)^n P_0$$

Since, $$\sum_{n=0}^{\infty} P_n = 1$$

$\Rightarrow$ $$P_0 + \frac{\lambda}{\mu} P_0 + \left(\frac{\lambda}{\mu}\right)^2 P_0 + \ldots = 1$$

$$P_0\left[1 + \frac{\lambda}{\mu} + \left(\frac{\lambda}{\mu}\right)^2 + \ldots\right] = 1$$

i.e., $$P_0\left(\frac{1}{1 - \frac{\lambda}{\mu}}\right) = 1$$

Since, $\frac{\lambda}{\mu} < 1$, sum of infinite G.P. is valid.

$$P_0 = 1 - \frac{\lambda}{\mu} = 1 - \rho$$

Also,
$$P_n = \left(\frac{\lambda}{\mu}\right)^n P_0 = \left(\frac{\lambda}{\mu}\right)^n \left(1 - \frac{\lambda}{\mu}\right)$$

$$P_n = \rho^n (1 - \rho)$$

Measures of Model I

1. Expected (average) number of units in the system L_S.

$$L_S = \sum_{n=1}^{\infty} nP_n$$

$$= \sum_{n=1}^{\infty} n\left(\frac{\lambda}{\mu}\right)^n \left(1 - \frac{\lambda}{\mu}\right)$$

$$= \left(1 - \frac{\lambda}{\mu}\right)\frac{\lambda}{\mu}\sum_{n=1}^{\infty} n\left(\frac{\lambda}{\mu}\right)^{n-1}$$

$$= \left(1 - \frac{\lambda}{\mu}\right)\frac{\lambda}{\mu}\left(1 + 2\left(\frac{\lambda}{\mu}\right) + 3\left(\frac{\lambda}{\mu}\right)^2 + \ldots\right)$$

$$= \left(1 - \frac{\lambda}{\mu}\right)\left(\frac{\lambda}{\mu}\right)\left(1 - \frac{\lambda}{\mu}\right)^{-2}$$

$$= \frac{\frac{\lambda}{\mu}}{1 - \frac{\lambda}{\mu}} = \frac{\rho}{1 - \rho}, \rho = \frac{\lambda}{\mu} < 1.$$

$$\boxed{L_S = \frac{\rho}{1 - \rho}}$$

2. Expected (average) queue length L_q.

$$L_q = L_s - \frac{\lambda}{\mu} = \frac{\rho^2}{1 - \rho}$$

$$\boxed{L_q = \frac{\rho^2}{1 - \rho}}$$

3. Expected waiting line in the queue,

$$\boxed{W_q = \frac{\lambda}{\mu(\mu - \lambda)} = \frac{\rho}{1 - \rho}}$$

4. Expected waiting line in the system,

$$W_S = W_q + \frac{1}{\mu}$$

$$= \frac{\lambda}{\mu(\mu-\lambda)} + \frac{1}{\mu} = \frac{1}{\mu-\lambda}$$

$$\boxed{W_S = \frac{1}{\mu-\lambda}}$$

5. Expected waiting time of a customer who has to wait $(W/W>0)$

$$\boxed{(W/W>0) = \frac{1}{\mu-\lambda} = \frac{1}{\mu(1-\rho)}}$$

6. Expected length of non-empty queue,

$$(L/L>0) = \frac{\mu}{\mu-\lambda} = \frac{1}{1-\rho}$$

7. Probability of queue size $\geq N = \rho^N$

$$= \int_t^{\infty} \rho(\mu-\lambda)e^{-(\mu-\lambda)W}\,dW$$

8. Probability of waiting time in the queue $\geq t$

$$= \int_t^{\infty} \lambda(1-\lambda)e^{-(\mu-\lambda)W}\,dW$$

9. Probability (waiting time in the system $\geq t$)

$$= \int_t^{\infty} \rho(\mu-\lambda)e^{-(\mu-\lambda)W}\,dW$$

10. Traffic intensity, $\rho = \frac{\lambda}{\mu}$

Inter-relationship between L_S, L_q, W_S, W_q (Littles formula)

We know,

$$L_S = \frac{\frac{\lambda}{\mu}}{1-\frac{\lambda}{\mu}} = \frac{\lambda}{\mu-\lambda}$$

$$W_S = \frac{1}{\mu-\lambda}$$

$\therefore$ $\boxed{L_s = \lambda W_s}$

Similarly, $L_q = \lambda W_q$ hold in general,

$$W_q = \frac{\lambda}{\mu(\mu-\lambda)}$$

$$W_S = \frac{1}{\mu-\lambda}$$

$$\therefore \quad W_S - \frac{1}{\mu} = \frac{1}{\mu-\lambda} - \frac{1}{\mu} = \frac{\mu-(\mu-\lambda)}{\mu(\mu-\lambda)} = \frac{\lambda}{\mu(\mu-\lambda)}$$

$$\therefore \quad W_q = W_S - \frac{1}{\mu}$$

Multiplying both sides by λ, we have,

$$\lambda W_q = \lambda\left(W_S - \frac{1}{\mu}\right)$$

$$L_q = \lambda W_S - \frac{\lambda}{\mu} = L_S - \frac{\lambda}{\mu}$$

$$\boxed{L_q = L_S - \frac{\lambda}{\mu}}$$

Example 18.1 A T.V. mechanic finds that the time spent on his jobs has an exponential distribution with mean 30 minutes, if he repairs sets in the order in which they come in. If the arrival of sets is approximately Poisson with an average rate of 10 per eight-hour day, what is the mechanic's expected idle time each day? How many jobs are ahead of the average set just brought in?

Solution

Here, $\mu = 1/30, \quad \lambda = \dfrac{10}{8\times 60} = \dfrac{1}{48}$

Expected number of jobs are,

$$L_S = \frac{\frac{\lambda}{\mu}}{1-\frac{\lambda}{\mu}} = \frac{\lambda}{\mu-\lambda}$$

$$= \frac{\frac{1}{48}}{1/30 - 1/48} = 1\frac{2}{3} \text{ jobs.}$$

Since the fraction of the time the machanic is busy equals to $\dfrac{\lambda}{\mu}$, the number of hours for which the repairman remains busy in an eight-hour day,

$$= 8\left(\frac{\lambda}{\mu}\right) = 8 \times \frac{30}{48} = 5 \text{ hours}$$

Therefore, the time for which the machanic remains idle in an eight-hour day = (8 – 5) hours = 3 hours.

Example 18.2 At what average rate must a clerk at a supermarket work, in order to insure a probability of 0.90 that the customers will not have to wait longer than 12 minutes? It is assumed that there is only one counter, to which customers arrive in a Poisson fashion at an average rate of 15 per hour. The length of service by the clerk has an exponential distribution.

Solution

Here, $\lambda = \dfrac{15}{60} = \dfrac{1}{4}$ customer/minute $\mu = ?$

Prob. (waiting time ≥ 12) $= 1 - 0.9 = 0.10$

$$\int_t^{\infty} \lambda(1-\lambda)e^{-(\mu-\lambda)\omega}\, d\omega$$

$$\therefore \quad \int_{12}^{\infty} \lambda\left(1-\frac{\mu}{\lambda}\right)e^{-(\mu-\lambda)\omega}\, d\omega = 0.1$$

$$\lambda\left(1-\frac{\mu}{\lambda}\right)\left(\frac{e^{-(\mu-\lambda)\omega}}{-(\mu-\lambda)}\right)_{12}^{\infty} = 0.1$$

$$\frac{\lambda}{\mu}(e^{-12(\mu-\lambda}) = 0.10$$

$$e^{(3-12\mu)} = 0.4\mu$$

$$\frac{1}{\mu} = 2.48 \text{ minutes per service.}$$

Example 18.3 Arrivals at a telephone booth are considered to be Poisson, with an average time of 10 minutes between one arrival and the next. The length of a phone call is assumed to be distributed exponentially with mean three minutes.

(*i*) What is the probability that a person arriving at the booth will have to wait?

(*ii*) What is the average length of the queue that forms from time to time?

(*iii*) The telephone department will install a second booth when convinced that an arrival would have to wait at least three minutes for the phone. By how much time must the flow of arrivals be increased in order to justify a second booth?

Solution

Given, $\lambda = 1/10$, $\mu = 1/3$

(*i*) Probability $(w > 0) = 1 - P_0 = \frac{\lambda}{\mu} = \frac{1}{10} \times \frac{3}{1} = 3/10 = 0.3$

(*ii*) $(L/L > 0) = \frac{\mu}{\mu - \lambda} = \frac{1/3}{1/3 - 1/10} = 1.43$ persons

(*iii*) $W_q = \frac{\lambda}{\mu(\mu - \lambda)}$

Since, $W_q = 3,\ \mu = \frac{1}{3},\ \lambda = \lambda'$ for second booth,

$$3 = \frac{\lambda'}{\frac{1}{3}\left(\frac{1}{3} - \lambda'\right)} \Rightarrow \lambda' = 0.16$$

Hence, increase in the arrival rate = 0.16 – 0.10 = 0.06 arrival per minute.

Example 18.4 As in example 18.3, in a telephone booth with Poisson arrivals spaced 10 minutes apart on the average and exponential call length averaging three minutes.

(*i*) What is the probability that an arrival will have to wait for more than 10 minutes before the phone becomes free?

(*ii*) What is the probability that it will take him more than 10 minutes in total to wait for the phone and complete his call?

(*iii*) Estimate the fraction of a day that the phone will be in use.

(*iv*) Find the average number of units in the system.

Solution Given,

$$n\lambda = 0.1 \text{ arrival/minute}$$

$$\mu = 0.33 \text{ service/minute}$$

(*i*) Probability (waiting time ≥ 10) $= \int_{10}^{\infty} \left(1 - \frac{\lambda}{\mu}\right) \lambda e^{-(\mu-\lambda)W} \, dW$

$$= -\frac{\lambda}{\mu}\left(e^{-(\mu-\lambda)\omega}\right)_{10}^{\infty}$$

$$= 0.3\, e^{-2.3} = 0.03$$

(*ii*) Probability (waiting time in the system ≥ 10)

$$= \int_{10}^{\infty} (\mu - \lambda)_e^{-(\mu-\lambda)W} \, dW$$

$$= e^{-10(\mu-\lambda)} = e^{-2.3} = 10$$

(*iii*) The fraction of a day that the phone will be busy = traffic intensity

$$\rho = \frac{\lambda}{\mu} = 0.3.$$

(*iv*) Average number of units in the system,

$$L_S = \frac{\lambda}{\mu - \lambda} = \frac{\frac{1}{10}}{\frac{1}{3} - \frac{1}{10}} = 3/7 = 0.43 \text{ customer.}$$

Example 18.5 Customers arrive at a one-window drive-in bank according to Poisson distribution with mean 10 per hour. Service time per customer is exponential with mean five minutes. The space in front of the window including that for the serviced car can accommodate a maximum of three cars. Others can wait outside this space.

(*i*) What is the probability that an arriving customer can drive directly to the space in front of the window?

(*ii*) What is the probability that an arriving customer will have to wait outside the indicated space?

(*iii*) How long is an arriving customer expected to wait before starting service?

Solution Given,

$$\lambda = 10 \text{ per hour}$$

$$\mu = \frac{1}{5} \times 60 = 12 \text{ per hour}$$

$$\rho = \frac{\lambda}{\mu} = \frac{10}{12}$$

(*i*) The probability that an arriving customer can drive directly to the space in front of the window,

$$P_0 + P_1 + P_2 = P_0 + \frac{\lambda}{\mu} P_0 + \left(\frac{\lambda}{\mu}\right)^2 P_0$$

$$= P_0 \left(1 + \frac{\lambda}{\mu} + \left(\frac{\lambda}{\mu}\right)^2\right)$$

$$= \left(1-\frac{\lambda}{\mu}\right)\left(1+\frac{\lambda}{\mu}+\left(\frac{\lambda}{\mu}\right)^2\right) \quad \because \quad P_0 = 1-\frac{\lambda}{\mu}$$

$$= \left(1-\frac{10}{12}\right)\left(1+\frac{10}{12}+\frac{100}{144}\right) = 0.42$$

(*ii*) Probability that an arriving customer will have to wait outside the indicated space,

$$S = 1-0.42 = 0.58$$

(*iii*) Average waiting time of a customer in a queue,

$$= \frac{\lambda}{\mu}\frac{1}{\mu-\lambda} = \frac{10}{12}\left(\frac{1}{12-10}\right) = \frac{5}{12}$$

$$= 0.417 \text{ hours.}$$

Example 18.6 In a supermarket, the average arrival rate of customers is 10 every 30 minutes, following Poisson process. The average time taken by a cashier to list and calculate the customer's purchase is two and a half minutes following exponential distribution. What is the probability that the queue length exceeds six? What is the expected time spent by a customer in the system?

Solution

$$\lambda = \frac{10}{30} \text{ per minute}$$

$$\mu = \frac{1}{2.5} \text{ per minute}$$

$$\rho = \frac{\lambda}{\mu} = \frac{\frac{1}{3}}{1/2.5} = 0.8333$$

(*i*) The probability of queue size $> 6 = \rho^6$

Expected waiting time $\quad W_S = \frac{1}{\mu-\lambda} = (0.8333)^6 = 0.3348.$

(*ii*)

$$W_S = \frac{L_S}{\lambda} = \frac{\frac{\rho}{1-\rho}}{\lambda} = \frac{0.833}{1-0.8333} \times 3$$

$$= 14.96 \text{ minutes.}$$

Example 18.7 On an average, 96 patients per 24-hour day require the service of an emergency clinic. Also, on an average a patient requires 10 minutes of active attention. Assume that the facility can handle only one emergency at a time. Suppose that it costs the clinic ₹ 100 per patient treated, to obtain an average servicing time of 10 minutes and thus, each minute of decrease in this average time would cost ₹ 10 per patient treated. How much would have to be budgeted by the clinic to decrease the average size of the queue from $1\frac{1}{3}$ patients to $\frac{1}{2}$ patients?

Solution

Given, $\quad \lambda = \frac{96}{24 \times 60} = \frac{1}{15}$ patient/minute

$$\mu = \frac{1}{10} \text{ patient/minute}$$

Average number of patients in the queue,

$$L_q = \frac{\lambda}{\mu}\frac{\lambda}{\lambda-\mu} = \frac{\left(\frac{\lambda}{\mu}\right)^2}{1-\frac{\lambda}{\mu}}$$

$$= \frac{\left(\frac{1}{15}\right)^2}{\left(\frac{1}{10}-\frac{1}{15}\right)\frac{1}{10}} = 1\frac{1}{3} \text{ patients}$$

But, $L_q = 1\frac{1}{3}$ is reduced to $L_q' = 1/2$

$\therefore$ Substituting $L_q' = 1/2, \lambda' = \lambda = \frac{1}{15}$ in the formula

$$L_q' = \frac{\lambda^{12}}{\mu'(\mu'-\lambda')}$$

$$\frac{1}{2} = \frac{\left(\frac{1}{15}\right)^2}{\mu'(\mu'-1/15)} \Rightarrow \mu' = 2/15 \text{ patients/minute}$$

Hence, the average rate of treatment required is, $\frac{1}{\mu'} = 7.5$ minutes. Decrease in time required by each patient

$$= 10 - \frac{15}{2} = \frac{5}{2} \text{ minutes}$$

$\therefore$ The budget required for each patient

$$= 100 + \frac{5}{2} \times 10 = ₹125$$

So, in order to get the required size of the queue, the budget should be increased from ₹ 100 to ₹ 125 per patient.

Example 18.8 In a public telephone booth, the arrivals on an average are 15 per hour. A call on an average takes three minutes. If there is just one phone, find (*i*) the expected number of callers in the booth at any time (*ii*) the proportion of the time, the booth is expected to be idle?

Solution

Given, $\lambda = 15$ per hour

$$\mu = \frac{1}{3} \times 60 \text{ per hour}$$

(*i*) Expected length of the non-empty queue

$$= \frac{\mu}{\mu-\lambda} = \frac{20}{20-15} = 4$$

(ii) The service is busy $= \frac{\lambda}{\mu} = \frac{15}{20} = \frac{3}{4}$

$\therefore$ the booth is expected to be idle for $1 - \frac{3}{4} = \frac{1}{4}$ hours = 15 minutes.

Example 18.9 In a railway marshalling yard, goods trains arrive at a rate of 30 trains per day. Assuming that inter-arrival time and service time distribution follows an exponential distribution with an average of 30 minutes, calculate the following.

(i) The mean queue size.
(ii) The probability that queue size exceeds 10.
(iii) If the input of the train increases to an average of 33 per day, what will be the changes in (i) and (ii)?

Solution

Given, $\lambda = \frac{30}{60 \times 24} = \frac{1}{48}$ trains/minute

$$\mu = \frac{1}{30} \text{ trains/minute}$$

$$\rho = \frac{\lambda}{\mu} = \frac{30}{48} = \frac{5}{8}$$

(i) $L_S = \frac{\rho}{1-\rho} = \frac{5/8}{1-5/8} = \frac{5/8}{3/8} = \frac{5}{3} = 1.66$ trains = 2 trains (app.)

(ii) $P(\geq 10) = (0.75)^{10} = 0.056$

(iii) When the input increases to 33 trains per day,

we have, $\lambda = \frac{33}{60 \times 24} = \frac{11}{480}, \mu = \frac{1}{30}$ trains/min

$\Rightarrow$ $L_S = \frac{\rho}{1-\rho}$ where, $\rho = \frac{\lambda}{\mu} = \frac{11}{16}$

$$L_S = \frac{11/16}{5/16} = \frac{11}{5} = 2.1 \text{ trains}$$

also, $\rho(\geq 10) = \rho^{10} = \left(\frac{11}{16}\right)^{10} = 0.1460.$

EXERCISES

1. People arrive at a theatre ticket centre in a Poisson distributed arrival rate of 25 per hour. Service time is constant at two minutes. Calculate,

   (i) the mean number in the waiting line.
   (ii) the mean waiting time.
   (iii) utilization factor.

   [Ans. (i) 4 people, (ii) 10 minutes, (iii) r = 0.833]

2. At a one-man barber shop, customers arrive according to Poisson distribution, with a mean arrival rate of five per hour and the hair cutting time was exponentially distributed with an average hair cut taking 10 minutes. It is assumed that because of his excellent reputation, customers were always willing to wait. Calculate the following—

   (*i*) Average number of customers in the shop and the average number waiting for a hair cut.
   (*ii*) The per cent of time, an arrival can walk right in without having to wait.
   (*iii*) The percentage of customers who have to wait before getting into the barber's chair.

   [**Ans.** (*i*) 4.8, (*ii*) 83.3%, (*iii*) 16.7%]

3. Cars arrive at a petrol pump with exponential inter-arrival time having mean $\frac{1}{2}$ minute. The attendant on an average takes $\frac{1}{5}$ minute per car to supply petrol. The service time being exponentially distributed, determine,

   (*i*) the average number of cars waiting to be served.
   (*ii*) the average number of cars in the queue.
   (*iii*) the proportion of time, for which the pump attendant is idle.

   [**Ans.** (*i*) 2 cars, (*ii*) 4/3 cars, (*iii*) 0.34]

4. The mean arrival rate to a service centre is three per hour. The mean service time is found to be 10 minutes per service. Assuming Poisson arrival and exponential service time, find,

   (*i*) the utilization factor for this service facility.
   (*ii*) the probability of two units in the system.
   (*iii*) the expected number of units in the system.
   (*iv*) the expected time in minutes that a customer has to spend in the system.

   [**Ans.** (*i*) 1/2, (*ii*) 1/8, (*iii*) 1, (*iv*) 1/3]

5. At a public telephone booth in a post office, arrivals are considered to be Poisson, with an average inter-arrival time of 12 minutes. The length of the phone call may be assumed to be distributed exponentially with an average of four minutes. Calculate the following.

   (*i*) What is the probability that a fresh arrival will not have to wait for the phone?
   (*ii*) What is the probability that an arrival will have to wait more than 10 minutes before the phone is free?
   (*iii*) What is the average length of the queue that forms from time to time?

   [**Ans.** (*i*) = 0.67, (*ii*) = 0.063, (*iii*) = 1.5]

6. Consider a self-service store with one cashier. Assume Poisson arrivals and exponential service time. Assuming nine customers arrive on the average of every five minutes and the cashier can serve 10 of them in five minutes, find,

   (*i*) (*a*) the average number of customers queueing for service.
   (*b*) the average time a customer spends in the system.
   (*c*) the average time a customer waits before being served.
   (*ii*) the probability of having more than 10 customers in the system.
   (*iii*) the probability that a customer has to queue for more than 20 minutes. If the service can be increased up to 12 in every five minutes by using a different cash register, what will be the effect on the quantities (*a*), (*b*) and (*c*).

   [**Ans.** Case (*i*) (*a*) 3 customers; (*b*) $P(\geq 10) = (0.9)^{10}$; (*c*) $P(W \geq 2) = 0.67$.
   Case (*ii*) (*a*) 3 customers; (*b*) $P(\geq 10) = (0.75)^{10}$; (*c*) $P(W \geq 2) = 0.3$]

18.4.2 MODEL II (M/M/1): (N/FCFS)

This model differs from model I in the sense that, the maximum number of customers in the system is limited to *N*. Therefore, the difference equations of model I are valid for this model as long as $n < N$. Arrivals will not exceed *N* in any case. The various measures of this model are,

1. $P_0 = \dfrac{1-\rho}{1-\rho^{N+1}}$ where, $\rho = \dfrac{\lambda}{\mu}\left(\dfrac{\lambda}{\mu} > 1 \text{ is allowed}\right)$ 2. $P_N = \dfrac{1-\rho}{1-\rho^{N+1}}\rho^n$, for $n = 0, 1, 2, \ldots N$

3. $L_q = \dfrac{\lambda}{\mu}$ 4. $L_S = \rho_0 \sum_{n=0}^{N} n\rho^n$

5. $L_q = L_S - \dfrac{\lambda}{\mu}$ 6. $W_S = L_S/\lambda$

7. $W_q = L_q/\lambda$

Example 18.10 In a railway marshalling yard, goods trains arrive at the rate of 30 trains per day. Assume that the inter-arrival time follows an exponential distribution and the service time is also to be assumed as exponential with mean of 36 minutes.Calculate,

(*i*) the probability that the yard is empty.
(*ii*) the average queue length, assuming that the line capacity of the yard is nine trains.

Solution for model II

Given,
$$\lambda = \frac{30}{60 \times 24} = \frac{1}{48}, \quad \mu = \frac{1}{36} \text{ trains per minute}$$
$$\rho = \frac{\lambda}{\mu} = \frac{36}{48} = 0.75$$

(*i*) The probability that the queue is empty is given by,
$$P_0 = \frac{1-\rho}{1-\rho^{N+1}} \quad \text{where } N = 9$$
$$= \frac{1-0.75}{1-(0.75)^{9+1}} = \frac{0.25}{0.90} = 0.28.$$

(*ii*) Average queue length is given by,
$$L_s = \frac{1-\rho}{1-\rho^{N+1}} \sum_{n=0}^{N} n\rho^n$$
$$= \frac{1-0.75}{1-(0.75)^{10}} \sum_{n=0}^{9} n(0.75)^n$$
$$= 0.28 \times 9.58 = 3 \text{ trains.}$$

Example 18.11 A barber shop has space to accommadate only 10 customers. He can serve only one person at a time. If a customer comes to his shop and finds it full, he goes to the next shop. Customers randomly arrive at an average rate $\lambda = 10$ per hour and the barber's service time is negative exponential with an average of $1/\mu = 5$ minutes per customer. Find P_0 and P_n.

Solution

Given,
$$N = 10, \lambda = \frac{10}{60}, \mu = \frac{1}{5}$$
$$\rho = \frac{\lambda}{\mu} = \frac{5}{6}$$

$$P_0 = \frac{1-\rho}{1-\rho^{11}} = \frac{1-5/6}{1-(5/6)^{11}}$$

$$= \frac{0.1667}{0.8655} = 0.1926$$

$$P_n = \left(\frac{1-\rho}{1-\rho^{n+1}}\right)\rho^n$$

$$= (0.1926) \times \left(\frac{5}{6}\right)^n \qquad [n=0, 1, 2, ... 10]$$

Example 18.12 A car park contains 5 cars. The arrival of cars is Poisson, at a mean rate of 10 per hour. The length of time each car spends in the car park is exponential distribution with mean of 0.5 hours. How many cars are in the car park on an average?

Solution

Given, $N = 5, \lambda = \frac{10}{60}, \mu = \frac{0.5}{60} = \frac{1}{2 \times 60}$

$$\rho = \frac{\lambda}{\mu} = 20$$

$$P_0 = \left(\frac{1-\rho}{1-\rho^{N+1}}\right) = \frac{1-20}{1-20^6} = \frac{-19}{-63999999}$$

$$= 2.9692 \times 10^{-7}$$

$$L_s = P_0 \sum_{n=0}^{N} nP^n = (2.9692 \times 10^{-7}) \sum_{n=0}^{5} n(2.9692 \times 10^{-7})^n$$

$$= 4 \text{ (approximately)}.$$

Example 18.13 Assuming for a period of two hours in a day (8–10 am), trains arrive at the yard every 20 minutes, then calculate for this period.

(*i*) The probability that the yard is empty.

(*ii*) Average queue length, assuming that the capacity of the yard is 4 trains only.

Solution

Given, $\rho = \frac{36}{20} = 1.8, \quad N=4$

(*i*) $\rho_0 = \frac{\rho - 1}{\rho^5 - 1} = 0.04$

(*ii*) Average queue size

$$= \rho_0 \sum_{n=0}^{4} n \cdot \rho^n$$

$$= 0.04(\rho + 2\rho^2 + 3\rho^3 + 4\rho^4) = 0.04\,(67.77) = 2.9 = 3 \text{ trains.}$$

EXERCISES

1. Patients arrive at a clinic according to a Poisson distribution at the rate of 30 patients per hour. The waiting room does not accommodate more than 14 patients. Examination time per patient is exponential with mean rate 20 per hour.
   (*i*) Find the effective arrival rate at the clinic.
   (*ii*) What is the probability that an arriving patient will not wait? Will he find a vacant seat in the room?
   (*iii*) What is the expected waiting time until a patient is discharged from the clinic?

   [Ans. (*i*) 19.98 (*ii*) 0.67 (*iii*) 0.65]

2. A stenographer has 5 persons for whom she performs stenographic work. Arrival rate is Poisson and service times are exponential. Average arrival rate is 4 per hour with an average service time of 10 minutes. Find,
   (*i*) the average waiting time of an arrival.
   (*ii*) the average length of waiting line.
   (*iii*) the average time on arrival spent in the system.

   [Ans. (*i*) 12.4 minutes (*ii*) 0.79 person (app.) (*iii*) 22.4 minutes]

3. Customers arrive at a one-window drive-in bank according to Poisson distribution with mean 10 per hour. Service time per customer is exponential with mean 5 minutes. The car space in front of the window, including that for the service, can accommodate a maximum of 3 cars. Other cars can wait outside this space.
   (*i*) What is the probability that an arriving customer can drive directly to the space in front of the window?
   (*ii*) What is the probability that an arriving customer will have to wait outside the indicated space?
   (*iii*) How long is an arriving customer expected to wait before starting the service?

   [Ans. (*i*) 0.42, (*ii*) 0.48 (*iii*) 0.417]

18.4.3 Model III: (Multiservice Model) (M/M/S): (∞/FCFS)

When there are n units in the system, difference equations may be obtained in the following two situations.

(*i*) if $n \leq s$, all the customers may be served simultaneously. There will be no queue. $(s-n)$ number of servers may remain idle and then,

$$\mu n = n\mu,\ n = 0, 1, 2, \ldots S;$$

(*ii*) if $n \geq s$, all the servers are busy, and the maximum number of customers waiting in queue will be $(n - s)$, then, $\mu_n = s_\mu$

Also, $\lambda_n = \lambda\ [n = 0, 1, 2 \ldots]$

The steady state difference equations are,

$$P_0(t+\Delta t) = P_0(t)(1-\lambda\Delta t) + P_1(t)\mu\Delta t + 0(\Delta t)$$

for $n = 0$

$$P_n(t+\Delta t) = P_n(t)[1-(\lambda+n\mu)\Delta t] + P_{n-1}(t)\lambda\Delta t$$
$$+ P_{n+1}(t)(n+1)\mu\Delta t + 0(\Delta t) \text{ for } n = 1, 2 \ldots S-1$$

$$P_n(t+\Delta t) = P_n(t)[1-(\lambda+S\mu)\Delta t] + P_{n-1}(t)\lambda\Delta t$$
$$+ P_{n+1}(t)S\mu\Delta t + 0(\Delta t) \text{ for } n = S, S+1, S+2 \ldots$$

Now, dividing these equations by Δt and taking limit as $\Delta t \to 0$, the difference equations are,

$$P_0^1(t) = -\lambda P_0(t) + \mu P_1(t) \text{ for } n = 0$$

$$P_n^1(t) = -(\lambda+n\mu)P_n(t) + \lambda P_{n-1}(t) + (n+1)\mu P_{n+1}(t)$$

for, $$n = 1, 2 \ldots S-1.$$

$$P_n^1(t) = -(\lambda + S\mu)P_n(t) + \lambda P_{n-1}(t) + S\mu P_{n+1}(t)$$

for, $$n = S, S+1, S+2 \ldots$$

Considering the case of steady state, i.e., when $t \to \infty$, $P_n(t) \to P_n$ and hence, $P_n{}^1(t) \to 0$ for all n, above equations become,

$$0 = -\lambda\, \rho_0 + \mu P_1 \text{ for } n = 0 \tag{1}$$

$$0 = -(\lambda + n\mu)P_n + \lambda P_{n-1} + (n+1)\mu P_{n+1} \tag{2}$$

$$\text{for, } 1 \le n \le S-1$$

$$0 = -(\lambda + S\mu)P_n + \lambda P_{n-1} + S\mu P_{n+1} \text{ for } n \le S \tag{3}$$

Here, $$P_0 = P_0 \text{ initially,}$$

$$P_1 = \frac{\lambda}{\mu} P_0 \text{ from (1)}$$

$$P_2 = \frac{\lambda}{2\mu} P_1 = \frac{\lambda^2}{2!\mu^2} P_0 \text{ (Put } n = 1 \text{ in (2))}$$

$$P_3 = \frac{\lambda}{3\mu} P_2 = \frac{\lambda^3}{3!\mu^3} P_0 \text{ (Put } n = 2 \text{ in (2))}$$

In general, $$\boxed{P_n = \frac{\lambda}{n\mu} P_{n-1} = \frac{1}{n!}\left(\frac{\lambda}{\mu}\right)^n P_0 \quad 1 \le n \le S}$$

$$P_S = \frac{\lambda}{S\mu} P_{S-1} = \frac{1}{S!}\left(\frac{\lambda}{\mu}\right)^S \cdot P_0$$

$$P_{S+1} = \frac{\lambda}{S\mu} P_S = \frac{1}{S}\frac{1}{S!}\left(\frac{\lambda}{\mu}\right)^{S+1} \cdot P_0$$

$$P_{S+2} = \frac{\lambda}{S\mu} P_{S+1} = \frac{1}{S^2}\frac{1}{S!}\left(\frac{\lambda}{\mu}\right)^{S+2} .P_0$$

In general, $$\boxed{P_n = P_{S+(n-S)} = \frac{1}{S^{n-S}}\frac{1}{S!}\left(\frac{\lambda}{\mu}\right)^n P_0 \quad n \ge S}$$

Now, find P_n using the fact,

$$\sum_{n=0}^{\infty} P_n = 1$$

i.e., $$\sum_{n=0}^{S-1} P_n + \sum_{n=S}^{\infty} P_n = 1$$

This gives the steady state distribution of arrivals (n) as,

$$P_n = \begin{cases} \dfrac{1}{n!}\left(\dfrac{\lambda}{\mu}\right)^n P_0, \; n = 0, 1, 2 \ldots S-1 \\ \dfrac{1}{S!}\dfrac{1}{S^{n-S}}\left(\dfrac{\lambda}{\mu}\right)^n P_0, \text{ if } n = S, S+1 \ldots \end{cases}$$

Measures of Model III

1. Length of the queue,

$$L_q = P_S \frac{\rho}{(1-\rho)^2}$$

$$\text{where, } P_S = \frac{\left(\dfrac{\lambda}{\mu}\right)^S P_0}{S!}$$

2. Length of the system,

$$L_S = \frac{\lambda}{\mu} + L_q$$

3. Waiting time in the queue,

$$W_q = \frac{L_q}{\lambda}$$

4. Waiting time in the system,

$$W_S = \frac{L_s}{\lambda}$$

5. The mean number of individuals who actually wait is given by,

$$L(L>0) = \frac{1}{1-\rho}$$

6. The mean waiting time in the queue for those who actually wait is given by $W(W>0)$,

$$= \frac{1}{S\mu - \lambda}$$

7. Probability $P\,(W>0) = \dfrac{P_S}{1-\rho}$

8. Probability that there will be someone waiting $= \dfrac{P_S\,\rho}{1-\rho}$

9. Average number of idle servers $= S -$ (Average number of customers served)

10. Efficiency of M/M/S model $= \dfrac{\text{Average number of customers served}}{\text{Total number of customers served}}$

Example 18.14 A supermarket has two girls ringing up sales at the counters. If the service time for each customer is exponential with mean four minutes and if people arrive in a Poisson fashion at the counter, at the rate of 10 per hour, then calculate,

(*i*) the probability of having to wait for service.
(*ii*) the expected percentage of idle time for each girl.
(*iii*) if a customer has to wait, find the expected length of his waiting time.

Solution

(*i*) Probability of waiting time for service is,

$$P(W>0) = \frac{\left(\frac{\lambda}{\mu}\right)^S}{S!(1-\rho)} P_0$$

$$\lambda = \frac{1}{6}, \mu = 1/4, S = 2$$

$$\rho = \frac{\lambda}{\mu S} = \frac{1}{3}$$

$$\rho_0 = \left[\sum_{n=0}^{S-1} \frac{(S\rho)^n}{n!} + \frac{(S\rho)^S}{S!(1-\rho)}\right]^{-1}$$

$$= \left[\sum_{n=0}^{1} \frac{\left(2 \cdot \frac{1}{3}\right)^n}{n!} + \frac{\left(2 \cdot \frac{1}{3}\right)^2}{2!(1-1/3)}\right]^{-1}$$

$$= 1 + 2/3 + \left[\frac{\frac{4}{9}}{2 \times 2/3}\right]^{-1} = \frac{1}{2}$$

$$\text{Thus, probability } (W>0) = \frac{(4/6)^2 \cdot \frac{1}{2}}{2!(1-1/3)} = 1/6$$

(*ii*) The fraction of the time the service remains busy,

(i.e., traffic intensity) is given by, $\rho = \dfrac{\lambda}{S\mu} = \dfrac{1}{3}$

$\therefore$ The fraction of the time the service remains idle is,

$$\left(1 - \frac{1}{3}\right) = \frac{2}{3} = 67\% \text{ (approximately)}$$

(*iii*) $(W/W>0) = \dfrac{1}{1-\rho} \cdot \dfrac{1}{S\mu} = \dfrac{1}{1-\frac{1}{3}} \cdot \dfrac{1}{2 \times \frac{1}{4}} = 3$ minutes.

Example 18.15 A petrol station has two pumps. The service time follows the exponential distribution with mean four minutes and cars arrive for service in a Poisson process at the rate of 10 cars per hour. Find the probability that a customer has to wait for service. What proportion of time do the pumps remain idle?

Solution

Given, $S = 2, \lambda = 10$ per hour

$$\mu = \frac{1}{4} \text{ per minute} = \frac{60}{4} = 15 \text{ per hour}$$

$$\rho = \frac{\lambda}{S\mu} = \frac{10}{2\times 15} = \frac{1}{3}$$

(*i*) Probability $\quad (W > 0) = \dfrac{P_S}{1-\rho}, P_S = \dfrac{\left(\dfrac{\lambda}{\mu}\right)^S}{S!} P_0$

where, $\quad P_0 = \left[\sum_{n=0}^{S-1} \dfrac{(S\rho)^n}{n!} + \dfrac{(S\rho)^S}{S!(1-\rho)}\right]^{-1}$

$$= \left[\sum_{n=0}^{1} \frac{(\rho S)^n}{n!} + \frac{(\rho S)^2}{2!(1-\rho)}\right]^{-1}$$

$$= \left[1 + \frac{(\rho S)^1}{1!} + \frac{(\rho S)^2}{2!(1-\rho)}\right]^{-1}$$

$$= \left[1 + \frac{1}{3}\times 2 + \frac{\left(\frac{1}{3}\cdot 2\right)}{2!\left(1-\frac{1}{3}\right)}\right]^{-1} = \frac{1}{2}$$

$$P(W > 0) = \frac{P_S}{1-\rho} = \frac{1}{1-\rho}\frac{\left(\frac{\lambda}{\mu}\right)^S}{S!} P_0$$

$$= \frac{1}{1-\frac{1}{3}}\left[\frac{\left(\frac{2}{3}\right)^2 \frac{1}{2}}{2!}\right] = \frac{1}{9}\times\frac{3}{2} = 0.167 \text{ (approximately)}.$$

(*ii*) The duration of time for which the pumps are busy $= \dfrac{\lambda}{S\mu} = \dfrac{1}{3}$

$\therefore$ The duration of time for which the pumps remain idle

$$= 1 - \frac{1}{3} = \frac{2}{3} = 67\% \text{ (approximately)}$$

Example 18.16 A telephone exchange has two long distance operators. The telephone company finds that during the peak load, long-distance calls arrive in a Poisson fashion at an average rate of 15 per hour. The length of service on these calls is approximately distributed with mean length five minutes.

(*i*) What is the probability that a subscriber will have to wait for his long distance call during the peak hours of the day?

(*ii*) If the subscribers will wait and be serviced in turn, what is the expected waiting time?

Establish the formula used.

Solution

Here, $$\lambda = \frac{15}{60} = \frac{1}{4},\ \mu = \frac{1}{5},\ S = 2$$

$\therefore$ $$\rho = \frac{\lambda}{\mu S} = \frac{5}{8}$$

First, calculate $$P_0 = \left[\sum_{n=0}^{S-1} \frac{(S\rho)^n}{n!} + \frac{(S\rho)^S}{S!(1-\rho)}\right]^{-1}$$

$$= \left[\sum_{n=0}^{1} \frac{(5/4)^n}{n!} + \frac{(5/4)^2}{2!(1-5/8)}\right]^{-1}$$

$$= \frac{1}{1+5/4+(5/4)^2\cdot\frac{1}{2}\cdot 8/3} = 3/13$$

(*i*) $$P(W>0) = \frac{\left(\frac{\lambda}{\mu}\right)^S}{S!(1-\rho)}\cdot P_0$$

$$= \frac{\left(\frac{5}{4}\right)^2\cdot 3/13}{2!(1-5/8)} = 25/52 = 0.48$$

(*ii*) $$W_q = L_q/\lambda$$

$$= \frac{1}{\lambda}\frac{\rho(S\rho)^S}{S!(1-\rho)^2}P_0$$

$$= 4\frac{5/8\cdot(5/4)^2}{2!(1-5/8)^2}\cdot\frac{3}{13} = \frac{125}{39} = 3.2 \text{ minutes.}$$

Example 18.17 Four counters are being run on the frontier of a country to check the passports and necessary papers of the tourists. The tourists choose any counter at random. If the arrival at the frontier is Poisson at the rate λ and the service time is exponential with parameter $\lambda/2$, what is the steady state average queue at each counter?

Solution

Here, $$S = 4,\ \lambda = \lambda,\ \mu = \lambda/2$$

$$\rho = \frac{\lambda}{\mu S} = \frac{1}{2}$$

$$P_0 = \left[\sum_{n=0}^{3} \frac{2^n}{n!} + \frac{4^4}{4!}\frac{\left(\frac{1}{2}\right)^4}{(1-1/2)}\right]^{-1}$$

$$= \left[\frac{2^0}{0!} + \frac{2^1}{1!} + \frac{2^2}{2!} + \frac{2^3}{3!} + \frac{256}{24} \times \frac{1}{8}\right]^{-1}$$

$$= [1+2+2+8/6+4/3]^{-1} = [5+8/3]^{-1} = 3/23$$

But, the expected queue length λq is,

$$= \frac{(\lambda/\mu)^S}{S!} \frac{\rho}{1-\rho^2} P_0 = \frac{2^4}{4!} \frac{\frac{1}{2}}{\left(\frac{1}{2}\right)^2} \cdot \frac{3}{23} = 4/23.$$

EXERCISES

1. A two-channel waiting line with Poisson arrivals has a mean arrival rate of 50 per hour and exponential service with a mean service rate of 75 per hour for each channel. Find,
   (*i*) the probability of an empty system.
   (*ii*) the probability that an arrival in the system will have to wait. **[Ans.** (*i*) 0.83, (*ii*) 0.167]
2. There are two clerks in a university, to receive dues from the students. If the service time for each student is exponential with mean four minutes and if the boys arrive in a Poisson fashion at the counter at the rate 10 per hour, determine,
   (*i*) the probability of having to wait for service.
   (*ii*) the expected percentage of idle time for each clerk. **[Ans.** (*i*) 0.167, (*ii*) 0.67%]
3. A general insurance company has three claim adjusters in its branch office. People with claims against the company are found to arrive in a Poisson fashion at an average rate of 20 per eight-hour day. The amount of time that an adjuster spends with a claimant is found to have a negative exponential distribution with mean service time 40 minutes. Claimants are processed in the order of appearance.
   (*i*) How many hours a week can an adjuster expect to spend with the claimants?
   (*ii*) How much time on an average does a claimant spend in the branch office?
   [Ans. (*i*) 22 hours, (*ii*) 49 minutes]
4. A railway-goods traffic station has four claims assistants. Customers with claims against the railway are observed to arrive in a Poisson fashion at an average rate of 24 per eight-hour day for six days. The amount of time the claims assistant spends with the claimant is found to have an exponential distribution with a mean service time of 40 minute. Service is given in the order of appearance of the customers.
   (*i*) How many hours/week can a claim assistant expect to serve the claimant?
   (*ii*) On an averagee, how much time does a claimant spend in the goods traffic office?
   [Ans. (*i*) 72 hours (*ii*) 47.2 minutes]

18.4.4 Model IV (M/M/S) : (M/FCFS)

This model is essentially the same as model III, except that the maximum number of customers in the system is limited to N, where $N > S$(S = Number of channels)

$$\therefore \quad \lambda_n = \begin{cases} \lambda, & 0 \le n \le N \\ 0, & n \ge N \end{cases}$$

$$\mu_n = \begin{cases} n\mu, & 0 \le n \le S \\ S\mu, & S \le n \le N \end{cases}$$

$$P_n = \begin{cases} \dfrac{1}{n}\left(\dfrac{\lambda}{\mu}\right)^n P_0, 0 \le n \le S \\ \dfrac{1}{S^{n-S}S!}\left(\dfrac{\lambda}{\mu}\right)^n P_0, S \le n \le N \end{cases}$$

$$P_0 = \left[\sum_{n=0}^{S-1}\frac{1}{n!}\left(\frac{\lambda}{\mu}\right)^n + \sum_{n=S}^{N}\frac{1}{S^{n-S}S!}\left(\frac{\lambda}{\mu}\right)^n\right]^{-1}$$

$$L_q = \frac{(S\rho)^C \rho}{S!(1-\rho)^2}[1-\rho^{N-S+1} - (1-\rho)(N-S+1)\rho^{N-S}]P_0$$

$$L_S = L_q + S - P_0 \sum_{n=0}^{S-1}\frac{(S-n)(S\rho)^n}{n!}$$

$$W_S = \frac{L_S}{\lambda'}, \text{ where } \lambda' = \lambda(1-P_N)$$

$$W_q = W_S - \frac{1}{\mu}$$

Example 18.18 A barber shop has two barbers and three chairs for customers. Assume that the customers arrive in a Poisson fashion at a rate of five per hour and each barber services customers according to an exponential distribution with mean 15 minutes. Further, if a customer arrives and there are no empty chairs in the shop, he will leave. What is the expected number of customers in the shop?

Solution

Here, $S = 2, N = 3, \lambda = \dfrac{5}{60} = \dfrac{1}{12}$ customer/min

$$\mu = \frac{1}{15}/\text{min}$$

$$P_0 = \left[\sum_{n=0}^{2-1}\frac{1}{n!}\left(\frac{\lambda}{\mu}\right)^n + \sum_{n=2}^{3}\frac{1}{2^{n-2}}\frac{1}{2!}\left(\frac{\lambda}{\mu}\right)^n\right]^{-1}$$

$$= \left[1 + 1.\frac{5}{4} + \frac{1}{2!}\left(\frac{5}{4}\right)^2 + \frac{1}{2.2!}\left(\frac{5}{4}\right)^3\right]^{-1}$$

$$= \left[1 + \frac{5}{4} + \frac{1}{2}(5/4)^2 + \frac{1}{4}(5/4)^3\right]^{-1}$$

$$= \frac{256}{901} = 0.28$$

$$P_n = \begin{cases} \dfrac{1}{n!}(5/4)^n \times 0.28 & 0 \le n < 2 \\ \dfrac{1}{2^{n-2}2!}(5/4)^n \times 0.28 & 2 \le n \le 3 \end{cases}$$

$$= \begin{cases} \dfrac{1}{n!}(1.25)^n \times 0.28 & 0 \le n < 2 \\ \dfrac{1}{2^{n-2}2!}(1.25)^n \times 0.28 & 2 \le n \le 3 \end{cases}$$

$$L_S = L_q + S - P_0 \sum_{n=0}^{S-1} \frac{(S-n)\left(\dfrac{\lambda}{\mu}\right)^n}{n!}$$

$$= \sum_{n=2}^{3}(n-2)P_n + 2 - P_0 \sum_{n=0}^{2-1} \frac{(2-n)(1.25)^n}{n!}$$

$$= P_3 + 2 - 3.2\,P_0$$

$$= \left[\frac{1}{2.2!}(1.25)^3 \times 0.28\right] + 2 - 3.2 \times 0.28 = 1.226 \text{ customers.}$$

EXERCISE

1. Let there be an automobile inspection site with three inspection stalls. Assume that cars wait in such a way that when a stall becomes vacant, the car at the head of the line pulls up to it. The station can accommodate four cars at the most, to be waiting (seven in station) at one time. The arrival pattern is Poisson with a mean of one car every minute during peak hours. The service time is exponential with mean six minutes. Find the average number of cars in the site during peak hours, the average waiting time and the average number of cars per hour that cannot enter the station because of full capacity.

[**Hint:** S = 3, N = 7, l = 1 car per minute, m = $\frac{1}{6}$ car/min]

[**Ans.** (*i*) 3.09 cars, (*ii*) 6.06 cars, (*iii*) 12.3 minutes, (*iv*) 30.3 cars per hour]

SUMMARY

The Queue Discipline

- First come first served (FCFS)
- First in first out (FIFO)
- Last in first out (LIFO)
- Selection for service in random order (SIRO)

Customer's Behaviour

(*i*) ***Balking*** A customer who leaves the queue because it is too long and he has no time to wait or does not have sufficient waiting space.

(*ii*) ***Reneging*** This occurs when a waiting customer leaves the queue due to impatience.

(*iii*) ***Priorities*** In certain applications, some customers are served before others regardless of their arrival. These customers have priority over others.

(*iv*) ***Jockeying*** Customers may jockey from one waiting line to another. This is most common in a supermarket.

Kendall's Notation for Representing Queueing Models

a = probability law for the arrival (inter-arrival) time

b = probability law according to which the customers are being served.

c = number of channels (or service stations)

d = capacity of the systems, i.e., the maximum number allowed in the system (in service and waiting)

e = queue discipline

Models of Queuing Theory

Model I: (M/M/1): (∞ /FCFS) (Birth and Death Model)

(*i*) Probability (that there is no unit in the system at time *t* and no arrival in time Δt) $= P_0(t)\,(1-\lambda\,\Delta t)$

(*ii*) Probability (that there is one unit in the system at time *t*, one unit serviced in Δt and no arrival in Δt).

$$= P_i(t)\, n\,\Delta t\,(1-\lambda\Delta t)$$
$$= P_n = \rho^n (1-\rho)$$

Measures of Model I:

1. $L_S = \dfrac{\rho}{1-\rho} = \dfrac{\lambda}{\mu-\lambda}$

2. $L_q = \dfrac{\rho^2}{1-\rho} = \dfrac{\lambda^2}{\mu(\mu-\lambda)}$

3. $W_q = \dfrac{\rho}{1-\rho} = \dfrac{\lambda}{\mu(\mu-\lambda)}$

4. $W_S = \dfrac{1}{\mu-\lambda}$

5. $(W/W>0) = \dfrac{1}{\mu-\lambda} = \dfrac{1}{\mu(1-\rho)}$

6. $(L/L>0) = \dfrac{\mu}{\mu-\lambda} = \dfrac{1}{1-\rho}$

7. Probability of queue size $\geq N = \rho^N = \int_t^{\infty} \rho(\mu-\lambda)\, e^{(\mu-\lambda)^w}\, dw$

8. Probability (waiting time in the queue $\geq t$) $= \int_t^{\infty} \lambda(\mu-\lambda)\, e^{-(\mu-\lambda)^w} dw$

9. Probability (waiting time in the system $\geq t$) $= \int_t^{\infty} \rho(\mu-\lambda) e^{-(\mu-\lambda)w} dw$

10. Traffic intensity $\rho = \dfrac{\lambda}{\mu}$.

Model II: (M/M/1): (N/FCFS)

1. $P_0 = \dfrac{1-\rho}{1-\rho^{N+1}}$, where $\rho = \dfrac{\lambda}{\mu}\left(\dfrac{\lambda}{\mu} > 1 \text{ is allowed}\right)$

2. $P_N = \dfrac{1-\rho}{1-\rho^{N+1}}\,\rho^n$ for $n = 0\,1, 2, ..., N.$

3. $L_q = \dfrac{\lambda}{\mu}$

4. $L_S = \rho_0 \sum_{n=0}^{N} n\rho^n$

5. $L_q = L_S - \dfrac{\lambda}{\mu}$

6. $W_S = L_S/\lambda$

7. $W_q = L_q/\lambda$

Model III: (Multiservice model) (M/M/S): (∞/FCFS)

$$P_n = \begin{cases} \dfrac{1}{n!}\left(\dfrac{\lambda}{\mu}\right)^n P_0, & n = 0, 1, 2, ..., S-1, \\[2ex] \dfrac{1}{S!}\dfrac{1}{S^{n-S}}\left(\dfrac{\lambda}{\mu}\right)^n P_0, & \text{if } n = S, S+1, ... \end{cases}$$

Measures of Model III:

1. $L_q = P_S \dfrac{\rho}{(1-\rho)^2}$, where $P_S = \dfrac{\left(\dfrac{\lambda}{\mu}\right)^S P_0}{S!}$

2. $L_S = \left(\dfrac{\lambda}{\mu}\right) + L_q$

3. $W_q = \dfrac{L_q}{\lambda}$

4. $W_S = \dfrac{L_S}{\lambda}$

5. $L(L>0) = \dfrac{1}{1-\rho}$

6. $W(W>0) = \dfrac{1}{S\mu - \lambda}$

7. Prob $(W>0) = \dfrac{P_S}{1-\rho}$

8. Probability that there will be someone waiting $= \dfrac{P_S \rho}{1-\rho}$

9. Average number of idle servers = $S -$ (average number of customers served).

10. Efficiency of $M/M/$S model $= \dfrac{\text{Average number of customers served}}{\text{Total number of customers served}}$

Model IV: (M/M/S): (N/FCFS)

1. $\lambda_n = \begin{cases} \lambda, & 0 \le n \le N \\ 0, & n \ge N \end{cases}$

2. $\mu_n = \begin{cases} n\mu, & 0 \le n \le S \\ S\mu, & S \le n \le N \end{cases}$

3. $P_n = \begin{cases} \dfrac{1}{n}\left(\dfrac{\lambda}{\mu}\right)^n P_0, & 0 \le n \le S \\ \dfrac{1}{S^{n-S}} S!\left(\dfrac{\lambda}{\mu}\right)^n P_0, & S \le n \le N \end{cases}$

4. $P_0 = \left[\displaystyle\sum_{n=0}^{s-1} \frac{1}{n!}\left(\frac{\lambda}{\mu}\right)^n + \sum_{n=C}^{N} \frac{1}{S^{n-s} S!}\left(\frac{\lambda}{\mu}\right)^n\right]^{-1}$

5. $L_q = \dfrac{(S\rho)^c \rho}{S!(1-\rho)^2}\left[1-\rho^{N-S+1} - (1-\rho)(N-S+1)\rho^{N-S}\right] P_0$

6. $L_S = L_q + S - P_0 \displaystyle\sum_{n=0}^{S-1} \frac{(S-n)(S\rho)^n}{n!}$

7. $W_S = \dfrac{L_S}{\lambda'}$ where $\lambda' = \lambda(1-P_N)$

8. $W_q = W_S - \dfrac{1}{\mu}$

□□□

Chapter 19

Game Theory

19.1 INTRODUCTION

Competition is the watchword of modern life. We can say that a competitive solution exists, if two or more individuals make decisions in a situation that involves conflicting interests, and in which the outcome is controlled by the decision of all the concerned parties. A competitive situation is called a *game*. The term *game* represents a conflict between two or more parties. A situation is termed as game when it possesses the following properties.

(*i*) The number of competitors is finite.
(*ii*) There is a conflict in interests between the participants.
(*iii*) Each of the participants has a finite set of possible courses of action.
(*iv*) The rules governing these choices are specified and known to all players. The game begins when each player chooses a single course of action from the list of courses available to him.
(*v*) The outcome of the game is affected by the choices made by all the players.
(*vi*) The outcome for all the specific set of choices, by all the players, is known in advance and is numerically defined.

The outcome of a game consists of a particular set of courses of action undertaken by the competitors. Each outcome determines a set of payments (positive, negative or zero), one to each competitor.

19.1.1 Definition

The term '*strategy*' is defined as a complete set of plans of action specifying precisely what the player will do under every possible future contigency that might occur during the play of the game, i.e., strategy of a player is the decision rule he uses for making a choice, from his list of courses of action. Strategy can be classified as:

(*i*) Pure strategy (*ii*) Mixed strategy

A strategy is called *pure* if one knows in advance of the play that it is certain to be adopted, irrespective of the strategy the other players might choose.

The optimal strategy mixture for each player may be determined by assigning to each strategy, its probability of being chosen. The strategy so determined is called *mixed strategy* because it is a probabilistic combination of the available choices of strategy. Mixed strategy is denoted by the set, $S = \{X_1, X_2...X_n\}$ where, X_j is the probability of choosing the course j such that $X_j > 0, j = 1, 2...n$ and $X_1 + X_2 + ... X_n = 1$. It is evident that a pure strategy is a special case of mixed strategy.

In the case where all but one X_j is zero, a player may be able to choose only n pure strategy, but he has an infinite number of mixed strategies to choose them.

19.2 PAY-OFF

Pay-off is the outcome of playing the game. A pay-off matrix is a table showing the amount received by the player named at the left hand side after all possible plays of the game. The payment is made by the player named at the top of the table.

If a player *A* has *m* courses of action and player *B* has *n* courses, then a pay-off matrix may be constructed using the following steps.

(*i*) Row designations for each matrix are the courses of action available to *A*.
(*ii*) Column designations for each matrix are the courses of action available to *B*.
(*iii*) With a two-person zero-sum game, the cell entries in *B*'s pay-off matrix will be the negative of the corresponding entries in *A*'s pay-off matrix and the matrices will be as shown below.

$$
\begin{array}{cc}
 & \text{Player } B \\
 & \begin{array}{ccccccc} 1 & 2 & 3 & \cdots & j & \cdots & n \end{array} \\
\text{Player } A \quad \begin{array}{c} 1 \\ 2 \\ \\ \vdots \\ m \end{array} &
\begin{bmatrix}
a_{11} & a_{12} & a_{13} & \cdots & a_{1j} & \cdots & a_{1n} \\
a_{21} & a_{22} & a_{23} & \cdots & a_{2j} & \cdots & a_{2n} \\
a_{31} & a_{32} & a_{33} & \cdots & a_{3j} & \cdots & a_{3n} \\
 & & & \cdots & & & \\
a_{m1} & a_{m2} & a_{m3} & \cdots & a_{mj} & \cdots & a_{mn}
\end{bmatrix}
\end{array}
$$

A's pay-off matrix.

$$
\begin{array}{cc}
 & \text{Player } B \\
 & \begin{array}{ccccccc} 1 & 2 & 3 & \cdots & j & \cdots & n \end{array} \\
\text{Player } A \quad \begin{array}{c} 1 \\ 2 \\ \vdots \\ i \\ \vdots \\ m \end{array} &
\begin{bmatrix}
-a_{11} & -a_{12} & a_{13} & \cdots & -a_{1j} & \cdots & -a_{1} \\
-a_{21} & -a_{22} & a_{23} & \cdots & -a_{2j} & \cdots & a_{2} \\
\vdots & & & & & & \\
-a_{i1} & -a_{i2} & -a_{i3} & \cdots & -a_{ij} & \cdots & a_{in} \\
\vdots & & & & & & \\
-a_{m1} & -a_{m2} & -a_{m3} & \cdots & -a_{mj} & \cdots & a_{mn}
\end{bmatrix}
\end{array}
$$

19.3 TYPES OF GAMES

(*i*) ***Two-person games and n-person games*** In two-person games, the players may have many possible choices open to them for each play of the game but the number of players remain only two. Hence, it is called a *two-person game*. In case of more than two persons, the game is generally called *n*-person game.

(*ii*) ***Zero-sum game*** A *zero-sum game* is one in which the sum of the payments to all the competitors is zero, for every possible outcome of the game if the sum of the points won, equals the sum of the points lost.

(*iii*) ***Two-person zero-sum game*** A game with two players, where the gain of one player equals the loss of the other, is known as a *two-person zero-sum game*. It is also called a *rectangular game* because their pay-off matrix is in the rectangular form. The characteristics of such a game are:

(*a*) Only two players participate in the game.
(*b*) Each player has a finite number of strategies to use.
(*c*) Each specific strategy results in a pay-off.
(*d*) Total pay-off to the two players at the end of each play is zero.

19.4 THE MAXIMIN-MINIMAX PRINCIPLE

This principle is used for the selection of optimal strategies by two players. Consider two players *A* and *B*. *A* is a player who wishes to maximize his gains, while player *B* wishes to minimize his losses. Since *A* would like to maximize his minimum gain, we obtain for player *A*, the value called *maximin value* and the corresponding strategy is called the *maximin strategy*.

On the other hand, since player *B* wishes to minimize his losses, a value called the *minimax value*, which is the minimum of the maximum losses is found. The corresponding strategy is called the *minimax strategy*. When these two are equal (maximin value = minimax value), the corresponding strategies are called *optimal strategies* and the game is said to have a *saddle point*. The value of the game is given by the saddle point.

The selection of maximin and minimax strategies by *A* and *B* is based upon the so-called maximin-minimax principle, which guarantees the best of the worst results.

Saddle point A saddle point is a position in the pay-off matrix where, the maximum of row minima coincides with the minimum of column maxima. The pay-off at the saddle point is called the *value* of the game.

We shall denote the maximin value by $\underline{\gamma}$, the minimax value of the game by $\overline{\gamma}$ and the value of the game by γ.

Notes:

(*i*) A game is said to be fair if,
maximin value = minimax value = 0, i.e., if $\overline{\gamma} = \underline{\gamma} = 0$

(*ii*) A game is said to be strictly determinable if,
maximin value = minimax value ≠ 0. $\underline{\gamma} = \gamma = \overline{\gamma}$.

Example 19.1 Solve the game whose pay-off matrix is given by,

$$\text{Player } A \quad \begin{array}{c} \\ A_1 \\ A_2 \\ A_3 \end{array} \overset{\text{Player } B}{\begin{array}{c} \begin{array}{ccc} B_1 & B_2 & B_3 \end{array} \\ \begin{bmatrix} 1 & 3 & 1 \\ 0 & -4 & -3 \\ 1 & 5 & -1 \end{bmatrix} \end{array}}$$

Solution

Player *B*

		B_1	B_2	B_3	Row minima
Player *A*	A_1	1	3	1	1
	A_2	0	–4	–3	–4
	A_3	1	5	–1	–1
Column maxima		1	5	1	

$$\text{Maxi (minimum)} = \text{Max}(1, -4, -1) = 1$$
$$\text{Mini (maximum)} = \text{Min}(1, 5, 1) = 1.$$

i.e., Maximin value $\underline{\gamma} = 1 =$ Minimax value $\overline{\gamma}$

$\therefore$ Saddle point exists. The value of the game is the saddle point, which is 1. The optimal strategy is the position of the saddle point and is given by, (A_1, B_1).

Example 19.2 For what value of 1, is the game with the following matrix strictly determinable?

$$\begin{array}{cc} & \text{Player } B \\ & \begin{array}{ccc} B_1 & B_2 & B_3 \end{array} \\ \text{Player } A \begin{array}{c} A_1 \\ A_2 \\ A_3 \end{array} & \begin{bmatrix} \lambda & 6 & 2 \\ -1 & \lambda & -7 \\ -2 & 4 & \lambda \end{bmatrix} \end{array}$$

Solution Ignoring the value of l, the pay-off matrix is given by,

$$\begin{array}{ccc} & \text{Player } B & \\ & \begin{array}{ccc} B_1 & B_2 & B_3 \end{array} & \text{Row minima} \\ \text{Player } A \begin{array}{c} A_1 \\ A_2 \\ A_3 \end{array} & \begin{bmatrix} \lambda & 6 & 2 \\ -1 & \lambda & -7 \\ -2 & 4 & \lambda \end{bmatrix} & \begin{array}{c} 2 \\ -7 \\ -2 \end{array} \\ \text{Column maxima} & \begin{array}{ccc} -1 & 6 & 2 \end{array} & \end{array}$$

The game is strictly determinable if,

$$\underline{\gamma} = \gamma = \overline{\gamma}.\ \text{Hence, } \underline{\gamma} = 2, \qquad \overline{\gamma} = -1$$

$\Rightarrow$ $-1 \leq \lambda \leq 2.$

Example 19.3 Determine which of the following two-person zero-sum games are strictly determinable and fair. Given the optimum strategy for each player in the case of strictly determinable games.

(*i*)
$$\begin{array}{cc} & \text{Player } B \\ & \begin{array}{cc} B_1 & B_2 \end{array} \\ \text{Player } A \begin{array}{c} A_1 \\ A_2 \end{array} & \begin{bmatrix} -5 & 2 \\ -7 & -4 \end{bmatrix} \end{array}$$

(*ii*)
$$\begin{array}{cc} & \text{Player } B \\ & \begin{array}{cc} B_1 & B_2 \end{array} \\ \text{Player } A \begin{array}{c} A_1 \\ A_2 \end{array} & \begin{bmatrix} 1 & 1 \\ 4 & -3 \end{bmatrix} \end{array}$$

Solution

$$\text{Maxi (minimum)} = \underline{\gamma} = \text{Max}(-5, -7) = -5$$
$$\text{Mini (maximum)} = \overline{\gamma} = \text{Min}(-5, 2) = -5$$

(*i*)

$$\begin{array}{ccc} & \text{Player } B & \\ & \begin{array}{cc} B_1 & B_2 \end{array} & \text{Row minima} \\ \text{Player } A \begin{array}{c} A_1 \\ A_2 \end{array} & \begin{bmatrix} -5 & 2 \\ -7 & -4 \end{bmatrix} & \begin{array}{c} -5 \\ -7 \end{array} \\ \text{Column maxima} & \begin{array}{cc} -5 & 2 \end{array} & \end{array}$$

Since $\underline{\gamma} = \overline{\gamma} = -5 \neq 0$, the game is strictly determinable. There exists a saddle point $= -5$. Hence, the value of the game is -5. The optimal strategy is the position of the saddle point given by, (A_1, B_1).

(*ii*)

$$\begin{array}{ccc} & \text{Player } B & \\ & \begin{array}{cc} B_1 & B_2 \end{array} & \text{Row minimum} \\ \text{Player } A \quad \begin{array}{c} A_1 \\ A_2 \end{array} & \begin{bmatrix} 1 & 1 \\ 4 & -3 \end{bmatrix} & \begin{array}{c} 1 \\ -3 \end{array} \\ \text{Column maximum} & \begin{array}{cc} 4 & 1 \end{array} & \end{array}$$

Maxi (minimum) = $\underline{\gamma}$ = Max (1, –3) = 1.

Mini (maximum) = $\overline{\gamma}$ = Min (4, 1) = 1.

Since $\underline{\gamma} = \overline{\gamma} = 1 \neq 0$, the game is strictly determinable. Value of the game is 1. The optimal strategy is, (A_1, B_2).

Example 19.4 Solve the game whose pay-off matrix is given below.

$$\begin{bmatrix} -2 & 0 & 0 & 5 & 3 \\ 3 & 2 & 1 & 2 & 2 \\ -4 & -3 & 0 & -2 & 6 \\ 5 & 3 & -4 & 2 & -6 \end{bmatrix}$$

Solution

$$\begin{array}{ccc} & \begin{array}{ccccc} B_1 & B_2 & B_3 & B_4 & B_5 \end{array} & \text{Row minima} \\ \text{Player } A \quad \begin{array}{c} A_1 \\ A_2 \\ A_3 \\ A_4 \end{array} & \begin{bmatrix} -2 & 0 & 0 & 5 & 3 \\ 3 & 2 & 1 & 2 & 2 \\ -4 & -3 & 0 & -2 & 6 \\ 5 & 3 & -4 & 2 & -6 \end{bmatrix} & \begin{array}{c} -2 \\ 1 \\ -4 \\ -6 \end{array} \\ \text{Column maxima} & \begin{array}{ccccc} 5 & 3 & 1 & 5 & 6 \end{array} & \end{array}$$

Maxi (minimum) = $\underline{\gamma}$ = Max (–2, 1, –4, –6) = 1.

Mini (maximum) = $\overline{\gamma}$ = Min (5, 3, 1, 5, 6) = 1.

Since, $\underline{\gamma} = \overline{\gamma} = 1$, there exists a saddle point. Value of the game is 1. The position of the saddle point is the optimal strategy and is given by, $[A_2, B_3]$.

EXERCISES

1. For a game with the following pay-off matrix,

$$\begin{array}{cc} & \text{Player } A \\ \text{Player } B & \begin{bmatrix} -1 & 2 & -2 \\ 6 & 4 & -6 \end{bmatrix} \end{array}$$

determine the best strategies as well as the value of the game for players *A* and *B*. Is this game (*i*) fair, (*ii*) strictly determinable?

[Ans. Value of game is = 2. Game is not fair, but strictly determinable]

2. Determine the optimal minimax strategies for each player in the following game.

$$\begin{array}{cc} & \begin{array}{cccc} B_1 & B_2 & B_3 & B_4 \end{array} \\ \begin{array}{c} A_1 \\ A_2 \\ A_3 \end{array} & \begin{bmatrix} -5 & 2 & 0 & 7 \\ 5 & 6 & 4 & 8 \\ 4 & 0 & 2 & -3 \end{bmatrix} \end{array}$$

[Ans. g = 4, (A_2, B_3) is the optimum strategy]

19.5 GAMES WITHOUT SADDLE POINTS (MIXED STRATEGIES)

A game without saddle point can be solved by various solution methods.

19.5.1 2 × 2 Games without Saddle Point

Consider a 2 × 2 two-person zero-sum game without any saddle point, having the pay-off matrix for player *A* as,

$$\begin{array}{c} \\ A_1 \\ A_2 \end{array}\begin{array}{c} \begin{array}{cc} B_1 & B_2 \end{array} \\ \begin{bmatrix} a_{11} & a_{12} \\ a_{21} & a_{22} \end{bmatrix} \end{array}$$

The optimum mixed strategies,

$$S_A = \begin{bmatrix} A_1 & A_2 \\ p_1 & p_2 \end{bmatrix} \text{ and } S_B \begin{bmatrix} B_1 & B_2 \\ q_1 & q_2 \end{bmatrix}$$

where,
$$p_1 = \frac{a_{22} - a_{21}}{(a_{11} + a_{22}) - (a_{12} + a_{21})}, p_1 + p_2 = 1 \Rightarrow p_2 = 1 - p_1$$

$$q_1 = \frac{a_{22} - a_{12}}{(a_{11} + a_{22}) - (a_{12} + a_{21})}, q_1 + q_2 = 1 \Rightarrow q_2 = 1 - q_1$$

$$\text{The value of the game } (\gamma) = \frac{a_{11}\, a_{22} - a_{12}\, a_{21}}{(a_{11} + a_{22}) - (a_{12} + a_{21})}$$

Example 19.5 Solve the following pay-off matrix. Also determine the optimal strategies and value of the game.

$$A \overset{B}{\begin{bmatrix} 5 & 1 \\ 3 & 4 \end{bmatrix}}$$

Solution

$$A \overset{B}{\begin{bmatrix} 5 & 1 \\ 3 & 4 \end{bmatrix}}. \text{ Let this be,}$$

$$\begin{array}{c} \\ A_1 \\ A_2 \end{array}\begin{array}{c} \begin{array}{cc} B_1 & B_2 \end{array} \\ \begin{bmatrix} a_{11} & a_{12} \\ a_{21} & a_{22} \end{bmatrix} \end{array}. \text{ The optimum mixed strategies,}$$

$$S_A = \begin{pmatrix} A_1 & A_2 \\ p_1 & p_2 \end{pmatrix} \text{ and } S_B = \begin{pmatrix} B_1 & B_2 \\ q_1 & q_2 \end{pmatrix}$$

where,
$$p_1 = \frac{a_{22} - a_{21}}{(a_{11} + a_{22}) - (a_{12} + a_{21})} = \frac{4 - 3}{(5 + 4) - (1 + 3)} = \frac{1}{5}$$

$$p_2 = 1 - p_1 \Rightarrow p_2 = 1 - \frac{1}{5} = \frac{4}{5}$$

$$q_1 = \frac{a_{22} - a_{12}}{(a_{11} + a_{22}) - (a_{12} + a_{21})} = \frac{4 - 1}{(5 + 4) - (1 + 3)} = \frac{3}{5}$$

$$q_2 = 1 - q_1 \Rightarrow q_2 = 1 - \frac{3}{5} = \frac{2}{5}$$

value of game, $$\gamma = \frac{(5 \times 4) - (1 \times 3)}{(5 + 4) - (1 + 3)} = \frac{17}{5}$$

∴ The optimum mixed strategies,

$$S_A = \left(\frac{1}{5}, \frac{4}{5}\right); S_B = \left(\frac{3}{5}, \frac{2}{5}\right)$$

$$\text{Value of game} = \frac{17}{5}.$$

Example 19.6 Solve the following game and determine its value.

$$\begin{array}{c} \quad B \\ A\begin{bmatrix} 4 & -4 \\ -4 & 4 \end{bmatrix} \end{array}$$

Solution It is clear that the pay-off matrix does not possess any saddle point. The players will use mixed strategies. The optimum mixed strategy for the players are,

$$S_A = \begin{pmatrix} A_1 & A_2 \\ p_1 & p_2 \end{pmatrix}, p_1 + p_2 = 1$$

$$S_B = \begin{pmatrix} B_1 & B_2 \\ q_1 & q_2 \end{pmatrix}, q_1 + q_2 = 1.$$

$$p_1 = \frac{a_{22} - a_{21}}{(a_{11} + a_{22}) - (a_{12} + a_{21})} = \frac{4 - (-4)}{4 + 4 - (-4 - 4)} = \frac{8}{16} = \frac{1}{2}$$

$$p_2 = 1 - p_1 \Rightarrow p_2 = 1 - \frac{1}{2} = \frac{1}{2}$$

$$q_1 = \frac{a_{22} - a_{12}}{(a_{11} + a_{22}) - (a_{12} + a_{21})} = \frac{4 - (-4)}{4 + 4 - (-4 - 4)} = \frac{8}{16} = \frac{1}{2}$$

$$q_2 = 1 - q_1 = 1 - \frac{1}{2} = \frac{1}{2}.$$

The optimum strategy is, $S_A = \left(\frac{1}{2}, \frac{1}{2}\right); S_B = \left(\frac{1}{2}\ \frac{1}{2}\right)$

The value of the game is, $$\gamma = \frac{a_{22}\, a_{11} - a_{12}\, a_{21}}{(a_{22} + a_{11}) - (a_{12} + a_{21})}$$

$$= \frac{(4 \times 4) - [-4 \times (-4)]}{(4 + 4) - [-4 + (-4)]} = 0.$$

Example 19.7 In a game of matching coins with two players, suppose A wins one unit of value when there are two heads, wins nothing when there are two tails and losses 1/2 unit of value when there are one head and one tail. Determine the pay-off matrix, the best strategies for each player and the value of the game to A.

Solution The pay-off matrix for the player A is given by,

$$\text{Player } A \quad \begin{array}{c} \\ H \\ T \end{array} \overset{\text{Player } B}{\begin{array}{cc} H & T \\ \end{array}} \begin{bmatrix} 1 & -\frac{1}{2} \\ -\frac{1}{2} & 0 \end{bmatrix}$$

Let this be,

$$\begin{array}{c} \\ A_1 \\ A_2 \end{array} \begin{array}{c} \begin{array}{cc} B_1 & B_2 \end{array} \\ \begin{pmatrix} a_{11} & a_{12} \\ a_{21} & a_{22} \end{pmatrix} \end{array}$$

The optimum mixed strategies, $S_A = \begin{pmatrix} A_1 & A_2 \\ p_1 & p_2 \end{pmatrix}, p_1 + p_2 = 1$

$$S_B = \begin{pmatrix} B_1 & B_2 \\ q_1 & q_2 \end{pmatrix}, q_1 + q_2 = 1.$$

$$p_1 = \frac{a_{22} - a_{21}}{(a_{11} + a_{22}) - (a_{12} + a_{21})} = \frac{0 - \left(-\frac{1}{2}\right)}{1 + 0 - \left(-\frac{1}{2} - \frac{1}{2}\right)}$$

$$= \frac{\frac{1}{2}}{2} = \frac{1}{4}$$

$$p_2 = 1 - p_1 = 1 - \frac{1}{4} = \frac{3}{4}.$$

$$q_1 = \frac{a_{22} - a_{12}}{(a_{11} + a_{22}) - (a_{12} + a_{21})} = \frac{0 - \left(-\frac{1}{2}\right)}{1 + 0 - \left(-\frac{1}{2} - \frac{1}{2}\right)} = \frac{1}{4}$$

$$q_2 = 1 - q_1 = 1 - \frac{1}{4} = \frac{3}{4}$$

$$\text{Value of the game} = \frac{1 \times 0 - \left(-\frac{1}{2}\right)\left(-\frac{1}{2}\right)}{1 + 0 - \left(-\frac{1}{2} - \frac{1}{2}\right)} = \frac{\frac{-1}{4}}{2}$$

$$\gamma = -\frac{1}{8}$$

∴ The optimum mixed strategy is given by,

$$S_A = \left(\frac{1}{4}, \frac{3}{4}\right);\ S_B = \left(\frac{1}{4}, \frac{3}{4}\right)$$

and the value of game is –1/8.

EXERCISES

1. For a game with the following pay-off matrix, determine the optimal strategy and the value of the game.

(*i*)

$$\begin{array}{cc} & B \\ A & \begin{pmatrix} 6 & -3 \\ -3 & 3 \end{pmatrix} \end{array}$$

$$\left[\textbf{Ans. } S_A = \left(\frac{1}{4}, \frac{3}{2}\right), S_B = \left(\frac{1}{4}, \frac{3}{4}\right), \text{Value of game} = \frac{3}{4}\right]$$

(*ii*)

$$\begin{array}{cc} & B \\ A & \begin{pmatrix} 2 & 5 \\ 4 & 1 \end{pmatrix} \end{array}$$

$$\left[\textbf{Ans. } S_A = \left(\frac{1}{2}, \frac{1}{2}\right), S_B = \left(\frac{2}{3}, \frac{1}{3}\right), \text{Value of game} = 3\right]$$

2. Two players, *A* and *B* match coins. If the coins match, then *A* wins two units of value. If coins do not match, then *B* wins two units of value.

Determine the optimum strategies for the players and the value of the game.

$$\left[\textbf{Ans. } S_A = S_B = \left(\frac{1}{2}, \frac{1}{2}\right), \text{Value of game} = 0\right]$$

3. Consider a 'modified form' of matching-based coins game problem. The matching player is paid ₹ 800 if both the coins turn heads and ₹ 1 if both the coins turn tails. The non-matching player is paid ₹ 300 when the two coins do not match. Given the choice of being the matching or non-matching player, which one would you choose and what would be your strategy?

$$\left[\textbf{Ans. } S_{\text{match}} = \left(\frac{4}{5}, \frac{11}{15}\right), S_{\text{Non-match}} = \left(\frac{4}{5}, \frac{11}{5}\right)\ \text{Value of game} = -\frac{1}{5}, \text{Non-matching player}\right]$$

Hint: Pay-off matrix for matching player is, Non-matching (*B*)

$$\text{Matching player } (A) \quad \begin{array}{c|cc} & H & T \\ \hline H & 8 & -3 \\ T & -3 & 1 \end{array}$$

19.5.2 Graphical Method for 2 × *n* or *m* × 2 Games

Consider the following 2 × *n* games.

$$\text{Strategy for player } A \quad \begin{array}{c} \text{Strategy for player } B \\ \begin{array}{cc} & \begin{array}{cccc} B_1 & B_2 & \cdots & B_n \end{array} \\ \begin{array}{c} A_1 \\ A_2 \end{array} & \begin{bmatrix} a_{11} & a_{12} & \cdots & a_{1n} \\ a_{21} & a_{22} & \cdots & a_{2n} \end{bmatrix} \end{array} \end{array}$$

Let the mixed strategy for player *A* be given by,

$$S_A = \begin{pmatrix} A_1 & A_2 \\ p_1 & p_2 \end{pmatrix} \text{ such that, } p_1 + p_2 = 1, p_1,\ p_2 \geq 0$$

Now, for each of the pure strategies available to B, expected pay-off for player A would be as follows.

B's pure move	A's expected pay-off $E(p)$
B_1	$E_1(p) = a_{11}p_1 + a_{21}p_2$
B_2	$E_2(p) = a_{12}p_1 + a_{22}p_2$
	$\vdots$
B_n	$E_n(p) = a_{1n}p_1 + a_{2n}p_2$

The player B would like to choose that pure move B_j against S_A for which $E_j(p)$ is a minimum for $j = 1, 2 \ldots n$. Let us denote this minimum expected pay-off for A by,

$$\gamma = \text{Min}\,(E_j(p))\, j = 1, 2 \ldots n.$$

The objective of player A is to select p_1 and p_2 in such a way that, γ is as large as possible. This may be done by plotting the straight lines,

$$Ej(p) = a_{1j}p_1 + a_{2j}p_2 = (a_{1j} - a_{2j})\, p_1 + a_{2j}$$
$$j = 1, 2 \ldots. n.$$

as linear functions of p_1.

The highest point on the lower boundary of these lines will give the maximum value among the minimum expected pay-offs on the lower boundary (lower envelope) as well as the optimum value of probability p_1 and p_2.

Now the two strategies of player B corresponding to the lines that pass through the maximin point can be determined. It helps in reducing the size of the game to (2×2).

Similarly, we can treat $m \times 2$ games in the same way and get the minimax point, which will be the lowest point on the upper boundary (upper envelope).

Example 19.8 Solve the following 2×3 game graphically.

$$\begin{array}{cc} & \text{Player } B \\ \text{Player } A & \begin{bmatrix} 1 & 3 & 11 \\ 8 & 5 & 2 \end{bmatrix} \end{array}$$

Solution Since the problem does not possess any saddle point, let player A play by the mixed strategy

$$S_A = \begin{pmatrix} A_1 & A_2 \\ p_1 & p_2 \end{pmatrix} \text{ with, } p_2 = 1 - p_1$$

against player B.

A's expected pay-off against B's pure move is given by,

B's pure move	A's expected pay-off $E(p_1)$
B_1	$E_1(p_1) = p_1 + 8(1 - p_1) = -7p_1 + 8$
B_2	$E_2(p_1) = 3p_1 + 5(1 - p_1) = 5 - 2p_1$
B_3	$E_3(p_1) = 11P_1 + 2(1 - P_1) = 9p_1 + 2.$

These expected pay-off equations are then plotted as functions of P_1 as shown in the Fig. 19.1, which shows the pay-offs of each column represented as points on two vertical axes 1 and 2, of unit distance apart.

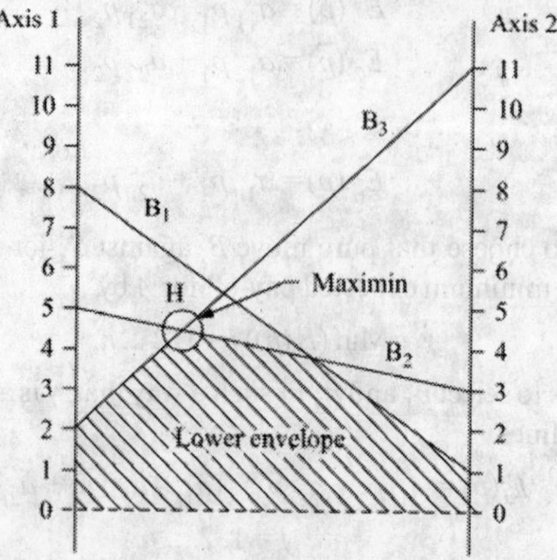

Fig. 19.1

Now, since player A wishes to maximize his minimum expected pay-off, we consider the highest point of intersection H on the lower envelope of A's expected pay-off equation. The lines B_2 and B_3 passing through H define the relevant moves that B_2 and B_3 alone need to play. The solution to the original 2×3 game reduces to,

$$\begin{array}{c} \\ A_1 \\ A_2 \end{array} \begin{array}{c} \begin{array}{cc} B_2 & B_3 \end{array} \\ \begin{bmatrix} 3 & 11 \\ 5 & 2 \end{bmatrix} \end{array}$$

The optimum strategy for A and B is given by,

$$S_A = \begin{pmatrix} A_1 & A_2 \\ p_1 & p_2 \end{pmatrix} \quad p_1 + p_2 = 1$$

$$S_B = \begin{pmatrix} B_1 & B_2 & B_3 \\ 0 & q_1 & q_2 \end{pmatrix} \quad q_1 + q_2 = 1$$

$$p_1 = \frac{2-5}{3+2-(11+5)} = \frac{-3}{-11} = \frac{3}{11}$$

$$p_2 = 1 - p_1 = 1 - \frac{-3}{-11} = \frac{8}{11}$$

$$q_1 = \frac{2-11}{-11} = \frac{-9}{-11} = \frac{9}{11}$$

$$q_2 = 1 - \frac{9}{11} = \frac{2}{11}$$

$$A_1 \, A_2 \, B_1 \, B_2 \, B_3$$

$$S_A = \left(\frac{3}{11}, \frac{8}{11}\right) \text{ and } S_B \left(0, \frac{9}{11}, \frac{2}{11}\right)$$

Value of the game,

$$\gamma = \frac{6-55}{-11} = \frac{49}{11}.$$

Example 19.9 Solve the 6 × 2 game problem graphically.

$$\begin{bmatrix} 1 & -3 \\ 3 & 5 \\ -1 & 6 \\ 4 & 1 \\ 2 & 2 \\ -5 & 0 \end{bmatrix}$$

Solution The given problem does not possess any saddle point. Therefore, let player B play by the mixed strategy

$$S_B = \begin{pmatrix} B_1 & B_2 \\ q_1 & q_2 \end{pmatrix} \text{ with, } q_2 = 1 - q_1$$

against player A.

The expected pay-off equations are plotted in the Fig. 19.2 with two axes I and II vertically at unit distance apart.

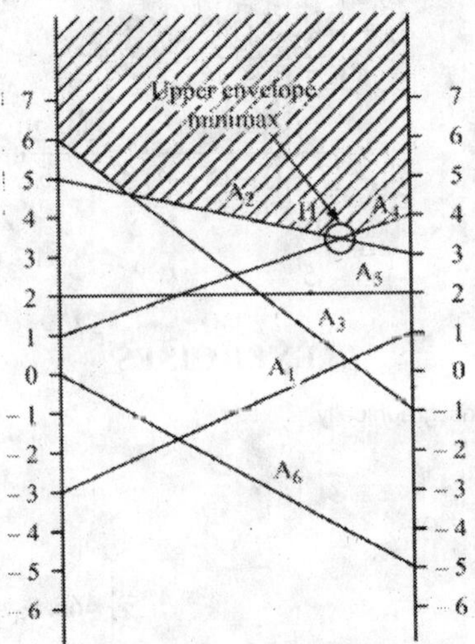

Fig. 19.2

Since player B wishes to minimize his maximum expected pay-off, we consider the lowest point of the upper boundary of B's expected pay-off equation. The point H (intersection of lines A_2 and A_4) represents the minimax expected value of the game for player B. Hence, the solution to the original 6 × 2 game reduces to the 2 × 2 pay-off matrix.

$$\begin{array}{cc} & \text{Player } B \\ & \begin{array}{cc} B_1 & B_2 \end{array} \\ \text{Player } A \begin{array}{c} A_2 \\ A_4 \end{array} & \begin{pmatrix} 3 & 5 \\ 4 & 1 \end{pmatrix} \end{array}$$

The optimal mixed strategy for A and B is given by,

$$S_A = \begin{pmatrix} A_1 & A_2 & A_3 & A_4 & A_5 & A_6 \\ 0 & p_1 & 0 & p_2 & 0 & 0 \end{pmatrix} \text{ with, } p_1 + p_2 = 1$$

$$S_B = \begin{pmatrix} B_1 & B_2 \\ q_1 & q_2 \end{pmatrix} \quad q_1 + q_2 = 1$$

$$p_1 = \frac{1-4}{3+1-(5+4)} = \frac{-3}{-5} = \frac{3}{5}$$

$$p_2 = 1 - \frac{3}{5} = \frac{2}{5}$$

$$q_1 = \frac{1-5}{-5} = \frac{-4}{-5} = \frac{4}{5}$$

$$q_2 = 1 - q_1 = 1 - \frac{4}{5} = \frac{1}{5}$$

$$S_A = \begin{pmatrix} A_1 & A_2 & A_3 & A_4 & A_5 & A_6 \\ 0 & \frac{3}{5} & 0 & \frac{2}{5} & 0 & 0 \end{pmatrix}$$

$$S_B = \begin{pmatrix} B_1 & B_2 \\ \frac{4}{5} & \frac{1}{5} \end{pmatrix}$$

Value of the game, $$\gamma = \frac{3\times1-5\times4}{(3+1)-(5+4)} = \frac{3-20}{-5} = \frac{-17}{-5}$$

$$\gamma = -\frac{17}{5}$$

EXERCISES

1. Solve the following problems graphically.

(*i*) $\text{Player } A \overset{\text{Player } B}{\begin{bmatrix} 3 & -3 & 4 \\ -1 & 1 & -3 \end{bmatrix}}$

$$\left[\textbf{Ans. } S_A = \left(\frac{4}{11}, \frac{7}{11}\right); S_B = \begin{pmatrix} B_1 & B_2 & B_3 \\ 0 & \frac{7}{11} & \frac{4}{11} \end{pmatrix}; \gamma = -\frac{5}{11}\right]$$

(*ii*) $\text{Player } A \overset{\text{Player } B}{\begin{pmatrix} 1 & 3 & -3 & 7 \\ 2 & 5 & 4 & -6 \end{pmatrix}}$

$$\left[\textbf{Ans. } S_A = \left(\frac{1}{2}, \frac{1}{2}\right); S_B = \begin{pmatrix} B_1 & B_2 & B_3 & B_4 \\ 0 & 0 & \frac{13}{20} & \frac{7}{20} \end{pmatrix}; \gamma = \frac{1}{2}\right]$$

(*iii*) $\text{Player } A \overset{\text{Player } B}{\begin{bmatrix} 1 & 2 \\ 5 & 4 \\ -7 & 9 \\ -4 & -3 \\ 2 & 1 \end{bmatrix}}$

$$\left[\textbf{Ans. } S_A \begin{bmatrix} A_1 & A_2 & A_3 & A_4 & A_5 \\ 0 & \frac{16}{17} & \frac{1}{17} & 0 & 0 \end{bmatrix}\right.$$

$$\left. S_B = \begin{bmatrix} B_1 & B_2 \\ \frac{5}{17}, & \frac{12}{17} \end{bmatrix}; \gamma = \frac{73}{17}\right]$$

(iv) Player A, Player B

$$\begin{bmatrix} -6 & 7 \\ 4 & -5 \\ -1 & -2 \\ -2 & 5 \\ 7 & 6 \end{bmatrix}$$

$$\left[\textbf{Ans. } S_A = \begin{pmatrix} A_1 & A_2 & A_3 & A_4 & A_5 \\ 0 & 0 & 0 & \frac{13}{20} & \frac{9}{20} \end{pmatrix}\right.$$

$$\left. S_B = \begin{pmatrix} B_1 & B_2 \\ \frac{11}{20} & \frac{9}{20} \end{pmatrix}; \gamma = \frac{23}{30}\right]$$

2. The companies A and B are competing for the same product. Their different strategies are given in the following pay-off matrix.

Company A, Company B

$$\begin{pmatrix} 4 & -3 & 3 \\ -3 & 1 & -1 \end{pmatrix}$$

Determine the best strategies for the two companies.

$$\left[\textbf{Ans. } S_A = \begin{pmatrix} A_1 & A_2 \\ \frac{4}{11}, & \frac{7}{11} \end{pmatrix}; S_B = \begin{pmatrix} B_1 & B_2 & B_3 \\ \frac{4}{11} & \frac{7}{11}, & 0 \end{pmatrix}; \gamma = -\frac{5}{11}\right]$$

19.5.3 Dominance Property

Sometimes it is observed that one of the pure strategies of either player is always inferior to at least one of the remaining. The superior strategies are said to dominate the inferior ones. In such cases of dominance, we reduce the size of the pay-off matrix by deleting those strategies, which are dominated by others. The general rules for dominance are:

(i) If all the elements of a row, say kth row, are less than or equal to the corresponding elements of any other row, say rth row, then kth row is dominated by the rth row.

(ii) If all the elements of a column, say kth column, are greater than or equal to the corresponding elements of any other column, say rth column, then the kth column is dominated by the rth column.

(iii) Dominated rows and columns may be deleted to reduce the size of the pay-off matrix as the optimal strategies will remain unaffected.

(iv) If some linear combinations of some rows dominate ith row, then the ith row will be deleted. Similar arguments follow for columns.

Example 19.10 Using the principle of dominance, solve the following game.

Player A, Player B

$$\begin{bmatrix} 3 & -2 & 4 \\ -1 & 4 & 2 \\ 2 & 2 & 6 \end{bmatrix}$$

Solution In the given pay-off matrix, all the elements in the third column are greater than or equal to the corresponding elements in the first column. Therefore, column three is dominated by first column. Delete column three. The reduced pay-off matrix is given by,

Player A, Player B

$$\begin{bmatrix} 3 & -2 \\ -1 & 4 \\ 2 & 2 \end{bmatrix}$$

Since no row (or column) dominates another row (or column). The 3 × 2 game can now be solved by the graphical method. Since player B wishes to minimize his maximum loss, we find the lowest point of the upper boundary. The expected pay-off equations are then plotted as shown in Fig. 19.3.

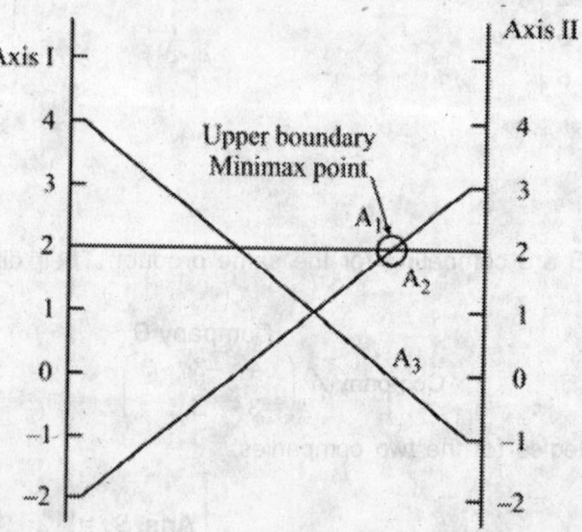

Fig. 19.3

The lowest point in the upper boundary is given by the intersection of lines A_1 and A_2. The solution in the original game is reduced to a 2 × 2 matrix.

$$\begin{array}{cc} & \begin{array}{cc} B_1 & B_2 \end{array} \\ \begin{array}{c} A_1 \\ A_3 \end{array} & \begin{bmatrix} 3 & -2 \\ 2 & 2 \end{bmatrix} \end{array}$$

The optimum strategy for A and B is given by,

$$S_A = \begin{pmatrix} A_1 & A_2 & A_3 \\ p_1 & 0 & p_2 \end{pmatrix} \quad p_1 + p_2 = 1$$

$$S_B = \begin{pmatrix} B_1 & B_2 \\ q_1 & q_2 \end{pmatrix} \quad q_1 + q_2 = 1$$

$$p_1 = \frac{2-2}{3+2-(-2+2)} = 0$$

$$p_2 = 1 - p_1 = 1 - 0 = 1$$

$$q_1 = \frac{2-2}{3+2-(-2+2)} = \frac{4}{5}$$

$$q_2 = 1 - q_1 = 1 - \frac{4}{5} = \frac{1}{5}$$

$$S_A = \begin{pmatrix} A_1 & A_2 & A_3 \\ 0 & 0 & 1 \end{pmatrix} \text{ and } S_B = \begin{pmatrix} B_1 & B_2 \\ \frac{4}{5} & \frac{1}{5} \end{pmatrix}$$

$$\text{Value of the game, } \gamma = \frac{3 \times 2 - (-2) \times (2)}{3+2-(-2+2)} = \frac{10}{5} = 2.$$

Example 19.11 Solve the following game.

$$\text{Player } A \begin{array}{c} \text{Player } B \\ \begin{bmatrix} 1 & 7 & 2 \\ 6 & 2 & 7 \\ 5 & 1 & 6 \end{bmatrix} \end{array}$$

Solution Since all the elements in the third row are less than or equal to the corresponding elements of the second row, therefore, the third row is dominated by the second row. Delete this dominated row. The reduced pay-off matrix is given by,

$$\text{Player } A \begin{array}{c} \text{Player } B \\ \begin{bmatrix} 1 & 7 & 2 \\ 6 & 2 & 7 \end{bmatrix} \end{array}$$

The elements of the third column are greater than or equal to the corresponding elements of the first column, which give that column third is dominated by column one. This dominated column is deleted and the reduced pay-off matrix is given by,

$$\text{Player } A \begin{array}{c} \text{Player } B \\ \begin{bmatrix} 1 & 7 \\ 6 & 2 \end{bmatrix} \end{array}$$

The reduced pay-off matrix is a 2×2 matrix. The optimal strategy for players A and B is given by,

$$S_A = \begin{pmatrix} A_1 & A_2 & A_3 \\ p_1 & p_2 & 0 \end{pmatrix} \quad p_1 + p_2 = 1$$

$$S_B = \begin{pmatrix} B_1 & B_2 & B_3 \\ q_1 & q_2 & 0 \end{pmatrix} \quad q_1 + q_2 = 1$$

$$p_1 = \frac{2-6}{2+1-(7+6)} = \frac{-4}{-10} = \frac{2}{5}$$

$$p_2 = 1 - \frac{2}{5} = \frac{3}{5}$$

$$q_1 = \frac{2-7}{2+1-(7+6)} = \frac{-5}{-10} = \frac{1}{2}$$

$$q_2 = 1 - q_1 = 1 - \frac{1}{2} = \frac{1}{2}$$

Value of the game, $\gamma = \dfrac{2 \times 1 - 7 \times 6}{2+1-(7+6)} = \dfrac{-40}{-10} = 4.$

The optimal strategy is given by,

$$S_A = \begin{pmatrix} A_1 & A_2 & A_3 \\ \frac{2}{5} & \frac{3}{5} & 0 \end{pmatrix}$$

$$S_B = \begin{pmatrix} B_1 & B_2 & B_3 \\ \frac{1}{2} & \frac{1}{2} & 0 \end{pmatrix}$$

Value of the game is, $\gamma = 4.$

EXERCISES

1. Using dominance, solve the pay-off matrix, given by,

(*i*) Player *A* (rows), Player *B* (columns)

$$\begin{bmatrix} 2 & -2 & 4 & 1 \\ 6 & 1 & 12 & 3 \\ -3 & 2 & 0 & 6 \\ 2 & -3 & 7 & 7 \end{bmatrix}$$

$$\left[\textbf{Ans. } S_A = \begin{pmatrix} A_1 & A_2 & A_3 & A_4 \\ 0 & \frac{1}{2} & \frac{1}{2} & 0 \end{pmatrix}; S_B = \begin{bmatrix} B_1 & B_2 & B_3 & B_4 \\ \frac{2}{7} & \frac{1}{2} & 0 & \frac{5}{7} \end{bmatrix}; \text{Value of the game, g} = \frac{3}{7}\right]$$

(*ii*) Player *A* (rows), Player *B* (columns)

$$\begin{bmatrix} 1 & 7 & 3 & 4 \\ 5 & 6 & 4 & 5 \\ 7 & 2 & 0 & 3 \end{bmatrix}$$

$$\left[\textbf{Ans. } S_A = \begin{pmatrix} A_1 & A_2 & A_3 \\ 0 & 1 & 0 \end{pmatrix}; S_B = \begin{pmatrix} B_1 & B_2 & B_3 & B_4 \\ 0 & 0 & 1 & 0 \end{pmatrix}; \text{Value of the game, g} = 4\right]$$

(*iii*)

$$\begin{array}{c} \\ A_1 \\ A_2 \\ A_3 \end{array}\begin{array}{c} \begin{array}{ccccc} B_1 & B_2 & B_3 & B_4 & B_5 \end{array} \\ \begin{bmatrix} 4 & 4 & 2 & -4 & -6 \\ 8 & 6 & 8 & -4 & 0 \\ 10 & 2 & 4 & 0 & 12 \end{bmatrix} \end{array}$$

$$\left[\textbf{Ans. } S_A = \begin{pmatrix} A_1 & A_2 & A_3 \\ 0 & \frac{4}{9} & \frac{5}{9} \end{pmatrix}; S_B = \begin{pmatrix} B_1 & B_2 & B_3 & B_4 & B_5 \\ 0 & \frac{7}{9} & 0 & \frac{2}{9} & 0 \end{pmatrix}; \text{Value of the game, } \gamma = \frac{8}{3}\right]$$

2. The following matrix represents the pay-off to P_1 in a rectangular game between two persons P_1 and P_2.

P_1 (rows), P_2 (columns)

$$\begin{bmatrix} 8 & 15 & -4 & -2 \\ 19 & 15 & 17 & 16 \\ 0 & 20 & 15 & 5 \end{bmatrix}$$

By the notion of dominance, reduce the game to a 2 × 4 game and solve it graphically.

$$\left[\textbf{Ans. } S_{P_1} \begin{bmatrix} 1 & 2 & 3 \\ 0 & \frac{15}{6} & \frac{1}{16} \end{bmatrix}; S_{P_2} = \begin{bmatrix} 1 & 2 & 3 & 4 \\ 0 & \frac{11}{6} & 0 & \frac{5}{16} \end{bmatrix}; \text{Value of the game, } \gamma = \frac{245}{16}\right]$$

3. Solve the following game.

$$\text{Player } A \begin{array}{c} \\ I \\ II \\ III \\ IV \end{array}\begin{array}{c} \text{Player } B \\ \begin{array}{cccc} I & II & III & IV \end{array} \\ \begin{bmatrix} 3 & 2 & 4 & 0 \\ 3 & 4 & 2 & 4 \\ 4 & 2 & 4 & 0 \\ 0 & 4 & 0 & 8 \end{bmatrix} \end{array}$$

$$\left[\textbf{Ans. } S_A = \begin{pmatrix} I & II & III & IV \\ 0 & 0 & \frac{2}{3} & \frac{1}{3} \end{pmatrix}; \; S_B = \begin{pmatrix} I & II & III & IV \\ 0 & 0 & \frac{2}{3} & \frac{1}{3} \end{pmatrix}; \text{Value of the game, } \gamma = \frac{8}{3}\right]$$

SUMMARY

Types of Games

(*i*) ***Two-person games and n-person games*** In two-person games, the players may have many possible choices open to them for each player of the game but the number of players remains only two. Hence, it is called a *two-person game*. In case of more than two persons, the game is generally called *n*-person game.

(*ii*) ***Zero-sum game*** A zero-sum game is one in which the sum of the payment to all the competitors is zero for every possible outcome of the game if the sum of the points won equals the sum of the points lost.

(*iii*) ***Two-person zero-sum game*** A game with two players, where the gain of one player equals the loss of the other is known as a two-person zero-sum game. It is also called a *rectangular game* because the pay-off matrix is in a rectangular form.

The Maximin-Minimax Principle

Consider two players *A* and *B*. Player *A* wishes to maximize his gain, while player *B* wishes to minimize his losses. Since player *A* would like to maximixe his minimum gain, we obtain the value called maximin value and the corresponding strategy is called the maximin strategy.

On the other hand, since player *B* wishes to minimize his losses, a value called the *minimax value*, which is the minimum of the maximum losses, is found. The corresponding strategy is called the *minimax strategy.*

Saddle point A saddle point is a position in the pay-off matrix, where the maximum of row minima coincides with the minimum of column maxima. The pay-off at the saddle point is called the '*value of the game*'.

2 × 2 Games without saddle point

Consider a 2 × 2 two-person zero-sum game without any saddle point, having the pay-off matrix for player *A*

$$\begin{array}{c} \\ A_1 \\ A_2 \end{array}\begin{array}{c} \begin{array}{cc} B_1 & B_2 \end{array} \\ \begin{bmatrix} a_{11} & a_{12} \\ a_{21} & a_{22} \end{bmatrix} \end{array}$$

The optimum mixed strategies,

$$S_A = \begin{bmatrix} A_1 & A_2 \\ p_1 & p_2 \end{bmatrix} \text{ and } S_B = \begin{bmatrix} B_1 & B_2 \\ q_1 & q_2 \end{bmatrix}$$

where,
$$p_1 = \frac{a_{22} - a_{21}}{(a_{11} + a_{22}) - (a_{12} + a_{21})}, p_1 + p_2 = 1 \Rightarrow p_2 = 1 - p_1.$$

$$q_1 = \frac{a_{22} - a_{12}}{(a_{11} + a_{22}) - (a_{12} + a_{21})}, q_1 + q_2 = 1 \Rightarrow q_2 = 1 - q_1.$$

The value of the game is, $\nu = \dfrac{a_{11}a_{22} - a_{12}a_{21}}{(a_{11} + a_{22}) - (a_{12} + a_{21})}$

Graphical method for 2 × n or m × 2 games

Consider the following $2 \times n$ games.

$$A \begin{array}{c} \\ A_1 \\ A_2 \end{array} \overset{\displaystyle B}{\overset{\begin{array}{cccc} B_1 & B_2 & \cdots & B_n \end{array}}{\begin{bmatrix} a_{11} & a_{12} & \cdots & a_{1n} \\ a_{21} & a_{22} & \cdots & a_{2n} \end{bmatrix}}}$$

Let the mixed strategy for player A be given by,

$$S_A = \begin{pmatrix} A_1 & A_2 \\ p_1 & p_2 \end{pmatrix} \text{ such that, } p_1 + p_2 = 1, p_1, p_2 \geq 0.$$

Now for each of the pure strategies available to B, expected pay-off for player A would be as follows.

B's pure move	A's expected pay-off $E(p)$
B_1	$E_1(p) = a_{11}p_1 + a_{21}p_2$
B_2	$E_2(p) = a_{12}p_1 + a_{22}p_2$
	$\vdots$
B_n	$E_n(p) = a_{1n}p_1 + a_{2n}p_2$

Dominance property

Sometimes it is observed that one of the pure strategies of either player is always inferior to at least one of those remaining. The superior strategies are said to dominate the inferior ones. In such cases of dominance, we reduce the size of the pay-off matrix by deleting those strategies which are dominated by others. The general rules for dominance are:

(*i*) If all the elements of a row, say kth row, are less than or equal to the corresponding elements of any other row say rth row, then kth row is dominated by the rth row.

(*ii*) If all the elements of a column, say kth column, are greater than or equal to the corresponding elements of any other column, say rth column, then the kth column is dominated by the rth column.

(*iii*) Dominated rows and columns may be deleted to reduce the size of the pay-off matrix, as the optimal strategies will remain unaffected.

(*iv*) If some linear combinations of certain rows dominate ith row, then the ith row will be deleted. Similar arguments follow for columns.

Chapter 20

Simulation

Simulation is a representation of reality through the use of a model or other device, which will react in the same manner as reality under a given set of conditions.

Simulation is also defined as the use of a system model that has the designed characteristics of reality, in order to produce the essence of an actual operation.

20.1 TYPES OF SIMULATION

Simulation is mainly of two types:

(*i*) Analogue (environmental) simulation
(*ii*) Computer (system) simulation

Some examples of simulation models are given below:

(*i*) Testing an aircraft model in a wind tunnel.
(*ii*) Children cycling in a park with various signals and crossings—to model a traffic system.
(*iii*) Planetarium.

To determine the behaviour of a real system in actual environment, a number of experiments are performed on simulated models either in the laboratories or on the computer itself.

20.2 RANDOM VARIABLE

The random variable is a real-valued function, defined over a sample space associated with the outcome of a *conceptual* chance experiment. Random variables are classified according to their probability density function.

Random number It refers to a uniform random variable or a numerical value assigned to a random variable, following uniform probability density function. In other words, it is a number in a sequence of numbers, whose probability of occurrence is the same as that of any other number in that sequence.

Pseudo-random numbers Random numbers are called *pseudo-random numbers* when they are generated by some deterministic process, but have already qualified the pre-determined statistical test for randomness.

20.3 MONTE-CARLO TECHNIQUE OR MONTE-CARLO SIMULATION

The Monte-Carlo method is a simulation technique in which statistical distribution functions are created by using a series of random numbers. The method is generally used to solve the problems that cannot be adequately represented by the mathematical models or where the solution of the model cannot be arrived at, by analytical method.

Monte-Carlo simulation yields a solution very close to the optimal solution, but not necessarily the exact solution. The Monte-Carlo simulation procedure can be summarized in the following six steps.

Step 1 Clearly define the problem.

(*a*) Identify the objectives of the problem.
(*b*) Identify the main factors which have the greatest effect on the objectives of the problem.

Step 2 Construct an appropriate model.

(*a*) Specify the variables and parameters of the model.
(*b*) State the conditions under which the experiment is to be performed.
(*c*) Define the relationship between the variables and parameters.

Step 3 Prepare the model for experimentation.

(*a*) Define the starting conditions for the simulation.
(*b*) Specify the number of runs of simulation to be made.

Step 4 Using steps 1 to 3, experiment with the model.

(*a*) Define a coding system that will correlate the factors defined in step 1 with the random numbers to be generated for the simulation.
(*b*) Select a random number generator and create the random numbers to be used in the simulation.
(*c*) Associate the generated random numbers with the factors identified in step 1 and coded in step 4 (*a*).

Step 5 Summarize and examine the results obtained in step 4.

Step 6 Evaluate the results of the simulation.

20.3.1 Generation of Random Numbers

Monte-Carlo simulation needs the generation of a sequence of random numbers, which constitute an integral part of the simulation model and also help in determining random observations from the probability distribution.

Random numbers may be found through a computer using random tables or manually. The most common method to obtain random numbers is to generate them through a computer program.

Example 20.1 A sample of 100 arrivals of a customer at a retail sales depot is according to the following distribution.

Time between arrival (min.)	*Frequency*
0.5	2
1.0	6
1.5	10
2.0	25
2.5	20
3.0	14
3.5	10
4.0	7
4.5	4
5.0	2

A study of the time required to service customers by adding up the bills, receiving payments and placing packages, yields the following distribution.

Time between arrival (min.)	*Frequency*
0.5	12
1.0	21
1.5	36
2.0	19
2.5	7
3.0	5

Estimate the average percentage of customer waiting time and average percentage of idle time of the server, by simulation, for the next 10 arrivals.

Solution Tag-numbers are allocated to the events in the same proportions as indicated by the probabilities.

Arrivals	*Frequency*	*Probability*	*Cumulative Probability*	*Tag-numbers*
0.5	2	0.02	0.02	00–01
1.0	6	0.06	0.08	02–07
1.5	10	0.10	0.18	08–17
2.0	25	0.25	0.43	18–42
2.5	20	0.20	0.63	43–62
3.0	14	0.14	0.77	63–76
3.5	10	0.10	0.87	77–86
4.0	7	0.07	0.94	87–93
4.5	4	0.04	0.98	94–97
5.0	2	0.02	1.00	98–99

Service time (min.)	*Frequency*	*Probability*	*Cumulative Probability*	*Tag-numbers*
0.5	12	0.12	0.12	00–11
1.0	21	0.21	0.33	12–32
1.5	36	0.36	0.69	33–68
2.0	19	0.19	0.88	69–87
2.5	7	0.07	0.95	88–94
3.0	5	0.05	1.00	95–99

The random numbers are generated and linked to the appropriate events. The first 10 random numbers, simulating arrival, the second 10, simulating service times. The results are incorporated in Table 20.1, on the assumption that the system starts at 0.00 am.

Average waiting time per customer is, $\frac{4.5}{10} = 0.45$ minutes.

Average waiting time (or) idle time of the servers = $\frac{7.00}{10} = 0.7$ minutes.

Table 20.1

Arrival no.	*Random number*	*Inter-arrival time (min.)*	*Arrival time (min.)*	*Random no.*	*Service time (min.)*	*Service Start*		*Waiting time of end customer server*	
			a		*e*	*b*	*f*	*c = b – a Customer*	*d = f – a Server*
1	93	4.0	4.0	78	2.0	4	6	–	4.0
2	22	2.0	6.0	76	2.0	6	8	–	–
3	53	2.5	8.5	58	1.5	8.5	10.0	–	0.5
4	64	3.0	11.5	54	1.5	11.5	13	–	1.5
5	39	2.0	13.5	74	2.0	13.5	15.5	–	0.5
6	07	1.0	14.5	92	2.5	15.5	18	1.0	–
7	10	1.5	16.0	38	1.5	18.0	19.5	2.0	–
8	63	3.0	19.0	70	2.0	19.5	21.5	0.5	–
9	76	3.0	22.0	96	3.0	22.0	25.0	–	0.5
10	35	2.0	24.0	92	2.5	25.0	27.5	1.0	–
							Total	4.5	7.0

Example 20.2 A tourist car operator finds that during the past few months, the car's use has varied so much that the cost of maintaining the car varied considerably. During the past 200 days the demand for the car fluctuated as below.

Trips per week	*Frequency*
0	16
1	24
2	30
3	60
4	40
5	30

Using random numbers, simulate the demand for a 10-week period.

Trips/week or Demand/week	*Frequency*	*Probability*	*Cumulative Probability*	*Tag-numbers*
0	16	0.08	0.08	00–07
1	24	0.12	0.20	08–19
2	30	0.15	0.35	20–34
3	60	0.30	0.65	35–64
4	40	0.20	0.85	65–84
5	30	0.15	1.00	85–99

Solution The tag-numbers allotted for the various demand levels are shown in the table above.

Week	*Random number*	*Demand*
1	82	4
2	96	5
3	18	1
4	96	5
5	20	2
6	84	4
7	56	3
8	11	1
9	52	3
10	03	0
		Total = 28

The simulated demand for the cars for the next 10 weeks period is given in the table above.
Total demand = 28 cars.

$$\text{Average demand} = \frac{28}{10} = 2.8 \text{ cars per week.}$$

Example 20.3 A manufacturing company keeps stock of a special product. Previous experience indicates the daily demand as given below.

Daily demand	*5*	*10*	*15*	*20*	*25*	*30*
Probability	0.01	0.20	0.15	0.50	0.12	0.02

Simulate the demand for the next 10 days. Also find the daily average demand for the product on the basis of simulated data.

Solution

Demand	*Probability*	*Cumulative probability*	*Tag-numbers*
5	0.01	0.01	00–00
10	0.20	0.21	01–20
15	0.15	0.36	21–35
20	0.50	0.86	36–85
25	0.12	0.98	86–97
30	0.02	1.00	98–99

Day	*Random number*	*Demand*
1	82	20
2	96	25
3	18	10
4	96	25
5	20	10
6	84	20
7	56	20
8	11	10
9	52	20
10	03	10
		Total = 170

$$\therefore \quad \text{Average demand} = \frac{170}{10} = 17 \text{ units/day.}$$

Example 20.4 An automobile production line turns out about 100 cars a day but deviations occur owing to many causes. The production is more accurately described by the probability distribution given below.

Production/day	*Probability*	*Production/day*	*Probability*
95	0.03	101	0.15
96	0.05	102	0.10
97	0.07	103	0.07
98	0.10	104	0.05
99	0.15	105	0.03
100	0.20	106	0.60
			1.00

Finished cars are transported across the bay at the end of each day by a ferry. If the ferry has space for only 101 cars, what will be the average number of cars waiting to be shipped and what will be the average number of empty space on the ship?

Solution The tag-numbers are established in the table below.

Production/day	*Probability*	*Cumulative probability*	*Tag-numbers*
95	0.03	0.03	00–02
96	0.05	0.08	03–07
97	0.07	0.15	08–14
98	0.10	0.25	15–24
99	0.15	0.40	25–39
100	0.20	0.60	40–59
101	0.15	0.75	60–74
102	0.10	0.85	75–84
103	0.07	0.92	85–91
104	0.05	0.97	92–96
105	0.03	1.00	97–99

The simulated production of cars for the next 15 days is given in the following table.

Day	Random number	Production per day	No. of cars waiting	No. of empty space in the ship
1	97	105	4	–
2	02	95	–	6
3	80	102	1	–
4	66	101	–	–
5	96	104	3	–
6	55	100	–	1
7	50	100	–	1
8	29	99	–	2
9	58	100	–	1
10	51	100	–	1
11	04	96	–	5
12	86	103	2	–
13	24	98	–	3
14	39	99	–	2
15	47	100	–	1
		Total	10	23

Average number of cars waiting to be shipped $= \frac{10}{15} = 0.67$ per day.

Average number of empty spaces on the ship $= \frac{23}{15} = 1.53$ per day.

Example 20.5 Suppose that the sales of a particular item per day is Poisson with mean five, then generate 20 days of sales by the Monte-Carlo method.

Solution The probability for the sales is given by,

$$P(X=r) = \frac{e^{-\lambda}\lambda^r}{r!} = \frac{e^{-5}5^r}{r!} \quad (\because \lambda = 5)$$

γ	*Cumulative probability*	*Tag-numbers*
0	0.01	00–00
1	0.04	01–03
2	0.13	04–12
3	0.27	13–26
4	0.44	27–43
5	0.62	44–61
6	0.76	62–75
7	0.87	76–86
8	0.93	87–92
9	0.97	93–96
10	0.98	97–97
11	0.99	98–98
12	1.00	99–99

The simulated sales for the next 20 days is given in the table below.

Day	*Random number*	*Sales*	*Day*	*Random number*	*Sales*
1	49	05	11	99	12
2	55	05	12	89	08
3	89	08	13	10	02
4	15	03	14	27	04
5	12	02	15	50	05
6	94	09	16	93	09
7	85	07	17	92	08
8	34	04	18	57	05
9	07	02	19	50	05
10	53	05	20	78	07

EXERCISES

1. The following data is observed in a tea serving counter. The arrival is at one minute interval.

No. of persons arriving	***0***	***1***	***2***	***3***	***4***	***5***
Probability	0.05	0.15	0.40	0.20	0.15	0.05

The service is taken as 2 persons for one minute interval. Using the following random numbers, simulate for 15 minutes period. 09, 54, 94, 01, 80, 73, 20, 26, 90, 79, 25, 48, 99, 25, 89. Calculate also the average number of persons waiting in the queue per minute. **[Ans.** 0.71 persons/minute]

2. A special purpose drill bores holes having a mean diameter of 1 cm. The process is normally distributed. Simulate a sequence of 10 diameters, if the standard deviation of the process is 0.002 cm.
3. At a toll office, a sample of 100 arrivals of vehicles gives the following frequency distribution of the inter-arrival and service time.

Inter-arrival time (min.)	***Frequency***	***Service time***	***Frequency***
1.0	2	1.5	10
1.5	5	–	–
2.0	9	2	22
2.5	25	–	–
3.0	22	2.5	40
3.5	11	–	–
4.0	10	3.0	20
4.5	6	–	–
5.0	3	3.5	8
5.5	2	–	–

There is a clerk at the office. Simulate the process for 20 arrivals and estimate the average percentage of vehicle waiting time and average per cent of the idle time available to the clerk.

SUMMARY

Types of simulation

(*i*) Analogue (environmental) simulation
(*ii*) Computer (system) simulation

Random variable: The random variable is a real valued function defined over a sample space associated with the outcome of a conceptual chance experiment.

Random number: A numerical value assigned to a random variable following the uniform probability density function.

Pesudo-random numbers: Random numbers are called pseudo-random numbers when they are generated by some deterministic process but have already qualified the pre-determined statistical test for randomness.

Monte-Carlo technique for Monte-Carlo simulation

Step 1 Clearly define the problem.
- (*a*) Identify the objectives of the problem.
- (*b*) Identify the main factors which have the greatest effect on the objectives of the problem.

Step 2 Construct an appropriate model.
- (*a*) Specify the variables and parameters of the model.
- (*b*) State the conditions under which the experiment is to be performed.
- (*c*) Define the relationship between the variables and parameters.

Step 3 Prepare the model for experimentation.
- (*a*) Define the starting conditions for the simulation.
- (*b*) Specify the number of runs of simulation to be made.

Step 4 Using steps 1 to 3, experiment with the model.
- (*a*) Define a coding system that will correlate the factors defined in step 1. with the random numbers to be generated for the simulation.
- (*b*) Select a random number generator and create the random numbers to be used in the simulation.
- (*c*) Associate the generated random number with the factors identified in step 1 and coded in step 4 (*a*).

Step 5 Summarize and examine the results obtained in step 4.

Step 6 Evaluate the results of the simulation.

Chapter

21

Decision Theory

21.1 INTRODUCTION

Decision theory is concerned with the theory about decisions. Only some aspects of human activity are mainly focused on this theory. In particulars how we use our freedom has been emphasized. In other words, goal-directed behaviour in the presence of options is the main factor in decision theory.

21.1.1 Basic Terminologies in Decision Theory

The following terms are used in decision theory.

1. ***Decision-maker*** Decision-maker is a person who is responsible for making decisions.
2. ***Acts*** They are the alternative courses of action or strategies that are available for decision-making. The objective is to choose the best alternative from those available. Decision alternatives are also called 'action', 'strategies' or 'courses of action'.
3. ***Events*** They are the occurrences that affect the achievement of the objectives. Events are also called 'stages of nature' or 'outcomes for the decision problem'. In any decision table, rows represent the 'decision alternatives' and columns represent the 'states of nature'.
4. ***Payoff tables*** Decision analysis tools which represent the pros and cons of a decision in tabular form are called Payoff tables. Payoffs (positive or negative returns) which are related to all possible combinations of alternative actions and external conditions are listed in pay-off tables. A pay-off table represents the profits of a problem.
5. ***Opportunity loss table*** It is a pay-off table, which represents the cost or loss incurred because of failure to take the best possible action. It is the numerical difference between the optimal outcome and the actual outcome for a given decision.
6. ***Utilities*** It is the individual's satisfaction level over a risky decision and its outcomes.

21.1.2 Steps in the Decision-Making Process

The decision-making process involves the following steps.

1. Determine the various alternatives or courses of action from which the final decision is to be made.
2. Identify the possible outcomes called the 'states of nature', which are available to the decision-maker.
3. Tabulate the pay-off function for all the decision alternatives with respect to the states of nature from the different combinations. The pay-off matrix is given in the table below.

States of nature	*Decision alternatives* A_1	A_2	...	*(Course of action)* A_m
S_1	a_{11}	a_{12}	...	a_{1m}
S_2	a_{21}	a_{22}	...	a_{2m}
$\vdots$	$\vdots$			
S_n	a_{n1}	a_{n2}	...	a_{nm}

4. Construct the regret or opportunity loss table. It is the difference between the highest possible (optimal) outcome and the actual outcome for a given course of action.
5. Select the optimum decision criterion, which results in the largest pay-off.

21.2 DECISION-MAKING ENVIRONMENT

Decisions are made under three types of environments.

21.2.1 Decision-making Under Conditions of Certainty

In this environment, there exists only one outcome for a decision as there is complete certainty about the future. The decision environment is perfect and deterministic. For example, in a replacement problem, if the annual maintenance cost and the swap value of the equipment are known in advance, then these quantities are called 'deterministic quantities', and the corresponding economic age to replace the equipment is an example of decision under certainty.

21.2.2 Decision-making Under Uncertainty

Here, more than one states of nature i.e. when there are two or more possible future events exist, but the decision-maker lacks sufficient knowledge that will allow him to assign probabilities to the various states of nature. Situations like launching a new product fall under this category.

21.2.3 Decision-making Under Conditions of Risk

If the availability of information for a decision environment is partial, then a decision under such an environment is called 'decision under risk'. The available information will be given in the form of probability distribution. The probability of various outcomes may be determined objectively from the past data.

Three approaches can be used to deal with the decision environment with risk. They are,

(*i*) Expected Money Value (EMV) criterion
(*ii*) Expected Opportunity Loss (EOL) criterion
(*iii*) Expected Value of Perfect Information (EVPI) criterion.

(*i*) *Expected Money Value (EMV) Criterion*
In this approach, first construct a pay-off table listing the alternative decisions and the various states of nature. Enter the conditional profit for each decision-event combination along with associated probabilities.

Compute the EMV for each alternative by multiplying the conditional profits by assigned probabilities and adding the resulting conditional values. Select the alternative that yields the highest EMV.

Example 21.1 A newspaper boy has the following probabilities of selling a magazine.

No. of copies sold	10	11	12	13	14
Probability	0.10	0.15	0.20	0.25	0.3

Cost of a copy is 30 paise and the sale price is 50 paise. He cannot return unsold copies. How many copies should he order?

Solution

1. Compute the conditional profit table resulting from any possible combination of supply and demand. Stocking of 10 copies each day will always result in a profit of 200 paise, irrespective of the demand. (50 – 30 × 10 = 200 paise). When the demand on a particular day is 13 copies, he can sell only 10 and then, the conditional profit is 200 paise.
Payoff = 20 × copies sold – 30 × copies unsold. With this we form the following conditional profit table.

Possible demand (No. of copies)	Probability	Possible stocks				
		10 copies	11 copies	12 copies	13 copies	14 copies
10	0.10	200	170	140	110	80
11	0.15	200	220	190	160	130
12	0.20	200	220	240	210	180
13	0.25	200	220	240	260	230
14	0.30	200	220	240	260	280

2. Compute the expected value of each decision or alternative by multiplying the conditional profit by the associated probability and adding the resulting values. The expected profit table is shown below.

Expected Profit Table

Possible demand (No. of copies)	Probability	Possible stocks				
		10 copies	11 copies	12 copies	13 copies	14 copies
10	0-10	20	17	14	11	8
11	0-15	30	33	28.5	24	19.5
12	0.20	40	44	48	42	36
13	0.25	50	55	60	65	57.5
14	0.30	60	66	72	78	84
Total exp. profit (paise)		200	215	222.5	220	205

3. From the above table, it is observed that the highest possible profit is paise 222.5 per day.

∴ The newspaper boy should purchase 12 copies per day, in order to get his maximum profit.

(ii) *Expected Opportunity Loss (EOL) Criterion: An Alternative Approach*

In this approach, first construct a conditional profit table for each decision-event combination along with the associated probabilities. For each event, compute the conditional opportunity loss (COL) by subtracting the corresponding pay-off from the maximum pay-off for that event. Calculate the expected opportunity loss (EOL) for each alternative by multiplying the conditional opportunity losses by the assigned probabilities and summing up their product. The alternative that yields the lowest EOL is selected.

Example 21.2 A department store with a bakery section is faced with the problem of how many cakes to buy in order to meet the day's demand. The departmental store prefers not to sell day-old cakes left over cakes are therefore, a complete loss. On the other hand, if a customer desires a cake but all of them have been sold, he will buy elsewhere and the sales will be lost. The store has therefore, collected information on the past sales based on selected 100-day period as shown in the table below.

Sales per day	15	16	17	18
No. of days	20	40	30	10
Probability	0.2	0.4	0.3	0.1

Construct the conditional profit and the opportunity loss tables. What is the optimal numbers of cakes that should be bought each day. A cake costs ₹ 2 and sells for ₹ 2.50.

Solution

1. Compute the conditional profit table resulting from any possible combination of supply and demand. Stocking of 15 cakes each day will always result in a profit of $0.5 \times 15 = ₹7.5$, irrespective of the demand. When the demand on some day is 18 cakes but the stock is only 15 cakes, the profit is still ₹7.50 only.

   If the demand on a particular day is 17 but the stock is of 18 cakes, the profit is

   $$17 \times 2.5 - 18 \times 2 = ₹6.5$$

   Thus, the conditional profit is given in Table 1. Payoff = 2.5 × cakes sold – 2 × cakes unsold

Table 21.1

Conditional Profit Table (₹)

Possible demand (No. of cakes)	*Probability*	*Possible stocks (Alternative)*			
		15	*16*	*17*	*18*
15	0.2	7.5	5.5	3.5	1.5
16	0.4	7.5	8	6	4
17	0.3	7.5	8	8.5	6.5
18	0.1	7.5	8	8.5	9

2. Compute the conditional opportunity loss for each stock alternative. This is obtained by subtracting each pay-off value in a row from the maximum pay-off of that row. The resulting conditional opportunity loss (COL) table is shown in Table 21.2.

Table 21.2

Conditional Loss Table (₹)

Possible demand (No. of cakes) (Event)	*Probability*	*Possible stocks (Alternative)*			
		15	*16*	*17*	*18*
15	0.2	0	2	4	6
16	0.4	0.5	0	2	4
17	0.3	1	0.5	0	2
18	0.1	1.5	1	0.5	0

3. Compute the expected opportunity loss of each decision alternative by multiplying its conditional loss values by the associated probability and then summing the resulting values. The expected loss table is shown in Table 21.3.

Table 21.3

Expected Loss Table

Possible demand (No. of cakes) (Event)	*Probability*	*Possible stocks (Alternative)*			
		15	*16*	*17*	*18*
15	0.2	0	0.4	0.4	0.4
16	0.4	0.2	0	1	2
17	0.3	0.3	0.15	0	0.6
18	0.1	0.15	0.1	0.05	0
Expected opportunity loss (₹)		0.65	0.65	1.45	3

4. From the above table, it is observed that the minimum expected loss is ₹ 0.65 per day, which is for stocks 15 and 16. Therefore, the optimum purchase of cake is 15 or 16.

Note: The above problem can also be solved by using the EMV method. In the EMV method, the problem is of maximizing expected profit, whereas in the EOL method, the problem is of minimizing expected loss. However, the optimal answer will remain the same.

(iii) Expected Value of Perfect Information (EVPI) Criterion

In the EMV criterion, the expected monetary value is calculated without perfect information. If we have the right information before a decision is made, we can obtain a maximum attainable EMV (i.e.) EMV*. Perfect (accurate) information will increase the expected profit from EMV* up to the value of expected profit with perfect information (EPPI). The amount of increase will be equal to the expected value of perfect information (EVPI). Thus we have,

EVPI = Expected profit with perfect information – Maximum EMV.

Example 21.3 Calculate the expected value with perfect information for Example 21.1.

Solution

1. Calculate the conditional profit table under certainty, i.e., the demand is known in advance. Under such circumstances, the newspaper boy will stock up the exact number of papers that are required each day. The following table shows the conditional profit values under perfect information.

Conditional Profit Table Under Certainty (₹)

Possible demand (No. of papers) (Event)	***Probability***	***Possible stocks (Alternative)***				
		10	***11***	***12***	***13***	***14***
10	0.1	24	–	–	–	–
11	0.15	–	25.5	–	–	–
12	0.2	–	–	27	–	–
13	0.25	–	–	–	28.5	–
14	0.3	–	–	–	–	30

2. Compute the expected profit with perfect informations by multiplying the conditional profit under certainty by its associated probability and summing up the resulting values. The sum value is called the 'expected profit under perfect information'.

Expected Profit Table with Perfect Information (₹)

Possible demand (No. of papers)	***Conditional profit under certainty***	***Probability of demand***	***Expected profit with perfect information***
16	24	0.1	2.4
17	25.5	0.15	3.825
18	27	0.2	5.4
19	28.5	0.25	7.125
20	30	0.3	9
			EPPI = 27.75

3. The best expected daily profit without information was found to be ₹ 25.775

$\therefore$ EVPI = EPPI − Max EMV

EVPI = 27.75 − 25.775 = ₹ 1.975

This is the maximum amount the newspaper boy should pay to get additional information, so that he can increase his maximum expected daily profit.

When the given problem is solved by EOL criterion, the minimum expected loss will be equal to EVPI.

(iii a) Expected Value Criterion

In this approach, first compute the expected value of each alternative and then select the alternative with the best expected value for implementation. The alternative, which has the higher expected value in the decision column is selected as the best one.

Example 21.4 The details for two competing alternatives are shown in the table below.

Annual Revenue of alternative

Alternative-I		*Alternative-II*	
Annual Revenue	*Probability*	*Annual Revenue*	*Probability*
2000	0.15	4000	0.3
3000	0.2	2500	0.4
5000	0.4	3500	0.2
4000	0.25	1200	0.1

Find the best alternative, when the interest rate is 0 per cent.

Solution

Compute the expected annual revenue of the alternative by using the formula,

$$ER = \frac{\sum_{j=1}^{4} C_{ij}P_{ij}}{\sum_{j=1}^{4} P_{ij}}$$

where, C_{ij} = Annual revenue of jth alternative during ith year.

P_{ij} = Associated probability of occurrence of jth alternative during the year i

$$\therefore \quad ER_1 = \frac{2000 \times 0.15 + 3000 \times 0.2 + 5000 \times 0.4 + 4000 \times 0.25}{1}$$

$$= ₹\,3900$$

$$ER_2 = 4000 \times 0.3 + 2500 \times 0.4 + 3500 \times 0.2 + 1200 \times 0.1$$

$$= ₹\,3020$$

Result Since the expected annual revenue of alternative 1 is higher than that of alternative 2, the former is the best.

(iii b) Expected Value Combined with Variance Criterion

In this approach, the expected annual revenue and the variance of annual revenue will be given. The best alternative is selected by comparing the coefficient of variation of different alternatives.

Example 21.5 The details for three competing alternatives are shown in the table below.

Mean and Variance of Each Alternative

	Alternative j (₹)		
	1	2	3
Expected annual revenue $(\bar{x}_j)$	5000	6000	7000
Variance of annual revenue $(\sigma_j)^2$	10000	2000	4000

Find the best alternative, when the interest rate is 0 per cent.

Solution

Compute the coefficient of variations ($CV_j = j = 1, 2$ and 3) of the annual evenues of the alternatives. Then,

$$CV_j = \frac{\sigma_j}{x_j}$$

$$CV_1 = \frac{\sqrt{10000}}{5000} = 0.02$$

$$CV_2 = \frac{\sqrt{2000}}{6000} = 0.00745$$

$$CV_3 = \frac{\sqrt{4000}}{7000} = 0.00903$$

Result Since the coefficient of variation of alternative 2 is lesser than that of alternatives 1 and 3, alternative 2 should be selected as the best alternative.

21.3 DECISION UNDER UNCERTAINTY

If the available information for a decision environment is insufficient, then a decision taken under such an environment is called *decision under uncertainty*. This available information of the decision environment cannot be described in the form of a probability distribution. Such a situation arises when a new product is launched in the market.

Under conditions of uncertainty, there are five criteria available for making a decision.

(*i*) Maximin gain criterion or Minimax loss criterion
(*ii*) Maximax gain criterion or Minimin loss criterion
(*iii*) Laplace criterion
(*iv*) Savage minimax regret criterion
(*v*) The Hurwicz criterion

21.3.1 Maximin Criterion

In this criterion the decision-maker achieves the maximum possible pay-off or the minimum possible cost. The steps involved in this are,

Step 1 Determine the minimum outcome of each alternative row, irrespective of the column.

Step 2 Select the highest maximum outcomes of the decision alternatives.

Note: If it is a minimax loss criterion, choose the maximum in each row and select the minimum alternative of the maximum loss.

Example 21.6 A businessman has four alternatives, each of which can be followed by any of the four possible events. The conditional pay-offs (in ₹) for each action-event combination are given below.

Alternatives	*Payoff conditional on events*			
	P	*Q*	*R*	*S*
A_1	8	4	14	–6
A_2	–4	10	12	7
A_3	14	6	0	4
A_4	13	8	6	–3

Determine which alternatives should be selected if the businessman adopts,

(*i*) Maximin criterion
(*ii*) Minimax criterion

Solution

(*i*) *Maximin criterion*

1. Compute the minimum assured pay-off for each alternative.

$$A_1 = -6, A_2 = -4, A_3 = 0, A_4 = -3$$

2. Since the maximum of these minimum pay-offs is 0, the corresponding alternative A_3 is selected according to the maxmin principle.

(*ii*) *Minimax criterion*

1. Since the pay-off numbers designate the costs, compute the maximum possible costs for each alternative.

$$A_1 = 14, A_2 = 12, A_3 = 14, A_4 = 13$$

2. Since the minimum of these maximum costs is 12, the alternative A_2 is selected.

21.3.2 Maximax Gain Criterion or Minimin Loss Criterion

In this criterion, the decision-maker selects a particular alternative, which corresponds to the maximum pay-off for each alternative. If the cost is given, then the least minimum cost for each alternative is selected.

Step 1 Select the highest maximum outcomes of the decision alternatives.

Note: If it is a minimax loss criterion, choose the maximum in each row and select the minimum alternative of the maximum loss.

Refer to previous problem on pay-off table. Determine which alternative should be selected, if the salesman adopts,

(*a*) Maximax gain criterion
(*b*) Minimin loss criterion

(*a*) Maximax criterion

1. Compute the maximum assumed pay-off for each alternative.

$$A_1 = 14, \quad A_2 = 12, \quad A_3 = 14, \quad A_4 = 13.$$

2. Since the highest of these maximum pay-offs is 14, the corresponding alternatives A_1 and A_3 are selected, according to the maximax principle.

(b) Minimin criterion

1. Compute the minimum possible costs of each alternative.

$$A_1 = -6, \quad A_2 = -4, \quad A_3 = 0, \quad A_4 = -3.$$

2. Since the least of these minimum costs is – 6, the corresponding alternative A_1 is selected, according to the minimum principle.

21.3.3 Laplace Criterion

In this criterion, the decision-maker uses all the information by assigning equal probabilities to the pay-off for each action and then the alternative, which corresponds to the maximum expected pay-off is selected as the best alternative. If the cost is given in the problem, the alternative corresponding to the minimum cost is selected as the best alternative.

Example 21.7 The estimated sales of proposed types of perfumes are as under.

Types of perfumes	*Estimated levels of sales (Units)*		
	₹ 20,000	*₹ 10,000*	*₹ 25,000*
A	25	15	10
B	40	20	5
C	60	25	3

What will be the best alternative if a person adopts the Laplace criterion?

Solution Laplace principle assumes that the estimated levels of sales are equally likely. Thus, the associated probabilities are given by, $P(i) = \frac{1}{3}$ $(j = 1, 2, 3)$ and the expected costs due to deviations from the best level are:

$$E(A) = \frac{1}{3}\ (25 + 15 + 10) = 16.6667$$

$$E(B) = \frac{1}{3}\ (40 + 20 + 5) = 21.6667$$

$$E(C) = \frac{1}{3}\ (60 + 25 + 3) = 29.333$$

Result Since the expected pay-off for perfume C is higher, it is the one that should be selected.

21.3.4 Savage Minimax Regret Criterion

Sometimes, minimax or maximin criterion may yield a misleading result because of selecting the alternative actions with respect to the minimum of the maximum values or maximum of the minimum values of the rows. This can be avoided by using savage minimax regret criterion. It is based on the concept of regret (after selecting a wrong decision) and calls for selecting the course of action that minimizes the maximum regret. The steps involved in this are as follows:

Step 1 From the given pay-off matrix, construct a regret (opportunity loss) table of each alternative for every state of nature.

Step 2 Choose the maximum pay-off in each column (states of nature) and subtract all the elements in that column from this maximum value.

Step 3 For each decision alternative (row), choose the maximum row value and enter this in the last decision column.

Step 4 Select the decision alternative with the smallest value in the decision column.

Example 21.8 Consider the following pay-off profit matrix.

Alternatives	*Expected levels of sales (₹)*		
	I	*II*	*III*
A	30	20	15
B	40	50	20
C	70	50	5

Solve this using savage minimax regret criterion.

Solution

1. The opportunity loss table for each alternative with the states of nature is shown below.

Alternatives	*Expected levels of sales (₹)*		
	I	*II*	*III*
A	70 – 30 = 40	50 – 20 = 30	20 – 15 = 5
B	70 – 40 = 30	50 – 50 = 0	20 – 20 = 0
C	70 – 70 = 0	50 – 50 = 0	20 – 5 = 15
Column Maximum	70	30	20

2. The opportunity loss table and the maximum loss in each row is entered in the next table.

Alternatives	*Expected levels of sales (₹)*			*Decision column (Max. loss)*
	I	*II*	*III*	
A	40	30	5	40
B	30	0	0	30
C	0	0	15	15

Result Since the minimum of maximum loss is in alternative *C* = ₹ 15, this alternative should be selected.

21.3.5 The Hurwicz Criterion

In this criterion, the decision-maker's view falls between that of extreme pessimism and extreme optimism of the maximum criterion. It is made by assigning weights with certain degrees of optimism and pessimism. The basic steps involved in this criterion are:

Step 1 Find the largest and smallest pay-off for each alternative.

Step 2 Assign weights for largest and smallest as α and $(1-\alpha)$ respectively, i.e., $0 \leq \alpha \leq 1$.

Step 3 Compute the expected value of decision alternatives = α (Max. pay-off) + $(1-\alpha)$ Minimum pay-off.

Step 4 Choose the decision alternative with the highest expected value as the optimal decision alternative.

Example 21.9 Consider the following pay-off (profit) matrix.

States of Nature

		1	*2*	*3*	*4*
Alternative	A_1	5	10	18	25
	A_2	8	7	8	23
	A_3	21	18	12	21
	A_4	30	22	19	15

Solve this using Hurwicz criterion with $\alpha = 0.75$.

Solution

1. Find the largest and smallest pay-off for each alternative and compute the expected value of the decision alternative.

$\alpha = 0.75$

Alternatives	*Largest pay-off*	*Smallest pay-off*	*Expected value of decision alternative*
A_1	25	5	$25 \times 0.75 + 5 \times 0.25 = 20$
A_2	23	7	$23 \times 0.75 + 7 \times 0.25 = 19$
A_3	21	12	$21 \times 0.75 + 12 \times 0.25 = 18.75$
A_4	30	15	$30 \times 0.75 + 15 \times 0.25 = 26.25$

Result Since the pay-offs here represent profits according to Hurwicz principle, the optimum solution is to choose the alternative A_4.

21.4 DECISION TREE ANALYSIS

A decision tree is a graphical representation of various decision alternatives, states of nature, probabilities attached to the states of nature and the conditional profits as well as losses. In constructing a tree diagram, two types of nodes are used:

(*i*) Decision node represented by a square, and (*ii*) State of nature node (chance node) represented by a circle. Alternative courses of action (strategies) start from the decision node as main branches. At the end of each main branch, there is a state of nature node from which emerge chance events in the form of sub-branches.

The corresponding pay-offs and the associated probabilities with alternative courses as well as the chance events are shown on these branches. At the end of the chance branches, the expected values of the outcome are shown.

The general approach used in decision tree analysis is to work backwards through the tree from right to left, computing the expected value of each chance node. Then select the particular branch having a decision node, which leads to the chance node with the maximum expected value.

Steps in Decision Tree Analysis

1. Identify the decision points and alternatives at each point systematically.
2. At each decision point, determine the probability and the associated pay-off with each course of action.
3. Compute the expected pay-off (EMV) for each course of action. Start from the extreme right and move towards the left.
4. Choose the course of action that yields the best pay-off for each of the decisions. Proceed backward to the next stage of decision points.
5. Repeat the above steps till the first decision point is reached.
6. Identify the best course of action to be adopted from the beginning to the end, under various possible outcomes as a whole.

Example 21.10 A company is going to develop a new product in the market. Three alternative decisions are available for the management.

A_1: Advertising on television, where advertising cost is ₹ 3,000 per day.
A_2: Appointing salesmen for marketing. The cost is ₹ 1,200 per day.
A_3: Conducting an exhibition, where the cost is ₹ 900 per day.

The unit price is fixed at ₹ 25, product and the cost of units associated with the respective decision alternatives are 9, 5 and 11. The expected demand for the product is as follows.

Demand	200	300	400	500
Probability	0.3	0.2	0.4	0.1

The company has to decide upon the best alternative among the three decisions.

Solution

1. Formulate the pay-off table for the three alternative decisions and the state of nature by using,

Profit = (Fixed price – Cost of units) × Demand

Alternatives	*State of nature (Demand)*			
	200	*300*	*400*	*500*
A_1 (9)	(25 – 9) × 200 = 3200	(25 – 9) × 300 = 4800	(25 – 9) × 400 = 6400	(25 – 9) × 500 = 8000
A_2 (5)	(25 – 5) × 200 = 4000	(25 – 5) × 300 = 6000	(25 – 5) × 400 = 8000	(25 – 5) × 500 = 10000
A_3 (11)	(25 – 11) × 200 = 2800	(25 – 11) × 300 = 4200	(25 – 11) × 400 = 5600	(25 – 11) × 500 = 7000

2. Construct a decision tree by using the above pay-off values with their associated probabilities.

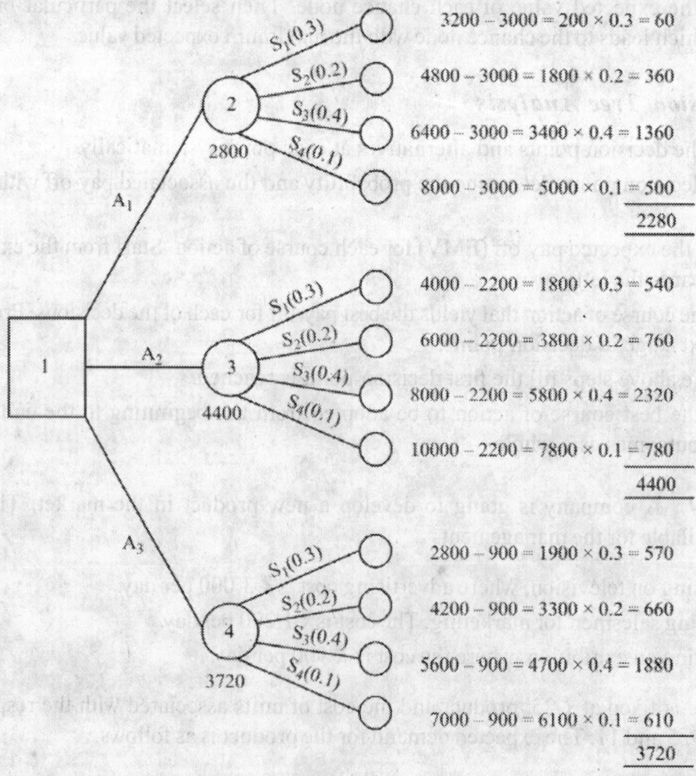

Result Since the maximum pay-off for alternative 2 = ₹ 4,400, it is the best alternative and should be selected.

Example 21.11 A manager has two independent investments *A* and *B* available to him, but he lacks the capital to undertake both of them simultaneously. He can choose to take *A* first and then stop, or if *A* is successful only then take *B* or vice versa. The probability of success for *A* is 0.7, while for *B* it is 0.4. Both investments require an initial capital outlay of ₹ 2,000 and both return nothing if the venture is unsuccessful. Successful completion of *A* will return ₹ 3,000 and successful completion of *B* will return ₹ 5,000. Draw the decision tree and determine the best strategy.

Solution

1. Compute the various action-event combinations and tabulate the resulting pay-offs of the problem. The net EMV corresponding to various event decision points are indicated in the decision tree.

Decision alternative	***Decision***	***Event***	***Probability***	***Conditional value***	***Expected value***
3	Accept *A*	Success	0.7	3000	2100
		Failure	0.3	(–) 2000	(–) 600
				Net EMV	1500
	Stop	0	0	0	0

(Contd...)

2	Accept B	Success Failure	0.4 0.6	5000 (–) 2000	2000 1200
				Net EMV	(–) 800
	Stop	0	0	0	0
1	Accept A	Success Failure	0.7 0.3	3800 (–) 2000	2660 (–) 600
					2060
	Accept B	Success	0.4	6500	2600
		Failure	0.6	(–) 2000	(–) 1200
				Net EMV	1400
	Stop	0	0	0	0

Result Since the EMV is maximum in decision 1, the optimal decision is to accept investment A, and if it is successful, then accept B.

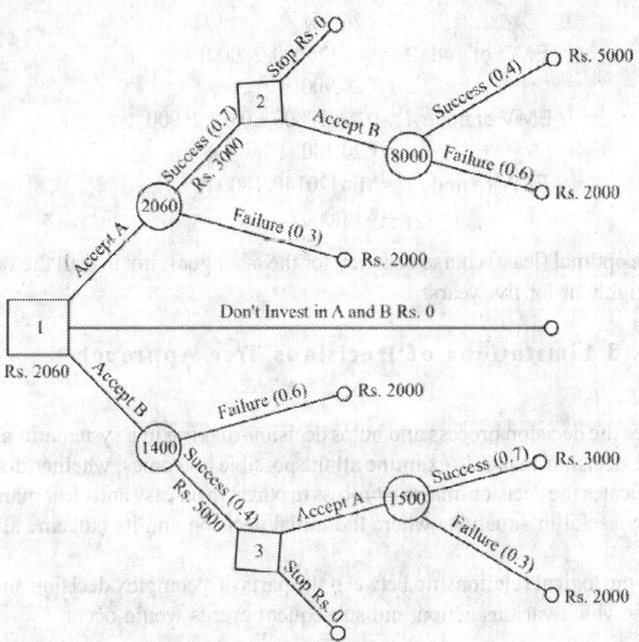

Example 21.12 A finance manager has to decide whether or not to drill a well on his farm. In his village, only 40 per cent of the wells drilled were successful at 200 feet of depth. Some of the farmers who did not get water at 200 feet , drilled further upto 250 feet but only 20 per cent struck water. Cost of drilling is ₹ 50 per foot. The finance manager estimated that he would pay ₹ 18,000 during a five year period on the present value terms, if he continues to buy water from the neighbour rather than go for the well, which would have a life of five years. He has three decisions to choose from: (a) Should he drill up to 200 feet, (b) If no water is found at 200 feet, should he drill up to 250 feet? (c) Should he continue to buy water from his neighbour?

Solution

1. Draw the decisions tree diagram for the given problem.

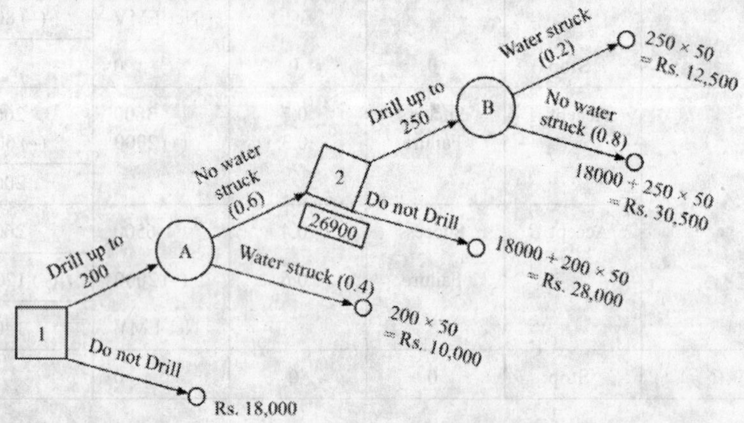

2. Compute the associated cost of each outcome and enter these values on the decision tree.

$$\begin{aligned}
\text{EMV of node } B &= 0.2 \times 12500 + 0.8 \times 30500 \\
&= ₹\,26{,}900. \\
\text{EMV of node 2} &= \text{Min}\,[26900, 28000] \\
&= ₹\,26{,}900. \\
\text{EMV of node } A &= 0.4 \times 10000 + 0.6 \times 26900 \\
&= ₹\,20{,}140. \\
\text{EMV of node 1} &= \text{Min}\,[20140, 18000] \\
&= ₹\,18{,}000.
\end{aligned}$$

Result Thus the optimal (least) course of action for the manager is not to drill the well and pay ₹ 18,000 for water to his neighbour for five years.

Advantages and Limitations of Decisions Tree Approach

Advantages

1. It structures the decision process and helps decision-making in a systematic and sequential order.
2. It helps the decision-maker to examine all the possible outcomes, whether desirable or not.
3. It communicates the decision-making process to others in an easy and clear manner about the future.
4. It is mainly useful in situations where the initial decision and its outcome affects the subsequent decisions.
5. It displays the logical relationship between the parts of a complex decision and identifies the time sequence is which various action and subsequent events would occur.

Limitations

1. Decision tree diagrams become more complicated as the number of decision alternatives and variables increase.
2. It becomes highly complicated when interdependent alternatives and dependent variables are present in the problem.
3. It analyzes the expected values and gives an average solution only.
4. Often there is inconsistency in assigning probabilities for different events.

SUMMARY

Decision may be classified into two categories, tactical and strategic. Tactical decisions are those which affect the business in the short run. Strategic decisions are those which have far-reaching effects on the business.

(*i*) ***The decision-maker*** The decision-maker is charged with responsibility of making the decision. That is, he has to select one from a set of possible courses of action.

(*ii*) ***The acts*** The acts are the alternative courses of action or strategies that are available to the decision-maker. The decision involves a selection among two or more alternative courses of action. The problem is to choose the best of these alternatives to achieve an objective.

(*iii*) ***Event*** Events are the occurrences that affect the achievements of the objectives.

(*iv*) ***Pay-off Table*** A pay-off table represents the economics of a problem.

(*v*) ***Opportunity loss table*** An opportunity loss is the loss incurred because of failure to choose the best possible action.

Types of Decision-making Situations

(*i*) Decision-making under certainty
(*ii*) Decision-making under uncertainty
(*iii*) Decision-making under risk
(*iv*) Decision-making under conflict.

Laplace criterion As the decision-maker has no information about the probability of occurrences of various events, he makes a simple assumption that each probability is equally likely.

Hurwicz alpha criterion This method is a combination of maximum criterion and maximax criterion. In this method, the decision-maker's degree of optimism is represented by α, the coefficient of optimism. α varies between 0 and 1. When $\alpha = 0$, there is total pessimism and when $\alpha = 1$, there is total optimism.

$D_i = \alpha M_i + (1 - \alpha) m_i$, where M_i is the maximum pay-off of '*i*' strategy and m_i is the minimum pay-off of '*i*' strategy. The strategy with highest of $D_1, D_2, \ldots$ is chosen. The decision-maker will specify the value of α, depending upon his level of optimism.

Chapter

22 Non-Linear Programming Problem

22.1 INTRODUCTION

Non-linear programming (NLP) is an extension of linear programming (LP). The principal differences between NLP and LP is that in NLP, the variables which are either in objective function and/or in the constraints occur in higher powers such as (x^2) or in the multiplication form such as ($x_1, x_2 \ldots$) with a greater number of variables, i.e., non-linear.

Generally, if the objective function $f(x)$ is a function of a single variable say x, the problem of finding maximum/minimum of $f(x)$ is elementary. If x is a function of two variables (x_1, x_2), we can find maximum/minimum for $f(x)$. However, if $x = (x_1, x_2, \ldots x_n)$ then for finding maximum/minimum NLP techniques such as Wolfe's method, Beale's method, and Separable programming are used.

If the objective function $f(x)$ is not continuous or differentiable, then search methods, whose only requirement is $f(x)$ should be compatible are used to find the extreme. Each of these problems requires different solution procedure.

In this chapter a set of NLP like the following are explained:

- Non-linear programming problem of general nature
- Quadratic programming problem
- Separable programming problem

22.2 LAGRANGE MULTIPLIER METHOD

This method is used to optimize a continuous and differentiable function subject to equality constraints.

Consider the non-linear programming problem

Optimize $\qquad Z = f(x)$

Subject to, $\qquad G_i(x_1, x_2, \ldots x_n) = b_i, i = 1, 2, \ldots m.$

A modified form of the above model is shown below

Optimize $\qquad Z = f(x_1, x_2, \ldots x_n)$

Subject to, $\qquad g_i(x_1, x_2, \ldots x_n) = 0, i = 1, 2, \ldots m.$

$\qquad x_j \geq 0, j = 1, 2, \ldots n.$

Where $\qquad g_i(x_1, x_2, \ldots x_n) = G_i(x_1, x_2, \ldots x_n) - b_i, i = 1, 2, \ldots m.$

This problem consists of n variables with m constraints. Multiply each constraint with an unknown variable λ_i ($i = 1, 2, \ldots m$) and subtract each from the objective function $f(x)$ to be optimized. The new objective function is

$$L(x, \lambda) = f(x) - \sum_{i=1}^{m} \lambda_i g_i(x), \quad x = (x_1, x_2, \ldots x_n)^T$$

Where $m < n$. The function $L(x, \lambda)$ is called the *Lagrange function.*

Steps of Lagrange Method

Step 1: Form the Lagrange function as $L(x, \lambda) = f(x_1, x_2, \ldots x_n) - \sum_{i=1}^{n} \lambda_i g_i(x_1, x_2, \ldots x_n)$

Step 2: Find the partial derivatives of L with respect to x_j and λ of $L(x, \lambda)$ and equal to zero given by

$$\frac{\partial L}{\partial x_j} = 0, \quad j = 1, 2, \ldots n$$

$$\frac{\partial L}{\partial \lambda_i} = 0, \quad i = 1, 2, \ldots m$$

So, the system consists of $n + m$ unknown variables with $n + m$ simultaneous equations of the first order partial derivatives.

Step 3: Find the solution of the system of equation $(n + m)$ obtained from step 2.

Step 4: Form the Bordered Hessian matrix $[H^B]$ of size $n + m$.

General form of the Bordered Hessian matrix

	1	2	..	I	..	m	1 2 .. j .. n
1	0	0				0	Coefficients of $\frac{\partial L}{\partial \lambda_i} = 0, \quad i = 1, 2, \ldots m$
2	0	0		0		0	Written row wise
:	:						
i	0	0		0		0	
:	:						
m	0	0		0		0	
1	Coefficients of						$\frac{\partial L}{\partial x_i} \frac{\partial L}{\partial x_j}$
	$\frac{\partial L}{\partial \lambda_i} = 0, \quad i = 1, 2, \ldots m$						for $i = 1, 2, \ldots m$
2	written columnwise						$j = 1, 2, \ldots n$
:							
j							
:							
n							

Step 5: In this step using the sufficient conditions for maxima and minima, the testing for the stationary point $(x_1, x_2, \ldots x_n)$ to be optimal solution is given as:

i. Find the last $(n-1)$ principal minors of the Bordered Hessian matrix.

ii. The stationary point will give the maximum objective function value, if the sign of each of the last $(n-m)$ principal minor determinants of the Bordered Hessian matrix is same as that of $(-1)^{m+1}$, ending with the $(2m+1)^{th}$ principal minor determinant.

iii. The stationary point will give the minimum objective function value, if the sign of each of the last $(n-m)$ principal minor determinants of the bordered Hessian matrix is same as that of $(-1)^m$ ending with the $(2m+1)^{th}$ principal minor determinant.

Example 1 Solve the non-linear programming problem.

Optimize $\quad Z = 4x_1^2 + 2x_2^2 + x_3^2 - 4x_1x_2$

Subject to, $\quad x_1 + x_2 + x_3 = 15,\ 2x_1 - x_2 + 2x_3 = 20;\ x_1, x_2, x_3 \geq 0$

Solution

$$f(x) = 4x_1^2 + 2x_2^2 + x_3^2 - 4x_1x_2$$
$$g_1(x) = x_1 + x_2 + x_3 - 15$$
$$g_2(x) = 2x_1 - x_2 + 2x_3 - 20$$

Construct the Lagrangian function

$$L(x, \lambda) = f(x) - \lambda_1 g_1(x) - \lambda_2 g_2(x) = (4x_1^2 + 2x_2^2 + x_3^2 - 4x_1x_2) - \lambda_1(x_1 + x_2 + x_3 - 15) - \lambda_2(2x_1 - x_2 + 2x_3 - 20)$$

Using necessary conditions

$$\frac{\partial L}{\partial x_1} = 0 \Rightarrow 8x_1 - 4x_2 - \lambda_1 - 2\lambda_2 = 0$$

$$\frac{\partial L}{\partial x_2} = 0 \Rightarrow 4x_2 - 4x_1 - \lambda_1 + \lambda_2 = 0$$

$$\frac{\partial L}{\partial x_3} = 0 \Rightarrow 2x_3 - \lambda_1 - 2\lambda_3 = 0$$

$$\frac{\partial L}{\partial \lambda_1} = 0 \Rightarrow -(x_1 + x_2 + x_3 - 15) = 0$$

$$\frac{\partial L}{\partial \lambda_2} = 0 \Rightarrow -(2x_1 - x_2 + 2x_3 - 20) = 0$$

Solving these simultaneous equations, we get $(x_1, x_2, x_3) = \left(\frac{33}{9}, \frac{10}{3}, 8\right)$ and $\lambda_1 = \frac{40}{9}, \lambda_2 = \frac{52}{9}$.

The bordered Hessian matrix at this solution is given by

$$\left[H^B\right] = \begin{bmatrix} 0 & 0 & 1 & 1 & 1 \\ 0 & 0 & 2 & -1 & 2 \\ 1 & 2 & 8 & -4 & 0 \\ 1 & -1 & -4 & 4 & 0 \\ 1 & 2 & 0 & 0 & 2 \end{bmatrix}$$

$$n = 3, m=2$$

$$\therefore \quad n-m = 1, 2m+1=5$$

$$|H^B| = 72>0.$$

The sign of this value $|H^B|$ is same as that of $(-1)^{1+1}$. Hence the solution (x_1, x_2, x_3) corresponds to the maximum point.

$\therefore$ The optimal results are presented as $(x_1, x_2, x_3) = \left(\frac{33}{9}, \frac{10}{3}, 8\right)$

$$Z_{\text{Max}} = \frac{7380}{81} = 91.1$$

Example 2 Solve the following problem by using the method of Lagrangian multiplier.

Minimize $Z = x_1^2 + x_2^2 + x_3^2$

Subject to the constraints

(i) $x_1 + x_2 + 3x_3 = 2$

(ii) $5x_1 + 2x_2 + x_3 = 5$ and $x_1, x_2 \geq 0$.

Solution

$$f(x) = x_1^2 + x_2^2 + x_3^2$$

$$g_1(x) = x_1 + x_2 + 3x_3 - 2$$

$$g_2(x) = 5x_1 + 2x_2 + x_3 - 5$$

Construct the Lagrangian function

$$L(x, T\lambda) = f(x) - \lambda_1 g_1(x) - \lambda_2 g_2(x)$$

$$= x_1^2 + x_2^2 + x_3^2 - \lambda_1(x_1 + x_2 + 3x_3 - 2) - \lambda_2(5x_1 + 2x_2 + x_3 - 5)$$

Using the necessary condition

$$\frac{\partial L}{\partial x_1} = 0 \Rightarrow 2x_1 - \lambda_1 - 5\lambda_2 = 0$$

$$\frac{\partial L}{\partial x_2} = 0 \Rightarrow 2x_2 - \lambda_1 - 2\lambda_2 = 0$$

$$\frac{\partial L}{\partial x_3} = 0 \Rightarrow 2x_3 - 3\lambda_1 - \lambda_2 = 0$$

$$\frac{\partial L}{\partial \lambda_1} = 0 \Rightarrow -(x_1 + x_2 + 3x_3 - 2) = 0$$

$$\frac{\partial L}{\partial \lambda_2} = 0 \Rightarrow -(5x_1 + 2x_2 + x_3 - 5) = 0$$

Solving these simultaneous equations, we get the solution

$$(x_1 x_2 x_3) = \left(\frac{37}{46}, \frac{16}{46}, \frac{13}{46}\right) \text{ and } (\lambda_1 \lambda_2) = \left(\frac{3}{23}, \frac{7}{23}\right)$$

$$Min\ Z = \frac{897}{1058}$$

Apply sufficient condition to check for the minimum of Z for which form the bordered Hessian matrix

$$[H^B] = \begin{bmatrix} 0 & 0 & 1 & 1 & 3 \\ 0 & 0 & 5 & 2 & 1 \\ 1 & 5 & 2 & 0 & 0 \\ 2 & 2 & 0 & 2 & 0 \\ 3 & 1 & 0 & 0 & 2 \end{bmatrix}$$

Since $m = 2, n = 3, n - m = 1, 2m + 1 = 5.$

One minor of H^B of order 5 is $H^B \mid H^B| = 460 > 0$.

The sign of this value $|H^B|$ is same as that of $(-1)^m = (-1)^2 = 1$.

$\therefore$ The extreme point (x_1, x_2, x_3) corresponds to minimum of Z.

Optimum solution in Min $Z = \frac{897}{1058}$.

Exercise 22.1 Obtain the solution of the following problems by using the method of Lagrangian multipliers.

1. Min $Z = -2x_1^2 + 5x_1x_2 - 4x_2^2 + 18x_2$

   Subject to, $x_1 + x_2 = 7,\ x_1, x_2 \geq 0$

   Ans. $x_1 = 4.95$

   $x_2 = 2.045$

   Min $Z = 10.5$

2. Maximize $Z = x_1^2 + 2x_2^2 + x_3^2$

   Subject to, $2x_1 + x_2 + 2x_3 = 30$

   $x_1, x_2, x_3 \geq 0$

Ans. $\left(\frac{120}{17}, \frac{30}{17}, \frac{120}{17}\right)$

$$\text{Max } Z = 105.88$$

3. Minimize $Z = 4x_1^2 + 2x_2^2 + x_3^2 - 4x_1x_2$

Subject to,

$$x_1 + x_2 + x_3 = 15$$

$$2x_1 - x_2 + 2x_3 = 20$$

$$x_1, x_2, x_3 \geq 0$$

Ans. $\left(x_1 = \frac{11}{3}, x_2 = \frac{10}{3}, x_3 = 8\right)$

$$\text{Max } Z = 91.111.$$

22.3 KUHN-TUCKER CONDITIONS

The necessary and sufficient conditions for a local optimum of the general non-linear programming problem, with both equality and inequality constraints is called Kuhn-Tucker conditions.

Consider the following general form of NLP in which the objective function is to be maximized with all the constraints of $\leq$ type.

Example Maximize $Z = f(x_1, x_2, \ldots x_n)$

Subject to, $G(x_1, x_2, \ldots x_j \ldots x_n) \leq b_i, i = 1, 2, \ldots, m$

$$j = 1, 2, \ldots n$$

$$x_j \geq 0$$

The modified form of the above problem is

Max $Z = f(x_1, x_2 \ldots x_n)$

Subject to, $g_i(x_1, x_2 \ldots x_n) \leq 0, i = 1, 2 \ldots n$

$$x_j \geq 0, j = 1, 2, \ldots n$$

Where $g_i(x_1, x_2 \ldots x_n) = G(x_1, x_2 \ldots x_n) - b_i$

By adding slack variable to the constraints, the above problem can be modified as

$$\text{Maximize } Z = f(x_1, x_2, \ldots x_n)$$

Subject to $g_i\left(x_1, x_2 \ldots x_n\right) + s_i^2 = 0, \quad i = 1, 2, \ldots m \quad x_j \geq 0, \quad j = 1, 2, \ldots n$

where s_i^2 are slack variables added to the constraint.

This problem consists of $n + m$ variables and m constraints. Let L be the Lagrangian function and λ_i be the Lagrangian multiplies of the ith constraints.

Then the Lagrangian function is given as

$$L(x, s, \lambda) = f(x) - \sum_{i=1}^{m} \lambda_i \left[g_i(x) + s_i^2\right]$$

where $\lambda = (\lambda_1, \lambda_2, \ldots \lambda_m)$ is the vector of the Lagrangian multiplier.

The necessary conditions for an extreme point to be local optimum (maxima or minima) can be obtained by solving the frequency equations.

$$\frac{\partial L}{\partial x_j} = \frac{\partial f(x)}{\partial x_j} - \sum_{i=1}^{M} \lambda_i \frac{\partial g_i(x)}{\partial x_j} = 0 \qquad j = 1,2,...n$$

$$\frac{\partial L}{\partial \lambda_i} = -\left(g_i(x) + s_i^2\right) = 0 \qquad i = 1,2,...m$$

$$\frac{\partial L}{\partial s_i} = -2x_i\lambda_i = 0 \qquad i = 1,2,...m$$

The equation $\frac{\partial L}{\partial \lambda_i} = 0$ gives back the original set of constraints $g_i(x) + s_i^2 = 0$.

The equation $\frac{\partial L}{\partial s_i} = 0$ provides the set of rules $-2\lambda_i x_i = 0$ or $\lambda_i s_i = 0$ for finding the unconstrained optimum. The condition $\lambda_i s_i = 0$ implies that either $\lambda_i = 0$ or $s_i = 0$.

If $s_i = 0$ and $\lambda_i > 0$ then the equation $\frac{\partial L}{\partial \lambda_i} = 0$ gives $g_i(x) = 0$.

This means either $\lambda_i = 0$ or $g_i(x) = 0$ which in turn can be written as

$$\lambda_i g_i(x) = 0$$

Since $s_i^2 \geq 0 \Rightarrow g_i(x) \geq 0$, the equation $\lambda_i g_i(x) = 0$

$\Rightarrow$ when $g_i(x) < 0, \lambda_i = 0$ and when $g_i(x) = 0, \lambda_i > 0$. Also, if $\lambda_i = 0, s_i^2 > 0$ then the ith constraint is inactive. This constraint will not change the optimum value of Z'' because

$$\lambda = \frac{\partial z}{\partial b_j} = 0 \text{ and hence can be discarded.}$$

To maintain the relation of λ_i, Kuhn-Tucker has established the following necessary conditions.

i. $\lambda_i \geq 0 \; i = 1,2,...m$

ii. $\frac{\partial L}{\partial x_j} = 0 \quad (j = 1,2,...n)$

iii. $\lambda_i g_i(x_1, x_2, \ldots, x_n) = 0 \quad i = 1,2,\ldots m$

iv. $g_i(x_1, x_2, \ldots, x_n) = 0 \quad i = 1,2,\ldots m$

Note:

For a minimization problem, with concave objective function and with all ≥ type constraints (concave type constraints), the value of λ_i should be ≥ 0. If L is concave, in the case of maximization problem and convex in the case of minimization problem. The different possibilities of λ_i are given below.

i. For maximization objective function ≤ type constraints $\lambda_i \geq 0 \quad i = 1, 2 \ldots m$

ii. For maximization objective function, with ≥ type constraints $\lambda_i \leq 0 \quad i = 1, 2 \ldots m$

iii. For maximization objective function with = type constraints λ_i is unrestricted in sign, $i = 1, 2, \ldots$ m

iv. For minimization objective function with ≤ type of constraints $\lambda_i \leq 0 \quad i = 1, 2, \ldots m$

v. For minimization objective function and with ≥ type constraints $\lambda_i \geq 0 \quad i = 1, 2, \ldots m$

vi. For minimization objective function and with = constraints, λ_i is unrestricted in sign, i = 1, 2…*m*.

Summary of Kuhn-Tucker Conditions

	F(x)	*g(x)*	λ_i
Maximum	Concave	Convex	≥ 0
		Concave	≤ 0
		Linear	No restriction
Minimum	Convex	Convex	≤ 0
		Concave	≥ 0
		Linear	No restriction

If $f(x)$ and $g(x)$ are indefinite then K.T. conditions are necessary but not sufficient for stationary points.

Example 1 Solve the following NLP using Kuhn-Tucker conditions.

Maximize $\quad Z = x_1^2 - x_1x_2 - 2x_2^2$

Subject to,
$$4x_1 + 2x_2 \leq 24$$
$$5x_1 + 10x_2 \leq 20$$
$$x_1, x_2 \geq 0$$

Solution The Lagrangian function $\lambda(x, \lambda) = x_1^2 - x_1x_2 - 2x_2^2 - \lambda_1(4x_1 + 2x_2 - 24) - \lambda_2(5x_1 + 10x_2 - 20)$

The Kuhn-Tucker conditions are

$$\lambda_1 \geq 0, \quad \lambda_2 \geq 0 \qquad (1)$$

$$\frac{\partial L}{\partial x_1} = 2x_1 + x_2 - 4\lambda_1 - 5\lambda_2 = 0 \qquad (2)$$

$$\frac{\partial L}{\partial x_2} = x_1 - 4x_2 - 2\lambda_1 - 10\lambda_2 = 0 \quad (3)$$

$$\lambda_1(4x_1 + 2x_2 - 24) = 0 \quad (4)$$

$$\lambda_2(5x_1 + 10x_2 - 30) = 0 \quad (5)$$

$$4x_1 + 2x_2 - 24 \le 0 \quad (6)$$

$$5x_1 + 10x_2 - 30 \le 0 \quad (7)$$

From (4) if $\lambda_1 = 0$, x_1 and x_2 must be equal too which is not true.

$$4x_1 + 2x_2 - 24 = 0 \quad (8)$$

Similarly from (5) if $\lambda_2 = 0$, x_1 and x_2 must be equal too which is not true.

$$5x_1 + 10x_2 - 30 = 0 \quad (9)$$

Solving (8) and (9), (2) and (3), we get the optimum solution

$$x_1 = 6, \quad x_2 = 0, \quad \lambda_1 = 0, \quad \lambda_2 = 0, \quad Z_{\max} = 36$$

Example 2 Determine x_1 and x_2 so as to

Maximize $\quad Z = 12x_2 + 21x_1 + 2x_1x_2 - 2x_1^2 - 2x_2^2$

Subject to the constraints

(*i*) $x_2 \le 8$, (*ii*) $x_1 + x_2 \le 10, x_1, x_2 \ge 0$

Solution

$$f(x_1, x_2) = 12x_1 + 21x_2 + 2x_1x_2 - 2x_1^2 - 2x_2^2$$

$$g_1(x_1, x_2) = x_2 - 8 \le 0$$

$$g_2(x_1, x_2) = x_1 + x_2 - 10 \le 0$$

Define Lagrangian function as

$$\lambda(x, s, \lambda) = f(x) - \lambda_1(g_1(x) + s_1^2) - \lambda_2(g_2(x) + s_2^2)$$

The Kuhn-Tucker necessary conditions can be stated as:

(i) $$\frac{\partial f}{\partial x_j} - \sum_{i=1}^{2} \lambda_i \frac{\partial g_i}{\partial x_i}, = 0 \quad j = 1, 2$$

$$\Rightarrow \quad 12 + 2x_2 - 4x_1 - \lambda_2 = 0$$

$$21 + 2x_1 - 4x_2 - \lambda_1 - \lambda_2 = 0$$

(ii) $$\lambda_i g_i(x) = 0 \quad j = 1, 2$$

$$\lambda_1(x_2 - 8) = 0$$

$$\lambda_2(x_1 + x_2 - 10) = 0$$

(iii) $$g_i(x) \le 0$$

$$\Rightarrow \quad x_2 - 8 \le 0, \quad x_1 + x_2 - 10 \le 0$$

(iv) $$\lambda_i \ge 0 \quad i = 1, 2$$

There are 4 cases.

Case I

If $$\lambda_1 = 0, 1 = 0, \text{ then from condition (1)}$$

$$12 + 2x_2 - 4x_1 = 0$$

$$21 + 2x_1 - 4x_2 = 0$$

Solving these equations, we get $x_1 = 15/2, x_2 = 9$. This solution violates condition (iii) and therefore it should be discarded.

Case II

$\lambda_1 \ne 0$, $\lambda_2 = 0$, then from condition (ii)

we have $x_2 - 8 = 0$ or $x_2 = 8$

$$x_1 + x_2 - 10 = 0 \text{ or } x_1 = 2$$

Substituting these values in conditions (i) we get

$\lambda_1 = -27$ and $\lambda_2 = 20$. However this solution violates the condition (iv) and therefore may be discarded.

Case III

$\lambda_1 \ne 0$, $\lambda_2 = 0$, then from conditions (ii) and (i) we have

$$x_1 + x_2 = 10$$

$$2x_1 - 4x_2 = -12 + \lambda_1$$

Solving these equations we get $x_1 = 2, x_2 = 8$ and $\lambda_1 = -16$.

This solution violates the condition (iv) and therefore may be discarded.

Case IV

$$\lambda_1 = \lambda_2 \ne 0, \text{ then from conditions (i) and (ii)}$$

$$2x_1 - 4x_2 = -12 + \lambda_2$$

$$2x_1 - 4x_2 = -21 + \lambda_2$$

$$x_1 + x_2 = 0.$$

Solving these equations, we get $x_1 = 17/4, x_2 = 23/4, \lambda_2 = 13/4$. This solution is the optimum solution as it does not violate any of the Kuhn-Tucker conditions.

$$x_1 = 17/4, x_2 = 23/4, \lambda_1 = 0, \lambda_2 = 13/4$$

$$\text{Max } Z = 1894/16.$$

Example 3 Determine x_1, x_2, x_3 so as to

Maximize $$Z = -x_1^2 - x_2^2 - x_3^2 + 4x_1 + 6x_2$$

Subject to the constraints,

$$x_1 + x_2 \le 2$$

$$2x_1 + 3x_2 \le 12$$

$$x_1, x_2 \ge 0$$

Solution Given $$f(x) = -x_1^2 - x_2^2 - x_3^2 + 4x_1 + 6x_2$$

$$g_1(x) = x_1 + x_2 - 2$$

$$g_2(x) = 2x_1 + 3x_2 - 12$$

Define Lagrangian function $L(x, \lambda, S)$

$$= f(x) - \lambda_1\left(g_1(x) + s_1^2\right) - \lambda_2\left(g_2(x) + s_2^2\right)$$

Where s_1, s_2 are slack variables and λ_1, λ_2 are Lagrangian multipliers.

The Kuhn-Tucker conditions are given by:

(1) $$\frac{\partial f}{\partial x_j} - \sum_{i=1}^{2} \lambda_i \frac{\partial g_i}{\partial x_j} = 0 \quad j = 1,2,3$$

(i) $$-2x_1 + 4 = \lambda_1 + 2\lambda_2$$

(ii) $$-2x_2 + 6 = \lambda_1 + 3\lambda_2$$

(iii) $$-2x_2 = 0$$

(2) $$\lambda g_i(x) = 0$$

gives

(i) $$\lambda_1\left(x_1 + x_2 - 2\right) = 0$$

(ii) $$\lambda_2\left(2x_1 + 3x_2 - 12\right) = 0$$

(3) $$g_i(x) \le 0$$

(i) $$x_1 + x_2 - 2 \le 0$$

(ii) $$2x_1 + 3x_2 - 12 \le 0$$

(4) $$\lambda_1 \ge 0 \; \lambda_2 \ge 0$$

We have four different cases.

Case I: $\lambda_1 = 0, \lambda_2 = 0$ (i), (ii), (iii) of (1) yield $x_1 = 2, x_2 = 3, x_3 = 0$. This solution violates the inequalities of (3).

Case II: $\lambda_1 = 0, \lambda_2 \neq 0$. In this case (ii) of (2) will give $2x_1 + 3x_2 = 12$ and (i) and (ii) of (1) gives

$-2x_1 + 4 = 2\lambda_2, -2x_2 + 6 = 3\lambda_2$. The solution to these simultaneous equation gives

$x_1 = 2/13, x_2 = 3/13, \lambda_2 = 24/13 > 0$ also (iii) of (1) gives $x_3 = 0$. However this solution violates (i) of (3). So this solution is discarded.

Case III: . $\lambda_1 \neq 0, \lambda_2 \neq 0$. In this case (2) (i) and (ii) gives $x_1 + x_2 = 2$ and $2x_1 + 3x_2 = 12$. These equations give $x_1 - 6, x_2 = 8$. Then (1) (i), (ii) and (iii) yield $x_3 = 0, \lambda_1 = 68, \lambda_2 = -26$.

Since $\lambda_2 = -26$ violates the condition (4) so this solution is also discarded.

Case IV: $\lambda_1 \neq 0, \lambda_2 = 0$. In this case (2) (i) gives $x_1 + x_2 = 0$. Along with (1) (i) and (ii) $-2x_1 + 4 = \lambda_1 + 2\lambda_2$ $-2x_2 + 6 = \lambda_1 + 3\lambda_2$ give $x_1 = 1/2, x_2 = 3/2$ and $\lambda_1 = 3 > 0$. Further from (3) (iii) $x_3 = 0$. This solution does not violate any of the Kuhn-Tucker conditions.

Hence the optimum solution is $x_1 = \frac{1}{2}, x_2 = \frac{3}{2}, x_3 = 0, \lambda_1 = 3, \lambda_2 = 0$. Max $Z = \frac{17}{2}$.

Exercise 1. Solve the following non-linear programming problem using Kuhn-Tucker conditions.

Maximize $Z = x_1^2 + x_1 x_2 - 2x_2^2$

Subject to, $4x_1 + 2x_2 \leq 24$

$x_1, x_2 \geq 0$

(**Ans:** $x_1 = 6,\ x_2 = 0, \lambda_1 = 3, Z = 36$)

2. Solve the following non-linear programming problem using Kuhn-Tucker conditions.

Maximize $Z = 8x_1 + 10x_2 - x_1^2 - x_2^2$

Subject to, $3x_1 + 2x_2 \leq 6$

$x_1, x_2 \geq 0$

(**Ans:** $x_1 = \frac{4}{3}, x_2 = \frac{33}{13}$ Max $Z = 21.3$)

Quadratic Programming Problem (QPP)

An NLPP with non-linear objective function and linear constraints is called quadratic programming problem. It is a special type of mathematical optimization problem in which quadratic functions of several variables are optimized subject to linear constraints on these variables:

The general structure of QPP is stated as follows.

Max or Min $Z = \left[\sum_{j=1}^{n} c_j x_j + \frac{1}{2} \sum_{j=1}^{n} \sum_{k=1}^{n} x_j x_{jk} x_k \right]$

Subject to the constraints

$$\sum_{j=1}^{n} a_{ij}x_j \leq b_i \;\; x_j \geq 0\text{, for all } i \text{ and } j.$$

In matrix notation, the QPP is given as

Optimize (Max or min) $\quad Z = cx + \frac{1}{2}x^T Dx.$

Subject to the constraints,

$$Ax \leq b\,(1)\;\; x \geq 0 \qquad (2)$$

Where $\quad x = (x_1 x_2 \ldots x_n)^T, c = (c_1 c_2 \ldots c_n)\, b = (b_1 b_2 \ldots b_n)^T$

$$D = \{d_{jk}\}_{n\times n} \text{ symmetric matrix } (d_{jk} = d_{kj}).$$

$$A = \{a_{ij}\}_{n\times n} \text{ matrix.}$$

The matrix D is symmetric and positive definite (i.e., the quadratic term $x^T Dx$ in x is positive for all values of x except at $x = 0$). In this case, the problem is of minimization type. If $x^T Dx$ in x is negative definite for all values of x except for $x = 0$, in this case the problem is of maximization type.

Also the objective function of the QPP is strictly convex in x for minimization and concave in x for maximization. If the matrix D is null, the QPP reduces to the standard LPP.

Kuhn-Tucker Conditions

The necessary and sufficient Kuhn-Tucker conditions to get an optimal solution to the problem of maximizing the given quadratic objective function subject to linear constraints is derived below.

Step 1: Introducing slack variables s_i^2 and r_j^2 to constraints (1) and (2) the problem becomes

$$\text{Max } f(x) = \sum_{j=1}^{n} c_j x_j - \frac{1}{2}\sum_{j=1}^{n}\sum_{k=1}^{n} x_j d_{jk} x_k$$

Subject to constraints,

$$\sum_{j=1}^{n} a_{ij}x_j + S_i^2 = b_i i = 1,2,\ldots,n$$

$$-x_j + r_j^2 = 0\; j = 1,2,\ldots,n.$$

Step 2: Forming Lagrangian function

$$L(x, s, r, \lambda, \mu) = f(x) - \sum_{j=1}^{n}\lambda_i\left(a_{ij}x_j + s_i^2 - b_i\right) - \sum_{j=1}^{n}\mu_j\left(-x_j + r_j^2\right)$$

Step 3: Differentiate $L(x, s, r, \lambda, \mu)$ partially with x, s, r, λ and equating to zero in order to get the required Kuhn-Tucker necessary conditions.

(i) $\quad c - \frac{1}{2}\left(2x^T D\right) - \lambda A + \mu = 0$

or

$$c_j - \sum_{k=1}^{n} x_k d_{jk} - \sum_{i=1}^{m} \lambda_i a_{ij} + \mu_j = 0$$

$$j = 1, 2, \ldots, n.$$

(ii) $$-2\lambda_s = 0 \text{ or } \lambda_i s_i^2 = 0 \text{ or}$$

$$\lambda_i \left[\sum_{j=1}^{n} a_{ij} x_j - b_i \right] = 0, i = 1, 2, \ldots, n.$$

(iii) $$-2\mu r = 0 \text{ or } \mu_j r_j = 0, j = 1, 2, \ldots, n.$$

$$\mu_j x_j = 0, j = 1, 2, \ldots, n.$$

(iv) $$Ax + s^2 - b = 0, \text{ i.e., } Ax \le b \text{ or}$$

$$\sum_{j=1}^{n} a_{ij} x_i \le b_i \; i = 1, 2, \ldots, n.$$

(v) $$-x + r^2 = 0, \text{ i.e., } x \ge 0 \text{ or}$$

$$x_j \ge 0, j = 1, 2, \ldots, n.$$

(vi) $$\lambda_i, \mu_j, x_j, s_j, r_j \ge 0$$

These conditions except (ii) and (iii) are linear constraints involving $2(n + m)$ variables. The condition $\mu_j x_j = \lambda_i s_i = 0$ implies that both x_j and μ_j as well as s_i and λ_i cannot be basic variables at a time in a non-degenerate basic feasible solution. The condition $\mu_j x_j = 0$ and $\lambda_i s_i = 0$ are also called *Complementary Slackness Conditions*.

22.4 WOLFE'S MODIFIED SIMPLEX METHOD

The iterative procedure for the solution of a quadratic programming problem by Wolfe's method is described as follows:

Step 1: Convert the inequality constraints into equations by introducing the slack variables s_i^2 in the ith constraint $i = 1, 2, \ldots, m$ and slack variable in the jth non-negativity constraint $j = 1, 2, \ldots, n$.

Step 2: Construct the Lagrangian function

$$L(x, s, r, \lambda, \mu) = f(x) - \sum_{j=1}^{m} \lambda_i \left(\sum_{j=1}^{n} a_{ij} x_j - b_i + s_i^2 \right) - \sum_{j=1}^{n} \mu_j \left(-x_j + r_j^2 \right)$$

where $x = (x_1, x_2, \ldots, x_n), s = (s_1, s_2, \ldots, s_n), r = (r_1, r_2, \ldots, r_n), \lambda = (\lambda_1 \lambda_2, \ldots, \lambda_n),$
$\mu = (\mu_1 \mu_2 \ldots \mu_n),$

Differentiate $L(x, s, r, \lambda, \mu)$ partially w.r. to x, s, r, λ, and μ and equate the first order partial derivatives to zero. Derive the Kuhn-Tucker conditions from the resulting equations.

Step 3: Introduce artificial variables $A_j (j = 1, 2, \ldots, n)$ in the Kuhn-Tucker conditions (i). Then we have

$$c_j - \sum_{k=1}^{n} x_k d_{jk} - \sum_{i=1}^{m} \lambda_i a_{ij} + \mu_j + A_j = 0$$

and construct an objective function $Z = A_1 + A_2 + \ldots + A_n$.

Step 4: Apply phase I of the simplex method to check the feasibility of the Constraint $AX \le b$. If there is no feasible solution terminate the procedure. Otherwise get an initial basic feasible solution for phase II. To get the desired feasible solution solve the following problem

$$\text{Minimize } Z = A_1 + A_2 + \ldots + A_n.$$

$$\text{Subject to, } \sum_{k=1}^{n} a_{jk} x_k + \sum_{i=1}^{m} \lambda_i a_{ij} - \mu_i + A_j,\ j = 1, 2, \ldots, n$$

$$\sum_{j=1}^{n} a_{ij} x_j + S_i^2 = \lambda_i i = 1, 2, \cdots n.$$

and $\lambda_i, x_j, \mu_j, s_i, A_j \ge 0$ for i and j.

$$\left.\begin{aligned} \lambda_i s_i &= 0 \\ \mu_j x_j &= 0 \end{aligned}\right\} \text{Complementary Slackness Condition.}$$

Thus, while deciding for a variable to enter into the basis at each iteration, the Complementary Slackness Conditions are satisfied.

This problem has $2(m+n)$ variables and $(m+n)$ linear constraints, together with $(m+n)$ Complementary Slackness Conditions.

Step 5: Apply phase II of simplex method to get an optimal solution to the problem given in step 4. The solution obtained in step 5 is an optimum solution of the QPP.

Example Apply Wolfe's method to solve QPP.

Maximize $Z = 2x_1 + 3x_2 - 2x_1^2$

Subject to,

$$x_1 + 4x_2 \le 4$$

$$x_1 + x_2 \le 2,\ x_1, x_2 \ge 0.$$

Solution Consider non-negativity conditions $x_1, x_2 \ge 0$ as inequality constraints. Add slack variables to all inequality constraints in order to express them as equations. The Standard form of QPP becomes

Maximize $Z = 2x_1 + 3x_2 - 2x_1^2$

Subject to,

$$x_1 + 4x_2 - s_1^2 = 4$$

$$x_1 + x_2 - s_2^2 = 2$$

$$-x_1 + r_1^2 = 0$$

$$-x_2 + r_2^2 = 0$$

Step 1: Construct the Lagrangian function

$$L(x_1, x_2, s_1, s_2, \lambda_1, \lambda_2, \mu_1, \mu_2, r_1, r_2)$$

$$= \left(2x_1 + 3x_2 - 2x_1^2\right) - \lambda_1\left(x_1 + 4x_2 - s_1^2 - 4\right) - \lambda_2\left(x_1 + x_2 - s_2^2 - 2\right) - \mu_1\left(-x_1 + r_1^2\right) - \mu_2\left(-x_2 + r_2^2\right)$$

The necessary and sufficient condition for the maximum of L and hence of Z are.

$$\frac{L}{\partial x_1} = 2-4x_1-\lambda_1-\lambda_2+\mu_1=0$$

$$\frac{\partial L}{\partial x_2} = 3-4\lambda_1-\lambda_2+\mu_1=0$$

$$\frac{\partial L}{\partial s_1} = -2\lambda_1 s_1=0 \qquad \frac{\partial L}{\partial \lambda_1}=x_1+4x_2+s_1^2-4=0$$

$$\frac{\partial L}{\partial s_2} = -2\lambda_2 s_2=0 \qquad \frac{\partial L}{\partial \lambda_2}=x_1+x_2+s_2^2-2=0$$

$$\frac{\partial L}{\partial r_1} = 2\mu_1 r_1=0 \qquad \frac{\partial L}{\partial \mu_1}=-x_1+r_1^2=0$$

$$\frac{\partial L}{\partial r_2} = 2\mu_2 r_2=0 \qquad \frac{\partial L}{\partial \mu_2}=-x_2+r_2^2=0$$

After simplifying these conditions, we get

$$4x_1+\lambda_1+\lambda_2+\mu_1 = 0 \quad (1)$$

$$4\lambda_1+\lambda_2-\mu_2 = 3 \quad (2)$$

$$x_1+4x_2-s_1^2 = 4 \quad (3)$$

$$x_1+x_2+s_2^2 = 2 \quad (4)$$

$$x_1, x_2, s_1^2, s_2^2, \lambda_1, \lambda_2, \mu_1\mu_2 \geq 0$$

$$\left.\begin{aligned}\mu_1 x_1 &= \mu_2 x_2 = 0\\ \lambda_1 s_1 &= \lambda_2 s_2 = 0\end{aligned}\right\}\text{Complementary Slackness Condition.}$$

By introducing artificial variables A_1 and A_2 in the first two constraints.

Step 2 The modified LPP becomes

Max $Z = -A_1 - A_2$

Subject $4x_1+\lambda_1+\lambda_2-\mu_1+A_1 = 2$

$$4\lambda_1+\lambda_2-\mu_2+A_1 = 3$$

$$x_1+4x_2+x_3 = 4$$

$$x_1+x_2+x_4 = 2$$

$x_1x_2x_3x_4 \geq 0,\ A_1, A_2, \lambda_1, \lambda_2, \mu_1, \mu_2 \geq 0$, satisfying the Complementary Slackness Condition.

$$\lambda_1 s_1 = \lambda_2 s_2 = 0$$

$$\mu_1 x_1 = \mu_2 x_2 = 0$$

The initial basic feasible solution to the LPP is shown in the table below.

		c_j	0	0	0	0	0	0	0	0	−1	−1
C_B	y_B	x_B	x_1	x_2	x_3	x_4	λ_1	λ_2	μ_1	μ_2	A_1	A_2
−1	A_1	2	4	0	0	0	1	1	−1	0	1	0
−1	A_2	3	0	0	0	0	4	1	0	−1	0	1
0	x_3	4	1	4	1	0	0	0	0	0	0	0
0	x_4	2	1	1	0	1	0	0	0	0	0	0
	$z_j - c_j$	−5	−4	0	0	0	5	2	−1	−1	0	0

From the above table, it is observed that $x_1, \lambda_1, \lambda_2$ can enter the basis. But λ_1 and λ_2 will not enter the basis because $x_3\left(s_1^2\right)$ and $x_4\left(s_2^2\right)$ are in the basis. Introduce x_1 and drop A_1.

First iteration

		c_j	0	0	0	0	0	0	0	0	−1
C_B	y_B	x_B	x_1	x_2	x_3	x_4	λ_1	λ_2	μ_1	μ_2	A_2
0	x_1	$\frac{1}{2}$	1	0	0	0	$\frac{1}{4}$	$\frac{1}{4}$	$\frac{-1}{4}$	0	0
−1	A_2	3	0	0	0	0	4	1	0	−1	1
0	x_3	$\frac{7}{2}$	0	4	1	0	$\frac{-1}{4}$	$\frac{-1}{4}$	$\frac{1}{4}$	0	0
0	x_4	$\frac{3}{2}$	0	1	0	1	$\frac{-1}{4}$	$\frac{-1}{4}$	$\frac{1}{4}$	0	0
	$z_j - c_j$	−3	0	0	0	0	−4	−1	0	1	0

From the above table, it is observed that either λ_1 or λ_2 can't enter the basis as x_3 and x_4 are still in the basis in order to satisfy Complementary Slackness Condition. Since μ_2 is not in the basis, x_2 can enter the basis (as $\mu_2 x_2 = 0$).

Second iteration

Introduce x_2 and drop x_3.

C_B	y_B	x_B	x_1	x_2	x_3	x_4	λ_1	λ_2	μ_1	μ_2	A_2
0	x_1	$\frac{1}{2}$	1	0	0	0	$\frac{1}{4}$	$\frac{1}{4}$	$\frac{-1}{4}$	0	0
–1	A_2	3	0	0	0	0	4	1	0	–1	1
0	x_2	$\frac{7}{8}$	0	1	$\frac{1}{4}$	1	$\frac{-1}{16}$	$\frac{-1}{16}$	$\frac{1}{16}$	0	0
0	x_4	$\frac{5}{8}$	0	0	$\frac{-1}{4}$	0	$\frac{-3}{16}$	$\frac{-3}{16}$	$\frac{3}{16}$	0	0
	$z_j - c_j$	–3	0	0	0	0	–4	–1	0	1	0

Since $x_4\left(s_2^2\right)$ is in the basis, λ_2 can't enter the basis. Hence λ_1 enter the basis.

Third iteration

Drop A_2 and introduce λ_1.

C_B	y_B	x_B	x_1	x_2	x_3	x_4	λ_1	λ_2	μ_1	μ_2
0	x_1	$\frac{5}{16}$	1	0	0	0	0	$\frac{3}{16}$	$\frac{-1}{4}$	$\frac{1}{16}$
0	λ_1	$\frac{3}{4}$	0	0	0	0	1	$\frac{1}{4}$	0	$\frac{-1}{4}$
0	x_2	$\frac{59}{64}$	0	1	$\frac{1}{4}$	0	0	$\frac{-3}{64}$	$\frac{1}{16}$	$\frac{-1}{64}$
0	x_4	$\frac{49}{64}$	0	0	$\frac{-1}{4}$	1	0	$\frac{-9}{64}$	$\frac{3}{16}$	$\frac{-3}{64}$
	$z_j - c_j$	0	0	0	0	0	0	0	0	0

Hence the optimum solution

$$x_1 = \frac{5}{16},\ x_2 = \frac{59}{64} \text{ and}$$

$$\text{Max } Z = 2\left(\frac{5}{16}\right) + 3\left(\frac{59}{64}\right) - 2\left(\frac{5}{16}\right)^2 = 3.19$$

Example 2 Use the Wolfe's method to solve the QPP.

$$\text{Maximize } Z = 2x_1 + x_2 - x_1^2$$

Subject to the constraints,

(i) $2x_1 + 3x_2 \le 6$

(ii) $2x_1 + x_2 + s_2^2 = 4$, and $x_1, x_2 \ge 0$.

Solution Considering non-negative conditions $x_1, x_2 \ge 0$ as inequality constraints and add slack variables to all inequalities to express them as equations. After adding slack variables the problem becomes

Maximize $\quad Z = 2x_1 + x_2 - x_1^2$

Subject to,

(i) $2x_1 + 3x_2 + s_1^2 = 6$

(ii) $2x_1 + x_2 + s_2^2 = 4$

(iii) $-x_1 + r_1^2 = 0$

(iv) $-x_2 + r_2^2 = 0$

From the Lagrangian function $L(x, s, \lambda, r, \mu)$

$$= \left(2x_1 + x_2 - x_1^2\right) - \lambda_1\left(2x_1 + 3x_2 + s_1^2 - 6\right) - \lambda_2\left(2x_1 + x_2 + s_2^2 - 4\right) - \mu_1\left(-x_1 + r_1^2\right) - \mu_2\left(-x_2 + r_2^2\right)$$

The necessary and sufficient condition for the Maximum of L and hence of Z are

$$\frac{\partial L}{dx_1} = 2 - 2x_1 - 2\lambda_1 - 2\lambda_2 + \mu_1 = 0$$

$$\frac{\partial L}{\partial x_2} = 1 - 3\lambda_1 - \lambda_2 + \mu_1 = 0$$

$$\frac{\partial L}{\partial s_1} = -2\lambda_1 s_1 = 0$$

$$\frac{\partial L}{\partial s_2} = -2\lambda_2 s_2 = 0$$

$$\frac{\partial L}{\partial r_1} = 2\mu_1 r_1 = 0$$

$$\frac{\partial L}{\partial r_2} = 2\mu_2 r_2 = 0$$

$$\frac{\partial L}{\partial \lambda_1} = 2x_1 + 3x_2 + s_1^2 - 6 = 0$$

$$\frac{\partial L}{\partial \lambda_2} = 2x_1 + x_2 + s_2^2 - 4 = 0$$

$$\frac{\partial L}{\partial \mu_1} = -x_1 + r_1^2 = 0 \qquad \frac{\partial L}{\partial \mu_2} = -x_2 + r_2^2 = 0$$

After simplifying the conditions, we get

(i) $2x_1 + 2\lambda_1 + 2\lambda_2 - \mu_1 = 2$

(ii) $3\lambda_1 + \lambda_2 - \mu_2 = 1$

(iii) $2x_1 + 3x_2 + s_1^2 = 6$

(iv) $2x_1 + x_2 + s_2^2 = 4$

(v) $\lambda_1 s_1 = \lambda_2 s_2 = 0,\ \mu_1 x_1 \neq \mu_2 x_2 = 0$

and $x_1, x_2, \lambda_1, \lambda_2, \mu_1 \mu_2, s_1, s_2 \geq 0$.

Introduce artificial variables A_1 and A_2 in the first two constraints. The modified QPP becomes

$$\text{Minimize } Z = A_1 + A_2$$

or

$$\text{Minimize } Z = -A_1 - A_2$$

Subject to the Constraints

(i) $2x_1 + 2\lambda_1 + 2\lambda_2 - \mu_1 + A_1 = 2$

(ii) $3\lambda_1 + \lambda_2 - \mu_2 + A_2 = 1$

(iii) $2x_1 + 3x_2 + s_1^2 = 6$

(iv) $2x_1 + x_2 + s_2^2 = 4$ where $\begin{bmatrix} \lambda_1 s_1 = \lambda_2 s_2 = 0 \\ \mu_1 x_1 = \mu_2 x_2 = 0 \end{bmatrix}$

and $x_1, x_2, s_1, s_2, A_1, A_2 \lambda_1, \lambda_2, \mu_1, \mu_2 \geq 0$.

The initial basic feasible solution to the LPP is shown in the table below.

		c_j	0	0	0	0	0	0	0	0	–1	–1
C_B	y_B	x_B	x_1	x_2	λ_1	λ_2	μ_1	μ_2	s_1	s_2	A_1	A_2
–1	A_1	2	2	0	2	2	–1	0	0	0	1	0
–1	A_2	1	0	0	3	1	0	–1	0	0	0	1
0	s_1	6	2	3	0	0	0	0	1	0	0	0
0	s_2	4	2	1	0	0	0	0	0	1	0	0
	$z_j - c_j$	–2	0	0	–5	–3	1	1	0	0	0	0

From the above table, it is observed that λ_1 to enter the basis (or λ_2). Due to Complementary Slackness Condition $\lambda_1 s_1 = \lambda_2 s_2 = 0$, it is not possible. Since $\mu_1 = 0$, x_1 can be entered into the basis with A_1 as leaving variable.

First iteration: Introduce x_1 and drop A_1.

		c_j	0	0	0	0	0	0	0	0	−1
C_B	y_B	x_B	x_1	x_2	λ_1	λ_2	μ_1	μ_2	s_1	s_2	A_2
−1	x_1	1	1	0	1	1	$\frac{1}{2}$	0	0	0	0
−1	A_2	1	0	0	3	1	0	−1	0	0	1
← 0	s_1	4	0	(3)	−2	2	1	0	1	0	0
0	s_2	2	0	1	−2	−2	1	0	0	1	0
		$z_j - c_j$	0	0↑	−3	−1	0	1	0	0	0

From the above table, it is observed λ_1, λ_2 cannot enter the basis and also μ_1 due to Complementary Slackness Condition. Hence we enter x_2 to the basis because $\mu_2 = 0$.

Second iteration: Introduce x_2 and drop s_1.

		c_j	0	0	0	0	0	0	0	0	−1
C_B	y_B	x_B	x_1	x_2	λ_1	λ_2	μ_1	μ_2	s_1	s_2	A_2
0	x_1	1	1	0	1	1	$\frac{-1}{2}$	0	0	0	0
← −1	A_2	1	0	0	3	1	0	−1	0	0	1
0	x_2	$\frac{4}{3}$	0	1	$\frac{-2}{4}$	$\frac{-2}{3}$	$\frac{1}{3}$	0	$\frac{1}{3}$	0	0
0	s_2	$\frac{2}{3}$	0	0	$\frac{-4}{3}$	$\frac{-4}{3}$	$\frac{2}{3}$	0	$\frac{-1}{3}$	1	0
	$z_j - c_j$	0	0	0	−3↑	−1	0	1	0	0	0

Since $s_1 = 0$, λ_1 can be entered into the basis with A_2 as leaving variable.

Third iteration. Introduce λ_1 and drop A_2.

		c_j	0	0	0	0	0	0	0	0
x_B	C_B	y_B	x_1	x_2	λ_1	λ_2	μ_1	μ_2	s_1	s_2
$\frac{2}{3}$	0	x_1	1	0	0	$\frac{2}{3}$	$\frac{-1}{2}$	$\frac{1}{3}$	0	0
$\frac{1}{3}$	0	λ_1	0	0	1	$\frac{1}{3}$	0	$\frac{-1}{3}$	0	0
$\frac{14}{9}$	0	x_2	0	1	0	$\frac{-4}{9}$	$\frac{1}{3}$	$\frac{-2}{9}$	$\frac{1}{3}$	0
$\frac{10}{9}$	0	s_2	0	0	0	$\frac{-8}{9}$	$\frac{2}{3}$	$\frac{-4}{9}$	$\frac{-1}{3}$	1
0		$z_j - c_j$	0	0	0	0	0	0	0	0

Since all $z_j - c_j = 0$ an optimum solution for phase I is reached. Solution is given by $x_1 = \frac{2}{3}$,

$$x_2 = \frac{14}{9},\ \lambda_1 = \frac{1}{3},\ \lambda_2 = 0,\ \mu_1 = \mu_2 = 0,\ s_1 = 0,\ s_2 = \frac{10}{9}.$$

The solution also satisfies Complementary Slackness Condition. Also Max $Z = 0$. The current solution is also feasible. The max value of the objective function of the given Q.P. is

$$\text{Max Z} = 2\left(\frac{2}{3}\right) + \left(\frac{14}{9}\right) - \left(\frac{2}{3}\right)^2 = \frac{22}{9}.$$

EXERCISES

1. Use Wolfe's method to solve

$$\text{Maximize Z} = 4x_1 + 6x_2 - 2x_1^2 - 2x_1x_2 - 2x_2^2$$

Subject to the constraints, $x_1 + x_2 \le 2,\ x_1, x_2 \ge 0$.

(**Ans.** $x_1 = \frac{1}{3},\ x_2 = \frac{5}{6},\ \lambda_1 = 1,\ \mu_1 = \mu_2 = 0,$ Max $Z = \frac{75}{18}$.)

2. Use Wolfe's method to solve

$$\text{Maximize Z} = 2x + y - x^2$$

Subject to,
$$2x + 3y \le 6$$
$$2x + y \le 4,\ x_1, x_2 \ge 0$$

(**Ans.** $x = \frac{2}{3}$, $y = \frac{14}{9}$, Max $Z = \frac{22}{9}$.)

3. Solve the following QPP using Wolfe's method.

$$\text{Maximize Z} = 6x_1 + 3x_2 - 2x_1^2 - 3x_2^2 - 4x_1x_2$$

Subject to the constraints, $x_1 + x_2 \le 1$

$$2x_1 + 3x_2 \le 4;\ x_1, x_2 \ge 0.$$

(Ans. $x_1 = 1, x_2 = 0$, Max $Z = 4$.)

4. $$\text{Max Z} = 4x_1 + 6x_2 - 2x_1^2 - 2x_1x_2 - 2x_2^2$$

Subject to, $x_1 + 2x_2 \le 2$

and $x_1, x_2 \ge 0$.

(**Ans.** $x_1 = \frac{1}{3}, x_2 = \frac{5}{6}$, Max $Z = \frac{25}{6}$.)

5. $$\text{Min z} = x_1^2 + x_2^2 + x_3^2$$

Subject to,

$$x_1 + x_2 + 3x_3 = 2$$

$$5x_1 + 2x_2 + x_3 = 5,\ x_1, x_2, x_3 \ge 0$$

(**Ans.** $x_1 = \frac{81}{100}$, $x_2 = \frac{7}{20}$, $x_3 = \frac{7}{20}$, Min $Z = \frac{17}{20}$).

22.5 UNCONSTRAINED OPTIMIZATION

Search Methods

The methods used to find the maximum/minimum of function *f*(*x*) depending on whether *f*(*x*) is a single variable of *f*(*x*), $x = (x_1, x_2 \ldots x_n)$ has several variables are one dimensional

1. Search method (1-D).
2. Direct search methods (Interal halving)
3. Fibonacci sequence method
4. Golden section search method

The 1-D search method is also known as *univariate search method*, where variables in *x* are varied one at a time and the iterations are stopped, if successive values of *f*(*x*) yield the same value. It is also called the *step method*.

In Fibonacci sequence method, we specify the limit of accuracy and calculate the end points of the intervals using the Fibonacci sequence.

A slightly modified form of Fibonacci sequence method is the Golden section search method, where the distance of the points of uncertainty intervals are determined using a standard formula.

22.5.1 Fibonacci Search

Fibonacci search is a univariate search technique that can be used to find the maximum (or minimum) of an arbitrary unimodal, univariate objective function. This method is a sequential search technique that successfully reduces the interval in which the maximum (or minimum) of an arbitrary nonlinear function must lie. To apply this technique, the assumption of unimodality must be invoked or the technique may locate a stationary point or completely fail. This method gives an optimal solution in the minimax case in a sequence of N functional evaluations.

Definition: The interval of uncertainty is defined as the interval in which the optimum solution is known to exist.

Consider the following successive relationship which generates an infinite series of numbers

$$x_n = x_{n-1} + x_{n-1}, \quad n = 2, 3...$$

Define $x_0 = 0$ and $x_1 = 1$

The above equation generates a series of numbers that are known as *Fibonacci numbers* given in the following table. The Fibonacci sequence is defined as

$$F_N = F_{N-1} + F_{N-2}, N > 1$$

Identifier	*Sequence*	*Fibonacci Number*
F_0	0	1
F_1	1	1
F_2	2	2
F_3	3	3
F_4	4	5
F_5	5	8
F_6	6	13
F_7	7	21
F_8	8	34
F_9	9	55
F_{10}	10	89
F_{11}	11	144

Interval Length of Fibonacci Method

Define the initial interval of search to be of Length L_0. This interval is critical interval of uncertainty. This interval must lie between points A and B. To reduce the initial interval of uncertainty to some finite length L_N using exactly N functional evaluations.

L_0 = Length of the interval of uncertainty after n functional evaluation.

X_n = Value of the variable X after N functional evaluations.

f_n = Value of the objective function using X_n, $n = 1, 2, \ldots, N$

$\in$ = the Minimum separation allowed between any points over the interval L_0.

It represents the resolution that can be obtained between the points X_n and X_{n-1}. The calculation of this parameter ε is essential as the optimum solution is based on the elimination of the regions in which the optimum solution can't lie.

Steps Involved in Fibonacci Sequence Method

Step 1: Define the end points of the search A and B.
Step 2: Define the number of functional evaluations N, that are to be used in the search.
Step 3: Define the minimum resolution parameter $\in$.
Step 4: Define the initial interval and first interval of uncertainty as $(B - A)$.
Step 5: Define the second interval of uncertainty as follows:

$$L_2 = \frac{1}{F_n}\left(L_0 F_{N-1} + \in(-1)^n\right)$$

where F_N and F_{N-1} are Fibonacci numbers.

Step 6: Locate the first two functional evaluations as the two symmetric points x_1 and x_2 defined as follows: $x_1 = A + L_2$, $x_2 = B - L_1$.

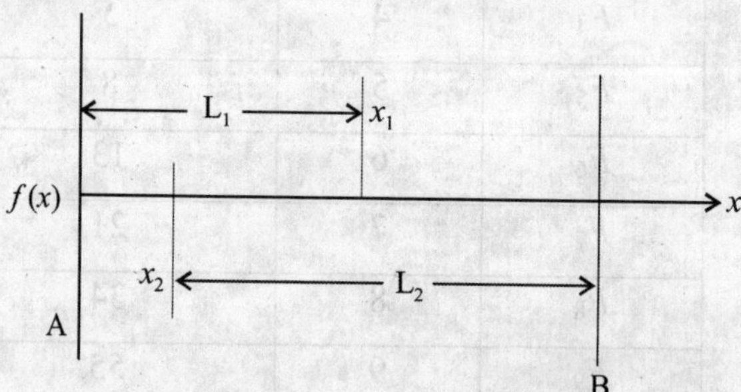

Step 7: Calculate $f(x_1)$ and $f(x_2)$ and eliminate the interval in which the optimum cannot lie.

Step 8: Use the relationship $L_n = L_{n-2} - L_{n-1}$ to locate subsequent points of evaluation within the remaining interval of uncertainty.

Repeat steps 7 and 8 until N fractional evaluations have been executed. The final solution can be either an average of the two points evaluations (x_N and x_{N-1}) or the best (max/min) functional evaluation.

Example 1: Find the minimum of $f(x) = x^2 - 2x$ by Fibonacci method. Take interval $0 \leq x \leq 1.5$ and $\in = 0.25$.

Solution: Fibonacci sequence is defined as

$$F_2 = F_0 + F_1, F_3 = F_1 + F_2 \text{ and so on.}$$

$$\{F_0, F_1, F_2, F_3, F_4, F_5\} = \{1, 1, 2, 3, 5, 8\}$$

Step 1:
Find Fibonacci number F_n using

$$\in = \frac{1}{F_N} \leq 0.25 \Rightarrow N \geq 4.$$

Take $\qquad N = 4$

Step 2:
End points of the interval are (0, 1.5)
$\therefore A = 0, B = 1.5;\ L_0 = B - A = 1.5 - 0 = 1.5$

Step 3:
Calculate $x_1 = A + L_2, x_2 = B - L_2$

$$L_2 = \frac{1}{F_N}\left(L_0 F_{N-1} + \in(-1)^N\right)$$

$$= \frac{1}{F_N}\left(1.5F_3 + \in(-1)^4\right)$$

$$= \frac{1}{5}(1.5(3) + 0.25)$$

$$= 0.95$$

$$x_1 = 0 + 0.95 = 0.95$$

$$x_2 = 1.5 - 0.95 = 0.55$$

Step 4:
Plot point x_2 in the figure at a distance 0.55 from (0) and x_4 at a distance 0.95 from the end points.

$$f(x_1) = f(0.95) = -0.9975$$

$$f(x_2) = f(0.55) = -0.7975$$

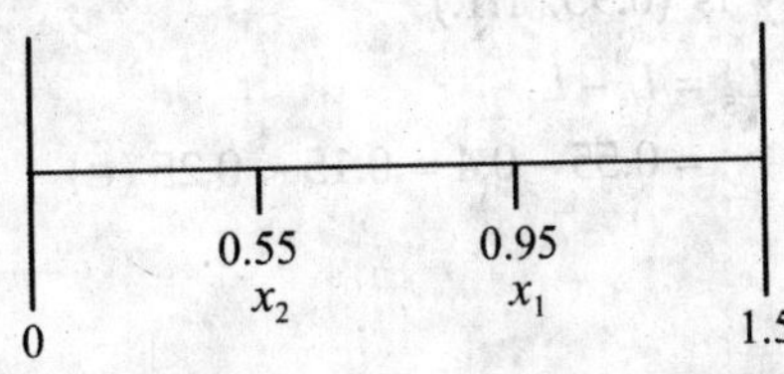

Step 5:

Since $f(x_2) > f(x_1)$ *i.e.* $f(0.55) > f(0.95)$

Optimum lies in the interval (0.55, 1.5)

Step 6: Take $A = 0.55$, $B = 1.5$

Redetermine a new point $x_3 = A + L_3$

$$x_4 = B - L_3$$

$$L_3 = L_2 - L_1 = 1.5 - 0.95 = 0.55$$

$$x_3 = 0.55 + 0.55 = 1.1$$

$$x_4 = 1.5 - 0.55 = 0.95$$

0.55	x_4	x_3	1.5
x_2	0.95	1.1	

Step 7:

Find $f(0.95) = -0.9975$ since $f(1.1) > f(0.95)$

$f(1.1) = -0.99$

Also $f(0.55) > f(0.95)$

Reject the interval (1.1, 1.5).

The new interval of uncertainty is (0.55, 1.1)

$$A = 0.55, \; B = 1.1$$

$$L_4 = L_2 - L_3 = 0.95 - 0.55 = 0.4$$

$$x_5 = 0.55 + 0.4 = 0.95$$

$$x_6 = 1.1 - 0.4 = 0.7$$

0.55	0.7	0.95	1.1
x_2	x_6	x_5	x_3

$$f(0.95) = -0.9975$$

$$f(0.7) = -0.91$$

$$f(0.7) > f(0.95)$$

$$f(1.1) > f(0.95)$$

$$f(0.7) > f(0.95)$$

New interval of uncertainty is (0.95, 1.1.)

$$L_5 = L_3 - L_4$$

$$= 0.55 - 0.4 = 0.15 < 0.25 \; (\epsilon)$$

The following table shows the progression through three functional evaluations.

Functional Evaluations(n)	Interval of uncertainty	x_{n-1}	$F(x_{n-1})$	x_n	$F(x_n)$
1	$0.95 \geq x \geq 0$	0.55	–0.7975	0.95	–0.9975
2	$0.55 \geq x \geq 0.95$	0.95	–0.9975	1.1	–0.99
3	$0.7 \geq x \geq 0.95$	0.7	–0.91	0.95	–0.9975

At the 3rd functional evaluation, the interval of uncertainty is established as I_3 = 0.95.

The best optimal solution is $\frac{1.1+0.95}{2} = 1.025$

$$f(1.025) = -0.999375 = -1.0$$

Example 2 Maximize the function $f(x) = -3x^2 + 21.6x + 1.0$ with a minimum resolution of 0.50 over six functional evaluations. The optimal value of $f(x)$ is assumed to be in the range $25 \geq x \geq 0$.

Solution

Given $\in = 0.50$

End points A = 0

$$N = 6$$

$$B = 25$$

$$L_{10} = L_1 = B - A = 25$$

$$L_2 = \frac{1}{F_N}\left(L_1 F_{N-1} + \in(-1)^N\right)$$

$$L_2 = \frac{1}{F_6}\left(L_1 F_5 + \in(-1)^6\right)$$

$$= \frac{1}{13}(25(8) + 0.5) = 15.4231$$

$$L_2 = 15.4231$$

$$x_1 = A + L_2 = 15.4231$$

$$x_2 = B - L_2 = 9.5769$$

$$f(x_1) = f(15.4231)$$

$$= -3(15.4231)^2 + 21.6(15.4231) + 1.0 = -379.477$$

$$f(x_2) = f(9.5769)$$

$$= -3(9.5769)^2 + 21.6(9.5769) + 1.0 = -67.233$$

Since $f(x_2) > f(x_1)$, the region of uncertainty is 0 to 15.4321, i.e., region to the right of $x_1 = 15.42$ is eliminated.

0 $x_2 = 9.58$ $x_1 = 15.42$ 25

$$L_0 = 25$$
$$L_1 = 25$$
$$L_2 = 15.4231$$

Here end points are $A = 0$, $B = 15.42$

$$L_3 = L_1 - L_2 = 25 - 15.4231 = 9.5769$$
$$x_3 = A + L_3 = 0 + 9.5769 = 9.5769$$
$$x_4 = B - L_3 = 15.42 - 9.5769 = 5.8462$$
$$f(x_3) = f(9.5769) = -67.233$$
$$f(x_4) = f(5.8462) = 24.744$$
$$f(x_4) > f(x_3) \text{ i.e., } f(5.8462) > f(9.5769)$$

the region of uncertainty is 0 to 9.5769.

i.e., region to the right of $x_3 = 9.5769$ is eliminated.

The following table shows the progression through the six functional evaluations.

Fibonacci search

Functional Evaluations	*Interval of uncertainty*	x_{n-1}	$F(x_{n-1})$	x_n	$F(x_n)$
1	$0 \le x \le 2.5$	0	1	25	–1938.8
2	$0 \le x \le 15.4231$	9.5769	–67.233	15.4231	–379.477
3	$0 \le x \le 9.5769$	5.8462	24.744	9.5769	–67.233
4	$0 \le x \le 5.8462$	3.731	39.83	5.8962	24.744
5	$2.115 \le x \le 5.8462$	2.115	32.26	3.731	39.83
6	$2.115 \le x \le 4.2304$	3.731	39.83	4.2304	38.688

At the sixth functional evaluation, the interval of uncertainty is established as $I_6 = 2.115$.

The optimal solution is $x_5 = 3.731$.

$$f(x_5) = 39.83$$
$$\in = 4.2304 - 3.731 = 0.4994 < 0.5$$

Exercise: Find the minimum of $f(x) = x^3 - 3x - 5$, $0 \le x \le 1.2$ and level of uncertainty is $x = 0.35$.

22.5.2 Golden Section Search

In performing a Fibonacci search, a prior specification of the resolution factor ($\in$) and the number of experiments to be performed (N) are required. In search methods to have a proper functioning, the successive experiments will gradually reduce the interval of uncertainty, i.e., the final interval of uncertainty will converge to zero as the number of functional evaluation increases to infinity provided that $\in$ is small.

$$\lim_{\substack{N\to\infty \\ \in\to 0}} \{L_2\} = \lim_{\substack{N\to\infty \\ \in\to 0}} \left\{ \frac{1}{F_N}\left(L_0 F_{N-1} + \in(-1)^N\right) \right\}$$

$$= L_0 \left\{ \frac{F_{N-1}}{F_N} \right\}$$

In the above limit, the ratio of $\frac{F_{N-1}}{F_N}$ goes to 0.618 which is known as *golden ratio or golden section*. The modified version of Fibonacci method with this golden ratio is known as *golden section search.* In comparison to the Fibonacci method, the golden section search is less efficient as it is derived from Fibonacci method. In golden section search method, the minimax principle is lost for early searches as the solution in each search is neither dependent upon resolution considerations nor on the number of functional evaluations. In practice, the golden section search is often used because it requires less information to implement each search and is by construction self-starting.

The general procedure for this method is given below:

Step 1: Define the initial interval of uncertainty as $L_0 = B - A$, and A and B are the end points of the search.

Step 2: Determine the first two functional evaluations at points x_1 and x_2 defined by

$$x_1 = A + 0.618\ (B - A)$$

$$x_2 = B - 0.618\ (B - A)$$

Step 3: Eliminate the appropriate region in which the optimum cannot lie.

Step 4: Determine the region of uncertainty defined by

$$L_{j+1} = L_{j-1} - L_j \quad j = 2, 3.......$$

Where

$$L_0 = B - A$$

$$L_1 = B - A$$

$$L_2 = x_1 - A \text{ or } L_2 = B - x_2$$

depending upon the region eliminated in step 3.

Step 5: Establish a new functional evaluation using the result of step 4. Evaluate $f(x)$ at this point, and then go to step 3. Repeat this procedure until a specified convergence criteria is satisfied.

Example 1 Minimize $f(x) = x^4 - 15x^3 + 72x^2 - 1135x$.

Terminate the search when $|f(x_n) - f(x_{n-1})| \leq 0.50$.

The initial range of x is $1 \leq x \leq 15$.

Solution

Given $A = 1$, $B = 15$

$$L_0 = B - A = 14$$
$$x_1 = 1 + 0.618(14) = 9.652$$
$$x_2 = 15 - 0.618(14) = 6.348$$

x — 1, 6.348, 9.652, 15

$$f(x_1) = 595.70, \quad f(x_2) = -168.82$$

Since $f(x_1) > f(x_2)$ the region to the right of $x = 9.652$ can be eliminated and the interval of uncertainty after two functional evaluations is given by $1 \le x \le 9.652$.

The following table shows the progression of the golden section search method.

Finctional Evaluations (n)	X_{n-1} *(right)*	$f(x_{n-1})$	X_n *(left)*	$f(x_n)$	*Interval of uncertainty*	*Length*
2	9.652	595.70	6.348	–168.82	$1 \le x \le 9.652$	8.652
3	6.346	–168.80	4.304	–100.06	$4.304 \le x \le 9.652$	5.348
4	7.609	–114.64	6.346	–168.80	$4.304 \le x \le 7.609$	3.305
5	6.346	–168.80	5.566	–147.61	$5.566 \le x \le 7.609$	2.043
6	6.828	–166.42	6.346	–168.80	$5.566 \le x \le 6.828$	1.262
7	6.346	–168.80	6.048	–163.25	$6.048 \le x \le 6.828$	0.780
8	6.530	–169.83	6.346	–168.80	$6.346 \le x \le 6.828$	0.482
9	6.643	–169.34	6.530	–169.83	$6.346 \le x \le 6.643$	0.297

$$|f(x_9) - f(x_8)| = -169.34 - (-169.83)$$
$$= 0.49$$

Since termination criterion are satisfied, the golden section search will stop at this point.

The optimum solution is given by $x = 6.643$, $f(x) = -169.34$

Exercises Find the minimum of $x^2 - 2x$ in (1, 2) within an interval of uncertainty $0.13 < 0$ where L_0 is the original interval of uncertainty. Solve by Golden section search method.

Short Questions and Answers

1. Basics of Operations Research

1. **What is operations research?**
There are many definitions of operations research. According to one such definition
"Operations Research is the application of scientific methods to complex problems arising from operations involving large systems of men, machines, materials and money in industry, business, government and defence."

2. **What are the various types of models?**
The various types of models are
   (*i*) Iconic or physical models
   (*ii*) Analogue or schematic models
   (*iii*) Symbolic or mathematical models.

3. **What is an analogue model?**
Analogue model can represent dynamic situations. They are analogous to the characteristic of the system under study. They use one set of properties to represent some other set of properties of the system. After the model is solved, the solution is reinterpreted in terms of the original system.

4. **What is an iconic model?**
Iconic models are the pictorial representations of real systems and have the appearance of the real structure. Examples of such models are city maps, houses, blueprints, etc.

5. **What is a symbolic model?**
Symbolic model is one which employs a set of mathematical symbols to represent the decision variables of the system. These variables are related together by mathematical equations which describe the properties of the system.

6. **Name some characteristics of a good model.**
   (*i*) It should be simple and coherent.
   (*ii*) It should be open to parametric type of treatment.
   (*iii*) There should be less number of variables.
   (*iv*) Assumptions made in the model should be clearly mentioned and should be as small as possible.

7. **What are the main characteristics of operations research?**
Some of the main characteristics of operations research are:
   (*i*) its system orientation.
   (*ii*) the use of inter-disciplinary forms.
   (*iii*) application of scientific method.
   (*iv*) uncovering of new problems.

8. **State any four applications of operations research.**
   (*i*) Assignment of jobs to applicants to maximize the total profits or minimize total costs.

(*ii*) Replacement techniques are used to replace the old machines with new ones.
(*iii*) Inventory control techniques are used in industries to purchase optimum quantity of raw materials.
(*iv*) Before executing a project, activities are sequenced and scheduled using the PERT chart.

9. **What are the methods used for solving operations research models?**
(*i*) Analytic procedure
(*ii*) Iterative procedure
(*iii*) Monte-Carlo technique.

10. **Explain the principles of modelling?**
(*i*) Models should be validated prior to implementation.
(*ii*) Models are only aids in decision-making.
(*iii*) Models should not be complicated. They should be as simple as possible.
(*iv*) Models should be accurate as possible.

3. Graphical Method

11. **What do you mean by a general LPP?**

The general LPP is given by,

Max or Min $Z = C_1X_1 + C_2X_2 + ... + C_nX_n$ ...(1)

Subject to,

$$\left.\begin{array}{l} a_{11}X_1 + a_{12}X_2 + ... + a_{1n}X_n \ (\leq = \geq) b_1 \\ a_{21}X_1 + a_{12}X_2 + ... + a_{2n}X_n \ (\leq = \geq) b_2 \\ \vdots \\ a_{m1}X_1 + a_{m2}X_2 + ... + a_{mn}X_n \ (\leq = \geq) b_m \end{array}\right\} \quad ...(2)$$

$$X_1, X_2 ... X_n \geq 0. \quad ...(3)$$

Equation (1) is called the objective function, (2) is the constraints obtained from the available resources and (3) is the non-negativity restriction.

12. **Give the matrix form of representing a general LPP.**

$$\text{Max or Min } Z = CX$$

$$\text{Subject to, } AX \begin{pmatrix} \leq \\ = \\ \geq \end{pmatrix}$$

$$X \geq 0$$

$$C = (C_1\, C_2 \, ... \, C_n) \times \begin{pmatrix} X_1 \\ X_2 \\ \vdots \\ X_n \end{pmatrix}, b = \begin{pmatrix} b_1 \\ b_2 \\ \vdots \\ b_m \end{pmatrix},$$

$$A = \begin{pmatrix} a_{11} & a_{12} & ... & a_{1n} \\ a_{12} & a_{22} & ... & b_{2n} \\ \vdots & \vdots & & \\ a_{m1} & a_{m2} & ... & a_{mn} \end{pmatrix}$$

13. **Define a feasible region.**
A region in which all the constraints are satisfied simultaneously is called a feasible region.

14. **Define a feasible solution.**
Any solution to a LPP which satisfies the non-negativity restrictions of the LPP is called its feasible solution.

15. **What is a redundant constraint?**
A constraint that does not form boundary of feasible region and has impact on the solution of the problem, remodel of which, does not alter the solution is called a redundant constraint.

16. **Define optimal solution.**
Any feasible solution which optimizes (minimizes or maximizes) the objective function is called its optimal solution.

17. **What is the difference between feasible solution and basic feasible solution?**
The solution of *m* basic variables when each of the *(n – m)* non-basic variables is set to zero is called basic solution.

A basic solution in which all the basic variables are 0 is called a basic feasible solution.

18. **Define the following:**
(*i*) Basic solution
(*ii*) non-degenerate solution
(*iii*) degenerate solution.

(*i*) Basic solution
Given a system of *m* linear equations with *n* variables (*m*/*n*), any solution which is obtained by solving for *m* variables keeping the remaining *n* – *m* variables as zero is called a basic solution.

Such *m* variables are called basic variables and *n* – *m* variables are called non-basic variables.

(*ii*) Non-degenerate solution
A non-degenerate basic feasible solution is the basic feasible solution which has exactly *m* positive X_i (i = 1, 2 . . . . *m*), i.e., none of the basic variables are zero.

(*iii*) Degenerate solution
A basic feasible solution is said to be degenerate if one or more basic variables are zero.

19. **Define unbounded solution.**
If the value of the objective function *Z* can be increased or decreased indefinitely. Such solutions are called unbounded solutions.

20. **What are the two forms of an LPP?**
The two forms of LPP are (*i*) Standard form and (*ii*) Canonical form.

21. **What do you mean by canonical form of a LPP?**
In canonical form, if the objective function is of maximization, then all the constraints other than non-negativity conditions are '≤' type. Similarly, if the objective function is of minimization, all the constraints are '≥' type.

22. **What do you mean by the standard form of LPP?**
In standard form, irrespective of the objective function namely maximize or minimize, all the constraints are expressed as equations, also right hand side constants are non-negative, *i.e.* all the variables are non-negative.

23. **State the characterstics of canonical form and write the canonical form of LPP in matrix form.**
Characteristics of canonical form

(*i*) The objective function is of maximization type.
(*ii*) All constraints are '≤' type.
(*iii*) All variables X_i are non-negative.

Matrix form

Max $Z = CX$			Min $Z = CX$
Subject to,	$AX \leq b$	Or	Subject to, $AX \geq b$
	$X \geq 0$		$X \geq 0$

24. State the characteristics of standard form and write the standard form of LPP in matrix form?

Characteristics of standard form

(*i*) The objective function is of maximization type.
(*ii*) All constraints are expressed as equations.
(*iii*) RHS of each constraint is non-negative.
(*iv*) All variables are non-negative.

Matrix form

Max Z = CX

Subject to, $AX = b$

$X \geq 0$

25. What are the limitations of LPP?

(*i*) For larger problems having many limitations and constraints, the computational difficulties are enormous even when computers are used.
(*ii*) Many times it is not possible to express both the objective function and constraints in linear form.
(*iii*) The solution variables may have any values. Sometimes the solution variables are restricted to take only integer values.
(*iv*) This method does not take into account the effect of time.

26. What are slack and surplus variables?

The non-negative variable which is added to LHS of the constraint to convert the inequality ≤, into an equation is called slack variable.

$$\sum_{j=1}^{n} a_{ij} x_i + s_i = b_i \; (i = 1, 2 \dots m)$$

where s_i are called *slack variables.*

The non-negative variable which is removed from the LHS of the constraint to convert the inequality into an equation is called a *surplus variable.*

27. What are decision variables in the construction of operation research problems?

While making mathematical modelling of operations research problems, the variables which are used and the value of which gives the solution are the decision variables.

28. How many basic feasible solutions are there to a given system of 4 simultaneous equations in 5 unknowns?

$$5C_4 = 5$$

29. What is the test of optimality in the simplex method?

Compute the net evaluation $Z_j - C_j$ (j = 1, 2, ... n) by using the relations

$$Z_j - C_j = C_B (a_j - c_j)$$

If all $Z_j - C_j \geq 0$, then the current feasible solution is optimal, which is the test of optimality.

30. What is key column and how is it selected?

Key column is the column which gives the entering variable column and is selected by finding the most negative value of $Z_j - C_j$.

31. What is key row and how is it selected?

The leaving variable row is called the *key row* and is selected by finding the ratio

$$\text{Min}\left(\frac{x_{Bi}}{a_{ir}}, a_{ir} > 0\right)$$

i.e., the ratio between the solution column and the entering variable column by considering only the positive Dr.

32. **When does the simplex method indicate that the LPP has unbounded solution?**
The indication of unbounded solution of LPP can be obtained if all the variables in the key column are negative.

33. **What is meant by optimality?**
By performing optimality test we can find whether the current feasible solution can be improved or not, which is possible by finding the $Z_j - C_j$ row.

34. **How will you find whether a LPP has got an alternative optimal solution or not, from the optimal simplex table?**
In optimal simplex table, in $Z_j - C_j$ row, if zero occurs for non-basic variables, it indicates that the LPP has an alternate solution.

5. Artificial Variables Technique

35. **What are the methods used to solve an LPP involving artificial variables?**
(*i*) Big M method or penalty cost method
(*ii*) Two-phase simplex method

36. **Define artificial variable.**
Any non-negative variable which is introduced in the constraint in order to get the initial basic feasible solution is called artificial variable.

37. **When does an LPP possess a pseudo-optimal solution?**
An LPP possesses a pseudo-optimal solution, if at least one artificial variable is in the basis at positive level even though the optimality conditions are satisfied.

38. **What are the disadvantages of Big M method over two-phase method?**
Although Big M method can always be used to check the existence of a feasible solution, it may be computationally inconvenient because of the manipulation of the constant M. Also when the problem is to be solved on a digital computer, M must be assigned some numerical value which is greater than C_1, C_2.... in the objective function. But a computer has only a fixed number of digits. In two-phase method, these difficulties are overcome as it eliminates the constant M from calculations.

39. **What is degeneracy?**
The concept of obtaining a degenerate basic feasible solution in a LPP is known as degeneracy.

40. **Define the phenomenon of cycling.**
The phenomenon of repeating the same sequence of simplex iterations endlessly, without improving the value of the objective function is known as cycling.

41. **How can we resolve degeneracy in a LPP?**
(*i*) Divide each element of the rows by the positive coefficients of the key column in that row.
(*ii*) Compare the resulting ratios, column by column, first in the identity and then in the body from left to right.
(*iii*) The row which first contains the smallest ratio contains the leaving variable.

6. Duality in Linear Programming

42. **Define dual of LPP.**
For every LPP, there is a unique LPP associated with it involving the same data and closely related optimal solution. The original problem is then called *the primal problem* while the other is called its *dual problem.*

43. **What are the advantages of duality?**
(*i*) If primal contains a large number of constraints and a smaller number of variables, then the process of computations can be considerably reduced by converting it into the dual problem.
(*ii*) Since the optimal solution to the objective function is the same for both primal and dual, a dual solution can be used to check the accuracy of the primal solution.

44. **State the fundamental theorem of duality.**
If either the primal or the dual problem has a finite optimal solution, then the other problem also has finite optimal solution and the values of the objective function are equal, i.e., Max Z = Min Z'. The solution of the other problem can be obtained from $Z_j - C_j$ row of the optimal simplex table below the slack and surplus variables.

45. **What is the difference between regular simplex method and dual simplex method?**
In regular simplex method we first determine the entering variables and then the leaving variables while in the case of dual simplex method we first determine the leaving variables and then the entering variables.

46. **What do you mean by the shadow prices?**
The values of the decision variable of dual of a LPP represents the shadow prices of a resource.

47. **What is the advantage of dual simplex method?**
The advantage of dual simplex method is to avoid introducing the artificial variables along with the surplus variable as the '≥' type constraint is converted into '≤' type.

48. **State the optimality condition in dual simplex method.**
In dual simplex method, if all $Z_j - C_j \geq 0$ and also all $x_{Bi} \geq 0$ then the current solution is an optimum feasible solution.

49. **State the feasibility condition in dual simplex method.**
In dual simplex method, in finding the variable which enters the basis, we find Max $\{Z_j - C_j / a_i K, a_i K < 0\}$. If there is no ratio with negative denominator then the procedure does not have a feasible solution.

50. **State the existence theorem of duality.**
If either the primal or the dual problem has an unbounded solution, then the other problem has no feasible solution.

51. **State the complementary slackness theorem of duality.**
   (*i*) If a primal variable is positive, then the corresponding dual constraints is an equation at the optimum and vice versa.
   (*ii*) If a primal constraint is a strict inequality then the corresponding dual variable is zero at the optimum and vice versa.

52. The maximization problem in the primal becomes the <u>minimization</u> problem in its dual.

53. The dual of the dual is <u>primal</u>.

54. The method used to solve LPP without the use of artificial variables is called <u>dual simplex</u> method.

55. What are the two important forms of primal-dual pairs?
The two important forms of primal-dual pairs are (*i*) symmetric form (*ii*) non-symmetric form.

56. If either the primal or the dual problem has an unbounded solution then the other problem has <u>no feasible solution</u>.

57. If a dual constraint is strict inequality then the corresponding primal variable is <u>zero</u> at the optimum.

7. Revised Simplex Method

58. **What are the advantages of revised simplex method?**
   (*i*) There is less accumulation of round-off errors, since no calculation is done on a column unless it is ready to enter the basis.
   (*ii*) The data can be stored more accurately and compactly, since the revised simplex table works only with the original data.
   (*iii*) This method is more economical on the computer as it computes and stores only the relevant information needed currently for testing and/or updating the current solution.

8. Transportation Problem

59. **What do you understand by transportation problem (T.P.)?**
T.P. is a special class of Linear Programming Problem in which we transport a commodity (single product) from the source to a destination in such a way that the total transportation cost is minimum.

60. **Define feasible, basic feasible, non-degenerate solution of a T.P.**
Refer to the definitions in the chapter.

61. **Give reasons as to why the LPP solution techniques are not made use of while solving a T.P.**
As there are $m + n - 1$ equations in a T.P. with m origins and n destinations, by adding an ...cial variable to each equation, a large number of variables are involved.
   (*i*) If the problem has m sources and n destinations and $m + n - 1$ equations can be formed. Hence, computation may exceed the capacity of the computer. So LPP technique is not made use of while solving a T.P.
   (*ii*) The coefficient x_{ij} in the constraints are all in unity. For such a technique, transportation technique is easier than simplex method.
   (*iii*) T.P. is minimization of objective function, whereas, simplex method is suitable for maximization problem.

62. **List any three approaches used with T.P. for determining the starting solution.**
   (*i*) North-west corner rule
   (*ii*) Least cost method (Matrix Minima)
   (*iii*) Vogel's approximation method.

63. **Define the optimal solution to a T.P.**
The basic feasible solution to a T.P. is said to be optimal, if it minimizes the total transportation cost.

64. **State the necessary and sufficient condition for the existence of a feasible solution to a T.P.**
The necessary and sufficient condition for the existence of a feasible solution is a solution that satisfies all the conditions of supply and demand.

65. **What is the purpose of MODI method?**
The purpose of MODI method is to get the optimal solution of a T.P.

66. **When does a T.P. have a unique solution?**
A T.P. has a unique solution, if the net evaluation given by $C^*_{ij} = C_{ij} - (u_i + v_j)$ of all the empty cells are positive, i.e., of all $\Delta_{ij} > 0$.

67. **What do you mean by degeneracy in a T.P.?**
If the number of occupied cells in a $m \times n$ T.P. is less than $m + n - 1$, then it is called a degeneracy in a T.P.

68. **Explain how degeneracy in a T.P. may be resolved?**
This degeneracy in a T.P. can be resolved by adding one (more) empty cell having the least cost and is of independent position with a non-negative allocation ($\varepsilon > 0$).

69. **What do you mean by an unbalanced T.P.?**
Any T.P. is said to be unbalanced if

$$\sum_{i=1}^{m} a_i \neq \sum_{j=1}^{n} b_j$$

i.e., if the total supply is not equal to the total demand.

70. **How do you convert an unbalanced T.P. into a balanced one?**
The unbalanced T.P. can be converted into a balanced one by adding a dummy row (source) with cost zero and the excess demand is entered as a rim requirement, if total supply < total demand. On the other, hand if the total supply > total demand, we introduce a dummy column (destination) with cost 0 and the excess supply is entered as a rim requirement for the dummy destination.

71. List the merits and limitations of using North-west corner rule.
Merits This method is easy to follow because we need not consider the transportation cost.
Limitations The solution obtained may not be the best solution, as the allocations have been made without considering the cost of transportation. While performing optimality test, it may need more iterations to get the optimal solution.

72. Vogel's approximation method results in the most economical initial basic feasible solution. Why?
Yes, it is true. In this method we take into account not only the least cost c_{ij} but also the costs that just exceed c_{ij}. This method considerably reduces the number of iteration required to arrive at the optimal solution. Also it gives near optimal solution that may, at times, be the optimal solution.

73. How will you identify that a T.P. has got an alternate optimal solution?
While performing optimality test, if some of Δ_{ij} value, where $\Delta_{ij} = C_{ij} - (u_i + v_j)$ for empty (non-basic) cell is zero, then it is the indication of an alternate solution.

74. The number of non-basic variables in the balanced T.P. with m rows and n columns is $\underline{mn - (m + n - 1)}$.

75. The number of non-basic variables in the balanced T.P. with 4 rows and 5 columns is <u>12</u>.

76. In the north-west corner rule, if the demand in the column is satisfied, one must move to the <u>right</u> cell in the next <u>column</u>.

77. For any T.P., the coefficients of all x_{ij} in the constraints are <u>unity</u>.

78. An optimum solution results when net change value of all unoccupied cells are <u>non-negative</u>.

79. A solution that satisfies all the conditions of supply and demand but it may or may not be optimal is called an <u>initial feasible solution</u>.

80. Degeneracy in a $m \times n$ T.P. occurs when the number of occupied cell is less than $m + n - 1$.

81. When do you say that the occupied cell is in independent position?
An occupied cell is in independent position, when no closed path can be drawn from the allocations.

82. The transportation model is restricted to dealing with a single commodity only. Is it true or false. (False.)

83. If a constant value is added to every cost element c_{ij} in the transportation table, the optimal values of the variable x_{ij} will change. Is it true or false. (False.)

9. Transhipment and Assignment Problems

84. **What is an assignment problem? Give two applications.**
The problem of assigning the number of jobs to equal number of facilities (machines or persons or destinations) at a minimum cost or maximum profit is called an assignment problem.
Applications:

(*a*) If n jobs have to be assigned to n workers or machines with unit cost or unit time of performing the job, we can use assignment model to get minimum cost.

(*b*) Travelling salesmen problem, i.e., a salesman has to visit a number of cities, not visiting the same city twice and return to the starting place.

85. **What do you mean by an unbalanced assignment problem?**
If the number of rows is not equal to the number of columns in the cost matrix of the assignment problem or if the cost matrix of the given assignment problem is not a square matrix, then the given assignment problem is said to be unbalanced.

86. **Why can the transportation technique or the simplex method not be used to solve the assignment problem?**
The transportation technique or simplex method cannot be used to solve the assignment problem because of degeneracy.

87. **State the difference between the T.P. and the A.P.**

The major differences between T.P. and A.P. are,

(*i*) The cost matrix in T.P. is not necessarily a square matrix, whereas in A.P., it is a square matrix.

(*ii*) Supply and demand at any source and at any destination may be positive quantity a_i, b_j in T.P. whereas in A.P. it will be 1, i.e., $a_i = b_j = 1$.

(*iii*) The allocations X_{ij} in the case of T.P. can take any positive values satisfying the rim requirements, whereas in A.P., X_{ij} will take only two possible values 1 or 0.

88. **How is the presence of an alternate optimal solution established?**

If the final cost matrix contains more than a required number of zeros at independent positions, then it indicates the presence of an alternate optimal solution.

89. **What is the objective of the travelling salesman problem?**

The objective of the travelling salesman problem is that the salesman has to visit various cities, not visiting the same place twice and return to the starting place by spending minimum transportation cost.

90. **How do you convert the maximization assignment problem into a minimization one?**

The maximization A.P. can be converted into minimization assignment problem by subtracting all the elements in the given profit matrix from the highest element in that matrix.

91. **If each entry is increased by 3 in a 4 × 4 assignment problem, what is the effect on the optimal value?**

The effect in the optimal value when each entry is increased by 3 is given by

New optimal value = Original optimal value + 3 × 4, where 4 is the order of matrix.

92. **Give the linear programming form of the A.P.**

The A.P. can be expressed as

$$\text{Minimize } Z = \sum_{i=1}^{n} \sum_{j=1}^{n} C_{ij} X_{ij}$$

where C_{ij} is the cost of assigning i^{th} machine to the jth job, subject to the constraints

$$X_{ij} = \begin{cases} 1 \text{ if } i\text{th machine is assigned to the } j\text{th job} \\ 0 \text{ if not.} \end{cases}$$

93. **Why is A.P. a completely degenerate form of a T.P.?**

Since the units available at each source and the units demanded at each destination are equal, we get exactly one occupied cell in each row and each column. Hence, we get only n occupied cells in the place in the required $n + n - 1 = 2n - 1$ occupied cells. Hence, an A.P. is a completely degenerate form of a T.P.

94. **The optimum assignment schedule remains unnoticed, if we add or subtract a constant from all the elements of a row or column of the assignment cost matrix. Is this statement true?**

The above statement is true, optimal schedule will not be altered. But the optimal value will be changed (refer to Q. No. 91).

95. **What is the name of the method used in getting the optimum assignment?**

Hungarian method.

96. **When is an A.P. said to be unbalanced? How do you make it a balanced one?**

If the cost matrix or profit matrix is not a square matrix, then the problem is said to be unbalanced. To make it balanced, we add a row or column accordingly with all the entries zero.

97. An A.P. is a completely degenerate form of a T.P.

98. An A.P. represents a T.P. with all demands and supplies equal to 1.

99. The transportation technique or simplex method cannot be used to solve the A.P. because of Degeneracy.

100. The A.P. can be stated in the form of a $n \times n$ matrix (C_{ij}) called Cost matrix or effective matrix.

101. **How do you solve an A.P., if the profit is to be maximised?**

The given profit matrix can be converted into a loss matrix or minimization type by subtracting all the elements from the highest element of the given matrix. For this minimization problem, apply steps of the Hungarian method to get an optimal assignment.

102. **State whether the following are true or false.**

(*i*) A.P. is a completely degenerated form of a T.P. (True)

(*ii*) Assignment technique is essentially a minimization technique. (True)

(*iii*) If for an A.P. all $C_{ij} \geq 0$ then an assignment schedule (X_{ij}) which satisfies $\Sigma\Sigma C_{ij} X_{ij} = 0$ must be optimal. (True)

(*iv*) The transportation technique or simplex method cannot be used to solve the A.P. because of degeneracy. (True)

(*v*) In a travelling salesmen problem no assignment should be made along the diagonal line of the cost matrix. (True)

(*vi*) In a travelling salesmen problem, the salesman cannot visit a city twice, until he has visited all the cities once. (True)

(*vii*) In A.P., if the final cost matrix contains more than one zero at independent positions then the problem will have a unique solution. (False)

11. Integer Programming Problems

103. **What do you mean by integer programming problem?**
An LPP in which some or all of the variables in the optimal solution are restricted to assume non-negative integer values is called an integer programming problem.

104. **Define a pure integer programming problem.**
In a LPP, if all the variables in the optimal solution are restricted to assume non-negative integer values, then it is called a pure IPP.

105. **Define a mixed integer programming problem.**
In an LPP, if only some of the variables in the optimal solution are restricted to assume non-negative integer values, while the remaining variables are free to take any non-negative values, then it is called a mixed integer programming problem.

106. **Differentiate between pure and mixed IPP.**
In a pure IPP all the variables in the optimal solution are restricted to assume non-negative integer values. Whereas in mixed IPP, only some of the variables in the optimal solution are restricted to assume non-negative integer values.

107. **Give some applications of IPP.**

(*i*) In product mix problem

(*ii*) Sequencing and routing decisions

(*iii*) All allocation problems involving the allocation of goods, men and machine.

108. **What are the methods used in solving IPP?**
There are two methods, namely,

(*i*) Cutting methods (Gomary's cutting plane algorithm)

(*ii*) Search method (Branch and bound technique).

109. **Explain Gomarian constraint or fractional cut constraint. Also explain its geometrical interpretation.**
A new constraint introduced to the problem such that the new set of feasible solution includes all the original feasible integer solutions but does not include the optimum non-integer solution initially found. This new constraint is called fractional cut or Gomarian's constraint.

110. **Why should the optimum values not be rounded off instead of resorting to integer programming? Explain.**
If the non-integer variable is rounded off, then it violates the feasibility and also there is no guarantee that the rounded solution will also be optimal.

Example

Max $Z = 20x_1 + 8x_2$

Subject to, $3x_1 + 4x_2 \leq 8$

$x_1, x_2 \geq 0$ and are integers.

The solution $x_1 = \frac{8}{3}, x_2 = 0$ and Max Z $= \frac{160}{3}$

If the variable is rounded off to $x_1 = 3, x_2 = 0$. In such a case, it does not satisfy the constraint $3x_1 + 4x_2 \leq 8$. Hence, the solutibn $x_1 = 3, x_2 = 0$ is not feasible. Thus, a new rounded solution may not be feasible. Also, if we round the solution to $x_1 = 2$, then the solution is feasible but Max Z = 40 which is far away from the optimal solution

$$\text{Max Z} = \frac{160}{3}.$$

Hence, there is no guarantee that the rounded solution will be optimum.

111. **Can we apply the Branch and Bound method for both pure and mixed IPP?**
Yes.

112. **Every integer program, mixed or pure can be expressed in terms of zero-one variables. Is it true or not?**
True.

113. **What is Gomary constraints that is included in the simplex otherwise known as?**
Fractional cut constraint is the other name for Gomary constraint.

114. **Where is Branch and Bound method used?**
This method is an enumeration method which is used when all the feasible integer points are not enumerated.

115. **In the optimal solution of an IPP by simplex method the basic variable x_1 is not an integer.** The corresponding row in the table is

x_B	x_1	x_2	x_3	x_4	x_5	x_6	x_7
$x_1 = 3\frac{1}{4}$	1	$\frac{3}{2}$	$-\frac{5}{3}$	0	2	0	$-\frac{11}{4}$

Construct a Gomary's constraint for this.
From the source row, we have the Gomarian constraint as

$$\frac{3}{2}x_2 + \frac{1}{3}x_3 + \frac{1}{4}x_7 \geq \frac{1}{4}$$

$$\Rightarrow \quad -\frac{3}{2}x_2 - \frac{1}{3}x_3 - \frac{1}{4}x_7 + G_1 = -\frac{1}{4}$$

where, G_1 is the Gomarian slack.

116. **What is the fractional part of the negative number $-\frac{98}{19}$?**

The fractional part of the negative number $-\frac{98}{19}$ is given by $+\frac{16}{19}$

as the number can be expressed as $-\frac{98}{19} = -6 + \frac{16}{19}$

117. **What is the fractional part of $-\frac{2}{3}$?**

The fractional part can be expressed as $-\frac{2}{3} = -1 + \frac{1}{3}$

$\therefore$ The fractional part of $-\frac{2}{3}$ is $\frac{1}{3}$.

118. **Explain the importance of the IPP.**
In LPP, all the decision variables were allowed to take any non-negative real values as it is quite possible and appropriate to have fractional values in many solution and which are meaningless in the context of the actual decision problem. This is the main reason why IPP is so important for marginal decisions.

13. Dynamic Programming

119. **What is dynamic programming?**

Many decision-making problems involve a process that takes place in multiple stages in such a way that at each stage, the process is dependent on the strategy chosen. Such types of problems are called dynamic programming problems (DPP).

120. **Define the following terms in dynamic programming: stage, state, state variables.**

(*i*) **Stage** A stage may be defined as the portion of the problem that possesses a set of mutually exclusive alternatives from which the best alternative is to be selected.

(*ii*) **State** States are various possible conditions in which the system may find itself at that stage of the problem.

(*iii*) **State variables** The current situation (state) of the system at a stage is described by a set of variables called state variables.

121. **Give a few applications of DPP.**

(*i*) It is used to determine the optimal combination of advertising media (TV, Radio, Newspapers) and the frequency of advertising.

(*ii*) Spare part level determination to guarantee high efficiency of utilization of expensive equipment.

(*iii*) It has been used to determine the inventory level, and for formulating the inventory recording.

(*iv*) Other areas of application: Scheduling methods, Markovian decision, decision models, infinite stage system, probabilistic decision problems, etc.

122. **Stale Bellmans principle of optimality.**

It states that "An optimal policy (set of decisions) has the property that whatever be the initial state and initial decisions, the remaining decisions must constitute an optimal policy for the state resulting from the first decision."

123. **What are the advantages of dynamic programming?**

The decision-making process consists of selecting a combination of plans from a large number of alternative combinations, which also need a lot of computational work, where too much time is involved. Also, the number of combinations is very large. These drawbacks can be avoided by using DPP as it divides the given problem into sub-problems or stages. Only one stage is considered at a time and various infeasible combinations are eliminated by reducing the volume of computations.

14. Sequencing Problems

124. **When can we apply Johnson's algorithm in finding the optimal ordering of *n* jobs through 3 machines?**

The Johnson's algorithm in finding the optimal ordering of *n* jobs through 3 machines can be applied, if the problem is converted into two-machine problem.

125. If there are 4 tasks to perform, each of which requires processing on 2 different machines, the number of theoretically possible sequence is <u>$(4!)^2$</u>.

126. The algorithm used to find an optimal sequence of *n* jobs through two or three machines is due to <u>Johnson.</u>

127. **Write the condition for Johnson's algorithm to be applicable in finding the optimal sequencing order of *n* jobs through 3 machines.**

The conditions for applying Johnson's algorithm for finding the optimal sequencing *y* on 3 machines *A*, *B*, *C* in the order *ABC* is

Min time on machine $A \geq$ Max time on machine *B*

or

Min time on machine $C \geq$ Max time on machine *B*.

15. Network Scheduling by PERT/CPM

128. **What do you mean by a project?**
A project is defined as a combination of inter-related activities all of which must be executed in a certain order for its completion.

129. **What are the two basic planning and control techniques in a network analysis?**
(*i*) Programme Evaluation Review Technique (PERT)
(*ii*) Critical Path Method.

130. **What are the three main phases of a project?**
The three phases of a project are planning, scheduling and control.

131. **What is a network?**
It is the graphic representation of logically and sequentially connected arrows and nodes representing activities and events of a project.

132. **What do you mean by an activity of a project?**
An activity represents some action and as such is a time consuming effort necessary to complete a particular part of the overall project.

133. **What is a dummy activity and when is it needed?**
Certain activities which neither consume time nor resources, but are used simply to represent a connection between events are known as dummies. When two activities have the same head and tail events, they cannot be represented in a network diagram without using dummy activity.

134. **What are the three common errors in the construction of network?**
The three common errors are (*i*) Formation of loops (*ii*) Dangling (*iii*) Redundancy.

135. **What is dangling in a network?**
To disconnect an activity before the completion of all activities in a network diagram is known as dangling.

136. **How is dangling avoided in the network?**
The dangl:ng can be avoided by adding a dummy activity. This can be connected to the end event.

137. **Distinguish between float and slack.**
The basic difference between slack and float is that slack is used for the difference between the latest and earliest event time whereas float is the same difference used for the activity.

138. **What are the three types of floats?**
The three types of floats are (*i*) Total float (*ii*) Free float (*iii*) Independent float.

139. **What is the name of the activity whose total float is zero?**
Critical activity.

140. **What is the name of the rule used for numbering the events?**
Fulkerson rule.

141. **Define total float.**
The amount of time by which the completion of an activity could be delayed beyond the earliest expected completion time without affecting the overall project duration time is called the total float.

142. **Define critical activity.**
An activity is said to be critical if a delay in its start will cause a further delay in the completion of the entire project.

143. **What is the critical path?**
The sequence of critical activities in a network is called the critical path.

144. **Can the total float be negative?**
No.

145. Earliest finish of an activity can be calculated by a formula $Es_j - \text{Max}_i = (E_{si} + t_{ij})$ where Es_j is the earliest start time and t_{ij} is the normal time.

146. **Can a dummy activity appear on the critical path of a project network?**

Yes.

147. **If the total float of an activity 3 – 4 is 18, the latest and the earliest occurrence of the events 3 and 4 are 15, 12 and 22, 10 respectively. What is free float?**

$$FF = TF - \text{Head event slack} = 18 - (22 - 10) = 6.$$

148. **What is the independent float of the activity 3 – 4 in question 147?**

$$IF = FF - \text{Tail event slack} = 6 - (15 - 12) = 6 - 3 = 3.$$

149. **Distinguish between PERT and CPM.**

PERT	***CPM***
(*i*) Event oriented.	(*i*) Activity oriented.
(*ii*) Probabilistic.	(*ii*) Deterministic.
(*iii*) Three time estimates namely optimistic, pessimistic, most likely are given.	(*iii*) Time is fixed.
(*iv*) Resourcess such as labour, equipments, materials are limited.	(*iv*) No limitation of resources.

150. **Define the expected variance of a project length.**

The expected variance of a project length, also called the variance of the critical path, is the sum of the variances of all the critical activities.

151. **Express the expected duration of an activity of a project in terms of t_o, t_m and t_p.**

The expected duration of an activity in terms of the three time estimates is given by

$$t_e = \frac{t_e + 4t_m + t_p}{6}$$

152. **What is the formula for finding the variance of an activity in terms of optimistic and pessimistic time estimates?**

The formula for variance σ^2 in terms of t_o and t_p is given by

$$\sigma^2 = \left(\frac{t_p - t_o}{6}\right)^2$$

153. The name of the probability distribution used in PERT which estimates the expected duration and the expected variance of the activity is β-distribution.

154. Write down at least two main assumptions in PERT network calculation.

(*i*) The activity durations are independent, i.e., the time required to complete an activity will have no bearing on the completion times of any other activity of the project.

(*ii*) The activity durations follow β-distribution.

155. **For a standard normal variable Z, $P(0 \le z \le 1) = 0.4313$, if the expected duration of a project is 40 days and the standard deviation of the critical path is 5 days, what is the probability of completing the project in 35 days?**

The probability of completing the project within 35 days is given by $P(Z \le D)$

$$D = \frac{T_s - T_e}{\sigma} = \frac{35 - 40}{5} = -1$$

Given,

$$T_s = 35$$
$$T_e = 40$$
$$\sigma = 5$$

$$\therefore \quad P(Z \leq -1) = 0.5\ \phi\,(1)$$
$$= 0.5 - 0.3413 = 0.1587$$

156. **PERT takes care of uncertain durations. How far is this statement true?**
In research projects or design of gearbox or a new machine, various activities are based on judgement. It is difficult to get a reliable time estimate because of the rapidly changing technology.
Time values are subject to chance variations. For such cases where the activities are non-deterministic in nature, PERT was developed. It takes care of uncertain durations.

157. **A critical activity must have its total and free float equal to zero. Is it true?**
Yes, the total and free float of a critical activity will be zero.

158. **What are the two kinds of cost of any project?**
The two kinds of cost of any project are direct cost and indirect cost.

159. **Give the difference between direct and indirect cost.**
Direct costs are directly associated with the activity and because of this factor, the project duration is reduced with increase in total cost.
Indirect costs are associated with overhead expenses, managerial services, etc., i.e., these costs are not directly associated with the activity, due to which the project duration is reduced with decreased total cost.

160. **Define crashing.**
The process of reducing the activity duration by putting an extra effort is called crashing the activity.

161. **Define the cost time slope of an activity.**
The cost slope indicating the increase in cost per unit and reduction in time, is defined as

$$\text{Cost slope} = \frac{\text{Crash cost} - \text{Normal cost}}{\text{Normal time} - \text{Crash time}}$$

162. **What is the name you give for activities which have zero total float?**
The name of the activity which has zero total float is called critical activity.

163. **Define crash time and crash cost.**
The crash time represents the minimum activity duration time, that is possible and any attempts to further crash would only raise the activity cost without reducing the time. The activity cost corresponding to the crash time is called the crash cost.

164. **What is resource scheduling?**
Resource scheduling implies the task of allocation of resources to various activities in such a manner that the allocation is considered as acceptable under the given situation.

165. **What is resource levelling?**
Resource levelling refers to the scheduling of activities within the limits of the available floats in such a way that the variations in resource requirements are minimized.

166. **What is resource smoothing?**
Resource smoothing involves rescheduling of the activities of a project in such a way as to utilize the resource in a fairly uniform manner and achieving the minimum project duration.

167. **Define optimum duration of a project.**
Optimum duration of a project is the duration, for which the total cost associated with it is minimum.

168. **Define the least duration of a project.**
Least duration of a project is the minimum duration beyond which no more crashing of the activity is possible. Here, the total cost associated with it is not necessarily minimum.

169. **If all the paths of a network are critical paths then the project duration cannot be reduced further. Is it true or false?**
False.

170. **What do you mean by parallel paths?**
When some critical activities are crashed, some non-critical paths also become critical. These are called parallel paths.

171. **In PERT analysis the variance of a job having optimistic time 5, most likely time 8 and pessimistic time 17 is**

$$\left(\frac{17-5}{6}\right)^2 = 4$$

172. The cost time slope of an activity having normal time 4 hours, crash time 2 hours, normal cost ₹ 150 and crash cost ₹ 350 is 350 – 150/4 – 2 = ₹ 100

16. Inventory Control

173. **What is meant by inventory?**
Inventory is defined as idle resources of an enterprise. It is the physical stock of goods kept for future use.

174. **What are the main objectives of an inventory model?**
(*i*) It provides adequate service to the customers.
(*ii*) It reduces the possibility of duplication of orders.
(*iii*) It helps in minimizing the loss due to deterioration, obsolescence, damage, etc.
(*iv*) It optimizes the cost associated with inventory.
(*v*) It helps in deciding whether to avail price discount or bulk purchases.

175. **What are the different types of inventories?**
The different types of inventories are:
(*i*) Transportation inventories, (*ii*) Buffer inventories, (*iii*) Anticipation inventories, (*iv*) Decoupling inventories, (*v*) Lot-size inventories.

176. **What are the different costs that are involved in the inventory problem?**
The different costs involved in the inventory problem are (*i*) item (purchase or production) cost, (*ii*) ordering or set-up cost, (*iii*) carrying or holding cost, (*iv*) Shortage or stock out cost.

177. **Define holding cost and set-up cost.**
The cost associated with carrying or holding the goods in stock is known as holding cost or carrying cost which is denoted by C_1 per unit of goods for a unit time. (e.g). invested capital cost, record keeping cost, taxes and insurance, etc.

The cost which includes the fixed cost associated with obtaining goods through placing of an order or purchasing or manufacturing or setting up a machinery before starting the production is called set-up cost and is denoted by C_3.

178. **Define shortage cost.**
The penalty costs that are incurred as a result of running out of stock (i.e. shortage) are known as shortage costs and are denoted by C_2.

179. **What are the two types of variables in the inventory?**
(*i*) Controlled variable
(*ii*) Uncontrolled variables.

180. **Define lead time.**
The time gap between placing of an order and its actual arrival in the inventory is known as lead time.

181. **Define order cycle.**
The time period between placement of two successive orders is referred to as an order cycle.

182. **Define time horizon.**

The time period over which the inventory level will be controlled is known as time horizon.

183. **Define re-order level.**

The level between maximum and minimum stock at which purchasing activities must start for replenishment is known as re-order level. ROL = $Ld \times R$

184. **Define buffer stock or safety stock.**

Buffer stock means the extra inventory maintained in addition to the inventory required corresponding to normal consumption levels. Optimum buffer stock = (max. lead time – min. lead time.) × R.

185. **What is total inventory cost?**

Total inventory cost = Purchase cost of inventory items + Ordering cost + Carrying cost + Shortage cost.

186. **What is economic order quantity?**

It is that size of order which minimizes total annual cost of carrying inventory and cost of ordering under the assumed conditions of certainty and that annual demands are constant.

187. **What are the different classifications of inventory model?**

The inventory model can be classified into two categories:

(*i*) Deterministic inventory model

(*ii*) Probabilistic inventory model

188. **Write the EOQ formula under purchasing model without shortages.**

$$\text{EOQ} = \sqrt{\frac{2C_3R}{C_1}}$$

where, R is the demand rate

C_1 is the holding cost per unit per time

C_3 is the set-up cost per order.

189. **Write the formula for finding the minimum inventory cost under the purchasing model without shortages.**

$$C_{\text{min}} = \sqrt{2RC_1C_3}$$

190. **Write the EOQ formula under deterministic demand with shortages where lead time is zero.**

$$q^* = \sqrt{\frac{C_1 + C_2}{C_2}}\sqrt{\frac{2C_3R}{C_1}}$$

where, C_2 is the shortage cost.

C_1 and C_3 are the holding cost and set-up cost.

R is the demand rate.

191. **State the formula for EOQ under manufacturing model where**

(*i*) shortages are allowed (*ii*) shortages are not allowed.

$$(i)\ q^* = \sqrt{\frac{C_1 + C_2}{C_2}}\sqrt{\frac{K}{K - R}}\sqrt{\frac{2C_3R}{C_1}} \qquad (ii)\ q^* = \sqrt{\frac{K}{K - R}}\sqrt{\frac{2C_3R}{C_1}}$$

192. **Distinguish between deterministic model and probabilistic model.**

Deterministic	*Probabilistic*
(*i*) Demand is either static or dynamic. (*ii*) Lead time is constant. (*iii*) Lead time demand is known and fixed.	(*i*) Demand is stationary or non-stationary. (*ii*) Lead time is not constant. (*iii*) Lead time demand is assumed to follow normal distribution.

193. **Briefly explain probabilistic inventory model.**

Demand can be classified into stationary demand, i.e., single period model and non-stationary demand, i.e., multiperiod with variable lead time model. Stationary demand can be further classified into:

(*i*) Model with instantaneous demand, no set-up cost.
(*ii*) Model with continuous demand, no set-up cost.
(*iii*) Model with instantaneous demand and set-up cost.

194. **The optimum order quantity decreases with the increase in shortage cost. Is it ture?**

Yes, it is true.

195. **What is the EOQ formula with different rates of demand in different cycle?**

$$\text{Consider EOQ} = \sqrt{\frac{2RC_3}{C_1}}\sqrt{\frac{C_1 + C_2}{C_2}} \quad \text{where, } C_2 \text{ is the shortage cost.}$$

$$= a \text{ Constant} \times \sqrt{\frac{C_1 + C_2}{C_2}}$$

If C_2 increases $\sqrt{\frac{C_1 + C_2}{C_2}}$ decreases, thus EOQ $q^* = \sqrt{\frac{2C_3P/T}{C_1}}$ decreases

where, the demand rate $R = D/T$, D is the total demand to be satisfied during the period T.

196. **If the average inventory is 250 units and the maximum inventory is 300 units then find the safety stock.**

Maximum inventory $= B + q^* = 300$ units

Average inventory $= B + q^*/2 = 250$ units

On adding we get, $2B + 3q^*/2 = 550$ units

On subtracting we get, $q^*/2 = 50$ units

$q^*/100$ units

$$\therefore \quad 2B = 500 - \frac{3q^*}{2}$$

$$= 550 - 150 = 400$$

$$\therefore \quad B = \frac{400}{2} = 200$$

The safety stock = 200 units

197. **What are the two main decisions to be made in inventory control?**

(*i*) Size of the order (*ii*) The time of placing an order.

198. **Write the formula for optimum value of z under stochastic inventory model (z = discrete).**

$$\sum_{d=0}^{z-1} p(d) < \frac{C_2}{C_1 + C_2} < \sum_{d=0}^{z-1} p(d)$$

199. **Write the formula for Q_0 stochastic inventory model with demand as continuous variable.**

$$\int_0^Q f(x)\,dx = \frac{C_2}{C_1 + C_2}$$

200. The formula for average inventory is $\frac{\text{EOQ}}{2}$ + Safety stock.

201. The ordering cost is independent of ordering quantity.

202. The newspaper boy problem is discussed under stochastic demand in discrete units.

203. EOQ decreases when the cost of the item decreases.

204. EOQ results in equalization of carrying cost and procurement costs.

205. With usual notation $t^* = \frac{1}{N^*}$ where, N^* is the optimum number of order given by R/q^*.

206. When large quantities of buffer stock is maintained the inventory cost would be high.

17. Replacement Models

207. **What is replacement?**

Efficiency of certain items decreases due to wear and tear and require expensive maintenance cost. Certain items like bulbs fail suddenly. In such cases the old items have to be replaced by new ones to prevent any further increase in expenditure. This is called replacement.

208. **When should the replacement be done?**

For an item, its depreciation resulting in decrease in efficiency, operating or maintenance cost is calculated and added. This sum is then divided by the number of years to find the average annual cost, the year in which it reaches the minimum value is the year of replacement.

209. **What are the categories into which the replacement of items are classified?**

The different categories of replacement policies are:

(*i*) Replacement of items like truck, machine whose efficiency decreases with advancement of time.

(*ii*) Replacement of items which do not deteriorate but fail after a certain amount of use, which includes both individual and group replacement policy.

210. **When do we replace a machine considering the time t as a discrete variable and ignoring changes in the value of money?**

Replace the machine at the end of n years, if the maintenance cost in the $(n + 1)$ year is more than the average total cost in the nth year, i.e., average cost in $(n + 1)$ year > average cost in n years.

211. **When do we go in for probabilities replacement model?**

There are certain items which fail completely after some period of use. The period between installation and failure is not constant, but follows some probability distribution. In such case we go in for probabilities replacement model.

212. **Describe briefly some of the replacement policies?**

(*i*) Replacement policy for items whose maintenance cost increases with time and money is not counted.

(*ii*) Replacement policy for items whose maintenance cost increases with time and the money value changes with constant rate.

(*iii*) Replacement policy for items that fail completely, which includes,

(*a*) Individual replacement policy

(*b*) Group replacement policy.

213. **Define group replacement.**

Under this policy, we take decisions as to when all the items should be replaced, irrespective of whether they have failed or not, with a provision that if any item fails before/the replacement time it may be replaced individually.

214. **Define individual replacement.**

Under this policy an item is replaced as soon it fails.

215. **State the conditions under which group replacement is superior to individual replacement.**

Let group replacement be made at the end of *i*th period. If the cost of individual replacement for *i*th period is greater than the average cost per period by the end of period *t*, then group replacement is superior to individual replacement.

216. Differentiate between group replacement and individual replacement.

217. **Define replacement model for items that fail completely.**

Individaul replacemnet	*Group replacement*
(*i*) Items are replaced as and when they fail.	(*i*) All items are replaced after certain period irrespective of their condition in addition to individual replacement as and when they fail.
(*ii*) Cost of individual replacement is high.	(*ii*) Cost is low.
(*iii*) Failure probability is not needed for replacement.	(*iii*) Failure probaility is used to find replacement period.

For items that fail completely, we can use either individual replacement or group replacement whichever is cheaper.

218. **Define discount factor.**

Let *r* per cent be the rate at which money value decreases. The present worth factor of unit amount to be spent after one year is given by

$V = (1+r)^{-1}$ where V is called the discount rate or discount factor.

219. **What is present worth factor?**

Let the money value decrease by *r* per cent per year, then one rupee spent a year from now is $(1+r)^{-1}$ today.

One rupee spent two years from now is $\left(\frac{1}{1-r}\right)^2 (1+r)^{-2}$ today.

In general one rupee spent *n* years from now is $(1+r)^{-n}$ today.

$(1+r)^{-n}$ is called the present worth factor (pwt).

220. **Write the formula for optimum replacement when salvage value is negligible whose money value changes with time.**

The formula for the weighted average cost is given by

$$W(n) = \frac{C + \sum\limits_{n=1} R_n V^{n-1}}{\sum\limits_{n=1} V^{n-1}}$$

where, C is the capital cost of the item, R_n is the running cost, V is the discount rate given by $V = (1+r)^{-1}$, and r is the rate of interest per year.

221. **Write the formula for optimum replacement when salvage is considered.**

$$W(n) = \frac{C + \sum_{n=1} R_n V^{n-1} - S_n V^n}{\sum_{n=1} V^{n-1}}$$

222. **What is preventive replacement?**
Preventive replacement is a procedure which provides for replacement after a time when the effect of ageing has become sufficiently critical even if the actual failure has not yet occurred. It will reduce the number of sudden failures or break downs.

223. **What is the advantage of preventive replacement over routine replacement?**
Preventive replacement attempts to optimize the trade-off between the cost of preventive replacement and the cost of failure. Cost of preventive replacement is cheaper than the cost of routine replacement.

224. **What are the situations which make the replacement of items necessary?**
(*i*) When equipment or machine becomes worse with time.
(*ii*) When items like light bulbs, electronic resistors etc. fail completely.
(*iii*) Problems of mortality and staffing.

225. If all items are replaced irrespective of whether they have failed or not is known as group replacement policy.

226. If the money carries a rate of interest of 12 per cent per year, the present worth factor of one rupee due in one year is 0.89285.

227. What are the major limitations while dealing with replacement situation? The major limitations for replacement situation are cost and time.

228. What is the other name for resale value?
The other name for resale value is salvage value.

229. **What are the types of failures?**
Gradual failure The failure mechanism when as the life of an item increases, its efficiency decreases causing decrease in the value of equipment and increase in expenditure on operating cost.
Sudden failure This type of failure is applicable to those items that do not deteriorate considerably with service but which ultimately fail after some period of use. The period between installation and failure is not constant and follows probability distribution.

230. **Name the three categories of replacement items which follow sudden failure mechanism.**
(*i*) Progressive failure, (*ii*) Regressive failure, (*iii*) Random failure.

231. **What is meant by running cost?**
The cost which is required to maintain and run or to operate the machine is called running cost.

232. **What is replacement?**
When the age of a machine increases, its efficiency decreases. This results in an increase in maintenance or operating cost and a decrease in the scrap or resale value of the machine, Therefore, it is necessary to replace the old machine with a new one. The problem is to determine the best age (optimum) at which the machine should be replaced.

233. **What is 'salvage value'?**
Salvage or resale value is the actual worth or cost of any machine at a given period of time. When the age of the machine increases, the salvage value decreases.

234. **State the conditions under which group replacement is superior to individual replacement.**
We compute the cost of individual replacement per period and then calculate the optimum group replacement cost per period, if the resulting cost of group replacement is less than the cost of individual replacement, group replacement will become preferable.

18. Queueing Theory

235. **Define a queue.**

The flow of customers from finite/infinite population towards service facility is called a queue (waiting line).

236. **Define a customer.**

The arriving unit that requires some service to be performed is called a customer.

237. **What are the basic characteristics of a queueing system?**

The basic characteristics of a queueing system are

(*i*) the input (arrival pattern)
(*ii*) the service mechanism (service pattern)
(*iii*) the queue discipline
(*iv*) customer behaviour.

238. **Define the following:**

(*i*) **Balking** A condition in which a customer may leave the queue because the queue is too long and he has no time to wait or there is insufficient waiting space.
(*ii*) **Reneging** This occurs when a waiting customer leaves the queue due to impatience.
(*iii*) **Jockeying** Customers may jockey from one waiting line to another.

239. **Define transient and steady state.**

A system is said to be in a transient state when its operating characteristics are dependent on time. When the operating characteristics of a system are independent of time, it is called a steady state.

240. **Define traffic intensity or utilization factor.**

An important measure of a simple queue is its traffic intensity given by

$$\rho = \frac{\text{Mean arrival rate}}{\text{Mean service rate}} = \frac{\lambda}{\mu}$$

241. **Explain Kendall's notation.**

Kendall's notation is used for representing queueing models. Generally queueing model may be completely specified in the following symbol form (*a*/*b*/*c*); (*d*/*e*)

a = inter-arrival time (arrival pattern)
b = service pattern
c = number of channels
d = capacity of the system
e = queue discipline

242. **Give the formula for probability of *n* units in the system under single server, FCFS discipline.**

$$P_n = \left(\frac{\lambda}{\mu}\right)^n P_0, P_0 = 1\left[\frac{\lambda}{\mu}\right]$$

where, λ and μ are mean arrival and mean service rate respectively.

243. **What is the distribution for service time?**

The distribution for service time is exponential with mean $\frac{1}{\mu}$.

244. The inter-arrival time under queue follows a Poisson distribution.

245. **Write Little's formula.**

$L_s = \lambda w_s$
$L_q = \lambda w_q$
$L_q = L_s - \lambda/\mu.$

246. Constant service time is a special case of Erlang service time.

247. The time interval between consecutive arrivals generally follows <u>exponential distribution.</u>

248. **What do you understand by explosive state?**

If $\frac{\lambda}{\mu} > 1$, then the state is referred as explosive state.

249. M/M/1 model is also known as <u>Birth-Death</u> model.

19. Game Theory

250. **Define a game.**

The competitive situation will be called a game, if it has the following properties:

(*i*) There is a finite number of participants called players.

(*ii*) Each player has a finite number of strategies available to him.

(*iii*) Every game results in an outcome.

251. **Define strategy.**

The strategy of a player is the decision rule he uses for making the choice from his list of courses of action.

252. **What are the classification of strategy?**

The classifications of strategy are:

(*a*) Pure strategy and (*b*) Mixed strategy.

253. **When do players apply mixed strategies?**

Players apply mixed strategy when there is no saddle point.

254. **Define a saddle point.**

A saddle point is the position in the pay-off matrix, where the maximum of row minima coincides with the minimum of column maxima.

255. **Define two-person zero sum game.**

A game with two players, where a gain of one player equals the loss of the other is known as a two-person zero sum game.

256. **Distinguish between Pure and Mixed strategies.**

(*i*) A strategy is called pure, if one knows in advance of the play that it is certain to be adopted irrespective of the strategy the other may choose. The optimal strategy mixture for each player may be determined by assigning to each strategy its probability of being chosen. These strategies are called mixed strategy.

(*ii*) A pure strategy is a special case of mixed strategy. A player may be able to choose only *n* pure strategies, whereas he had infinite number of mixed strategies.

257. Games without saddle point require players to play <u>Mixed</u> strategies.

258. <u>Saddle point</u> is the point of intersection of pure strategies.

259. **A pure strategy game is one in which each player has only one optimal strategy—True or False.**

True.

260. **Define pay-off.**

The gains resulting from a game is called pay-off, and when it is presented in the form of a table, it is called pay-off matrix.

261. **What type of games are solved graphically?**

The games in which the pay-off matrix is of the form $m \times 2$ or $2 \times n$ are solved graphically.

262. **Define value of the game.**

The value of the game is defined as the expected gain to a player.

263. **What is meant by minimax, maximin?**

Minimax is maximum of row minima, and Maximin is minimum of column maxima.

264. **When do you say a game is stable?**

A game is stable when there is a saddle point.

265. **When is the game fair?**
A game is fair if minimax value = maximin value = 0.
266. A game wherein the gain of one player equals the loss of other is called zero-sum game.
267. One of the methods for simplifying $m \times n$ game with mixed strategy is Dominance.
268. **A game can have more than one saddle point. (True/false)**
True.
269. **A game is said to be zero sum game if all the elements in the principal diagonal of the pay-off matrix are zero. (True/False)**
True.
270. **A $n \times n$ game can be solved by the matrix method only if row oddments = column oddments. (True/False)**
True.
271. **What is the limitation of the method of matrices?**
This method can be applied only when the sum of column oddments is equal to the sum of row oddments, i.e., if both players use all their plays in their best strategies.
272. **Distinguish between 'pure and mixed strategies'.**
If a player decides to use only one particular course of action with probability of 1, then the strategy is known as pure strategy. If a player decides to play more than one strategy then the player is said to follow a situation known as mixed strategy. Here the probability of selection of the individual strategies will be less than one.

20. Simulation

273. **Define simulation. Why is it used?**
The representation of reality in some physical form or in some form of mathematical equations may be called simulation, i.e., simulation is imitation of reality. This is used because one is satisfied with suboptimal results for decision-making and also representation by a mathematical model is beyond the capabilities of the analyst.
274. **Define random number.**
Random number is a number whose probability of occurrence is the same as that of any other number in the collection.
275. **Define Pseudo-random number.**
Random numbers are called Pseudo-random numbers when they are generated by some deterministic process and they qualify the predetermined statistical test for randomness.
276. **Explain Monte-Carlo technique.**
It is a simulation technique in which statistical distribution functions are created by using a series of random numbers. This is generally used to solve problems which cannot be adequately represented by the mathematical models.
277. **What are the advantages of simulation?**
The advantages of simulation are:
(*a*) mathematically less complicated
(*b*) flexible
(*c*) modified to suit the changing environments of the real situation
(*d*) can be used for training purposes.
278. **What are the limitations of simulation?**
(*i*) Quantification of the variables may be difficult.
(*ii*) Simulation may not yield optimum results.
(*iii*) Simulation may not always be cheap.
(*iv*) Simulation may not always be less time consuming.
(*v*) The results obtained from simulation models cannot be completely relied upon.
279. **What are the uses of simulation?**
(*i*) Inventory problems (*ii*) Queueing problems
(*iii*) Training programs etc.

21. Decision Theory

280. What are the classifications of decision?

The classifications of decision are:

(*i*) Tactical decision (*ii*) Strategic decision

281. What are the types of decision-making situations?

(*i*) Decision-making under certainty. (*ii*) Decision-making under uncertainty.
(*iii*) Decision-making under risk. (*iv*) Decision-making under conflict.

282. What is Expected Monetary Value (EMV)?

The conditional value of each event in the pay-off table is multiplied by its probability and the product is summed up. The resulting number is the EMV for the act.

283. What is Expected Opportunity Loss (EOL)?

The difference between the greater pay-off and the actual pay-off is known as opportunity loss.

284. What is Expected Value of Perfect Information (EVPI)?

The expected value with perfect information is the average (expected) return in the long run, if we have perfect information before a decision is to be made.

285. What is Bayesian rule?

Bayesian rule of decision theory is an approach in which the decision-maker selects a course of action on rational basis by using subjective evaluation of probability based on experience, past performance, judgement, etc.

286. Define Decision tree.

Decision tree is one of the devices for representing a diagrammatic presentation of sequential and multi-dimensional aspects of a particular decision or problem for systematic analysis and evaluation.

287. Describe some methods which are useful for decision-making under uncertainty.

(*i*) Maximax Criterion
(*ii*) Minimax Criterion
(*iii*) Maximin Criterion
(*iv*) Laplace Criterion (Criterion of Equal Likelihood)
(*v*) Hurwicz Alpha Criterion (Criterion of Realism)

288. What is decision-making?

Decision-making is an integral part of any business organization. It involves choosing the best decisions through proper evaluations of the parameters, to get desired outcome.

289. Define (*i*) Pay-off table (*ii*) Opportunity loss table

(*i*) **Pay-off table** A table that represents the profits of a problem is called a pay-off table.
(*ii*) **Opportunity loss table** It is a pay-off table which represents the cost or loss incurred because of failure to take the best possible action. It is the numerical difference between the optimal outcome and actual outcome for a given decision.

290. Define utility in decision theory.

It is the individual's satisfaction level over a risky decision and its outcome.

291. What are the various types of decisions?

The various types of decisions can be categorized as follows:

(*i*) Decision under certainty (*ii*) Decision under risk
(*iii*) Decision under uncertainty (*iv*) Decision-making under conflict.

292. What are the approaches that are used in a decision-making environment where the following risks exist?

(*i*) Expected money value criterion (EMV)
(*ii*) Expected opportunity loss criterion (EOL)
(*iii*) Expected value of perfect information criterion (EVPI)

293. **Write the steps involved while selecting the alternative in EMV criterion.**

(*i*) Construct a pay-off table, listing the alternative decisions and the various states of nature.

(*ii*) Enter the conditional profit for each decision event combination along with the associated probabilities.

(*iii*) Compute the EMV for each alternative by multiplying the conditional profits by assigned probabilities and summing up their products.

(*iv*) The alternative that yields the highest EMV is selected.

294. **What is expected opportunity loss criterion?**

In this approach, first construct a conditional profit table for each decision event combination along with the associated probabilities. For each event, compute the conditional opportunity loss by subtracting the pay-off from the maximum pay-off for that event. Calculate the expected opportunity loss for each alternative by multiplying the conditional opportunity losses by the assigned probabilities and summang up their products. The alternative that yields the lowest EOL is selected.

295. **What is expected value of perfect information criterion?**

EVPI = Expected profit with perfect information—Max. EMV.

296. **What is expected in the value criterion?**

In this approach, first compute the expected value of each alternative. Then select the alternative with the best expected value for implementation. The alternative that has the highest value in the decision column is selected as the best alternative.

297. **What are the methods used for decision-making under certainty?**

(*i*) Maximin gain criterion

(*ii*) Minimax gain criterion

(*iii*) Laplace criterion

(*iv*) Savage minimax regret criterion

(*v*) Hurwicz criterion.

298. **Define the following:**

(*i*) Maximin gain criterion

(*ii*) Minimax gain criterion

(*iii*) Laplace criterion.

(*i*) **Maximin gain criterion (or) Minimax loss criterion** In this criterion, the decision maker achieves the maximum possible pay-off or the minimum possible cost.

(*ii*) **Minimax gain or Maximin loss criterion** In this criterion, the decision-maker selects a particular alternative, which corresponds to the maximum pay-off for each of the alternative. When cost is given, the minimal cost for each alternative is selected.

(*iii*) **Laplace criterion** In this criterion, the decision-maker uses all the information by assigning equal probabilities to the pay-off for each action and then the alternative, which corresponds to the maximum expected pay-off is selected as the best. If the cost is given in the problem, the alternative that corresponds to the minimum cost is selected as the best.

299. **Define the following.**

(*i*) Savage minimax regret criterion

(*ii*) Hurwicz criterion.

(*i*) **Savage minimax regret criterion** When the minimax or maximin criterion are not able to yield an optimal solution, the savage minimax regret criterion method is used. It is based on the concept of regret (after selecting a wrong decision) and calls for selecting the course of action that minimizes the maximum regret.

(*ii*) **Hurwicz criterion** In this criterion, the decision-maker's view lies between that of extreme pessimism and extreme optimism with regard to the maximum criterion. It is made by assigning weights with certain degrees of optimism as well as pessimism.

300. **Define a decision tree.**

A decision tree is a graphical representation of various alternatives, states of nature, probabilities attached to the states of nature and the conditional benefits and losses. It is used for the systematic analysis and evaluation of a particular decision problem.

Index

L

M

N

O

P

Q

R

S

T

U

V